# Lecture Notes in Artificial Intelligence

Subseries of Lecture Notes in Computer Science
Edited by J. Siekmann

# Lecture Notes in Computer Science

Edited by G. Goos and J. Hartmanis

## Editorial

Artificial Intelligence has become a major discipline under the roof of Computer Science. This is also reflected by a growing number of titles devoted to this fast developing field to be published in our Lecture Notes in Computer Science. To make these volumes immediately visible we have decided to distinguish them by a special cover as Lecture Notes in Artificial Intelligence, constituting a subseries of the Lecture Notes in Computer Science. This subseries is edited by an Editorial Board of experts from all areas of AI, chaired by Jörg Siekmann, who are looking forward to consider further AI monographs and proceedings of high scientific quality for publication.

We hope that the constitution of this subseries will be well accepted by the audience of the Lecture Notes in Computer Science, and we feel confident that the subseries will be recognized as an outstanding opportunity for publication by authors and editors of the AI community.

Editors and publisher

# Lecture Notes in
# Artificial Intelligence

Edited by J. Siekmann

Subseries of Lecture Notes in Computer Science

## 482

Y. Kodratoff  (Ed.)

# Machine Learning – EWSL-91

European Working Session on Learning
Porto, Portugal, March 6–8, 1991
Proceedings

# Springer-Verlag

Berlin Heidelberg New York London
Paris Tokyo Hong Kong Barcelona

**Volume Editor**

Yves Kodratoff
CNRS and Université Paris Sud
LRI, Building 490
F-91405 Orsay, France

CR Subject Classification (1987): I.2.6

ISBN 3-540-53816-X Springer-Verlag Berlin Heidelberg New York
ISBN 0-387-53816-X Springer-Verlag New York Berlin Heidelberg

© Springer-Verlag Berlin Heidelberg 1991
Printed in Germany

Printing and binding: Druckhaus Beltz, Hemsbach/Bergstr.
2145/3140-543210 – Printed on acid-free paper

# Editor's Foreword

During the last decade numerous learning techniques, such as empirical induction, explanation-based learning, version spaces, etc., have been developed and tested on a variety of applications. It appears that each method leads to interesting results, but that real applications require a combination of the various methods in order to solve practical problems. This is why Part 1 of this book is concerned with a topic which has been emerging during the very last few years in Machine Learning (ML), **multi-strategy learning**, also called **constructive learning**. This part of the book starts with a kind of discussion between a theoretical approach as given by Giordana et al., and Tecuci's more intuitive approach. Part 1 goes on with several instances of a multi-strategic approach to ML, and ends up with a discussion on representation changes steered by F. Bergadano. The topic called **discovery** can be said to be an application of multi-strategy learning, since it tends to use a combination of inductive and deductive techniques in order to discover functional relationships among sets of numeric data. This topic has been already extensively dealt with in statistics. The point of view of ML in that matter, as shown by papers of Part 2, brings to the fore the importance of using the symbolic information implicitly contained in the data, rather than the raw data alone.

Part 3 deals with the **numeric and statistical approaches,** including techniques using information compression as the key to learning, also often called **inductive construction of decision trees** by ML specialists. The last paper in this part is the only representative of **genetic algorithms** that passed the criticism of our referees.

Part 4 brings us back to purely symbolic techniques stemming from **theorem proving** techniques, including **explanation-based learning**, which have become so important since the middle of the last decade. Part 5 deals with **inversion of resolution,** which is of course an inductive technique, but the origin of which is so much embedded within logic programming that it counts as the very first inductive technique to be as well formalized as the deductive ones.

In Part 6, **analogy and case-based reasoning**, we come back to more intuitive learning methods that have been undergoing a continuous progress during this last decade. Part 7, **multi-agents**, contains two papers describing how agents may interact in order to improve their learning. This last topic has received very little attention up to now. Together with multi-strategy approaches they may well become the great research topics of the 1990s. Last part, **applications**, describes some applications to ML.

The reader may complain about the scarcity of such applications in this volume. This is due to the fact that the content of the book stems from the proceedings of the fifth European Working Session on Learning (EWSL-91, the programme of which is given at the end of this volume) which deals more with recent advances in the field than with applications.

It is my pleasure to acknowledge the help I received from the EWSL programme committee in the selection of the papers accepted for this volume. The choices were made during a vivid discussion conducted almost entirely through electronic mail, which leads to a combination of an informal discussion where quick ideas are put forward, together with a bit more care than in ordinary meetings, since everything leaves a trace and is communicated to everyone else. If our European electronic mail could work a little bit better, this would certainly improve the ease with which such discussions take place. Some of our European PC members gathered information through replies from US members, while I was unable to reach them directly! EWSL-91 PC members are Ivan Bratko (Yugoslavia), Pavel Brazdil (Organization chair, Portugal), Peter Clark (UK), Kenneth De Jong (USA), Luc De Raedt (Belgium), Jean-Gabriel Ganascia (France), Yves Kodratoff (Programme chair, France), Nada Lavrac (Yugoslavia), Ramon Lopez de Mantaras (Spain), Katharina Morik (FRG), Igor Mozetic (Austria), Stephen Muggleton (UK), Lorenza Saitta (Italy), Alberto Segre (USA), Jude Shavlik (USA), Derek Sleeman (UK), Gheorghe Tecuci (Rumania and USA), Maarten Van Someren (The Netherlands).

The discussions of the programme committee, hence the composition of this volume, have been strongly inspired by a large selection of the members of the ML community, mainly if not exclusively a European one. I warmly thank all these referees for their careful job. I also take the opportunity of noticing that the number of referees has been larger than the number of papers accepted for publication, allowing each paper to be reported upon four times. This shows well that the European community of ML is growing at a steady rate, that the field is now quite mature, and ready to start working on large applications. Here is a list of the people who acted as referees for EWSL-91:
J. Aguilar, A. Arigoni, M. Bain, Jerzy Bala, Francesco Bergadano, R. Bisio, Gilles Bisson, Marko Bohanec, Damjan Bojadziev, Pierre Bonelli, Robin A. Boswell, Ivan Bratko, Pavel Brazdil, Maurice Bruynooghe, Cao Feng, Claudio Carpineto, Bojan Cestnik, Peter Clark, Helen G. Cobb, William Cohen, Antoine Cornuejols, Susan Craw, Kenneth De Jong, Luc De Raedt, Danny De Schreye, L. Di Pace, Bojan Dolsak, Kejitan Dontas, Saso Dzeroski, Peter Edwards, Werner Emde, F. Esposito, F. Fabrocini, Bogdan Filipic, Doug Fisher, Marta Franova, Jean-Gabriel Ganascia, R. Gemello, A. Giordana, Diana Gordon, Nicolas Graner, Haym Hirsh, Simon Holland, Dimitar Hristovski, Aram Karalic, Joerg-Uwe Kietz, Kenneth Kaufman, Saliha Khouas, Yves Kodratoff, Igor Kononenko, Matevz Kovacic, Nada Lavrac, Ramon Lopez de Mantaras, F. Malerba, F. Mana, P. Meseguer, Simos Metaxas, J. Millan, Ray Mooney, Eduardo Morales, Katharina Morik, Marjorie Moulet, Igor Mozetic, Stephen Muggleton, Yves Niquil, M. Nunez, Rudiger Oehlmann, Peter W. Pachowicz, Jan Paredis, Alexandre Parodi, Bernhard Pfahringer, Enric Plaza, Jean-Francois Puget, Connie Ramsey, Michael Rissakis, Celine Rouveirol, Gunther Sablon, Lorenza Saitta, Alan C. Schultz, Alberto Segre, V. Semeraro, Sunil Sharma, Jude Shavlik, Derek Sleeman, William N. Spears, Martin Stacey, Jan Talmon, Michael Tanner, Gheorghe Tecuci, P. P. Terpstra, Luis Torgo, C. Torras, Tanja Urbancic, Bozo Urh, Bradley W. Utz, Walter Van de Velde, Maarten W. Van Someren, Alen Varsek, Harry Vassilev, Gilles Venturini, Christel Vrain, Gerhard Widmer, Bob J. Wielinga, Janusz Wnek, Stefan Wrobel, Jianping Zhang, Renata Zupanc.

# Contents

# Part 4: Theorem Proving and EBL

# Part 5: Inversion of Resolution

## Part 6: Analogy and Case-Based Learning

## Part 7: Multi-agents

## Part 8: Applications

# ABSTRACTING BACKGROUND KNOWLEDGE FOR CONCEPT LEARNING

A. GIORDANA(*)  D. ROVERSO(**)  L. SAITTA(*)

(*) Dip. di Informatica, Università di Torino, C.so Svizzera 185, 10149 Torino. Italy
Email: attilio@pianeta.di.unito.it.
(**) Computing Science Dpt., University of Aberdeen, Aberdeen, Scotland, UK
Email:davide@uk.ac.abdn.cs

## Abstract

In this paper the current approach to automatic concept acquisition is criticized. In particular, it is argued that using only generalization, coupled with a simplicity criterion for selecting hypotheses, generates concept descriptions which are poor with respect to their information content, difficult to agree upon by humans and strictly task dependent.

A new framework is proposed instead, based on notion of abstraction, in the sense of Plaisted and Tenenberg. The novelty of this paper, with respect to previous ones, occasionally mentioning abstraction in machine learning, is that it gives a precise definition of abstraction, shows its relation with generalization and also offers a computational framework. Moreover, a special type of abstraction, particularly useful for the learning task, is defined, and an algorithm for computing it is also presented. This type of abstraction can be applied to a body of background knowledge (domain theory), allowing EBG to be performed in a more synthetic representation space. This transformation can (at least partially) offer a solution to the problem of domain theory intractability.

A complete example of domain theory abstraction is also worked out, for the sake of exemplification.

**Keywords**: Abstraction, concept learning, explanation based learning.

## 1. Introduction

In the last decade, many learning systems have been built up. However, if we consider their capabilities, these systems appear deceivingly far from our idea of learning, even when they succeed in solving particular problems. For instance, it may happen that learned concept descriptions turn out to be incoprehensible to a human expert, even though they proved effective in characterizing or discriminating concepts for a specific task.

In this paper we are mostly concerned with the problem of acquiring concept descriptions, but several of the points made also apply to other machine learning tasks, such as learning in planning or machine discovery. In previous papers, we have pointed out some weaknesses inherent in the very philosophy of the current approaches to machine learning (Giordana, Roverso &Saitta, 1990; Giordana &Saitta, 1990). In order to make this paper self-consistent, a brief résumé of that discussion is reported in this section.

Since ever, automated concept acquisition has been based on three unquestioned assumptions (Michalski, Carbonell &Mitchell, 1983,1985; Michalki & Kodratoff, 1990; Carbonell, 1989):

- The basic process for acquiring concepts is **generalization**.
- A concept coincides with its **description**.

- Good concept descriptions are **simple** and **effective**.

Up to now, some kind of *more-general-than* relation has always been the skeleton of both inductive (Michalski, 1983; Bergadano, Giordana & Saitta, 1988; Mitchell, 1982; Buntine, 1988) and deductive (Mitchell, Keller & Kedar-Cabelly, 1986; DeJong & Mooney, 1986) concept learning; moreover, to learn a concept usually means to learn its description, i.e., a relation between the name of the concept and a given set of features. Finally, simplicity, as a requirement for the entities involved in human thought, has always been an appealing criterion (Pearl, 1978), while effectiveness is usually equated to correctness of the concept description with respect to a given task. Effectiveness and simplicity are often considered as opposite criteria, which are to be traded-off (Iba, Wogulis & Langley, 1988). In (Giordana, Roverso & Saitta, 1990) we proposed to replace the above assumptions with the following ones:

- The basic mechanism for concept acquisition is **abstraction**.

The idea of abstraction is well known in software engineering; in Artificial Intelligence abstraction has been frequently mentioned in problem-solving literature, since in (Newel & Simon, 1972). However, its meaning was mostly left to the intuition of the reader until Plaisted introduced a formal definition, based on predicate mapping (Plaisted, 1981). Other authors followed Plaisted's approach in the field of automated reasoning. Particularly interesting is Tenenberg's work, which deals with the problem of preserving the consistency of a theory being abstracted (Tenenberg, 1987).

In Machine Learning, abstraction has been fruitfully used by Knoblock to learn high level operators in hierarchical planning (Knoblock, 1989a, 1989b). Some others have occasionally used the word in concept acquisition (Van de Velde, 1989; Drastal, Czako & Raatz, 1989), but no one has either attributed to it a formal meaning or investigated the relationship between abstraction and generalization.

- A concept should be represented as an **abstract data type**.

The description of a concept is only a particular aspect of its definition; more important are the relationships between it and other concepts (Amsterdam, 1988) and the operations that can be defined over it.

- Complexity has to be a **semantic** notion, not just a syntactic one.

We notice that while it is true that humans are not good at handling long and intricate descriptions, it is also true that they can deal with concepts of very high semantic complexity, such as, for instance, "liberty". Hence, the simplicity criterion has to be related only to the structure of a description, not to its semantic content; in other words, a simple description may involve however semantically complex components, provided that they are arranged into a simple surface structure. By restricting the notion of complexity to syntactic entities, such as number of conjuncts in a formula, has the effect that a *simple* description turns out to be a *poor* one, whereas a rich description is associated to over-fitting (Watanabe, 1969). The way out is that details have not to be trown away, but synthesized into intermediate concepts (i.e., abstracted), allowing concept descriptions to be at the same time syntactically simple and robust.

The idea of introducing intermediate levels in concept descriptions is not new; in fact, it underlies the *contructive* learning approach (Muggleton & Buntine, 1988; Matheus & Rendell, 1989; Utgoff, 1985). However, this approach has been mostly heuristic and intuitive in nature and needs suggestions from an oracle. As an alternative, constructive learning can be modeled as an abstraction process, and then, a theoretical framework for abstraction can help to automatize the choice of the most suitable representation level. As we will see in the next section, we require that abstractions be both instance and generalization preserving transformations; these properties guarantee that learning can occur at the most suitable level and, then, concept descriptions can be transformed into more abstract or less abstract ones, without bothering about loosing consistency and/or completeness.

Notice that, while generalization is a transformation process local to a particular description, abstraction is a global change of representation, involving the whole representation language; it is then easy to move from one level to another, according to the current task needs. This possibility of reasoning at different level of details is particularly important in EBG, when the domain theory is large and the tractability problem emerges. In this case, abstracting the theory can let large deduction subtree collapse into single nodes, which can be expanded afterwards only if needed. This point was the one mainly exploited by Plaisted (Plaisted,1981) and Knoblock (Knoblock, 1989a, 1989b).

Abstraction can be used, in learning concepts, in two different ways. In the first one (direct abstraction problem), a hierarchy of representation spaces (abstraction levels) is given, together with an abstraction theory allowing descriptions to be translated from one level to another. The background knowledge, possibly available, should be also translatable from one level to another, without loosing consistency. Chosen a given abstraction level, whatever inductive and/or deductive learning algorithm can be used for searching the concept description space at that level, using, as usual, generalization. The main problem in this approach is the choice of the most suitable abstraction level. Examples of this use of abstraction have already been presented in (Drastal Czago & Raatz, 19889; Giordana, Roverso & Saitta, 1990). The second way (inverse abstraction problem), has been mentioned before, corresponding to the constructive learning approach: in this case, the abstraction hierarchy is not given and has to be learned at the same time as the concept descriptions. In this case, the main difficulty is how to choose the intermediate concepts among the large number of potentially definable ones.

In (Giordana, Roverso & Saitta, 1990) we have been mostly interested in term abstractions, i.e., in transformations of the instance descriptions to ease the inductive task. In this paper, we are more concerned with the problem of abstracting a body of background knowledge, to be used in deductive or inductive/deductive approaches. A special kind of abstraction theory, constrained to preserve both concept instances and formula generalization, is defined in Section 2, whereas an inference rule to compute it is given in Section 3. An example, taken from an artificial domain, is completely worked out, for the sake of clarification, in Section 4. Finally, some conclusions are reported in Section 5.


## 2. Semantic Abstraction

In this section, a more precise definition of the notions, informally introduced before, will be given. In particular we will define a form of semantic abstraction which will be said completeness preserving and we will show that it benefit of the properties of preserving concept instances and the *more-general-than* relation.

In order to be precise, we need to introduce the meaning of some symbols that will be used in the following. The symbol $L = <T, P, F, C>$ denotes a Horn clause language, where T, P, F and C are the sets of terms, predicates, functions and logical connectives, respectively. Moreover, the symbol $\Theta$ will denote a set of sentences in $L$ describing a learning problem; specifically, $\Theta = T \cup X$, where $T$ is a set of Horn clauses representing a body of *background knowledge,* and $X$ is a set of ground clauses representing the examples. Finally we will call a model (or interpretation) of $\Theta$ a structure $M = \; < A, R_1, \dots , R_n, F_1, \dots ,F_m, \{c_j | j \in J\}>$. In $M$, A is a non-empty set containing the objects of the domain, the $R_h$'s $(1 \le h \le n)$ are subsets of $A^{r_h}$ (basic $r_h$-ary relations) and are associated to the predicates names P of $L$ occurring in $\Theta$, the $F_k$'s $(1 \le k \le m)$ are mapping from $A^{s_k}$ to A (elementary functions of arity $s_k$) and are associated to the function names F of $L$ and the $c_j$'s are constants belonging to A and are associated to terms T of $L$. We remember that $M$ is a model for $\Theta$ iff: $M \; |- \varphi, \; \forall \varphi \in \Theta$.

## 2.1.  Abstraction

In AI, the first formal definition of abstraction was given by Plaisted (Plaisted, 1981) in terms of a mapping between languages preserving instances and negation. Abstraction is firstly defined as a *predicate mapping* associating a single predicate of the more abstract space to a predicate of the less abstract one, and then the definition is extended to clauses.

However, predicate mappings, or, in general, abstractions based only on syntactic transformations, they can generate an inconsistent set of abstract clauses, even if applied to an originally consistent one. Tenenberg discussed this problem and showed that renaming the predicates in the abstraction mapping can cause positive and negative assertions to collide, possibly generating contradictions (Tenenberg, 1987). In order to overcome this problem, Tenenberg defines a *restricted predicate mapping*, which is no longer a purely syntactic mapping. Specifically, given a set of clauses $\Theta$, a restricted predicate mapping $g(\Theta)$ is a subset of the corresponding predicate mapping $f(\Theta)$; $g(\Theta)$ maps only that subset $\Theta'$ of $\Theta$, for which consistency is preserved. The set $\Theta'$ is determined by checking consistency on the model. However, the restricted predicate mapping is no longer an abstraction mapping in Plaisted's sense. As a consequence, not every proof derivable from $\Theta$ has a correspondent proof in $g(\Theta)$, as it happens for an abstraction mapping. Nevertheless, restricted predicate mappings proved useful in problem solving (Tenenberg, 1987; Knoblock, 1989a, 1989b).

In this paper we extend Tenenberg's framework to include abstraction schemes more complex than predicate mappings. To this aim, we adopt a different definition of abstraction, which explicitly uses the models associated to the languages. In fact, predicate mappings  become cumbersome when one want to abstract terms of the language or to map formulae to predicates, preserving consistency at the same time. As Tenenberg pointed out, the consistency requirement cannot be satisfied without using models and, hence, abstraction implicitly becomes a mapping between models. In other words, this form of  abstraction is semantic and must be evaluated using a deductive mechanism instead of a purely syntactic rewriting.

However, the kind of abstraction introduced here is explicitly considered a mapping between models (and not between languages as in predicate mapping), which is defined through an abstraction theory $T_A$ defining the semantics of the relations in the abstract model from the ones in the ground model. In particular, given a set of sentences $\Theta \subseteq L$, a language $L'$ and an abstraction theory $T_A$ defining the predicates of $L'$ in terms of the predicates in $L$, the set of sentences $\Theta'$ of $L'$, such that $:\Theta , T_A \; |- \; \Theta'$, will be called the *abstraction of $\Theta$ through $T_A$*. Therefore, whatever minimal model $M'$ of $\Theta'$ will be considered as the abstraction of a model $M$ of $\Theta$. Notice that $T_A \subseteq L \cup L'$.

In order to have abstractions preserving instances, the form of the generic abstraction theory $T_A$ is restricted to be a set of axioms having the form:

$$\psi \leftrightarrow D_1 \vee D_2 \vee .... \vee D_n \qquad\qquad (2.1)$$

where $\psi$ is an atomic formula in the language $L'$ and $D_1, D_2,..., D_n$ are conjunctions of predicates in the language $L \cup L'$. Moreover, let $\overline{x}$ be the set of variables occurring in $\psi$ and $\overline{y}$ the set of variables occurring in $D_1 \vee D_2 \vee .... \vee D_n$, as commonly made in logic programming, we assume that: (a) $\overline{x} \subseteq \overline{y}$; (b) The variables $\overline{x}$ are implicitly universally quantified; (c) The variables $\overline{y} - \overline{x}$ are implicitly existentially quantified.

In order to understand how this form of abstraction works, we will introduce a simple example, in a block world domain, where the basic components can be only bricks (of different length) and wheels (of identical size). The initial world $\mathcal{M}$, in Fig. 1(a), consists of a very schematic instance of the concept of CAR together with some disconnected elements non pertaining to the concept instance. The description of the scene is given by means of the factual knowledge $\mathcal{X}$ in Table I. Moreover, in the world $\mathcal{M}$ composite objects, consisting of chains of adjacent bricks, are defined through the theory $\mathcal{T}$.

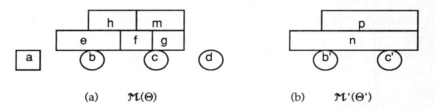

(a)    $\mathcal{M}(\Theta)$                  (b)    $\mathcal{M}'(\Theta')$

**Fig. 1** - An example of term abstraction. The object chains in the model $\mathcal{M}(\Theta)$ are merged into a single object in the abstract model $\mathcal{M}'(\Theta')$, whereas the isolated objects are deleted.

**Table I**
Axiomatization of the abstraction from
the world of Fig. 1(a) to the world of Fig. 1(b)

$\Theta = \mathcal{X} \cup \mathcal{T}$

$\mathcal{X} = \{$ brick(a), wheel(b), wheel(c), wheel(d), brick(e), brick(f), brick(g), brick(h), brick(m), on(e,b), on(g,c), on(h,e), on(h,f), on(m,f), on(m,g), adj(e,f), adj(f,g), adj(h,m) $\}$

$\mathcal{T}$ = { chain([x,y]) ← brick(x) ∧ right-most(y) ∧ brick(y) ∧ adj(x,y),
       chain([x,y]) ← brick(x) ∧ chain(y) ∧ adj(x,y) }

$T_A$ = { WHEEL(x) ↔ [wheel(x) ∧ on(y,x)] ∨ [wheel(x) ∧ on(x,y)],
       BRICK(x) ↔ [left-most(x) ∧ right-most(x) ∧ on(x,y)] ∨
             [left-most(x) ∧ right-most(x) ∧ on(y,x)] ∨ [chain(x) ∧ left-most(x)] }

$\Theta' = \mathcal{X}' = \{$ WHEEL(b'), WHEEL(c'), BRICK(p), BRICK(n) $\}$

The abstracted world $\mathcal{M}'$, reported in Fig. 1(b), is obtained by deduction through the theory $T_A$ (in Table I). It consists of a simplified scene where the boundaries between bricks chained togheter disappear and the isolated objects have been deleted. In Table I the predicates of the language $L$ are in lower cases whereas those in the language $L'$ are in capital letters.

## 2.2 Properties of Semantic Abstraction

Semantic Abstraction, as defined in (2.1), preserves the *more-general-than* relation between formulas. This is an essential property in the task of learning concept descriptions, because guarantees that concept descriptions learned on an abstract model are still consistent in the ground model and viceversa. In order to verify this property we need to define what we mean by *more-general-than* relation.

Generalization can be defined either in an extensional (in the sense of set inclusion) or in an intensional way. We use the intensional definition and restrict ourself to define it only between Horn clauses sharing the head; this is because we are interested in comparing in generality only descriptions of the same concept. Let $\gamma_1: \xi \leftarrow \varphi$ and $\gamma_2: \xi \leftarrow \psi$ be two clauses belonging to $L$. Then, $\gamma_2$ will be said *more-general-than* $\gamma_1$ (denoted by $\gamma_1 |< \gamma_2$ or $\varphi |< \psi$)) iff either $\psi$ can be derived from $\varphi$ and $\Theta$ (if $\varphi$ is not a ground clause), or $\gamma_2$ subsumes $\gamma_1$, (if $\gamma_1$ is a ground clause), i.e.: $\gamma_1 |< \gamma_2 \Leftrightarrow \Theta \vdash \{\neg\varphi, \psi\}$ or $\exists\sigma | \gamma_2 \sigma \subseteq \gamma_1$, being $\sigma$ a substitution on the terms of $\gamma_2$. This definition is a special case of Buntine's definition of generalization (Buntine, 1988).

Denoting by EXT($\varphi$) the extension of $\varphi$ on $\mathcal{M}$, namely the set of objects in the model $\mathcal{M}$ satisfying $\varphi$, the usual extensional relationship is obtained: $\varphi |< \psi \Rightarrow \text{EXT}(\varphi) \subseteq \text{EXT}(\psi)$. Then, moving from one clause to a more general one, the corresponding extension usually increases. However, it is easy to prove that the semantic abstraction preserves the relation "$|<$". In other words, semantic abstraction preserves implication and then also *more-general-than* relation, according to the given definition.

## 3. Completeness Preserving Abstraction

In general, computing semantic abstraction is a semi-decidable problem and it is practically intractable also in many cases where it is decidable. Then, we need to restrict the types of abstraction theories to be used in practice. We will focus our attention toward a form of abstraction which we call *Completeness Preserving Abstractions* (CP-abstraction), which is particularly relevant to the task of learning concept descriptions and that in many practical cases is tractable. CP-abstraction preserves the correspondence between equivalence relations; in particular, given an axiom of the type $\varphi \leftrightarrow \psi$, a CP-abstraction generates, in the abstract world, at least one axiom of the type $\varphi' \leftrightarrow \psi'$, being $\varphi'$ an abstraction of $\varphi$ and $\psi'$ an abstraction of $\psi$. It follows that, given a concept description obtained by Explanation-Based Generalization (Mitchell, Keller & Kedar-Cabelli, 1986) in the ground world, there exists a corresponding description in the abstract world.

Given a theory $T$ in the ground world and an abstraction theory $T_A$, the existence of a CP-abstraction depends exclusively upon $T$ and $T_A$. In the following an algorithm is described for computing a CP-abstraction of $T$, provided that $T_A$ be completeness-preserving with respect to $T$. The same algorithm can be used to decide whether $T_A$ is completeness-preserving (w.r.t. $T$) or not.

Before introducing the formal algorithm we will illustrate CP-abstraction through an example. The theory $\mathcal{T}$ in the example of Table I in Section 2 can be put in the form:

$\mathcal{T}$: {chain(z) ↔ [brick(x) ∧ right-most(y) ∧ brick(y) ∧ adj(x,y) ∧ z = [x y]] ∨

[brick(x) ∧ chain(y) ∧ adj(x,y) ∧ z = [x y]]}    (3.1)

according to (Clark, 1978), by making the closed world assumption (Reiter, 1978).

Consider, moreover, the abstraction theory:

$T_A$: {CHAIN(x) ↔ chain(x), R-BRICK(x) ↔ right-most(x) ∧ brick(x),

C-BRICK(x,y) ↔ brick(x) ∧ adj(x,y)}

It is easy to verify that from $\mathcal{T}$ and $T_A$ the sentence:

CHAIN(z) ↔ [C-BRICK(x,y) ∧ R-BRICK(y) ∧ z = [x y]] ∨

[ C-BRICK(x,y) ∧ CHAIN(y) ∧ z = [x,y]]    (3.2)

stating a recursive definition of the predicate CHAIN(x) in the abstract world, can be derived. The abstraction (3.2) is completeness preserving with respect to $\mathcal{T}$ because a complete definition of the predicate CHAIN(x) in terms of the predicates C-BRICK(x,y) and R-BRICK(y) has been obtained, as well as, in the ground world, the predicate chain(x) was completely defined in terms of the predicates brick(x), adj(x,y) and right-most(x). On the contrary, if we consider another theory $T_A'$ of the form:

$T_A'$: {CHAIN(x) ↔ chain(x), R-BRICK(x) ↔ right-most(x) ∧ brick(x) ∧ small(x),

C-BRICK(x,y) ↔ brick(x) ∧ adj(x,y)}

where the predicate small(x) has been added to the second axiom, from $\mathcal{T}$ and $T_A'$ we will derive the sentence:

CHAIN([x,y]) ← C-BRICK(x,y) ∧ R-BRICK(y) ∨ C-BRICK(x,y) ∧ CHAIN(y)

where the bi-implication is no more true. In fact, the extension of CHAIN(x) can be deduced (in the abstract world) only for the chains beginning with a small brick. The others chains are also present in the abstract world as ground assertions, abstracted through the first axiom in $T_A'$, but the possibility of deducing them has been lost.

Given a Horn clause theory $\mathcal{T}$ and an abstraction theory $T_A$, we will state the inference rules for computing CP-abstraction for the axioms in $\mathcal{T}$ when it is possible. As it appears from the examples given above, the semantic abstraction basically consists in applying the absorption rule, but with a substantial difference with respect to previous works (Muggleton & Buntine, 1988) where generalization is performed. As abstraction is non-generalizing, the absorption must be properly restricted in order to avoid generalization.

The algorithm we describe makes use of absorption and works on equivalence relations of the type (3.1) where the functors appear only in equality relations; the axioms of a Horn theory can always be transformed in this way (Clark, 1978). Moreover, it is supposed that before applying abstraction some deduction steps have beee performed on the axiom to abstract and on the abstraction theory in order to have the rhs of the axioms expressed with of a common set of predicates such that absorption can be applied, when is possible, without further deduction. This point is a crucial one because of the possible intractability. As the deduction occurs only through theories $\mathcal{T}$ and $T_A$, which, in general, consist of universal assertions, this risk results quite reduced in practice.

We will now define the rule for deriving semantic abstraction and then we will restrict it in order to obtain CP-abstractions.

Let $\mathbf{A}$: $[R(\bar{x}) \leftrightarrow \mathbf{D}_1 \vee \mathbf{D}_2 \vee ... \vee \mathbf{D}_n]$ and $\mathbf{B}$: $[P(\bar{y}) \leftrightarrow \mathbf{C}_1 \vee \mathbf{C}_2 \vee ... \vee \mathbf{C}_m]$ be two axioms in $\mathbf{T} \cup T_A$, being the $\mathbf{C}_i$'s and $\mathbf{D}_j$'s conjunctions of atomic formulae and equality relations. If, for a disjunct $\mathbf{C}_i$ of the definition of P there exists a corresponding disjunct $\mathbf{D}_j$ of the definition of R such that:

$$\mathbf{C}_i = \alpha_i \wedge \beta_i, \quad \mathbf{D}_j = \alpha_j \wedge \varphi, \quad \alpha_i \sigma = \alpha_j \tag{3.3}$$

being, $\sigma$ a unifier, restricted to be a consistent renomination of variables (i.e. such that it doesn't rename different variables with the same name), $\varphi$ a conjunction where the variables occurring in $\alpha_j$ but not in $P(\bar{y})$ $\sigma \wedge \xi_i \sigma$ must not appear neither in $\varphi$ nor in $R(\bar{x})$ and $\xi_i$ represents the set of equality relations of $\mathbf{C}_i$, then the new disjunct $\mathbf{D}_j' = \varphi \wedge P(\bar{y}) \sigma \wedge \xi_i \sigma$ represents the usual absorption as it could be applied between the clauses $R(\bar{x}) \leftarrow \mathbf{D}_j$ and $P(\bar{y}) \leftarrow \mathbf{C}_i$. If for all the $\mathbf{C}_i$ in $\mathbf{B}$ there exist a corresponding disjunct $\mathbf{D}_j$ in $\mathbf{A}$ satisfying the relation (3.3) with the same unifier $\sigma$ and the same conjunction $\varphi$, the sentence $\mathbf{A}'$: $[R(\bar{x}) \leftarrow \mathbf{D}_1' \vee \mathbf{D}_2' \vee ... \vee \mathbf{D}_n']$, obtained by applying the absorption rule simultaneously on all the disjunct in $\mathbf{A}$, will be called the $(\sigma\varphi)$-abstraction $\mathcal{A}_{(\sigma\varphi)}(\mathbf{A},\mathbf{B})$ of $\mathbf{A}$ through $\mathbf{B}$.

An abstraction $\mathcal{A}_{(\sigma\varphi)}(\mathbf{A},\mathbf{B}) = \mathbf{A}'$ is a Completeness Preserving Abstraction $CPA_{(\sigma\varphi)}(\mathbf{A},\mathbf{B})$ and can be written as $\mathbf{A}'$: $[R(\bar{x}) \leftrightarrow \mathbf{D}_1' \vee \mathbf{D}_2' \vee ... \vee \mathbf{D}_n']$ if for every pair of disjuncts $[\mathbf{C}_i, \mathbf{D}_j]$ selected for the abstraction $\beta_i \sigma$ subsumes $\alpha_i \sigma$ (Buntine, 1988).

Completeness-Preserving abstractions, can be obtained by applying CPA-transformations, iteratively. In the Next section, the behaviour of an abstraction algorithm, based on CPA-transformation, is illustrated in a block world domain.

Finally, it is worth noting that, given the two sets of axioms $\mathbf{T}$ and $T_A$, if $\mathbf{T} \vdash \{\varphi \rightarrow h\}$ and $\{\varphi' \rightarrow h\}$ is a CP-abstraction of $\varphi \rightarrow h$ through $T_A$, the extension on the ground world of $\varphi$ must be equal to the extension of $\varphi'$ in the abstract world. This guarantees that, if we obtain a theory $\mathbf{T}'$ by applying a CP-abstraction to a domain theory $\mathbf{T}$, all the concept descriptions, obtainable by EBG in the basic world, will have at least a correspondent one in the abstract world.

## 4. An Example of CP-abstraction in the Block World

In order to illustrate how the abstraction procedure, described in Section 3, works, we will consider a simple example in the block world domain. Suppose that the basic world be a block world, where the basic components can be only bricks (of different length) and wheels (of identical size). Using this basic components, it is possible to build up simplified models of objects of the real world, such as cars, arches and so on.

We selected four classes of concepts, namely: CAR, TREE, ARCH and TRAILER; some possible instances of them are shown in Fig. 2. Moreover, a theory T describing the given concepts in term of complex features, such as brick-stack and brick-chain, defined recursively, is given in Table II. It easy to verify that the instances described in Fig. 2 satisfy the definitions in Table II.

Finally, an abstraction theory $T_A$, reported in Table III has been supplied, defining intermediate level concepts such as car-body, trailer-body, pillar and so on. By abstracting the theory of Table I through the theory of Table III by means of the algorithm CP-abstraction, we will obtain the abstracted domain theory reported in Table IV.

## Table II

Theory defining the concepts of CAR, TREE, ARCH and TRAILER. The predicates immediately verifiable in the basic world, two composition functions and a set of axioms defining the concepts, are reported.

### Predicates of the initial world

| | | |
|---|---|---|
| obj(x) | = | x is an object |
| brick (x) | = | object x is a brick; |
| wheel(x) | = | object x is a wheel; |
| l-brick(x) | = | object x is a long brick; |
| s-brick(x) | = | object x is a short brick; |
| m-brick(x) | = | object x is a medium-length brick; |
| onground(x) | = | object x is at ground level; |
| overlaps(x1,x2) | = | there is at least one point P in the object x1, such that the perpendicular from P to the ground intersects object x2; |
| touch(x1,x2) | = | object x1 shares at least one point with x2; |
| higher(x1,x2) | = | the center of gravity of x1 is higher than that of x2; |
| adj(x1,x2) | = | the object x1 touches x2 on the right of x1; |
| sep-bottom(x1,x2) | = | objects x1 and x2 do not overlap and to not touch themselves; |
| m-brick-bottom(x) | = | object x is a medium-lenght brick or it is a compound object whose bottomless component is a medium-length brick. |

### Composition Functions

stack (x1,x2) = creates a new object by stacking x1 on x2 when x1 is on the top of x2;
chain (x1,x2) = creates a new object by concatenating x1 and x2 when x1 is adj to x2.

### Domain Theory

brick-stack(x) $\leftrightarrow$ [brick(x)] $\lor$ [x=*stack(y,z)* $\land$ brick(y) $\land$ brick-stack(z) $\land$ touch(y,z) $\land$ overlaps(y,z)]

brick-chain(x) $\leftrightarrow$ [brick(x)] $\lor$ [x=*chain(y,z)* $\land$ brick(y) $\land$ brick-chain(z) $\land$ adj(y,z)]

car $\leftrightarrow$ [l-brick(x) $\land$ wheel(y) $\land$ wheel(z) $\land$ onground(y) $\land$ onground(z) $\land$ touch(x,y) $\land$ overlaps(x,y) $\land$ touch(x,z) $\land$ overlaps(x,z) $\land$ obj(w) $\land$ touch(w,x) $\land$ overlaps(w,x) ]

arch $\leftrightarrow$ [brick-stack(x) $\land$ brick-stack(y) $\land$ m-brick-bottom(x) $\land$ m-brick-bottom(y) $\land$ onground(x) $\land$ onground(y) $\land$ sep-bottom(x,y) $\land$ brick-chain(z) $\land$ touch(z,x) $\land$ overlaps(z,x) $\land$ touch(z,y) $\land$ overlaps(z,y)]

tree $\leftrightarrow$ [s-brick(x) $\land$ s-brick(y) $\land$ onground(x) $\land$ touch(y,x) $\land$ overlaps(y,x) $\land$ brick-stack(z) $\land$ touch(z,y) $\land$ overlaps(z,y)]

trailer $\leftrightarrow$ [l-brick(x) $\land$ wheel(y) $\land$ onground(y) $\land$ s-brick(z) $\land$ onground(z) $\land$ touch(x,y) $\land$ overlaps(x,y) $\land$ touch(x,z) $\land$ overlaps(x,z) $\land$ obj(w) $\land$ touch(w,x) $\land$ overlaps(w,x)]

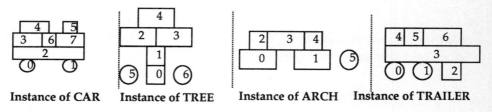

Instance of CAR    Instance of TREE    Instance of ARCH    Instance of TRAILER

**Fig.2** - Instances of car, trees, arches and trailers in the block world.

## Table III
### Example of Completeness- Preserving Abstraction Theory

### Predicates of the abstract world

| | | |
|---|---|---|
| obj(x) | = | x is an object ; |
| brick (x) | = | object x is a brick; |
| adj(x1,x2) | = | the object x1 touches x2 on the right of x1; |
| sep-bottom(x1,x2) | = | objects x1 and x2 do not overlap and to not touch themselves; |
| m-brick-bottom(x) | = | object x is a medium-lenght brick or it is a compound object which bottomless component is a medium-length brick; |
| ontop(x1,x2) | = | the object x1 lies on the top of the object x2; |
| useful-wheel(x) | = | object x is a wheel that lies on the ground; |
| car-body(x) | = | the object x is a body of a car; |
| trailer-body(x) | = | the object x is a body of a trailer; |
| trunk(x) | = | the object x is a part of a trunk ; |
| pillar(x) | = | the object x is a pillar. |

### Composition Functions

| | | |
|---|---|---|
| stack (x1,x2) = | | creates a new object by stacking x1 on x2 when x1 is on the top of x2; |
| chain (x1,x2) = | | creates a new object by concatenating x1 and x2 when x1 is adj to x2. |

### Axioms

ontop(x,y) $\leftrightarrow$ [touch(x,y) $\land$ overlaps(x,y)]

useful-wheel(x) $\leftrightarrow$ [wheel(x) $\land$ onground(x)]

car-body(x) $\leftrightarrow$ [useful-wheel(y) $\land$ useful-wheel(z) $\land$ l-brick(x) $\land$ ontop(x,y) $\land$ ontop(x,z)]

trailer-body(x) $\leftrightarrow$ [useful-wheel(y) $\land$ s-brick(z) $\land$ onground(z) $\land$ l-brick(x) $\land$ ontop(x,y) $\land$ ontop(x,z)]

trunk(x) $\leftrightarrow$ [s-brick(x) $\land$ s-brick(y) $\land$ onground(y) $\land$ ontop(x,y)]

pillar(x) $\leftrightarrow$ [brick-stack(x) $\land$ m-brick-bottom(x) $\land$ onground(x)]

## Table IV
### Abstracted Domain Theory

| | | |
|---|---|---|
| brick-stack(x) | $\leftrightarrow$ | [brick(x)] $\lor$ [x=*stack(y,z)* $\land$ brick(y) $\land$ brick-stack(z) $\land$ ontop(y,z)] |
| brick-chain(x) | $\leftrightarrow$ | [brick(x)] $\lor$ [x=*chain(y,z)* $\land$ brick(y) $\land$ brick-chain(z) $\land$ adj(y,z)] |
| car | $\leftrightarrow$ | [car-body(x) $\land$ obj(w) $\land$ ontop(w,x) ] |
| arch | $\leftrightarrow$ | [pillar(x) $\land$ pillar(y) $\land$ sep-bottom(x,y) $\land$ brick-chain(z) $\land$ ontop(z,x) $\land$ ontop(z,y)] |
| tree | $\leftrightarrow$ | [trunk(x) $\land$ brick-stack(z) $\land$ ontop(z,x)] |
| trailer | $\leftrightarrow$ | [trailer-body(x) $\land$ obj(w) $\land$ ontop(w,x)] |

In the following, the way the algorithm CP-Abstract-Axioms works, when applied to the axioms defining the concept TREE, is illustrated step-by-step.

**Inputs to the algorithm**

**A**: tree ↔ [s-brick(x) ∧ s-brick(y) ∧ onground(x) ∧ touch(y,x) ∧ overlaps(y,x) ∧ brick-stack(z) ∧
  touch(z,y) ∧ overlaps(z,y)]

**B**1: ontop(x1,y1) ↔ [touch(x1,y1) ∧ overlaps(x1,y1)]

**B**2: useful-wheel(x2) ↔ [wheel(x2) ∧ onground(x2)]

**B**3: car-body(x3) ↔ [useful-wheel(y3) ∧ useful-wheel(z3) ∧ l-brick(x3) ∧ ontop(x3,y3) ∧ ontop(x3,z3)]

**B**4: trailer-body(x4) ↔ [useful-wheel(y4) ∧ s-brick(z4) ∧ onground(z4) ∧
  l-brick(x4) ∧ ontop(x4,y4) ∧ ontop(x4,z4)]

**B**5: trunk(x5) ↔ [s-brick(x5) ∧ s-brick(y5) ∧ onground(y5) ∧ ontop(x5,y5)]

**B**6: pillar(x6) ↔ [brick-stack(x6) ∧ m-brick-bottom(x6) ∧ onground(x6)]

**Deduction steps performed by applying CPA-transformation.**

σ1 = [y/x1, x/y1]    φ1=s-brick(x)∧s-brick(y)∧onground(x)∧ brick-stack(z)∧touch(z,y) ∧ overlaps(z,y)
**A**1: tree ↔ [s-brick(x)∧s-brick(y)∧onground(x)∧ontop(y,x)∧brick-stack(z)∧ touch(z,y)∧ overlaps(z,y)]

σ2 = [z/x1, y/y1]     φ2 = s-brick(x)∧s-brick(y)∧onground(x)∧touch(y,x)∧overlaps(y,x)∧brick-stack(z)
**A**2: tree ↔ [s-brick(x)∧s-brick(y)∧onground(x)∧touch(y,x)∧overlaps(y,x) ∧ brick-stack(z) ∧ ontop(z,y)]

σ3 = [z/x1, y/y1]    φ3 = s-brick(x) ∧ s-brick(y) ∧ onground(x) ∧ ontop(y,x) ∧ brick-stack(z)
**A**3: tree ↔ [s-brick(x) ∧ s-brick(y) ∧ onground(x) ∧ ontop(y,x) ∧ brick-stack(z)∧ ontop(z,y)]

σ4 = [y/x1, x/y1]    φ4 = s-brick(x) ∧ s-brick(y) ∧ onground(x) ∧ brick-stack(z) ∧ ontop(z,y)
**A**4: tree ↔ [s-brick(x) ∧ s-brick(y) ∧ onground(x) ∧ ontop(y,x) ∧ brick-stack(z)∧ ontop(z,y)]

σ5 = [y/x5]    φ5 = brick-stack(z) ∧ touch(z,y) ∧ overlaps(z,y)
**A**5 =   tree ↔ (∃ y,z)[trunk(y) ∧ brick-stack(z) ∧ touch(z,y) ∧ overlaps(z,y)]

σ6 = [y/x5]    φ6 = brick-stack(z) ∧ ontop(z,y)
**A**6: tree ↔ [trunk(y) ∧ brick-stack(z) ∧ ontop(z,y)]

# 5. Conclusions

In this paper, we emphasize the benefits obtainable from an approach to learning based on the the idea of abstraction. A formal definition of abstraction is given, the abstraction mechanism is axiomatized by means of a theory and the abstraction itself can be obtained by deduction.

In the past, we have already shown how this mechanism for computing abstraction can be applied in order to improve the results of an induction algorithm. Here we investigated the possibility of abstracting also a domain theory and, in particular, we proposed an algorithm for computing completeness-preserving abstractions. This form of abstraction is very useful in learning, because it preserves the possibility of obtaining a complete concept description by EBG, in the abstract world.

12

However, the potential utility of this type of abstraction and of the algorithm we propose, can go far beyond this aspect. More in general, CP-abstraction can preserve universal properties stated through a set of axioms $\mathcal{T}$. On the other hand the algorithm described in Section 3 can be seen both as a tool for computing CP-abstraction and as a tool for deciding whether an abstraction theory is Completeness-Preserving or not with respect to $\mathcal{T}$. Now, one of the most interesting problem involving abstraction in machine learning is that of generating automatically an abstraction theory. This is the subject investigated, for instance, by Knoblock and most of the work developed in constructive learning can be cast into this framework. Therefore, the possibility of checking the Completeness-Preserving property of an abstraction theory with respect to a theory $\mathcal{T}$ can prove a good mechanism for filtering the abstraction theories, generated by same oracle, by asking that the corresponding abstract world mantain the universal properties stated by $\mathcal{T}$. The proposed algorithm seems fast enough to be applied, in practical applications, to this purpose.

# References

Amsterdam J. Some Philosophical Problems with Formal Learning Theories. In *Proc. AAAI-88*, pp. 580-584, 1989

Bergadano F., Giordana, G. & Saitta L. (1988). Automated Concept Acquisition in Noisy Environments. *IEEE Trans. on Pattern Analysis and Machine Intelligence*, 10, 555-578, 1988.

Buntine W. Generalized Subsumption and its Applications to Induction and Redundancy. *Artificial Intelligence*, 36, 149-176, 1988.

Carbonell J. (Ed). *Artificial Intelligence*. Special Issue on Machine Learning, 40, 1989.

Clark K.L. Negation as failure. In Gallaire H. and Minker J. (Eds) *Logic and Databases*, Plenum Press, New York, pp. 293-372, 1978.

Dejong G. & Mooney R. Explanation-Based Learning: An Alternative View.*Machine Learning*, 1, 145-176, 1986.

Drastal G., Czako G. & Raatz S. Induction in an Abstraction Space. *Proc. IJCAI-89*, Detroit, MI, pp. 708-712, 1989.

Giordana A., Roverso D. & Saitta L. Abstraction: An Alternative Approach to Concept Acquisition. *In Proceedings of ISMIS-90* , pp. 379-387, Knoxville, TN, 1990.

Giordana A. & Saitta L. Abstraction: A General Framework for Learning. In *Proceedings of AAAI Workshop on Automatic Generation of Abstraction and Approximation* , pp. 245-256, Boston, MA,1990

Iba W.,Wogulis J. & Langley P. Trading-off Simplicity and Coverage in Incremental Concept Learning. *Proc. 5th Int. Conf. on Machine Learning*, Ann Arbor, MI, pp. 73-79, 1988.

Knoblock C. A Theory of Abstraction for Hierachical Planning. in D.P. Benjamin (Ed.), *Change of Representation and Inductive Bias*, Kluwer Publ. Co., Boston, MA, 1989a.

Knoblock C. Learning Hierarchies of Abstraction Spaces. *Proc. 6th Int. Workshop on Machine Learning* Ithaca, NY, 1989b.

Matheus C. & Rendell L. Constructive Induction in Decision Trees. In *Proc. IJCAI-89*, Detroit, MI, pp. 645-650, 1989.

Michalski R. A Theory and Methodology of Inductive Learning. In Michalski R., Mitchell T. & Carbonell J.(Eds), pp. 83-134, Morgan Kaufmann, Palo Alto, CA, 1983.

Michalski R., Carbonell J. & Mitchell T.(Eds). *Machine Learning: An AI Approach, Vol. I*. Morgan Kaufmann, Los Altos, CA, 1983.

Michalski R., Carbonell J. & Mitchell T.(Eds). *Machine Learning: An AI Approach, Vol. II*. Morgan Kaufmann, Los Altos, CA, 1985.

Michalski R. & Kodratoff Y. (Eds). *Machine Learning: an Artificial Intelligence Approach, Vol. III*. Morgan Kaufmann, Los Altos, CA, 1990.

Mitchell T. Generalization as Search. *Artificial Intelligence*, 18, 203-226, 1982.

Mitchell T., Keller R.M. & Kedar-Cabelli S. Explanation based generalization: A unifying view. *Machine Learning*, 1, 47-80, 1986.

Muggleton S. & Buntine W. *Machine Invention of First-order Predicates by Inverting Resolution*. In Proc. Fifth International Conference on Machine Learning, Ann Arbor, MI, pp.339-352, 1988.

Newell A., Simon H. *Human Problem Solving*. Prentice-Hall (Eds), Englewood Cliffs, NJ, 1972.

Pearl J. On the Connection between the Complexity and Credibility of Inferred Models. *Int. J. of General Systems*, 4, 255-264, 1978.

Plaisted D. Theorem Proving with Abstraction. *Artificial Intelligence*, 16, 47-108, 1981.

Reiter R. On Closed World Databases. In Gallaire H. and Minker J. (Eds) *Logic and Databases*, Plenum Press, New York, pp. 55-76, 1978.

Tenenberg J. Preserving Consistency across Abstraction Mappings. *Proc IJCAI-87*, pp. 1011-1014, Milano, Italy, 1987.

Utgoff P. Shift of Bias in Inductive Concept Learning. In R. S. Michalski, J. Carbonell, and T. Mitchell (Eds) *Machine Learning, An Artificial Intelligence Approach, Vol. II*, Morgan Kaufmann, Los Altos, CA, pp. 107-148, 1985.

Van de Velde W. Representation Issues in Second Generation Expert Systems. In K. Morik (Ed), *Knowledge Representation and Organization in Machine Learning*, Lecture Notes in Artificial Intelligence, Vol. 347, Springer-Verlag, pp. 17-49, 1989.

Watanabe S. *Knowing and Guessing, A formal and Quantitative Study*. Wiley Publ. Co, 1969.

# A MULTISTRATEGY LEARNING APPROACH TO DOMAIN MODELING AND KNOWLEDGE ACQUISITION

Gheorghe Tecuci*

Center for Artificial Intelligence, Department of Computer Science, George Mason University,
4400 University Drive, Fairfax, VA 22030, USA. Email: tecuci@gmuvax2.gmu.edu

**Abstract**

This paper presents an approach to domain modeling and knowledge acquisition that consists of a gradual and goal-driven improvement of an incomplete domain model provided by a human expert. Our approach is based on a multistrategy learning method that allows a system with incomplete knowledge to learn general inference or problem solving rules from specific facts or problem solving episodes received from the human expert. The system will learn the general knowledge pieces by considering all their possible instances in the current domain model, trying to learn complete and consistent descriptions. Because of the incompleteness of the domain model the learned rules will have exceptions that are eliminated by refining the definitions of the existing concepts or by defining new concepts.

**Keywords:** domain modeling, knowledge acquisition, multistrategy learning, rule and concept learning

## 1. Motivation and related work

The behavior of an expert system is based on an internal model of a real world domain. The model is composed of representations of different entities from the real world, as well as of procedures for manipulating these representations. In order to solve a real world problem, the user has to represent it into the language of the domain model. Then the system will look for a solution by using the model and will show the found solution to the user which will interpret it in the real world. The better this model approximates the real world domain, the more adequate is the system's behavior. Traditionally, such a domain model is built by the knowledge engineer and the human expert. With few exceptions (Morik, 1989), the current knowledge acquisition tools support the modeling task only by helping the human expert to express his knowledge (Boose, Gains and Ganascia, 1989). The built domain model is often

---

*On leave from Research Institute for Informatics, Bucharest, Romania

only a crude approximation of the represented domain: it incorporates defaults, omits details, and abstracts the represented entities. The causes for this situation are multiple: the representation language is inherently imprecise, the information from the human expert is incomplete, the represented domain has not a well defined theory (Bhatnagar and Kanal, 1986). To cope with these problems, the human expert is often asked to express his knowledge in the form of uncertain knowledge pieces, for instance, in the form of uncertain rules characterized by certainty factors which are more or less justified. This, however, results in a degradation of the knowledge provided by the human expert because he is asked questions to which he does not know precise answers. Moreover, because the resulting expert system lacks the capability of self-improving its knowledge through experience, the domain model has to be, from the very beginning, complete enough and correct enough for determining reasonable functioning of the system. All of these make the current approaches to building expert systems complex, time-consuming and error-prone.

We believe that the methods and the techniques developed in the field of machine learning (e.g., Michalski, Carbonell and Mitchell, 1983, 1986; Segre, 1989; Kodratoff and Michalski, 1990; Porter and Mooney, 1990) are applicable for partially automating the domain modeling and knowledge acquisition process (Morik, 1989; Wrobel, 1989). For instance, by using empirical induction, a system can learn general concepts or rules characterizing a set of examples. By applying analogical learning, a system may acquire knowledge about an unknown entity by transferring and modifying prior knowledge about a similar entity. By using explanation-based learning, a system may transform inefficient knowledge into efficient rules or concepts. Until now, however, these single-strategy learning methods did not have a significant impact on the field of knowledge acquisition because each strategy requires specific conditions in order to be applicable. For instance, empirical learning typically needs many input examples, though it does not need much background knowledge. Explanation-based learning needs only one example, but requires complete background knowledge. Learning by analogy needs background knowledge analogous with the input. Real-world applications rarely satisfy the requirements of single-strategy learning methods. This explains an increasing interest in building systems that integrate different learning strategies (e.g., Lebowitz, 1986; Wilkins et al., 1986; Tecuci et al., 1987; Minton et al., 1987; Danyluk, 1987; Pazzani, 1988; Dietterich and Flann, 1988).

In this paper we propose an approach to domain modeling and knowledge acquisition based on a synergistic integration of different learning strategies: explanation-based learning, learning by analogy, empirical inductive learning, learning by asking questions and by being told, abduction and conceptual clustering.

## 2. Toward a methodology for domain modeling and knowledge acquisition

One may distinguish two phases in the development of a domain model. The first one consists of defining a suitable framework for modeling the domain, by choosing a knowledge representation formalism and an associated problem solving method. The second one consists of effectively building the model by representing the entities of the application domain, in the defined framework.

An expert system shell, like EMYCIN (van Melle et al., 1981) for instance, is a framework for representing diagnostic models. Research in expert systems has elaborated different frameworks for different expertise domains like planning, design, diagnosis, monitoring, prediction, interpretation, and expert system shells for such expertise domains have been built.

Choosing (or building) a suitable expert system shell solves the first part of building the model of an application domain. Effectively building the model with the expert system shell represents the second and the much more difficult part of modeling.

The methodology we are presenting is concerned with the automation of the second part of modeling. This methodology is a development of our previous work on learning expert knowledge (Tecuci, 1988; Tecuci and Kodratoff, 1990) and is experimentally implemented in a learning system that may be associated with an expert system shell. The goal of the learning system is to learn directly from the human expert. In other words, the traditional role of the knowledge engineer is taken by the system itself that is building and improving the domain model through successive interactions with the expert. A direct consequence of this goal is that the interaction with the human expert should be as natural for the human expert as possible. A human expert may provide an elementary description of his domain. He is particularly good at providing solutions to problems and to judge if a solution to a problem is good or not. He is less good at providing explanations of why the solutions are good or not but can easily accept or reject tentative explanations. What is particularly difficult for the human expert is to provide general pieces of information as, for instance, general problem solving rules. It is, therefore, the task of the learner to learn such general pieces of information and to iteratively develop and update the world model. Such an update is done through an interaction with the expert in which the expert is asked only the types of questions he is expected to answer correctly.

The scenario for building the domain model is the following one. First, the human expert will define (within the chosen framework) an initial model of his domain. Because he is requested to define only that knowledge which he may easily express, we assume that this initial world model is incomplete. In general, it will consist of incomplete descriptions of some basic object concepts from the domain to be modeled, object concepts that define an initial language for representing new object concepts, facts, rules etc. This initial model will allow the system to learn new knowledge from the expert and thus to develop its model. The validity of the learned knowledge strongly depends of the validity of the initial knowledge. Therefore it is preferable to start with few and valid knowledge than to start with much and imperfect knowledge.

Once an initial model has been defined, the system may react to new inputs from the expert (or, in general, from the real world) with the goal of developing and updating the model so that to become consistent with the inputs. Whenever the system receives an input, it will try to understand and assimilate it into the world model. For instance, if the input is a new fact, the system will try to justify that it is a consequence of the knowledge explicitly represented into the model. To this purpose, it may need to update the model (by abducting new facts or rules, or by explicitly storing the input). Based on the understanding of the input fact, the system may learn a general inference rule allowing the direct derivation of the input (as well as of other related facts). If the input is a problem solving episode, then the system will try to explain to itself the validity of this episode (by building a proof or at least a justification of it) and based on this understanding it may learn a general problem solving rule. If the input consists of several examples of a concept, the system will try to understand the commonalties of these examples in the context of its background knowledge, thus learning the definition of the concept. In order to improve the consistency of the domain model, the system will learn the general knowledge pieces by considering all their possible instances in the current domain model, trying to learn complete and consistent descriptions. However, because of the incompleteness of the domain model (that, for instance, does not contain some necessary concepts), the learned rules will have exceptions. For instance, they may cover invalid problem solving episodes. Therefore, in order to eliminate the exceptions of the learned rules, new concepts have to be defined, or the definitions of the existing concepts have to be refined. In this way, the domain model is iteratively developed in a goal-driven manner.

The next sections illustrate this methodology with a very simple example from robotics.

## 3. Modeling the world of a simple robot

We shall briefly illustrate the model building methodology with a very simple example of a robot able to perform simple domestic tasks. The robot receives commands from its master and executes them. A command is executed by performing a single robot action or a sequence of such actions.

### 3.1 The framework for the domain model

One may model the world of such a robot in terms of object-concepts, states, action-concepts, and problem solving rules.

An object-concept represents a set of objects having similar properties and relations to other object-concepts. The object-concepts may be of different degrees of generality.

An instance of an object-concept represents a specific object from the real world, together with its properties and relations to other objects. One may assimilate an instance with a very specific concept representing only one element.

A specification of all the objects in the world, together with their current properties and relations, represents the current state of the world.

The action-concepts are representations of the actions by which the robot can change the state of the real world. Such an action-concept is represented by the following elements:
- the name of the action and the object-concepts that may have certain roles in the action (the object on which the action is performed, the instrument used, etc.);
- the preconditions: the set of states in which the action may be applied;
- the effects: the state resulted after the execution of the action.

We distinguish between elementary actions and complex actions. An elementary action is directly executable by the robot. A complex action is one that is executed by a sequence of elementary actions.

A problem solving rule is a kind of schemata that indicates a decomposition of a complex action into simpler actions.

The robot receives commands for executing actions. If such an action is an elementary one then the robot is executing it. If the action is a complex one, then the robot has to first decompose it into a sequence of elementary actions.

All these elements constitute the framework for representing the model of the robot world. To build the model, one has to effectively define the object-concepts, the action-concepts, and the problem solving rules.

In the following sections we shall show how such a model is incrementally developed by the human trainer and the learning system.

## 3.2 Providing an initial domain model

First, the human expert defines the initial model of the domain. This model may be, for instance, the one represented in figure 1.

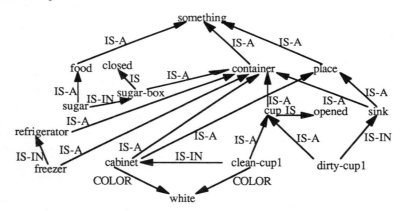

Figure 1. The initial domain model.

This initial model is composed of incomplete descriptions of concepts representing some of the objects from the robot world.

## 3.3 Incremental development of the model

Once the expert has provided the system with an initial model, he will start teaching it to solve problems by presenting examples of problem solving episodes like the one in figure 2. From such a problem solving episode the system will try to learn a general problem solving rule of the form presented in figure 3.

**Example1:**

| | |
|---|---|
| *The problem* | ; to take clean-cup1 |
|         TAKE clean-cup1 | ; the robot has to |
| *has the solution* | ; open the cabinet |
|         OPEN cabinet | ; and to take the cup |
|         TAKE clean-cup1 FROM cabinet | ; from it |

Figure 2. An example of problem solving episode.

| | |
|---|---|
| IF | ; If x and y are two |
|         x and y satisfy certain constraints | ; objects satisfying |
| THEN | ; certain constraints |
| *the problem* | ; then to TAKE x |
|         TAKE x | ; the robot has to |
| *has the solution* | ; OPEN y and to |
|         OPEN y | ; TAKE x FROM y |
|         TAKE x FROM y | |

Figure 3. The general rule to be learned from **Example 1**.

As a by-product of learning such a rule the domain model may be improved by:
- completing the definitions of the object-concepts that cover positive or negative instances of the rule's variables (as shown in section 3.5.1);
- defining new object-concepts that cover positive instances of the rule's variables (as shown in section 3.5.2);
- improving the models of the actions from the rule (as shown in section 3.6).

Therefore, rule learning is in fact an opportunity for a goal-driven improvement of the domain model.


## 3.4 Learning problem solving rules

Table 1 presents the method of learning a general problem solving rule starting from one example. A detailed description of this learning method is given in (Tecuci and Kodratoff, 1990). Therefore here we shall only briefly illustrate it.

As mentioned in Table 1, the learning steps depend of the system's current knowledge. In this section we shall suppose that all system's knowledge is the one from figure 1. In section 3.6, however, we shall show how learning proceeds when the domain model contains also (incomplete) descriptions of the actions "TAKE x", "OPEN y", and "TAKE x FROM y".

First the system will try to understand the problem solving episode received from the expert (Example1), where by understanding we mean proving (or at least justifying) its correctness. It uses heuristics to propose plausible pieces of explanations in terms of the features and the relationships between the objects from the problem solving episode (Tecuci and Kodratoff, 1990), pieces of explanations requiring the user's validation, as shown in figure 4.

---

Table 1. The rule learning method.

• *Find an explanation of the validity of the input*
Depending of the system's knowledge, the process of finding the explanation may involve deduction, induction and/or analogy.

• *Generalize the found explanation to an analogy criterion*
Depending of the system's knowledge, the analogy criterion is an inductive, a deductive or an inductive and deductive generalization of the explanation.

• *Use the analogy criterion to generate examples analogous with the input*
The instances of the analogy criterion in the domain model represent explanations similar with the explanation of the input. From each such explanation the system may generate a problem solving episode analogous with the input. These episodes represent positive examples (if they are correct) or negative examples (if they are not correct) of the rule to be learned.

• *Learn from the generated examples*
Learn a general rule that covers as many of the positive examples as possible and as few of the negative examples as possible.

---

*The problem solving episode is correct because:*
(clean-cup1 IS-IN cabinet) ? Yes
(clean-cup1 COLOR white) & (cabinet COLOR white) ? No

Figure 4. Finding a justification of Example1.

The found piece of explanation is (clean-cup1 IS-IN cabinet). This explanation is inductively generalized by turning all the contained objects into variables and this generalization is taken as an analogy criterion. The instances of this analogy criterion in the domain model are similar explanations that may account for problem solving episodes similar with Example1. Because analogy is a weak inference, these problem solving episodes could be, however, correct or incorrect (see figure 5). The goal of the system is to learn a general rule that covers the correct problem solving episodes and rejects the incorrect ones.

First of all, from the initial problem solving episode, its explanation and the analogy criterion, the system builds an initial version space for the rule to be learned. This version space is shown in figure 6. As may be noticed, this representation keeps all the knowledge that may be useful for learning the rule: the initial example, the explanation, and the features of the covered objects that are not relevant for the rule learning (and should not be used in the condition of the rule).

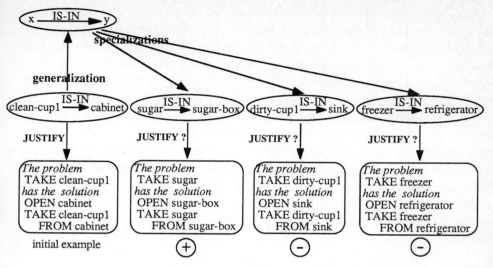

Figure 5. Generation of problem solving episodes analogous with the input one.

```
IF
        upper bound
        (x IS-A something) & (y IS-A something) & (x IS-IN y)   ; the analogy criterion
        lower bound
        (x IS-A clean-cup1) & (y IS-A cabinet) & (x IS-IN y)       ; the explanation
THEN
the problem
        TAKE x
has the solution
        OPEN y
        TAKE x FROM y
with the positive example:
        (x IS-A clean-cup1) & (y IS-A cabinet)
with the irrelevant features:
        (x COLOR z) & (y COLOR z)
```

Figure 6. The initial version space for the rule to be learned.

Next the system applies the analogy criterion to the domain model in figure 1 and generates, one after the other, the problem solving episodes from figure 5, asking the expert to validate them:

> *Let us consider the problem*
> TAKE sugar
> *Is the following a correct solution*
> OPEN sugar-box
> TAKE sugar FROM sugar-box ? <u>Yes</u>

Figure 7. A problem solving episode generated by the system.

Each such generated problem solving episode is used to shrink the version space from figure 6 (Tecuci and Kodratoff, 1990).

For each positive example there are two possible cases:
- if the current upper bound is more general than the positive example, then generalize the lower bound of the rule, as little as possible, so that to cover the example and to remain less general than the upper bound;
- if the current upper bound does not cover the positive example then keep this example as a positive exception of the rule being learned.

For each negative example the system tries to find an explanation of the failure. If such an explanation is found then it is used to particularize both bounds of the current version space for no longer covering the negative example. If no explanation is found then two cases are possible:
- if the current lower bound does not cover the negative example then particularize the upper bound as little as possible so that not to cover the negative example and to remain more general than the lower bound;
- if the current lower bound covers the negative example then keep it as a negative exception of the rule being learned.

Let us suppose that the problem solving episodes from figure 5 are generated in the order from the left to the right. The first generated problem solving episode is accepted by the user and is therefore a new positive example for the rule to be learned. Its explanation (sugar IS-IN sugar-box) is expressed in terms of the variables 'x' and 'y' as

(x IS-A sugar) & (y IS-A sugar-box) & (x IS-IN y)

and is used to generalize the lower bound in figure 6 to

*new lower bound*
(x IS-A something) & (y IS-A container) & (x IS-IN y)

The next two problem solving episodes generated by the system are rejected by the user. However, their corresponding explanations

(x IS-A dirty-cup1) & (y IS-A sink) & (x IS-IN y)

(x IS-A freezer) & (y IS-A refrigerator) & (x IS-IN y)

are covered by the *new lower bound* of the version space. Therefore these two instances represent negative exceptions for the rule being learned:

IF
    *upper bound*
    (x IS-A something) & (y IS-A something) & (x IS-IN y)
    *lower bound*
    (x IS-A something) & (y IS-A container) & (x IS-IN y)
THEN
*the problem*
    TAKE x
*has the solution*
    OPEN y
    TAKE x FROM y
*with the positive examples:*
    (x IS-A clean-cup1) & (y IS-A cabinet)
    (x IS-A sugar) & (y IS-A sugar-box)
*with the negative exceptions:*
    (x IS-A dirty-cup1) & (y IS-A sink)
    (x IS-A freezer) & (y IS-A refrigerator)
*with the irrelevant features:*
    (x COLOR z) & (y COLOR z)

Figure 8. Version space with negative exceptions.

## 3.5 Improving the domain model

The existence of the rule's exceptions is due to the incompleteness of the domain model the language of which does not contain the expression distinguishing between the positive examples and the negative examples of the rule. But this is an excellent opportunity to develop the domain model by completing the descriptions of the existing concepts or even by defining new concepts. The definition of new concepts for the elimination of the rule's exceptions was called demand-driven concept formation by (Wrobel, 1989). In the following, we shall present two methods for the elimination of the negative exceptions of the rules. In what regards the positive exceptions, they are treated as positive examples of new rules to be learned.

### 3.5.1 Turning negative exceptions into negative examples by refining the descriptions of the known concepts

A negative exception of a rule may be transformed into a negative example by identifying (or defining) a new object feature that discriminates between the positive examples and the negative exception, as it is presented in Table 2.

---

Table 2. Refining object descriptions.

• Find a feature F of an object Oij from one positive example Ej such that:
 - F may be a feature of the corresponding objects Oi1,...,Oin, from ALL the positive examples;
 - F is not a feature of the corresponding objects O'ik,...,O'il from SOME of the negative exceptions Nk,...,Nl.

• Refine the descriptions of the objects Oi1,..., Oin by adding the feature F.

• Refine the descriptions of O'ik ,..., O'il by adding the feature NOT-F.

• Particularize the lower bound of the rule by adding the feature F (which is now shared by all the current positive examples)

• Remove Nk,...,Nl from the list of negative exceptions and add them to the list of negative examples.

• Repeat this procedure as long as such features could be found or could be defined by the user.

---

Let us consider the following negative exception from the version space in figure 8

(x IS-A dirty-cup1) & (y IS-A sink)

together with the positive examples

(x IS-A clean-cup1) & (y IS-A cabinet)

(x IS-A sugar) & (y IS-A sugar-box)

To transform this negative exception into a negative example, the system may analyze all the features of clean-cup1 in order to find one that may be a feature of sugar without being a feature of dirty-cup1. Or, it may analyze all the features of sugar in order to find one that may be a feature of clean-cup1 without being a feature of dirty-cup1. It may also look for a feature of cabinet or for a feature of sugar-box that is not a feature of sink.

In the domain model from figure 1 sugar-box has the feature (sugar-box IS closed), which is not a feature of cabinet and sink. Therefore, the system makes the hypothesis

(cabinet IS closed)

NOT(sink IS closed), rewritten as (sink IS opened)

and asks the user to validate them.

Let us suppose that the user validates these hypothesis. This means that (y IS closed) is a feature that discriminates between the known positive examples and the analyzed negative exception. By introducing the discriminating feature into the rule's conditions, the considered negative exception becomes a negative example (see figure 13).

Also, the descriptions of the sink and the cabinet are refined by adding the discovered properties:

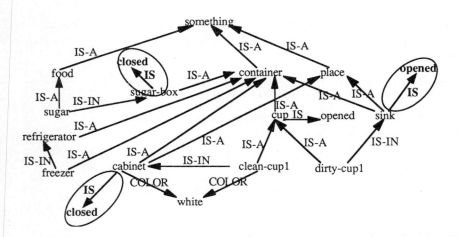

Figure 9. Goal-driven transfer of the property IS from sugar-box to cabinet and sink.

This is a case of goal-driven property transfer from one concept to another. It is quite often for an expert to define a feature of a concept but to forget to specify it when describing another concept. With the above presented method, the learner may discover and remove such an incompleteness.

### 3.5.2 Turning negative exceptions into negative examples by defining new concepts

Another method of transforming a negative exception of a rule into a negative example consists of defining a new concept that discriminates between the positive examples and the negative exception, as shown in Table 3.

---

Table 3. Definition of new concepts.

• Define a new concept C that
- covers corresponding objects Oi1,...,Oin from ALL the positive examples;
- does not cover the corresponding objects O'ik,...,O'il from SOME of the negative exceptions Nk,...,Nl;
- is less general than the concept from the lower bound that covers Oi1,...,Oin;
- may be given a meaningful name by the user.

• Replace with C the concepts from the upper bound and the lower bound that cover Oi1,...,Oin.

• Remove Nk,...,Nl from the list of the negative exceptions and add them to the list of the negative examples.

• Repeat this procedure as long as there are negative exceptions and meaningful concepts can be defined.

---

Let us consider the second negative exception from the version space in figure 8
$$(x \text{ IS-A freezer}) \& (y \text{ IS-A refrigerator})$$
together with the positive examples
$$(x \text{ IS-A clean-cup1}) \& (y \text{ IS-A cabinet})$$
$$(x \text{ IS-A sugar}) \& (y \text{ IS-A sugar-box})$$
One may define a concept covering clean-cup1 and sugar, not covering freezer, and being less general than something:

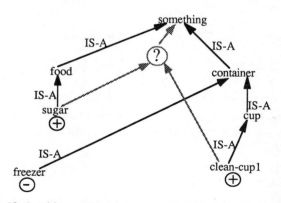

Figure 10. An object concept that would eliminate a negative exception.

One may also define a concept covering cabinet and sugar-box, not covering refrigerator, and being less general than container:

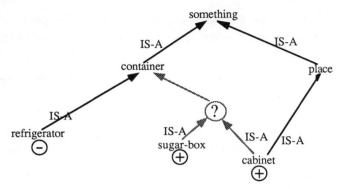

Figure 11. Another object concept that would eliminate a negative exception.

Analyzing the features of the covered and the uncovered objects (in the context of the problem solving episode from figure 2) the expert may realize, for instance, that sugar and clean-cup1 are objects that could be moved by the robot while freezer is not such an object. Therefore, he may name the corresponding intermediate concept movable-obj (i.e. object that could be moved by the robot) and may approve its introduction into the domain model. In such a case, however, the expert should also analyze the other concepts from the model in order to find the correct place for the new concept:

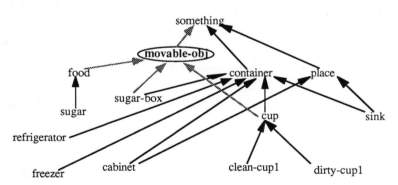

Figure 12. Definition of the concept movable-obj.

One may notice that this is a case of goal-driven conceptual clustering in which known concepts are clustered under newly defined ones, in order to improve the consistency of the learned rules.

By defining the 'movable-obj' concept the version space of the rule to be learned becomes the one shown in figure 13.

IF

> *upper bound*
> (x IS-A movable-obj) & (y IS-A something) & (x IS-IN y) & (y IS closed)
>
> *lower bound*
> (x IS-A movable-obj) & (y IS-A container) & (x IS-IN y) & (y IS closed)

THEN
*the problem*
> TAKE x

*has the solution*
> OPEN y
> TAKE x FROM y

*with the positive examples:*
> (x IS-A clean-cup1) & (y IS-A cabinet)
> (x IS-A sugar) & (y IS-A sugar-box)

*with the negative examples:*
> (x IS-A dirty-cup1) & (y IS-A sink)
> (x IS-A freezer) & (y IS-A refrigerator)

*with the irrelevant features:*
> (x COLOR z) & (y COLOR z)

Figure 13. The version space after turning the negative exceptions into negative examples.

A similar method is used by BLIP (Wrobel, 1989). The main difference is that BLIP always defines only one concept that discriminates between the objects from the positive examples and the corresponding objects from the exceptions of a rule. Our method may define several concepts, each eliminating at least one exception, if they are meaningful concepts in the modelled domain. If we want the domain model to approximate the real world as close as possible, there is no reason to believe that one has always to define only one concept for eliminating all the exceptions. Moreover, it may not be always desirable to eliminate all the exceptions because this may result in a complicated domain model.

## 3.6 The use of the action models

In the above sections we have supposed that the system does not have any models of the actions involved in the initial problem solving episode. However, if the system has even incompletely learned action models then the learning of the new rule is speeded up and at the same time with learning the rule the system is also improving the action models.

Let us suppose, for instance, that the system disposes of the incompletely learned action models from figure 14. By using these action models the system may build the tree in figure 15 which "proves" that the sequence of actions

OPEN cabinet, TAKE clean-cup1 FROM cabinet

achieves the goal of the action

TAKE clean-cup1.

The tree in figure 15 is, however, only a plausible proof. Indeed, to build this tree, the system used the upper bounds of the applicability conditions of the action models from figure 14, upper bounds that may cover situations in which the corresponding actions are not applicable. Also, the system had to abduct the fact (cabinet IS closed), which is not present in the domain model from figure 1. Therefore this tree has to be validated by the user.

IF
    *upper bound*
    (x IS-A something)

    *lower bound*
    (x IS-A bottle)
THEN
*the action*
    TAKE x
*has the effect*
    (Roby HAS x)
*with the positive examples*
    (x IS-A wine-bottle1)
    (x IS-A whisky-bottle1)

IF
    *upper bound*
    (x IS-A something) &(y IS-A something) &
    (x IS-IN y) & (y IS opened)

    *lower bound*
    (x IS-A fruit) & (y IS-A fruit-basket) &
    (x IS-IN y) & (y IS opened)
THEN
*the action*
    TAKE x FROM y
*has the effects*
    (Roby HAS x)
    NOT(x IS-IN y)
*with the positive examples*
    (x IS-A apple) & (y IS-A fruit-basket)
    (x IS-A banana) & (y IS-A fruit-basket)

IF
    *upper bound*
    (x IS-A something) & (x IS closed)

    *lower bound*
    (x IS-A bottle) & (x IS closed)
THEN
*the action*
    OPEN x
*has the effects*
    (x IS opened)
    NOT(x IS closed)
*with the positive example*
    (x IS-A wine-bottle1)
    (x IS-A whisky-bottle1)

Figure 14. Incompletely learned action models.

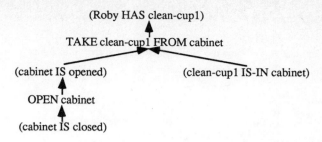

Figure 15. A plausible proof of the correctness of Example1 in figure 2.

The validation of the plausible proof from figure 15 has the following important consequences:
- the leaves of the tree represent the explanation of the problem solving episode in figure 2

(cabinet IS closed) & (clean-cup1 IS-IN cabinet)

- the abducted fact (cabinet IS closed) is introduced into the domain model;
- each action instance from the tree represents a new positive example for the corresponding action model that could be generalized to cover it. For instance, the lower bound of the precondition of 'OPEN x' is generalized to cover (x IS-A cabinet) & (x IS closed):

```
IF
        upper bound
        (x IS-A something) & (x IS closed)

        lower bound
        (x IS-A container) & (x IS closed)
THEN
the action
        OPEN x
has the effects
        (x IS opened)
        NOT(x IS closed)
with the positive examples
        (x IS-A wine-bottle1)
        (x IS-A whisky-bottle1)
        (x IS-A cabinet)
```

Figure 16. Improving the model of the action OPEN.

The action models may also be used to generalize the plausible proof in figure 15 (Tecuci and Kodratoff, 1990):

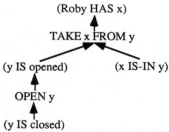

Figure 17. Generalization of the plausible proof in figure 15.

The leaves of this tree represent the analogy criterion to be used for generating new problem solving episodes: (y IS closed) & (x IS-IN y).

Therefore, the system is able to define the initial version space shown in figure 18 and may search the rule in this space by following the steps indicated in Table 1.

IF

upper bound
(x IS-A something) & (y IS-A something) &
(x IS-IN y) & (y IS closed)

lower bound
(x IS-A clean-cup1) & (y IS-A cabinet) &
(x IS-IN y) & (y IS closed)

THEN
the problem
TAKE x
has the solution
OPEN y
TAKE x FROM y
with the positive example:
(x IS-A clean-cup1) & (y IS-A cabinet)

Figure 18. A version space defined with the help of incomplete action models.

If the domain model contains complete action models then the method presented in Table 1 becomes explanation based learning. In such a case, the generalized tree from figure 17 would be a logical proof and the leaves of this tree would be the condition of the rule in figure 3 (Tecuci and Kodratoff, 1990).

## 4. Conclusions

We have presented a methodology for domain modeling and knowledge acquisition that involves a synergistic combination of different learning strategies. This methodology was implemented in Common Lisp on Macintosh. After using it to build experimental domain models in several domains (manufacturing, geography, chemistry, etc.) we have concluded that it has a high potential for partially automating the process of building expert systems.

There are several directions of improvement and development of this methodology. One direction consists of developing methods for automating the construction of the initial domain model. A interesting approach is provided by the BLIP and MOBAL systems (Morik, 1989; Wrobel, 1989) which are able to build such an initial domain model from user provided facts. Another direction of research concerns the development of methods for restructuring the domain model. The system should be able not only to define new concepts and to add new features at the known concepts but also to delete concepts or to remove features from the known concepts, managing all the consequences of such changes in the domain model. Also the multistrategy rule learning method may be improved by better integrating the existent learning strategies and by adding new ones, in order to increase the learning capabilities of the system. This research direction is closely related to an on going effort at the Center for Artificial Intelligence to define a unifying theory of machine learning and a general multistrategy task-adaptive learning methodology based on this theory (Michalski, 1990; Tecuci and Michalski, 1990).

## Acknowledgements

The author thanks Yves Kodratoff, Ryszard Michalski and Katharina Morik for useful discussions that influenced this work, Michael Hieb, Ken Kaufman and the referees for useful comments and criticisms, and Janet Holmes for help in the preparation of this report.

This research was partly done in the Artificial Intelligence Center of George Mason University. Research activities of the Center are supported in part by the Defence Advanced Research Projects Agency under grant No. N00014-87-K-0874, administrated by the Office of Naval Research, and in part by the Office of Naval Research under grants No. N00014-88-K-0226 and No. N00014-88-K-0397.

The initial research was done  under the support from the Romanian Academy, the Research Institute for Informatics in Bucharest and the French National Research Center.

## References

Bhatnagar, R.K., and Kanal L.N. (1986) Handling Uncertain Information: A Review of Numeric and Non-numeric Methods, in Kanal L.N. and Lemmer J.F. (eds) *Uncertainty in Artificial Intelligence*, Elsevier Science Publishers, North-Holland, 3-26.

Boose, J.H., Gaines, B.R., and Ganascia, J.G.(eds), *Proceedings of the Third European Workshop on Knowledge Acquisition for Knowledge-based Systems*, Paris, July, 1989.

Danyluk, A.P., The Use of Explanations for Similarity-Based Learning, *Proceedings of IJCAI-87*, pp. 274-276, Milan, Italy, 1987.

Dietterich, T.G., and Flann, N.S., An Inductive Approach to Solving the Imperfect Theory Problem, *Proceedings of 1988 Symposium on Explanation-Based Learning*, pp. 42-46, Stanford University, 1988.

DeJong G., and Mooney R., Explanation-Based Learning: An Alternative View, in *Machine Learning*, vol.1, no. 2, pp. 145-176, 1986.

Kodratoff Y., and Ganascia J-G., Improving the Generalization Step in Learning, in Michalski R., Carbonell J. & Mitchell T. (eds) *Machine Learning: An Artificial Intelligence Approach*, Vol. 2, Morgan Kaufmann 1986, pp. 215-244.

Kodratoff Y., and Tecuci G., Techniques of Design and DISCIPLE Learning Apprentice, *International Journal of Expert Systems: Research and Applications*, vol.1, no.1, pp. 39-66, 1987.

Kodratoff, Y., and Michalski, R.S. (eds), *Machine Learning: An Artificial Intelligence Approach,* Morgan Kaufmann, vol.III, 1990.

Lebowitz, M., Integrated Learning: Controlling Explanation, *Cognitive Science,* Vol. 10, No. 2, pp. 219-240, 1986.

Michalski, R.S., Carbonell J.G., and Mitchell T.M. (eds), *Machine Learning: An Artificial Intelligence Approach,* Morgan Kaufmann, vol.I, 1983, vol.II, 1986.

Michalski R.S., Theory and Methodology of Inductive Learning, *Readings in Machine Learning,* Dietterich T., and Shavlik J. (eds.) Morgan Kaufmann 1990.

Michalski R. S., Toward a Unified Theory of Learning: Multistrategy Task-adaptive Learning, Submitted for publication in *Machine Learning Journal,* 1990.

Minton, S., Carbonell, J.G., Etzioni, O., Knoblock C., Kuokka D.R., Acquiring Effective Search Control Rules: Explanation-Based Learning in the PRODIGY System, *Proceedings of the 4th International Machine Learning Workshop,* pp. 122-133, University of California, Irvine, 1987.

Mitchell T.M., Version Spaces: An Approach to Concept Learning, Doctoral dissertation, Stanford University, 1978.

Mitchell T.M., Keller R.M., and Kedar-Cabelli S.T., Explanation-Based Generalization: A Unifying View, *Machine Learning,* vol.1, no.1, pp. 47-80, 1986.

Morik K., Sloppy modeling, in Morik K. (ed), *Knowledge Representation and Organization in Machine Learning,* Springer Verlag, Berlin 1989.

Pazzani M.J., Integrating Explanation-based and Empirical Learning Methods in OCCAM, in Sleeman D. (ed), *Proceedings of the Third European Working Session on Learning,* Glasgow, 1988.

Porter B., & Mooney R. (eds), *Proceedings of the Seventh International Workshop on Machine Learning,* Texas, Austin, 1990, Morgan Kaufman.

Segre, A.M. (ed.), *Proceedings of the Sixth International Workshop on Machine Learning,* Cornell University, Ithaca, New York, June 26-27, 1989.

Tecuci G., Kodratoff Y., Bodnaru Z., and Brunet T., DISCIPLE: An expert and learning system, Expert Systems 87, Brighton, December, 14-17, in D. S. Moralee (ed): *Research and Development in Expert Systems IV,* Cambridge University Press, 1987.

Tecuci G., DISCIPLE: A Theory, Methodology, and System for Learning Expert Knowledge, Ph.D. Thesis, University of Paris-Sud, 1988.

Tecuci, G. and Kodratoff Y., Apprenticeship Learning in Imperfect Theory Domains, in Kodratoff Y., and Michalski R.S. (eds), *Machine Learning: An Artificial Intelligence Approach,* vol. III, Morgan Kaufmann, 1990.

Tecuci, G. and Michalski R., A Method for Multistrategy Task-Adaptive Learning Based on Plausible Justification, to appear in *Reports of Machine Learning and Inference Laboratory,* George Mason University, 1991.

van Melle, W., Scott, A.C., Bennett, J.S., and Peairs, M., The EMYCIN Manual, Report no. HPP-81-16, Computer Science Department, Stanford University, 1981.

Zhang, J. Learning Flexible Concepts from Examples: Employing the Ideas of Two-Tiered Concept Representation, PhD Thesis, University of Illinois at Urbana-Champaign, 1990.

Wilkins, D.C., Clancey, W.J., and Buchanan, B.G., *An Overview of the Odysseus Learning Apprentice,* Kluwer Academic Press, New York, NY, 1986.

Wrobel S., Demand-Driven Concept Formation, in Morik K.(ed), *Knowledge Representation and Organization in Machine Learning,* Springer Verlag, Berlin 1989.

# Using Plausible Explanations to Bias Empirical Generalization in Weak Theory Domains

Gerhard Widmer

Department of Medical Cybernetics and Artificial Intelligence, University of Vienna,
and
Austrian Research Institute for Artificial Intelligence
Schottengasse 3, A–1010 Vienna, Austria
e–mail: gerhard@ai–vie.uucp

**Abstract:** The paper argues for the usefulness of plausible explanations not just for analytical learning, but also for empirical generalization. The larger context is an implemented system that learns complex rules (for a musical task) on the basis of a qualitative theory of the domain. It learns by generalizing and compiling plausible explanations, but it can also incrementally modify learned rules in reaction to new evidence. The paper shows how this incremental modification (generalization) becomes more effective if it is based on an analysis of the explanations underlying learned rules; these explanations support a notion of 'deep' similarity and can provide substantial bias on the empirical modification of concepts. Several criteria that implement this bias are described, and an extended example illustrates how they lead to intelligent generalization behaviour.

## 1 Introduction

In an attempt to overcome some of the weaknesses of Explanation–Based Learning (Mitchell *et al.*, 1986) – especially the need for a complete and consistent domain theory – some authors have recently proposed to generalize the EBL approach to domains with weaker theories by moving from *logically sound* explanations to *plausible* ones. In particular, G. DeJong has presented a system that performs 'plausible EBL' on the basis of a *qualitative theory* of the domain (DeJong, 1989). However, his system has several shortcomings. To mention just two, it does not try to rate the (relative) plausibility of competing explanations, which is crucial with a domain theory that supports multiple explanations, and it does not empirically modify learned concepts in the face of new evidence (it just abandons a concept and looks for an alternative explanation – there must always be a complete explanation). The second limitation is particularly serious, since one of the explicit assumptions of this kind of research is that the qualitative domain theory may be incomplete and support incorrect explanations.

The system described here is also based on a qualitative domain theory. The learning task is a quite complex musical problem: harmonizing given melodies. The system tries to overcome both of the above mentioned limitations. It can heuristically assess the *relative plausibility of explanations*, which leads to faster convergence towards the correct concepts, and it can *empirically modify* learned concepts in the face of new evidence. The system in its entirety (plausible reasoner, learner, problem solver) is very complex. So this article will concentrate on one particular issue: the possibilities of using plausible explanations to bias empirical generalization of learned rules. We will describe the criteria used by the system in this process. Work on analogous methods for empirical specialization is currently under way.

As the test domain in this project is tonal music, the given examples will be musical ones. However, this should not deter the reader unfamiliar with music theory and notation. It is not necessary to understand the musical details of the examples in order to appreciate the general mechanism and the implications for a broader class of learning problems.

## 2  Learning task and domain theory

The system's task consists in learning rules for harmonizing given melodies, i.e., placing chords (chord symbols) underneath a melody as in the popular song literature. Training instances are correctly harmonized pieces provided by a teacher. Fig.1 shows a simple harmonized melody; it is the beginning of the well-known Christmas song 'Silent Night'.

*Fig.1: Part of a harmonized melody*

The system learns mainly by finding plausible explanations of the correctness of training instances and compiling the explanations into general rules. The *domain theory* that allows the construction of plausible explanations is a *qualitative model* describing in abstract terms how people perceive, i.e., 'hear', simple tonal music. We cannot present the details of the qualitative model here; the interested reader can find a detailed description in (Widmer, 1990). The model is rather complex; it occupies about 1000 lines of Prolog code. Basically, it is an abstraction hierarchy that relates audible effects of musical events to more abstract perceivable effects via four different types of relationships:

1. *Deductive rules* (as in standard EBL domain theories); an example:

    relative_consonance( Chord, Note, extremely_high) :-
            chord_contains_note( Chord, Note).

    *("The relative consonance between a note and a simultaneously played chord is extremely high if the chord contains the note in its basic triad")*

2. *Qualitative proportionality relations;* these are dependency statements similar to the qualitative relations described in (Forbus, 1984). In our domain theory, a statement Q+(A,B) – read "feature A is positively qualitatively proportional to feature B" – means that there is some partial functional relationship between A and B that is monotonically increasing in its depend-

ence on A, or, less technically, "if A increases or has a high value, B will also, *all other things being equal*". Q+(A,B) does *not* mean that A is the only factor on which B depends, nor does it mean that A must always be present when B is. Q– is interpreted analogously for inverse proportionality. An example:

Q+ ( relative_chord_distance( Chord1, Chord2, D), contrast( Chord1, Chord2, C)).

*("Given a sequence of two chords (Chord1, Chord2), the listener may experience a feeling of contrast between the chords which is positively (qualitatively) proportionally related to the harmonic distance (along the circle of fifths) between the chords")*

3. *Additional proportionality relations*: statements of the form ADDQ+(A,B) and ADDQ–(A,B) are to be interpreted like Q+ and Q–, respectively, except that they specify only *additional influences*; that is, they are only relevant if there is already some reason to believe that B holds or has a particular value. An example:

ADDQ+ ( metrical_strength( Chord2, S), contrast( Chord1, Chord2, C)).

*("If there is some perceived contrast, it may be felt the more strongly the stronger Chord2's metrical position is")*

4. *General qualitative dependency relations*: statements of the form D(A,B) simply indicate that A has probably something to do with B; they do not say what this relationship looks like. In this sense, they are similar to S.Russell's *partial determinations* (Russell, 1986). An example from our domain theory:

D ( contrast( Chord1, Chord2, C), interestingness( sequence(Chord1,Chord2), I )).

*("Whether or not a sequence of two chords is heard as 'interesting' by a listener depends – among other things – on the degree of contrast between the chords")*

## 3 Plausible explanations

A vital part of the system is a *plausible reasoning component*; given the above domain theory, it can find plausible explanations of why given harmonizations may sound good and thus be correct. Plausible explanations are hierarchical trees just like in standard EBL. However, there are two important differences:

First, since they are based on various types of non–deductive knowledge, these explanations can involve different *types of explanatory links*. There are four possible types of links in our system, according to the four types of plausible inference that the qualitative domain theory allows the reasoner to draw. These are:

1. DED – deductive argument, based on a strict deductive rule in the domain theory (this is the typical explanation link in classical EBL)

2. QPLUS and QMINUS – plausible arguments, based on qualitative proportionality relations Q+ and Q–, respectively, in the domain theory

3. ADD.QPLUS and ADD.QMINUS – additional plausible arguments that further strengthen the plausibility of a QPLUS or QMINUS argument; they are based on additional proportionality relations ADDQ+ and ADDQ– in the domain theory

4. DEP – plausible argument, based on qualitative dependency relation D in the domain theory.

```
good(A7,bb)  <- DED (high) —                    type of explanatory link
                                                qualitative measure of plausibility
    characterization(A7)  <- DED (extremely_high) —
    chord_root(A7,a)  <- TRUE (extremely_high)
    chord_mode(A7,major)  <- TRUE (extremely_high)
    chord_type(A7,7)  <- TRUE (extremely_high)
    global_key(key(f,major))  <- TRUE (extremely_high)        qualitative value of
                                                              domain parameter
                                                              (from qualitative model)
    goodness(A7,bb,extremely_high)  <- QUAL (high) —
    goodness(A7,bb,extremely_high)  <- QPLUS (high) —

    interestingness(A7,bb,extremely_high)  <- QUAL (high) —
    interestingness(A7,bb,extremely_high)  <- DEP (moderate) —
    contrast(F,A7,moderate)  <- QUAL (extremely_high) —
    contrast(F,A7,moderate)  <- QPLUS (extremely_high) —
    previous_chord(A7,F)  <- TRUE (extremely_high)
    relative_chord_distance(F,A7,moderate)  <- DED (extremely_high) —
    distance_on_circle_of_fifths(F,A7,4)  <- TRUE (extremely_high)

    interestingness(A7,bb,extremely_high)  <- QPLUS (high) —
    tension_buildup(A7,bb,extremely_high)  <- QUAL (high) —
    tension_buildup(A7,bb,extremely_high)  <- QPLUS (high) —
    previous_chord(A7,F)  <- TRUE (extremely_high)
    local_tension_increase(F,A7,high)  <- DED (extremely_high) —
    intrinsic_chord_tension(F,low)  <- DED (extremely_high) —
    chord_type(F,triad)  <- TRUE (extremely_high)
    intrinsic_chord_tension(A7,high)  <- DED (extremely_high) —
    chord_type(A7,7)  <- TRUE (extremely_high)

    tension_buildup(A7,bb,extremely_high)  <- QMINUS (extremely_high) —
    relative_consonance(A7,bb,extremely_low)  <- DED (extremely_high) —
    not_chord_contains_note(A7,bb)  <- TRUE (extremely_high)
    chord_scale(A7,scale(a,mixolydian))  <- TRUE (extremely_high)
    not_scale_contains_note(scale(a,mixolydian),bb)  <- TRUE (extremely_high)

    tension_buildup(A7,bb,extremely_high)  <- ADD.QPLUS (moderate) —
    salience(bb,moderate)  <- DED (extremely_high) —
    structural_salience(bb,moderate)  <- TRUE (extremely_high)
    metrical_strength(bb,moderate)  <- TRUE (extremely_high)

    goodness(A7,bb,extremely_high)  <- QPLUS (high) —
    coherence(A7,bb,extremely_high)  <- QUAL (high) —
    coherence(A7,bb,extremely_high)  <- QPLUS (high) —
    harmonic_stability(A7,bb,extremely_high)  <- QUAL (high) —

    harmonic_stability(A7,bb,extremely_high)  <- QPLUS (high) —
    plausible_local_key(bb,key(d,minor))  <- TRUE (extremely_high)
    stability_of_chord_in_key(A7,key(d,minor),high)  <- DED (extremely_high) —
    dominant_7_chord(key(d,minor),A7)  <- TRUE (extremely_high)

    harmonic_stability(A7,bb,extremely_high)  <- ADD.QPLUS (moderate) —
    salience(bb,moderate)  <- DED (extremely_high) —
    structural_salience(bb,moderate)  <- TRUE (extremely_high)
    metrical_strength(bb,moderate)  <- TRUE (extremely_high)
```

*Fig.2: Training instance and plausible explanation*

The second difference to purely deductive explanations is that each branch of the explanation (i.e., each 'argument') is annotated with an assessed *degree of plausibility* of the argument. This measure is computed by the plausible reasoner according to various heuristics (see, e.g., Collins & Michalski, 1989). It expresses the degree of confidence with which the system is prepared to believe a particular argument. The measure enables the system to consider more plausible explanations before less plausible ones. These annotations are only very approximate; they can take qualitative values from the domain {extremely_high, high, moderate, low, extremely_low}.

Fig.2 gives an example of such an explanation. A training instance is a pair <note, accompanying chord>, and the goal concept is good( Chord, Note) (Chord is a good harmonization for Note). The additional explanatory link type QUAL is just an auxiliary label to group together in one subtree all the qualitative arguments for one feature. The structure of the explanation (if not the content) should be self–explanatory. Fig.3 shows the learned rule that results from generalization and compilation of the explanation.

---

```
RULE1:   good(Chord,Note)  :-  chord_root(Chord,Root),
                               chord_mode(Chord,major),
                               chord_type(Chord,7),
                               global_key(key(KRoot,KMode)),
                               previous_chord(Chord,PrevChord),
                               distance_on_circle_of_fifths(PrevChord,Chord,4),
                               chord_type(PrevChord,triad),
                               not_chord_contains_note(Chord,Note),
                               chord_scale(Chord,scale(SRoot,SMode)),
                               not_scale_contains_note(scale(SRoot,SMode),Note),
                               structural_salience(Note,moderate)
                               metrical_strength(Note,moderate),
                               plausible_local_key(Note,key(LRoot,LMode)),
                               dominant_7_chord(key(LRoot,LMode),Chord).
```

---

*Fig.3: Rule learned by compiling plausible explanation*

In general, since the underlying domain theory (qualitative model) is only approximate and not assumed to be entirely correct, an explanation may be both too specific – it may refer to features that are not really relevant to the current situation – and incorrect, i.e., too general – it may not include all the relevant conditions that are needed to discriminate positive from negative examples. That is where the need for empirical generalization and specialization arises.

## 4 Inductive bias afforded by plausible explanations

The straightforward way to react to new instances would be to empirically generalize or specialize learned rules in response to a new conflicting instance. That is how it was done in a predecessor of the current system (Widmer, 1989). However, by basing empirical generalization decisions not only on the *rule* to be generalized, but rather on the *explanation* that led to that rule, a much higher degree of effectiveness and context–sensitivity of the generalization process can be achieved. The plausible explanation can be used to *bias* empirical generalization of the rule. This observation was already made by A. Danyluk in (Danyluk, 1987; 1989), but only for strictly deductive explanations. Since our plausible explanations provide much more differentiated information – they are based on a richer set of types of explanatory links, and they include explicit plausibility information – the system can take even more advantage of them.

So far, we have developed criteria and heuristics for the situation when the system encounters a new positive instance that is not covered by any existing rule. The system then has to decide whether to generalize one of the rules (and if so, *which* rule to generalize, and *how* to generalize it) or create a new rule on the basis of the new instance. This decision is based on an analysis of the mismatches of the new instance with the explanations underlying each of the rules. (It should be mentioned here that the system is an interactive learning apprentice (Mitchell *et al.*, 1985; Tecuci & Kodratoff, 1989). Before committing a generalization to memory, the system can ask a human teacher for confirmation.)

Let X denote a condition in a rule – which corresponds to a leaf in the explanation underlying the rule – that is not satisfied by the current instance. The system takes into account the following criteria when deciding whether (and if so, how) to generalize:

1. Can X be generalized to apply to the new instance in such a way that the argument in the original explanation that depends on X still holds? If possible, such a generalization would be *safe* (at least with respect to the plausible explanation). Also, this criterion provides a strong *bias* on the *type* of generalization that is performed in cases where there are multiple ways to generalize X – only those will be considered that preserve the validity of the argument that depends on X.

2. The system considers the *type* of explanatory link of X (or of some higher–level node whose validity depends entirely on X): some types are intrinsically more important than others. For instance, ADD.QPLUS and ADD.QMINUS arguments are by definition less salient than QPLUS or QMINUS. Generalizing or dropping such a condition is less dangerous than dropping an entire QUAL branch, say.

3. The system looks at the *plausibility* with which X was thought to hold in the original explanation. An argument that was not very credible to begin with can more safely be dropped or generalized.

4. If X were to be dropped, how strong would the hypothesis depending on X (some ancestor of X in the explanation tree) still be? That is, how many arguments supporting it are still left, and how strong are they? Obviously, if there are still strong arguments left that support the original hypothesis, the overall integrity of the explanation is not compromised too much.

Information from these various heuristics is combined to yield one approximate value indicating how 'likely' it is that generalization of the explanation (and the rule derived from it) is justified. In summary, the explanations serve a dual purpose: first, they provide a measure of '*deep similarity*' – matches and mismatches between instances and rules are rated according to what role they play in an explanation structure; this is a better measure of similarity than just simple counting of syntactic matches. And second, they can provide bias on the type of generalization that seems most plausible.

# 5 An example

The following example illustrates the effect of some of these heuristics. From the training example shown in Fig.2 (the combination of chord A7 and note bb), the system has already learned good(C7,e)  <- DED (high) ––

   characterization(A7)  <- DED (extremely_high) ––
   chord(root(C7,c)  <- TRUE (extremely_high)
   chord_mode(C7,major)  <- TRUE (extremely_high)
   chord_type(C7,7)  <- TRUE (extremely_high)
   global_key(key(f,major))  <- TRUE (extremely_high)

   goodness(C7,e,extremely_high)  <- QUAL (high) ––
   goodness(C7,e,extremely_high)  <- QPLUS (high) ––
   interestingness(C7,e,extremely_high)  <- QUAL (high) ––

   > interestingness(C7,e,extremely_high)  <- DEP (moderate) ––
   > contrast(F,C7,moderate)  <- QUAL (extremely_high) ––
   > contrast(F,C7,moderate)  <- QPLUS (extremely_high) ––
   > previous_chord(C7,F)  <- TRUE (extremely_high)
   > relative_chord_distance(F,C7,moderate)  <- DED (extremely_high) ––
   > **distance_on_circle_of_fifths(F,A7,4)  <- TRUE (extremely_high)**

   interestingness(C7,e,extremely_high)  <- QPLUS (high) ––
   tension_buildup(C7,e,extremely_high)  <- QUAL (high) ––
   tension_buildup(C7,e,extremely_high)  <- QPLUS (high) ––
   previous_chord(C7,F)  <- TRUE (extremely_high)
   local_tension_increase(F,C7,high)  <- DED (extremely_high) ––
   intrinsic_chord_tension(F,low)  <- DED (extremely_high) ––
   chord_type(F,triad)  <- TRUE (extremely_high)
   intrinsic_chord_tension(C7,high)  <- DED (extremely_high) ––
   chord_type(C7,7)  <- TRUE (extremely_high)

   > tension_buildup(C7,e,extremely_high)  <- QMINUS (extremely_high) ––
   > relative_consonance(C7,e,extremely_low)  <- DED (extremely_high) ––
   > **not_chord_contains_note(C7,e)  <- TRUE (extremely_high)**
   > chord_scale(C7,scale(c,mixolydian))  <- TRUE (extremely_high)
   > **not_scale_contains_note(scale(c,mixolydian),e)  <- TRUE (extremely_high)**

   > tension_buildup(C7,e,extremely_high)  <- ADD.QPLUS (moderate) ––
   > salience(e,moderate)  <- DED (extremely_high) ––
   > structural_salience(e,moderate)  <- TRUE (extremely_high)
   > **metrical_strength(e,moderate)  <- TRUE (extremely_high)**

   goodness(C7,e,extremely_high)  <- QPLUS (high) ––
   coherence(C7,e,extremely_high)  <- QUAL (high) ––
   coherence(C7,e,extremely_high)  <- QPLUS (high) ––
   harmonic_stability(C7,e,extremely_high)  <- QUAL (high) ––

   harmonic_stability(C7,e,extremely_high)  <- QPLUS (high) ––
   plausible_local_key(e,key(f,major))  <- TRUE (extremely_high)
   stability_of_chord_in_key(C7,key(f,major),high)  <- DED (extremely_high) ––
   dominant_7_chord(key(f,major),C7)  <- TRUE (extremely_high)

   > harmonic_stability(C7,e,extremely_high)  <- ADD.QPLUS (moderate) ––
   > salience(e,moderate)  <- DED (extremely_high) ––
   > structural_salience(e,moderate)  <- TRUE (extremely_high)
   > **metrical_strength(e,moderate)  <- TRUE (extremely_high)**

*Fig.4: New training instance and match with old explanation*

the rule (Rule 1) depicted in Fig.3. When it analyzes the C7 chord in the same piece (Fig.4), it notices that this new instance is not covered by any existing rule; in particular, it is not covered by Rule 1. Four conditions of the rule are not satisfied by the new instance. They correspond to five leaves in the explanation tree from which Rule 1 was originally derived (one violated condition – metrical_strength (Note,moderate) – occurs twice in the explanation). Fig. 4 displays the explanation again, with unmatched leaves printed in boldface and higher–level compromised explanation branches enclosed in boxes. Let us look at each of the conflicts in turn to see how they are interpreted:

- distance_on_circle_of_fifths(PrevChord,Chord,4) is not satisfied; in the new instance, the harmonic distance between the Dmin chord and the subsequent C7 chord is only 2. While it might be possible to generalize this condition to something like distance >= 2 or distance <= 4, this would no longer support the superordinate argument relative_chord_distance moderate (2 is a low harmonic chord distance); also, as a consequence, the hypothesis that there is moderate contrast is no longer plausible, so that even if chord_distance were generalized, it would no longer be a plausible argument for interestingness. So the system decides to simply drop the condition. Since there is another strong argument left for interestingness (the branch immediately below), and since the original explanation branch supplied only moderate support for the interestingness hypothesis from the beginning (see Fig.2), dropping it seems not to compromise the overall character of the explanation too much.

- not_chord_contains_note(Chord,Note) is not satisfied; in the new instance, the C7 chord in question *does* contain the note (e) in the melody, i.e., chord and note are consonant. The same holds for not_scale_contains_note. These conditions cannot be generalized, so they would have to be dropped. Again, since there are other arguments left for tension_buildup, the two conditions (and the corresponding branch) are simply dropped.

- and finally, metrical_strength(Note,moderate) is not true in the current instance; the metrical strength of the e is strong (it is at the beginning of a measure). This, however, presents no problem: if this condition is generalized to at_least moderate, it covers the new instance as well and still supports the more general hypothesis that the salience of e is moderate (this is determined by the plausible reasoner). If the system could *not* find a sensible way to generalize this condition, it would not hesitate to drop it altogether: the explanation branch that is affected (tension_buildup in one case, harmonic_stability in the other) is of type ADD.QPLUS and is thus intrinsically not too important to the integrity of the entire explanation.

So in this case, the heuristics are in favour of generalizing the explanation, which results in the generalized version of rule 1 depicted in Fig. 5. (For the musically knowledgeable reader: the rule describes a class of situations where a new local tonic should be introduced with an appropriate dominant seventh chord).

There are a few observations that deserve attention here. They all testify to the importance of looking at the *explanation* underlying the rule to be generalized.

- The two training situations that led to Rule 1' look very different on the surface, and they are rather complex (the length of each of their descriptions is about 130 predicates). Which of the similarities they share are significant is only revealed by the plausible explanation.

- More specifically, when just looking at Rule 1, it would seem that the generalization necessary to accommodate the new instance is quite dramatic: five out of fourteen conditions have to be

---

```
RULE1':   good(Chord,Note)   :-   chord_root(Chord,Root),
                                   chord_mode(Chord,major),
                                   chord_type(Chord,7),
                                   global_key(key(KRoot,KMode)),
                                   previous_chord(Chord,PrevChord),
                                   chord_type(PrevChord,triad),
                                   structural_salience(Note,moderate)
                                   metrical_strength(Note,S),
                                   at_least(S,moderate),
                                   plausible_local_key(Note,key(LRoot,LMode)),
                                   dominant_7_chord(key(LRoot,LMode),Chord).
```

---

*Fig.5: Generalized rule*

dropped or generalized. A purely inductive generalizer that has some general heuristics and bounds to decide whether or not to accept a generalization might find this too drastic. Again, it is the analysis of the *explanation* behind the rule that reveals that the generalization is indeed quite safe.

- The above example gives a glimpse of how analysis of an explanation can bias the *kind of generalization* to be chosen from a number of possibilities: metrical_strength moderate and metrical_strength strong were generalized to at_least moderate. The straightforward way to generalize the two would have been a disjunction or an interval bounded at both ends. But an analysis of the explanation reveals that the generalization need not be constrained at the upper end; if metrical_strength is stronger than moderate or strong, this would even *strengthen* the argument in the explanation, so at_least is the best generalization. This kind of analytical bias is most effective in our system when musical intervals have to be generalized. These are organized in various (partly orthogonal) hierarchies, all of which are candidates for generalization.

Preliminary experiments have demonstrated that the system learns complex rules very effectively. For instance, from the two training pieces shown in Fig.6 it learned just 7 (quite general) rules of the type good(Chord,Note). They enabled it to harmonize a new, quite different piece (Fig.7). This solution is more than reasonable (the reader not familiar with musical notation will have to take my word for it). We have not as yet done any extended experiments comparing our system with a less sophisticated generalizer in order to measure, in precise terms, the increase in effectiveness resulting from explanation–sensitive generalization, but our experiences during the development and refinement of the system clearly indicated a substantial improvement as the generalizer was made more sophisticated.

## 6 Conclusion

The paper has presented a program that learns highly complex concepts on the basis of an *approximate, qualitative* domain theory. In particular, it has shown how *plausible explanations* can be used to *bias empirical generalization* of already learned rules when new instances are encountered. The advantage of this is threefold: analysis of the explanations underlying rules leads to more intelligent decisions as to *whether* some rule merits generalization, *which* rule is most

*Training piece 1 (key: d major):*

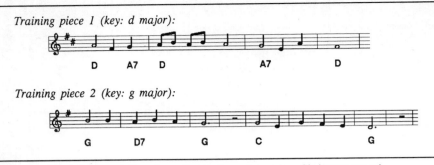

*Training piece 2 (key: g major):*

Fig.6: *Two training pieces (beginnings of Austrian Christmas songs)*

*Test piece (key: b flat major):*

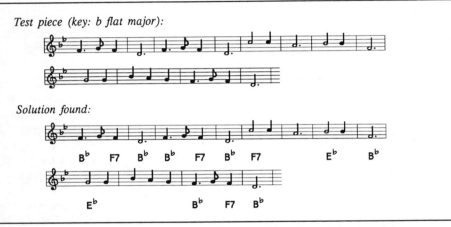

*Solution found:*

Fig.7: *Test piece and solution found after learning from pieces 1 and 2*

similar to the new instance – analysis of the explanation provides a 'deeper' similarity measure than simple syntactic match counting –, and *how* best to generalize some condition. The overall effect is that the information contained in the domain theory is more fully exploited and that the system converges more rapidly on the correct concept definitions.

The criteria and heuristics presented in this paper apply to the case of empirical *generalization*. The next step is to develop heuristics along similar lines for empirical *discrimination*. This will be needed to arrive at a truly flexible incremental learner. Also, as stated above, we will try to experimentally measure the quantitative advantage, in terms of learning effectiveness, of this approach over less sophisticated generalization strategies.

It may be worth noting once more that our musical test field is definitely not a toy domain; it approaches the complexity of real–world problems and thus points to the practicability of this approach (the system usually takes just a few seconds to respond). As qualitative theories are gaining more and more attention as devices for modelling various domains, research on combining qualitative reasoning, plausible reasoning, knowledge–based learning, and interactive apprenticeship techniques may lead to practically usable systems for complex applications.

## Acknowledgements

Comments by Bernhard Pfahringer greatly improved the quality of this paper. Thanks to Prof. Robert Trappl for his continuing support. This research is sponsored by the Austrian *Fonds zur Förderung der wissenschaftlichen Forschung* under grant P7082–PHY. Financial support for the Austrian Research Institute for Artificial Intelligence is provided by the Austrian Federal Ministry for Science and Research.

The program is implemented in Quintus Prolog on an Apollo DN3000 workstation.

## References

Collins, A. and Michalski, R. (1989). The Logic of Plausible Reasoning: A Core Theory. *Cognitive Science 13*, 1–49.

Danyluk, A. (1987). The Use of Explanations for Similarity–Based Learning. In *Proceedings of the Tenth International Joint Conference on Artificial Intelligence (IJCAI–87)*, Milano, Italy. Morgan Kaufmann.

Danyluk, A. (1989). Finding New Rules for Incomplete Theories: Explicit Biases for Induction with Contextual Information. In *Proceedings of the Sixth International Workshop on Machine Learning*, Ithaca, N.Y. Morgan Kaufmann.

DeJong, G. (1989). Explanation–Based Learning with Plausible Inferencing. In *Proceedings of the Fourth European Working Session on Learning (EWSL–89)*, Montpellier, France. Pitman Publishing.

Forbus, K.D. (1984). Qualitative Process Theory. *Artificial Intelligence 24(1–3) (special volume on qualitative reasoning about physical systems)*, 85–169.

Mitchell, T., Mahadevan, S. and Steinberg, L. (1985). LEAP: A Learning Apprentice for VLSI Design. In *Proceedings of the Ninth International Joint Conference on Artificial Intelligence (IJCAI–85)*, Los Angeles, CA. Morgan Kaufmann.

Mitchell, T., Keller, R. and Kedar–Cabelli, S. (1986). Explanation–Based Generalization: A Unifying View. *Machine Learning 1(1)*.

Russell, S. (1986). *Analogical and Inductive Reasoning*. Ph.D. Thesis, Report STAN–CS–87–1150, Stanford University, Stanford, CA.

Tecuci, G. and Kodratoff, Y. (1989). Multi–Strategy Learning in Nonhomogeneous Domain Theories. In *Proceedings of the Sixth International Workshop on Machine Learning*, Ithaca, N.Y. Morgan Kaufmann.

Widmer, G. (1989). A Tight Integration of Deductive and Inductive Learning. In *Proceedings of the Sixth International Workshop on Machine Learning*, Ithaca, N.Y. Morgan Kaufmann.

Widmer, G. (1990). *A Qualitative Model of the Perception of Melodies and Harmonizations*. Submitted. Available as Report TR–90–12, Austrian Research Institute for Artificial Intelligence, Vienna.

# THE REPLICATION PROBLEM:
# A CONSTRUCTIVE INDUCTION APPROACH[*]

**Der-Shung Yang      Gunnar Blix[†]      Larry A. Rendell**
Beckman Institute and Computer Science Department
University of Illinois at Urbana-Champaign
405 N. Mathews Ave., Urbana, IL 61801
yang@cs.uiuc.edu      blix@cs.uiuc.edu      rendell@cs.uiuc.edu

## Abstract

Pagallo's FRINGE and Symmetric FRINGE can improve learning by constructing new features based on the decision tree output of an induction algorithm. The new features help the replication problem. This paper examines the influence of replication problem in learning, and studies an refined version of Symmetric FRINGE called DCFringe. Like Symmetric FRINGE, DCFringe attacks both DNF and CNF problems using a dual heuristic. But unlike Symmetric FRINGE, DCFringe distinguishes between conjunctive and disjunctive replication, thus outperforming FRINGE for CNF-type concepts while equaling its performance for DNF-type concepts. We study the scope of the replication problem by relating it to other known characteristics of difficult concepts, such as concept dispersion, relative concept size, feature interaction and embedded parity. We discuss the generality of our solution in terms of its extensibility to other representations. We also suggest approaches to overcome some limitations of our approach such as its tendency to overfit the data and its susceptibility to noise.

**Keywords**      Empirical learning, constructive induction.

[*]This research was supported by grant IRI 8822031 from the National Science Foundation.
[†]Supported by a University of Illinois CS/AI Fellowship and a scholarship from the Royal Norwegian Research Council for Science and Humanities.

# 1 Introduction

Decision-tree approaches to learning concepts from examples have been reported successful by a number of researchers (e.g., Quinlan [1986], Rendell [1983] and Breiman *et al.* [1984]); yet recent research suggests that these approaches exhibit severe limitations for significant concept classes [Rendell and Seshu, 1990, Yang and Blix, 1990, Pagallo and Haussler, 1990, Matheus, 1989]. These limitations can be attributed to two factors: first, the partitioning approaches are greedy, disregarding the effects of interaction between features in the target concept; second, the algorithms assume an implicit bias towards concepts that can be described as a disjunction of a small number of conjoined attributes. The FRINGE and Symmetric FRINGE algorithms [Pagallo, 1989, Pagallo and Haussler, 1990] deal with these limitations by using feature construction to combat feature interactions manifested in the decision tree replication problem. We propose DCFringe—an enhancement of Symmetric FRINGE—as a more refined approach to these limitations.

The learning problem attacked in this paper is that of acquiring a *concept,* that is a description of an unknown *target concept* (i.e., a class of objects or events) of which we are given a set of attribute-vector *training examples,* labeled as either *positive,* (i.e., objects or events consistent with the target concept) or *negative* (i.e., belonging to some other class). The basis of DCFringe is typical of decision tree learners: it proceeds to construct a binary decision tree by iteratively determining the best binary single feature test according to some predetermined dissimilarity criterion; the decision to use only single feature tests rests on the assumption that feature interaction is unimportant in the target concept.

Pagallo and Haussler [1990] note that the decision tree approach fails to produce accurate and concise results for even moderate-sized $k$-term-$l$-DNF expressions, as well as target concepts such as parity and multiplexor. Rendell and colleagues [Rendell and Cho, 1990, Rendell and Seshu, 1990] quantify this effect and propose some characteristics of concepts that are hard to learn: a high dispersion in the instance space, relative size of the concept in its instance space, a high degree of feature interaction, or embedded parity problems [Seshu, 1989]. These problems can be overcome by considering tests on combinations of features when building the decision tree (a.k.a. lookahead) at the expense of exponentially increasing the number of tests considered; FRINGE and DCFringe represent alternatives in which the combinations of features to be considered are selected on the basis of previously built decision trees, thus significantly reducing the combinations to be considered.

Section 2 defines the replication problem, and determines its scope by relating it to concept difficulty as defined elsewhere; this section also introduces terminology and ways of characterizing concepts in order to quantify the severity of the problem and the effects of our solution. Section 3 introduces DCFringe in detail and relates it to Pagallo and Haussler's [1990] FRINGE. In section 4 we present and discuss empirical results of testing FRINGE[1] and DCFringe on different concept classes. Finally, section 5 discusses some limitations of DCFringe and suggests some ways of attacking these in future research.

## 2 Replication Problem

The replication problem was noted by Pagallo and Haussler [Pagallo and Haussler, 1990, Pagallo, 1989] as an inherent weakness of binary decision trees for representing Boolean concepts. The term *replication problem* refers to the duplication of a sequence of tests in different branches of a decision tree, leading to an inconcise representation that also tends to have low predictive accuracy. Pagallo and Haussler observed the problem in trees constructed for target concepts best represented as $k$-term-$l$-DNF expressions (figure 1).

However, the problem occurs for most concepts not representable as monomials.[2] Replications are inherent to the decision tree representation rather than the concept itself, although the problem can be attributed to underlying characteristics of the concept class (see section 2.2).

In this paper we distinguish between conjunctive and disjunctive replications: infor-

---

[1]The implementation of FRINGE used for these experiments is Yang's [1991] reconstruction according to the algorithm given by Pagallo and Haussler [1990]; the underlying partitioning learning system for both implementations is a decision tree version of PLS1 [Rendell, 1983].

[2]A monomial is a conjunction of literals, where a literal is an attribute or a negation of an attribute. Let $l$-monomial denote a monomial with $l$ literals: then a $k$-term-$l$-DNF (disjunctive normal form) expression is a disjunction of $k$ $l$-monomials. (This definition differs slightly from that of [Kearns *et al.*, 1987] in that they assume $k$ and $l$ as upper bounds.) Similarly, CNF is defined as conjunctions of clauses, where clauses are disjunctions of literals.

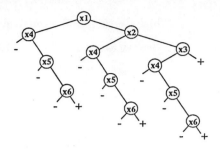

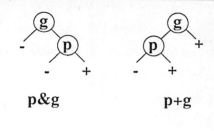

Figure 1: Decision tree representation for $x_1x_2x_3 + x_4x_5x_6$

Figure 2: Basic patterns for conjunctive and disjunctive replication

mally, conjunctive replications correspond to terms in DNF, while disjunctive replications correspond to CNF clauses. The resulting decision tree replication patterns are depicted in figure 2; a *disjunctive pattern is a pattern of two test nodes, one with two children leaves whose parent's sibling is a positive leaf.*[3] This distinction becomes important to understand the difference between FRINGE and DCFringe. In effect, DCFringe's superior performance for CNF-type[4] concepts can be attributed to its ability to handle disjunctive replications.

To further motivate the research presented in this paper, the following two sections relate the replication problem to characteristics of the class of the target concept. First, in order to capture these characteristics, section 2.1 introduces necessary terminology and ways of describing properties of these classes or their representations. Second, we review which concept properties make learning hard, and relate these to the replication problem through the introduced terminology.

## 2.1 Representation Properties

Any Boolean concept can be represented as a DNF expression, a CNF expression, and a decision tree, as well as any number of other representation schemes; however, one representation may be more appropriate than others for representing a particular con-

---

[3]This definition is restrictive, since there are larger patterns caused by disjunction as well; thus our use of this definition underestimates the effect of disjunctions on replication.

[4]Concepts can be represented both in DNF and CNF form; CNF-type refers to concepts whose CNF representation is more compact than the corresponding DNF form.

cept. First, we consider relationships between DNF and CNF form and develop some definitions to capture their differences. Next, we show how certain characteristics of difficult concepts are reflected in the corresponding DNF representation, and introduce a measure that captures this relationship. Finally, we consider some essential properties of the decision tree representation as well as its correspondence to the other forms.

For every concept, if we can discover the shortest Boolean expression for that concept in either form, we can compare the shortest expression in DNF with the shortest expression in CNF and decide which form is more suitable for representing the concept. Unfortunately, there is no known algorithm to find the shortest expression in either DNF or CNF. But we do know that disjunctive replication patterns are prevalent in the decision tree of *typical* CNF expressions. Therefore, we propose an alternative measure of *CNFness* as *the number of nodes in the disjunctive replication patterns divided by the total number of nodes in the tree.*[5]

Pagallo and Haussler [1990] note the limited success of FRINGE on the parity concept, but provide no explanation. We claim that the main difference between parity concepts and the DNF-type concepts that FRINGE learns successfully is the degree of feature interaction. Parity concepts cannot be expressed as $\mu$ DNF. A concept is $\mu$ DNF ($\mu$ CNF) if each feature occurs in at most one literal of the expression on DNF (CNF) form [Kearns *et al.*, 1987]. In essence, FRINGE is successful at learning concepts that can be expressed as $\mu$ DNF.

The degree of improvement in conciseness that can be expected from using FRINGE or DCFringe for a particular concept is related to the severity of the replication problem for that concept; for difficult concepts the trees typically exhibit a high degree of replication, but also a greater potential for improvement. The *replication rate* for a concept is *the number of replications of tests in a decision tree for the concept, divided by the total number of nodes in the tree*. Although this definition depends on the particular algorithm as well as the distribution of examples, it gives us a reasonably accurate assessment of the severity of the replication problem for a given concept.

---

[5]Our restrictive definition of what constitutes a disjunctive replication leads this measure to underestimate the cases where CNF is more appropriate.

## 2.2  Scope of the Problem

Pagallo and Haussler [1990] show that the replication problem occurs whenever a concept is easily expressed in DNF with a small number of terms each comprising several features. We claim the problem becomes more serious and more difficult when concept representation requires a larger number of disjuncts, e.g., if the concept is better expressed in CNF or is highly dispersed in the instance space. Rendell and colleagues [Rendell and Cho, 1990, Rendell and Seshu, 1990] identify a number of concept characteristics that affect the accuracy and conciseness of machine learning systems in general and decision tree learning algorithms in particular; some of the more important are concept dispersion in instance space, relative size of the concept, and embedded parity problems. In this section, we show that the immediate objective of solving the replication problem is general in that it is directly related to these problems associated with learning difficulties.

We can establish lower bounds for the replication rate of decision tree representations of concepts expressed in either DNF or CNF form based on the following theorem from [Pagallo and Haussler, 1990, p. 97]: Let $f$ be a $\mu$DNF formula over the set of variables $V$, where $f = C_1 + \ldots + C_m$, $k_i$ is the number of variables in $C_i$, then any decision tree equivalent has at least $k_1 \times \ldots \times k_m$ leaves. From this, and the definitions of the previous section, we develop the following lower bounds:

**Replication Rate Bound:** *A $\mu$ k-term-l-DNF expression represented as a binary decision tree has at least $l^k$ leaves and $l^k - 1$ tests, and the replication rate is at least $1 - \frac{lk}{l^k-1}$. The same lower bounds hold for a $\mu$ k-clause-l-CNF expression.*

These bounds follow from a consideration of tree structure. The lower bounds for the number of leaves is found by observing that $k_i = l$ for each term, and there are exactly $k$ terms. The number of tests can be derived from the number of leaves by observing that the tree is binary. With at least $l^k - 1$ tests in the tree, at least $l^k - 1 - lk$ are replicated, giving the $1 - \frac{lk}{l^k-1}$ rate; a higher number of tests leads to an equal increase in replications, thus increasing the rate. The results for CNF follow from the duality of DNF and CNF expressions and the corresponding decision trees.

Concept dispersion, roughly captured by the number of peaks [Rendell and Seshu, 1990] needed to represent the concept in instance space, affects both the accuracy and the conciseness of the description. In effect, the more peaks (or disjuncts) needed to represent the concept, the lower predictive accuracy and the less concise description. From the replication rate bound, we see that increasing the number $k$ of terms (clauses) exponentially increases the lower bound[6] as long as the concept is $\mu$ DNF (CNF); for non-$\mu$ concepts this does not always hold, because of overlap between the terms. Furthermore, note that any $\mu$ $k$-term-$l$-CNF expression translates into a non-$\mu$ $l^k$-term-$k$-DNF expression: the replication rate is unchanged; however, this shows that CNF-type concepts generally are more dispersed that DNF-type concepts.

By the relative size of a concept, we mean the proportion of the entire instance space belonging to the concept [Rendell and Seshu, 1990] (see also [Holte and Porter, 1989]). The relative size of the concept also has a subtle effect on the replication rate: when the peaks are relatively small, each peak (or disjunct) requires more features to describe it. From the replication rate bound, we see that an increase in the term size $l$ leads to a polynomially increased lower bound.

Seshu [1989] defines the generalized parity problem as a classical parity problem[7] embedded in a higher dimensional space, i.e., a set of positive and a set of negative examples that cannot be consistently distinguished on the basis of a single feature. In effect, this means that there is some interaction between features that prevents a greedy decision tree algorithm from finding a consistent tree. Equivalently, we see the concept in question is non-$\mu$, that is, it cannot be represented by a $\mu$ DNF, nor a $\mu$ CNF expression. That embedded parity leads to a high replication rate as well is evident from figure 3.

# 3 DCFringe

Pagallo and Haussler [1990] proposed FRINGE to tackle the replication problem. Section 2.2 shows that the replication problem is a manifestation of several characteristics that make concept learning hard. Their experiments have shown that FRINGE's simple feature construction mechanism outperforms other complicated mechanisms in terms of

---

[6]Since the replication rate bound only states lower bounds, we cannot claim that the actual replication rate increases; however, the lower bound increasing is a good indication that the rate increases as well, and empirical evidence supports this claim.

[7]The classical parity problem here denotes either $n$-ary parity or $n$-ary equivalence in an $n$-dimensional instance space; both create the same problems for decision tree learners.

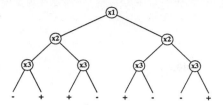

Figure 3: Decision tree for odd parity on three features

predictive accuracy. Furthermore, Matheus [1989] tried three choices of operands for binary conjunction: the two nodes at the *root* of a branch, the two at the *fringe*, and any two *adjacent* nodes. The best accuracy was usually attained using the FRINGE method, although in some cases Adjacent had slightly better accuracy (but poorer efficiency).

Typically, FRINGE performs best when learning small[8] DNF expressions. Nevertheless, it failed to learn a 5-parity concept.[9] Our experiments indicate other concepts for which FRINGE fails. Moreover, concept difficulty for typical decision tree approaches increases with the instance-space dimensionality [Seshu, 1989]. This reveals a limitation of FRINGE, i.e., its performance is subject to some characteristics of the target concept. Our experiments with FRINGE show that it not only fails to improve the predictive accuracy on concepts exhibiting a high degree of *disjunctive* replication, but it can in fact lead to degradation of performance.

Pagallo and Haussler [1990] note that FRINGE's feature construction operators, *negation* and *conjunction*, form a complete set of Boolean operators, ascribing FRINGE with the potential to generate all Boolean features. Nevertheless, we argue that negation and conjunction forms a complete set *only* as long as we *impose no restrictions on the operands*. As seen in the next section, FRINGE imposes a strong bias in selecting the operands for the feature construction process. Although it is important to bias the operand selection, FRINGE's bias is overly restrictive, which prevents the generation of useful disjunctive features. This motivates DCFringe [Yang, 1991].

Figure 4 depicts patterns occurring near the fringe of a decision tree. The crucial

---

[8]around 32 to 80 attributes with 6 to 10 terms of length 3 to 7
[9]The average error for the 5-parity concept went from 29.37% to 24.92%. In other cases, the average error can decrease to 1%.

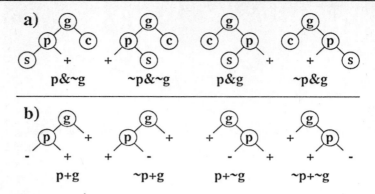

Figure 4: Patterns near the fringe of a decision tree; a) shows patterns recognized by FRINGE; b) shows additional patterns used in DCFringe

observation is that patterns reveal useful ways to combine features. Although both FRINGE and DCFringe make use of this observation, DCFringe considers more of the *context* in which the pattern occurs before selecting which feature to construct. FRINGE performs the constructions shown in figure 4a regardless of the node type of the sibling and the parent's sibling; as depicted in figure 4b DCFringe constructs a disjunctive feature in the case where the sibling is a leaf and the parent's sibling is a positive leaf.

Pagallo [1989] proposed that the CNF problem can be attacked with a dual heuristic for negative leaves, using disjunction instead of conjunction. Later, Pagallo [1990] implemented a combined algorithm Symmetric FRINGE that performs the constructions of FRINGE and dual FRINGE combined. Compared with DCFringe, Symmetric FRINGE is less selective because it forms all conjunctions and disjunctions, regardless of tree structure. Symmetric FRINGE produces more features, which can proliferate in multiple iterations. Our experiments have shown that, in general, DCFringe outperforms Symmetric FRINGE in terms of accuracy, conciseness, and efficiency [Yang *et al.*, 1991]. In the following section we examine the DCFringe algorithm and compare it to FRINGE.

## 3.1 Algorithm

Figure 5 shows the basic iterative learning procedure used at the top level of both FRINGE and DCFringe. The algorithm repeats a two-step process: building a decision tree and feeding it to the feature construction procedure. The construction procedure terminates when no more new features are generated, or a limit of iteration is reached.

---

```
INPUT TrainingSet, TestSet, Features
INPUT IterationLimit, DesiredAccuracy
Index = 0
REPEAT
  Index = Index + 1
  Tree = DecisionTree(TrainingSet, Features)
  Accuracy = ComputeAccuracy(Tree, TestSet)
  NewFeatures = ConstructFeatures(Tree)
  Features = Features + NewFeatures
UNTIL (Index = IterationLimit) OR
  (NewFeatures = NIL)
```

Figure 5: DCFringe algorithm

---

Figure 6 shows the core of DCFringe: the ConstructFeatures function. Given a decision tree learned by PLS1, ConstructFeatures generates new features by conjoining or disjoining features depending on their positions in the decision tree. This function performs the same conjunction operation as FRINGE *except* when the parent's sibling is a positive leaf and the sibling is a leaf; in this case a disjunctive feature is formed instead. The signs within the new conjunction or disjunction depends on whether the current node lies in the left hand side or the right hand side of its parent node, and also the relative position of its parent node to its grandparent node.

## 4   Results

In section 2.1 we showed the replication problem is a manifestation of underlying problems that make concepts difficult to learn. Here we investigate how these problems affect learning algorithms. First, we claim that FRINGE solves the replication problem only to the extent that the concept in question is easily expressible as $\mu$ (or near $\mu$) DNF; thus when the underlying concept is highly dispersed in the instance space, DCFringe's disjunctive operators are necessary to combat the disjunctive replications. Second, we claim that although the degree of replication has some effect on the final result, DCFringe

```
FUNCTION ConstructFeatures(Tree)
INIT Features = NIL
FOR every positive Leaf at depth ≥ 2 in Tree DO
   IF Sibling of Leaf is a negative leaf THEN
      IF ParentSibling of Leaf is a positive leaf THEN
         Feature = Disjoin(Parent, GrandParent, Leaf)
      ELSE (* ParentSibling is not a leaf *)
         Feature = Conjoin(Parent, GrandParent, Leaf)
      ENDIF
   ELSE (* Sibling is not a leaf *)
      Feature = Conjoin(Parent, GrandParent, Leaf)
   ENDIF
   Features = Features + Feature
END
RETURN Features

FUNCTION Conjoin(Parent, GrandParent, Leaf)
(* Disjoin is analogous *)
IF Leaf is left child of Parent THEN
   IF Parent is left child of Grandparent THEN
      RETURN (NOT Parent AND NOT GrandParent)
   ELSE
      RETURN (NOT Parent AND GrandParent)
   ENDIF
ELSE
   IF Parent is left child of Grandparent THEN
      RETURN (Parent AND NOT GrandParent)
   ELSE
      RETURN (Parent AND GrandParent)
   ENDIF
ENDIF
```

Figure 6: ConstructFeatures algorithm

is an effective solution to the replication problem. In this section we present empirical evidence to support both claims.

## 4.1 Experimental design

FRINGE and DCFringe were run on 160 randomly[10] generated concepts on 10 features. These concepts are generated from 16 pre-determined classes; the classes are 4/2 DNF

---

[10]Generation is random within predetermined classes, better described as *local randomness*. See [Yang, 1991] for more details.

and CNF[11] and 2/4 DNF and CNF, all either $\mu$ or non-$\mu$ as well as monotone[12] or non-monotone. For each of the 160 target concepts, 90 training examples and 200 testing examples were generated such that no two examples were the same; the number of training examples was determined empirically to be in the area where FRINGE and DCFringe are most effective [Yang, 1991].

Here we concentrate on the effects of CNF-type versus DNF-type concepts as well as the effects of increasing degree of replication; the effects of $\mu$ versus non-$\mu$ and monotonicity were tested separately and the results may be found in [Yang, 1991]. The experiments and results were partitioned according to CNFness in order to test our first claim. A $\mu$ 4-clause-2-CNF expression yields a CNFness of 0.52, while the CNFness of a $\mu$ 2-clause-4-CNF expression is 0.3. Note that the CNFness of any $\mu$ DNF expression is 0.

The same experiments were used to test our second claim, but the emphasis was shifted to replication rate rather than CNFness as the independent variable. Note that all $k/l$ $\mu$ expressions for given $k$ and $l$ will yield the same replication rate regardless of whether they are DNF or CNF; 4/2 expressions have replication rate 0.73 and 2/4 expressions 0.60. These two categories cover half of our experimental data, the remaining being from non-$\mu$ expressions yielding differing replication rates.

## 4.2 Experimental results

This section presents and discusses the most significant results from our experiments with FRINGE and DCFringe. First, we compare the performance of FRINGE and DCFringe with respect to the CNFness of the target concepts. Second, we show the significant improvement provided by DCFringe over a pure partitioning learning method, PLS1.

Figure 7 shows the influence of CNFness on the accuracy improvement of FRINGE: The histogram shows the percentage of concepts on which FRINGE results in accuracy improvement or degradation. When there are no disjunctive replication patterns at all (dark bars), FRINGE gains improvements of more than 5% for over half of the testing

---

[11]The notation $k/l$ is used to signify $k$-term-$l$-DNF and $k$-clause-$l$-CNF respectively.
[12]An expression is *monotone* if all the literals are positive.

concepts. However, using the same distribution of concepts with a high CNFness (light bars), we have a completely different picture: When the CNFness is 0.40,[13] only less than 5% of the concepts show a slight improvement in accuracy. On most of the testing concepts, using FRINGE results in a decrease in accuracy, showing that CNFness significantly affects the performance of FRINGE.

Figure 8 shows the corresponding results for DCFringe. Note that the distribution for the concepts with no disjunctive replications is similar, although not identical, to that of FRINGE; the two systems exhibit some minor differences in results for individual concepts, but the overall performance is similar for low CNFness. However, for CNF-type concepts (CNFness 0.40) the distribution for DCFringe is not significantly different from the distribution for DNF-type concepts, verifying that the ability of DCFringe to construct disjunctive features overcomes a major limitation of FRINGE.

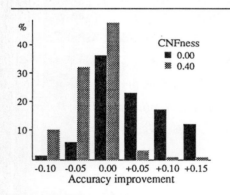

Figure 7: Effect of CNFness on the performance of FRINGE

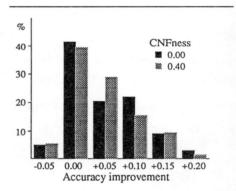

Figure 8: Effect of CNFness on the performance of DCFringe

Figure 9 shows the influence of the replication problem on the accuracy of a partitioning learning system, PLS1. We see a noticeable trend that as the replication rate increases, the accuracy for PLS1 decreases. When the replication rate is low, over 70% of the testing concepts are learned correctly. When the replication rate is between 0.60 and 0.80, most of the testing concepts are learned only to an accuracy of less than 0.85. This result validates the hypothesis that the replication problem strongly affects the performance in terms of accuracy of partitioning learning systems.

---

[13]These numbers are approximate, averaging several test concepts.

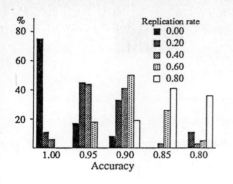

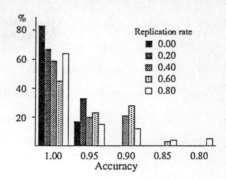

Figure 9: Effect of replications on the performance of PLS1

Figure 10: Effect of replications on the performance of DCFringe

The effect of applying DCFringe is demonstrated in figure 10; the figure shows the last pass accuracy of DCFringe when applied to the same concepts given to PLS1. DCFringe reaches accuracies between 0.95 and 1.00 almost regardless of replication rate; the figure suggests that high replication rate has some effect (although some irregularity should be attributed to sparse training data and approximations in calculating replication rates). Nevertheless, the salient movement from low accuracy to high accuracy for high replication rate concepts supports our claim that DCFringe effectively counteracts the replication problem.

# 5   Related Issues

Several important issues in concept learning have so far not been considered in this paper. In this section we consider some of the strengths and limitations of our approach with respect to handling noise as well as handling other classes of concepts. Furthermore we examine some issues related to the generality of the problem and our solution.

In order to reduce the effects of noise, increase the confidence and applicability, and reduce the size of a decision tree, the tree is often submitted to a post-pruning process [Breiman et al., 1984]; this process assumes that the important tests indeed occur at the top of the decision tree. DCFringe, on the other hand, is based on the assumption that features that interact will occur near the fringes of the tree because the greedy algorithm is unable to detect their significance earlier. This has two important implications: first, pruning decision trees before feature construction impedes the feature construction process; second, using DCFringe before pruning tends to reduce the effects of pruning by constructing complicated features that overfit the data.

Pruning decision trees before submitting them to feature construction removes the fringes DCFringe relies on for identifying feature interaction. However, Matheus [1989] has shown that deferring pruning until after feature construction is terminated is an effective means of reducing FRINGE's susceptibility to noise. We suspect the same result applies to DCFringe, although to a lesser degree because of DCFringe's ability to introduce disjunctive features. DCFringe has the potential for reducing one of the negative effects of pruning by identifying interacting features near the fringes of the tree: pruning is normally unable to distinguish these features from true noise.

Although the tendency of DCFringe to overfit the data for most concepts is dominated by its ability to identify essential features, DCFringe causes a degradation of accuracy for some concepts. More research is needed to understand the circumstances in which this problem occurs as well as how to counteract this behavior. Two possible approaches that need further study are applying additional restrictions on the construction of new features or applying constraints on the application of the constructed features; constraining feature construction by applying additional knowledge is a particularly promising approach in this respect [Matheus, 1989, Ragavan and Rendell, 1990].

This paper considers decision tree learning; thus both the problem and our solution is limited in its scope. However, we have shown that the replication problem is a manifestation of characteristics associated with concept learning difficulties of a more general nature. Although the feature construction mechanism of DCFringe is closely tied to the decision tree approach, the approach can be generalized by noting that the features are constructed based on distributional information in the example set. Features are constructed from others that yield a low conditional entropy on a subset of the instance space; they are retained if their combination yields a higher conditional entropy. Further study is needed to fully understand the relationship between the example distribution in instance space and the constructed features in order to make these results applicable to other representations.

The performance of DCFringe depends on the maturity of the decision tree passed to the feature construction procedure; this maturity is again related to the size of the training set. More research is necessary to understand the effects of the training set size on performance, particularly to assess the conditions under which DCFringe is most effective. It is likely that these conditions vary with certain concept characteristics, some of which have been identified in this paper; however, more study is also needed into the correspondences between the characteristics of concepts that are hard to learn, their representations, and the effects that these have on the learning system.

# 6   Conclusions

This paper presents feature construction as an effective solution to the decision tree replication problem. The replication problem is shown to be a manifestation of concept characteristics associated with learning difficulty, demonstrating the generality of the problem. We introduce two measures, CNFness and replication rate, that capture essential aspects of the correspondence between learning difficulty and representation. Furthermore, we show how this correspondence motivates the development of DCFringe—an enhancement of Pagallo and Haussler's [1990] FRINGE.

DCFringe distinguishes between disjunctive and conjunctive replications, thus considering more of the context in which replication occurs before constructing new features. In our experiments, DCFringe outperforms FRINGE in accuracy for learning concepts corresponding to CNF-type expressions, and equals the performance of FRINGE for DNF-type concepts. Furthermore, DCFringe yields a significant improvement in both accuracy and conciseness with respect to decision-tree learners such as PLS1 [Rendell, 1983].

DCFringe as presented in this paper is limited in its ability to handle noisy data, in part caused by the power of the feature construction mechanism; one possible remedy for this effect is the use of deferred pruning [Matheus, 1989]. Furthermore, DCFringe's powerful feature construction mechanism tends to overfit the data in certain cases; possible remedies include further constraining feature construction and the application of the constructed features, particularly through the use of knowledge.

# Acknowledgments

We appreciate the comments and criticism of Powell Benedict, Chris Matheus, Eduardo Perez, Harish Ragavan, Raj Seshu and Larry Watanabe on earlier presentations of this work. We also thank the anonymous reviewers of EWSL.

# References

[Breiman et al., 1984] Leo Breiman, Jerome H. Friedman, Richard A. Olshen, and Charles J. Stone. *Classification and Regression Trees.* Wadsworth, Belmont, CA, 1984.

[Holte and Porter, 1989] R. C. Holte and Bruce W. Porter. Concept learning and the problem of small disjuncts. In *Proceedings of the Eleventh International Joint Conference on Artificial Intelligence*, pages 813–824, 1989.

[Kearns et al., 1987] Michael Kearns, Ming Li, Leonard Pitt, and Leslie G. Valiant. Recent results on boolean concept learning. In *Proceedings of the Fourth International Workshop on Machine Learning*, Irvine, CA, 1987.

[Matheus, 1989] Christopher J. Matheus. *Feature Construction: An Analytical Framework and an Application to Decision Trees.* PhD thesis, University of Illinois at Urbana-Champaign, December 1989.

[Pagallo and Haussler, 1990] Giulia Pagallo and David Haussler. Boolean feature discovery in empirical learning. *Machine Learning*, 5:71–99, 1990.

[Pagallo, 1989] Giulia Pagallo. Learning DNF by decision trees. In *Proceedings of the Eleventh International Joint Conference on Artificial Intelligence*, 1989.

[Pagallo, 1990] Giulia Pagallo. *Adaptive Decision Tree Algorithms for Learning from Examples.* PhD thesis, University of California at Santa Cruz, June 1990.

[Quinlan, 1986] J. Ross Quinlan. Induction of decision trees. *Machine Learning*, 1(1):81–106, 1986.

[Ragavan and Rendell, 1990] Harish Ragavan and Larry A. Rendell. Context-based acquisition of difficult concepts. Unpublished manuscript., 1990.

[Rendell and Cho, 1990] Larry A. Rendell and Howard Cho. Empirical learning as a function of concept character. *Machine Learning*, 5(3):267–298, 1990.

[Rendell and Seshu, 1990] Larry A. Rendell and Raj Seshu. Learning hard concepts. *Computational Intelligence*, 1990. (To appear).

[Rendell, 1983] Larry A. Rendell. A new basis for state-space learning systems and a successful implementation. *Artificial Intelligence*, 20(4):369–392, 1983.

[Seshu, 1989] Raj Seshu. Solving the parity problem. In *Proceedings of the Fourth European Working Session on Learning*, pages 263–271, Montpellier, France, December 1989.

[Yang and Blix, 1990] Der-Shung Yang and Gunnar Blix. FRINGE, DCFringe and $\mu$ concepts. Presented at the Workshop on *Computational Learning Theory and Natural Learning Systems*, 1990.

[Yang et al., 1991] Der-Shung Yang, Larry A. Rendell, and Gunnar Blix. A scheme for feature construction and a comparison of empirical methods. Submitted to *the Thirteenth International Joint Conference on Artificial Intelligence*, 1991.

[Yang, 1991] Der-Shung Yang. Feature discovery in decision tree representation. Master's thesis, University of Illinois at Urbana-Champaign, May 1991.

# INTEGRATING AN EXPLANATION–BASED LEARNING MECHANISM INTO A GENERAL PROBLEM–SOLVER

F. ZERR (*) (**)  J.G. GANASCIA (***)

(*) L.R.I., Bât 490, Université Paris XI, 91405 ORSAY. FRANCE
(**) THOMSON–CSF DSE/DT/SEP/STI, 9 rue des mathurins 92223 BAGNEUX. FRANCE
(***) LAFORIA, URA 1095 du CNRS, Université Pierre et Marie CURIE, Tour 46–0, 4 place Jussieu 75252 Paris. FRANCE.

## Abstract

In this paper, we study the problem of integrating an *Explanation–Based Learning* mechanism into a general and industrial problem solver. During our investigations into *SOAR* we discovered a number of weaknesses related to its architecture and learning mechanism, known as *Chunking*. Using general concepts on which SOAR is based, we define a new learning system based, on the one hand, on a general and industrial problem solver, and, on the other hand, on an efficient learning mechanism known as *EBG* (*Explanation–Based Generalization*). Due to the fact that EBG sometimes learns production rules which are too general, we have introduced the possibility of restricting the generality of learned rules, in order to improve significantly the performances of industrial applications.

We have tested this system on an industrial application at *Thomson*. In this application, we had to find correct trajectories for planes through a network of valleys. This type of problem is complex and the search combinational, as the valleys were not properly interconnected. However, learning *327* production rules made the resolution *78* times faster and the system sometimes even found better solutions.

**Keywords:** Explanation–based learning, EBG, Chunking, problem solving, production systems.

# INTRODUCTION

The aim of this study is to show the contribution made by *EBL (Explanation–Based Learning)* in solving industrial applications. The integration of a learning mechanism into a general problem solver entails a number of difficulties. These are discussed in section *1*. Even though many EBL mechanisms exist, few general problem solvers integrate any of these. The *SOAR* [6] system has an EBL mechanism, called *Chunking*. Based on the concept of *Universal Subgoaling*, the system's architecture and the learning mechanism have considerable limitations. To obtain correct rules, Chunking should be used more for memorization purposes than as a general rule learning technique. Because of these weaknesses (*section 2*), SOAR is seldom used in industry. The study of this system allows us to extract general concepts, which will help us to integrate a learning mechanism into a general problem solver *(section 3)*. Contrary to Chunking, *EBG* creates general rules, which are sometimes far too general. Therefore, in the same section, we introduce the possibility of restricting the generality of learned rules, in order to improve significantly the performance of industrial applications. In section *4*, we present some results obtained with our new learning system. Applied to an interesting combinational application used at *Thomson*, very good results are obtained. Learning *327* production rules makes the solution *78* times faster and the system sometimes even finds better solutions. We conclude with a summary of our findings.

# 1 THE CONTEXT OF THE PROBLEM

When we want to integrate an EBL mechanism into an industrial problem solver, we are faced with one particular problem. On the one hand, rules cannot be created from the totality or any part of the proof tree, since they would be too specific. If they are too specific, a large number of rules have to be learned. On the other hand, if we learn general rules we decrease the time performances of the system. The cost of the learned production rules (i.e. the additional time required for their pattern matching) is linked to their generality. With an extensive data base, the more general the production rule is, the more time–consuming it is. Learning a single but very general rule may negate the advantages gained by learning. Thus we have to learn rules which are neither too specific nor too general.

If we want to integrate a learning mechanism, we have to modify the problem solver. But we must take care not to over-modify the problem solver, so that we keep the system general. For instance, to integrate an EBL mechanism into SOAR, the architecture has to be modified substantially. We will focus on this particular system in the next section.

# 2 SOAR

SOAR is one of the few architectures which integrate an explanation-based learning mechanism. The system is based on the concept of *Universal Subgoaling*. This characteristic enables the firing of the learning mechanism (*Chunking*) to be controlled. Both these ideas are interesting and worth further examination.

## 2.1 UNIVERSAL SUBGOALING

### 2.1.1 Subgoaling

In SOAR, a subgoal can be set up for any problem. For instance, a task can be broken down hierarchically into subtasks. Subgoals can also be set up for any control decision for which immediate knowledge is insufficient. In these subgoals we can reason about the behavior of the system.

A learning mechanism is added to the subgoaling, because at the end of each subgoal, its solution can be learned. Thus, when a similar subgoal occurs, the learned rule immediately provides the result. However, subgoals to be learned cannot be specified individually, since SOAR systematically learns each subgoal.

### 2.1.2 Universal Subgoaling

Subgoaling is universal in that SOAR systematically creates new subgoals. Subgoaling is not *deliberate*; it is the system rather than the user who decides on the creation of subgoals. To manage the creation, it was necessary to define a solid communication protocol between the user and the system. In order to do this, control knowledge called *preferences* was introduced. Implemented by facts, preferences represent knowledge of

SOAR's behavior and enable the user and the system (through production rules) to weight up different choices. Then, when a lack of knowledge (or preferences) arises, the system enters into a predefined situation called *impasse*. In this situation, the system creates a new subgoal to overcome the difficulty, then learn the solved subgoal.

This notion of universal subgoaling facilitates the implementation of *universal weak methods* (search strategies), such as *depth-first search*, *breadth-first search*, *means-ends search*, *etc.*. In SOAR, *57* default rules are encoded. They respond to impasses and cause the system to default weak methods.


## 2.2 CHUNKING

*Chunking* [7] belongs to the explanation-based learning system family. Unlike most of these mechanisms, chunking relies on a simplified proof tree, since it is only concerned with the facts of the proof tree. We will look at the effect of this on learned production rules in section *2.4*.

The chunking algorithm acquires new production rules (or *Chunks*) which summarize the processing that provides the subgoal's results. The conditions of a chunk, are the facts that existed before the subgoal's creation and that were relevant in determining the result. These conditions are determined by using the traces (only in terms of facts) of the rules that fire during the subgoal.

After obtaining the condition and the action facts of the chunk, the *variabilization* mechanism replaces, in all the facts, each *identifier* by a variable. Two identical identifiers are replaced by the same variable, whereas two different identifiers are not. All the other elements are retained. Thus, the *variabilization* process is related to the data representation. In SOAR, the facts are represented by the *(Class Object Attribute Value)* representation. An *object* is called an *identifier*, a temporary symbol. The *value* can be a constant value or the identifier of another object. All objects are interconnected. This means that the generalization process only turns objects into variables.


## 2.3 CRITICISM OF UNIVERSAL SUBGOALING IN SOAR

### 2.3.1 Handling subgoaling and preferences by facts

Handling subgoaling and preferences by control facts is unwieldy. To illustrate the point, we will use the *eight-puzzle* example [6]: Out of *1851* created facts, *868* are control facts, of which *332* correspond to preferences and *536* handle the hierarchy of subgoals.

Control conditions (conditions dealing with the access to subgoals) exist in the condition part of the production rules. Therefore, there are also control conditions in learned rules. In the *eight-puzzle* example, one of the learned rules includes *10* control conditions out of a total of *29* conditions.

In short, implementing subgoaling by facts is not the most effective way to proceed, since more facts are created. They make the rules less understandable for the user and decrease system performance.

## 2.3.2 Handling Universal Subgoaling

When presenting universal subgoaling, we mentioned a communication protocol between the user and the system, which requires uniform knowledge representation accessible to both the user and the system. Therefore, in order to achieve this, preferences were implemented by facts, a uniform data representation *(Class Object Attribute Value)* chosen and objects interlinked using identifiers.

Unfortunately, this type of data representation makes the rules less understandable and their execution more time-consuming. It increases the number of conditions both in the production rules and in the learned rules. In the *eight-puzzle* example, one of the learned rules has *40* conditions and its semantics are obscure.

## 2.4 CRITICISM OF CHUNKING

Historically, the first version of the SOAR system (*SOAR1* in *1982*) did not include a learning mechanism. SOAR was intended to be a universal problem solver. Chunking was implemented later (after *SOAR2* in *1984*). This integration proved useful, since some of the search methods are extremely unwieldy and may solve a given subgoal several times in solving a goal. Learning the result of subgoals prevents them from being computed several times. In this context, chunking is used more as for memorization purposes than as a learning technic.

In his paper *"Mapping Explanation-Based Generalization Onto SOAR"* [11], Rosenbloom showed that Chunking is equivalent to *Explanation-Based Generalization* (EBG), a powerful technic for learning by explanation [9]. Rosenbloom mentioned some of the most important differences between the two. These have not, unfortunately, been developed, hence their importance is under-estimated. We expanded on these differences in one of our papers [15]. Rules learned by chunking are often *over-specified* or *over-generalized*. The generality of learned rules is also related to the data representation and the architecture of SOAR. We will now focus on the weaknesses of Chunking which arise when more general rules are required.

### 2.4.1 Over-specification

Over-specification is a relatively unimportant problem, since it does not affect the consistency of the knowledge base. Nevertheless, it leads to the creation of further production rules and turns Chunking into a memorization mechanism rather than a learning mechanism. This over-specification is due to the variabilization algorithm, which only substitutes variables for identifiers and not for certain constants. *Variabilization* is an artificial process, since it does not rely on a proof tree but on a fact tree, and more precisely on the representation of these facts (potential presence of identifiers).

Another situation in which over-specification may arise is where the algorithm, which is based on a fact tree, loses the bindings between variables occurring in different conditions. When two different variables from two conditions of the proof tree (unused by Chunking) are instanciated by the same identifiers, the *variabilization* algorithm substitutes a single variable for this identifier in both conditions.

### 2.4.2 Over-generalization

Over-generalization is a more serious problem, relatively speaking, since it affects the consistency of the knowledge base. It is also due to the *variabilization* algorithm. This kind of mistake occurs when production rules contain *subterms* in their conditions or actions. A subterm can either be a restriction function on a variable, or an evaluation function on the right-hand side of a rule. The following rule includes both kinds of subterms in terms.

```
(Rule  Weight-of-object
     ( Object  <O1> ^Volume  <V0>  & ( > <V0>  50 ))  ; greater
     ( Object  <O1> ^Density <D0>  & ( <> <D0>  1 ))  ; not equal
     ( Object  <O1> ^Type     <T0>  & ( <> <T0>  Endtable)

→
     ( Object <O1> ^Weight  = ( Compute ( * <V0> <D0> ))))

          where <O1>,  <V0> ,  <D0>  and  <T0>   are variables
```

During the learning time, these subterms are lost in the fact tree. From the previous production rule only the instanciations (i.e. the facts) remain. The following facts belong to the fact tree. After *variabilization*, identifiers are replaced by variables. The associated subterms are lost and the learned production rules become over-general.

```
     ( Object   O12   ^Volume   100 )
     ( Object   O12   ^Density  0.9 )
     ( Object   O12   ^Type     T1  )
     ( Object   O12   ^Weight   90  )
          where O12  and  T1   are identifiers
```

## 2.4.3 How to prevent these weaknesses

In order to prevent these problems, the authors of SOAR propose that the use of restriction tests on variables and the use of evaluation instructions be avoided. This restriction is considerable, since it reduces the programming language to a much impoverished minimal subset, which is unlikely to be used in industry. The generality of rules is controlled by means of the data representation. Additional indirection should help to ensure the presence of identifiers in learned rules. These identifiers would be *variabilized* at learning time. For instance in the following example, the value of a *counter* fact must be generalized.

```
     ( Counter   C1   ^Value  0 )
          is transformed into:
     ( Counter   C1   ^Value  V0)
     ( Value     V0   ^Name  0 )
```

As a result, Chunking is correct only if considered as a process for memorizing results. When asked to learn more general rules, the loss of variable bindings or restriction tests leads to inconsistences in the knowledge base. We may prevent these weaknesses by creating intermediate subgoals or using a heavier data representation. Unfortunately, in using a heavier data representation, more conditions are included in production rules, whose pattern matching time will increase immediately. This affects system performance and knowledge base legibility.

## 2.5 IMPLEMENTATION EBG INSTEAD OF CHUNKING IN SOAR

EBG is a general technic for learning by explanation. We replaced Chunking by EBG, which we implemented on SOAR. We reached the following conclusions:
- The learned rules are correct. They are neither over-specified nor over-generalized. This characteristic is vital in a learning system.
- The generality of a production rule does not depend on the data representation.
- Production rules may contain restriction tests as well as evaluation instructions. EBG keeps these information in the learned production rules. The richness of the programming language is preserved.
- Unfortunately, in this implementation EBG is not independent of the SOAR architecture. The left-hand side of learned rules always contains a large number of control conditions. The data representation *(Class Object Attribute Value)* does not significantly improve system performance.

Despite these weaknesses, SOAR remains an interesting learning system from a theoretical point of view. We defined an efficient learning system by extracting and adjusting fundamental concepts of SOAR.

# 3 DEFINITION OUR LEARNING SYSTEM

In the previous section we saw that SOAR has a large number of constraints. These constraints prevents EBG from improving its performances significantly. That is why, we chose to define a new learning system based on SOAR's concepts. We thereby avoid implementing these in a time-consuming way. By integrating EBG into a general problem solver, we also try to keep it as general as possible and consider the learning module as independent. In this section we present the concepts on which our system is based and give an idea of their implementation.

## 3.1 SUBGOALING

Subgoaling is the main idea behind our learning mechanism. At the present time, a large number of problem solvers allow production rules to be structured into sets, known as *rulesets*. The possibility of associating them with one or several *conflict sets* (or *Agendas*) facilitates the control local to a problem space. Thus, as in SOAR, the firing of the learning mechanism can be confined to a specified subgoal. The benefit of an implementation of this type is that production rules are prevented from being overloaded with control conditions, thereby improving system performances. The user can also easily define new subgoals. This is known as *deliberate subgoaling*.

## 3.2 DELIBERATE SUBGOALING

In contrast with universal subgoaling, *deliberate subgoaling* is under the user's control. In controlling the subgoal creation, the user also controls the firing of the learning mechanism. From the point of view of implementation, deliberate subgoaling does not require any protocol specification in order to create subgoals. Handling by facts, the choice of a uniform data structure and the presence of a decision algorithm are no longer necessary. These simplifications save time (using a multi–attribute data representation) and improve the legibility of the knowledge base (rules contain fewer conditions). Deliberate subgoaling enables all the characteristics of the problem solver. It is adequate for solving most of the problems. Unfortunately, it does not allow the definition of default strategies. However, we should remember that our goal is not to obtain a universal problem solver.

## 3.3 CONTROL: NOTION OF PRIORITY

A learning system also has to learn control knowledge capable of modifying and improving the behavior of this system. This kind of knowledge can be learned through subgoals when a lack of control knowledge occurs during the reasoning process. SOAR creates these subgoals and learns their results, i.e. learns the creation of new preferences (implemented by facts).

In our system, the control knowledge will be expressed by the notion of *priority* (or *weight*) and learned the same way. A priority is directly associated with a rule instance. The action side of a learned control rule is a function, which modifies the priority of a rule instance in a given conflict set. This function can also be expressed as a very complex evaluation function (*weight, distance, etc.*). It is built by the learning algorithm so that all the variables it contains are substituted correctly (see example in *section 4.2.2.1*). The cost of this implementation is practically nil, since a priority is dealt immediately. Preferences in SOAR are recorded as control facts, so they must be reevaluated continuously.

## 3.4 SPECIFYING THE GENERALITY OF LEARNED RULES

On the one hand the SOAR system integrates Chunking, more as a memorization mechanism than a learning mechanism. This kind of mechanism is not very efficient in an industrial application. On the other hand, our new system integrates EBG, a general learning mechanism. Based on the generality of the rule from the knowledge base, the rules learned by EBG are as general. However, in some industrial applications the learned rules are too general or, more specifically, too time-consuming. The cost of these rules in time negates the advantage of learning. Hence, we have to control the generality of the learned rules. Contrary to SOAR, we will not have to modify the data representation in order to act on the generality of the rules. We will now look at how we propose that the user specialize his learned rules.

We will consider the industrial application written by *Thomson*, the purpose of which is to find a trajectory for planes through a network of valleys, moving from an objective to a given direction. It is a combinational problem. Let us suppose that the system has learned the following general rule:

```
(Rule General-rule
     . . .
     ( Valley   ?X-ccord-1  ?Y-coord-1  ?Name-1 )     ; first Valley
     ( Valley   ?X-coord-2  ?Y-coord-2  ?Name-2 )     ; second Valley
     (Test (connected-or-near ?Name-1  ?Name-2 )) ; restriction test
     . . .
  =>  . . . )

         where ?X-ccord-1, ?Y-coord-1 , ... and ?Name-2  are variables
```

The rule is general to every valley on the map, but is also too time–consuming. To make this rule less time–consuming, we can specify some variables. For instance, in specifying the name of the valleys, the rule becomes local. If the learned example includes *Valley–13* and *Valley–10*, the local rule will be as described follows.

```
(Rule Local–rule
     . . .
     ( Valley  ?X–ccord–1  ?Y–coord–1  Valley–13 )    ; first  Valley
     ( Valley  ?X–coord–2  ?Y–coord–2  Valley–10 )    ; second Valley
     (Test (connected–or–near Valley–13 Valley–10 )) ; restriction test
     . . .
  =>  . . . )
```

In order to specialize the learned rules, we allow the user to declare some attributes of some conditions to be specific. The next function defines the specialization of the attribute *Name* of the condition *Valley*. So after each EBG learning process, the variable in the specified condition is replaced by its instanciated value. To keep the learned rule correct, this variable is replaced by its instanciation in the whole rule.

```
( Specialization :Condition Valley :Attribute Name )
```

# 4 RESULTS

The general problem solver that we have chosen is CIME [1]. Written by Thomson, CIME is similar to the ART [3] problem solver. Moreover, this system is able to manage rulesets associated with conflict sets. These possibilities enabled us to implement easily the concepts examined earlier.

## 4.1 GAMES

Firstly, we solved, using CIME, the games previously executed on SOAR. Without learning, for all these examples, the solution speed is 5 to 100 times faster with CIME. Therefore in our system learning decreases the resolution time. The results are summarized in the following table.

| Solution time decrease \ Games | Eight–puzzle | Monkey and Bananas | Water Gauge | Missionary and Cannibals | Magic Square |
|---|---|---|---|---|---|
| On the **same** example | | 5 | 6 | 2.7 | 194 |
| On **other** examples | **5** (times faster) | | | | |

## 4.2 AN INDUSTRIAL APPLICATION: SEARCH FOR TRAJECTORIES

Thanks to the Thomson application, we were able to check that our system satisfies the needs of industry. The search for plane trajectories through a network of valleys (the valleys are not always interconnected) from an objective to a given direction, raises a combinational problem (Note: We tried to implement this application on SOAR, but did not succeed). This application was previously been written on CIME. When we implemented it on our system, we obtained very good results. We will devote the first part of the following section to discussing learning general rules and the second part to learning local but more efficient rules.

### 4.2.1 Learning general rules

In the first step, we have learned general rules from only one example (a given objective on the map). So the learned control rules direct the search to finding a solution. The meaning of the learned rules can be explained as follows:
– If there is **one** valley which leads to the solution of the goal, choose it.
– If there are **two** consecutive valleys (connected or with a *hole*) which leads to the solution of the goal, choose both.
– If there are **three** consecutive valleys (connected or with a *hole*) which leads to the solution of the goal, choose all three.
It is as if the system sees 1, 2 or 3 steps ahead. However, these rules are very time–consuming and decrease the performances of the system. The following graph shows that a fourth step production rule throws the resolution speed down.

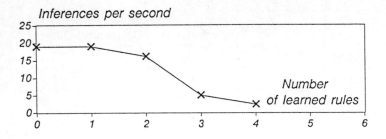

*Inferences per second*

*Number of learned rules*

Despite the increase in solution time, the system provides better solutions after learning. The following example illustrates a solution obtained without learning (*left*) and a solution obtained after learning (*right*).

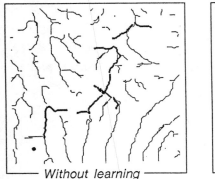

*Without learning*

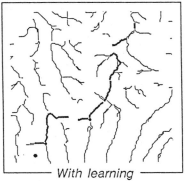

*With learning*

The bold-faced trajectory obtained without learning (left) is not acceptable. Because the map is incomplete and the valleys are not fully connected, adjacent valleys were included in the final result.To obtain a better solution without learning, the knowledge base should be enriched with more efficient control rules. This would avoid bad paths. But, as the network is not completely connected, it is difficult to write these rules. In this situation, learning production rules favors the building of a simplified rule base; the EBG mechanism constructs those complicated control rules.

### 4.2.2 Learning specific rules

We have seen that in our application general rules are costly. One solution for learning efficient rules is to specialize the time-consuming conditions. More precisely, we specialize the attribute *Name* of the condition *Valley* (*see section 3.4*). After specialization, the distance computation functions are kept, so that the learned rules stay general locally to learned valleys. It means that if an objective is placed in an area as follows, the learned rules fire.

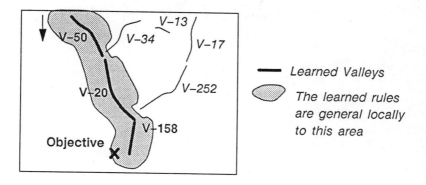

To learn everything about a given map, we chose *32* different objectives and learned their results. By breaking down the goal (finding a trajectory for an objective) hierarchically into subgoals (finding a trajectory from a valley to the right map board), all the best partial trajectories associated to valleys were learned. So, the whole map was covered by learning.

To choose between two different valleys, a distance has been introduced. This distance is transformed into a priority associated with the rule instance in the conflict set. The best plane trajectory is the one which has the shortest distance between the different valleys. As in the previous paragraph, learning control rules is as though the system counted before time the value of all the "jumps" between the valleys up to the goal. Thus learning everything about the map can be considered as preprocessing for finding the best solutions.

### 4.2.2.1 Execution results

We will now give an example of learned rules. The following shows the third step rule associated with the valleys *V–4*, *V–3* and *V–1* of the trajectory.

```
( Rule P12
      ( Declare (ruleset Valley) (type  learned ))
      ( objective ?o ?x ?y )
?c1◄─ ( possible-choice ?d  ?o  V-4  ?distance )      ; choice
      ( Valley  ?x1  ?y1  V-4 )                       ; first  Valley
      ( Valley  ?x2  ?y2  V-3 )                       ; second  Valley
      (Test (connected-or-near  V-4  V-3 ))
      ( Valley  ?x3  ?y3  V-1 )                       ; third  Valley
      (Test (connected-or-near  V-3  V-1 ))
      (Test (valley-near-right-bord  V-1 ))
   =>
      (change-priority :Agenda  Choices
                       :Rules    Create-new-connection
                       :instances   ?c1
                       :value    (+ 100000
                                    (-  ?distance )
                                    (-  (compute-distance  V-4  V-3))
                                    (-  (compute-distance  V-3  V-1))
```

With *32* objectives, *327* production rules are learned. The following maps illustrate the set of initial valleys (*left*) and the set of learned valleys (*right*). Unlearned valleys are insignificant in finding a solution, whereas the learned valleys are weighted with a function of priority computation. The map is preprocessed.

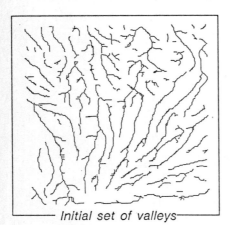

——— *Initial set of valleys*———

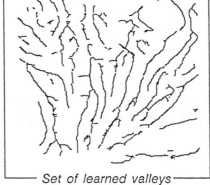

——— *Set of learned valleys*———

For each of the *32* other objectives, i.e. the objectives which are not used by the learning procedure, the following map gives the trajectory found with the *327* learned rules. These trajectories are **bold-faced** on the map. Some objectives do not have any trajectory towards the north side of the map.

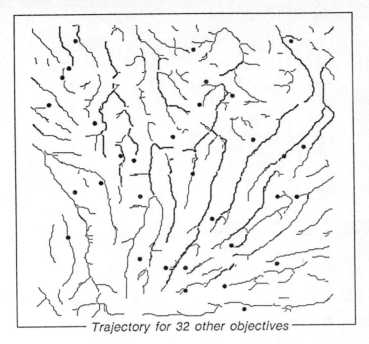

*Trajectory for 32 other objectives*

The two following tables give the results of the solution for the *32* objectives without and then with learned production rules. We also give an average value per objective. Learning *327* rules finds the solution with much greater speed. The solution speed is *78* times faster after learning. After learning, the solution time is always less than *300* seconds. This result is the more important one, as the solution without learning can sometimes take several hours.

| Objec-tive | Without After Learning | | Objec-tives | Without After Learning | | Objec-tives | Without After Learning | |
|---|---|---|---|---|---|---|---|---|
| 1 | 5 seconds | 9 | 12 | 15 | 33 | 23 | 5387 | 88 |
| 2 | 5 | 5 | 13 | 3633 | 81 | 24 | 1059 | 43 |
| 3 | 5 | 10 | 14 | 325 | 32 | 25 | 6355 | 162 |
| 4 | 16 | 11 | 15 | 21 | 43 | 26 | 6863 | 1689 |
| 5 | 30 | 13 | 16 | 4242 | 171 | 27 | 16768 | 4209 |
| 6 | 1244 | 50 | 17 | 1257 | 59 | 28 | 15346 | 284 |
| 7 | 451 | 42 | 18 | 4383 | 86 | 29 | 9715 | 59 |
| 8 | 1034 | 248 | 19 | 10045 | 86 | 30 | 12395 | 80 |
| 9 | 232 | 24 | 20 | 1730 | 43 | 31 | 10411 | 87 |
| 10 | 222 | 33 | 21 | 1748 | 78 | 32 | 14026 | 299 |
| 11 | 182 | 42 | 22 | 13366 | 121 | | | |

| Average Value | Number of Rules fired | Number of States created | Solution Time |
|---|---|---|---|
| Without Learned rules | 11220 | 2043 | 6314 s 1h 45' 14" |
| With Learned rules | 500 | 15 | 81 s 1' 21" |

## 4.2.2.2 Other results

The solutions obtained with learned rules are as good as those obtained without learning. In seven cases they were even better, because the system did not have enough time to explore the whole search tree. We deliberately limited the solution to 15,000 rule firings (around 3 hours).

We noted that the solution time decreases even during the learning process for the 32 first objectives. This means that the amount of time spent in constructing new rules is less than the advantage gained by their use. The construction time for one rule is about 18 seconds.

| AVERAGE value per objective | Number of Rules fired | Number of States created | Solution Time | EBG Learning Time |
|---|---|---|---|---|
| Without Learned rules | 5782 | 1041 | 3923 seconds | |
| During Learning | 1258 | 69 | 472 seconds | 188 seconds |

# 5 CONCLUSION

We succeeded in integrating a learning mechanism into a general problem solver. By implementing more effectively the different concepts extracted from SOAR and by using an efficient learning algorithm (EBG), we kept the problem solver general and useful. We also allow the user to control the generality of the learned rules, in order to improve significantly the performances of the learning system in an industrial context.

Because the problem solver is roughly the same, applications are easily portable and learnable from a general problem solver such as ART or CIME to our system. The learned production rules are not overloaded with control conditions so, it is possible to use the learned knowledge in another problem solver. This is not the case in SOAR.

Writing an application in our system is not restrictive. Quite the contrary; obliging the user to define sets of rules and offering him local conflict sets is a positive point. Indeed EBG deals with subterms into terms, but like other mechanisms based on explanation, it cannot deal with overly rich programming languages. For instance, the deletion of facts must be handled carefully. The creation of facts in a loop instruction on the action side of a rule will also be excluded.

We saw that learning decreases the solution time or provides better solutions. In other applications you can define fewer control rules, since the learning mechanism learns them for you. This justifies learning in an industrial context.

# REFERENCES

[1] W. Chehire, A. Combastel, D. Chouvet, J.Y. Quemeneur, F. Zerr. "*CIME: Une approche cohérente pour développer, intégrer et optimiser des modules experts dans un milieu opérationnel*" in Avignon 1989

[2] W. Chehire "*KIRK: Un environnement de développement de Systèmes Experts*" in Avignon 1988

[3] B. Clayton "*ART: Automated Reasoning Tool*" Inference Corporation 1985

[4] G. Dejong , R. Mooney "*Explanation-Based Learning: An alternative view*" In Machine Learning 1: 145-176,19. 1986

[5] C. L. Forgy "*RETE: A fast algorithm for many pattern/many object pattern match problem.*" In Artificial Intelligence 19:17-37, 1982

[6] J. Laird , A. Newell , P.S. Rosenbloom "*SOAR: An architecture for general intelligence*" In Artificial Intelligence 33, 1-64, 1987

[7] J. Laird , P.S. Rosenbloom , A. Newell  *"Chunking in SOAR: The anatomy of a general learning mechanism"*  in Machine Learning 1, 1986

[8] J. Laird  *"The SOAR Casebook"*  SOAR Project Papers  CMU. 1986

[9] T. Mitchell , R. Keller , S. Kedar-cabelli  *"Explanation-Based Generalization: A unifying view"*  in Machine Learning 1, 1986

[10] R. Mooney  S. Bennett  *"A domain independent explanation-based generalizer"*  In Proceedings AAAI 86  1986

[11] P.S. Rosenbloom , J. Laird  *"Mapping Explanation Based Generalization onto SOAR"*  in Proceedings AAAI 86 , Philadelphia, PA. 1986

[12] P.S. Rosenbloom , J. Laird, A. Newell  *"Knowledge-level learning in SOAR."*  in Proc. of Sixth National Conference on Artificial Intelligence Seattle. 1986

[13] D. J. Scales  *"Efficient Matching Algorithms for the SOAR / OPS5 Production System"*  Knowledge Systems Laboratory  Report No KSL 86-47, 1986

[14] M. Tambe, A. Newell  *"Why Some chunks Are Expensive"*  Carnegie Mellon Computer Science Departement,  Report No 103. 1988

[15] F. Zerr, J.G. Ganascia  *"Comparaison du Chunking avec l'EBG implémenté sur SOAR"*  5 ièmes Journées Françaises d'apprentissage,  LANNION 1990

# ANALYTICAL NEGATIVE GENERALIZATION AND EMPIRICAL NEGATIVE GENERALIZATION ARE NOT CUMULATIVE : A CASE STUDY

C. CARPINETO

Fondazione "Ugo Bordoni", Via B. Castiglione 59, 00142-Rome, Italy

## Abstract

This paper addresses the problem of using explanation-based generalizations of negative inputs in Mitchell's candidate elimination algorithm and in other more recent approaches to version spaces. It points out that a mere combination would produce a worse result than that obtainable without input pre-processing, whereas this problem was not perceived in previous work. Costs and benefits of the extra computation required to take advantage of prior EBL phase are analysed for a conjunctive concept languages defined on a tree-structured attribute-based instance space. Furthermore, this result seems to be independent of the particular inductive learning algorithm considered (i.e., version spaces), thus helping clarify one aspect of the ill-understood relation between analytical generalization and empirical generalization.

**Keywords**   Inductive generalization, analytical generalization, version spaces

## 1 Introduction

Recent work on integrated learning has shown that empirical learning methods and EBL methods can enhance each other in a number of ways. The overall utility of such a combination, however, often relies on heuristics for which little justification is provided, rather than being supported by theoretical or empirical evaluation. In this paper we shall analyse the use of analitycally generalized negative inputs in a version space approach [Mitc82a]. There are several reasons why this is an interesting problem.

First of all, since Mitchell presented the candidate elimination algorithm [Mitc78] most of attempts to improve his framework (e.g., [Mitc82b], [Utgo86]) have focused on using analytically generalized *positive* inputs in place of ground positive inputs. Pre-processing of the *negative* inputs by an EBL module has, by contrast received less attention. We show that, contrary to what is sometimes reported in the literature (e.g., [Char86], [Ellm89]), the use of generalized negative inputs in Mitchell's algorithm is not as straightforward as the use of generalized positive inputs.

Secondly, more recently Hirsh ([Hirs89], [Hirs90]) and Carpineto [Carp90] have investigated, with similar results, the suitability of version spaces as a problem structure whereby empirical and analytical learning can be tightly integrated. Both of these two approaches employ a learning algorithm somewhat different from Mitchell's one, and explicitly deal with generalized negative inputs. However, similarly to the former case, the direct use of the output of the negative EBL phase into such empirical frameworks seems to raise a problem that has not been perceived. Our research was, in fact, motivated by the difficulties uncovered during the development of the method presented in [Carp90].

Thirdly, the problem at hand is an instance of a typical combination pattern, i.e. using an EBL phase before doing empirical learning. The advantage of using version spaces is that the inductive bias is more explicit than that of other empirical learning algorithms. This makes it possible to better investigate the ill-understood relation between analytical generalization and empirical generalization. The result of our analysis suggests that analytical negative generalization and empirical negative generalization are not cumulative; more precisely, we will show that an inductive learning algorithm that makes use of generalized negative inputs may be slower than the same algorithm without prior generalization.

In the next sections we present the problem, as it raises in Mitchell's approach. Then we discuss how the algorithm has to be modified, and analyse the problem for a conjunctive concept language defined on a tree-structured attribute-based instance spaces. Finally we consider the generality of the question addressed here, and sketch the overall costs and benefits of this type of integrated approach to learning from negative examples.

## 2 Version spaces with generalized positive inputs

The idea behind Mitchell's approach [Mitc78] is to represent and update the set of all concept descriptions that are consistent (complete and consistent, according to other terminologies) with data. In order to do so efficiently, the user must provide the set of generalization terms, along with information about the partial order imposed by the relation more-general-than over the terms. This is usually done by representing the generalization language as a directed acyclic graph, in which each node is a term, and such that a node N is a successor of a node M if and only if the set of instances associated with N is a superset of the set of instances associated with M. In this way the space of consistent concepts at any given one time (i.e. the version space) can be represented by only two sets, S (the set of the most specific consistent concepts) and G (the set of the most general consistent concepts).

The procedure to update the version space is as follows. For each positive example, the algorithm removes the members of G that do not match the example, and generalizes the members of S that do not match the example only to the extent required so that they match the example and remain more specific than some term in G. For each negative example, the algorithm removes the members of S that match the example, and specializes the members of G that match the example only to the extent required so that they do not match the example and remain more general than some term in G. The computational requirements for this approach to work are that the sets S and G be finite, and the procedures to match instances to concepts and to test whether one concept is more general than another be tractable. After processing each example the version space shrinks; it may eventually reduces to the target concept, provided that the concept description language is consistent with tha data.

This framework has been later ([Mitch82b], [Utgo86]) improved by adding an EBL module for pre-processing the positive instances. It takes single positive instances, and uses its domain theory in an EBL fashion to construct generalized positive instances. The output of this module can then be directly submitted to the candidate elimination algorithm, as if it were a ground instance. In fact, since the result of EBL provides sufficient conditions for concept membership, every admissible concept description must be at least as general as the generalized instance (if the EBL module returned necessary and sufficient conditions for concept membership, we would get just the target concept.). In this way each instance has the effect of multiple instances; the advantage is that fewer instances are necessary for convergency.

# 3  Version spaces with generalized negative inputs

Although prior analytical generalization has been usually restricted to positive instances, there is a widely accepted opinion (e.g., [Char86], [Ellm89]) that a similar extension for negative instances would raise no difficulty. Here we shall critically examine this view. The point we want to make is that updating a version space with the explanation-based generalization of a negative instance, rather than with the ground instance, not only does not result in an improvement of efficiency, but will in general yield a bigger version space than that obtainable by using the ungeneralized instance, thus slowing down the convergency.

To illustrate this, consider a (ungeneralized) negative instance $u$ and its analytical generalization $g$. Let $c_u$ be the most specific concept of the generalization language that includes $u$ (suppose, for simplicity, that there is only one), and let $c_g$ be the most specific concept that includes $g$ (suppose again, for simplicity, that there is only one). $C_g$ will be linked to $c_u$ with a path of edges of the type more-general-than. If the version space is updated with $u$, the sets G and S are modified in such a way that the new version space will contain only concepts that do not include $u$; therefore all the concepts equal to or more general than $c_u$ will be automatically removed from the space of admissible concepts. If we suppose that the graph shown in fig. 1 is a fragment of the current version space, the concepts dropped as a consequence of presentation of the ungeneralized instance $u$ are those contained in the subgraph rooted in $c_u$.

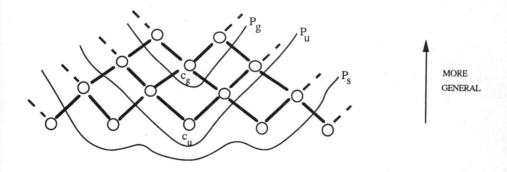

Fig. 1  Pruning of the space of admissible concepts after presentation of :

$P_u$ - Ungeneralized negative instance

$P_g$ - Generalized negative instance

$P_s$ - Generalized negative instance  with later specialization

Likewise, if the version space is updated with $g$, the concepts pruned away from the space of candidate descriptions will be the concepts *above* $c_g$. These concepts, as can be seen in fig. 1, are only a subset of the concepts removed after presentation of $u$. The convergency of the algorithm is therefore slower when using the generalized input.

This result is only apparently paradoxical. Because the concepts are represented in a generalization hierarchy, and because any concept is dropped from the generalization space if it contains *at least* one negative example, it turns out that in a version space approach the more specific negative concepts are the more informative. In this case, in fact, the existence of a negative instance is stated with respect to a smaller instance set.

If we want to take advantage of prior analytical generalization we have to make the greater amount of information carried by $g$ explicit. The information is that *every* instance that has the same explanation as the generalized instance is a negative instance. The two key consequences are that (a) all the concepts of the generalization language more specific than $c_g$ cannot be candidate concept descriptions, and (b) all the concepts that are more general than *any* concept more specific than $c_g$ cannot be candidate concept descriptions either. In order to exploit this fact in the version space updating, a two-step procedure is necessary. In the first step all the maximally specific concepts that are more specific than $c_g$ must be found (there may or may not be singletons among them). This can be done by specializing the term $c_g$ over the generalization graph. In the second step each of the concepts previously computed must be submitted to the candidate elimination algorithm. In this way, updating the version space with the generalized instance will in general result in the elimination of a much greater subgraph than that eliminated after presentation of the ungeneralized instance (fig. 1).

The difference can be more accurately evaluated if we make some hypothesis about the partial order. In the next section we consider one particular concept language, along with its associated partial order.

### 3.1 Some results with a conjunctive concept language

Consider an instance space based on tree-structured attributes, each attribute with l levels and branching factor b (the case can be easily extended to nominal and linear attributes, considering that a nominal attribute can be converted in a tree-structured attribute using a dummy root 'any-value', and that a linear attribute can be considered as a tree-structured attribute with branching factor = 1). Also, let n be the number of attributes. In the following we will use, as an illustration, an example with n = 2, l = 3, b = 2 :

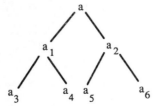 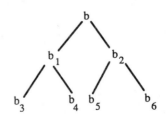

Consider a conjunctive concept language in which each term is a conjunction of n values, one for each attribute. As each attribute can take on $b^l - 1$ values, the number of concepts included in such a language is $(b^l - 1)^n$. In our example, the language contains 49 concepts.

The number of concepts that are eliminated from the concept space in each of the three cases we have considered - namely ungeneralized instance, generalized instance, generalized instance with later specialization - can be computed as follows.

1) <u>Ungeneralized instance</u>. For this concept language $c_u = u$. Each attribute value in $c_u$ can be generalized in l different ways (along the path from the leaf to the root in the corresponding attribute tree). The number of concepts more general than or equal to $c_u$ is therefore $l^n$. In our example, assuming $u = a_3b_3$, there are 9 concepts more general than or equal to $a_3b_3$ (see fig. 2).

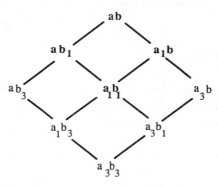

Fig. 2   The concepts more general than $a_3b_3$ and $a_1b_1$ (in bold)

2) <u>Generalized instance</u>. If $g$ is such that each attribute value in $g$ is placed x levels $(0 \le x \le l - 1)$ above the leaves in the corresponding attribute tree, there are $(l - x)^n$ concepts more general than or equal to $c_g$ ($c_g = g$ for this concept language). In our example, assuming $g = a_1b_1$ ($x = 1$), there are 4 such concepts (see fig. 2).

3) <u>Generalized instance with later specialisation.</u> The number of concepts eliminated at the end of the three phases - analytical generalization of the example, specialization, empirical generalization of the previously found concept leaves - can be easily computed considering for each attribute a reduced tree, in which there are only and all of the values that can be generated during the three phases. Assume that each attribute value in $g$ is placed x levels above the leaves in the corresponding attribute tree, and be $a_i*$ the value of the i-th attribute. During the specialization of $g$, each attribute will be specialised in all possible ways. For the i-th attribute, there are $1 + b + b^2 + \ldots + b^x = b^{x+1} - 1$ values more specific than or equal to ($\le$) $a_i*$. In our example $g = a_1b_1$; the concepts $\le a_1b_1$ are shown in fig. 3.

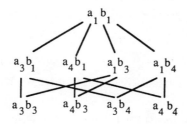

Fig. 3 The concepts more specific than $a_1b_1$

The successive empirical generalization of the leaves found in the specialisation step will produce, for the i-th attribute, all the values $\leq a_i*$ (obtained reversing the previous specialisation) plus all the values more general than $a_i*$ (obtained keeping generalizing the value $a_i*$ along the path from $a_i*$ to the root). In all, there are $[(b^{x+1} - 1) + (1 - x - 1)] = (b^{x+1} + 1 - x - 2)$ admissible values for the i-th attribute, and therefore $(b^{x+1} + 1 - x - 2)^n$ conjunctive concepts will be generated (removed). This expression does not hold for $b = 1$, or for $x = 0$; in either case the number of removed concepts is $1^n$. In our example there are 16 removed concepts; they are not shown here, but they can be easily obtained computing the union of the sets of concepts more general than each of the concept leaves shown in fig. 3.

## 4 Generality of the problem

As mentioned earlier, a similar problem seems to be of direct concern of two other recent version space approaches, [Hirs89]-[Hirs90] and [Carp90]. Here we shall refer to Hirsh, but similar considerations can be applied to [Carp90]. The idea in [Hirs89]-[Hirs90] is to compute the new version space by merging the version spaces associated to each instance, rather than by updating the S and G sets of the current version space. The version space corresponding to each negative instance ranges from the empty concept (i.e., nothing is an example of the concept) to all the minimal specializations of the universal concept (i.e., everything is an example of the concept) that do not cover the instance. If we use a generalized instance, the set of maximally general concepts of the associated version space will contain members that would be discarded using just the ground instance, namely the parents (recall that the graph is directed in such a way that each concept is more specific than its successors) of the maximally specific concept that covers the generalized instance. Therefore the version space associated to the generalized instance would be larger, the overall version space after merging would also be larger, and the covergency would be slowed down. Yet this problem is not mentioned in [Hirs89]-[Hirs90].

More generally, the problem addressed here seems to be independent of the particular inductive learning algorithm considered. We used the version space approach because the explicit use of the partial order relation over the generalization terms makes the underlying mechanisms of negative generalization much clearer; however, the use made of negative information by most other inductive algorithm is analogous. In fact, negative instances are used to implicitly remove from the concept space all the elements that contain at least one of them. In [Wins75], for instance, each negative instance is used to specialize the current candidate concept in such a way that it no longer includes the negative example. In [Mich83] the negative examples provide boundaries on the extent to which each positive example can be generalized. Therefore the use of generalized negative inputs in such algorithms seems to have the same inconveniences as in the version space approach(es).

## 5 Overall utility of the integrated schema and future work

In this paper we have considered using the results of EBL from negative examples as inputs of an inductive learning algorithm. We have shown that it is possible to exploit the greater amount of information carried by a generalized instance only at cost of extra computation.

It is worth considering the overall utility of this type of integrated approach to learning from negative examples.

The advantage is that a large portion of the candidate concept space may be removed after presentation of one single negative example. Furthermore, this approach may be particularly useful if only few examples are available.

The disadvantage is that the computational cost of this approach may be high. There are two components : the cost of specialising the output of EBL and the cost of EBL.

The cost of specializing the output of the EBL phase depends on the generalization language. For the simple case when the generalization language can be represented as a finite directed acyclic graph, accessing the successors of a concept takes constant time, and finding the maximally specific successor(s) of a concept takes therefore time proportional to the length of the path linking the concept to its more distant successor(s). This may be true of propositional concept representations as well as first-order concept representations. In [VanL89], for instance, the concepts dealt with by the version space algorithm are represented as conjunctions of literals, a concept $c_1$ being more general than a concept $c_2$ if there exists a substitution for the variables of $c_1$ such that every literal in $c_1$ is equal to some literal in $c_2$. In this case, the lattice used to specialize a generalized instance would contain all the possible combinations of a given set of literals, including also the constraints that can be imposed over the variables. This is also the case in [Hirs90], where the concept language is enriched using taxonomic information on the predicates that describe each instance. If the generalization language is instead defined by a context-free grammar, as in LEX [Mitc82b], the problem would be that of generating all the strings that can be derived from a given string of the language applying the rewrite rules of the grammar. This problem is, in general, exceedingly hard.

Besides the cost of applying the result of EBL, it must be considered the cost of the analytical learning itself. It turns out that explanations of negative instances may be very expensive to analyze. In learning plans, for instance, analytical generalization of a failure trace requires not only reasoning about states along the trace, as in EBL from success; it also requires to make sure that alternative paths branching off the failure path do not lead to any problem solution.

The kind of trade-off described here is probably too difficult for a theoretical evaluation; perhaps, clues to the answer may be found experimentally. One direction for future work is to evaluate, in the blocks world domain, the utility of prior analytical generalization of failure traces that are input to a version space algorithm. For this purpose we want to utilize a version space algorithm - similar to that of [VanL89] - which is able to process STRIPS-like concepts, and charge the EBL module with a failure theory similar to that used in [Mint87].

## Acknowledgements

This work was carried out within the framework of the agreement between the Italian PT Administration and the Fondazione Ugo Bordoni. Part of the research was done while at the Computing Science Department of the University of Aberdeen, partially supported by CEC SS project SC1.0048.C(H). I would like to thank Gianni Romano in Rome and Derek Sleeman and Peter Edwards at Aberdeen for helpful discussions on this and related topics.

# References

[Carp90]     Carpineto, C. (1990). Combining EBL from success and EBL from failure with parameter
             version spaces. *9th European Conference on Artificial Intelligence*. Stockholm.

[Char86]     Charniak, E., McDermott, D. (1986). *Introduction to Artificial Intelligence*. Addison-Wesley

[Ellm89]     Ellman, T. (1989). Explanation-Based Learning: A Survey of Programs and   Perspectives.
             *ACM Computing Surveys,* 21(2), 163-221.

[Hirs89]     Hirsh, H. (1989). Combining Empirical and Analytical Learning with Version Spaces.
             *6th International Workshop on Machine Learning*. Syracuse, New York.

[Hirs90]     Hirsh, H. (1990). Incremental Version-Space Merging *7th International Conference on
             Machine Learning*. Austin, Texas.

[Mich83]     Michalski, R.S. (1983). A theory and methodology of inductive learning.*Artificial
             Intelligence*, 20, 111-161

[Mint87]     Minton, S., Carbonell, J. G. (1987). Strategies for Learning Search Control Rules:An
             Explanation-based Approach. *10th IJCAI*, Milan, Italy.

[Mitc78]     Mitchell, T. M. (1978). *Version Spaces : An Approach to Concept learning*. PhDthesis,
             Stanford University.

[Mitc82a]    Mitchell, T.M. (1982). Generalization as Search. *Artificial Intelligence*, 18, 203-226.

[Mitc82b]    Mitchell, T.M., Utgoff, P. E., Banerji, R.B. (1982). Learning problem-solving heuristics by
             experimentation. In R.S. Michalski et al. (Eds), *Machine Learning*. Tioga Press, Palo Alto,
             California.

[Utgo86]     Utgoff, P.E. (1986). Shift of Bias for Inductive Concept Learning. In R.S. Michalski et al.
             (Eds), *Machine   Learning.Vol.II* Morgan Kaufmann, Los Altos, California.

[VanL89]     VanLehn, K. (1989). Efficient Specialization of Relational Concepts. *Machine   Learning* 4
             (1), 99-106.

[Wins75]     Winston, P. H. (1975). Learning structural descriptions from examples. In P.H. Winston
             (Ed.), *The psychology of computer vision*. New York: McGraw-Hill.

# Evaluating and Changing Representation in Concept Acquisition

F. Bergadano [(*)], F. Esposito [(**)], C. Rouveirol [(***)] and S. Wrobel [(****)]

[(*)] University of Torino [(**)] University of Bari

[(***)] LRI, Université de Paris Sud [(****)] GMD, Bonn

## Abstract

Adequate representation of examples and hypotheses is a key issue in concept learning. Simplistic representations may fail to allow for discriminant classification rules, while over-detailed inductive hypotheses may turn out to perform badly on new examples. If a representation is evaluated to fall in one of these two extremes, both causing poor performance, it is then necessary to change it. Change often depends on our knowledge of the predicates that are relevant in the application domain, but may also be automated in some cases. All of the above issues are analyzed in the present paper and methods for evaluating and changing a given representation are reviewed.

## 1  Introduction

Concept acquisition systems produce concept descriptions starting from examples and a-priori knowledge. It is very important and sometimes essential to the success of learning that a suitable representation formalism be chosen both for the input information and for the language describing the concepts. Thus, three kinds of problems arise.

*Representation of the examples*:

It is often the case that the concept instances cannot be processed in their original form, but have to be transformed into a suitable representation, i.e. it is necessary to develop a language for representing the examples (Mitchell, 1982). Transforming examples from a given representation into a desired one is a process which itself can be enhanced using machine learning. Depending on the learning system and on the concepts and rules that are to be learned the instances must be represented appropriately. Relevant choices are:

- is a list of attribute-value pairs sufficient or are we to allow for related components in every example?

- how many and which attributes and/or relations do we include in this representation?

- is the target concept an attribute's value, or a unary predicate, or can it be a predicate's argument?

*Form of the background knowledge*:
Information related to attribute compatibility and relevance is included in the background knowledge. It may be useful, for instance, to state that some combination of attributes or some relations can never occur in a given context, or that some other combinations are useful for describing some concepts. Preference criteria (Michalski, 1983) and inductive bias (Utgoff, 1986) are included in this kind of information. The background knowledge may be wired in the learning procedure or may be given in an explicit logical form. The latter case is the one we consider in particular, with the awareness that even a logical representation of previous knowledge may be given at different levels of detail. This kind of knowledge can itself be learned if it is represented explicitly. Representation change has to involve background knowledge as well as the format of the input events.

*Representing the learned concept descriptions*:
The concept descriptions learned by an automated procedure need not be simply arithmetic or logical combinations of the attributes originally present in the examples; they may involve higher level predicates defining complex conditions on the basic attributes, as well as variables and quantifiers. It must be possible to match the concept representation with the examples, but the concept representation may be more abstract and allow for synthetic formulas that cover many possible instantiations.

For every one of the above problems, two actions are of interest: evaluation and change.

# 2   Evaluating a representation framework

In choosing, evaluating and changing the representations for all these three kinds of informations, several basic concerns come into place:

- complexity of learning,

- predictivity of what has been learned,

- comprehensibility of what has been learned

The first issue is quite intuitive: if the attributes in the examples are too many and the language for representing the concepts is too low level, if on top of this the bias in the background knowledge is insufficient or wrong, then the number of inductive hypotheses to be explored is far too large, and learning will have a prohibitive computational complexity. The second issue is nevertheless also important: if the number of possible inductive hypotheses is too large and the hypotheses are semantically diverse, then the information available in the examples may not be statistically sufficient for making an appropriate (= predictive) choice. Predictiveness may be evaluated both by theoretical analysis and by experimental measures.

## 2.1 Theoretical and a-priori measures

If we were given a concept description and were asked how predictive it is, that is to say, how well it could distinguish independent examples and counterexamples, we could use Bernoulli's limitation:

$$Pr\{|observed\_error - true\_error| > \epsilon\} < 2e^{-\frac{m\epsilon^2}{2}} \tag{1}$$

where $m$ is the number of examples and counterexamples that we have seen, the ones the *observed_error* is computed from. *True_error* is the recognition error that would be observed on all the possible examples. If the number of examples is sufficiently large, the above limitation states that, with high probability, the performance of the given concept description as measured on the available examples is quite close to the performance that we may expect on new examples.

Unfortunately, this is not what we call induction in Machine Learning. This would just be the testing of a hypothesis supplied by an oracle. Normally, this hypothesis is not given and we must search for the best one in a very large number of possibilities. If we are asked how predictive we expect this best hypothesis to be, we cannot use Bernoulli's limitation, which is valid when the recognition rule is fixed, but we must modify it into the following (Vapnik, 1982):

$$Pr\{Max_{\phi \in \Phi}|observed\_error(\phi) - true\_error(\phi)| > \epsilon\} < 2|\Phi|e^{-\frac{m\epsilon^2}{2}} \tag{2}$$

where $\Phi$ is the set of hypotheses that are possible. Better limitations (also applicable to an infinite number of hypotheses) may be found, but this is the basic idea. From the above formula, we see that a large number of possible rules has very bad effects on predictivity. In general, the more varied and expressive the language that we use for learning the concept descriptions, the worse the correspondence between the observed and the unknown.

When deciding about representation issues, one cannot ignore this fact, which is constantly observed in Machine Learning experiments. As a consequence, much emphasis has been given to the importance of "bias" or preference criteria for choosing only the hypothesis that are deemed plausible *a priori*.

It is not sufficient that learning be predictive, it must also be performed efficiently. If the time needed for obtaining predictive concept descriptions grows exponentially with the size of the examples, then induction may turn out to be practically unfeasible. There has been a growing interest on these aspects of induction in Computational Learning Theory.

It turns out, and this is indeed very interesting, that predictiveness and complexity are closely interrelated. Here is the trade-off: if the language for expressing inductive hypotheses is simple and contains few alternatives, then we may not be able to find a description that discriminates the available examples, that is to say we cannot adequately describe the observations; if the language is too complex then it may take too long to find acceptable hypotheses and what we find may turn out to perform badly on new data, that is to say we cannot produce effectively reliable predictions of the unobserved.

From such a theoretical analysis it is sometimes possible to state whether some representation (of the examples, of the bias, of the concepts) is sufficiently simple in order to make learning both computationally feasible and predictive. The results of this analysis certainly also give hints as to how change should be performed. For instance, if a hierarchy of possible representations is given, an analysis of predictiveness may suggest that some representation is too specific and the examples should be described at the next level, into a more abstract representation language.

## 2.2   Experimental measures

Nevertheless, theoretical analysis provides bounds that are often too far away from reality (see, for instance, Bergadano and Saitta, 1989). Theories must be enhanced in order to allow for average case analysis (Pazzani and Sarrett, 1990). To this end, new research is needed. In addition to theoretical investigations we need the experimental study of techniques for evaluating representations. Standard cross-validation methods (such as leave-one-out) may be used to see whether some representation causes the learned descriptions to perform badly on examples used as test; again this will provide important suggestions for change.

Similarly, experiments sometimes tell us that the representation we have chosen is not sufficiently expressive. This is the case when the recognition rate is low for the learning examples, and does not improve when the learning examples increase in number. Needless to say, performance on the test examples will even be worse, and the representation of the concepts must be changed in order to include additional details.

Unfortunately, in some cases these forms of experimental and theoretical analysis will give us both advices: (1) make the representation simpler because predictiveness on test examples degrades too much w.r.t. the learning examples and (2) make the representation more expressive because the recognition rate is low even for the learning examples. In this case, either the learning problem is too difficult, or the features and the kind of predicates we have chosen are inadequate. Therefore the change of representation will not just need to address the level of detail, but will involve a thorough transformation in the form of the examples and in the language for describing the concepts.

# 3 A Pattern Recognition perspective

The expressiveness/predictivity trade-off described above is known in classical Pattern Recognition as *curse of dimensionality* and cautions us to use a limited number of attributes (descriptors) when only a small number of training examples is available. Despite the intrinsic interest of the mathematical problem of designing and improving classification algorithms, the real power (predictivity) often comes from the careful choice of the variables themselves, based on a good knowledge of the domain. It is fundamental to determine which descriptors should be employed for the best learning results, through a process of selection and extraction, the first being the choice of the best subset of size p from a given set of n descriptors (p<n), while the second being a data transformation, i.e. a process of mapping original descriptors into more effective new descriptors.

This mapping implies a change in representation and may be evaluated on the basis of its *fidelity*, i.e., on how much information was retained in the process of dimensionality reduction (Siedlecki et al., 1988). The most exciting feature of mapping techniques is that they belong to a small group of multivariate data analysis methods that are able to avoid the curse of dimensionality problem. Nevertheless, the effectiveness of the descriptors may be related to the representativeness of the training examples: often these are chosen by a degree of similarity to stereotypic events rather than by statistical frequency. Therefore the combination-of or correlation-between descriptors resulting from a proposed scenario may be less rich than in the actual situation. To increase the number and the variety of the learning examples may be a solution, but it causes a serious problem of complexity.

It is possible to reduce complexity by a strategy of symbolization and hierarchicalization (Chandrasekaran, 1988). This may be accomplished integrating techniques of multivariate data analysis with symbolic concept learning methods (Esposito, 1990). Instead of learning by a direct application of a symbolic method on the initial description of the examples, intermediate symbols can be constructed, which are then used as attributes into descriptions at a higher level. Symbols at each level are produced by a classificatory process using the symbols from the previous level as attributes. The process of abstraction by intermediate concepts may be performed by:

- identifying groups of attributes that contribute to an intermediate abstraction

- performing a change of representation, for example by mapping techniques, which, working efficiently on numerical descriptors, allow us to define powerful constructors.

- evaluating these intermediate concepts on the basis of an associated measure of "goodness" that may be expressed in terms of amount of information, in order to choose a small number of categories;

- Expressing these intermediate concepts, that are the output of the classifiers, in terms of qualitative attributes at the next level of abstraction

# 4 Representation change in symbolic learning

In principle, a representation change can involve the representation *formalism* or the representation *language*. The representation language syntactically defines the allowed representational expressions. It consists of elementary units of representation (eg., symbols), plus rules for combining them into larger structures (eg., the term and formula building rules of logic). The representation formalism determines how meaning is assigned to expressions in the representation language. For logical representations, this could be the standard Tarskian semantics, for a neural network it would have to be a suitable description of what such a network (regarded as a representational structure) means.

Representation changes on the formalism level are still the exclusive domain of the human system designer. On the language level, automatical approaches are more promising. Most existing approaches in Machine Learning have dealt with the first component of a representation language, i.e., its set of elementary symbols, and ways of extending it. This is usually referred to as the *new-term problem*. Less explored is the aspect of changing the rules for forming expressions.

Most automated approaches can usefully be analyzed in the framework of representation change *operators*. This means, those systems have one or more operators available that introduce or remove new terms, or change the syntax rules of the language. By basing representation change on operators, one is able to bypass the problem of evaluating an entire representation as it was discussed in the first section. Instead, one can often define heuristics that control the application of an operator, and (optionally) an evaluation of the operator's effect.

## 4.1 Constructive Learning and Inverse Resolution

Most of concept learning systems restrict their learning language in order to have a manageable set of candidate hypothesis. Then, when learning in this context becomes impossible, they shift their representation bias to a weaker one, extending their learning language in order to make learning possible (for example, the version space method introduces an intermediate concept when necessary, so that the concept to be learned becomes conjunctive in the learning language). We present in this section a different use of change of knowledge representation for learning. The representation shifts we describe are implemented in the N-IRES system, that is based on inversion of resolution (I.R.) (Muggleton and Buntine. 1988), but they may be applied to a broader range of concept learning systems.

The N-IRES system has a very weak representation bias: the examples (not necessarily ground), as well as the background knowledge and the outputs, are definite clauses, which is a rather powerful language. In this framework, representation shift does not aim at extending the expressive power of the learning language. It is rather used to make the learning task easier and more efficient. Here are two examples of such representation changes, the first one called *flattening* (together with its reverse, unflattening), and the second one called *saturation*.

Flattening transforms a set of clauses in first order logic with function symbols into an equivalent set of clauses without function symbols. The basic idea of flattening is to replace each function of arity n by a predicate of arity n+1, that has the same arguments as the function plus one for storing the result of the function. Each new predicate so introduced is defined in terms of the function it replaces. For example, the clause

member(a,cons(a,nil)).

where a and nil are constants (functions of arity 0) and cons is a function of arity 2, is replaced by the clause:

member(X,Z) :- a_p(X),nil_p(Y), cons_p(X,Y,Z).

together with the following clauses that define the new predicates a_p, nil_p and cons_p:


a_p(a).

nil_p(nil).

cons_p(X,Y,cons(X,Y)).


Flattening and its reverse representation change, unflattening do not change the semantics of the logic programs (the semantic is unchanged because of the definition of the new predicates introduced). It is thus interesting to notice that this representation change that does not restrict the range of things that can be represented makes learning easier (in our case, learning was inversion of resolution). It has kept us from restricting a priori our learning language. It would also allow learning systems that do not handle input with function symbols to extend their scope.

The second representation change (that can be described as inversion of resolution as well) is the saturation operator. Saturation, given one example clause and background knowledge, computes and adds to the body of the example clause all the possible generalizations of the body of this clause.

For instance, given the example clause:

sentence([sue,loves,a,man]).

and the following clauses as background knowledge:


sentence(S0,S) :- noun_phrase(S0,S1),
                  verb_phrase(S1,S).

noun_phrase(S0,S) :- determiner(S0,S1),

```
                    noun(S1,S).
noun_phrase(S0,S) :- name(S0,S).
verb_phrase(S0,S) :- transitive_verb(S0,S).
transitive_verb([loves,L],L).
noun([man,L],L).
determiner([a,L],L).
verb([loves,L],L).
name([sue,L],L).
```

it provides us with the clause:

```
sentence ([sue,loves,a,man],[]) :-
        noun_phrase([sue,loves,a,man],[loves,a,man]),
        name([sue,loves,a,man],[loves,a,man]),
        verb_phrase([loves,a,man],[]),
        transitive_verb([loves,a,man],[a,man]),
        noun_phrase([a,man],[]),
        determiner([a,man],[man]),
        noun_phrase([man],[]).
```

which is the parsing of the example clause. It contains in all the possible generalizations for the initial clause: for example, it contains the most general generalization of the input clause, given the domain theory, i.e.:

```
sentence ([sue,loves,a,man],[]) :-
        noun_phrase([sue,loves,a,man],[loves,a,man]),
        verb_phrase([loves,a,man],[]).
```

This representation change (it is done by the exhaustive application of deduction on the body of the example clause, for all the details about Saturation, see (Rouveirol, 1991)) allows one to simplify a lot the generalization process. The background knowledge is used once and for all to make all the possible generalizations explicit in the body of the clauses, and then can be left out of the generalization process. This least commitment strategy allows to postpone choices when performing purely inductive steps only, i.e. the dropping rule, and only when all the information is available. Saturation has been used in a generalization algorithm that is not based on I.R. (Bisson, 1990).

There are also in I.R. operators that reformulate knowledge bases by adding new terms to the vocabulary. Interconstruction takes as input a set of clauses that do not necessarily describe the same concept. It introduces a new concept whose preconditions are the generalization of the bodies of the input clauses. Intraconstruction takes as input a set of clauses also, but describing the same concept, and it introduces a new concept defined by as many clauses as there are in the input. Each defining clause for the new concept describes the literals of each input clause that do not match the common generalization of those clauses. In other words, the new concept describes the variation of the input clauses relatively to their common generalization. To sum up, the terms created by inversion of resolution stand either for the similarities or the dissimilarities for the input clauses. For example, with the two input clauses:

grandfather(X,Z) :- father(X,Y), father(Y,Z)

grandfather(X,Z) :- father(X,Y), mother(Y,Z)

intraconstruction builds, given the generalization of the clauses:

grandfather(X,Z) :- father(X,Y)

the new predicate

newp(Y,Z) :- father(Y,Z)

newp(Y,Z) :- mother(Y,Z)

Newp represents the parent predicate. Intraconstruction creates intermediate disjunctive concepts that allow us to index knowledge efficiently: disjunctions are moved to lower level concepts (here, from grandfather to parent). Intraconstruction performs exactly the reverse change than EBL. EBL sums up a proof with several intermediary steps into one rule to prove a given goal, whereas Intraconstruction introduces intermediate concepts that will increase the complexity of proofs. It is of course particularly interesting to introduce a new concept if it appears afterwards in the preconditions of several other concepts.

It must be noted that Intraconstruction is not a demand driven process, i.e. that the new term introduced is not strictly necessary to perform for learning. Learning procedures, after the introduction of the parent predicate will not necessarily perform better. Introduction of new predicates in this context has to be assessed and controlled following totally different criteria than in demand driven approaches, such as the information compression (Muggleton, 1988) of the resulting theory, the use of the new predicate (is it often used to reformulate other concept preconditions?), an oracle that validates it if it corresponds to a meaningful concept, etc ...

In learning systems that use a powerful representation language , it is interesting to develop automatic representation changes that make particular learning tasks easier. In this case, of course, shift of representation cannot be done independently from the learning goal.

## 4.2   Demand-driven approaches

A very simple and efficient control heuristic for representation change has been used in systems that learn concepts from examples: a representation change operator is applied whenever the existing representation does not allow for the formulation of a concept that separates the positive from the negative examples ("demand-driven"). This heuristic is especially powerful in learning systems that maintain a version space of possible concepts, since it is then trivial to decide when to apply the representation change operator: whenever the version space is empty. Utgoff's STABB (1986) used this strategy; the change operator introduced a most general disjunction that was consistent with the observed instances. In the concept learner CLINT (De Raedt and Bruynooghe, 1989), the same control heuristic was used with a different operator that changed the syntax rules of the language (eg. by allowing more variables in rules).

A modification of the basic heuristic was used in the non-version space concept learner STAGGER (Schlimmer, 1987), where new terms were added whenever the *current* concept misclassified a new example, i.e., no attempt was made to make sure that no other possible concept would suffice. The change operator in STAGGER also introduced boolean term combinations. Finally, the heuristic was applied in a learning-from-observation setting in the BLIP system (Wrobel, 1988) and its successor MOBAL, where a representation change was triggered whenever the domain of application of a learned rule could not be formulated with the existing concepts. MOBAL uses a powerful change operator that introduces new terms defined by sets of Horn clauses, and evaluates its results.

Independent of the power of the change operator, the control heuristic used in demand-driven approaches is easy to check and avoids complicated evaluations, but, on the other hand, it covers only a small part of representational problems: only those changes that are absolutely necessary for the system to reach its learning goal are performed, anything else that might be useful (eg. by improving the efficiency of learning or quality of the result) is left aside.

# 5    Future Issues

When summarizing the approaches to representation change in Machine Learning taken so far, certain commonalities are apparent, that define directions for future research:

- There is a strong focus on *extending* the representation language (with new terms or more powerful syntax rules) with little attention paid to the problem of reducing or reformulating a representation (but some work has been done on the problem of removing unnecessary distinctions by means of abstraction (Giordana and Saitta, 1990));

- Representation change is performed by local operators, instead of global restructuring;

- Evaluation of changes likewise is not global, but local to the effects of an operator application;

- The evaluation criteria are formulated with respect to the needs of the learning program (demand-driven systems) or to goal-free measures (like information compression); the intended use of the learning result, eg. for user inspection or problem solving, is not taken into account.

- All approaches define new terms with respect to already existing terms, i.e., they can never introduce truly new distinctions: they never leave the "closure" of existing symbols.

To address these issues, work on representation evaluation and change will have to be placed in a larger context that defines the quality of an acquired theory and its representation with respect to its intended use. This will require models that allow the relationship between a representation and the world it represents to be examined; Subramanian has presented first steps in this direction (1990). Finally, to overcome the symbol closure limitation, representation change will have to be studied in "grounded" systems with true access to the world, such as an autonomous agent with sensors and effectors (Wrobel, 1990).

# References

[Bis90] G. Bisson. K.b.g., a knowledge base generalizer. In *Proc. of the seventh Int. Conf. on Machine Learning*, pages 9–16, Austin, TX, 1990.

[BS89] F. Bergadano and L. Saitta. On the error probability of boolean concept descriptions. In K. Morik, editor, *EWSL89 – Proc. of the 4th Europ. Working Session on Learning*, pages 25 – 36, Pitman, London, 1989.

[Cha88] B. Chandrasekaran. From numbers to symbols to knowledge structures: Pattern Recognition and Artificial Intelligence Perspectives on the classification task. In E. S. Gelsema and L. N. Kanal, editors, *Pattern Recognition in Practice, Vol. 2*, North Holland, 1988.

[DB89] L. DeRaedt and M. Bruynooghe. Towards friendly concept-learners. In *Proc. of the 11th Int. Joint Conf. on Artif. Intelligence*, pages 849 – 854, Morgan Kaufman, Los Altos, CA, 1989.

[Esp90] F. Esposito. Automated Acquisition of Production Rules by Empirical Supervised Learning Methods. In M. Schader and W. Gaul, editors, *Knowledge, Data and Computer Assisted Decisions*, Springer-Verlag, 1990.

[GS90] A. Giordana and A. Saitta. Abstraction: a General Framework for Learning. In *Proc. AAAI Workshop on the Automatic Generation of Approximations and Abstractions*, pages 245–256, Boston, MA, 1990.

[MB88] S. Muggleton and W. Buntine. Machine invention of first order predicates by inverting resolution. In *Proc. of the Fifth Int. Conf. on Machine Learning*, pages 339–352, Ann Arbor, MI, 1988.

[Mic83] R. S. Michalski. A theory and methodology of inductive learning. *Artificial Intelligence*, 20:111–161, 1983.

[Mit82] T. M. Mitchell. Generalization as search. *Artificial Intelligence*, 18:203–226, 1982.

[Mug88] S. Muggleton. A strategy for constructing new predicates in first order logic. In *Proc. of the 3rd european working sessions on learning*, pages 123–130, Glasgow, UK, 1988.

[PS90] M. Pazzani and W. Sarrett. Average case analysis of conjunctive learning algorithms. In *Proc. of the seventh Int. Conf. on Machine Learning*, pages 339–347, Austin, TX, 1990.

[Rou91] Celine Rouveirol. *ITOU: Induction de Theories en Ordre 1 (Ph.D. Thesis*. Technical Report, Lri, 1991. to appear.

[Sch87] Jeffrey C. Schlimmer. Incremental adjustment of representations for learning. In *Fourth International Workshop on Machine Learning*, pages 79 – 90, Irvine, CA, June 1987.

[SSS88] W. Siedlecki, K. Siedlecka, and J. Sklansky. Mapping techniques for exploratory pattern analysis. In E. S. Gelsema and L. N. Kanal, editors, *Pattern Recognition and Artificial Intelligence*, North Holland, 1988.

[Sub90] Devika Subramanian. A theory of justified reformulations. In D. Paul Benjamin, editor, *Change of Representation and Inductive Bias*, pages 147 – 167, Kluwer, Boston, 1990.

[Utg86] Paul E. Utgoff. Shift of bias for inductive concept learning. In R.S. Michalski, J.G. Carbonell, and T.M. Mitchell, editors, *Machine Learning - An Artificial Intelligence Approach*, pages 107 – 148, Morgan Kaufman, Los Altos, CA, 1986.

[Vap74] V. Vapnik. *Estimation of dependencies based on empirical data*. Springer Verlag, New York, 1974.

[Wro88] S. Wrobel. Automatic representation adjustment in an observational discovery system. In D. Sleeman, editor, *Proc. of the 3rd Europ. Working Session on Learning*, pages 253 – 262, Pitman, London, 1988.

[Wro90] Stefan Wrobel. *Concepts and Concept Formation: Fundamental Issues*. Arbeitspapiere der GMD Subreihe KI, GMD (German Natl. Research Center for Computer Science), P.O.Box 1240, 5205 St. Augustin 1, FR Germany, 1990. to appear.

# Application of Empirical Discovery in Knowledge Acquisition

Jan M. Żytkow     Jieming Zhu

Computer Science Department, Wichita State University

Wichita, KS 67208     U.S.A.

e-mail: zytkow@wsuiar.wsu.ukans.edu

## ABSTRACT

There is no doubt that the most fundamental method of knowledge acquisition is discovery, but the AI subfield of Knowledge Acquisition neither studies nor uses discovery methods. We argue that machine discovery is approaching the stage at which it can be useful to knowledge acquisition in two ways: as a source of useful techniques, and as a model of unified knowledge representation and application. We present the discovery system FAHRENHEIT and we discuss its various real-world applications: automated experimentation and discovery in a chemistry laboratory, mining databases for useful knowledge, and others, demonstrating FAHRENHEIT's potential as a knowledge acquisition aid. Finally, we discuss the new developments in the area of discovering basic laws and hidden structure, and we note that automation of modeling would close the cycle of automated knowledge acquisition and application.

# 1   Introduction

Despite progress, the state of the art in knowledge acquisition is characterized by an amalgamation of incompatible techniques, lack of standards, and narrow applications (Boose & Gaines 1989). In our search for a solution to these problems, we should consider the best mechanism for knowledge acquisition developed by humanity: modern science and engineering. Science and engineering offer us a unifying knowledge organization spanning many levels: data, empirical regularities, models, basic laws, and principles. Science and engineering offer proven methods of acquiring and verifying knowledge. Although the scientific metaphor is becoming popular in the field of knowledge acquisition, and although researchers acknowledge that building a knowledge-based system resembles the construction of a scientific theory, the scientific method has been used only in a very limited way for knowledge acquisition and representation. There are several reasons. First, although separate elements of the scientific method have been reconstructed, many important elements are still missing. Second, although many attempts have been made at integration of various discovery capabilities (IDS: Nordhausen & Langley 1990; BLAGDEN: Sleeman, Stacey, Edwards, & Gray 1989; FAHRENHEIT: Zytkow 1987; Langley & Żytkow 1989), each integration is limited to only a few elements of the scientific method. Third, the applications of machine discovery are believed to be still in the research phase.

We concentrate on the third argument. Although no-one objects to the claim that science and the scientific method are worth understanding and automating, the feasibility of the task raises doubts, in both the short and long run. To show that practical results are possible we summarize the FAHRENHEIT project, which is focused on multi-dimensional experimentation and data analysis. We demonstrate the breadth and importance of real-world applications of FAHRENHEIT. Then, in response to the first argument, we summarize progress that has been made in the last few years on automation of other elements of scientific method. We concentrating especially on discovery of basic laws and discovery of hidden structure. Finally, we consider automation of knowledge application. Although automated model construction is the key to the acquisition of practical knowledge (Morik 1989; Żytkow & Lewenstam 1990), so far little has been done in that area and significant progress is needed.

In a short run, FAHRENHEIT can be viewed as another incompatible technique added to the repertoir of knowledge acquisition methods. But from a larger perspective, the results in the area of machine discovery fall into a master plan, as gradually reconstructed components of a unified method of experimental science. This approach is guaranteed to succeed because scientific method and scientific knowledge representation form a solid and proven theoretical platform for knowledge acquisition.

We concentrate on automated discovery rather than on user support, exemplified by systems such as BLIP (Morik 1989; Wrobel 1989), QuMAS (Mozetic 1987) and DISCIPLE (Kodratoff & Tecuci 1989).

# 2  Discovery of patterns in empirical data

In this section we review the research program in machine discovery based on FAHRENHEIT. Because we summarize a large research program and many results, the review will

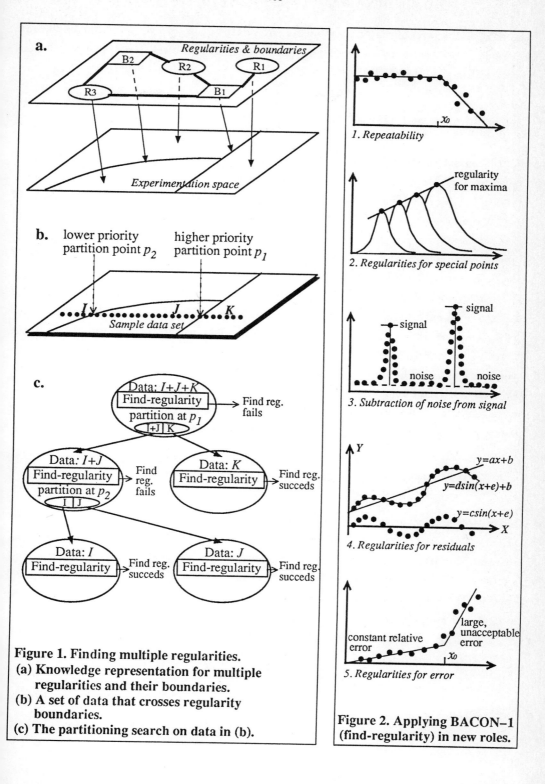

**Figure 1. Finding multiple regularities.**
(a) Knowledge representation for multiple regularities and their boundaries.
(b) A set of data that crosses regularity boundaries.
(c) The partitioning search on data in (b).

**Figure 2. Applying BACON–1 (find-regularity) in new roles.**

be done at the level of major components and related goals and we will make an unusual number of references to our own papers. FAHRENHEIT uses a well-known BACON system (Langley et al 1987), so we will use frequent comparisons with BACON.

## 2.1 The task of FAHRENHEIT

At the outset, FAHRENHEIT is given $N$ independent variables $x_1, ..., x_N$ and one dependent variable $y$ (also indicated as $x_0$), each limited in scope to a set of values $V_i, i = 0, 1, ..., N$.. The possible values of these variables form a cartesian product of $N + 1$ dimensions. FAHRENHEIT is given experimental control over the values of all independent variables and is supposed to find a regularity for the dependent variable y, which includes as many independent variables as possible. This has been the task of BACON, but while BACON has been able to succeed when there was one regularity in the whole block, FAHRENHEIT can discover several multidimensional regularities and the scope of each regularity within the block. The scope of each regularity is defined by a condition that must be satisfied by independent variables. Figure 1.a shows the space of two independent variables and three regularities $R_1, R_2, R_3$ divided by boundaries $B_1$ and $B_2$. The upper part of Figure 1.a shows the linked structure which is built by FAHRENHEIT to represent these regularities and their boundaries.

In addition to finding multiple regularities in data, FAHRENHEIT can also perform many other tasks in data analysis. We will discuss these in the next subsection.

## 2.2 Alternatives to regularity finding

Quantitative discovery systems were traditionally limited to regularity detection, whereas scientists are also interested in discovery of "special points" or patterns such as maxima, minima, discontinuities, and the like. Sometimes, finding a special point is more important than detecting a regularity. The maxima in data can indicate various chemical species; the maximum location indicates the type of ion, while the maximum height indicates the concentration. Discontinuity may indicate a phase change.

In addition to BACON's capability for detection of a single regularity for all data, FAHRENHEIT is capable of detection and analysis of such "patterns" in data as:

1. maxima and minima,

2. inflection points,

3. discontinuities,

4. changes of slope,

5. zeros and the values of x for which $y = a$,

6. boundaries of regularities.

This leads to a considerable growth of discovery power.

To understand the modularity of FAHRENHEIT it is important to notice that detection of special points is an alternative to regularity finding in formal terms of their inputs and outputs. Consider maxima as an example. A maximum is defined as a datapoint $(x, y)$ which is higher (has the $y$ value greater) than some points $x1$ and $x2$ on both sides of x by more than empirical error, and there are no points in between $x1$ and $x2$ higher than $y$. The input is a set of datapoints and their errors, in exactly the same format as required for the regularity finder. The output is a list of maxima. Each maximum is described by the location and error for location, and the height and error for the maximum height. The description of a regularity is analogous. It includes the values of parameters, such as slope and intercept, and the error of each parameter.

## 2.3 Goal structure

FAHRENHEIT combines several searches (Żytkow 1987). Each search corresponds to a particular goal. Our informal presentation is very close to the actual implementation of the system. We concentrate on the high level goals and we skip lower level details.

We will examine the circumstances in which different searches are called, starting from the situation in which BACON-3 has successfully completed the search for regularities for $M$ independent variables, $M < N$ ($N$ is the total number of independent variables):

1. Generalize to another dimension (cf. the Ordering search in the space of generalizations, Żytkow 1987). The instances of the generalization operator correspond to the remaining independent variables $x_{m+1}, ..., x_N$. They can be ordered by the use of the relevance relation between the dependent and independent variables).

2. Find a new non-investigated area in the M-dimensional subspace of independent variables. The Find-new-area search which is called to solve this problem returns several seeds which are M-tuples of independent values for which no regularity has yet been found. Each seed can be used to start the BACON-3 experiments in search for a new regularity for the given $M$ independent variables and for $y$.

In the situation in which the Find-regularity search (BACON-1) for $x_i$ or any module that detects special points has successfully returned to BACON-3 (Figure 3) the following goals can be invoked:

1. Generalize the regularity in the dimension $x_i$. Invoke the Boundary search (Żytkow 1987; Langley & Żytkow 1989) in order to find the scope of the regularity.

2. Apply Find-regularity to detect a regularity on maxima, or a regularity in the sequence of other special points.

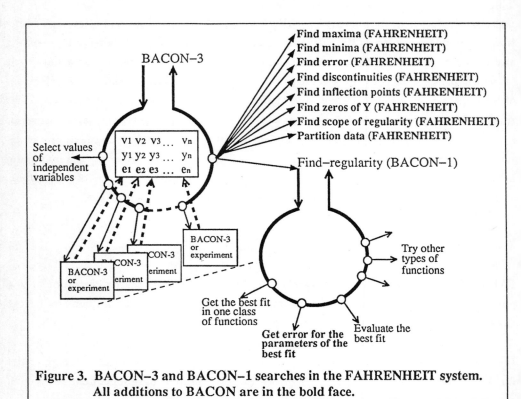

**Figure 3. BACON–3 and BACON–1 searches in the FAHRENHEIT system. All additions to BACON are in the bold face.**

In the case when the Find-regularity has been unsuccessful, FAHRENHEIT can take several steps.

1. Analyse the residuals, that is the differences $y - f(x)$ between predictions of the unsuccessful fit $f(x)$ and the actual data (Figure 2.4). Search for a regularity in residuals expands the curve fitting capability of FAHRENHEIT. The example in Figure 2.4 shows that Find-regularity, which can find a linear fit and $a \times sin(x + b)$, but not $a \times x \times sin(x + b) + c$, can discover the latter function as a result of the analysis of residuals.

2. Partition the data into several subsets and call Find-regularity on each. Figures 1.b and 1.c illustrate the Partition search in a situation in which the initial dataset

($I + J + K$ in Figure 1.b) belongs to three regularities. Find-regularity fails when called on the whole dataset. Search for the regularity in residuals also fails, but after the partitioning of data into subsets $I$, $J$, and $K$, three regularities are eventually detected (Figure 1.c).

The maxima, discontinuities, and the like, can be treated as patterns to be discovered in data, but they can be also treated instrumentally as hints for data partitioning. To consider all partitions of a large dataset into subsets would be a task of enormous complexity. The search can be reduced by hints about the likely partition points. Figures 1.b and 1.c illustrate our Partition search. Partition summarizes information about all types of special points. Each occurrence of a maximum, zero, or any other special point is counted as one reason for partitioning. As a result a list of likely partitioning points is returned, ordered by the number of reasons for partitioning data. In Figure 1.b, $p_1$ has the highest number of reasons, $p_2$ is the second. FAHRENHEIT partitions data gradually, starting at the points with the highest number of reasons. In our example, it uses $p_1$ first, and then $p_2$.

If the entire search for regularities in the given dataset for $x$ and $y$ fails, use Find-new-area for $x$ (described earlier) then take a seed and call BACON-3 again.

## 2.4   Recursion and modularity in goal generation

BACON-3 is a recursive mechanism which detects an N-dimensional regularity step after step. One independent variable is varied at each step, and the successful search adds one dimension to the regularity. FAHRENHEIT expands that recursive mechanism to include new modules for special points detection. As we discussed in section 2.2, all those modules are compatible with Find-regularity in terms of their inputs and outputs. Each can be substituted in BACON-3 for the call to Find-regularity, as illustrated in Figure 3, and the results can be used at higher levels of BACON-3 recursion. This is an important theoretical result, because by addition of modules for special points detection we expand considerably the discovery power without substantial changes to the control mechanism.

The recursive mechanism allows one to mix and match various goals in data analysis. For instance, FAHRENHEIT can search for the regularities on minima, or for regularity on a boundary of a regularity on maxima. The latter could be interpreted as an equation for a surface of a phase change.

# 3 Applications of FAHRENHEIT

Not only the whole FAHRENHEIT system but also individual modules can be applied in numerous ways. Before we present various applications of FAHRENHEIT, let us focus on applications of the Find-regularity module, which looks for one or more regularities on the values of $y$ as a function of $x$.

## 3.1 Different uses of one-dimensional regularity finder

The applications discussed below appear in the same order as the individual diagrams in Figure 2.

1. **Repeatability.** The scientific method requires that the repeatability analysis is conducted before the data can be used. If an experiment is repeated in the same circumstances, we expect the same results of measurements. In the real world, however, we cannot control all variables and some variables are expensive to control. We must accept limited repeatability, but it is essential to know the conditions within which experiments are approximately repeatable, and the measurement error specific to these conditions. We divide the independent variables given to FAHRENHEIT into two categories (Żytkow, Zhu, and Hussam 1990a): independent variables for which we want to build a theory and those independent variables which we want to abstract away but the values of which can be controlled. FAHRENHEIT starts from the repeatability analysis, concentrating on the latter class of variables. It performs experiments in which it varies the values of those variables, keeping constant the variables in the first category. Then it searches for regularities in data, paying particular attention to the constancy of the dependent variables. The scope of constancy is used as the range of repeatability. Figure 2.1 shows a considerable range of repeatability for all $x < x_0$. If no constant regularity can be discovered in a sequence of data for a particular independent variable, the value of that variable must be fixed to allow for repeatability.

2. **Regularities for special points.** Find-regularity can take a sequence of numbers that represent, for instance, heights of the maxima in data (plus error for each maximum height) as a function of an independent variable, and search for regularities on maxima.

3. **Noise estimate.** The heights of the maxima in Figure 2.3 could represent the concentration of several ions, but in order to obtain more precise data about con-

centration, we must find the noise and subtract it from the maxima heights. The noise can be detected as a regularity or regularities for the data points between peaks, indicated by a dashed line in Figure 2.3.

4. **Regularity for residuals.** Figure 2.4 illustrates the way in which the analysis of residuals expands the power of Find-regularity. Details have been described in section 2.3.

5. **Regularity for error.** As we discussed in item 1, above, repeatability analysis allows FAHRENHEIT to obtain the values of error. Find-regularity can detect a regularity on the size of error, such as constant absolute error, constant relative error, and the like. However, Find-regularity needs to know the error of error. The error of error is provided by the repeatability study as proportional to the error of standard deviation.

## 3.2 Discovery in a science laboratory

In virtually any physics or chemistry laboratory around the world we can find many tasks that can be interpreted as problems for FAHRENHEIT. All variables manipulated by the experimenter can be viewed as independent variables for FAHRENHEIT that form the N-dimensional product discussed in the introduction to section 2. The responses measured by the experimenter correspond to dependent variables.

FAHRENHEIT can be used as an automated system for data acquisition and analysis. Each independent variable must be physically interpreted by an output link to a particular manipulator, while each dependent variable by an input link from a sensor. This allows our discovery system to autonomously run a complete cycle in which it controls the experiments, collects data, and builds theories based on data analysis. Human intervention is reduced to the preparation of the initial experimental situation and occasional assistance.

We have conducted many experiments in the domain of differential pulse voltammetry, charging FAHRENHEIT with various tasks (Żytkow, Zhu, & Hussam 1990,1990a). Some experiments involved collection of many thousand data points and discovery of many regularities. The accuracy has been compatible with the accuracy achieved by human researchers. The values of error estimated in our tests are approximately the same as the values determined by a chemist and the regularities found by FAHRENHEIT were either equivalent to those of the chemist within empirical error or more accurate. In several cases our system detected a more complex and precise regularity than the chemist, or found a regularity (linear) in the cases in which the chemist did not look for it, believing that the results must be constant.

FAHRENHEIT returns the results in a much shorter time than human competitors. We found that what typically required several days of work for research assistants, FAHRENHEIT completed in 50 minutes.

Our results demonstrate that a quantitative discovery system can be used in a chemistry laboratory on an experimental problem of interest to a contemporary chemist and that a scientist might not only save enormously on time and effort spent on data analysis and derivation of empirical equations, but that the accuracy of results might improve.

## 3.3   Discovery of useful knowledge in databases

Any table of N attributes in a relational database allows us to define the N-dimensional space, which is the cartesian product of sets of values of all attributes. Finding regularities in such a block sounds like a typical task for FAHRENHEIT, but data in databases are sparse, no experiments can provide more data to allow for focussing on particularly interesting areas, and regularities are typically very poor, so they can be captured by contingency tables or weak correlations. Because of these differences, we constructed a descendent of FAHRENHEIT (Forty-niner: Żytkow & Baker 1991) and we applied it to the task of mining databases for useful Regularities. In a typical business, health-related, educational, scientific, or engineering enterprise, a large volume of data is available which represents knowledge accumulated over a long interval of time at considerable effort, and it is usually organized in a relational format. The data may be mined for useful trends and regularities. In a typical database, Forty-niner finds many regularities which are statistically significant, but much weaker than functional regularities satisfied within small error, which are entertained in physics and chemistry.

## 3.4   Experimental investigation of computational complexity

A computer program can be made available to FAHRENHEIT for the purpose of experimental study of computational complexity. Independent variables are the program parameters, while the dependent variables are the time or storage required for the computation. FAHRENHEIT can experiment with a given program in a similar way as it experiments with a physical situation, by changing the values of program parameters and recording the duration of each computation. Based on these data, FAHRENHEIT builds the theory that estimates computational complexity of the program in the same way as in the case of scientific data. The irregular time spent on garbage collection can cause problems which require the detection of outliers.

Phase changes are common in computer programs, similar to phase changes that occur in physical systems. Consider a parameter P which influences the program logarithmically starting from some threshold value $p_0$. For $p < p_0$, $C(p)$=const; for $p > p_0$, $C(p) = log(p)$. Both the Partition search in FAHRENHEIT (Figure 1.b, 1.c) and the Find-new-area search can handle phase changes in programs. For the worst case analysis, it will first find the maxima for time or storage, and then the regularity on maxima.

## 3.5 Analysis of abstract spaces

As a similar task, FAHRENHEIT can try to empirically analyse the function computed by a program. This may be very useful. When we define a particular altitude function to be used in hill climbing, the properties of that function relevant to the hill climbing search are often unclear. FAHRENHEIT can find useful information about the presence and distribution of local maxima, about their number and about the useful increment for the elementary step in hill climbing.

## 3.6 Automated knowledge acquisition by robots

Manipulatory skills can be developed as a result of experiments and theory formation. We applied FAHRENHEIT in a simulation in which a robot arm learns how to handle physical objects (Żytkow & Pachowicz 1989). Many regularities and many special points have been found, such as boundaries, maxima and minima. The center of gravity of solid objects has been discovered as a special point common in various experiments. The discovered theory can yield the rules which help to improve the efficiency and quality of future manipulations.

## 3.7 Discovery of patterns in sequences

Consider a sequence of numbers common to intelligence tests. MS.SPARC is another mutant descendent of FAHRENHEIT which handles regularities in sequences (Stefanski & Żytkow 1989). In order to avoid approximate solutions because they are not considered correct, MS.SPARC does not allow for any error in the fit.

## 3.8 Knowledge engineering aid

All previous applications can support expert knowledge acquisition. They can generate calibration curves and performance measurements such as complexity estimation. Rather than asking a human expert for his best guess of the values for certainty factors, we may apply FAHRENHEIT or Forty-niner on the relevant database to extract the precise values of coefficients, and to give a statistically sound estimation of the coefficient errors.

# 4   The cycle of knowledge discovery and application

Before we discuss our view of the full cycle of knowledge discovery and application, we briefly summarize the growth of discovery systems in the last three years. Many new systems have been developed, some of which are depicted at the top level in Figure 4. Several abilities lacking in earlier discovery systems have been introduced, primarily the ability to consider the empirical context of a law (IDS: Nordhausen and Langley, 1990; GALILEO: Zytkow 1990; Sleeman, Stacey, Edwards, and Gray, 1989), the ability to design experiments (KEKADA: Kulkarni and Simon, 1987; FAHRENHEIT: Zytkow, 1987; Langley and Żytkow 1989), the ability to represent objects, states and processes (Nordhausen and Langley, 1990; Żytkow 1990), and the ability to reason by analogy (Falkenhainer, 1987; Falkenhainer and Rajamoney, 1988). Several systems discover hidden components and their properties (REVOLVER: Rose 1989; GELL-MANN: Fischer and Zytkow 1990) or discover hidden properties of observable objects (BR-3: Kocabas 1991). Sleeman et al. (1989) propose an interesting search in the space of qualitative models of a chemical system. Progress has been made in the domain of discovering qualitative regularities (IDS; BLIP: Morik 1989, Wrobel 1989). Significant progress has been made also on the important issue of integration. Two systems, both descendents of BA-CON, reached a considerable integration: IDS and FAHRENHEIT, the latter augmented by the GALILEO system that generalizes knowledge by decomposing empirical equations into simpler expressions.

## 4.1   Transformation of empirical equations into basic laws

Many discovery systems, including BACON, FAHRENHEIT, and ABACUS (Falkenhainer & Michalski 1986), produce algebraic equations that summarize numerical data. Hereafter, we will call these BACON-like systems. Algebraic equations discovered by such

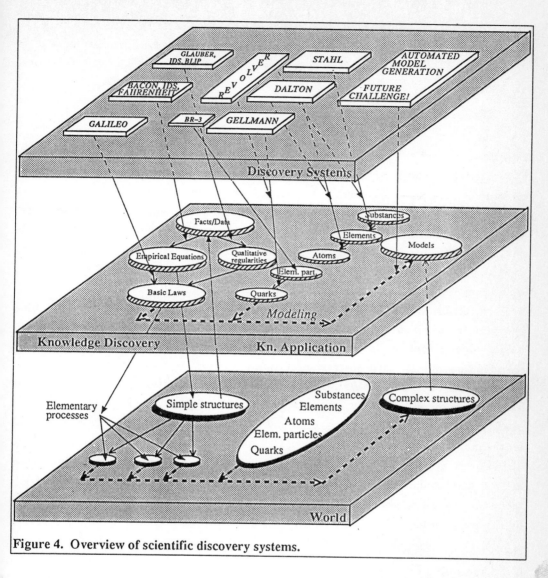

**Figure 4.** Overview of scientific discovery systems.

systems can be interpreted as quantitative laws of different sciences. Each law has been discovered by the empirical investigation of a particular situation. Physical situations can be varied in countless ways and different situations are usually described by different equations. If our discovery capability was limited to BACON-like systems we would have to discover the equations for each situation individually. GALILEO (Żytkow 1990) is a discovery system that has been developed to address this problem. It transforms equations generated by a BACON-like system into a form compatible with the structure of physical processes described by those equations, so that equations can be decomposed into expressions that describe elementary components of the physical structure, such as the expressions for kinetic or potential energy of a body, or energy disengaged during the change of phase. This type of analysis led scientists to a relatively small number of basic expressions which can be combined in countless ways to build models of new situations.

## 4.2  Discovery of hidden structure

Basic laws are not sufficient for knowledge application to a particular situation. Scientists must also know the structure for which to build an adequate model. Discovery of structure is the task complementary to finding laws and an autonomous discovery system must include both. Directly non-observable, hidden structure causes particular problems. Research on the discovery of hidden structure has resulted in many systems, each capable of dealing with limited, yet historically important cases in physics and chemistry (Figure 4). Among the systems that emerged from this research is REVOLVER (Rose 1989), which constitutes the first attempt at grasping generality in the process.

In the GELL-MANN system that discovers quarks (Fischer & Żytkow, 1990), hidden structure is described by hidden objects and their properties, by a pattern in which hidden objects combine to form observable particles, and by a particular combination of hidden objects for each observable particle. The earlier discovery systems, such as STAHL, DALTON, and REVOLVER did not postulate properties of hidden objects and have had a limited capability for postulating hidden objects. GELL-MANN finds the quark model that is accepted in physics and determines its uniqueness, which is critical for the model confirmation. Surprisingly, GELL-MANN has found a model that explains meson octet by two quarks and two antiquarks, and when allowed for multiples of 1/3 as strangeness values, it discovered the second quark model for the hadron octet. Both these new models do not, however, allow to reconstruct all particles which are explained by the accepted model.

## 4.3  Modeling

Knowledge of basic laws and knowledge of structure allow scientists efficient knowledge application in the form of model construction (Figure 4). To achieve substantial progress in the domain of **automated knowledge application, sharing, and interchange**, we must automate scientific modeling. Although modeling plays a major role in different areas of AI, applications are fragmented and the essence of scientific modeling is far from being understood. On average, scientists spend far more time on model construction than on development of basic theories, it is difficult to find a systematic account of modeling.

Żytkow (1990) argues that decomposition of knowledge into basic laws and basic structural components, and a capability for recombining them into models, will remedy the explosion in the size of the knowledge-bases. Moreover, Żytkow and Lewenstam (1990) provide a blueprint for automated model construction. Implementation of such a system would close the loop of automated knowledge discovery and application.

# 5    Conclusions

It is time to consider seriously machine discovery as a unifying schema for knowledge acquisition and representation. We demonstrated that FAHRENHEIT as a whole, and individual modules such as equation finder (BACON-1), can be used on many tasks, and that they can become tools for efficient and effective knowledge acquisition, especially when used in synergistic collaboration with a human knowledge engineer.

We noted the significant progress in automation of other discovery tasks, and we argued that the basic cycle of knowledge generation and application will be closed when we automate model generation.

**Acknowledgement:** The work described in this paper was supported by Office of Naval Research under the grants No. N00014-88-K-0226 and N00014-90-J-1603.

# References

Boose, J.H., & Gaines, B.R. (1989) Knowledge Acquisition for Knowledge-Based Systems: Notes on the State-of-the-Art. *Machine Learning, 4,* 377-394.

Falkenhainer, B.C. (1987) Scientific Theory Formation Through Analogical Inference, *Proceedings of Fourth International Workshop on Machine Learning*, Los Altos, CA: Morgan Kaufmann Publ., 218-229.

Falkenhainer, B.C., & Michalski, R.S. (1986) Integrating Quantitative and Qualitative Discovery: The ABACUS System, *Machine Learning, 1,* 367-401.

Falkenhainer, B.C., & Rajamoney, S. (1988) The Interdependencies of Theory Formation, Revision, and Experimentation, *Proceedings of the Fifth International Conference on Machine Learning.* Morgan Kaufmann Publ.: Los Altos, CA, 353-366.

Fischer, P., & Żytkow, J. (1990) Discovering Quarks and Hidden Structure, in: Ras Z. ed. *Methodologies for Intelligent Systems 5*, Elsevier, New York, NY, 362-370.

Kocabas, S. (1991) Conflict Resolution as Discovery in Particle Physics. To be published in *Machine Learning, 6*.

Kodratoff, Y. & Tecuci, G. (1989) The Central Role of Explanations in DISCIPLE, in Morik K. ed. *Knowledge Representation and Organization in Machine Learning*, Springer-Verlag, Berlin, 135-147.

Kulkarni, D., & Simon, H.A. (1987) The Processes of Scientific Discovery: The Strategy of Experimentation, *Cognitive Science, 12*, 139-175.

Langley, P.W., Simon, H.A., Bradshaw, G., & Żytkow J.M. (1987) *Scientific Discovery; An Account of the Creative Processes*. Boston, MA: MIT Press.

Langley, P.W., & Żytkow, J.M. (1989) Data-Driven Approaches to Empirical Discovery. *Artificial Intelligence, 40*, 283-312.

Morik, K. (1989) Sloppy Modelling, In Morik K. ed. *Knowledge Representation and Organization in Machine Learning*, Springer-Verlag, Berlin, 107-134.

Mozetic, I. (1987) The role of abstraction in learning qualitative models. *Proc. Fourth Int. Workshop on Machine Learning.* Morgan Kaufmann, 242-255.

Nordhausen, B., & Langley, P. (1990). An Integrated Approach to Empirical Discovery. in: J.Shrager & P. Langley eds. *Computational Models of Scientific Discovery and Theory Formation*, Morgan Kaufmann Publishers, San Mateo, CA, 97-128.

Rose, D. (1989) Using Domain Knowledge to Aid Scientific Theory Revision. *Proceedings of the Sixth Int. Workshop on Machine Learning*, Morgan Kaufmann Publishers, San Mateo, CA, 272-277

Sleeman, D.H., Stacey, M.K., Edwards, P., & Gray, N.A.B. (1989) An Architecture for Theory-Driven Scientific Discovery, *Proceedings of EWSL-89.*

Stefanski P. & Żytkow Jan M. (1989) A Multisearch Approach to Sequence Prediction, in: Ras Z. ed. *Methodologies for Intelligent Systems 4*, New York, NY: Elsevier, 359-366.

Wrobel, S. (1989) Demand-driven Concept Formation. In Morik K. ed. *Knowledge Representation and Organization in Machine Learning*, Springer-Verlag, Berlin, 289-319.

Żytkow, J.M. (1987) Combining many searches in the FAHRENHEIT discovery system. *Proceedings of Fourth International Workshop on Machine Learning.* Los Altos, CA: Morgan Kaufmann, 281-287.

Żytkow, J.M. (1990) Deriving basic laws by analysis of processes and equations, in: J.Shrager & P. Langley eds. *Computational Models of Scientific Discovery and Theory Formation*. Morgan Kaufmann Publishers, San Mateo, CA, 129-156.

Żytkow, J. & Baker, J. (1991) Interactive Mining of Regularities in Databases, To be published in: Piatetsky-Shapiro, G. and Frawley, W. eds. *Knowledge Discovery in Databases*, The AAAI Press, Menlo Park, CA.

Żytkow, J.& Lewenstam A. (1990) Analytical Chemistry: the Science of Many Models, *Fresenius Journal for Analytical Chemistry*, 225-233.

Żytkow, J. & Pachowicz, P. (1989) Fusion of vision and touch for spatio-temporal reasoning in learning manipulation tasks, in: *Proceedings of SPIE's Advances in Intelligent Robotic Systems*, 404-415.

Żytkow, J.M., Zhu, J. & Hussam, A. (1990) Automated Discovery in a Chemistry Laboratory, *Proceedings of the AAAI-90*, AAAI Press, 889-894.

Żytkow, J.M., Zhu, J. & Hussam, A. (1990a) Determining Repeatability and Error in Experimental Results by a Discovery System, in Ras Z. ed. *Methodologies for Intelligent Systems 5*, Elsevier, New York, NY, 438-445.

# USING ACCURACY IN SCIENTIFIC DISCOVERY

## M. MOULET

Equipe Inférence et Apprentissage
LRI, Bât 490, Université Paris-Sud
91405 Orsay Cedex. France
Email : marjorie@lri.lri.fr

## Abstract

Learning by discovery aims at bringing to light laws from a set of numerical or symbolic data. Our work deals with the improvement of the discovery system ABACUS created by Michalski and Falkenhainer, and in particular, with the way the system makes use of informative accuracy of the data. ABACUS, like most others current discovery systems does not use this information in the real physical sense, that means accuracy given by the measure device. However, in experimental domains accuracy cannot obviously be separated from the data. In this paper, we show how, when used in a more realistic manner, this information can significantly improve not only the accuracy of the results but also the efficiency of the search algorithm. Several additional modifications to ABACUS to improve the robustness of the system without losing generality will also be described.

## Key-words

Scientific discovery, learning by observation, numeric - symbolic integration.

# 1 Introduction

Our work is concerned with the field of learning by discovery and consists in the improvement of the discovery system **ABACUS** created by Falkenhainer (Falkenhainer & Michalski, 1986) and improved by Greene (1988). This system is well-known as one descendant of the **BACON** system created by Langley, Simon, Bradshaw and Zytkow (1985; 1986 and 1987). Without changing the algorithm itself and its basic heuristics, we add a new kind of information which improves the system's efficiency, especially its search algorithm. Moreover, this information is general enough to be applicable in most scientific domains. With this goal, we have integrated into the system the notion of uncertainty of data as an inherent part of the data.

Indeed, as soon as we have to deal with numerical data, whether it be the result of physical experiments or statistical results of a sociological study, the question of the accuracy associated with these data is raised. By accuracy, we mean the uncertainty of the data, expressed either with a **relative** value as in "the town contains 25 000 inhabitants, plus or minus two percent", or with an **absolute** value as in "it costs 400 pounds, plus or minus 20 pounds".

When the data is experimental, the accuracy associated with a measure is characterized most of the time by the quality of the **device used**. Consequently, the accuracy of these measures cannot be computed automatically from the data alone, but must be part of the data itself and given by the expert or the system's user.

Despite the fact that the necessity for specifying the accuracy of data during the acquisition step is self evident, we must emphasize that this requirement is not always observed by researchers in the learning community, even by those interested in data analysis or statistics. However, we can note one approach concerned with the problem of uncertainty. FAHRENHEIT, created by Zytkow (1987 ; Zytkow & Zhu & Hussam, 1990), is able to compute "errors" on the data by asking to the user for repeated experiments. However, these errors obviously correspond to a lack of fidelity of the device used, but they do not represent its sensibility (if a small change can be detected) or its rightness (with regard to a standard). Unfortunately, these two last properties can only be evaluated by a user experimentally.

In the majority of cases, only one value is chosen to represent the accuracy of all the numerical data. But this solution cannot be used in learning by discovery where data can frequently be provided by different measuring devices and moreover where the research is done by iterating computations, decreasing accuracy proportionately with the number of steps. In this context, there is no longer any justification for associating the same accuracy with all values.

In this paper, we want to introduce our new version of the system ABACUS and the improvements we have made concerning the use of uncertainty. We will first present ABACUS's aim and the general principles we have chosen to improve the system. Then, we describe in detail some definitions needed to manipulate uncertainty within ABACUS before we present the improvements. The first one and the most important of our work is based on our new approach to dealing with accuracy. The second one concerns mathematical cancellations and tautologies. Finally, we present a simple but useful way to improve the iterative search and to correct the drawbacks of the evaluation criteria used by ABACUS to control the search.

## 2 ABACUS's aim and algorithm

ABACUS deals with finding relations which are of interest to the experimenter, within a set of experimentations. This data set can be viewed as a matrix where each row represents an example and each column represents one measured parameter. In this context, the aim of the discovery system is to bring to light the mathematical relation(s) between all or some of the parameters such that all or a majority of the examples verify this (or one of these) relation(s). Thus, the search space to look through is constituted of all the mathematical formulas one can build from the initial parameters.

Let us precise that in the following, we will note either parameter or variable a column of the matrix, but *parameter* will rather represent the initial measured parameters and *variable* will rather represent the next columns created by the system.

ABACUS's discovery process cônsists in an iterative building of variables starting with the initial parameters as first variables. It chooses two among the four arithmetic operators (+, -, / and *) to apply to each pair of variables according to the existing monotonic dependency (the second variable increases or decreases when the first increases). As in BACON, the dependencies between two parameters can be computed only when all the other parameters are holding constant. The process stops when a variable is found which takes the same value for all examples. This variable will then represent the equation or law verified by the data set.

The main advantage ABACUS provides with regard to BACON is to propose to the user either one law as in BACON, or a collection of laws with each one summarizing a subset of the examples. Two solutions can be used to find the partition : the first one is to compute it with a clustering algorithm and then to search for an equation on each subset independently. The second is to search for only one variable such that all the examples can be gathered into different subgroups according to their value on this variable.

# 3    New principles

**1- The accuracy rate of each parameter is provided by the user** : only one **relative** uncertainty rate is provided if all the values of the parameter have been recorded with the same relative uncertainty, and if not, **absolute** uncertainty rates associated with each value. In the following, we will denote the relative and absolute uncertainty of a value $x_0$ by the respective expressions $\rho\ (x_0)$ et $\delta\ (x_0)$.

In spite of the fact that learning by discovery deals usually with experimental data, this work constitutes the first work where the user is allowed to provide along with the data their associated measures of accuracy. However, in an experimental field, like physics or chemistry, the uncertainty rates of the values are not only supplementary information but necessary and fundamental to the interpretation of the measures. These new values take the place in ABACUS of the previous parameter "uncertainty" initially used to represent the uncertainty rate of all the numerical values the system had to manipulate. We will show in the next parts how, as a contrast to this simpler way of dealing with uncertainty, our addition of the real uncertainties can improve the system.

**2-** One difficult problem in this kind of "blind" search, is how to avoid the generation of tautologies, that is to say equations which are self-evident like $y = y$, which are unfortunately often considered by the system as being good solutions. Although ABACUS have succeeded in controlling some of these tautologies, we have noticed that numerous tautologies were still not taken into account.

With this goal, we have integrated together with the notion of accuracy the one of negligibility, which definition is based on accuracy since a variable is negligible with regard to another according to the accuracy of the later. Moreover, we have implemented a simplification module, which is particularly useful to avoid the creation of tautologies. This has been done thanks to some additional computations based on arithmetical rules, quite simple when done "by hand" but quite problematic when done automatically, because of their complexity.

**3-** Finally, we have improved the search algorithm, by analyzing the way ABACUS evaluates variables in order to choose the best path in the search graph. At each step, the new variables are evaluated before the graph is splitted into two subgraphs which will be explored one after the other. Although this heuristic is useful in order to reduce combinatorial explosion, it is difficult to avoid a bad splitting of the search space. We propose a compromise, which is quite simple but has still proved to be useful, based on delaying the splitting.

# 4 Improvements based on new accuracies

We present now the principal definitions used to compare and manipulate different uncertain values, before we show the advantages of the use of accuracy for a discovery system.

## 4.1 Definition of a new equality

In the description of ABACUS above, we have described how the whole process relies on the finding of a variable which is constant on all or the majority of examples. We are therefore principally interested in detecting when two or more values of a same variable are equal. But once we are given the accuracy of these values, we can no longer use the standard definition of equality. In place of this standard definition, we introduce the notion of the **possibility** of two values being equal.

Note that in the previous version of ABACUS, the uncertainty parameter was also used to compare two values of a same variable, but it did not allow the values to have their own absolute uncertainty. Now, we have to generate a new comparison function that is valid for values taking different absolute or relative uncertainties. The simplest way is to define this comparison function from the absolute uncertainties.

Let us call *interval of definition of* $x$ the set $[x - \delta(x), x + \delta(x)]$, then two values $x_i$ and $x_j$ *have the possibility of being equal* if their two intervals of definition are not disjoint. Let us call this new property the $\delta$-**equality** and let us define it thus :

$$
\begin{array}{c}
x_i \text{ et } x_j \text{ are } \delta-\text{equal} \\
\textit{if and only if} \\
|x_j - x_i| \leq \delta(x_i) + \delta(x_j)
\end{array}
$$

Example : $x = 10 \pm 3$ is $\delta$-equal to $y = 12 \pm 1$ since $|10 - 12| = 2 \leq 3 + 1 = 4$

We can then generalize this property to p values. Let $x_0, x_1, ..., x_p$ be the values such that $x_0 \leq x_1 \leq ... \leq x_p$ (this condition helps simplifying the definition). If we have already verified that $x_0 ... x_{p-1}$ are $\delta$-**equal**, then

$$
\begin{array}{c}
x_p \text{ is } \delta-\text{equal to } x_0, ..., x_{p-1} \\
\textit{if and only if} \\
x_p - \delta(x_p) < \textit{min} \ \{ x_i + \delta(x_i) \} \\
0 \leq i \leq p-1
\end{array}
$$

Finally, when is found a variable which takes constant values for all the examples in fact we have to set which value will represent all of them, given that all the values of the variable are only δ-equal. Seeing that his value will only be used in the presentation of the result to the user, and not in the incremental process, and in order to avoid possible large mistakes, we choose to represent them by the most precise one (12 ± 1 in our example).

## 4.2 Accuracy computation formulas

One of the most important improvements to the initial version of ABACUS is its additional capacity to compute automatically the uncertainty rates of the variables the system generates. These new accuracies must obviously be computed according to the uncertainty rates of the previous variables and according to the function used to generate these new variables. It is then necessary to introduce the computation formulas able to provide the relative or absolute uncertainties of a function from either the absolute or the relative uncertainties of the previous variables.

We recall in the table 1 the computation formulas used to derive uncertainties when applying the different arithmetic operators to a pair of variables. Some of them can be found in the physics course of Joyal (1956) or Eurin and Guimiot (1953).

| op | $\rho \, (x \text{ op } y)$ (relative form) | $\delta \, (x \text{ op } y)$ (absolute form) |
|----|---------------------------------------------|-----------------------------------------------|
| + / - | $\dfrac{\delta \, (x + y)}{(x + y)}$ | $\delta \, (x) + \delta \, (y)$ |
| * | $\rho \, (x) + \rho \, (y)$ | $\delta \, (x) * y + x * \delta \, (y)$ |
| / | $\rho \, (x) + \rho \, (y)$ | $\dfrac{\delta(x)}{y} + \dfrac{x * \delta(y)}{y^2}$ |

Table 1. Formulas for the computation of accuracy

Concerning the trigonometric functions (we deal here with cosine and sine only), there are no formulas giving directly the uncertainty of the result of applying the function, given the uncertainty of the argument. We must therefore compute separately the uncertainty of each value, using the following principle :

Let $x_0$ be a value with the absolute uncertainty $\delta (x_0)$. Given a mathematical function $f$, the absolute uncertainty of $f(x_0)$ is the maximal difference observed between $f(x_0)$ and the values $f$ takes on the extreme values of $x_0$. This can be written as :

$$\delta (f(x0)) = max \; \{ \; |\; f(x0 + \delta (x0)) - f(x0) \; |\; ,\; |\; f(x0 - \delta (x0)) - f(x0) \; |\; \}$$

Note that this formula can, from now on, be easily used for any new operator which could be added to the system such as exponential, logarithm, etc.

## 4.3 Consequences on the final partitions and laws

ABACUS aims at splitting the example set into a partition such that the set of all the laws describing each group best describes the whole of the example set. One way to discover this partition is to find a variable which takes constant values on the subsets of a partition of the examples. It is then important to accurately compute these partitions that are "induced" by a variable, in order to find the right final partition.

The idea is therefore to compute these groups by comparing the values of a variable using the $\delta$-equality we have defined above. Given the initial accuracy rates, we can now compute the partitions with more accuracy. This allows for instance the discovery of new partitions where all data were gathered together before, because the accuracy was not high enough to allow a distinction to be made between some values.

We present in the sections below two aspects of the improvements due to our better conception of accuracy. The first one illustrates and justifies more precisely the influence of the accuracy rate on the resulting partitions and laws. The second emphasizes the role of the iterative computations of the uncertainty rates of the variables. In conclusion, these two improvements must be absolutely taken into account altogether in order to have the right reasoning.

## 4.3.1 influence of the accuracy rate

Table 2 illustrates the influence of accuracy on both the final laws and the final partitions. Experiments have been performed on the same example set changing accuracy rate (artificial one and assumed the same for all parameters for the sake of clearness and comprehension). The experiments are relative to the law of the speed of sound in air. There are fifteen examples described by four parameters : the speed V, the time T, the frequency FREQ and the atmospheric pressure P. Let us recall that the real law is : $V^2 = 401.32\ T$ (thus, the last two variables are not relevant) but small errors have been introduced. The results have been obtained with our new version of ABACUS, computing the uncertainty of each new variable.

| $\rho$ | partitions and laws | | |
|---|---|---|---|
| 5% | T = 0.836 V $\qquad$ ( ± 10% ) | | |
| 2% | T = 250 or 273 $\quad$ V = 1.232 T<br>T = 330 $\qquad\quad$ V = 1.107 T $\quad$ ( ± 4%) | | |
| 0.5% | T = 250 $\qquad$ V = 1.267 T<br>T = 273 $\qquad$ V = 1.212 T<br>T = 330 $\qquad$ V = 1.107 T $\quad$ ( ± 1% ) | | |
| 0.1% | $V^2 = 401.32\ T$ $\qquad$ ( ± 3.10$^{-1}$ % ) | | |
| 5.10$^{-5}$% | T = 0.00249 $V^2$ $\qquad$ ( ± 2.10$^{-3}$ % )<br>(after simplification of V + T/V divided by V ) | | |

Table 2. Influence of the accuracy on the laws and the partitions.

In order to understand these results, it must not be forgotten that each solution corresponds to a constant variable. The first result (for $\rho = 5\%$) means that the values of the variable $\frac{T}{V}$ on the 15 examples are found $\delta$-equal. In the two following cases, where the accuracy rate $\rho$ is decreased, the 15 are no more $\delta$-equal altogether but are $\delta$-equal when they are splitted into 2 or 3 groups. In the two last cases, the accuracy rate was obviously too high to allow all the values of $\frac{T}{V}$ to be $\delta$-equal, even by intervals. The system was able by generating the new variable $\frac{V^2}{T}$, to find an approximation of the right law. However, in the last case, $\frac{V^2}{T}$ was not found constant with regard of the error rate of 2 10$^{-3}$% but found it all the same by simplification of a formula obtained by combining next variables, according to the new improvement we will see in section 4.

Moreover, if we had increased the accuracy rate, there exists some value of the accuracy for which $\frac{V^2}{T}$ like $\frac{T}{V}$ will no more be found constant, nor the right law will be found. Generally, increasing accuracy does not necessarily improve the solution : a too high accuracy may lead to a solution other than the one desired, or even none at all.

The results shown in table 2 have been performed by varying the uncertainty rate. It must be pointed out that the user cannot in reality choose the accuracy rates, since they are provided by the measurements devices, and that each parameter has only one given accuracy that cannot be changed anymore. Actually, all solutions proposed by the system are correct, and one uncertainty is not better than another. The estimation of a result can then be done only according to the user's point of view. We assume then that in the user's interest it is better to give effectively each accuracy rate of the initial parameters than to choose randomly one accuracy rate.

In the law of the speed of sound, for instance, if we give the following right uncertainty rate: $\rho(T) = 0.3\%$, $\rho(V) = 0.001\%$, $\rho(P) = 1\%$ and $\rho(FREQ) = 3\%$, the law $V^2 = 401.206 * T$ is correctly found with an approximation of 0.202%.

### 4.3.2 influence of the accuracy computation

We have shown how the uncertainty rate can have an important influence on the final partitions. Furthermore, this influence is not relied to the treatment of the accuracy along the search : the good relationship can be pointed out using the initial version of ABACUS with an accuracy rate well chosen. However, in a different way, automatic computation of the accuracies on all variables, by influencing the variable accuracy, also influences how the values of the examples on this variable are δ-equal and thus the final partition. The most important is not therefore to choose the right initial accuracies but also to update the accuracies in the course of the generation of the new variables.

For instance, let us compare the percentage of values constant for the variable $\frac{V^2}{T}$ according to the uncertainty rate chosen. The minimum observed value is 400.69612 and the maximum one is 401.32234. With an uncertainty rate of 0.09%, all the values are found δ-equal, whereas it is no more true with an uncertainty rate of 0.03% for which only 60% of the values are found δ-equal. Therefore, if the uncertainty rate is fixed by the user at 0.03%, in the initial version in which the accuracy rate stays constant, the law will not be found. On the contrary, by updating the uncertainty rate according to the number and type of the operations involved, the variable $\frac{V^2}{T}$ will be found constant and the law will be discovered.

In our new version of the algorithm, high accuracy rates clearly may occur on the initial parameters, but we know in this case that it corresponds effectively to the noise in the experiments, and we are insured to be right when comparing the values of this parameter. Moreover, high accuracy rates stay being a problem just when the law to discover is quite simple and does not need many computations. Indeed, as the accuracy rates are decreasing proportionally to the number of steps of the algorithm, if the law is quite complex, the variable representing it will never in fact now take this large accuracy rate. Even in this case, the problem (high accuracy preventing discovering a solution) that appeared in the initial version have therefore been eliminated.

## 5    Dealing with tautologies

Tautologies are the source of new difficulties. Since at each step the system does not memorize the functions already applied but it keeps only the result under the form of a sum of products, there exits a definite chance to be stopped discovering a formula which is by simplification (the user must do) equivalent to a tautology. We present in the following two important ways we have added to the previous version of ABACUS in order to avoid such uninteresting solutions.

## 5.1 Pruning negligible terms

Since $\delta$-equality must take the place of the standard equality, we must exchange the standard definition of negligibility with a new one taking into account the interval of definition of the values. We consider now that $x_0$, with $\delta(x_0)$ as its absolute accuracy is negligible with regard to $y_0$ if $\forall x_i \in [x_0 - \delta(x_0), x_0 + \delta(x_0)]$ , $y_0 + x_i \in [y_0 - \delta(y_0), y_0 + \delta(y_0)]$. Thus, we obtain this theorem :

> $x_0$ **is negligible with regard to** $y_0$
> *if and only if*
> $$| x_0 | \leq \delta (y_0) - \delta (x_0)$$

This theorem is then used to determine if a given variable is negligible with regard to another thanks to the definition :

> $x$ **is negligible with regard to** $y$
> if and only if **for all** examples E,
> **the value of x at E is negligible with**
> **regard to the value of y at E.**

This notion of negligibility between two variables is from now on used to control the generation of new variables. It is forbidden now to add or subtract two variables when one is negligible regarding the other. Consequently, when x is negligible regarding y, we exclude the possibility of finding a solution such as $y = y + x$, or even of the type $1 + x/y = 1$ (obtained by dividing $y + x$ by y), those are unfortunately sometimes proposed as solutions by the initial version of ABACUS. In this way, we reduce the search graph significantly by pruning numerous uninteresting paths.

We have introduced a new concept which allows us to control this kind of tautology and even to avoid logical errors (or that may be seen as logical errors by the user). Moreover, although this notion of negligibility can be considered as an improvement independent of the one due to accuracy, it is unsafe to use it without knowing the correct accuracy of the variables. For instance, pruning the space search according to this concept within the initial version of ABACUS where the uncertainty can be 2% (default value) for all values can lead to eliminating interesting variables. The robustness of the pruning is thus increased by taking into account the accuracy of the parameters.

## 5.2 Simplifying formulas

An intermediary step in the building of equations is relative to their simplification, or numerical cancellation. As the desired law becomes more complex, more numerous variables are generated and thus, higher is the chance for ABACUS to fail by finding a tautology. Thus, this phase of simplification is needed not only in the user's interest but essentially to eliminate the tautologies.

### 5.2.1 the problem

In the ABACUS system, the form used to express the equations is a sum-of-products. For instance, $\frac{x}{y} * (a-b)$ is expressed in the system as $\frac{ax}{y} - \frac{bx}{y}$. An algorithm based on this notation to test whether a new term contains a partial cancellation already exists in the initial version of ABACUS and when the test is fulfilled, the system does not create the candidate term. ABACUS thus already deals with numerical cancellations such as : $\frac{a}{b} * (bc)$ simplified to ac.

Unfortunately, numerous tautologies remain that the initial version of ABACUS cannot detect. One family of them can be represented by : $\frac{X_1.A}{X} + \frac{X_2.A}{X}$ with $X_1 + X_2 = X$.

For instance, $\frac{x}{x-y} - \frac{y}{x-y} = 1$ is obviously a tautology.

The reason why the initial version of ABACUS cannot recognize it is the following. In order to follow the sum-of-products format, when it subtracts two quotients $\frac{x}{x-y}$ and $\frac{y}{x-y}$, it seems sufficient to generate directly the form $\frac{x}{x-y} - \frac{y}{x-y}$, and therefore, the system does not test if any cancellation is possible.

More generally, let us compare ABACUS' way of dealing with formulas and computer algebra rules indicated by Davenport, Siret and Tournier (1986) in order to have a canonic representation. There are four of these rules :

1- no rational in the expression of a quotient.
2- no integer must divide both the numerator and the denominator.
3- the main coefficient of the denominator must be positive.
4- no common divisor between the numerator and the denominator.

Unfortunately, in the initial version of ABACUS, just the first condition is verified.

## 5.2.2 a solution

Our work has therefore consisted in improving the system such that all formulas also verify the last three rules. The solution we propose is to apply to quotients well-known arithmetical rules :

- In all cases, we execute if needed the self-evident simplification, like when subtracting or dividing two identical terms.
If there is no quotient in all the involved terms, go to the third thereafter step. Otherwise,
- firstly, we transform all the terms such that they get the same quotient. In general, that needs to compute the smaller common multiple of all the quotients.
- Secondly, we simplify the dividend if needed, and if the result is a constant, we note that it is indeed a tautology, else, we simplify the quotient.
- Thirdly, if it is not a tautology, we reconstruct the equation as a sum-of-products.

Example : let us perform $\frac{a}{x+y} - \frac{a}{y}$ .

We start with computing the common denominator : $(x+y) \cdot y = xy + y^2$, then, we compute the dividend : $a.y - a (x + y) = a.y - a.x - a.y$, we simplify into $-a.x$, and finally we return the final quotient $\frac{-a.x}{xy + y2}$ . Since it is already in the sum-of-products form, the simplification stops.

The last rule is unfortunately not completely verified since we do not deal with factorization. That implies that $\frac{x^2 -2x + 1}{x^2 -1}$ and $\frac{x-1}{x+1}$ are not still recognized as been equal. But since our aim is only not to encounter tautologies, the main important point to make sure is that none solution of the form $\frac{x^2 -2x + 1}{x^2 -1} = \frac{x-1}{x+1}$ will be found. To obtain this solution, the system must perform the subtraction between the two terms. Now, the system must transform the expression by putting the them on the same denominator, we know that it will obtain 0 and thus it will not create any tautology.

### 5.2.3 additional improvement

In ABACUS initial, when two variables are combined in order to attempt the generation of a third one, a simplification check is performed, and as soon as a first simplification occurs, the generation of the third variable is disowned.

In our approach, we do not use this heuristic for the mean reason that it either forbids or slowly delays the generation of powerful variables. Furthermore, another interesting aspect of this improvement is the possible creation of squares of variables. Indeed, if the initial parameters are $x$ and $y$, ABACUS has just two ways to create the square of $x$ : firstly when there exists two groups such that the monotonic dependency between $x$ and $y$ is different for each of them. As these groups do not always appear, it may sometimes be impossible to generate the square of $x$.

A second way to obtain $x^2$ is doing a product of the form $(x+y) * (x+z)$. By development, $x^2 + xz + xy + yz$ will be found. Unfortunately, by this way and if the system does not allow simplifications, it is impossible to obtain the square of $x$ alone. Now, by simplifying equations, it is possible to create in an additional way, the square of $x$ (for instance, by subtracting xy from x $(x+y)$). An illustration of the improvement is given by the law : $x^2 + y + z$, which can be discovered only applying simplifications. Indeed, with the initial version of ABACUS, a solution is obtained, but only at the 998th variable and is a tautology :

$$x * y^2 / (x^2 * y^2 / (x + y) + x^4 / (x + y) + x * y^3 / (x + y) + x^3 * y / (x + y)$$
$$+ x^3 / (x^2 * y^2 / (x + y) + x^4 / (x + y) + x * y^3 / (x + y) + x^3 * y / (x + y)) = 1.0$$

which can be simplified to : $\dfrac{(xy^2 + y^3) * (x + y)}{(x^2y^2 + x^4 + xy^3 + x^3y)}$ .

Now, by simplifying $x(x + y) - xy$, we obtain the square of x alone and the solution is obtained when the 86th variable is generated. This shows a huge improvement on the original version of ABACUS.

# 6    Improving the search algorithm

The search is done through a directed graph where each generation is the result of all the possible combinations of all the couples of all the previous generations. Since for each couple of variables two functions are created (according to the monotonic dependencies), if $n$ is the number of initial parameters, each generation can be composed at most of twice the number of combinations of two elements between $n$, which corresponds to $2n(n - 1)$.

In average, only half of the possible combinations are realized, but the complexity of the search remains equal to $O(n^{2^p})$ if p is the maximal depth of the graph. The problem is then how to decrease the size of this graph.

One way to limit combinatorial explosion would be to find an evaluation function predicting which variable leads the quickest to the solution. Unfortunately, there are no known functions able to perform this test. We will describe the function chosen by ABACUS, its drawbacks and the principal improvement we have added which help to reduce each time the complexity.

One of the most important heuristic used by ABACUS is to split (according to a given evaluation function) at each generation the resulting nodes (or variables) into the a-nodes set containing the most "interesting" nodes or active nodes and the s-nodes set containing the others which can be viewed as "sleeping" nodes. The exploration starts then developing the a-nodes, returning to develop the s-nodes only when no solution has been found. A maximum depth can be fixed by the user and helps to prevent combinatory explosion. The order of development of the nodes is illustrated the figure 1 below by the numbers above the nodes.

## 6.1 Evaluation function of ABACUS

ABACUS' choice of evaluation function is the "degree of constancy" which represents for a function the percentage of the data for which the function evaluates to a constant. This choice is justified by the construction of the data which consists in gathering the examples by doing successive experiments for which the variations of two parameters are examined while all the others parameters are held constant.

For instance, if the law is $ab/c = cte$, a group of examples will be built to examine the dependencies between $a$ and $b$. When the system computes the new variables, it finds that the values of $a$ increase when those of $b$ decrease, and it will build $a+b$ and $a*b$ according to the basic heuristics.

Once the new variables being generated, the system will have to sort them according to their degree of constancy and to cut the ordered set in half to obtain the a-nodes set and s-nodes set. But here $a*b$ will be found constant on at least one group while $a+b$ has a small chance to be constant on some examples. We can see here that the choice is directly dependant on the groups built by the user.

## 6.2 The problem

Unfortunately, the user does not always provide all the groups characterizing all the couples of parameters. Furthermore, especially if there are numerous data, it can happen that variables not leading to the solution can present a degree of constancy greater than those of "good" variables. All these conditions can lead the system to split the variables badly.

Another instance of splitting the variables badly is presented in figure 1. This figure represents the initial tree built by the system on a set containing 13 examples which describes the conservation of momentum. Eight parameters M1, V1, M2, V2, M1P, V1P, M2P, V2P, representing the mass and the velocity of the two objects before and after a collision.

We recall that the real law is : M1V1 + M2V2 = M1PV1P + M2PV2P.

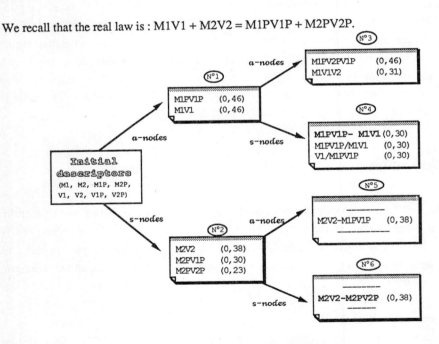

Figure 1. Variables splitting according to their degree of constancy
(numbers in parentheses give the accuracy of the variables)

We can note two important points :

- in the example, four among five variables are needed to create the equation and they must be gathered in the same set to be considered at the same time. Here, as the system is constrained to choose, it necessary splits the variables into two subsets, separating all the necessary variables. For this reason, the solution will be discovered only after the system has developed the subtree the root of which is the a-node n°1, after have exploring almost a hundredth of nodes. It is clear that systematically splitting the variables is not a good solution, especially when there are few of them.

- we can see an instance of a variable (M2PV1P in s-node n°2) which is not useful for discovering the solution which has however a better degree of constancy than a "good" variable (M2PV2P). That illustrates the well-known characteristic of an heuristic, that is to say, that a heuristic has a definite chance to fail in helping to solve a problem. Here, that implies that the known best nodes (necessary for building the solution) are not always those estimated with the higher degrees of constancy.

## 6.3 A new heuristic as a solution

To overcome these drawbacks of the algorithm, we restrict the heuristic of splitting the variables according to their degree of constancy by the following condition :

> *"If the variables of the generation are not too numerous,*
> *do not split them into a-nodes and s-nodes."*

We will estimate when the variables are too numerous not in absolute way, but with respect to the number of variables in the antecedent generation. For instance, hundred variables in the first generation may be considered as a great amount if there are only 20 parameters, but not in the case of 60 parameters. In this aim, we choose to set the minimum threshold for splitting to twice the number of variables in the previous generation. In this way, we are sure to reduce significantly the combinatorial explosion.

Furthermore, when there are few initial parameters, 10 or 15 for instance, even twice the number of them may be easily tractable. It is thus necessary to represent by a parameter the absolute minimum of variables under which it is not necessary to split. Let us call it *min-split*. The splitting of a generation $gen_k$ will be controlled by the two hereunder rules :

$$\text{" if } count\ (gen_k) \leq min\text{-}split \Rightarrow do\ not\ split\text{ "}$$

and

$$\text{" if } count\ (gen_k) > min\text{-}split\ \&\ count\ (gen_k) < 2 * count\ (gen_{k-1}) \Rightarrow do\ not\ split\text{ "}$$

The results this new heuristic are shown in the table 3, which compares the number of nodes created when it is used with the number of nodes generated when it is not used.

| discovered law | initial version | with new heuristic |
|---|---|---|
| $m1.v1 + m2.v2 = m1p.v1p + m2p.v2p$ | 250 | 107 |
| $N1.\sin(\theta 1) = N2.\sin(\theta 2)$ | 47 | 82 |
| $E = I.\cos(i) / r^2$ | 152 | 37 |
| $I = V0.\cos(\omega t) / r$ | 25 | 35 |
| $F = mv^2 \cos(\theta) / r$ | 146 | 121 |
| $S = (x+y).(z+w)$ | out of bound | 65 |

Table 3. Results of the heuristic "do not split if not too numerous"

In the previous example of the conservation of momentum, the number of new variables (5) is even less than the number of initial parameters (8), thus the system will not split them. This corresponds to delaying the choice between these variables. Applying this heuristic to the example, we observe that the number of nodes created until the law is found is decreased from 250 to 183.

We can note that the importance of the addition of this new heuristic cannot be evaluated from the number of nodes. The last example is the most representative case : on one hand, a bad choice without heuristic leads to the impossibility to find a solution inside the boundary of thousand nodes, and on the other hand, the new heuristic has allowed a delayed choice which then leads to the solution within a hundredth nodes.

On the other extreme, two examples in this table show that when the choice was already the best one, the added heuristic does not improve the rapidity but on the contrary delays the discovery of the law. As we are interested in improving the system to diminish the search such that the number of nodes and the time spent stays reasonable, we consider that the addition of research the heuristic sometimes lead to is negligible compared to the large improvement it adds when the laws are complex and when the evaluation function is inefficient to sort the variables correctly.

With this heuristic, we have automatically eliminated a high proportion of failure due to a bad initial choice. Since these bad choices avoid a law to be found in the threshold of hundred nodes, the efficiency of this heuristic is self evident.

# 7 Conclusion and future work

We have presented here three complementary aspects of our improvement of the system ABACUS. These improvements do not change the basic principles used in the system but integrate simple and useful notions independent of the application domain, quality which is one of the most principal aim of our system. Moreover, these improvements can not only be applied to ABACUS, but to all systems belonging to the BACON family like FAHRENHEIT or IDS (Nordhausen & Langley, 1990). Unfortunately, we have not resolved completely the problem of finding the law in only one step. However, we think that numerous improvements can be still added. Therefore, we present some different aspects which worth been further analyzed and improved :

1- The research axis we have presented here concerning accuracy seems worth exploring further. Firstly, some problems are still not resolved : for example, the problem of dealing with trigonometric values, always belonging to the interval [-1, 1] and easy to confuse even with a small degree of accuracy.

An additional point remains to be studied : as the graph search is explored, variables appear which have more and more values such that they have an absolute accuracy rate higher than the value itself. Intuitively, when we are provided a value like $10 \pm 20$, we decide that it does not merit much attention. Let us then consider a variable such that all its values verify $\delta(x_0) > x_0$. Even if it leads to a solution, we are practically guaranteed that the solution proposed will verify a very low accuracy rate, and if another solution is provided with more reasonable accuracies, the former will be rejected.

We propose to fix a percentage T (it could be a parameter of the system) which would indicate that when the accuracies becomes higher than T times $x_0$, it is not worth keeping the variable. This heuristic could reduce in an important way the search graph, but needs to be carefully examined to avoid errors.

2- In the same way that we have introduced accuracy, we will continue examining which kind of knowledge could be integrated without restricting the application field. For instance, an interesting knowledge used in ABACUS is constituted by the measure units. Their importance is such that when they are not used, the complexity is increased in such a way that generally, the system cannot find a solution within the threshold of thousand nodes. It would therefore be interesting to find analogical information so much powerful.

Now, when looking at qualitative physics, we can verify that a lot of knowledge are also available in every domain : for instance, the relations or laws already known between the parameters, or even incompatibilities between different types of variables, others than the compatibility rules. For instance, the expert knows whether it is worth multiply the length of the cube and the temperature or not. Dealing with this kind of information, we would in some way relate qualitative physics to scientific discovery. Now, the problem is an acquisition one : how to gather all this information?

## Acknowledgments

I would like to thank the following people who helped me a lot during this work : my thesis adviser Y. Kodratoff, M. Sebag and M. Schoenauer working at Polytechnic, H. Ralambondrainy who has worked at the INRIA in Diday's team, and all the mebers in the team Inférence et Apprentissage who helped me in the correction this paper, G. Bisson, K. Causse and A. Gordon.

## References

Davenport J., Siret Y., Tournier E. *Calcul formel. Systèmes et algorithmes de manipulations algebriques.* Collection etudes et recherche en informatique, Eds Masson, Paris, 1986.

Eurin M., Guimiot H. *Physique*, Classiques HACHETTE, 1953.

Falkenhainer B.C., Michalski R.S. Integrating Quantitative and Qualitative Discovery: The ABACUS system. *Machine Learning Journal,* vol. 3, 1986.

Falkenhainer B.C., Michalski R.S. Integrating Quantitative and Qualitative Discovery. *Machine Learning: An Artificial Intelligence Approach*, vol III, R.S. Michalski, J.G. Carbonell, T.M. Mitchell (Eds.), 1990.

Greene G.H. The ABACUS.2 system for quantitative discovery : Using dependencies to discover non-linear terms, MLI 88-17 TR-11-88, 1988.

Joyal M. *Cours de physique*, Vol. 3 Electricite, Eds Masson & Cie, 1956.

Langley P., Bradshaw G.L., Simon H. BACON.5: the discovery of conservation laws. *Proceedings of the seventh International Joint Conference on Artificial Intelligence*, p 121-126, 1985.

Langley P., Zytkow J., Simon H.and Bradshaw G.L. The search for regularity : Four aspects of scientific discovery in *Machine Learning: An Artificial Intelligence Approach*, volume II, Michalski R.S., Carbonell J.G., Mitchell T.M.(Eds.), Tioga, Palo Alto, Calif., 1986.

Langley P., Zytkow J., Simon H. and Bradshaw G.L. *Scientific discovery . Computational explorations of the creative process.* MIT press, Cambridge, MA, 1987.

Nordhausen B., Langley P. A robust approach to Numeric Discovery", *Proceedings of the seventh International Conference on Machine Learning*, p 411-418, edited by B.W. Porter and R.J.Mooney, Morgan Kauffman Publishers, Austin, 1990.

Zytkow J. M. Combining many searches in the FAHRENHEIT discovery system. *Proceedings of the fourth International Workshop on Machine Learning*, p 281-287, Morgan Kauffman Publishers, Irvine, 1987.

Zytkow J. M., Zhu J and Hussam, A., Automated discovery in a chemistry laboratory. *Proceedings of the AAAI-90*, AAAI Press, p 889-894, 1990.

# KBG : A GENERATOR OF KNOWLEDGE BASES[1]

GILLES BISSON
LRI, Equipe Inférence et Apprentissage
Université Paris-sud, Bâtiment 490
91405 Orsay Cedex France
email : bisson@lri.lri.fr, phone : (33) 69-41-63-00

## Abstract

A learning tool is often the result of a compromise between the capacity of the knowledge representation language used and the efficiency of the learning mechanisms dealing with this language. In this way, if systems based on attribute value representation are able to learn efficiently a set of diagnostic rules (or decision trees), they are unable to represent relations existing between several objects. On the contrary, the systems using first order logic are well adapted to express some complex links between objects, but they cannot deal with numerical knowledge.

Our system, KBG[2], is an inductive tool belonging to the family of "Constructive Learning" systems. The knowledge representation language used, both for input and output, is based on *first order logic* with some extensions allowing one to manipulate easily both *numerical* values and *procedural* knowledge. From a set of examples and a domain theory, KBG is able to learn a set of diagnostic rules usable by an external inference engine, or by the system itself in the frame of an incremental learning of concepts. The generation of the diagnostic rules is performed by iterative use of generalization and clustering operators. The generalization method is based on a specific similarity measure, allowing one to provide some explanations about the learning process : these explanations can be used by the expert to refine the initial knowledge. By using a classification phase, it becomes possible to point out some new sub-concepts in the learning set and to use them to index automatically the learned knowledge. Therefore, the learned rules are not built independently the ones from the others, but are directly organized in the form of a *hierarchical system of rules*, which is an important point to increase both the readability of the knowledge and its efficiency.

**Keywords :** Similarity Based Learning, Hierarchical System of Rules, First Order Logic Representation, Generalization, Structural Matching, Clustering, Knowledge Acquisition.

---

[1] This work is partially supported by CEC through the ESPRIT-2 contract MLT 2154 ("Machine Learning Toolbox") and also by MRT through PRC-IA.

[2] "Learning of Rule Systems in a First Order Representation", Université Paris-sud, Laboratoire de Recherche en Informatique, Internal Report 1991.

# ON ESTIMATING PROBABILITIES
# IN TREE PRUNING

Bojan Cestnik[1]  Ivan Bratko[1,2]

[1] Jožef Stefan Institute, Jamova 39, 61000 Ljubljana, Yugoslavia
E-mail: cestnik@ijs.ac.mail.yu

[2] Faculty of Electrical Eng. and Computer Science
Tržaška 25, 61000 Ljubljana, Yugoslavia

## Abstract

In this paper we introduce a new method for decision tree pruning, based on the minimisation of the expected classification error method by Niblett and Bratko. The original Niblett-Bratko pruning algorithm uses Laplace probability estimates. Here we introduce a new, more general Bayesian approach to estimating probabilities which we call *m-probability-estimation*. By varying a parameter $m$ in this method, tree pruning can be adjusted to particular properties of the learning domain, such as level of noise. The resulting pruning method improves on the original Niblett-Bratko pruning in the following respects: apriori probabilities can be incorporated into error estimation, several trees pruned to various degrees can be generated, and the degree of pruning is not affected by the number of classes. These improvements are supported by experimental findings. *m-probability-estimation* also enables the combination of learning data obtained from various sources.

## 1   Introduction

The importance of tree pruning and rule simplification in machine learning (ML) from incomplete and unreliable data has been widely acknowledged within the ML community. Several approaches to tree pruning have been developed in the last few years including (Breiman *et al*, 1984) , (Quinlan, 1986, 1987), (Niblett & Bratko, 1986), (Cestnik *et al*, 1987), (Clark & Niblett, 1987), (Smyth *et al*, 1990). The approaches differ in their use of various criteria for deciding whether to prune at a certain stage or not. That is the reason why they are difficult to compare. An attempt to summarise and empirically compare five tree pruning methods was made by Mingers (1989).

In this article we present a new method for tree pruning. It is based on the minimisation of the total expected classification error method by Niblett and Bratko (1986) and improved with a new Bayesian approach for estimating probabilities (Cestnik, 1990). Niblett and Bratko used Laplace's law of succession to estimate the required probabilities. For a $k$-class problem, this law states that if in the sample of $N$ trials there were $n$ outcomes of a class $c$, the probability of $c$ in the next trial is $(n+1)/(N+k)$. This assumes that the apriori probability distribution is uniform and equal for all classes. Laplace's law of succession is only a special case of a more general Bayesian method for estimating probabilities that assumes the beta prior probability distribution (Good, 1965; Berger, 1985). For the $k$-class problem, after $n$ successes in $N$ trials, the probability $p$ of $c$ in the next trial is, according to this Bayesian method, the following:

$$p = \frac{n + p_a m}{N + m} \tag{1}$$

where $p_a$ is apriori probability of $c$ and $m$ is a parameter of the estimation method.

This formula, developed in (Cestnik, 1990), will be called *m-probability-estimation*, and the resulting probability estimates *m-estimates*. The new method for tree pruning, using $m$-estimates, inherits the theoretical clarity from the original Niblett-Bratko method. By introducing one additional degree of freedom (parameter $m$) it alleviates some problems with the Niblett-Bratko method found by Cestnik *et al* (1987) and Mingers (1989). First, instead of assuming a uniform initial distribution of classes, which is seldom true in practice, prior probabilities can be incorporated in the estimation. Second, by varying the parameter $m$, several trees, pruned to different degrees, can be obtained. And third, the number of classes no longer affects the degree of pruning; the degree of pruning is determined by the choice of $m$. $m$ can be adjusted to some essential properties of the learning domain, such as the level of noise in the learning data.

In section 2 the approach to generating and pruning trees with $m$-probability-estimation is presented. Section 3 describes the experiments with the new method. In section 4, the obtained results are discussed and interpreted. The $m$-probability-estimation method also enables a new method for combining evidence from various sources. This is described in section 5. Finally, in section 6, the conclusions are drawn and some directions for further research are presented.

# 2   Generating and pruning with $m$-probability-estimates

The Bayesian approach to estimating a probability $p$ can be summarised in the following way (Good, 1965): first, one has to assume an initial (apriori) probability distribution for $p$. Then, the evidence $E$ converts this distribution into a final (aposteriori) distribution, from which the expectation and the variance of $p$ can be taken. Usually, a class of initial density functions is given by the beta form, proportional to $p^a(1-p)^{m-a}$, where $a > -1$ and $m-a > -1$. The initial distribution depends on the initial expectation and variance (Good, 1965), and can be practically determined with parameters $a$ and $m$. In (Cestnik, 1990) it is shown that $a$ and $m$ should satisfy the constraint $a = p_a m$, where $p_a$ is the initial expectation of $p$. The parameter $m$ is related to the initial variance. In fact,

$m$ determines the impact of the apriori probability $p_a$ to the estimation of $p$. Further interpretation of parameter $m$ is given at the end of this section.

In general, the need for manual estimation is considered as a basic limitation of the Bayesian approach. In the case when multiple attributes interact, a large number of parameters must be estimated in a subjective manner (Pearl, 1988). On the other hand, in the context of learning rules from data, a modified Bayesian approach can be used. Namely, the probability estimate of a given class in the whole learning set can be used as apriori probability in the estimation of conditional probabilities (given some attributes) of the class. This approach turned out to work very well in the framework of the "naive" Bayes formula (Cestnik, 1990). However, the problem of determining the value of $m$ still remains. For the sake of simplicity we will assume that $m$ is equal for all attributes and their combinations in a given domain. Yet, in practice, this might not be the case; $m$ might depend on a particular attribute or even a particular value of an attribute.

When building classifiers in the form of a decision tree from incomplete and unreliable data (class probability trees) there are three stages in which probability estimates are needed: first, in the tree construction, when selecting an attribute for the root of a subtree according to some criterion (eg. information gain); second, in the tree pruning phase, when the branches with little statistical validity have to be identified and removed; and third, in the classification phase, when, based on the examples in a given leaf, probabilities have to be assigned to the classes. Once we have decided upon the method for estimating apriori probabilities, we have to select a suitable $m$ for each of the three phases.

As a general scheme, we propose $m = 0$ in the tree construction phase, because a constructed full-sized tree is only a new form of representing the learning data set. Therefore, there is no need to incorporate "apriori information" since it may unnecessarily complicate the tree. On the other hand, in the tree pruning phase we want to adjust the constructed tree to the whole domain of learning (i.e. also to previously unseen objects – independent data set). At this stage, we have to consider apriori probabilities; consequently, $m$ has to be greater than 0. The actual value of $m$ depends on the level of noise in a given domain (larger $m$ for more noise). So, $m$ can be proposed by the domain expert. On the other hand, one can use heuristics to set $m$; for example, $m$ can be set so as to maximise the classification accuracy on an independent data set. A similar approach to determining the parameter $\alpha$ for pruning in $CART$ is described in (Breiman $et$ $al$, 1985).

With $m$-probability-estimates, the "static error" $E_s$ in a given node is given by the following formula:

$$E_s = 1 - \frac{n_c + p_{ac}m}{N + m} = \frac{N - n_c + (1 - p_{ac})m}{N + m} \tag{2}$$

where $N$ is the total number of examples in the node, $n_c$ is the number of examples in class $c$ that minimises $E_s$ for the given $m$, $p_{ac}$ is the apriori probability of class c, and $m$ is the parameter of the estimation method.

Note that if $m$ is equal to the number of classes and $p_{ac} = 1/m$ then the formula (2) is equivalent to Laplace's law of succession used by Niblett and Bratko.

The backed-up error $E_b$ of a given node is computed considering the error estimates for the subtrees. In the case of a binary tree $E_b$ is computed as follows:

$$E_b = p_1 E_1 + p_2 E_2 \tag{3}$$

where $p_i$ is the probability that an object will fall in the $i$-th subtree, and $E_i$ is the error estimate for the $i$-th subtree.

Again, (3) is the combination formula from the Niblett-Bratko approach. However, the difference is in the estimation of $p_i$. Instead of previously used relative frequency estimate we propose the $m$-estimates with $m = 2$. It should be admitted that here $m$ is chosen arbitrarily. However, we found out that the results do not depend much on the choice of $m$ in this formula.

The pruning algorithm is presented in (Niblett & Bratko, 1986). It basically states that if, in a given node, the backed-up error $E_b$ is greater than the static error $E_s$, the tree is pruned at this node.

When adjusting a constructed full-sized tree to the whole domain, the tree is pruned so as to minimise the expected classification error given a certain value of $m$. The same value of $m$ must then be used also in the classification of a new object with the pruned tree. It might happen that, with changing the value of $m$, the class that minimises the estimated error for some $m$ is different from the "minimal error" class for another $m$. A situation like this is presented in Figure 1. There are two classes, $'+'$ and $'-'$. Their apriori probabilities are: $p_a('+') = 0.4$ and $p_a('-') = 0.6$. Now, suppose that there is a leaf with 10 examples, 7 $'+'$ and 3 $'-'$. Figure 1 shows that for $m < 20$ the $m$-estimate probability of $'+'$ is higher than 0.5, when $m = 20$ both estimates are equal, and for $m > 20$ the probability estimate of $'-'$ takes over the lead. As a result, an object, fallen in this leaf, would be classified as $'+'$ if $m < 20$, undecided if $m = 20$, and as $'-'$ if $m > 20$.

To obtain a clearer understanding of the meaning of $m$, we will consider how $m$ affects the combination of evidence from data and apriori probabilities. The formula (1) can be rewritten in the following way:

$$p = \frac{N}{N + m} \hat{p} + \frac{m}{N + m} p_a \tag{4}$$

where $N$ is the number of examples, $\hat{p}$ is the relative frequency estimation $n/N$, $p_a$ is apriori probability and $m$ is the parameter of the estimation method.

From (4) it can be seen that if $m = 0$ then $p$ is equal to relative frequency estimate $\hat{p} = n/N$. When $m = N$ ($m$ is equal to the number of examples) $p$ is equal to the average of $\hat{p}$ and apriori probability $p_a$. In the limit, when $m$ is infinite, $p$ is equal to $p_a$. So, by varying the parameter $m$ one actually determines the effect of the

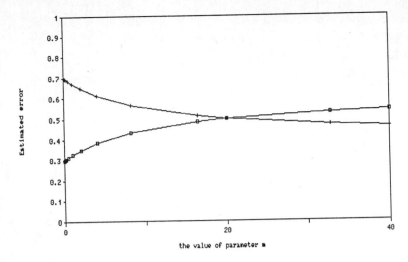

Figure 1: Estimated static errors for the classes $'+'$ and $'-'$ in a leaf with 10 examples (7 $'+'$ and 3 $'-'$). Apriori probabilities for $'+'$ and $'-'$ are 0.4 and 0.6 respectively. At $m = 20$ the estimated errors for the two classes are equal.

apriori probability and the relative frequency on the final probability estimate. A further interpretation of formula (4) is possible: the formula combines the apriori probability and the new evidence obtained from $N$ examples. The combination is such as if the apriori probability was obtained from $m$ prior examples and estimated with relative frequency.

# 3    Experiments and empirical findings

We did two sets of experiments: one with artificial, synthetic trees, and one with trees generated from learning data from eight natural domains. We will first describe the experiments with synthetic trees.

To measure the impact of the number of classes, the class distribution and the value of $m$ on the degree of pruning with the new method the following experiment was performed. First, complete binary tree of depth 10 (1024 leaves) was constructed. Second, each leaf was randomly assigned one example from a given class distribution. And third, the tree was pruned according to the value of $m$. In each experiment the size of the final tree and its accuracy on the "learning" examples (from the original tree) were measured. In experiments we varied the number of classes, the class distribution and parameter $m$. For each combination of these three variables, 10 experiments were performed to obtain the average values for the above-mentioned measured parameters. We repeated this experiment with complete binary trees of other depths between 8 and 12, and found that the relative degree of pruning (in percents) does not depend on the depth of the tree.

In the experiment we selected the following values for the parameters: The values for the number of classes were 2, 4, 8, 16 and 32. There were three different class distributions: uniform (0), where $p_i = c_0$ for all $i$; linear (1), where $p_i = p_{i-1} + c_1$ for $i > 1$ and $p_1 = c_1$; and geometric (2), where $p_i = p_{i-1}c_2$ for $i > 2$ and $p_1 = c_2$. The constants $c_0$, $c_1$ and $c_2$ are adjusted so that the sum of $p_i$ over all classes equals to 1 for each distribution. For the value of $m$ values 0, 0.01, 0.5, 1, 2, 3, 4, 8, 12, 16, 32, 64, 128 and 999 were selected.

The results obtained for uniform, linear and geometric class distribution are shown in Figures 2, 3 and 4, respectively. In each figure the points (labeled x) for the same class and different $m$, are connected with lines. The circle ○ represents the result of pruning with original Niblett-Bratko method. These experimental results will be interpreted in section 4.

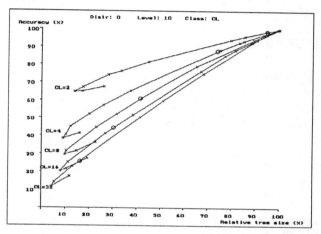

Figure 2: Accuracy vs. size of the tree for uniform distribution of classes

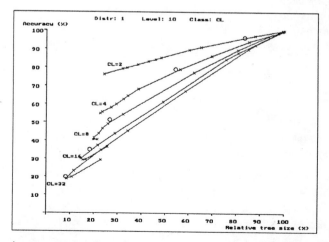

Figure 3: Accuracy vs. size of the tree for linear distribution of classes

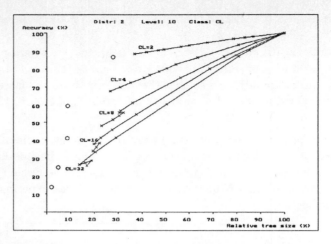

Figure 4: Accuracy vs. size of the tree for geometric distribution of classes

The new method was also tested on eight real-world domains. The domains are described in Table 1. The four rheumatology domains are essentially equal except for the number of classes that are hierarchically decomposed from three to six, eight and finally twelve classes. The first four domains are described in more detail in (Bratko & Kononenko, 1986).

| Domain | | #clas. | #attr. | #exam. | %maj.class |
|---|---|---|---|---|---|
| Hepatitis | HEPA | 2 | 19 | 155 | 79.4 |
| Lymphography | LYMP | 4 | 18 | 148 | 54.7 |
| Breast cancer | BREA | 2 | 10 | 288 | 79.9 |
| Primary tumor | PRIM | 22 | 17 | 339 | 24.8 |
| Rheumatology 3 | RE03 | 3 | 58 | 462 | 66.5 |
| Rheumatology 6 | RE06 | 6 | 58 | 462 | 61.9 |
| Rheumatology 8 | RE08 | 8 | 58 | 462 | 34.2 |
| Rheumatology 12 | RE12 | 12 | 58 | 462 | 34.2 |

Table 1: Description of eight medical domains

The results, presented in Table 2, are averaged over 10 experiments. Each time 70% of examples were randomly taken for learning and the rest 30% for testing. All the methods were tested on the same learning-testing partition.

In Table 2 there are three numbers for each error estimate $(m)$ in each domain. The first number stands for the number of leaves in the tree. The second one shows classification accuracy on the learning data set and the third one classification accuracy on the testing data set. The results are presented graphically in Figures 5 and 6.

| | HEPA | | | LYMP | | | BREA | | | PRIM | | |
|---|---|---|---|---|---|---|---|---|---|---|---|---|
| Laplace | 12.1 | 89.0 | 82.1 | 16.9 | 98.2 | 77.1 | 51.6 | 88.7 | 77.8 | 33.5 | 31.9 | 30.6 |
| 0.0 | 13.2 | 91.3 | 79.8 | 17.8 | 100.0 | 77.5 | 63.8 | 94.0 | 73.6 | 90.5 | 70.5 | 40.3 |
| 0.01 | 13.1 | 91.3 | 79.8 | 17.8 | 100.0 | 77.3 | 64.3 | 94.0 | 74.1 | 90.3 | 70.5 | 40.4 |
| 0.5 | 13.0 | 90.9 | 81.5 | 17.8 | 100.0 | 77.3 | 61.3 | 94.0 | 74.3 | 82.6 | 69.6 | 40.1 |
| 1 | 12.7 | 90.4 | 81.1 | 17.8 | 100.0 | 77.3 | 55.5 | 93.9 | 74.3 | 74.3 | 67.6 | 40.7 |
| 2 | 12.1 | 89.0 | 82.1 | 17.4 | 99.0 | 77.3 | 51.6 | 88.7 | 77.8 | 61.4 | 63.8 | 40.6 |
| 3 | 12.5 | 88.5 | 83.6 | 17.0 | 98.8 | 77.3 | 47.9 | 88.5 | 77.9 | 54.9 | 61.3 | 41.4 |
| 4 | 10.8 | 88.3 | 84.5 | 16.9 | 98.2 | 77.1 | 47.4 | 84.3 | 78.8 | 50.2 | 58.4 | 40.3 |
| 8 | 10.4 | 86.4 | 84.0 | 15.7 | 94.6 | 76.8 | 41.3 | 81.7 | 79.3 | 39.9 | 47.0 | 36.8 |
| 12 | 9.4 | 85.5 | 85.5 | 13.5 | 90.8 | 75.9 | 40.0 | 80.2 | 80.0 | 39.6 | 41.3 | 35.1 |
| 16 | 9.4 | 85.0 | 85.5 | 11.8 | 88.3 | 75.0 | 37.7 | 79.8 | 80.0 | 35.6 | 35.0 | 31.4 |
| 32 | 9.7 | 77.4 | 83.8 | 7.6 | 82.6 | 75.9 | 29.9 | 79.8 | 80.0 | 37.9 | 30.5 | 29.0 |
| 64 | 9.7 | 77.4 | 83.8 | 7.4 | 81.1 | 74.8 | 26.3 | 79.8 | 80.0 | 44.4 | 26.4 | 25.0 |
| 128 | 9.4 | 77.4 | 83.8 | 7.8 | 74.8 | 69.1 | 22.2 | 79.8 | 80.0 | 47.5 | 24.8 | 24.6 |
| 999 | 9.4 | 77.4 | 83.8 | 9.1 | 54.1 | 56.1 | 21.6 | 79.8 | 80.0 | 46.4 | 24.8 | 24.6 |

| m | RE03 | | | RE06 | | | RE08 | | | RE12 | | |
|---|---|---|---|---|---|---|---|---|---|---|---|---|
| Laplace | 40.4 | 79.5 | 70.0 | 46.3 | 66.8 | 64.5 | 49.1 | 64.4 | 47.7 | 44.2 | 58.0 | 47.6 |
| 0.0 | 60.4 | 86.2 | 67.6 | 70.2 | 80.3 | 56.8 | 87.0 | 81.7 | 47.0 | 86.3 | 78.0 | 45.6 |
| 0.01 | 59.8 | 86.1 | 67.8 | 70.2 | 80.3 | 56.8 | 87.0 | 81.7 | 46.6 | 86.3 | 78.0 | 45.6 |
| 0.5 | 52.5 | 84.5 | 68.1 | 66.0 | 79.6 | 57.2 | 85.2 | 81.3 | 46.3 | 85.4 | 77.2 | 46.0 |
| 1 | 49.4 | 83.5 | 69.2 | 63.2 | 78.6 | 58.5 | 83.0 | 79.9 | 46.2 | 81.5 | 76.4 | 45.6 |
| 2 | 44.1 | 82.5 | 69.7 | 56.5 | 76.5 | 60.4 | 74.9 | 77.2 | 46.2 | 76.7 | 74.5 | 46.0 |
| 3 | 40.4 | 79.5 | 70.0 | 50.4 | 72.9 | 62.0 | 67.2 | 75.0 | 46.6 | 71.8 | 73.0 | 46.5 |
| 4 | 36.7 | 77.4 | 70.3 | 44.9 | 70.2 | 63.0 | 61.8 | 72.2 | 47.6 | 64.4 | 70.0 | 47.7 |
| 8 | 32.5 | 76.4 | 71.4 | 46.1 | 65.8 | 64.0 | 49.1 | 64.4 | 47.7 | 48.3 | 60.7 | 47.9 |
| 12 | 31.7 | 73.8 | 70.8 | 43.6 | 64.3 | 63.0 | 42.4 | 60.0 | 48.4 | 44.2 | 58.0 | 47.6 |
| 16 | 32.3 | 71.0 | 69.8 | 43.8 | 62.6 | 63.5 | 41.1 | 58.1 | 48.9 | 41.8 | 56.0 | 47.8 |
| 32 | 33.0 | 69.0 | 68.9 | 40.7 | 61.2 | 63.5 | 44.1 | 52.0 | 46.3 | 40.4 | 50.3 | 45.1 |
| 64 | 32.5 | 66.0 | 67.5 | 34.8 | 61.2 | 63.5 | 40.3 | 46.6 | 43.5 | 42.2 | 46.1 | 43.6 |
| 128 | 30.2 | 66.0 | 67.5 | 35.1 | 61.2 | 63.5 | 39.2 | 44.3 | 42.9 | 40.8 | 43.9 | 43.5 |
| 999 | 28.3 | 66.0 | 67.5 | 35.1 | 61.2 | 63.5 | 36.0 | 33.5 | 35.9 | 35.8 | 33.5 | 35.9 |

Table 2: Results of pruning with the Laplace's estimates and with $m$-estimates for different values of $m$. The three numbers are the number of leaves in the tree, classification accuracy on the training set and classification accuracy on the independent testing set, respectively.

# 4 Phenomena and interpretation

The original Niblett-Bratko pruning method with Laplace's error estimate was empirically observed to occasionally over-prune (Cestnik *et al*, 1987) or under-prune (Mingers, 1989). Results from the previous section (see Figures 2, 3 and 4) explain the effect of over-pruning when apriori probabilities of classes are unequal (linear or geometric) in combination with high number of classes. In those cases Laplace's estimates prune too much, much more than the $m$-error-estimates with properly selected $m$. Similarly, the effect of under-pruning can be observed in the cases with uniform class distribution and small number of classes. In general, we view $m$ as a domain parameter, and believe that it should be set so as to correspond to the amount of noise in the domain.

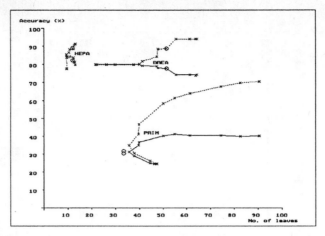

Figure 5: Results from Table 2 for domains HEPA, BREA and PRIM, presented in a graphical form

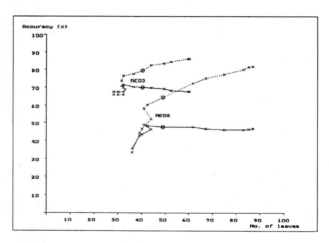

Figure 6: Results from Table 2 for domains RE03 and RE08, presented in a graphical form

The ideal pruning procedure should, when $m$ approaches infinity, prune maximally with only the root left (because all estimated probabilities would then be equal to the prior probabilities). However, the computed error estimates are only almost equal to the apriori probabilities and the pruning criterion $E_s \leq E_b$ is satisfied in about 50% of cases. Propagating this criterion upwards leaves about half of the tree unpruned. So, with very large $m$, only about half of a binary tree is pruned due to the random statistical behavior of the criterion $E_s \leq E_b$. This explains the irregularities at the left ends of some of the curves in Figures 2–4. It also suggests an obvious improvement that would prevent this anomalous behaviour: the pruning criterion should be "stabilised" by changing it to $E_s \leq E_b + \varepsilon$ where $\varepsilon$ is some small positive number.

Mingers in his study (1989) argues that various trees, pruned to different degrees, would be desirable in practice in knowledge acquisition for expert systems. This was considered as a drawback of the Niblett-Bratko method producing one tree only. As an improvement in this respect, the sequence of trees of different sizes can now be generated by varying the value of parameter $m$.

Mingers also found that in Laplace's error estimation a change in the number of classes drastically affects the degree of pruning. This paper quantitatively supports this conclusion. However, with properly setting the parameter $m$ the degree of pruning becomes stable. Our results also show the effect of prior class probabilities to the degree of pruning. Regarding the observed correlation between the degree of pruning in the Niblett-Bratko method and the number of classes, we believe the following. One should expect more pruning when there are more classes. This can be simply explained by the fact that with more classes and equally sized learning set the majority class estimates become less reliable and therefore more pruning is warranted. However, the degree of pruning with Laplace's estimate seems to exaggerate in this respect, and it also wildly varies with different apriori probability distributions for classes, which is not appropriate.

In some machine learning applications, some learning examples are designed by the expert simply to introduce known facts about the domain. This is typical of some engineering applications. How can such "absolute examples" be handled in this framework? In such situations we want to make sure that one example of class $c$ is enough to estimate $p_c = 1$ in the corresponding leaf. This can be handled by setting $m$ to 0. In a way, this setting ($m = 0$) corresponds to perfect data (no noise, no uncertainty, and complete information, i.e. sufficient set of attributes and examples to determine the class completely). On the other hand, large $m$ would correspond to very uncertain, noisy data.

The results in eight real-world domains show that the reality itself is very complicated. Usually, the distribution of classes is neither uniform, nor any other simple function. In addition, it seems that the optimal value for $m$ critically depends on noise (incomplete and unreliable data, missing data, etc.). The number of classes that is implicitly taken for $m$ in Laplace's estimate can only be viewed as an unsuccessful guess. For example, the best $m$ for Hepatitis (2 classes) is 12, the best $m$ for Lymphography (4 classes) is 0, and the best $m$ for Primary tumor (22 classes) is 3 (see Table 2).

# 5  Combination of various sources of evidence

The formula (4), that was used to interpret the parameter $m$, represents a way of combining the evidence from data (relative frequency estimation) and prior belief (apriori probability). Now, the question arises whether data from various sources can be combined using the same principle. For example, in a medical domain we may have some examples from patient histories (unreliable, incomplete, noisy) and some special cases constructed by an expert and supplied as absolute truth. Such situations can be handled according to the following generalisation of formula (4):

$$p = \sum_i \frac{w_i N_i}{\sum_j w_j N_j} p_i \tag{5}$$

where $p_i$ is the probability from $i$-th source, $N_i$ is the number of examples from $i$-th source, and $w_i$ is the weight of $i$-th source.

In the above mentioned medical case we might have three sources of information: apriori probability, patient histories and expert supplied examples. Suppose that we have 100 patient histories and 10 expert supplied cases. From the patient histories we estimate relative frequency probability $p_1$ and from expert supplied cases probability $p_2$. Suppose that the weight of expert cases is 10 and the weight of patient histories is 1. For the apriori probability $p_a$ we set $m$ $(= N_3)$ to 5. In such a case we can compute the combined probability estimate in the following way:

$$p = \frac{1 \times 100}{205} p_1 + \frac{10 \times 10}{205} p_2 + \frac{5}{205} p_a$$

Note that the total weight of expert supplied probability is equal to the weight of the probability based on patient histories, in spite of the different number of examples in both cases.

# 6 Conclusion

In this paper we presented a new method for minimal-error pruning of decision trees that is based on the Niblett and Bratko (1986) method and modified with the $m$-probability-estimation. Our main aim was to upgrade the above-mentioned approach so as to preserve the desirable theoretical properties and to alleviate some shortcomings observed by Cestnik *et al* (1987) and Mingers (1989).

The main improvements with respect to the original Niblett-Bratko method are the incorporation of apriori probabilities in the error estimation and a new degree of freedom represented by a choice of parameter $m$. The advantages, resulting from these two improvements, are the following: first, instead of assuming the uniform initial distribution of classes, which is seldom true in practice, prior probabilities can be incorporated in the error estimation. Second, by varying the parameter $m$, several trees, pruned to different degrees, can be obtained, which is useful in mechanised knowledge acquisition. And third, the number of classes no longer affects the degree of pruning; the degree of pruning is determined by the choice of $m$. Experimental results in synthetic and natural domains, presented in section 3, confirm the contributions of the new approach.

The proposed method for estimating probabilities (Cestnik, 1990) can be used at various stages: tree construction, tree pruning and classification. We propose a general scheme regarding the choice of $m$: generate a tree with $m = 0$, prune with $m' > 0$ and classify with $m' > 0$. The scheme is explained and justified in section 2. The fine adjustment of $m$ for pruning depends on the properties of the domain and degree of noise, and can be left to the domain expert.

The $m$-probability-estimation method also enables a new method for combining evidence from various sources which was presented in section 5.

For further work, we plan to design a method to automatically select the "best" $m$. There are various possibilities how it can be done. First, the selection can be based on an independent data set (to measure classification accuracy). The shortcoming of this is that it requires a separate data set. Next, the selection can be based on heuristics taking into account properties of the learning set (observing the slope of classification accuracy with respect to the size of a tree). Last but not least, domain expert can supply important information regarding the choice of $m$, such as: how much noise there is in the data, how truthworthy particular sources of data are, etc.

# Acknowledgments

The data for lymphographic investigation, primary tumor, breast cancer recurrence and rheumatology were obtained from the University Medical Center in Ljubljana. We would like to thank M.Zwitter, M.Soklic and V.Pirnat for providing the data. We thank G.Gong from Carnegie-Mellon University for providing the data for hepatitis problem. Long-term efforts of I.Kononenko and his colleagues were significant in turning these data into easy-to-use experimental material. This work was financially supported by the Research Council of Slovenia and carried out as part of European project ESPRIT II Basic Research Action No. 3059, Project ECOLES.

# References

Berger, J.O. (1985), *Statistical Decision Theory and Bayesian Analysis*, Springer-Verlag, New York.

Bratko, I., Kononenko, I. (1986), Learning diagnostic rules from incomplete and noisy data, AI Methods in Statistics, UNICOM Seminar, London, December 1986. Also in *Interactions in AI and Statistics* (ed. B.Phelps) London; Gower Technical Press, 1987.

Breiman, L., Friedman, J.H., Olshen, R.A., Stone, C.J. (1984), *Classification and Regression Trees*, Belmont, California: Wadsworth Int. Group.

Cestnik, B., Kononenko, I., Bratko, I. (1987), ASSISTANT 86: A Knowledge-Elicitation Tool for Sophisticated Users, *Progress in Machine Learning*, Eds. I.Bratko & N.Lavrac, Sigma Press, Wilmslow.

Cestnik, B. (1990), Estimating Probabilities: A Crucial Task in Machine Learning. In *Proceedings of ECAI 90*, Stockholm, August 1990.

Clark, P., Niblett, T. (1987), Induction in Noisy Domains, *Progress in Machine Learning*, Eds. I.Bratko & N.Lavrac, Sigma Press, Wilmslow.

Good, I.J. (1965), *The Estimation of Probabilities*, M.I.T. Press, Cambridge, Massachusetts.

Mingers, J. (1989), An Empirical Comparison of Pruning Methods for Decision Tree Induction, *Machine Learning* vol. 4, no. 2, Kluwer Academic Publishers.

Niblett, T., Bratko, I. (1986), Learning decision rules in noisy domains, Expert Systems 86, Cambridge University Press (*Proceddings of Expert Systems 86 Conf.*, Brighton 1986).

Pearl, J. (1988), *Probabilistic Reasoning in Intelligent Systems: Networks of Plausible Inference*, Morgan Kaufmann: San Mateo, CA.

Quinlan, J.R. (1986), Learning from noisy data, *Machine Learning* vol. 2, Eds R.Michalski, J.Carbonell and T.Mitchel, Palo Alto, CA: Tioga.

Quinlan, J.R. (1987), Simplifying decision trees, *International Journal of Man-Machine Studies*, 27, pp. 221–234.

Smyth, P., Goodman, R.M., Higgins, C. (1990), A Hybrid Rule-based/Bayesian Classifier, In *Proceedings of ECAI 90*, Stockholm, August 1990.

# Rule Induction with CN2:
# Some Recent Improvements

Peter Clark     Robin Boswell

The Turing Institute, 36 N.Hanover St., Glasgow

email: {pete,robin}@turing.ac.uk

## Abstract

The CN2 algorithm induces an ordered list of classification rules from examples using entropy as its search heuristic. In this short paper, we describe two improvements to this algorithm. Firstly, we present the use of the Laplacian error estimate as an alternative evaluation function and secondly, we show how unordered as well as ordered rules can be generated. We experimentally demonstrate significantly improved performances resulting from these changes, thus enhancing the usefulness of CN2 as an inductive tool. Comparisons with Quinlan's C4.5 are also made.

**Keywords:** learning, rule induction, CN2, Laplace, noise

## 1   Introduction

Rule induction from examples has established itself as a basic component of many machine learning systems, and has been the first ML technology to deliver commercially successful applications (eg. the systems GASOIL [Slocombe et al., 1986], BMT [Hayes-Michie, 1990], and in process control [Leech, 1986]). The continuing development of inductive techniques is thus valuable to pursue.

CN2 is an algorithm designed to induce 'if...then...' rules in domains where there might be noise. The algorithm is described in [Clark and Niblett, 1989] and [Clark and Niblett, 1987], and is summarised in this paper. The original algorithm used entropy as its search heuristic, and was only able to generate an ordered list of rules. In this paper, we demonstrate how using the Laplacian error estimate as a heuristic significantly improves the algorithm's performance, and describe how the algorithm can also be used to generate unordered rules. These improvements are important as they enhance the accuracy and scope of applicability of the algorithm.

# 2 An Improved Evaluation Function

## 2.1 The Original Entropy Function

The CN2 algorithm consists of two main procedures: a search algorithm performing a beam search for a good rule (shown in Appendix 2) and a control algorithm for repeatedly executing the search (shown later in Figure 1).

During the search procedure, CN2 must evaluate the rules it finds to decide which is best. One possible metric of rule quality is its accuracy on training data (eg. an option for AQ15 [Michalski et al., 1986]). An alternative is entropy, used by ID3 and the original CN2, which behaves very similarly to apparent accuracy. Entropy also prefers rules which cover examples of only one class.

The problem with these metrics is that they tend to select very specific rules covering only a few examples, as the likelihood of finding rules with high accuracy on the training data increases as the rules become more specific. In the extreme case, a maximally specific rule will just cover one example and hence have an unbeatable score using the metrics of accuracy (scores 100% accuracy) or entropy (scores 0.00, a perfect score). This is undesirable as rules covering few examples are unreliable, especially with noise in the domain. Their accuracy on the training data does not adequately reflect their true predictive accuracy (ie. accuracy on new test data) which may appear.

## 2.2 Significance Testing: A Partial Solution

To avoid selecting highly specific rules, CN2 uses a significance test (see [Clark and Niblett, 1989]) which ensures that the distribution of examples among classes covered by the rule is *significantly different* from that which would occur by chance. In this way, many rules covering only a few examples are eliminated, as the significance test deems their apparent high accuracy likely to be simply due to chance.

However, while a significance test eliminates rules which are below a certain threshold of significance, there is still the problem that rules which just pass the significance test will tend to be preferred over more general and reliable but less apparently accurate rules. Consider a domain with two equally likely classes C1 and C2, and consider three rules R1, R2 and R3, where:

R1 covers 1000 examples of class C1 and 1 of C2 (we denote this by [1000, 1])
R2 covers 5 examples of C1 and 0 of C2 (ie. [5, 0])
R3 covers [1, 0])

Here, the algorithm should ideally prefer R1 as its accuracy on new test data is likely to be the best – rules R2 and R3 only cover a few examples and their apparent accuracies of 100% are not fully reflective of performance on new test data. However, although a 99% significance test eliminates R3, R2 will just pass and be selected in preference to R1. Raising the significance level further does not solve the problem as a rule R1.5 (say) may exist which again just passes the raised significance threshold.

We can describe the metrics of apparent accuracy/entropy as having an undesirable 'downward bias', ie. preference for rules low down in the general (top) to specific (bottom) search space. Raising the significance threshold causes the level of specificity at which the search terminates to raise, but does not eliminate the downward bias itself.

## 2.3   The Use of Laplace

In fact, as reported by other authors (eg. [Niblett, 1987]) an approximate measure does exist to measure the expected accuracy directly, namely 1 - the Laplace expected error estimate. This expected accuracy is given by the formula:

$$\texttt{LaplaceAccuracy} = (n_c + 1)/(n_{tot} + k) \qquad (1)$$

where

$k$ is the number of classes in the domain

$n_c$ is the number of examples in the predicted class $c$ covered by the rule

$n_{tot}$ is the total number of examples covered by rule

When generating a rule list, the predicted class $c$ for a rule is simply the class with the most covered examples in it.

This formula is a special case of the m-probability-estimate developed by Cestnik [Cestnik, 1990]:

$$\texttt{mPAccuracy} = (n_c + p_o(c)\ m)/(n_{tot} + m)$$

where uniform prior probabilities $p_o$ for classes are assumed (ie. $p_o(c) = 1/k$) and the tunable parameter $m$ is set to $k$. The m-probability-estimate is analysed further in [Cestnik and Bratko, 1991].

For our example above the Laplace accuracy estimates for predicting the class with the most covered examples in are 99.8% for R1, 85.7% for R2 and 66.6% for R3. Thus Laplace avoids the undesirable 'downward bias' of entropy, and which significance testing only partly overcame.

A final check must be included to ensure the expected accuracy is at least better than that of a default rule predicting the class for all examples.

## 2.4   The New Role of Significance Testing

Significance testing can still be included to prune out the most specialised (and hence less frequently applicable) rules in the rule list. This reduces the complexity of the rule list, but at a slight cost in predictive accuracy. Interestingly, the behaviour of significance testing with Laplace is qualitatively different to that with entropy. With entropy, raising the significance threshold causes CN2 to select slightly more general rules during induction. With Laplace, general rules tend to be favoured anyway, and significance testing instead alters the point at which CN2 stops searching for further rules. In other words, with entropy the test affects which rules are chosen as 'best', but with Laplace acts solely as a termination criterion for the algorithm.

Table 1: Details of Experimental Domains

| Domain† | Description | Number of | | |
|---|---|---|---|---|
| | | Exs | Atts | Classes |
| lymphography | disease diagnosis | 148 | 18 | 4 |
| pole-and-cart | predict human balancing action from exs | 1044 | 4 | 2 |
| soybean | disease diagnosis | 307 | 35 | 19 |
| heart-diseaseC | disease diagnosis (data from Cleveland) | 303 | 13 | 2 |
| heart-diseaseH | disease diagnosis (data from Hungary) | 294 | 13 | 2 |
| glass | predict glass type from chem. content | 194 | 7 | 9 |
| primary-tumour | predict tumour type | 330 | 17 | 15 |
| voting-records | predict democrat/republican from votes | 435 | 16 | 2 |
| thyroid | disease diagnosis | 1960 | 29 | 3 |
| breast-cancer | predict if recurrence is likely | 286 | 9 | 2 |
| hepatitis | predict if survival likely | 157 | 19 | 2 |
| echocardio | predict if survival from heart problem likely | 131 | 7 | 2 |

† (Sources: Lymph, prim-tumour, breast-cancer from Ljubljana, 1985. Pole-&-cart from Turing Inst., 1990. Remainder from UCI, 1989. See end of paper for details of any data conversions made.)

## 2.5  Experimental Comparison

### 2.5.1  Experimental Method

Experiments were performed to measure the improvement in predictive accuracy using the Laplace heuristic. As demonstrated by previous authors (eg. [Buntine and Niblett, 1990]), tests on a single domain are not sufficient to draw reliable conclusions about the relative performance of algorithms. Thus experiments on twelve domains shown in Table 1 were conducted.

CN2 using entropy and Laplace were compared. Also, comparisons with Quinlan's C4.5 [Quinlan et al., 1987, Quinlan, 1987] were performed. Data was split into 67% for training and 33% for testing, and the results averaged over 20 runs. For CN2, a star size of 20 was used and significance testing was switched off. (The effect of significance testing is examined later). For C4.5 a single, pruned tree was generated for each run.

### 2.5.2  Results: Comparative Accuracies

Table 2 shows the average accuracies obtained over the above domains. To make an overall comparison between the algorithms, a paired, two-tailed t-test was used, whose results are also shown in this table. From this t-test, it can be seen that using the Laplacian heuristic significantly (>99% significant, from the 2-tail prob.) improves CN2's accuracy, with an average improvement of 6.4%. The comparison between CN2 (Laplace) and C4.5 did not reveal any significant difference in accuracy. Additionally, the average size of the rule lists induced by CN2 (Laplace) was smaller than for CN2 (Entropy). The sizes are tabulated in Appendix 1.

Table 2: Percentage Accuracies of Algorithms

The table shows percentage accuracies ($\sigma$ denotes their standard deviations). The graph schematically re-presents the data as follows: Each line corresponds to a different domain, and connects the observed accuracy using one algorithm with another. Thus an upward slope reflects an improvement in accuracy, and a downward slope a worsening. The average improvement of CN2 (Laplace), and the significance of this improvement, is summarised in the second table.

| Domain | Algorithm | | | | |
|---|---|---|---|---|---|
| | CN2 | | C4.5 | Default | |
| | (Entropy) | (Laplace) | | | |
| lymphography | 71.5 $\sigma$6.3 | 79.6 $\sigma$5.7 | 76.4 $\sigma$6.2 | 54.2 $\sigma$6.7 | |
| pole-and-cart | 52.5 $\sigma$1.9 | 70.6 $\sigma$3.1 | 74.3 $\sigma$2.0 | 48.8 $\sigma$1.0 | |
| soybean | 74.7 $\sigma$6.7 | 82.7 $\sigma$3.9 | 80.0 $\sigma$3.6 | 10.3 $\sigma$1.5 | |
| heart-diseaseC | 66.3 $\sigma$8.5 | 75.4 $\sigma$3.6 | 76.4 $\sigma$4.5 | 53.1 $\sigma$3.8 | |
| heart-diseaseH | 73.0 $\sigma$4.6 | 75.0 $\sigma$3.8 | 78.0 $\sigma$5.5 | 64.9 $\sigma$3.5 | |
| glass | 45.2 $\sigma$8.1 | 58.5 $\sigma$5.0 | 64.2 $\sigma$5.1 | 34.0 $\sigma$4.4 | |
| primary-tumour | 35.6 $\sigma$5.2 | 49.7 $\sigma$9.8 | 39.0 $\sigma$4.0 | 24.5 $\sigma$2.8 | |
| voting-records | 93.6 $\sigma$1.8 | 94.8 $\sigma$1.7 | 95.6 $\sigma$1.1 | 61.6 $\sigma$2.9 | |
| thyroid | 95.6 $\sigma$0.7 | 96.3 $\sigma$0.7 | 96.4 $\sigma$0.9 | 95.4 $\sigma$0.8 | |
| breast-cancer | 69.0 $\sigma$3.6 | 65.1 $\sigma$5.3 | 72.1 $\sigma$3.7 | 71.3 $\sigma$2.3 | |
| hepatitis | 71.3 $\sigma$5.2 | 77.6 $\sigma$5.9 | 79.3 $\sigma$5.8 | 78.0 $\sigma$4.6 | |
| echocardio | 63.9 $\sigma$5.4 | 62.3 $\sigma$5.1 | 63.6 $\sigma$5.3 | 64.4 $\sigma$4.9 | |

Comparison of mean accuracies using paired, two-tailed t-test on the above data:

| Algorithms Compared: | Mean Improvement (Mean X - Y) | Significance of improvement |
|---|---|---|
| CN2 (Laplace) - CN2 (Entropy) | 6.4% | 99.3% |
| CN2 (Laplace) - C4.5 | -0.5% | 30.0% |

## 2.5.3 Results: Effect of Pruning

In the original CN2 (ie. using entropy), using a significance test caused the algorithm to select a smaller number of more general rules (possibly with counter-examples against them) in preference to a large number of highly specific rules. The Laplace heuristic, however, is sufficient on its own to bias the search towards those general rules with higher predictive accuracy, tending to find rules of highest predictive accuracy (and thus also high significance) first. It would thus be expected that removing less significant rules using a significance test would have a different effect, namely that CN2 would still select the same rules early on during the search but would terminate earlier. This was indeed observed (see Appendix 1) with the same early rules tending to appear in the rule list but with the number of rules decreasing and the overall accuracy also slightly decreasing.

# 3 Generating Unordered Rules

## 3.1 The Disadvantage of Ordered Rules

The original CN2 algorithm generates rules assembled in a particular order, described as a rule list by Rivest [Rivest, 1987]. During classification of a new example, each rule is tried in order until one fires. The algorithm then exits, assigning the class which that rule predicted to the example.

Rule lists have the nice property of being 'logical', in the sense that clashes between rules cannot occur as only one rule can ever fire. Thus there is no need to include probabilistic machinery for resolving clashes between rules.

However, there is also a corresponding problem in understanding the rules, in that the meaning of any single rule is dependent on all the other rules which precede it in the rule list. Consider, for example, a rule list:

```
        If      feathers = yes      then    class = bird
else    if      legs = two          then    class = human
else    ...
```

The rule "if legs=two then class=human", when considered alone, is not correct as birds also have two legs. Thus to understand the rule, all the previous rules in the list must also be taken into consideration. This problem becomes acute with a large number of rules, making it difficult for an expert to understand the true meaning of a rule far down in the list. As induced rules must generally be validated by experts before their use in applications, this is a significant disadvantage.

## 3.2 Generating Unordered Rules Using CN2

### 3.2.1 The CN2 (unordered) Algorithm

CN2 consists of a search procedure and a control procedure. Fortunately CN2 can be easily modified to generate an *unordered* rule set by changing only the control procedure, leaving the beam search procedure unchanged (apart from the evaluation function, described below). The original control procedure for ordered rules is shown in Figure 1, and the control procedure for unordered rules is shown in Figure 2. (The search procedure is shown in Appendix 1).

The main modification to the algorithm is to iterate the search for each class in turn, removing only covered examples *of that class* when a rule has been found. Unlike for ordered rules, the negative examples remain because now each rule must independently stand against all negatives. The covered positives must be removed to stop CN2 repeatedly finding the same rule.

To effect this rule search for each class in turn, the Laplace heuristic (Equation 1) must be applied differently: with ordered rules the predicted class $c$ is taken simply as the one with the most covered examples in it, but with unordered rules the predicted class is fixed to be the class selected by the revised control procedure.

Figure 1: The CN2 Ordered Rules Algorithm

```
procedure CN2ordered(examples, classes):
let rulelist = []
repeat
    call FindBestCondition(examples) to find bestcond
    if    bestcond is not null
    then let class be the most common class of exs. covered by bestcond
        & add rule 'if bestcond then predict class' to end of rulelist
        & remove from examples all examples covered by bestcond
until bestcond is null
return rulelist
```

Figure 2: The CN2 Unordered Rules Algorithm

```
procedure CN2unordered(allexamples, classes):
let ruleset = {}
for each class in classes:
    generate rules by CN2ForOneClass(allexamples,class)
    add rules to ruleset
return ruleset.

procedure CN2ForOneClass(examples,class):
let rules = {}
repeat
    call FindBestCondition(examples, class) to find bestcond
    if    bestcond is not null
    then add the rule 'if bestcond then predict class' to rules
        & remove from examples all exs in class covered by bestcond
until bestcond is null
return rules
```

## 3.3   Applying Unordered Rules

With an unordered rule list, all rules are tried and those which fired collected. If a clash occurs (ie. more than one class predicted), some probabilistic method is needed to resolve clashes. The method used here is to tag each rule with the distribution of covered examples among classes, and then to sum these distributions to find the most probable class should a clash occur. For example, consider the three rules:

```
if   legs=two and feathers=yes  then class=bird,     covers [13,0].
if   size=large and flies=no    then class=elephant, covers [2,10].
if   beak=yes                   then class=bird,     covers [20,0].
```

Here the two classes are [bird, elephant], [13, 0] denoting that the rule covers 13 (training) examples of bird and 0 of elephant. Given a new example of a large, beaked, two-legged,

Table 3: Percentage Accuracies of Algorithms

(See Table 2 for explanation of graph and tables)

| Domain | Algorithm | | | | |
|---|---|---|---|---|---|
| | CN2 (Laplace) | | C4.5 | Default | |
| | unordered | ordered | | | |
| lymphography | 81.7 $\sigma$4.3 | 79.6 $\sigma$5.7 | 76.4 $\sigma$6.2 | 54.2 $\sigma$6.7 | |
| pole-and-cart | 72.0 $\sigma$2.9 | 70.6 $\sigma$3.1 | 74.3 $\sigma$2.0 | 48.8 $\sigma$1.0 | |
| soybean | 81.6 $\sigma$3.8 | 82.7 $\sigma$3.9 | 80.0 $\sigma$3.6 | 10.3 $\sigma$1.5 | |
| heart-diseaseC | 76.7 $\sigma$3.9 | 75.4 $\sigma$3.6 | 76.4 $\sigma$4.5 | 53.1 $\sigma$3.8 | |
| heart-diseaseH | 78.8 $\sigma$4.1 | 75.0 $\sigma$3.8 | 78.0 $\sigma$5.5 | 64.9 $\sigma$3.5 | |
| glass | 65.5 $\sigma$5.6 | 58.5 $\sigma$5.0 | 64.2 $\sigma$5.1 | 34.0 $\sigma$4.4 | |
| primary-tumour | 45.8 $\sigma$3.6 | 49.7 $\sigma$9.8 | 39.0 $\sigma$4.0 | 24.5 $\sigma$2.8 | |
| voting-records | 94.8 $\sigma$1.8 | 94.8 $\sigma$1.7 | 95.6 $\sigma$1.1 | 61.6 $\sigma$2.9 | |
| thyroid | 96.6 $\sigma$0.9 | 96.3 $\sigma$0.7 | 96.4 $\sigma$0.9 | 95.4 $\sigma$0.8 | |
| breast-cancer | 73.0 $\sigma$4.5 | 65.1 $\sigma$5.3 | 72.1 $\sigma$3.7 | 71.3 $\sigma$2.3 | |
| hepatitis | 80.1 $\sigma$5.7 | 77.6 $\sigma$5.9 | 79.3 $\sigma$5.8 | 78.0 $\sigma$4.6 | |
| echocardio | 66.6 $\sigma$7.3 | 62.3 $\sigma$5.1 | 63.6 $\sigma$5.3 | 64.4 $\sigma$4.9 | |

Comparison of mean accuracies using paired, two-tailed t-test on the above data:

| Algorithms Compared: | Mean Improvement (Mean X - Y) | Significance of improvement |
|---|---|---|
| CN2 (unordered) - CN2 (ordered) | 2.0% | 95.0% |
| CN2 (unordered) - C4.5 | 1.5% | 94.0% |

feathered, non-flying thing, all three rules fire. The clash is resolved by summing the covered examples (sum is [35, 10]) and then predicting the most common class in the sum (bird).

## 3.4 Comparative Performance

### 3.4.1 Experimental Method

The same experimental method as performed for the earlier experiments on ordered rules (Section 2.5.1) was followed in order to compare the performances of ordered and unordered rule sets. Additionally, a comparison with C4.5 was again made.

### 3.4.2 Results: Comparative Accuracies

The results are shown in Table 3. Surprisingly, the CN2 (unordered) algorithm had an even higher accuracy than that of CN2 (ordered), with a small (2%) but significant (at the 95% level) higher average accuracy. The comparison also showed a slight (1.5%) but again significant (at the 94% level) improvement over C4.5.

One possible explanation for this high performance is that, with unordered rules, several rules may contribute to the classification of one example thus reducing effects of noise and an occasional poorly performing rule. Spreading of the classification decision over several rules has been termed using 'multiple knowledge' [Gams et al., 1991] and algorithms specifically designed to generate 'extra' rules have been designed elsewhere (eg. [Gams, 1989, Cestnik and Bratko, 1988]). Cestnik and Bratko report this technique resulted in significantly improved accuracies, and it seems likely a similar phenomenon is occurring here. The possible presence of extra classificational information in the unordered rules, compared with the ordered rules and C4.5's trees, is supported by examination of the rule set sizes. Unordered rule sets were about twice the size of ordered rule lists, and about four times the size of C4.5 trees, as tabulated in Appendix 1. Pruning the unordered rule sets by significance testing using a significance threshold of 99.5% reduced them to a size similar to C4.5's trees, but also slightly reduced the accuracy to one no longer significantly different from that of C4.5.

### 3.4.3   Effect of Pruning

As for ordered rules, applying a significance test reduced the number of rules found by the algorithm while also slightly reducing the predictive accuracy (see Appendix 1).

### 3.4.4   Worse-than-Default Domains

An interesting finding, worthy of brief comment, was that CN2 (ordered), in the breast-cancer and echocardio domains, induced rules performing significantly (ie. outside the bounds of one standard error) worse than the default rule (confirmed by repeating the experiments over 250 runs). The simple explanation for this is that, in these cases, CN2 was still slightly overfitting the rules to the data. To understand how induced rules can actually do worse than the default rule, consider the worst case of overfitting where a ruleset/decision tree is grown so every rule/leaf covers only one training example. Given 70% of examples are in class c1 and 30% in class c2, and the classes are completely independent of the attributes (ie. 100% noise), the overfitted rules/tree will be correct with probability 0.7 for rules predicting c1 and 0.3 for c2. With 70% of the examples in c1 and 30% c2, the overall probability correct will thus be $0.7 \times 0.7 + 0.3 \times 0.3 = 0.58$, worse than the default accuracy of 0.7. The overfitting observed in our experiments reflects behaviour between these two extremes, and suggests the pruning of ordered rules could still be slightly improved.

# 4   Conclusion

In this paper we have described two important extensions to the CN2 algorithm. Most importantly, we has shown how the algorithm can be extended to generate unordered as well as ordered rules, thus contributing to the comprehensibility of the induced rule set. Secondly, we have described a different evaluation function for CN2, and experimentally demonstrated a significantly improved performance resulting from this change. These two extensions thus contribute to CN2's utility as a tool for inductively building knowledge-based systems.

## Acknowledgements

This work was funded under the Esprit MLT project, Number 2154. Thanks to Ivan Bratko, Tim Niblett, Matjaž Gams and Donald Michie for their valuable comments on the paper, and to Tim Niblett for his assistance in analysing the experimental data. We are grateful to G. Klanjšček, M. Soklič and M. Zwitter of the University Medical Center, Ljubljana for the use of the lymphography, breast-cancer and primary-tumour data sets and to I. Kononenko for their conversion to a form suitable for the induction algorithms. We are also grateful to David Aha (UCI) for the compilation and use of the UCI Repository of Machine Learning Databases.

## Availability of CN2

As part of Esprit MLT project 2154, CN2 has been implemented in C and runs on Sun workstations. To request copies of the algorithm, please contact Robin Boswell at robin@turing.ac.uk.

## References

Buntine, W. and Niblett, T. A further comparison of splitting rules for decision-tree induction. (Submitted to the Machine Learning Journal), 1990.

Cestnik, B. Estimating probabilities: A crucial task in machine learning. In *ECAI-90*, 1990.

Cestnik, B. and Bratko, I. Learning redundant rules in noisy domains. In Kodratoff, Y., editor, *ECAI-88*, pages 348–350, London, Pitman, 1988.

Cestnik, B. and Bratko, I. On estimating probabilities in tree pruning. In Kodratoff, Y., editor, *Proc. EWSL-91*, 1991.

Clark, P. and Niblett, T. Induction in noisy domains. In Bratko, I. and Lavrač, N., editors, *Progress in Machine Learning (proceedings of the 2nd European Working Session on Learning)*, Sigma, Wilmslow, UK, 1987.

Clark, P. and Niblett, T. The CN2 induction algorithm. *Machine Learning Journal*, 3(4):261–283, 1989.

Gams, M. New measurements highlight the importance of redundant knowledge. In Morik, K., editor, *EWSL-89*, pages 71–79, London, Pitman, 1989.

Gams, M., Bohanec, M., and Cestnik, B. A schema for using multiple knowledge. (submitted to IJCAI-91), 1991.

Hayes-Michie, J. E., editor *Pragmatica: Bulletin of the Inductive Programming Special Interest Group*, volume 1. Turing Institute Press, Glasgow, UK, 1990.

Leech, W. J. A rule-based process control method with feedback. *Advances in Instrumentation*, 41:169–175, 1986.

Michalski, R., Mozetic, I., Hong, J., and Lavrac, N. The multi-purpose incremental learning system AQ15 and its testing application to three medical domains. In *AAAI-86*, volume 2, pages 1041–1045, Ca. Kaufmann, 1986.

Niblett, T. Constructing decision trees in noisy domains. In Bratko, I. and Lavrač, N., editors, *Progress in Machine Learning (proceedings of the 2nd European Working Session on Learning)*, pages 67–78. Sigma, Wilmslow, UK, 1987.

Quinlan, J. R. Simplifying decision trees. *Int. Journal of Man-Machine Studies*, 27(3):221–234, 1987.

Quinlan, J. R., Compton, P. J., Horn, K. A., and Lazarus, L. Inductive knowledge acquisition: a case study. In *Applications of Expert Systems*, pages 157–173, Addison-Wesley, Wokingham, UK, 1987.

Rivest, R. L. Learning decision lists. *Machine Learning*, 2(3):229–246, 1987.

Slocombe, S., Moore, K., and Zelouf, M. Engineering expert system applications. In *Annual Conference of the BCS Specialist Group on Expert Systems*, 1986.

## Data Conversion Notes

Key: cl=classes, ex=examples, att=attributes. lymph: orig data 9cl/150ex reduced to 4cl/148ex by removing 3cl (populations 1,1,0) & merging 2 × 2cl (forms 'X' and 'maybe X'). p-tumour: orig data 22cl/339ex reduced to 15cl/330ex by removing 6cl (popns. 0,1,2,1,2,2,1). b-cancer: 8ex replaced illegal att val with 'unknown'. soybean: UCI file soybean-large.data. h-disease{C,H}: orig 5cl reduced to 2cl (0=absence, 1-4=presence). glass: remove att1 (ex no.). thyroid: 1960ex randomly drawn from UCI file allbp.data. echocardio: Predict for att 2 ('alive'/'dead'), delete atts 1 & 13 (alternative class vals), 10-12 (meaningless), delete 1ex with unknown cl val. Others: conversion straightforward.

# Appendix 1: Effect of Pruning on CN2

(See Table 2 for explanation of tables)

## Accuracy:

| Domain ↓ <br> Sig. Threshold → | CN2 (Entropy) <br> (Ordered rules) | | CN2 (Laplace) | | | | C4.5 |
|---|---|---|---|---|---|---|---|
| | 0% | 99.5% | Ordered Rules | | Unordered Rules | | |
| | | | 0% | 99.5% | 0% | 99.5% | |
| lymphography | 71.5 $\sigma$6.3 | 68.4 $\sigma$8.6 | 79.6 $\sigma$5.7 | 74.4 $\sigma$5.9 | 81.7 $\sigma$4.3 | 76.5 $\sigma$5.3 | 76.4 $\sigma$6.2 |
| pole-and-cart | 52.5 $\sigma$1.9 | 52.2 $\sigma$1.7 | 70.6 $\sigma$3.1 | 67.9 $\sigma$3.3 | 72.0 $\sigma$2.9 | 63.0 $\sigma$3.2 | 74.3 $\sigma$2.0 |
| soybean | 74.7 $\sigma$6.7 | 54.2 $\sigma$6.5 | 82.7 $\sigma$3.9 | 57.5 $\sigma$4.6 | 81.6 $\sigma$3.8 | 76.1 $\sigma$4.4 | 80.0 $\sigma$3.6 |
| heart-diseaseC | 66.3 $\sigma$8.5 | 67.1 $\sigma$9.2 | 75.4 $\sigma$3.6 | 76.1 $\sigma$4.4 | 76.7 $\sigma$3.9 | 76.6 $\sigma$3.7 | 76.4 $\sigma$4.5 |
| heart-diseaseH | 73.0 $\sigma$4.6 | 81.6 $\sigma$3.4 | 75.0 $\sigma$3.8 | 74.9 $\sigma$4.7 | 78.8 $\sigma$4.1 | 77.8 $\sigma$3.9 | 78.0 $\sigma$5.5 |
| glass | 45.2 $\sigma$8.1 | 44.4 $\sigma$7.7 | 58.5 $\sigma$5.0 | 56.9 $\sigma$7.7 | 65.5 $\sigma$5.6 | 61.6 $\sigma$8.3 | 64.2 $\sigma$5.1 |
| primary-tumour | 35.6 $\sigma$5.2 | 33.0 $\sigma$3.5 | 49.7 $\sigma$9.8 | 38.7 $\sigma$5.3 | 45.8 $\sigma$3.6 | 41.4 $\sigma$5.8 | 39.0 $\sigma$4.0 |
| voting-records | 93.6 $\sigma$1.8 | 94.0 $\sigma$1.8 | 94.8 $\sigma$1.7 | 92.8 $\sigma$1.8 | 94.8 $\sigma$1.8 | 93.3 $\sigma$2.1 | 95.6 $\sigma$1.1 |
| thyroid | 95.6 $\sigma$0.7 | 95.6 $\sigma$0.9 | 96.3 $\sigma$0.7 | 96.3 $\sigma$0.5 | 96.6 $\sigma$0.9 | 96.1 $\sigma$1.2 | 96.4 $\sigma$0.9 |
| breast-cancer | 69.0 $\sigma$3.6 | 68.7 $\sigma$4.3 | 65.1 $\sigma$5.3 | 64.2 $\sigma$7.6 | 73.0 $\sigma$4.5 | 70.8 $\sigma$3.5 | 72.1 $\sigma$3.7 |
| hepatitis | 71.3 $\sigma$5.2 | 77.5 $\sigma$5.6 | 77.6 $\sigma$5.9 | 78.1 $\sigma$5.9 | 80.1 $\sigma$5.7 | 80.8 $\sigma$4.5 | 79.3 $\sigma$5.8 |
| echocardio | 63.9 $\sigma$5.4 | 67.5 $\sigma$5.6 | 62.3 $\sigma$5.1 | 63.2 $\sigma$7.7 | 66.6 $\sigma$7.3 | 69.4 $\sigma$6.8 | 63.6 $\sigma$5.3 |
| Average | 67.7 | 67.0 | 74.0 | 70.1 | 76.1 | 73.6 | 74.6 |

## Rule list/rule set/decision tree size:

(Number of nodes inc. leaves in tree, or total number of att. tests in rule list/set)

| Domain ↓ <br> Sig. Thr. → | CN2 (Entropy) <br> (Ordered rules) | | CN2 (Laplace) | | | | C4.5 |
|---|---|---|---|---|---|---|---|
| | 0% | 99.5% | Ordered Rules | | Unordered Rules | | |
| | | | 0% | 99.5% | 0% | 99.5% | |
| lymph | 24.6 $\sigma$4.4 | 5.1 $\sigma$1.1 | 21.1 $\sigma$3.8 | 8.2 $\sigma$2.4 | 40.4 $\sigma$4.6 | 13.5 $\sigma$2.3 | 16.4 $\sigma$6.3 |
| pole-&-cart | 16.8 $\sigma$6.8 | 3.5 $\sigma$2.8 | 133.6 $\sigma$6.3 | 80.3 $\sigma$15.3 | 255.8 $\sigma$8.3 | 46.5 $\sigma$8.2 | 90.2 $\sigma$10.2 |
| soybean | 213.2 $\sigma$38.8 | 21.6 $\sigma$1.7 | 55.8 $\sigma$7.4 | 31.3 $\sigma$2.7 | 113.9 $\sigma$9.7 | 83.5 $\sigma$6.3 | 65.9 $\sigma$8.4 |
| heart-disC | 60.0 $\sigma$10.3 | 9.1 $\sigma$2.7 | 35.1 $\sigma$2.5 | 28.4 $\sigma$3.2 | 68.6 $\sigma$5.4 | 22.8 $\sigma$4.1 | 22.7 $\sigma$4.6 |
| heart-disH | 37.0 $\sigma$7.7 | 6.1 $\sigma$2.6 | 40.9 $\sigma$4.0 | 26.1 $\sigma$5.4 | 83.4 $\sigma$7.5 | 20.7 $\sigma$4.5 | 7.2 $\sigma$3.7 |
| glass | 79.0 $\sigma$9.4 | 4.7 $\sigma$2.3 | 32.8 $\sigma$3.0 | 17.2 $\sigma$3.0 | 49.8 $\sigma$3.6 | 30.8 $\sigma$3.5 | 30.9 $\sigma$5.8 |
| p-tumour | 313.9 $\sigma$24.7 | 5.4 $\sigma$2.1 | 85.2 $\sigma$9.6 | 23.0 $\sigma$5.2 | 351.0 $\sigma$23.4 | 131.4 $\sigma$9.3 | 55.9 $\sigma$13.1 |
| voting | 11.8 $\sigma$3.4 | 8.1 $\sigma$2.0 | 41.6 $\sigma$8.2 | 15.8 $\sigma$5.2 | 64.8 $\sigma$12.1 | 19.9 $\sigma$3.1 | 7.7 $\sigma$3.4 |
| thyroid | 1.3 $\sigma$0.8 | 1.1 $\sigma$0.5 | 48.4 $\sigma$5.8 | 37.2 $\sigma$7.1 | 95.6 $\sigma$9.9 | 30.6 $\sigma$4.5 | 15.5 $\sigma$7.4 |
| b-cancer | 27.9 $\sigma$6.0 | 3.8 $\sigma$1.5 | 53.7 $\sigma$5.4 | 25.8 $\sigma$7.4 | 100.5 $\sigma$6.7 | 18.0 $\sigma$5.6 | 13.0 $\sigma$7.0 |
| hepatitis | 18.2 $\sigma$4.9 | 2.2 $\sigma$1.2 | 24.0 $\sigma$5.5 | 12.6 $\sigma$3.0 | 43.4 $\sigma$6.7 | 12.6 $\sigma$2.3 | 6.4 $\sigma$2.6 |
| echocardio | 16.5 $\sigma$5.0 | 1.9 $\sigma$0.9 | 26.4 $\sigma$4.0 | 13.3 $\sigma$4.4 | 48.6 $\sigma$3.6 | 13.1 $\sigma$2.1 | 9.2 $\sigma$4.7 |
| Average | 68.4 | 6.1 | 49.9 | 26.6 | 109.7 | 37.0 | 28.4 |

# Appendix 2: The CN2 Rule Search Algorithm

---

**procedure** FindBestCondition(examples[,class][a]):

let mgc = the most general condition ('true')

let star initially contain only the mgc (ie. = { mgc })

let newstar = {}

let bestcond = null

**while** star is not empty

    **for** each condition cond in star:

        **for** each possible attribute test not already tested on in cond

            **let** cond' = a specialisation of cond, formed by adding test

                as an extra conjunct to cond (ie. cond' = 'cond & test')

            **if**     cond' is better than bestcond

              && cond' is statistically significant

            **then let** bestcond = cond'.

            add cond' to newstar

            **if**     size of newstar > maxstar (a user-defined constant)

            **then** remove the worst condition in newstar.

    **let** star = newstar

**return** bestcond

---

[a]class is only required for generating unordered rules

# ON CHANGING CONTINUOUS ATTRIBUTES INTO ORDERED DISCRETE ATTRIBUTES

J. CATLETT

Basser Department of Computer Science, University of Sydney, N.S.W. 2006, Australia
Email: jason@cs.su.oz.au

**Abstract**

The large real-world datasets now commonly tackled by machine learning algorithms are often described in terms of attributes whose values are real numbers on some continuous interval, rather than being taken from a small number of discrete values. Many algorithms are able to handle continuous attributes, but learning requires far more CPU time than for a corresponding task with discrete attributes. This paper describes how continuous attributes can be converted economically into ordered discrete attributes before being given to the learning system. Experimental results from a wide variety of domains suggest this change of representation does not often result in a significant loss of accuracy (in fact it sometimes significantly improves accuracy), but offers large reductions in learning time, typically more than a factor of 10 in domains with a large number of continuous attributes.

**Keywords**    Discretisation, empirical concept learning, induction of decision trees

## 1. Introduction

As Subramanian (1989) concisely stated, "Present day learners depend on careful vocabulary engineering for their success." Many authors since Amarel (1968) have demonstrated the critical importance of the framework used to represent a given learning task, and the benefits to be gained from an appropriate change of representation. Recent work such as Rendell (1989) has advanced the state of the art of constructive induction, where the attributes given to a selective induction system such as ID3 (Quinlan 1979, 1983) are transformed into better attributes. Usually "better" is taken to mean "higher level", allowing the target concept to be expressed more concisely, making the product of the learning more accurate. The transformations often involve investigation of many complex combinations of the raw attributes, and can be computationally expensive, but this work may be rewarded by error rates lower than could be obtained from induction directly on the raw attributes.

This paper too addresses the question of changing the representation of tasks given to an inductive learning system, but with the aim of lowering the computational cost of the learning rather than improving the accuracy of the product. The ideal representation would be one that allows the learner both to express the final concept most accurately (or concisely, or comprehensibly), and to compute that concept in the least time possible, but these two goals are in conflict. Thus the client for whom the learning is performed faces a trade-off between speed and accuracy. Changing the representation complicates this decision, because any change entails a computational cost.

The situations in which the client would want to reduce the cost of learning are becoming increasingly common as machine learning becomes a commercial technology. The main spur comes from problems of scale: training set of hundreds of thousands of instances are now being attacked (e.g. Sejnowski 1987), making learning time a limiting factor. As commercial knowledge acquisition tools that interface learning systems to corporate databases become popular, the management of the extraction and transformation of learning data will become a difficult logistic task, much of it needing to be transformed from numeric to symbolic form. Finally, in the past three years a class of applications that use incremental learning has come under the spotlight (for example, Utgoff 1988). Where this is done in real time with new examples becoming available during the induction, it may be advantageous to finish the induction earlier.

Various researchers have attacked the question of how to speed up the learning task. Selective induction algorithms such as ID3 that partition the instance space are generally very efficient and difficult to improve. Quinlan's first descriptions of ID3 (1979) included a method called windowing to speed up ID3 on large training sets, but Wirth & Catlett (1988) showed that on noisy data it usually costs rather than saves CPU time. Breiman, Friedman, Olshen & Stone (1984, pp 163-7) proposed a method of choosing the attribute to partition the space based on a random subset of the available instances, but this still retains much of the cost of dealing with continuous attributes.

The algorithm we describe for discretising a dataset could be used as before a variety of learning algorithms; here we use ID3, to provide a familiar basis for comparison. However, the rationale for some of the design decisions in the algorithm is based on the assumption that the learning system partitions the training set, and may not be appropriate for learners that build around a seed example, such as AQ15 (Michalski,

Mozetic, Hong, & Lavrac 1986).

ID3 is reviewed briefly in Section 2, with emphasis on continuous attributes. Other work related to continuous attributes is reviewed in Section 3. Section 4 introduces the algorithm for discretising continuous attributes. Section 5 describes domains used in experiments to evaluate this algorithm, and gives their results. We conclude with a statement of the areas to be explored further.

## 2. ID3

ID3 (Quinlan, 1979, 1983) is an inductive learning program that constructs classification rules in the form of decision trees. It is perhaps the most commonly found ML algorithm in both the scientific literature and in commercial systems; for illustrations of real-world applications see (Michie, 1987) or (Carter & Catlett, 1987). For a comprehensive introduction to the induction of decision trees see (Quinlan 1986). The following oversimplified summary aims merely to establish terminology and to emphasise some detail concerning continuous attributes.

The input to ID3 is a set of objects called the *training set*. The objects are described in terms of a fixed set of *attributes*, each attribute taking its value from a given set, and each object is assigned to one of a small fixed set of classes. The output is a decision tree that can be used to classify any object from that attribute space. Typically the tree has a low error rate on the training set, but is less accurate on unseen examples.

We can distinguish *continuous* attributes, whose values are real numbers on some interval, from *discrete* attributes, restricted to some finite (usually small) number of values. Discrete attributes can be further divided into *ordered* attributes, such as cold, tepid, warm, hot, or *unordered* attributes, such as Africa, America, Australia, Europe. Continuous attributes were not described in Quinlan's original ID3 paper (1979, 1983), nor were ordered discrete attributes, which were first reported in ASSISTANT (Kononenko, Bratko & Roskar, 1984). These simple extensions are now widespread in implementations.

ID3 builds its trees by progressively partitioning the training set: it chooses an attribute to split the set on, and then recursively builds a tree for each subset, until all the members of the subsets are of the same class. For each subset it must decide which is the best attribute to split on, which it does using an formula that assesses the gain in information theoretic terms of all possible splits. ID3 is a greedy algorithm with no lookahead, so making a bad choice of an attribute fragments the training set and reduces accuracy.

In choosing a continuous attribute to split the set, a *threshold* or *cutpoint* must also be selected. (These two terms are synonyms.) Computationally, this entails sorting the set on each attribute in turn, for each subset produced as the training set divides. Each sort takes time $O(n\log n)$ where $n$ is the number of elements in the subset.

When all the attributes are discrete (whether ordered or not) no sorting is required, merely space proportional to the number of values (which is quite small) and time $O(n)$. Overall the algorithm takes time proportional to the product of the training set size, the number of attributes, and the size of the final tree. With continuous values the growth is superlinear, because sorting of the relevant subset of the training set must be done for every attribute at every node created during the building of the tree. With discretisation, sorting is done only once per attribute. As an illustration of the relative costs, Figure 1 shows for a single run the CPU time taken to build a tree from continuous versus discretised binary attributes (i.e. single threshold) for the waveform domain (described in the next section). The floating figures plot on a log scale the accuracy of the trees built from discretised data for various sized training sets. The corresponding accuracies for the original continuous data are not shown; they are approximately the same. The figures for CPU time are joined with a dashed line for the discretised version, and a solid line for the continuous version. The line marked linear is simply a straight line that approximates the early part of the continuous attributes curve, showing the latter to be superlinear.

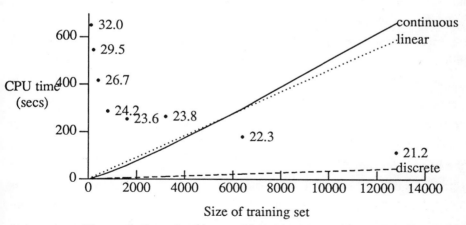

**Figure 1.** Learning time on discretised vs continuous attributes

This substantial difference in the CPU cost is the main motivation for changing continuous attributes into discrete ones. In the case of the wave domain illustrated above the learning time is reduced by a factor of about 14.

A further saving, in terms of space, comes from the fact that a floating point number typically takes four bytes to represent, while a discrete ordered attribute takes only one byte. (The implementation reported here reads in the data and converts it *in situ*, so space savings are not realised.) In very large domains (such the Heart domain, with 92 continuous attributes), memory requirements may be a limiting factor on the size of induction tasks that can be performed.

It may turn out that discretising attributes offers cognitive benefits as well as computations ones. In the thyroid domain, the discretising algorithm chose to a high degree of accuracy almost all the thresholds used by domain experts. Human experts may prefer to look at the set of thresholds chosen, and thereafter work from a tree labelled with symbolic values such as low, high, and very high, rather than using a tree with a large number of (sometimes very close) thresholds.

## 3. Relationship to other work on continuous attributes

The idea of discretising (or "quantizing") an attribute has appeared previously in the pattern recognition and statistics literature. (Wong & Chiu 1987) compare two techniques for discretising data. Their motivation for discretisation is not to reduce learning time, but to convert the real-valued data into a form suitable for their clustering algorithms. Their techniques do not require (or use) a distinguished class, as ID3 does. This would put them at a disadvantage in some applications, but makes them more widely applicable. Both techniques require the user to specify the number of intervals into which each attribute will be divided. Their first technique, called *equal width discretisation,* simply involves calculating the difference between the largest and smallest values for the attribute and placing the desired number of equal-width intervals between them. Their second technique, called *maximum marginal entropy discretisation,* requires sorting of the values, and basically allocates an equal number of examples to each interval. Where repeated values would cause that value to belong to more than one interval, the boundaries are adjusted so as to minimise an information theoretic measure on the discretised attribute. Note that this is not the same as ID3's measure because it is "class-blind"; it does not take into account the class of the examples, only the attribute values. For this reason we believe that such methods for discretisation may not be the best match for ID3; the results of experiments discussed at the end of Section 5 corroborate this.

Most of the commonly used additions to ID3, such as pruning and the treatment of unknown values (Quinlan 1989), are not affected by discretisation, but the implementation of one less common addition, *soft thresholds*, requires care. Its motivation comes from a distaste for the "knife-edge" threshold used by ID3, that can make a small change in an attribute's value cause a large change in the class or class probability estimate given by the tree. A more "fuzzy" threshold has obvious appeal. A little inspection shows that the methods devised to do this are not excluded by discretisation, although choices arise which are not evaluated in this paper. The idea of soft thresholds was first suggested by Catlett to Carter, and details of Carter's implementation were published in (Carter & Catlett, 1987). The basic idea is choose in addition to each threshold, a subsidiary threshold either side of it; examples falling between these two thresholds are considered sufficiently close to warrant "fuzzy" treatment from both of the subtrees below that attribute choice. The method of choosing the two subsidiary thresholds was subsequently improved by (Quinlan 1987). When using discretisation, we could calculate the subsidiary thresholds at the time of discretisation. The alternative is to determine them after the tree is built. This would entail re-traversing it, splitting the training set according to the attribute at each node, and calculating the subsidiary thresholds in the normal manner. The cost of doing this would still be small compared to building the whole tree from undiscretised data.

## 4. Algorithm for discretising continuous attributes

This section describes the algorithm that chooses the thresholds. Although it can be thought of logically as a preprocessor to ID3, the most economical implementation would include it as part of the learning program because the setup chores of getting the data in place are the same, and most of the necessary routines are already in ID3.

The algorithm given here decides on the thresholds for each attribute without reference to the others. A more advanced version might take into account a situation where, for example, even the best threshold on an attribute gives a gain that is so poor compared to other attributes that it might be deemed not worth spending more CPU time on. That question is related to the task of eliminating irrelevant attributes, and has appeared in the constructive induction literature.

The first threshold is computed in the same way as ID3 chooses its thresholds. Thus we are guaranteed that the attribute and cutpoint of the root of the tree built will be the same in both the continuous and discrete versions. After this we face a question: whether to go on and choose another threshold, and if so, how to choose it.

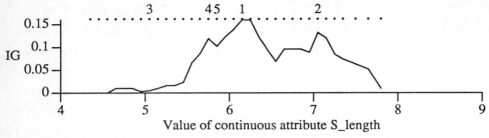

**Figure 2.** Initial information gain for Top cutpoints

Given that we are going to choose a second cutpoint, we must not make the obvious choice of the value with the second highest gain. Making this mistake typically results in a large number of cutpoints near the original one, offering very little additional discriminating power because the difference between them and the first cutpoint involves only a few examples. Instead we take the view that the situations where we will need the second cutpoint during the tree building occur where the set has already been split on the first cutpoint (or on some other attribute with a similar effect). Accordingly, we choose the subsequent cutpoints based on the subsets between the cutpoints already chosen. To illustrate this distinction, Figure 2 plots the information gain for all cutpoints on an attribute from the Iris domain. Each possible cutpoint is marked with a dot; the best five cutpoints are distinguished with a numeral above the dot denoting their rank. The third such cutpoint appears near-useless on the initial ranking, but after the population to the right of the best cutpoint is removed, it happens to become the best choice for the left subset.

Although the algorithms sounds like the same computation as goes on during the building of the tree, we are really avoiding the expensive $O(n \log n)$ operation of resorting the values. This is because we select all the thresholds for an attribute in one step, rather than jumping back and forth. We merely have to adjust the counts to the left and right of the last threshold to remove the influence of the examples on the other side of the threshold. The procedure can then be applied recursively. This method has the reassuring property that for a learning task with just one continuous attribute the discretised version would yield the same tree as the the discretised form, provided that a sufficient number of thresholds is used.

As with all recursive procedures, there must be a condition to determine when to stop, when we have enough thresholds in an interval. This decision is very like the decision of when to stop splitting the training set when growing a tree, so techniques from ID3 such as the chi-squared cutoff (Quinlan 83) or Fisher's test (Quinlan 87) could be used.

Another possibility is to look at the information gain offered by the split versus the number of examples, and to use some statistical test that determines a confidence level that the gain is not due to chance. Finally, the simplest method is to set some crude absolute cutoffs, which is what was used to produce the figures shown in this paper. (For future reference we will call this version D-2, for Discretiser 2). But even the extremely crude criterion of "stop after the first threshold" (i.e. the "discretised" version of every continuous attributes is always binary) was enough to produce trees of approximately the same accuracy in two domains, Hyper and Wave.

The stopping condition of D-2 comprises the following four broad sub-conditions. (Following the goal of reporting experiments in sufficient detail to allow them to be reproduced, we give the specific parameters used in D-2. We are not claiming that these are the best such values, merely that they are reasonable.)

1. If the number of examples represented in the interval is sufficiently small, we should stop, because estimates made based on very small samples may not be reliable. The smallest number we could divide is two; D-2's cutoff is currently 14.

2. Given that our motivation is to reduce CPU time, it seems reasonable to place some overall maximum on the number of thresholds produced for any attribute. If this is not imposed, some larger domains, such as Heart, produce hundreds of thresholds on what looks like reasonable data to split, and could consume more time finding thresholds that will never be used than is saved by the conversion to discrete attributes. D-2 limits the number of thresholds (or actually the number that are likely to be produced by the depth-first recursion) to seven.

3. D-2 stops if the gain on all possible thresholds is equal. (This happens quite often with the value 0, suggesting that further splitting may be ineffective.) This presumption is theoretically unsound (it would be easy to contrive a domain where this costs accuracy), but in practice it usually means that further splitting on the attribute would be unfruitful.

4. If all the examples in an interval belong to the same class, there is no need to split it, so no further thresholds need be established. This sub-condition logically implies the previous condition, but the converse does not hold.

When the number of classes is greater than two, one more complication is necessary to stop thresholds that split off less frequent classes from being swamped by thresholds that discriminate well between the most frequent classes. Experimentation with some of the thyroid domains, which contain some very unusual disorders, showed that this step was necessary. D-2 looks at an $n$ class decision as $n$ binary decisions by considering each class in turn is made the positive class with the others considered negative. At the end all the thresholds found are used. It would probably be possible to merge very close thresholds without loss of accuracy, but this was not tried; we doubt it would save very much time since an extra discrete value entails only a small amount of space and time.

## 5. Description of the domains and results of experiments

To test the effect of discretising on classification accuracy, we ran the following experiment on all the large domains with real valued attributes available to us. For each domain, we split the data randomly at least 20 times and, for each split, ran ID3 on the raw continuous data, then discretised the training and test data using thresholds calculated from the training data, and ran it on the discretised data. In both cases the trees were pruned on the training data using pessimistic pruning (Quinlan 1987). For each pair of data we recorded the original accuracy and the difference in accuracy due between the continuous and discrete data. The domains are described below.

1. Waveform: this was adapted from (Breiman et. al 1984). Although it is less popular than the discrete-valued faulty LED problem from the same book, it has been used in several comparison papers. Our implementation produces 42 real-valued attributes, half of them irrelevant but with the same distribution as the relevant ones. There are three classes, representing combinations of waveforms to which various kinds of noise is added to obtain the attributes.

2. Thyroid: this large and widely used dataset from the Garvan Institute in Sydney is described in (Quinlan, Compton, Horn & Lazarus 1988). It consists of case data and diagnoses for many disorders concerning thyroid hormones, of which the following were suitable for our experiments here (the number of classes is indicated in brackets): Hypo (5), Hyper (5), Binding Protein (3), Replacement (4) and Sick Euthyroid (2). The case data is described in terms of 29 attributes, of which six are real-valued: the patient's age and five assay readings. One unusual bonus offered by this domain is the knowledge of the actual thresholds used by specialists in interpreting the assays; almost all of them were found by D-2 (among many other thresholds).

3. Demon: this domain was deliberately contrived as the worst possible domain to give to this algorithm. Because the selection criterion looks at the relationship

between the mix of classes under its possible divisions, a division will appear useless if the subsets either side of a threshold have the same mix of classes. More formally, this occurs when the probability that an example's value for attribute $A$ is above a threshold $T$ is independent of its class:

$$P(A > T \mid C) = P(A > T)$$

Normally this is a good reason to ignore the attribute, but if we make its value effectively a "switch" on the thresholds relevant to other attributes, it becomes important to use it in combination with the other attributes. We chose three attributes A1 (the switch), A2, and A3, all with real values uniformly distributed on [0, 1], and the class being positive if the following expression hold true:

A1 < 0.5 & A2 < 0.8 & A3 > 0.2 or A1 > 0.5 & A2 > 0.2 & A3 < 0.8

Since there is no noise in this domain ID3 finds a highly accurate tree after a few hundred training instances.

The ML literature has seen switching in parity checkers and multiplexers on boolean attributes (Wilson 1987), and the example of the boolean function A1 > A2 is often trotted out as an illustration of the importance of the correct formulation of attributes to ID3, but we know of no real domain where this sort of switching occurs naturally on real-valued attributes, let alone on an attribute that is perfectly independent of the class. This domain is of course very contrived; the point was to devise a worst case monster to pit the algorithm against.

4.  Heart: this domain benefits most from discretising, because it consists of several thousand examples, each with 92 real-valued attributes, and takes about half an hour to produce a tree on a VAX-11/780. Discretising speeds up the induction by a factor of more than 50. The examples consist of measurements from heart patients over consecutive 30 second epochs, with the class indicating whether the heart was ischemic at that time. The application is described in (Oates, Cellar, Bernstein, Bailey & Freedman 1989).

5.  Othello: the generator for this data was provided by Paul Utgoff, and is described briefly in (Utgoff 1988) and in more detail in (Utgoff & Heitman 1988). The examples represents successive board positions in a game of Othello, and are described in terms of 14 integer-values attributes (with only 29 distinct values per attribute). The class indicates whether the position described by by the first seven attributes can be shown to be better than the position described by the last seven.

The object is to be learn preference predicates.

Because the examples within a game are strongly related, it is in some ways fairer to take the test set from a different game. The results reported below call the latter "Othello B", and the usual practice of splitting a single uniform sample randomly into test and training sets "Othello A".

Table 1 shows the the results of the comparison experiments. The column headed "Error rate mean" gives the percentage error on the test set by ID3 for continuous attributes. The training set is also used to compute thresholds for converting the attributes to ordered discrete versions, and the difference in error rate between the continuous and discrete versions is given in the next column. For example, the first line shows that on the Iris database, the error rate was the same in the two versions, and the second line shows that for the Demon domain the discrete version averaged error rate more than 10 percentage points higher than the continuous version. This mean figure and standard deviation relate to the mean of the differences, not the difference of the means. The column headed $N$ gives the number of trials. The column headed conclusion give the result of a two-sided t-test at the 5% level, with NSD denoting no significant difference (i.e. we accept the null hypothesis that the mean of the differences is zero, showing that there is no difference in error between the original continuous and the discretised version).

**TABLE 1.** Comparison experiments

| Domain | Training set size | Test set size | Error rate mean | Difference of errors mean | Difference of errors stddev | Number of trials | Concl. |
|---|---|---|---|---|---|---|---|
| Iris | 100 | 50 | 5.800 | 0.000 | 0.000 | 20 | NSD |
| Demon | 5000 | 3000 | 0.265 | -10.083 | 11.127 | 50 | worse |
| Wave | 300 | 200 | 29.231 | 0.712 | 3.470 | 26 | NSD |
| Wave | 3000 | 2000 | 24.881 | 0.922 | 1.262 | 29 | better |
| Heart | 3000 | 2039 | 2.555 | -0.061 | 0.494 | 20 | NSD |
| Oth. A | 3000 | 2022 | 15.574 | -5.349 | 0.943 | 20 | worse |
| Oth. B | 3000 | 6248 | 35.606 | 0.297 | 3.869 | 20 | NSD |
| Hypo | 5000 | 2438 | 0.744 | 0.051 | 0.095 | 20 | better |
| Hyper | 5000 | 2012 | 1.260 | 0.119 | 0.159 | 20 | better |
| Binding | 5000 | 2147 | 3.372 | 0.078 | 0.315 | 50 | NSD |
| Replace | 5000 | 2126 | 1.261 | -0.103 | 0.237 | 50 | worse |
| Euthy | 5000 | 2218 | 0.874 | -0.410 | 0.231 | 50 | worse |

The identical performance of the two methods in the case of Iris is not surprising; the pruned trees consist of only about seven nodes and the number of distinct values of the attributes is typically only about 30. The demon database delivered the expected result of turning a negligible error rate into a large one, with a very high standard deviation.

Several of the domains were slightly improved by discretisation; this may be due to the fact that the discretised trees are typically smaller. Although all the trees were pruned in some cases further pruning may result in higher accuracy. Another possible explanation, more likely in the case of the thyroid domain, is that the thresholds can be more accurately determined from the full sample.

The differences on the Othello test (B) were insignificant; but when the test set is taken from the same game, predetermining the thresholds costs accuracy. This may be because there are very similar examples within a single game, which can be accurately classified by trees trees that use more complexity (additional tests on already tested attributes) than would be justified by what is true of the game in general. Ironically this domain does not really require further discretisation, ordered discrete attributes can be used directly, giving a large speedup with no loss of accuracy.

The binding domain was just within the null hypothesis with a lower bound for the confidence interval of -0.01. At a confidence level of 10% we can conclude that the discretised version was better. Two of the domains, replace and euthyroid, were significantly worse at the 5% level under discretisation, and the remaining two, hypo and hyper, were significantly better.

Some comparisons of learning time (including time to discretise) showed that in domains with only a few continuous attributes, learning time was approximately half in the discretised version. In the other domains (Othello, Wave & Heart), the speedup was by factors of more than 10.

Some comparisons with class-blind methods of discretisation largely gave the conclusion that their performance is inferior to D2 in these applications. The two methods tested were equal width discretisation (described in Section 3), and a simplification of maximum marginal entropy discretisation, which could be called "roughly equal population" discretisation; it simply entails sorting the $n$ values (including repeats), and taking as the $j$ thresholds the values of every $j/n$th value. We examined the performance of these methods with number of intervals arbitrarily chosen at 2, 7, and 24. For the wave domain, this gave much smaller trees at least as accurate as ID3's. (This is consistent with evidence from other sources that the trees grown by ID3 for the Wave domain are overly large, and should be pruned further. Binary discretisation is an extreme way of achieving this.) In almost all other domains the error rate for the class-blind methods were grossly higher than for D2, with the exception of Othello, which can by explained by the following analysis. In the case of an attribute with only a few distinct values, $n$ say, once the number of intervals reaches $n$, the discretised error rate (at least for "roughly equal population" discretisation) will become the same as the undiscretised version. In the case of Othello, the value of 24 is very close to $n = 29$. Learning time will of course be lowered by treating the attribute as ordered discrete.

A quick comparison between the two class-blind discretisation methods showed a strong difference only in the heart domain, where equal width discretisation performed very poorly, which is consistent with Wong & Chiu's preference.

## 6. Conclusion

We have shown that discretising continuous attributes can be achieved simply, offering very large savings in CPU time in domains where they abound. This change does not often result in a significant loss of accuracy (in fact it sometimes significantly improves accuracy).

Some work remains to be done to tune the basic algorithm for best performance. Evaluation should be extended to extremely large training sets. Here the the initial thresholding could be performed on a subset to cut down the computational cost of the thresholding.

### Acknowledgments

Many people deserve thanks for providing data: Jeff Schlimmer for the Iris data, Ross Quinlan for the Thyroid data, John Oates and Ben Freedman of Royal Prince Alfred Hospital for the Heart data, and Paul Utgoff for the Othello data. Thanks are also due to Ross Quinlan for his advice and guidance. The anonymous referees of the European Working Session on Learning (EWSL-91) gave many very helpful comments and suggestions. This research was supported in part by a grant from the Australian Research Council.

### References

Amarel, S. (1968). On the representation of problems of reasoning about action, In D. Michie (Ed.), *Machine Intelligence 3,* Edinburgh University Press.

Breiman, L., Friedman, J. H., Olshen, R. A., Stone C. J. (1984). *Classification and regression trees.* Belmont, CA: Wadsworth International Group.

Carter, C., & Catlett, J. (1987). Assessing credit card applications using machine learning. *IEEE Expert, Fall 1987,* 71-79.

Kononenko, I., Bratko, I., & Roskar, E. (1984). Experiments in automatic learning of medical diagnostic rules, *Technical Report, Jozef Stefan Institute, Ljubljana.*

Michie, D. (1987). Current developments in expert systems. In J. R. Quinlan, (Ed.), *Applications of Expert Systems.* Maidenhead: Addison Wesley.

Michalski, R., Mozetic, T., Hong, J., Lavrac, N. (1986). The multi-purpose incremental learning system AQ15 and its testing application to three medical domains *Proceedings of AAAI-86,* Morgan Kaufmann.

Oates, J., Cellar, B., Bernstein, L., Bailey, B. P., Freedman, S. B. (1989). Real-time detection of ischemic ECG changes using quasi-orthogonal leads and artificial intelligence, *Proceedings, IEEE Computers in Cardiology Conference, 1989,* IEEE Computer Society.

Quinlan, J. R. (1979). Discovering rules by induction from large numbers of examples: a case study. In D. Michie (Ed.), *Expert systems in the micro-electronic age.* Edinburgh University Press.

Quinlan, J. R. (1983). Learning efficient classification procedures and their application to chess endgames (p. 469). In R. S. Michalski, J. R. Carbonell, T. M. Mitchell (Eds.), *Machine learning: an Artificial Intelligence approach* (pp. 463-82). Los Altos, CA: Morgan Kaufmann.

Quinlan, J. R. (1986). Induction of decision trees. *Machine Learning, 1,1.*

Quinlan, J. R., Compton, P.J., Horn, K.A. & Lazarus, L. (1988). Inductive knowledge acquisition: a case study In J. Quinlan (Ed.), *Applications of expert systems,* Maidenhead: Addison-Wesley

Quinlan, J. R. (1987). Simplifying decision trees. *International Journal of Man-machine Studies, 27* (pp. 221-234).

Quinlan, J. R. (1987b). Decision trees as probabilistic classifiers, *Proceedings of the fourth international conference on machine learning,* (pp. 31-37) Morgan Kaufmann.

Quinlan, J. R. (1989). Unknown attribute values in induction *Proceedings of the sixth international conference on machine learning,* (pp. 164-168) Morgan Kaufmann.

Rendell, L. (1989). Comparing systems and analysing functions to improve constructive induction *Proceedings of the sixth international conference on machine learning* (pp. 461-464) Morgan Kaufmann.

Sejnowski, T. J., & Rosenberg, C. R., (1987). Parallel networks that learn to pronounce English text *Complex Systems 1.* (pp. 426-429).

Subramanian, D. (1989). Representational issues in machine learning *Proceedings of the sixth international conference on machine learning* (pp. 426-429) Morgan Kaufmann

Utgoff, P. & Heitman, P.S. (1988). Learning and generalizing move selection preferences *Proceedings of the AAAI symposium on computer game playing* pp. 36-40 (original not seen).

Utgoff, P. (1989). ID5: an incremental ID3 *Proceedings of the fifth international conference on machine learning* (pp. 107-120) Morgan Kaufmann.

Wilson, S. W. (1987). Classifier systems and the animat problem *Machine Learning, 2,4*.

Wirth, J., & Catlett, J. (1988). Costs and benefits of windowing in ID3 *Proceedings of the fifth international conference on machine learning* (pp. 87-99) Morgan Kaufmann.

Wong, A.K.C., Chiu, D.K.Y., (1987). Synthesizing statistical knowledge from incomplete mixed-mode data, IEEE Trans. Pattern Analysis and Machine Intelligence, November 1987, Vol PAMI-9, No. 6, pp. 796-805.

# A Method for Inductive
# Cost Optimization

Floor Verdenius

RIKS, Postbus 463, 6200 AL Maastricht, The Netherlands[*]

**Abstract**

In this paper we present a Method for Inductive Cost Optimization (MICO), as an example of induction biased by using background knowledge. The method produces a decision tree that identifies those setpoints that enable the process to produce in as cost-efficient a manner as possible. We report on two examples, one idealised and one real-world. Some problems concerning MICO are reported.

**Keywords:** Machine Learning, Biased Inductive Learning, Cost Optimization, Decision Trees

## 1. Introduction

Inductive learning, deriving knowledge from a real-world dataset, has been the subject of much work in artificial intelligence. Top Down Induction of Decision Trees (TDIDT) is a well known class of induction algorithms. Algorithms in this class recursively partition a dataset, forming a tree that describes decision points; a typical example being ID3 (Quinlan 1986). ID3 generates decision trees for nominal valued data-records. The resulting tree gives a representation that can be used to classify new instances. One of the derivatives of ID3 is NPPA (Talmon, 1986) which generates binary decision trees for real-valued data. Both ID3 and NPPA use information gain as the criterion to find the best partition. In this paper we will use NPPA as our standard induction algorithm.

TDIDT techniques originally are developed as tools for automatic knowledge acquisition. They are also used as a tool for data-analysis in research and industry, for example Cosemans & Samyn (1990) used induction to identify the most significant parameters in several industrial production processes. They showed that induction can achieve good practical results, where statistical techniques are very time-consuming, and sometimes unable to identify all the determining parameters.

---

[*] Now at: SMR, Jacob van Lennepkade 334 m, 1053 NJ Amsterdam, The Netherlands

It has been reported (e.g. Shapiro, 1987; Nunez, 1988; Tan & Schlimmer, 1989; Bergadano et. al., 1990) that the applicability of induction is improved by using background knowledge. Particularly, it results in more realistic decision trees that provide appropriate answers to specific questions. In this paper we discuss one application of background knowledge in induction: optimization of production costs in industrial environments. The structure of this text is as follows: section 2 introduces the use of background knowledge as an instrument to improve induction and survey existing literature on this topic. In section 3 we introduce cost optimization as one example of the use of background knowledge in induction. In section 4 an application of this algorithm is discussed. We end with conclusions and plans for further research.

## 2. Context

Let us start with an example of a company, mass-producing some product in a batch production process. Two process parameters, the percentage P1 of some chemical element in a raw material and the temperature P2 in an oven are measured. Both these values can be controlled. At the end of the process the products are labeled relative to their quality. They are either saleable or unsaleable. The unsaleable product is considered to be waste, and has no economic value. The relation between the parameter-values and the labels is unknown.

Given this situation, different departments in this company typically require answers to different questions. For example:
(a) the research department: what are the the optimal setpoints for P1 and P2 from the point of view of quality control?
(b) the technical department: how can we diagnose a production failure as soon as possible, if we know the values of P1 and P2?
(c) the technical department again: and how can we diagnose a production failure as cheap as possible, including the costs of measuring P1 and P2?
(d) the production department: we have some heuristics about how P1 and P2 determine the quality label of our product. If we assume these heuristics to be correct, what additional knowledge can we derive from a dataset?
(e) the financial department: what setpoints for P1 and P2 should be used to produce with the lowest cost price and what is this cost price?

An important point to note is that in establishing this relationships no one analysis is sufficient for all requirements. Induction may answer the questions (a) and (b) (e.g. Cosemans & Samyn, 1990). It establishes relationships between input and output, e.g. between attributes and (quality) labels. By using background knowledge to bias induction, the questions (c) and (d) can be answered as showed by Nunez (1988) and Bergadano et. al. (1990) respectively. As we will show in this paper, by using background knowledge on production costs in induction, we can answer questions such as (e).

TDIDT programs search in the space of all possible decision trees that describe a given dataset. An algorithm chooses one specific tree out of this set. Utgoff (1986) shows that several factors influence the selection of the decision tree, e.g. the formalism or language in which hypothesis are described and the problem space considered. All influencing factors constitute the total bias of induction. These biasing factors can't be avoided, but they can be influenced. It is well known that information gain has a specific bias: it favours attributes with many different values above attributes with only a few different values. Criteria that are closely related to information gain, such as covariability (Cosemans & Samyn, 1990) or geometric distance (e.g. Spangler et. al., 1989) select trees that may be close to the one that is found using information gain. We must use the appropriate bias to be able to answer specific questions.

The decision trees that are constructed using information gain are very efficient, but they lack logical structure for experts (Arbab & Michie, 1985). Shapiro (1987) and Buntine & Stirling (1988) show how expert background knowledge can be used to bias the induction, producing trees that are easier to understand for humans. These methods, however, need the presence of an expert during the process of induction, and may be time consuming. Nunez (1988) automated the use of knowledge on diagnosis cost in the induction, and showed that by using this knowledge the constructed trees are easier to understand. We think, in accordance with the other authors mentioned, that the use of background knowledge in induction may enable us to answer the questions mentioned above and that it may produce trees with a structure that is close(r) to the way an expert reasons.

## 3. Cost Optimization

### 3.1 Why Cost Optimization

Several authors report the application of induction to data from industrial processes (e.g. Cosemans & Samyn, 1990; Bergadano et. al., 1990). Most examples are concerned with quality control. As we showed in section 2 however, not all questions that may be asked in industry can yet be answered by means of induction. We use induction to answer question (e) (the one that asks for the cheapest products). The reason for choosing to deal with this particular problem is threefold. Firstly, this question may be interesting for industry. Identifying the optimal setpoints from a cost price point of view enables industry to optimize profit. Second, background knowledge on cost optimization (in the way we use it) can be represented formally. Such a representation may not be available for some other types of background knowledge. Finally, it is a clear example of how the use of background knowledge may influence the partition criterion.

Our main goal was to develop an algorithm that was able to find a tuning of the process delivering cheap end products, by means of induction. This implied three changes in the process of induction. Decision trees on real valued parameters, as produced by TDIDT algorithms, contain choice points of the form: either make $P_x < p$, or $P_x > p$. Most process controllers work differently. A process set-point can be set, being the mean value to be reached in the process, and the controller has a specific accuracy, being the (standard) deviation of the values in the process. We adopt this process control method of representing choice points. In addition the partition criteria considers cost gain instead of information gain, and the produced tree contains an optimal path.

## 3.2  Assumptions

In accordance with other induction algorithms we assume that:
• the dataset is representative for the problem space
• the noise is kept within reasonable norms
• the dataset contains no missing values
• all quality determining parameters are represented in the dataset

In addition we assume that:
• all parameters in the dataset can be controlled
• controlling a parameter consists of controlling both the mean value and standard deviation
• the costs involved in controlling a parameter $P_i$ can be represented in two functions, $\mu P_i$ and $\sigma P_i$, for controlling the mean value and the standard deviation of $P_i$ respectively. These functions, which represent the functional relation between costs and setpoints, form the background knowledge to be used in the partition criterion.

## 3.3 Cost Gain as a Partition Criterion

To start with, we need the following data for optimizing the costs:
• A set of parameters P : { $p_1$, $p_2$, $p_3$, .....}.

- Mean and standard deviation cost functions $\mu P_i(\mu_o, \mu_n)$ and $\sigma P_i(\sigma_o, \sigma_n)$, one of them for each parameter $P_i$. These functions indicate how the cost of one single end-product is influenced when the mean value and standard deviation of parameter $P_i$ are changed from $\mu_o$ to $\mu_n$ and $\sigma_o$ to $\sigma_n$ respectively.

- A set of data-records $D : \{ d_1, d_2, d_3, .... \}$. Each data-record $d_x$ consists of: $\{k_x, v_{1x}, v_{2x}, ...., l_x\}$, with $k_x$ a key for $d_x$, $v_{jx}$ being the value of parameter $j$ for record $d_x$, and $l_x$ being the label of record $d_x$. The label is a member of a set $L : \{$ saleable, unsaleable $\}$. An unsaleable product represents waste.

- The initial costs of one individual product IC, as it is derived for the entire dataset.

The result of the algorithm should be a cost decision tree (CDT). In a CDT a path from the root to a leaf node represents a tuning of the production process (In this paper, for ease of understanding only the tuning of the most optimal path is shown). Such a tuning consists of a set of parameter/setpoint/accuracy combinations. Also attached to each tuning is a cost price $C_i$ of a saleable product.

Our aim is to minimize $C_i$. Let us first calculate $C_i$ for a certain node $i$. We assume that this node contains $x$ saleable and $y$ unsaleable products. Then $C_i$ is defined as follows:

$$(1) \qquad C_i = \frac{(x+y) * (IC + C_c)}{x},$$

where $C_c$ are the accumulated control costs of each node from the root of the tree down to the current node. To calculate $C_c$ we have to calculate the control costs generated by a branching node, $C_{ci}$. We assumed before that there are costs related to controlling the mean value and standard deviation of a parameter. If $P_i$ is a parameter, then $\mu P_i(\mu_o, \mu_n)$ is the function that gives the total costs of controlling $P_i$ from the old setpoint $\mu_o$ to the new setpoint $\mu_n$. Accordingly, $\sigma P_i(\sigma_o, \sigma_n)$ gives the costs resulting from changing the control accuracy from $\sigma_o$ to $\sigma_n$. The control costs in a node $i$ can now be expressed as:

$$(2) \qquad C_{ci} = \mu P_i(\mu_o, \mu_n) + \sigma P_i(\sigma_o, \sigma_n)$$

Our aim, minimizing the unit product costs for a saleable product can be reformulated as maximizing the cost gain. If $C_i$ is the cost at branching node $i$, by partitioning this node for $P_x = p$, we can calculate the new cost price for the child nodes: $C_{left}$ and $C_{right}$. The costgain then becomes:

$$(3) \qquad CG\ (P_x = p) = C_i - Min\ (C_{left}, C_{right})$$

Our algorithm now should find a parameter $P_x$ and related value $p$ such that CG is maximized.

Once a CDT has been derived, we have to find the optimal leaf. This of course is very simple: the path from the root to the leaf with the minimal cost price indicates the most optimal group of setpoints. In the branching points the setpoints are available, both as border values (as is the case in ID3/NPPA) and as mean and sigma values.

## 3.4 An Example

To illustrate the algorithm we generated a simplified two-dimensional space belonging to the example of section 2. Both the variables P1 and P2 take values from 0 to 9. The labels were attached: saleable (+) and unsaleable (-). The initial cost of a product, IC, was set to 11. This resulted in a cost price of a good product for the entire dataset, $C_i$ to be 14.86. A representation of the instance space is presented as a 10x10 grid (Figure 1). Figure 1a shows the areas that were recognized by NPPA. The region with the minimal cost price (region 1) has a cost price of 13.52, about 9 % cheaper than the cost price of the initial dataset.

Table 1 shows the cost functions for mean and standard deviation. The functions may stand for a process where the costs are inversely proportional to the standard deviation of the parameter values, and quadratic/linearly dependent on the mean value of the parameters (in real-world situations these functions may be far more complicated!). The partitioning MICO finds for this situation is shown in Figure 1b. A part of the related CDT can be found in Figure 2. MICO finds a partitioning in which only one unsaleable product is represented. The final cost price is 11.88, about 20 % cheaper than the original result, and 11% cheaper than the solution NPPA comes up with.

By varying cost functions and fixed product-costs, which are the background knowledge, the partitioning can be influenced. As might be expected induction biased this way follows certain rules: when the initial costs IC of one produced entity are relatively high, MICO seeks for an area with as little 'bad' products as possible (as in region 1 of Figure 1b). Lower IC leads to less partitioning: more 'bad' products are tolerated (as in region 1 of Figure 1c). This however also decreases the realative cost price reduction achieved by the partitioning (5% in Figure 1c). This may be illustrated by the following example: when producing airplanes (high IC), you want to be very sure that at the end of your process, a good plane is delivered, and so you are prepared to invest in process control. When you are producing chewing gum (low IC) you can afford to throw away some of your end products. The initial costs IC thus weights the importance of the unsaleable instances related to the saleable. Though the same effect can be reached in other ways, e.g. by duplicating the saleable and unsaleable instances so that their ratio is according to some weight, using the initial costs IC seems a better solution.

The cost functions weigh the preference for controlling certain parameters. If we vary the cost functions, we influence these weights. In Figure 1d we can see what happens when the cost functions for parameter P1 of Figure 1b are changed. The functions μP1 and σP1 are changed so that the effect of changing the setpoint and the standard deviation of P1 is 10 and 5 times as influential as in Figure 1b.

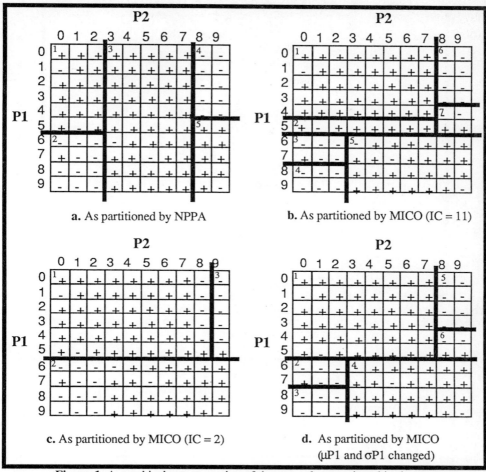

**Figure 1.** A graphical representation of the examples mentioned in the text

## 3.5 Information Gain versus Cost Gain

The performance of information gain and cost gain in some of the above examples can be seen in table 2. We see that the results MICO comes up with are at least as beneficial as the results of NPPA. This holds for all examples we have considered. The partitioning of the instance space as made by NPPA may differ significantly from the one found by MICO (see Figure 1).

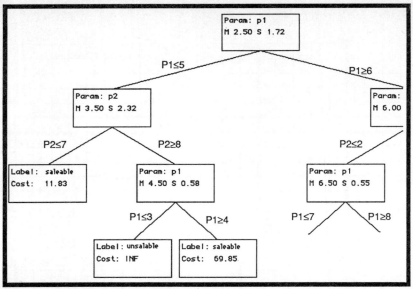

**Figure 2.** Part of the CDT belonging to Figure 1d (M = Mean value, S = standard deviation). In the branching nodes, the mean value and standard deviation that are needed to reach the descendant node with the minimum Ci are shown. The setpoints for the other branch are available in the program, and can be accessed through the interface

| Function type | Mean value cost | Standard deviation |
| | function | cost function |
| Parameter | $\mu P_x\ (o_\mu, n_\mu)$ | $\sigma P_x\ (o_\sigma, n_\sigma)$ |
| P1 | $0.01\ (n_\mu^2 - o_\mu^2)$ | $1/n_\sigma - 1/o_\sigma$ |
| P2 | $0.3\ (n_\mu - o_\mu)$ | $10\ (1/n_\sigma - 1/o_\sigma)$ |

**Table 1.** The mean and standard deviation functions of the example

CDT's produced according to MICO differ from the decision trees as produced by other TDIDT algorithms on several points. The first difference is that a CDT reflects a search space, where an optimal path can be found. The optimal path indicates the optimal tuning of the process. A decision tree on the other hand gives a classification of all instances in the dataset; it makes no sense to talk about an optimum here. When a CDT is used as a classification tree, it behaves as a probabilistic classifier (Quinlan 1987).

Another difference between CDT's and classical decision trees is the information provided by the branching points. In the branching points of NPPA-like decision trees conditions are stored in the form of an inequality on attribute values. In CDT's the branching points store a setpoint and a deviation.

| Used version | Initial cost price | Cost price of the NPPA solution | NPPA versus initial | Cost price of the MICO solution | MICO versus initial |
|---|---|---|---|---|---|
| IC = 11 (fig 1b) | 14.86 | 13.52 | 9.0% | 11.88 | 20.0% |
| IC = 2 (fig 1c) | 2.70 | 4.14 | -53.3% | 2.54 | 5.9% |
| μP1 10 times higher | 14.86 | 12.41 | 16.49% | 11.83 | 20.4% |

**Table 2.** A comparison of the NPPA and MICO in the examples of Figure 1

## 3.6 N-class Labeling

In section 3.4 we presented all requirements for the 2-class datasets, where one of the classes was waste. We will now sketch how the algorithm can be generalized to N-class situations and to situations where all products have some value, e.g. as scrap, or as a second class product. For the 2-class problems with one of the classes being waste, we can concentrate on costs. When we want to optimize the problem for more classes, with different values, costs are not sufficient. We have to find another way to compare two situations. This is solved by the introduction of a function representing the value of a product:

• Income-function $I(K_V, l)$; given a class-distribution $K_V$ and a specific label $l$, this function gives the total income for products of that label.

The partitioning criterion now becomes the maximization of the average benefits of a product. As argued before this does not change the basic algorithm. An extra calculation however is needed. Instead of minimizing the costs of a good product, we are now interested in maximizing the profit of a product. We now have to maximize the benefit gain:

(4)    $BG (P_x = p) = Max (B_{left}, B_{right}) - B_i$

(with $B_i$ the benefit in the parent node, and $B_{left}$ and $B_{right}$ the benefit for the child nodes). If we find a distribution of $[x_1, x_2, ... x_n]$ in a leaf node, the average benefit gain BG on a product can be calculated with the formula:

$$(5) \quad BG = \frac{(\sum_{i=1}^{n} x_i * I([x_1, x_2 .. x_n], x_i)) - (\sum_{i=1}^{n} x_i) * (IC + C_c)}{\sum_{i=1}^{n} x_i} .$$

The benefit of one product thus is calculated by taking the difference between total benefit and total cost, divided by the number of products. This extension is straightforward and introduces no new concepts. In many industrial cases 2-class labeling is sufficient.

## 4. Empirical Results

We have applied the algorithm to data gathered in an industrial company with a mass-production process. We received a small dataset from the factory, containing 52 records of 10 parameters. All parameters are real-valued. The initial costs, valid for the entire dataset, are 170. Given the distribution between saleable and unsaleable products in the dataset of 29 and 23 respectively, this resulted in a cost-price for the saleable products of 304.83. Good cost functions were not directly available. We therefore constructed cost functions on the basis of a factory-model we received from the company and on the basis of expert interviews.

We applied both NPPA and MICO on this dataset. The results are shown in table 3. Using the NPPA algorithm, we constructed a decision tree. The derived ruleset consists of 7 rules. The cheapest solution NPPA came up with was 174.98, which was valid for 6 examples. All examples in this rule were classified correctly. The CDT produced by MICO was larger, containing 10 rules. It contained a partition on a parameter that was not identified as quality determining by NPPA. Most of the rules were valid for a few examples, and thus were not very reliable. The cheapest set of setpoints reduced the total cost price from 304.83 to 171.46 (this rule incorporated 10 examples).

| Feature | Initial | NPPA | MICO |
|---|---|---|---|
| Number of rules | - | 7 | 10 |
| Lowest cost | 304.83 | 174.98 | 171.46 |
| Labeling accuracy (over all) | 55% | 86.5% | 78 % |
| Labeling accuracy (best) | 55% | 100 % | 100 % |

**Table 3.** Comparison between the initial dataset, NPPA and MICO on real world data

## 5. Conclusions

### 5.1. MICO

MICO is an algorithm that performs well in minimizing the costs and optimizing the benefits of a production process. The solutions it finds are at least as good as the ones NPPA finds, at least in two points: they represent production tunings for products with a low cost price, and they are understandable for operators of the production process, because they make choices that make sense.

If we try to understand how the information gain criterion works for these cases we see a reduction in uncertainty on the class label. In NPPA partitioning continues until no significant information gain can be reached. The way our cost optimizing algorithm works is very similar. MICO does not make use of information gain as its partitioning principle. The pragmatic condition of information gain, which is used in NPPA, is replaced by a well-defined one in MICO: the cost functions exactly quantify this criteria.

Algorithms like NPPA control the partitioning of the dataset by calculating some statistical feature of the information gain, e.g. the significance of the reached information gain. These control strategies are highly pragmatic. In MICO the control strategy is meaningful: as long as the cost price decreases, the process continues. The way the cost functions for standard deviation value of a parameter are formulated should guarantee that a partitioning up to individual records should not happen. Another view here is that the cost functions and the initial IC are the parameters controlling the partitioning. In other words this method of biasing induction uses a well-defined meaning in the real-world instead of a pragmatic measure.

## 5.2 Induction Biased by Background Knowledge

We have presented an algorithm that uses one specific form of background knowledge. Several other ways of using background knowledge however must be distinguished. The cost example uses background knowledge to partition the dataset.

One way of biasing induction is by manipulating the hypothesis space. The approach Utgoff (1986) took with STABB enlarges the space of hypothesis by weakening the bias. In TDIDT this use of weakening the bias can be found in Spangler et. al. (1989). Our approach of biasing induction doesn't weaken the bias, but shifts the bias to another part of the hypothesis space, thereby making it possible for other questions to be answered.

## 5.3 Acquiring Cost Functions

Applying MICO clearly creates a new problem: the acquisition of cost functions. As we explained in section 3.2 cost functions relate a change in parameter tuning with a change in the production costs of one product. In the industrial environments we visited, there were no such cost functions available, at least not formulated explicitly. However, there are very clear heuristics about them. For example, when talking about controlling a temperature gradient, a typical statement was: 'controlling this is very expensive, maybe it is cheaper to try influencing the temperature'.

This type of remarks was made very frequently. From that, we searched for formalization of the weights of the parameters. We found it to be hard for operators and engineers in industry to formulate the cost functions we needed in MICO. Our approach in acquiring the functions was to analyse the process on the basis of experts-interviews and to extract cost functions from this analysis. This resulted in cost functions of a type close to the heuristics of process experts.

## 6. Further research

We will continue developing the MICO algorithm. An interesting question is the effect of the dependency of parameters that appear in the cost functions. More experience is needed in constructing cost functions for real factory situations and we would like to compare MICO more extensively with existing methods for cost optimization as defined in the cost price analysis, and in engineering sciences. We should also search for better ways to represent cost functions. As we explained earlier, we adopted a representation for cost functions which is as close as possible to the heuristics that process experts use. This representation differs from the one used in business economics, where costs are considered to have a fixed and variable part. In this form, cost functions may be formulated more naturally, and better explicit formulation may take place. Other topics of research will be the significance of the cost optimizations as derived by MICO, and the possibilities for post-processing the produced trees (as in Payne & Meisel, 1977). This may enable us to further improve the solutions, of both optimality of costs and classification.

The main subject of our project is to develop appropriate strategies for applying background knowledge in induction. We find that this may enlarge the possibilities for using inductive learning techniques in practical situations, both in knowledge acquisition and in data analysis applications.

## Acknowledgements

I am indebted to Jan Talmon for making his NPPA version available for me, and to Hilde Thijsen for building the generic interface for my induction programs. I thank Jan Paredis, Jan Talmon and Gerry Kelleher for the useful suggestions and comments on earlier versions of this paper.

# References

Arbab & Michie 1985 **Arbab, B., and Michie, D.,** Generating Rules from Examples, in: Proceedings of IJCAI-85, pp. 631-633, Los Angeles , CA, 1985

Bergadano et. al. 1990 **Bergadano, F., Giordana, A. and Saitta, L.,** Biasing Induction by Using a Domain Theory: An Experimental Evaluation, in: Proceedings of ECAI-90, pp. 84-89, 1990

Buntine & Stirling 1988 **Buntine, W., and Stirling, D.,** Interactive Induction, in: Proceedings of the Fourth IEEE Conference on Artificial Intelligence Applications, pp. 320-326, San Diego, 1988

Cosemans & Samyn 1990 **Cosemans, G., and Samyn, J.,** Inductive Analysis of Datasets, paper presented at BeneLearn-90, Leuven 1990

Nunez 1988 **Nunez, M.,** Economic Induction: A Case Study, in:, Proceedings of EWSL-88, pp. 139-146, Glasgow, Scotland 1988

Payne & Meisel 1977 **Payne, H.J., and Meisel, W.S.,** An Algorithm for Constructing Optimal Binary Decision Trees, in: IEEE Transactions on computers, vol 26, pp. 905-916, 1977

Quinlan 1986 **Quinlan, J.R.,** Induction of Decision Trees, in: Machine learning, Vol. 1, No 1, pp. 81-106, 1986

Quinlan 1987 **Quinlan, J.R.,** Decision Trees as Probabilistic Classifiers, in: Proceedings of the 4th International Machine Learning Workshop, pp. 31-37, University of California, Irvine, 1987

Shapiro 1987 **Shapiro, A.,** Structured Induction in Expert Systems, Turing Institute, Glasgow, Scotland, 1987

Spangler et. al. 1989 **Spangler, S., Fayyad, U.M., and Uthurusamy, R.,** Induction of Decision Trees from Inconclusive Data, in: Proceedings of the 6th International Workshop on Machine Learning, pp. 146-150, Ithaca, NY, 1989

Talmon 1986 **Talmon, J.L.,** A Multiclass Nonparametric Partitioning Algorithm, in: Pattern recognition letters Vol. 4, pg 31-38, 1986

Tan & Schlimmer 1989 **Tan, M. and Schlimmer, J.C.,** Cost-Sensitive Concept Learning of Sensor Use in Approach and Recognition,in: Proceedings of the 6th International Workshop on Machine Learning, pp. 392-395, Ithaca, NY, 1989

Utgoff 1986 **Utgoff, P.E.,** Shift of Bias for Inductive Concept Learning, in: Machine Learning, An Artificial Intelligence Approach, Volume II, R.S. Michalski,, J.G. Carbonell and T.M. Mitchell (eds), Morgan Kaufman, Los Altos, California 1986

# When Does Overfitting Decrease Prediction Accuracy in Induced Decision Trees and Rule Sets?*

Cullen Schaffer
Departments of Computer Science and Statistics
Rutgers University
New Brunswick, NJ · 08903
201-932-3145 · schaffer@paul.rutgers.edu

### Abstract

Researchers studying classification techniques based on induced decision trees and rule sets have found that the model which best fits training data is unlikely to yield optimal performance on fresh data. Such a model is typically *overfitted*, in the sense that it captures not only true regularities reflected in the training data, but also chance patterns which have no significance for classification and, in fact, reduce the model's predictive accuracy. Various simplification methods have been shown to help avoid overfitting in practice. Here, through detailed analysis of a paradigmatic example, I attempt to uncover the conditions under which these techniques work as expected. One auxilliary result of importance is identification of conditions under which overfitting does *not* decrease predictive accuracy and hence in which it would be a mistake to apply simplification techniques, if predictive accuracy is the key goal.

*The research reported here was supported by a grant from the Robert Wood Johnson Pharmaceutical Research Institute.

# 1 Fitting and Overfitting: The Simplest Case

A certain fictitious kind of snail may have either one horn or two. A randomly selected snail has one horn and is observed to prefer apple mash to banana mash. A second randomly selected snail also has one horn and shows the same preference. A third randomly selected snail, however, has two horns and prefers banana mash. A fourth snail is now selected and we are asked to predict its taste preference on the basis of the three we have just observed.

If the new snail has two horns, we are faced with a dilemma. On the one hand, two of three observed snails prefer apple mash, suggesting that we should predict this preference. On the other hand, in our limited experience, two-horned snails have always been observed to prefer banana mash, suggesting the opposite answer.

On the basis of the evidence, we would estimate the probability that a randomly selected snail will prefer apple mash as $\frac{2}{3}$ and the probability that a randomly selected two-horned snail will prefer banana mash as 1. Of these two estimates, the first is more reliable, since it is based on more data, while the second is more pertinent to our prediction problem. The difficulty of the problem, from one perspective, is in weighing these incommensurable advantages.

A second, more familiar perspective is that the difficulty lies in deciding which patterns in the data reflect true regularities in snail behavior and which are due solely to chance. In effect, we have been asked to build a model on the basis of data. The question is how to capture true regularities in this model, while excluding spurious ones—that is, how best to *fit* the model without *overfitting* it.

The problem of overfitting is well documented in reports on decision tree and rule induction approaches to classification tasks; experience in practical applications has shown that the tree or rule set which best fits training data is rarely the one that will perform best in classifying new cases. Research has generally focused, however, on practical methods for avoiding overfitting rather than on deepening our understanding of it.

This paper concentrates, instead, on the latter goal and attempts to provide insight into the conditions under which overfitting adversely affects prediction accuracy. In approaching these questions, I have begun by isolating what I believe is the smallest rule induction or decision tree problem for which overfitting is a concern. An analysis of the snail problem—the result

| | Model | Prediction | Rule Set | Decision Tree |
|---|---|---|---|---|
| Simple Models | $M_1$ | $a$ | $T \Rightarrow a$ | $a$ |
| | $M_2$ | $b$ | $T \Rightarrow b$ | $b$ |
| Complex Models | $M_3$ | $a$ for 1, $b$ for 2 | $1 \Rightarrow a$ $2 \Rightarrow b$ | # with branches 1, 2 to $a$, $b$ |
| | $M_4$ | $b$ for 1, $a$ for 2 | $1 \Rightarrow b$ $2 \Rightarrow a$ | # with branches 1, 2 to $b$, $a$ |

Table 1: Models for the Snail Problem

of this distillation—is the main focus in what follows. By looking at overfitting in the small, however, I will argue that we learn about dealing with the problem as it arises in practice.

## 2 A First Result

Given a series of observations, each consisting of a number of horns (1 or 2) and a taste preference ($a$ or $b$), only four deterministic models of preference are possible. Table 1 lists these and shows that we may represent the models equally well as decision trees or rule sets.

In some cases, data may unambiguously support one of these four models. For example, the observations $\{<1, a>, <1, a>, <2, a>\}$ clearly favor $M_1$. In other cases, the evidence lends no special support to either of the complex models $M_3$ and $M_4$. Given the observations $\{<1, a>, <2, a>, <2, b>\}$ or $\{<1, a>, <1, a>, <1, b>\}$, for example, $M_1$ fits exactly as well as $M_3$. What remain are *equivocal* cases, exemplified by the case of the previous section, which lead to a choice between a simple hypothesis and a more tenuously supported, but better fitting complex hypothesis.

Employing this new term, I can state the concern of this paper precisely: I would like to ask about the conditions under which, in equivocal cases, choice of the best fitting complex model over the best fitting simple one leads to a decrease in prediction performance. In particular, I will be investigating this question for training sets of size three, since these are the smallest which may be equivocal.

Let $S_s$ be the strategy of choosing the best fitting simple model in equivocal cases and $S_c$ be the strategy of choosing the best fitting complex model.[1] The question, then, is to determine conditions under which $S_s$ is superior in predictive accuracy.

Let $p_1$ be the true probability of a one-horned snail preferring apple mash and let $p_2$ be the true probability of a two-horned snail preferring apple mash. Suppose, temporarily, that we have no prior knowledge about taste preferences in snails and, hence, none about the values of $p_1$ and $p_2$. We might model this state of ignorance by assuming, *a priori*, that any $(p_1, p_2)$ pair is as likely as any other, that is, that the prior joint distribution for these parameters is uniform on the unit square.

Given this assumption, a straightforward Bayesian analysis allows us to calculate the expected prediction accuracy of models chosen by $S_s$ and $S_c$ for three-observation, equivocal training sets, averaged over the possible values of $p_1$ and $p_2$.[2] This analysis shows that $S_c$ yields rules with a higher average prediction accuracy than $S_s$. That is, under the conditions described, over-fitting should *not* be a concern—the model which best fits the training data is the one which is likely to do best in future prediction.

Given the effort researchers have expended in devising techniques to avoid overfitting in inducing classification models, this result is rather striking at first. The catch is that it depends on the assumed prior distribution for $p_1$ and $p_2$. This implicitly entails an assumption that $p_1$ and $p_2$, considered as random variables, are independent and hence it necessarily makes observations of one-horned snails irrelevant to predictions about two-horned ones. In essence, we have assumed *a priori* that we must adopt the complex strategy of estimating the majority class for the two groups separately.

This initial result illustrates how we may study the effect of overfitting on prediction accuracy and specify conditions under which a bias toward simplicity is or is not desirable. It also shows that the choice of a prior distri-

---

[1]Note that, while the simplicity of models $M_1$ and $M_2$ is purely syntactic and hence arbitrary, the simplicity of $S_s$ relative to $S_c$ is not. To fit a model, $S_c$ estimates the majority class for each of two groups; $S_s$ does so for just one.

[2]I also assume, throughout the paper, that the probability of selecting a one-horned snail is .5 both for the training and the test sets.

bution for $p_1$ and $p_2$ is critical in weighing $S_s$ against $S_c$. The strongest lesson of this first result, however, is that the straightforward Bayesian approach of choosing a prior distribution and analyzing its implications may be dangerously unintuitive; assumptions entailed by a prior distribution are often less than obvious. Rather than burying such assumptions in a joint distribution, I have adopted a "disguised Bayesian" approach in the following which I believe is better suited to the goal of promoting intuitive understanding.

# 3    A Disguised Bayesian Analysis

Assume, then, that values for $p_1$ and $p_2$ are fixed, though unknown to us. Suppose, for example, that the values are, respectively, .6 and .8. In this case, the simple model $M_1$ is clearly optimal in prediction. It does not follow, however, that $S_s$ is the optimal model-selection strategy under the assumed conditions. Sheer chance may lead to the observation sequence $\{<1,b>, <1,b>, <2,a>\}$, in which case $S_s$ will select $M_2$ with accuracy .3 while $S_c$ will select $M_4$ with accuracy .6. Of course, for the assumed values of $p_1$ and $p_2$, we would not expect this sort of problem to arise very often; $S_s$ ought *normally* be superior. Formally, we may calculate the performance of models selected by the two strategies for each equivocal observation sequence and average these performance figures, weighting by the chance of the various observation sequences arising under the assumed values of $p_1$ and $p_2$. This calculation confirms our intuition; since it shows that models chosen by $S_s$ have an average prediction accuracy of .573 while those chosen by $S_c$ have an average prediction accuracy of .560.[3]

By making similar calculations for each possible pair of $p_1$ and $p_2$ values, we may construct the diagram shown in Figure 1. Boundary lines in the figure cover $(p_1,p_2)$ pairs for which $S_s$ and $S_c$ select models with the same average prediction accuracy. In the upper left and lower right regions, $S_c$ is superior; in the lower left and upper right, $S_s$ is superior.

Although it omits important details—such as the *degree* to which prediction accuracies for the two strategies differ at a given $(p_1, p_2)$ point—a diagram of this kind gives us a useful intuitive perspective on conditions under which the conventional bias toward simplicity is justified. Essentially, $S_s$

---

[3] Details of a more general calculation are described in Section 7.

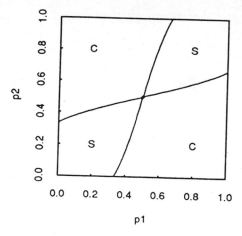

Figure 1: Comparing $S_s$ and $S_c$

is preferable only for $(p_1, p_2)$ pairs lying near the $p_1 = p_2$ line, though the acceptable distance grows as the parameters approach 0 or 1.

This result is easily explained. The more one- and two-horned snails are alike, the less is to be gained by treating them differently for purposes of prediction. At the same time, the risk incurred in considering the two types of snails separately remains constant. This risk is due to the fact that $S_c$ relies on less data in determining predictions for each snail type than $S_s$; for the observation sequence $\{<1, a>, <1, a>, <2, b>\}$, it bases predictions for two-horned snails on just one observation.

The striking point about Figure 1 is not, then, that the $S_s$ regions lie along the $p_1 = p_2$ line, but rather that they are so much smaller than those in which $S_c$ is preferable. This would seem to suggest that a bias toward simplicity increases prediction accuracy only in exceptional circumstances. Since practical experience has shown exactly the opposite, however, we must ask what it is about practical applications that leads to a prevalance of parameter vectors falling in $S_s$ regions. I will come back to this question in Section 5 after first discussing the effects of noise.

## 4 Noise

The analysis of the previous section implicitly assumes what Spangler, et al. (Spangler et al., 1988) have called "inconclusive data." If $p_1$ and $p_2$ are not taken from the set $\{0,1\}$, then the number of horns on a snail does not

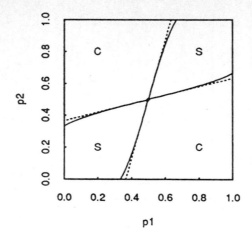

Figure 2: Comparing $S_s$ and $S_c$, $n_c = 0, .8$

entirely determine its taste preferences. Presumably, as in many realistic application, unobserved attributes account for this apparent deviation from determinism.

For additional realism, we may consider the possibility of influences compromising the validity of some observations. If a particular one-horned snail happens to prefer apple mash, for example, *noise* of various kinds might cause us mistakenly to treat the observation as either $<1, b>$ or $<2, a>$ or even $<2, b>$.

Let $n_d$ be the level of *description noise*, the probability that the true number of horns will be replaced by a random value equally likely to be 1 or 2. Let $n_c$ be the level of *classification noise*, the probability that the true taste preference of a snail will be replaced by a random value equally likely to be $a$ or $b$. For either of these kinds of noise, let a primed symbol denote the noise level in test (or performance) data, if this is different from the level in data on which a prediction model is based. Thus, $n_d'$ denotes the level of description noise in the test data.

Unexamined intuition might suggest that the increase in uncertainty resulting from introduction of noise would tend to favor selection of $S_s$ over $S_c$. Figure 2 shows, however, that this is only weakly so for the case of even extreme classification noise.[4]

This figure is, again, easy to explain. Adding classification noise has precisely the same effect as shifting the parameter pair $(p_1, p_2)$ in a straight

---

[4]Details of calculations supporting figures in this section are given in Section 7.

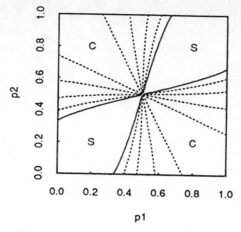

Figure 3: Comparing $S_s$ and $S_c$, $n_d = 0, .2, .4, .6$ and $.8$

line toward the point $(.5, .5)$. Examination of Figure 1 shows that very few points in the region where $S_c$ is preferred can be moved into the region where $S_s$ is preferred by such a translation. Hence, addition of classification noise expands the $S_s$ region only by annexation of these points.

Description noise, however, obliterates the distinction between *description groups*—identifiable subsets of the population which may be treated differently by a classification model—and makes it less profitable to consider the groups separately. While classification noise shifts $(p_1, p_2)$ in the direction of $(.5, .5)$, description noise shifts it toward the $p_1 = p_2$ line. Examination of Figure 1 indicates that *all* points in the $S_c$ region can eventually by moved into the $S_s$ region by such a translation. Hence, the intuition that simple models are best for weak data is justified in this case. Figure 3 illustrates the effect graphically. Note that noise must be increased to a level of roughly $n_d = .4$ to make the size of the $S_s$ and $S_c$ regions comparable.

A last point to note about description noise is that $n_d$ and $n_d'$ each have a significant effect on the relative merit of $S_s$ and $S_c$. Figure 4 shows first the effect of description noise in the test set (where it might most likely be expected to appear) and then the incremental effect of description noise in the training set.

# 5   Discussion

The results I have presented may be summarized as follows:

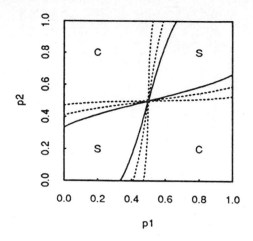

Figure 4: Comparing $S_s$ and $S_c$, $n_d = n'_d = 0$; $n_d = 0, n'_d = .4$; $n_d = n'_d = .4$

- Whether overfitting ought to be a concern depends critically on the distribution of problems over the $p_1$-$p_2$ unit square.

- In the absence of description and classification noise, the portion of this square in which $S_c$ is preferred is considerably larger than the one in which $S_s$ is preferred.

- Classification noise has a nearly negligible effect on the relative merit of $S_s$ and $S_c$.

- Description noise has a strong effect, however, even at moderate levels, and this is due in roughly equal measure to the effect of noise in the training and testing sets.

In response to the question posed in the title of this paper, then, we may tentatively generalize from the paradigmatic snail problem and answer that overfitting decreases prediction accuracy either (1) in the presence of significant description noise or (2) when classification patterns in description groups are not sharply distinguished in typical problems. The latter is just another way of stating the condition that available description attributes tend not to be very relevant to predicting classifications.

Given this summary, two questions are worth considering. First, since simplification strategies do generally help in practice, why is it that the conditions just stated normally hold?. Second, are there cases in which they do not hold and, hence, in which techniques for avoiding overfitting might actually yield inferior models?

Regarding the first question, description noise *is* certainly a common problem and, when present, may account for the fact that simplification techniques increase prediction accuracy. In many classification problems, however, description noise is insignificant. We may expect, for example, that a patient's vital signs will normally be measured correctly; the problem with using these to build a decision tree for diagnosis is that they do not entirely determine an illness.

If it pays to avoid overfitting in such cases, it must be because description attributes are not often highly relevant to classification. This may seem counter-intuitive at first, since we might expect analysts applying decision tree or rule induction techniques to choose attributes which they have good reason to believe *are* highly relevant. In fact, however, analysts often include a large number of description attributes, relying on the power of the induction technique to identify relevant ones. Also, perhaps more important, even relevant attributes are often highly interdependent, measuring similar qualities in a variety of ways. Hence, even if an attribute is highly relevant to classification taken by itself, it may be virtually valueless *after* other attributes have been taken into account. At the lower levels of a large decision tree, for example, the assumption that remaining attributes are unlikely to help might typically be justified.

These points lead to a natural answer to the second question posed above. In some cases, we may reasonably expect that description attributes are relevant and that description noise will not play a role. In these cases, some familiar and highly successful simplification techniques might be expected to lead to suboptimal classification procedures. For example, if we observe that two randomly selected dogs enjoy a certain food $F$, but a randomly selected person does not, it might well be reasonable to predict that people generally will not like $F$, despite the fact that two of three animals have been observed to enjoy it. Here, we are relying on our ability to distinguish reliably between dogs and people and on our common sense knowledge that an animal's species has a strong bearing on its taste preferences.

By contrast—to take a well-known example—Quinlan's (Quinlan, 1987) normally powerful technique of building a decision tree, converting it to a rule set and then simplifying this set would lead to the opposite prediction, since the observed difference between canine and human tastes is not statistically significant. The basic problem is that the statistical approach proceeds by assuming that attributes are irrelevant to classification unless proven otherwise. This null hypothesis is precisely the second condition I have identified as conducive to the success of simplification techniques.

# 6 Related Work and Comments

In their seminal work on CART, Breiman, et al. (Breiman et al., 1984) analyze the problem of overfitting nicely, identifying the basic tradeoff between model support and potential accuracy. Their analysis concentrates on explaining why overfitting is a problem rather than on when this problem arises. Others, notably (Niblett, 1987) and (Weiss, 1987), have also suggested powerful approaches to dealing with the problem of overfitting in practice and attempted mathematical analyses to support their work. Like Breiman et al., these authors concentrate in both algorithms and mathematical analyses on handling the kinds of cases normally faced in practice—in which overfitting is a concern—rather than distinguishing these from the less likely cases in which methods for avoiding overfitting might actually decrease predictive accuracy.

My distinction between description and classification noise is drawn from Quinlan's analysis of the effect of noise on decision tree performance (Quinlan, 1986). Quinlan does not, however, address the question of how noise affects overfitting and strategies for avoiding it.

A good review of such strategies is given in (Quinlan, 1987). As this review makes clear, there are other reasons than prediction accuracy to prefer simplicity in induced classification procedures.

Needless to say, the tiny problem I have analyzed here assumes away a host of important subtleties and we must be careful to consider the extrapolations I have offered as suggestive rather than conclusive. Large data sets, large attribute sets, problems involving continuous or multi-valued attributes, prior knowledge of relations between attributes—all these affect the analysis drastically and may in some cases render it inapplicable. On balance, however, I think even this small problem deepens our understanding of the problem of overfitting. In a word, it suggests (1) that methods for dealing with overfitting work only because of the validity of certain implicit assumptions and (2) that we may benefit by attempting to make these explicit.

# 7 Appendix

This appendix explains how to calculate the prediction accuracy of $S_s$ and $S_c$ on the basis of given values for $p_1, p_2, n_d, n'_d, n_c$ and $n'_c$.

If $n_d$ is the probability that a description value will be replaced at random, then the chance that the observed value will be erroneous is $n_d/2$. Define $e_d = n_d/2$ and $e'_d, e_c$ and $e'_c$ analogously. Then the probabilities of making any of four basic observations are:

$$
\begin{aligned}
P(<1,a>) &= [(1-e_d)(1-e_c)p_1 &+& (1-e_d)e_c(1-p_1) &+& \\
& \quad e_d(1-e_c)p_2 &+& e_d e_c(1-p_2)]/2 && \\
P(<1,b>) &= [(1-e_d)(1-e_c)(1-p_1) &+& (1-e_d)e_c p_1 &+& \\
& \quad e_d(1-e_c)(1-p_2) &+& e_d e_c p_2]/2 && \\
P(<2,a>) &= [(1-e_d)(1-e_c)p_2 &+& (1-e_d)e_c(1-p_2) &+& \\
& \quad e_d(1-e_c)p_1 &+& e_d e_c(1-p_1)]/2 && \\
P(<2,b>) &= [(1-e_d)(1-e_c)(1-p_2) &+& (1-e_d)e_c p_2 &+& \\
& \quad e_d(1-e_c)(1-p_1) &+& e_d e_c p_1]/2 &&
\end{aligned}
$$

As noted earlier, $P(<1,\cdot>)$ is assumed to be .5.

If we consider the order of observations, there are 12 possible equivocal three-observation training sets. Strategies $S_s$ and $S_c$ ignore the order of observations, however, and we can simplify calculations by recognizing just four equivocal observation sets:

$$
\begin{aligned}
O_1 &= \{<1,a>,<1,a>,<2,b>\} \\
O_2 &= \{<1,b>,<1,b>,<2,a>\} \\
O_3 &= \{<1,a>,<2,b>,<2,b>\} \\
O_4 &= \{<1,b>,<2,a>,<2,a>\}
\end{aligned}
$$

Each of these may appear in three equally likely permutations. Hence, if we let

$$
\begin{aligned}
k_1 &= P(<1,a>)^2 P(<2,b>) \\
k_2 &= P(<1,b>)^2 P(<2,a>) \\
k_3 &= P(<1,a>) P(<2,b>)^2 \\
k_4 &= P(<1,b>) P(<2,a>)^2
\end{aligned}
$$

and

$$n = k_1 + k_2 + k_3 + k_4$$

then we have $P(O_i) = k_i/n$ for $i = 1, 2, 3, 4$. Note that these probabilities are implicitly conditioned on observation of an equivocal training set, since we are only comparing the accuracy of $S_s$ and $S_c$ under these circumstances.

Let $A(M_i)$ be the accuracy of $M_i$ as measured by the probability of its predicting the observed class. Then

$$A(M_1) = (1 - e'_c)(p_1 + p_2)/2 + e'_c(1 - (p_1 + p_2)/2)$$
$$A(M_2) = e'_c(p_1 + p_2)/2 + (1 - e'_c)(1 - (p_1 + p_2)/2)$$

Since $S_s$ chooses $M_1$ given $O_1$ or $O_4$ and $M_2$ given $O_2$ or $O_3$, we have

$$A(S_s) = [P(O_1) + P(O_4)]A(M_1) + [P(O_2) + P(O_3)]A(M_2)$$

where the accuracy of a strategy is taken to be the average accuracy of the models it selects. Likewise, we have

$$
\begin{aligned}
A(M_3) \quad = \quad & [(1 - e'_d)(1 - e'_c)p_1 & + \quad & (1 - e'_d)e'_c(1 - p_1) & + \\
& e'_d(1 - e'_c)p_2 & + \quad & e'_d e'_c(1 - p_2) & + \\
& (1 - e'_d)(1 - e'_c)(1 - p_2) & + \quad & (1 - e'_d)e'_c p_2 & + \\
& e'_d(1 - e'_c)(1 - p_1) & + \quad & e'_d e'_c p_1]/2 & \\
A(M_4) \quad = \quad & [(1 - e'_d)(1 - e'_c)(1 - p_1) & + \quad & (1 - e'_d)e'_c p_1 & + \\
& e'_d(1 - e'_c)(1 - p_2) & + \quad & e'_d e'_c p_2 & + \\
& (1 - e'_d)(1 - e'_c)p_2 & + \quad & (1 - e'_d)e'_c(1 - p_2) & + \\
& e'_d(1 - e'_c)p_1 & + \quad & e'_d e'_c(1 - p_1)]/2 &
\end{aligned}
$$

and, since $S_c$ chooses $M_3$ given $O_1$ or $O_3$ and $M_4$ given $O_2$ or $O_4$,

$$A(S_c) = [P(O_1) + P(O_3)]A(M_3) + [P(O_2) + P(O_4)]A(M_4)$$

As I have noted, these calculations yield the expected *observed* accuracy of $S_s$ and $S_c$, counting a prediction model as successful when its predictions match the *apparent* class of new objects. To calculate the accuracy of these strategies in predicting the *true* class of new objects, simply let $n'_c = 0$.

# 8  Acknowledgements

Thanks to Tom Ellman, who suggested viewing noise as a model shift in the $p_1$-$p_2$ plane.

# References

Breiman, L., Friedman, J., Olshen, R., Stone, C. *Classification and Regression Trees.* Wadsworth and Brooks, 1984.

Niblett, T. Constructing decision trees in noisy domains. In *Proceedings of the Second European Working Session on Learning*, pages 67–78. Sigma Press, Bled., Yugoslavia, 1987.

Spangler, S., Fayyad, U., Uthurusamy, R. Induction of decision trees from inconclusive data. In *Proceedings of the Fifth International Workshop on Machine Learning*, pages 146–150, 1988.

Quinlan, J. The effect of noise on concept learning. In Michalski, R., Carbonell, J., Mitchell, T. *Machine Learning: An Artificial Intelligence Approach*, volume 2, chapter 6. Morgan Kaufmann, 1986.

Quinlan, J. Simplifying decision trees. *International Journal of Man-Machine Studies*, 27:221–234, 1987.

Weiss, S., Galen, R., Tadepalli, P. Optimizing the predictive value of diagnostic decision rules. In *Proceedings of the Sixth National Conference on Artificial Intelligence*, pages 521–526, 1987.

# SEMI-NAIVE BAYESIAN CLASSIFIER

Igor KONONENKO

University of Ljubljana, Faculty of electrical & computer engineering

Tržaška 25, 61001 Ljubljana, Yugoslavia

## Abstract

In the paper the algorithm of the 'naive' Bayesian classifier (that assumes the independence of attributes) is extended to detect the dependencies between attributes. The idea is to optimize the tradeoff between the 'non-naivety' and the reliability of approximations of probabilities. Experiments in four medical diagnostic problems are described. In two domains where by the experts opinion the attributes are in fact independent the semi- naive Bayesian classifier achieved the same classification accuracy as naive Bayes. In two other domains the semi-naive Bayesian classifier slightly outperformed the naive Bayesian classifier.

**Keywords:** machine learning, Bayesian classifier, approximations of probabilities, (in)dependence of events

## 1 Introduction

Let $A_i, i = 1 \ldots n$ be a set of attributes, each having values $V_{i,j}, j = 1 \ldots NV_i$. Let $C_j$ be one of $m$ possible classes. If the values of attributes for a given object are obtained in sequential order from $A_1$ to $A_k$, $1 \leq k \leq n$, the probability of class $C_j$ can be updated using the sequential Bayesian formula (Good 1950):

$$P(C_j|V_{1,J_1}, \ldots, V_{k,J_k}) = P(C_j) \prod_{i=1}^{k} \frac{P(C_j|V_{1,J_1}, \ldots, V_{i,J_i})}{P(C_j|V_{1,J_1}, \ldots, V_{i-1,J_{i-1}})} \tag{1}$$

where $J_i$ represents the index of the value of attribute $A_i$ for current object to be classified. The correctness of eq. (1) is obvious as the right hand side can be abbreviated to obtain the identity. If the values of all attributes are known then $k = n$. If in (1) the independence of attributes is assumed, the naive Bayesian formula is obtained:

$$\hat{P}(C_j | V_{1,J_1}, \ldots, V_{n,J_n}) = P(C_j) \prod_{i=1}^{n} \frac{P(C_j | V_{i,J_i})}{P(C_j)} \tag{2}$$

Both formulas, (1) and (2) can be used to classify new objects, given the set of training examples with known classes from which the prior probabilities can be approximated. An object is classified to class with maximal probability calculated with (1) or (2). In fact, formula (1) is appropriate for induction of decision trees, if the selection of the next attribute to be tested is assumed to be independent of an object to be classified (Kononenko 1989). In the case of a decision tree, the values $V_{1,J_1}, \ldots, V_{k,J_k}$ in (1) represent the path from the root to the leaf of a tree.

If a limited number of training data is available, the approximation of the probability with relative frequency:

$$\hat{P}(C_j | V_{1,J_1}, \ldots, V_{k,J_k}) = \frac{N_{C_j, V_{1,J_1}, \ldots, V_{k,J_k}}}{N_{V_{1,J_1}, \ldots, V_{k,J_k}}} \tag{3}$$

becomes unreliable due to small number of training instances having the same values of attributes as the new object to be classified. This is also the reason of applying various pruning techniques when generating decision trees. Smaller $k$ in (3) implies greater denominator which implies better approximation of probability.

On the other hand, in naive formula (2) the approximation of probabilities on the right hand side with relative frequencies is much more reliable. In addition, Cestnik (1990) has shown that instead of using relative frequencies it is better to use the following formula for approximation of probabilities on the right-hand side of (2) to still improve the reliability of approximations:

$$\hat{P}(C_j | V_{k,J_k}) = \frac{N_{C_j, V_{k,J_k}} + 2 \times P(C_j)}{N_{V_{k,J_k}} + 2} \tag{4}$$

where $P(C_j)$ is approximated using the Laplace's law of succession (Good 1950):

$$\hat{P}(C_j) = \frac{N_{C_j} + 1}{N + 2} \tag{5}$$

The same formula was used also by Smyth and Goodman (1990). It was experimentally verified, that the naive Bayesian formula achieves better classification accuracy than known inductive learning algorithms (Cestnik 1990) and, surprisingly, the explanation ability of naive Bayes, at least in inexact domains such as medical diagnostics, is better than the explanation ability of a decision tree (Kononenko 1990). The kind of explanation by naive Bayes is the *sum of information gains* by each attribute for/against each class for a given object, which appeared to be preferable by human experts than single if-then rule for a classified object.

However, the naivety of formula (2) can be too drastic in certain domains with strong dependencies between attributes. There is an obvious tradeoff between the 'non-naivety' and the reliability of the approximations of probabilities. In the paper an algorithm is defined that tries to optimize this tradeoff by detecting the dependencies between attributes' values.

In next section the kinds of dependencies between events are explored. In section 3 the algorithm of the semi-naive Bayesian classifier is described. In section 4 experiments in four medical diagnostic problems are described and in section 5 the results are discussed.

## 2   Dependence of events

By definition events $X_1$ and $X_2$ are independent if:

$$P(X_1X_2) = P(X_1) \times P(X_2) \tag{6}$$

The dependence between $X_1$ and $X_2$ is proportional to the difference between $P(X_1) \times P(X_2)$ and $P(X_1X_2)$. In the extreme we have $X_1 = X_2$ where $P(X_1X_2) = P(X_1) = P(X_2)$ or $X_1 = \overline{X_2}$, where $P(X_1X_2) = 0$. We are interested in the conditional dependence of events $X_1$ and $X_2$ with respect to class $C_j$. The events $X_1$ and $X_2$ are independent with respect to $C_j$ if:

$$P(X_1X_2|C_j) = P(X_1|C_j) \times P(X_2|C_j) \tag{7}$$

Again, the dependence between $X_1$ and $X_2$ with respect to $C_j$ is proportional to the difference between $P(X_1|C_j) \times P(X_2|C_j)$ and $P(X_1X_2|C_j)$. In the extreme we have $C_j = X_1 \vee X_2 = (X_1 \neq X_2)$ where $P(X_1X_2|C_j) = 0$ or $C_j = (X_1 = X_2)$ where $P(X_1X_2|C_j) = P(X_1|C_j) = P(X_2|C_j)$.

| A | B | C |
|---|---|---|
| 1 | 1 | 0 |
| 1 | 0 | 1 |
| 0 | 1 | 1 |
| 0 | 0 | 0 |

*Table 1:* XOR

XOR (exclusive 'or', see table 1) is the classical nonlinear problem, that cannot be solved by the naive Bayesian classifier. XOR can be solved in one of the following ways:

- the training examples are stored; such solution is appropriate only if XOR is known in advance to be present in the data and only in exact domains.

- the classes are split into subclasses; this solution has similar constraints like the previous one.

- attributes are joint; this solution seems to be most appropriate for the semi-naive Bayesian classifier as it naturally fits onto the formula, namely $P(C_j|X_1X_2)$ can be used instead of $P(C_j|X_1)$ and $P(C_j|X_2)$ separately. Besides, instead of joining whole attributes, only single values of different attributes can be joint, which is more flexible.

It remains to define the formula for detecting the dependencies between attributes. The following formula, that is valid for every attribute (variable) $A$, $B$ and $C$ could be used (Wan & Wong 1989):

$$H(A|C) + H(B|C) - H(AB|C) \geq 0 \qquad (8)$$

where

$$H(X) = -\sum_j P(X_j) \times log_2 P(X_j)$$

and

$$H(X|Y) = \sum_i P(Y_i) \times H(X|Y_i)$$

$$H(X|Y_i) = -\sum_j P(X_j Y_i) \times log_2 P(X_j Y_i)$$

and where $X_i, i = 1..n$ are possible values of attribute $X$.

The equality in (8) holds if attributes $A$ and $B$ are independent with respect to attribute $C$. In that case $C$ stands for the attribute that represents classes. The dependence of attributes $A$ and $B$ with respect to $C$ is proportional to the value of the left hand-side of (8).

However, eq. (8) cannot detect dependencies between single values of attributes, which could be more useful, as joining attributes' values is more flexible than joining whole attributes. Besides, eq. (8) needs a threshold above which it is useful to join attributes without loosing the reliability of approximations of probabilities. There is no obvious way to obtain such a threshold for optimizing the tradeoff between the 'non-naivety' and the reliability. In next section the formula is designed to include this tradeoff.

## 3  Semi-naive Bayesian classifier

When calculating the probability of class $C_j$ in (2) the influence of attributes $A_i$ and $A_l$ is defined with:

$$\frac{P(C_j|V_{i,J_i})}{P(C_j)} \times \frac{P(C_j|V_{l,J_l})}{P(C_j)} \tag{9}$$

If, instead of assuming the independence of values $V_{i,J_i}$ and $V_{l,J_l}$, the values are joint, the corrected influence is given with:

$$\frac{P(C_j|V_{i,J_i}V_{l,J_l})}{P(C_j)} \tag{10}$$

For joining the two values two conditions should be satisfied: the values of (9) and (10) should be sufficiently different while the approximation of $P(C_j|V_{i,J_i}V_{l,J_l})$ with relative frequency should be sufficiently reliable. For the estimation of the reliability of the probability approximation the theorem of Chebyshev (Vadnal 1979) can be used. The theorem gives the lower bound on the probability, that relative frequency $f$ of an event after $n$ trials differs from the factual prior probability $p$ for less than $\varepsilon$:

$$P(|f - p| \leq \varepsilon) > 1 - \frac{p(1 - p)}{\varepsilon^2 n} \tag{11}$$

The lower bound is proportional to $n$ and to $\varepsilon^2$. In our case we are interested in the reliability of the following approximation:

$$\hat{P}(C_j | V_{i,J_i} V_{l,J_l})) = \frac{N_{C_j V_{i,J_i} V_{l,J_l}}}{N_{V_{i,J_i} V_{l,J_l}}} \tag{12}$$

Therefore the number of trials $n$ in (11) is equal to $N_{V_{i,J_i} V_{l,J_l}}$, i.e. the number of training instances having values $V_{i,J_i}$ and $V_{l,J_l}$ of attributes $A_i$ and $A_l$, respectively. As prior probability $p$ is unknown, in our experiments for approximation of $p$ at the right-hand side of (11) the worst case was assumed, i.e. $p = 0.5$.

It remains to determine the value of $\varepsilon$. As we are interested also if the values of (9) times $P(C_j)$ and (12) are significantly different we will use $\varepsilon$ that is proportional to the difference between the two values. The joint values will influence all classes $C_j, j = 1 \ldots m$. Therefore, $\varepsilon$ will be the average difference between (9) times $P(C_j)$ and (12) over all classes:

$$\varepsilon = \sum_{j=1}^{m} P(C_j) \times \left| P(C_j | V_{i,J_i} V_{l,J_l}) - \frac{P(C_j | V_{i,J_i}) P(C_j | V_{l,J_l})}{P(C_j)} \right| \tag{13}$$

It is necessary to determine the threshold for the probability (11) above which it is useful to join two values of two attributes. In our experiments the threshold was set to 0.5. Therefore, the rule for joining two values states: join two values if the probability is greater than 0.5 that the theoretically correct (unknown) influence of values $V_{i,J_i}$ and $V_{l,J_l}$ differs, in average over all classes, from the used (approximated) influence for less than the difference between used influence and the influence of the two values without joining them:

$$1 - \frac{1}{4\varepsilon^2 N_{V_{i,J_i} V_{l,J_l}}} \geq 0.5 \tag{14}$$

The values can be iteratively joint so that more than two values can be joint together. In our experiments the exhaustive search was used. The number of iterations over the whole training set is approximately equal to the number of values of all attributes. The algorithm is as follows:

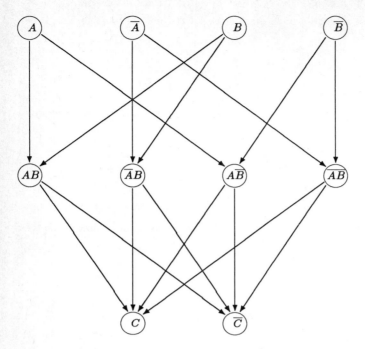

*Figure 1* XOR with 8 training instances (doubled training set) solved with the semi-naive Bayesian classifier.

Determine relative frequencies needed in equation (2);

**for** each value $V_{i,j}$ **do**

  **begin**

    each value $V_{k,l}$ join with $V_{i,j}$;

    from training set determine the relative frequencies for joint values;

    discard the pairs for which $\frac{1}{4e^2 N_{V_{i,J_i} V_{l,J_l}}} > 0.5$

  **end**

XOR as defined in table 1 is solved with the above algorithm by joining four pairs of values as shown on figure 1. However, for reliability of approximation of probabilities 8 training instances are needed obtained by doubling the training set from table 1.

| domain | primary tumor | breast cancer | thyroid | rheum. |
|---|---|---|---|---|
| # instances | 339 | 288 | 884 | 355 |
| # classes | 22 | 2 | 4 | 6 |
| # attributes | 17 | 10 | 15 | 32 |
| aver. # val./attribute | 2.2 | 2.7 | 9.1 | 9.1 |
| aver.# missing data/inst. | 0.7 | 0.1 | 2.7 | 0.0 |
| majority class | 25% | 80% | 56% | 66% |
| entropy (bit) | 3.64 | 0.72 | 1.59 | 1.70 |
| # all values | 59 | 29 | 141 | 298 |
| accuracy of physic. | 42% | 64% | 64% | 56% |

*Table 2*: Characteristics of data sets for four medical diagnostic problems

# 4   Experiments in medical diagnostics

The semi-naive Bayesian classifier, as defined in the previous section, was tested in four medical diagnostic problems: localization of primary tumor, prognostics of breast cancer recurrence, diagnostics of thyroid diseases and rheumatology. The data used in our experiments was obtained from University medical center in Ljubljana. Basic characteristics of four data sets are presented in table 2.

Diagnostic accuracy of physicians is the average of four physicians specialists in each domain from University medical center in Ljubljana tested on randomly selected subsets of patients. The diagnostic accuracy of physicians together with the number of classes and entropy roughly shows the difficulty of a classification problem. The average number of values per attribute together with the number of instances and the number of classes roughly shows the (un)reliability of relative frequencies obtained from data sets.

The percent of instances belonging to the majority class represents the classification accuracy of a simple classifier that classifies each object into the majority class. Such simple classifier

|  | primary tumor (%) (bit) |  | breast cancer (%) (bit) |  | thyroid (%) (bit) |  | rheumatology (%) (bit) |  |
|---|---|---|---|---|---|---|---|---|
| physicians | 42 | 1.22 | 64 | 0.05 | 64 | 0.59 | 56 | 0.26 |
| Assistant | 44 | 1.38 | 77 | 0.07 | 73 | 0.87 | 61 | 0.46 |
| naive Bayes | 51 | 1.58 | 79 | 0.18 | 70 | 0.79 | 67 | 0.51 |
| semi-naive Bayes | 51 | 1.58 | 79 | 0.18 | 71 | 0.81 | 68 | 0.55 |
| # accepted pairs | 0.4 | | 1.5 | | 32.3 | | 17.9 | |

*Table 3:* Results of the semi-naive Bayesian classifier in four medical diagnostic problems compared with the performance of other classifiers.

would significantly outperform physicians in rheumatology (for 10%) and in breast cancer (for 16%). This shows that the classification accuracy is not an appropriate measure for estimating the classification performance. For that reason the *average information score* of classifiers answers as defined in (Kononenko & Bratko 1991) was also measured. This measure eliminates the influence of prior probabilities of classes on the classification performance.

In our experiments the formulas (4) and (5) were used for approximating the probabilities in equation (2). In each experiment the whole data set was randomly split into 70% of instances for learning and 30% of instances for testing. The results in table 3 are averages of 10 experiments in each domain. In the table the number of accepted pairs of attributes' values is also presented. The results are compared with the performance of the naive Bayesian classifier, ID3 like inductive learning system Assistant (Cestnik et al. 1987) and physicians specialists.

It came out that joining of attributes' values in primary tumor and breast cancer is unnecessary as, by the opinion of physicians specialists, the attributes are in fact independent. The results of semi-naive and naive Bayes in these two domains are identical. However, in diagnostics

|  | naive Bayes | semi-naive Bayes | Assistant (non-naive Bayes) |
|---|---|---|---|
| generates | probabilities | probabilities | decision tree |
| knowledge | implicit | implicit | explicit |
| explanation | inf. gains | inf. gains | if-then rule |
| # atts used | all | all | few |
| missing data | insensitive | insensitive | sensitive |
| prob.approx. | reliable | reliable | unreliable |
| independence | assumed | not assumed | not assumed |
| speed | fast | slow | slow |
| incremental | yes | no | no |
| mulival. atts | sensitive | sensitive | insensitive |
| domains | inexact | inexact | exact |

*Table 4:* Characteristics of three classifiers

of thyroid diseases and in rheumatology joining of attribute's values slightly improves the performance.

Assistant achieved better performance in thyroid problem due to the binarization of attributes. In thyroid data most of attributes are continuous having initially 20 subintervals of values (see table 2) which are treated by Bayesian classifier as 20 discrete values. Therefore in the Bayesian classifier the data set is split into 20 subsets when approximating probabilities, which makes the approximation unreliable. On the other hand, in Assistant attributes are binarized (the values of each attribute are joint into two subsets) which leads to increased reliability of the probability approximation.

# 5 Discussion

In table 4 the characteristics of naive, semi-naive Bayes and Assistant (which represents non-naive Bayes, see section 1) are sketched. The generated knowledge by Assistant is in the form of a decision tree while naive and semi-naive Bayes generate probabilities. The top part of a decision tree typically shows the structure of the problem. The decision tree can be used without a computer to classify new objects, therefore it is the kind of *explicit knowledge*. On the other hand, the probabilities generated by naive and semi-naive Bayes cannot be directly used to classify new objects. This kind of knowledge is *implicit*. The physicians found both types of knowledge as interesting and useful information.

The explanation of classification of a new object in Assistant is simply the if-then rule used for the classification while in naive and semi-naive Bayes the explanation is the sum of information gains from all attributes for/against the conclusion. Physicians preferred the sum of information gains as more natural explanation, similar to the way physicians diagnose (Kononenko 1990).

While if-then rules typically include too few attributes for reliable classification (Pirnat et al. 1989), naive and semi-naive Bayes use all available attributes. Besides, learning of decision rules and classification with decision rules is very sensitive to missing data. Missing value of an attribute in naive and semi-naive Bayes is simply ignored.

The major advantage of naive and semi-naive Bayes is reliability of approximation of probabilities. Due to small number of training instances covered by single decision rule the final decision of a rule is unreliable. Pruning of decision trees partially overcomes this problem, however due to pruning rules are shortened and more attributes are discarded from diagnostic process.

If attributes are human defined (as was the case in medical data used in our experiments) attributes are usually relatively independent, as humans tend to think linearly. However, independence assumption is often unrealistic. Semi-naive Bayes overcomes the independence assumption while preserving the reliability of probability approximations. But learning is not as fast as with naive Bayes and it is not incremental. Incremental versions of semi-naive Bayes can be developed similarly to incremental versions of ID3 (Van de Velde 1989).

Assistant with on-line binarization of attributes successfully solves the problem of continuous and multivalued attributes (as shown in the case of thyroid diseases, see table 3). The naive Bayesian classifier assumes that all attributes are discrete. Therefore, continuous attributes must be converted to discrete by introducing a number of fixed bounds, loosing the integrity of training set and the order of values. The semi-naive Bayesian classifier is unable to join values of the same attribute in order to keep the training instances together for more reliable approximation of probabilities. There are two possibilities to overcome that problem:

- The use of XOR for joining the values of attributes besides AND as used in the algorithm described in section 3. XOR should join values $V_{i,l}$ and $V_{i,k}$ with similar $P(C_j|V_{i,l})$ and $P(C_j|V_{i,k})$. and small $N_{V_{i,l}}$ and/or $N_{V_{i,k}}$. Therefore, the aim of joining with XOR is opposite to that with AND: increasing the reliability of approximation of probabilities while unchanging the influence of attribute's values.

- The use of fuzzy bounds for continuous attributes can overcome both the loss of the information about the order of values as well as the loss of integrity of training set.

Semi-naive Bayes tries to optimize the tradeoff between the 'non-naivety' and the reliability of probability approximations. By lowering the threshold in (14) the reliability of probability approximations decreases and the 'non-naivety' increases, which can be useful for *exact* domains. For *inexact* (fuzzy) domains the threshold should be higher. Naive Bayes is due to independence assumption more appropriate for inexact domains while Assistant is appropriate for exact domains with, ideally, complete set of attributes *and* complete set of training instances.

An expert system shell based on the semi-naive Bayesian classifier can provide a useful tool for generating expert systems in domains, where training data is available. Dependencies between attributes can be determined automatically or, in case where there is not enough training instances for reliable probability approximations, the dependencies can be provided by human experts. Human expert can be consulted to determine also prior probabilities if not enough training data is available. The explanation ability of such a system seems powerful enough to assist experts or non-experts in their everyday work.

# Acknowledgements

Collecting and assembling the experimental data would not be possible without the invaluable help of physicians specialists Dr. Matjaž Zwitter, Dr. Sergej Hojker and Dr. Vlado Pirnat from the University Medical Center in Ljubljana. I thank them for providing and interpreting the data, for testing the diagnostic performance of physicians specialists from the University Medical Center, for the interpretation of results and for the estimation of the explanation abilities of the naive Bayesian classifier. I am grateful to Padhraic Smyth for his comments on the manuscript. This research was supported by Slovenian Research Community. The reported work was done in the Artificial Intelligence Laboratory at the Faculty of Electrical and Computer Engineering in Ljubljana. I would like to thank Prof. Ivan Bratko for providing the environment for efficient scientific work.

# References

Cestnik B. (1990) Estimating Probabilities: A Crucial Task in Machine Learning, *Proc. European Conference on Artificial Intelligence 90*, Stockholm, August 1990.

Cestnik, B., Kononenko, I., Bratko, I. (1987) ASSISTANT 86 : A Knowledge Elicitation Tool for Sophisticated Users. In: I. Bratko, N. Lavrač (eds.), *Progress in Machine learning*. Wilmslow, England: Sigma Press.

Good I.J. (1950) *Probability and the weighing of evidence.* London: Charles Griffin.

Kononenko, I. (1989) ID3, sequential Bayes, naive Bayes and Bayesian neural networks. *Proc. 4th European Working Session on Learning*, Montpellier, France, December 1989, pp.91-98.

Kononenko, I. (1990) Comparison of inductive and naive Bayesian learning approaches to automatic knowledge acquisition. In: B. Wielinga et al. (eds.) *Current Trends in Knowledge Acquisition*, Amsterdam: IOS Press.

Kononenko, I. & Bratko, I. (1991) Information Based Evaluation Criterion for Classifier's Performance. *Machine Learning*, Vol.6, pp.67-80 (in press).

Pirnat V., Kononenko I., Janc T., Bratko I. (1989) Medical Estimation of Automatically Induced Decision Rules, *Proc. of 2nd Europ. Conf. on Artificial Intelligence in Medicine*, City University, London, August 29-31 1989, pp.24-36.

Smyth P. & Goodman R.M. (1990) Rule Induction Using Information Theory. In: G.Piarersky

& W.Frawley (eds.) *Knowledge Discovery in Databases*, MIT Press.

Vadnal A. (1979) *Elementary Introduction to Probability Calculus* (in Slovene), Državna založba Slovenije, Ljubljana.

Van de Velde (1989) IDL, or Taming the Multiplexer, *Proc. 4th European Working Session on Learning*, Montpellier, France, December 1989, pp.211-225.

Wan S.J. & Wong S.K.M. (1989) A Measure for Concept Dissimilarity and its Applications in Machine Learning, *Proc. Int. Conf. on Computing and Information*, Toronto North, Canada, May 23-27 1989.

# DESCRIPTION CONTRASTING
## in
# INCREMENTAL CONCEPT FORMATION

Christine DECAESTECKER[*]

CADEPS Artificial Intelligence Research Unit, Université Libre de Bruxelles
Av. F.D.Roosevelt 50, C.P. 194/7, B-1050, Brussels, Belgium
Tel (+ 32 2) 650 2783; Email CADEPS@BBRNSF11(.BITNET)

**ABSTRACT**

This study evaluates the impact of concept descriptions on the behaviour and performance of concept formation processes (in which the data is either noisy or noise-free). Using a common architecture (ADECLU), different concept definitions are envisaged. These descriptions are of symbolic/numeric type, including statistical indices. The use of these indices introduces a "contrasting" between concept descriptions and reduces the effect of noise on predictive performance.

**KEYWORDS :**  Concept Formation, Incremental Conceptual Clustering, Attribute selection, Typical value.

## 1. INTRODUCTION

The general aim of incremental concept formation (Gennari & al, 1989) is to construct (on the basis of sequentially presented object descriptions) a (hierarchical) classification of objects where each class is provided with a definition which summarises its elements. Further aims are to condense (to summarise) information, to use the knowledge thus obtained to classify new objects, and to make predictions concerning unknown values of the objects. Thus, the performance of the acquired hierarchies is (predominantly) measured in terms of their ability to make predictions concerning unknown attributes. This ability is usually called the *"predictive power"* of the hierarchies (Gennari & al, 1989).

[*] This work is supported by the Belgian National incentive-program for fundamental research in Artificial Intelligence. The scientific responsibility is assumed by the author.

In earlier work (Decaestecker, 1989a,b), the author studied Incremental Concept Formation and developed ADECLU, an incremental hierarchical Conceptual Clustering system, which extends ideas from UNIMEM (Lebowitz, 1987) and COBWEB (Fisher, 1987). The aim of our research was to propose a process which selects attributes which best describe a concept.

A simple version (ADECLU1) (Decaestecker, 1989a) keeps only those characteristics which are common to the objects of the same class. A second version (ADECLU2)(Decaestecker, 1989b) keeps for each class, all the values observed, but uses association criterion from Data Analysis (especially the Goodman-Kruskal "Lambda" index), to select combinations of attributes which are more appropriate to describe a concept.

A new version (ADECLU/S) improves concept description by selecting, for each attribute, a set of typical values from all the values observed in the concept. The general aim is to obtain "contrasted" concept descriptions. This selection of typical values is also based on the optimisation of a statistical index (which guarantees good statistical properties to the selected values), and occurs together with the selection of the characteristics already used in ADECLU2. We observe that ADECLU/S seems better than ADECLU2, in recognizing and differentiating concepts with inter-class proximity (i.e. the elements of one class are close to the elements of another class), for which description contrasting is then useful. In this paper, we wish to show the influence of the knowledge representation (i.e. the concept descriptions) on the predictive power of the hierarchies produced by incremental processes such as ADECLU, in the presence and absence of noise in the data. Another point already mentioned in (Decaestecker, 1989a,b & 1990), concerns the quality of classification of the data (from the point of view of traditional Data Analysis).

Section 2 proposes a general description of ADECLU. In section 3, the formalism is specified for each of the 3 versions. This section aims to clarify the evolution of the knowledge representation between the different versions, as well as their inherent statistical properties. Section 4 clarifies a "cutoff" technique of the hierarchy. Section 5 presents the results obtained in the absence and present of noise for the different versions.

# 2. GENERAL DESCRIPTION

In this section, we recall the different characteristics of ADECLU, in a general formalism which is suitable for the 3 versions.

## 2.0 Description and Organisation of the Objects

The objects are described by a conjunction of attribute/value pairs. We will only treat qualitative attributes (or data translated into this qualitative format).

ADECLU organises a series of objects presented sequentially, into a hierarchy in which each node represents a concept and its description (only those descriptions occuring in the classification operation). The set of objects classified under a concept $C$ is partitioned into the subconcepts of $C$.

## 2.1 Description of the Concepts

Each concept is described by a conjunction of characteristics, where :

$$\text{characteristic} = \text{quadruplet} : (j, V_j, {}^cV_j, w_j)$$

where  $j$  is the attribute.

   $V_j$  is the set of values (of the attribute $j$) retained to describe (the objects integrated into) the concept.

   ${}^cV_j$  is the set of values (of the attribute $j$) observed in the concept but not retained to describe it.

   $w_j$  is the weight ($0 \leq w_j \leq 1$) which is a function of the information added by the characteristic to the concept definition. This weighting, called *"relevance"* of the characteristic, is expected to vary during the incremental process.

Later, we shall specify this general formalism for each of the versions of ADECLU. We shall see that for the first two versions (ADECLU1 and ADECLU2), the selection of $V_j$ is arbitrary (but consistent with common sense). However, the third version (ADECLU/S) performs a "statistical" selection of the values (called "typical") for the concept considered.

ADECLU is also characterised by its selection of conjunctions of relevant characteristics to describe a concept. This selection of attributes is realized by the weights $w_j$ which distinguish the *relevant* characteristics ($w_j > 0$) for classification and prediction, from the characteristics which are merely *descriptive* ($w_j = 0$). This selection is arbitrary in ADECLU1 and "statistical" in ADECLU2 and ADECLU/S. Hence the concepts provided by these two version can be labelled "*statistical*". They offer an interesting alternative to "probabilistic" concepts. The probabilistic concepts produced by COBWEB incorporate in the concept description, the conditional probabilities $P(O \in C \mid j(O) = v)$ and $P(j(O) = v \mid O \in C)$ ("predictiveness" and "predictability" of a value $v$ for a concept $C$) for each value of each attribute. As we shall see (section 3.2), the weights $w_j$ condenses these two notions and generalises them to the set $V_j$ of selected values for an attribute $j$ in a concept $C$. One advantage of this quality measure is the possibility to eliminate the inadequate internal disjunctions in a concept description ($w_j = 0$). An other is to can construct an internal disjunction of possible (but not all) values which optimises this measure. This possibility to increase the relevance of the characteristics, has motivated the selection of typical values in ADECLU/S.

## 2.2 Suitability criterion (evaluation function)

As with most Concept Formation systems (Fisher, 1987; Gennari & al, 1989), ADECLU uses a hill climbing search strategy in a space of concept hierarchies. When a new object $O$ is presented, a search is undertaken to find the most specific concept to classify the new object, based on the descriptions of the different concepts (partial matching). At each level of the hierarchy, a series of operators (creation, split, merge) is applied to an initial partition. The resulting partitions are compared using an evaluation function. The best concept and the corresponding partition are selected. Then, the process recurses for the subconcepts of the concept selected at the previous step.

We now present the evaluation function (used in ADECLU) called the *Suitability Criterion*. It is a context-dependent measure which is a function of the object description, the concept description and the partition which contains the concept.

**Definition :**     The suitability $S$ between an object $O$ and a concept $C_l$ of a partition $P$, is defined as follows:

$$S(O,C_l,P) = sc(O,C_l,P) - \sum_{k \neq l} sc(O,C_k,P)$$

where     the score $sc$ between an object $O$ and a concept $C_l$ is defined as

$$sc(O,C_l,P) = f(|C_l|) \sum_j p^O_{jl} w_{jl}$$

with     $f(|C_l|)$:   a function of the cardinal of $C_l$ (i.e. the number of objects in $C_l$ )

$w_{jl}$ :   the weighting of the characteristic $(j, V_{jl}, {}^cV_{jl}, w_{jl})$

$p^O_{jl}$ :   the matching factor which takes the value +1 or 0 or -1, depending on whether the attribute value of $O$ (i.e. $j(O)$) and the attribute value of $C_l$ ($V_{jl} \cup {}^cV_{jl}$), agree ($j(O) \in V_{jl}$) or are indifferent ($j(O) \in {}^cV_{jl}$) or disagree ($j(O) \notin (V_{jl} \cup {}^cV_{jl})$).

The factor $f(|C_l|)$ can take different forms. Details concerning its use and its effect on ADECLU2 can be found in (Decaestecker, 1989b).

# 3. EVOLUTION of the KNOWLEDGE REPRESENTATION

## 3.1 Specialising the general formalism for the different versions

The TABLE 1 below shows the general formalism introduced earlier, for each of the 3 versions of ADECLU.

| | $V_j$ | ${}^cV_j$ | $w_j$ |
|---|---|---|---|
| ADECLU1 | $\bigcap_{O \in C} j(O)$ | $\{ \bigcup_{O \in C} j(O)\} \setminus V_j$ | 0   if $V_j = \emptyset$<br>1   otherwise |
| ADECLU2 | $\bigcup_{O \in C} j(O)$ | $\emptyset$ | $L(V_j,C)$ |
| ADECLU/S | typical set | $\{ \bigcup_{O \in C} j(O)\} \setminus V_j$ | $L(V_j,C)$ |

TABLE 1 : 3 versions of ADECLU

ADECLU1 is the simplest of the versions, which initially can be used to show and to test the incremental strategy and the adequacy criterion presented in section 2.2. This simplified form produces good results on noise-free data (see section 5 and (Decaestecker, 1989a)), which justifies the general principles controlling the use of ADECLU. In ADECLU1, each concept $C$ is simply defined by a conjunction of characteristics which are common to all its objects (with inheritance rule).

In ADECLU2, the description of concepts becomes more general and allows multivalued characteristics, defined simply by the values observed in the concept, for a given attribute. The weights $w_j$, in the definition of the concept $C$ will reflect the degrees of association (in the Data Analytic sense (Andeberg, 1973)) which exist between the attribute $j$ (more precisely the subset of observed values) and the fact of belonging to the concept $C$ considered (cf section 3.2).

In the new version ADECLU/S, we introduce the notion of "typical values" from the values observed in the concept. The aim is to select, in each characteristic of a concept, a subset of typical values ($V_j$) which maximally "contrasts" the descriptions of "sybling" concepts (i.e. having the same parent in the hierarchy produced by ADECLU). The typicality of a value for a concept implies the notion of "distinctiveness" for this concept, i.e. that it will be observed in the majority of cases (with a superior frequency) in the concept relative to the others. This selection of values aims to increase the relevance of the characteristic and is based on a simple statistical index (cf section 3.3). With respect to the general formalism introduced in 2.1, only ADECLU/S actually uses $^cV_j$.

Both ADECLU2 and ADECLU/S use the value of an association criterion such as the definition of $w_j$. This criterion is the Lambda index of Goodman et Kruskal (represented as $L(V_j,C)$) between the memberships of $V_j$ and $C$ (cf section 3.2). This index seemed adequate to "summarise" two important aspects in the concept formation process, i.e. "classification" and "prediction of unknown values" (cf (Gennari & al, 1989)). More precisely, we are interested in:

1. the prediction that an object belongs to a concept $C$, given attribute values (for the classification of a new object)
2. the prediction that attributes have certain values, given that the object belongs to a concept $C$ (for the prediction of unknown values)

We will see in the following section how the Lambda index (a symmetric optimal class prediction index) meets these requirements. We will study it in the more general case of ADECLU/S, where not all the observed values are kept to describe a concept. (The definitions and properties presented in this paper, generalize those of ADECLU2 presented in (Decaestecker, 1989b)).

## 3.2 Selection of relevant characteristics (ADECLU2 and ADECLU/S)

Goodman and Kruskal (1954) suggested measuring the association between two variables X and Y by the *predictive power* of one variable as a predictor of the other and is defined as the relative decrease in the probability of error (in the prediction of $Y$), due to knowledge of the value of $X$. If the prediction of the value of $X$ from $Y$ is as important in the model as $Y$ from $X$, then these authors propose a symmetric relationship, by considering the prediction of $X$ half the time, and $Y$ the other half.

The probabilistic model is described in detail in (Goodman & al, 1954). The essence is as follows: For an object chosen at random in the population, one must predict at best, either the value of $X$ or the value of $Y$ (at random, with equal probabilities), given (case 1) no information or (case 2) the value of the other variable for this object (the value of $X$ to predict $Y$ and vice versa).

**Definition :** (Goodman & al, 1954)

$$\lambda = \frac{\text{(Prob. of error in case 1)} - \text{(Prob. of error in case 2)}}{\text{(Prob. of error in case 1)}}$$

If one only has a sample of the population (which is the case with incremental processes), one can estimate the value of $\lambda$ from the contingency table between $X$ and $Y$ (table of absolute frequencies) from the sample :

matrix $(n_{ij})_{pxq}$ where $n_{ij}$ is the number of objects for which $X = x_i$ and $Y = y_j$
with the marginal distributions $(n_{i.})$ and $(n_{.j})$ where $n_{i.} = \sum_j n_{ij}$ and $n_{.j} = \sum_i n_{ij}$

The maximum likelihood estimator of $\lambda$ between $X$ and $Y$ is :

$$L = \frac{\sum_i (\max_j n_{ij}) + \sum_j (\max_i n_{ij}) - (\max_j n_{.j}) - (\max_i n_{i.})}{2\, n_{..} - (\max_j n_{.j}) - (\max_i n_{i.})}$$

In ADECLU2 and /S, we define the *relevance* $(w_j)$ of the characteristics (when describing a concept) by the measure of the $L$ indices between each attribute $j$ and the membership of each concept $C$. Since we are dealing with incremental processes, we estimate, at each instant, the indices $\lambda$ for the objects already processed (integrated into the hierarchy). Since these processes are subject to numerous updates, we estimate $\lambda$ with a simplified 2x2 contingency table (see TABLE 2), between the variable "belonging to the concept" ($O \in C$ ?) and the variable "belonging to the set of values $V_j$ in $C$ for the attribute $j$ ($j(O) \in V_j$ ?). In a hierarchical organisation, the set of objects which will be used as a reference to measure the association criterion (and on which will be constructed the contingency table), will consist only of those objects integrated into the parent of the concept $C$ being considered.

In conclusion, for each characteristic of concept $C$, we will study the following contingency table :

| $j(O) \in V_j$ :<br>$O \in C$ : | yes | no | TOTAL |
|---|---|---|---|
| yes | $|C|-v$ | $v$ | $|C|$ |
| no | $N1-(|C|-v)$ | $N-N1-v$ | $N-|C|$ |
| TOTAL | $N1$ | $N-N1$ | $N$ |

where $|C|$ is the cardinal (card) of $C$ (i.e. the number of objects in $C$), $N$ is the card of the parent concept of $C$, $N1$ is the number of objects of the parent concept which match $j = V_j$ and $v$ is the number of objects of $C$ with $j(O) \notin V_j$.

TABLE 2 : Contingency table

The weight $w_j$ is then the estimation $L$ of the Lambda index applied to TABLE 2 :

$$w_j \equiv L = \frac{\max\,(|C|-v,\,v) + \max\,(N1-|C|+v,\,N-N1-v) + \max\,(|C|-v,\,N1-|C|+v) + \max\,(v,\,N-N1-v) - K}{2N - K}$$

where $K = \max\,(N1,\,N-N1) + \max\,(|C|,\,N-|C|)$

$w_j$ therefore measures the increase in good prediction of "$\in C$" or "$\in V_j$", given the knowledge of the other variable, relative to the absence of any information.

Property 3.1 below guides the choice of $L$, among the possible criteria.

**Property 3.1** : (2x2 table)

We have $L=1$ in the case of *"perfect association"* and *"perfect anti-association"* where the 2x2 tables have respectively the following forms :

| $a$ | $0$ |
|---|---|
| $0$ | $d$ |

association

| $0$ | $b$ |
|---|---|
| $c$ | $0$ |

anti-association

We have $L>0$ in the cases of "good" association or "good" anti-association where :

$$
\begin{array}{cc}
a \,>\, b & \qquad a \,<\, b \\
\vee \quad \wedge & \qquad \wedge \quad \vee \\
c \,<\, d & \qquad c \,>\, d
\end{array}
$$

$(a>b\,,a>c\,,d>c\,,d>b)$  
association

$(b>a\,,b>d\,,c>a\,,c>d)$  
anti-association

Also, $L > 0$ when one (and only one) of these relations is false.

We have $L=0$ when two of these relations are false. There are 4 possibilities (having the same relations in the two rows and in the two columns where, at most, two equalities are satisfied) which generalize the cases of independence (i.e. those having the same multiplicative factor between the two rows and between the two columns):

$$
\begin{array}{cccc}
a \le b & \quad a \ge b & \quad a \ge b & \quad a \le b \\
\wedge \quad \wedge & \quad \wedge \quad \wedge & \quad \vee \quad \vee & \quad \vee \quad \vee \\
c \le d & \quad c \ge d & \quad c \ge d & \quad c \le d
\end{array}
$$

The proof can be obtained by application of the definition of $L$.

Consequences for $w_j$ :

For each characteristic $(j,\,V_j,\,{}^cV_j,\,w_j)$ of a concept $C$,

$w_j = 1$     when $j = V_j\,(j \neq V_j)$ is a discriminating characteristic of $C$.

$w_j > 0$     explains (in the cases of association) a general tendency of the $C$ elements to have $j(O)$ in $V_j$ in contrast to the general tendency of the other elements (not in $C$) to have the value $j(O)$ out of $V_j$.

$w_j = 0$ when , for example,

a) $P(j(O) \in V_j \mid O \in C) \le 1/2$ and $P(O \in C \mid j(O) \in V_j) \le 1/2$

b) $P(j(O) \notin V_j \mid O \notin C) \le 1/2$ and $P(O \in C \mid j(O) \in V_j) \le 1/2$

c) $P(j(O) \notin V_j \mid O \notin C) \le 1/2$ and $P(O \notin C \mid j(O) \in V_j) \le 1/2$

d) $P(j(O) \in V_j \mid O \in C) \le 1/2$ and $P(O \notin C \mid j(O) \notin V_j) \le 1/2$

When $w_j = 0$, it is fully justifiable to eliminate the characteristic relative to the attribute $j$ from the definition of the concept $C$, because this characteristic is not relevant to the object classification nor to the attribute value prediction. Thus a characteristic of weight zero is not taken into account in the calculation of the score measuring the degree of "matching" between a new object and the concept being considered.

We must now distinguish (for $w > 0$) the cases of association from the cases of anti-association (between the two variables "$\in C$" and "$\in V_j$"). Since in ADECLU, the set $V_j$ is formed from the observed values of attribute $j$ in concept $C$, we will construct a set $V_j$ "in association" with the concept $C$. But, in ADECLU2, there are no "anti-association" cases, because the value set $V_j$ collects all the observed values and therefore the quantity "$v$" (of TABLE 2) is zero. In ADECLU/S, the selection of a set $V_j$ in association with $C$ is assured by the selection strategy itself.

### 3.3 Selection strategy of typical values in ADECLU/S

As announced in section 2.1, the selection values aims to increase the relevance of the characteristics. In TABLE 2 which defines the relevance $w_j$ of a characteristic, this motivation correspond to construct a set $V_j$ for which the quantities $v$ and $N_1-(|C|-v)$ are as smaller as possible. This notion can be assimilated to the notion of "contrast" between concept descriptions.

The contrast between a concept $C$ and its sibling concepts, with respect to the attribute $j$, is estimated by an index which is also defined using TABLE 2. This index (defined below) is called the "jContrast" (or simply $jC$) and is related to the Lambda index $w_j$. The jContrast is also the numerator of a measure credited to Hamann (Andeberg, 1973).

**Definition :**

| $j(O) \in V_j :$ <br> $O \in C :$ | yes | no | TOTAL |
|---|---|---|---|
| yes | $a$ | $b$ | $\|C\|$ |
| no | $c$ | $d$ | $N-\|C\|$ |
| TOTAL | $N1$ | $N-N1$ | $N$ |

where $a = |C|-v$
$b = v$
$c = N1-|C|+v$
$d = N-N1-v$

$$jContrast = 1/2\,[(a-b) + (a-c) + (d-b) + (d-c)] = a+d-b-c$$
$$= N + 2\,|C| - 2\,N1 - 4\,v$$

The aim of value selection is to construct (for each attribute $j$) a set $V_j$ for which jContrast ($jC$) is maximum. One can see (by a simple but long calculation) that the optimization of $jC$ corresponds generally with an increase of $w_j$. We have favoured the optimization of $jC$ because it can be made easily and economically in the incremental process and gives, for each set $V_j$ of selected values, good statistical properties.

We present now two properties of the jContrast index. The first shows that the sign of $jC$ characterises the type of association in a 2x2 table. The second guides the optimisation of $jC$ and characterises (see corollary) the set $V_j$ finally selected by ADECLU/S. For more details and proofs, see (Decaestecker, 1990).

## Property 3.2 :

For the 2x2 table before, we have:

| | | | |
|---|---|---|---|
| $jC = 0$ | when | $a + d = b + c$ | in the case of "indetermination" |
| $jC > 0$ | when | $a + d > b + c$ | in the case of "association" |
| $jC$ max $(= N)$ | when | $b + c = 0$ | in the case of "perfect association" |
| $jC < 0$ | when | $a + d < b + c$ | in the case of "anti-association" |
| $jC$ min $(= -N)$ | when | $a + d = 0$ | in the case of "perfect anti-association" |

## Property 3.3 :

Let $P$ be a set of disjoint concepts (a partition), and $C$ a concept of $P$.
For each characteristic $(j, V_j, {}^cV_j, w_j)$ of $C$,     if $jC \geq 0$,

the transfer of a value $k$ of ${}^cV_j$ to $V_j$ , increases the $jC$ value if
"frequency of $k$ in $C$" > "frequency of $k$ in $P\backslash\{C\}$"

the transfer of a value $k$ of $V_j$ to ${}^cV_j$ , increases the $jC$ value if
"frequency of $k$ in $C$" < "frequency of $k$ in $P\backslash\{C\}$"

**Definition :**     For each attribute $j$ found in the description of a concept $C$, we assert that :
The selected set of values $V_j$ or the division of the observed values by the pair $(V_j, {}^cV_j)$ is *optimal*, if the corresponding $jC$ is maximum for this selection of values in the total set of observed values (of $j$ in $C$).

## Corollary of Property 3.3 :

If $(V_j, {}^cV_j)$ is *optimal* then each selected value $k$ ($\in V_j$) verifies :
"frequency of $k$ in $C$" > "frequency of $k$ in $P\backslash\{C\}$"

which implies that (with $K$ the number of concepts in partition $P$) :
"frequency of $k$ in C" > $K/2$ "average frequency of $k$ in a concept of $P$"

and more particularly
"frequency of $k$ in $C$" = MAX ("frequency of $k$ in $C'$ ")     (with $C' \in P$)

Let $O$ be the new object that we have to classify, and let $(C, P)$ be the pair for which (at the level considered) the suitability $S(O, C, P)$ is maximum. Thus ADECLU/S integrates the object $O$ into concept $C$

(of the partition $P$). ADECLU/S must then adapt the description of $C$ i.e. for each characteristic, the value set $V_j$ and the weight $w_j$ must be adjusted.

For each characteristic $(j, V_j, {}^cV_j, w_j)$ and the corresponding value $j(O)$ of $O$,

if $j(O) \in V_j$:      first,    we can leave $V_j$ as it is,

                     and then,    transfer OR not $j(O)$ from $V_j$ to ${}^cV_j$

if $j(O) \notin V_j$:      first,    we can leave $V_j$ as it is and insert $j(O)$ into ${}^cV_j$ (if $j(O) \notin {}^cV_j$),

                     and then,    transfer OR not $j(O)$ from ${}^cV_j$ to $V_j$

We chose the case with jContrast maximum (and positive). It suffices to adjust the frequency of $j(O)$ in $C$ and to effect the transfer if the corresponding inequality of property 3.3 is satisfied. Then the quantities $|C|$, $N1$, $v$ are also updated and $w_j$ can be calculated for the resulting typical set. In each sybling concept $C'$ of $P\backslash\{C\}$, if $j(O) \in V_{jC'}$ and if the second inequality of property 3.3. is satisfied, then $j(O)$ must be transferred to ${}^cV_{jC'}$ (and the corresponding quantities $N1$ and $v$ adjusted). In (Decaestecker, 1990), can be found more details of this strategy. It occurs by simple transfer between $V_j$ and ${}^cV_j$ (for the concept considered <u>and</u> the sybling concepts) where the property 3.3 guides the choice.

## 4. CUTOFF IN THE CLASSIFICATION

In real world applications, a system which stores every object builds too large a hierarchy (to each object, corresponds a leaf of the hierarchy). Exhaustive trees, can have negative properties in noisy domains (Quinlan, 1986). To limit the number of concepts, several authors (e.g. (Gennari & al, 1989)) propose cutting the hierarchy. When the description of the object is similar enough to the description of the concept in which the object is classified, future descent (into subconcepts) is unnecessary, because enough information is already found in the concept description. In ADECLU(2 and /S), this possibility can be detected using the score function $sc(O,C,P)$. The rule is the following:

Let $(C, P)$ be the pair which optimizes the suitability criterion $S(O, C, P)$. Thus ADECLU integrates the object $O$ into the concept $C$ (of the partition $P$). Afterwards, we:

**"STOP DESCENT in the hierarchy IF"** :

$$\frac{sc(O,C,P)}{f(|C|)} \quad > \quad \text{"cutoff"} \ \#C$$

where $\#C$ is the total number of characteristics (with $w \geq 0$) in $C$

The left term of this inequality has a high value when :

1) the number of characteristics (with $w_j \neq 0$) which match between the descriptions of the object and the concept (i.e. $j(O) \in V_j$) is high.

2) $\#_{w\neq0}C$ (the number of characteristics in $C$ with $w_j \neq 0$) is high

3) the characteristics of $C$ are discriminant ($w_j \approx 1$).

The value of "$\#_{w \neq 0} C / \#C$" gives the percentage of characteristics which supply useful information to the concept description. If this percentage is small, few attributes are used at this level and it is thus necessary to pursue the specification of this concept. Thus the conditions 2) and 3) are satisfied when the concept description is *specific* and *contrasted* enough with respect to the other concepts. Examples (see (Decaestecker, 1990)) suggest taking a cutoff value of 0.5.

When the descent is stopped in $C$, the object $O$ is integrated into $C$, but not into its sub-concepts. At a later stage in the incremental process, the definition of $C$ and its location in the hierarchy can be changed. It would then be possible to continue (if necessary) the classification of $O$ into the lower levels of the concept hierarchy.

## 5. PREDICTIVE POWER (with and without NOISE)

Recall two principal aims of Concept Formation :
  – to condense (to summarise) information
  – to use this information to predict unknown values

The evaluation procedure to measure the predictive power (ability to make predictions concerning unknown attributes) of the hierarchies produced by Concept Formation systems, is inspired from the methods of supervised learning. (For further details, see (Fisher, 1987)(Gennari & al, 1989)). The system incorporates a number of cases (the so-called training set) of a data base. A hierarchy of concepts is thus created and will be used later to classify the remaining cases (the so-called test set), which do not include the value of one attribute. The value of this attribute is inferred from the result of the classification, by predicting the value taken from the concept into which the test case was classified. One can then calculate the percentage of correct predictions as a function of the number of cases present in the training set.

To investigate the effects of noise (i.e here, the incorrect reporting of an attribute's value) on the performances of ADECLU, we begin by randomly replacing attribute values in all the data base, with a fixed probability (e.g 25%). Then ADECLU is submitted to the same experiments as described before.

We will perform experiments on 4 classes (4 x 17 cases of 50 attributes), extracted from a data base of soybean diseases (Michalski & al, 1980). TABLES 3 and 4 below present the percentages of good predictions for the attribute $CL$ indicating the membership of one of the four classes, and the attribute $X8$, which is more difficult to predict in the presence of noise. The second data base studied has 140 descriptions of mushrooms classed according to degree of edibility. The third data base has 148 examples from the lymphography domain[1] with 4 possible final diagnostic classes. This data set was not submitted to a detailed checking and thus may contain errors in attribute values. TABLES 5 and 6 below present the percentages of good predictions for the attribute $CL$ indicating the membership of one of the different classes.

These predictions have been made either with or without noise in the data. The experiments have been repeated several times on each data base presented in different orders. The tables before summarise the

---

[1] The data was obtained from the University Medical Centre, Institute of Oncology, Ljubljana, Yugoslavia.

performances obtained, indicating, for each version, the average of the results as a function of the cardinal of the "training set".

To better visualise the effect of the selection of attributes, an other version of ADECLU was introduced (called ADECLU1-2) where all the weights $w_j$ of ADECLU2 are fixed at 1.0 (no selection of relevant characteristics). Note that this version gives worse results and its performance becomes mediocre in the presence of noise. ADECLU1 performs very well in the absence of noise, but its performance degrades in the presence of noise. This degradation increases with the growth of the training set (and therefor with the introduction of noise). The versions which behave the best, in the two cases, are ADECLU2 and ADECLU/S with a slight superiority of ADECLU/S for larger training sets (where "typicality" can be found and can play its role). The "statistical" selection of relevant attributes and of typical values, thus appears to be beneficial in its ability to predict unknown values.

| card of training set: | 5 | 10 | 15 | 20 | 25 | 30 |
|---|---|---|---|---|---|---|
| *WITHOUT NOISE* | | | | | | |
| ADECLU1: | 88 | 87 | 90 | 92 | 94 | 91 |
| ADECLU1-2: | 94 | 78 | 84 | 81 | 88 | 83 |
| ADECLU2: | 91 | 91 | 92 | 91 | 92 | 91 |
| ADECLU/S: | 90 | 87 | **98** | **97** | **95** | **97** |
| *25% of NOISE* | | | | | | |
| ADECLU1: | 85 | 80 | 81 | 78 | 80 | 76 |
| ADECLU1-2: | 85 | 55 | 56 | 56 | 55 | 54 |
| ADECLU2: | 85 | 85 | 87 | 78 | 79 | 80 |
| ADECLU/S: | 85 | 74 | 76 | **80** | **80** | **82** |

TABLE 3 : % (average) of good predictions
Data base "Soya", attribute *CL*

| card of training set: | 5 | 10 | 15 | 20 | 25 | 30 |
|---|---|---|---|---|---|---|
| *WITHOUT NOISE* | | | | | | |
| ADECLU1: | 83 | 92 | 93 | 94 | 92 | 91 |
| ADECLU1-2: | 83 | 88 | 81 | 83 | 84 | 72 |
| ADECLU2: | 84 | 89 | 95 | 90 | 97 | 95 |
| ADECLU/S: | 83 | 90 | 91 | **92** | **98** | **97** |
| *25% of NOISE* | | | | | | |
| ADECLU1: | 55 | 64 | 60 | 60 | 57 | 60 |
| ADECLU1-2: | 55 | 61 | 62 | 51 | 51 | 49 |
| ADECLU2: | 54 | 62 | 63 | 70 | 61 | 68 |
| ADECLU/S: | 54 | 62 | 62 | 67 | **65** | **69** |

TABLE 4 : % (average) of good predictions
Data base "Soya", attribute *X8*

| card of training set: | 20 | 40 | 60 | 80 | 100 |
|---|---|---|---|---|---|
| *WITHOUT NOISE* | | | | | |
| ADECLU1: | 63 | 78 | 84 | 74 | 80 |
| ADECLU1-2: | 58 | 56 | 58 | 54 | 54 |
| ADECLU2: | 68 | 82 | 79 | 89 | 87 |
| ADECLU/S: | 72 | 77 | 75 | 80 | **88** |
| *25% of NOISE* | | | | | |
| ADECLU1: | 48 | 55 | 45 | 46 | 59 |
| ADECLU1-2: | 35 | 41 | 25 | 38 | 37 |
| ADECLU2: | 48 | 60 | 65 | 69 | **69** |
| ADECLU/S: | 53 | 59 | 60 | 62 | **69** |

TABLE 5 : % (average) of good predictions
Data base "Mushroom", attribute *CL*

| card of training set: | 20 | 40 | 60 | 80 | 100 |
|---|---|---|---|---|---|
| *WITH NOISE* | | | | | |
| ADECLU1: | 66 | 63 | 69 | 66 | 69 |
| ADECLU1-2: | 61 | 56 | 67 | 60 | 67 |
| ADECLU2: | 67 | 76 | 73 | 71 | **73,6** |
| ADECLU/S: | 63 | 66 | 67 | 68 | **74,3** |

TABLE 6 : % (average ) of good predictions
Data base "Lympho", attribute *CL*

## 6. CONCLUSIONS and FUTURE DIRECTIONS

A central idea in ADECLU is that of "contrast". It occurs in the definition of the evaluation criterion and in the representation of concepts. In fact, a concept is an entity which is defined not only by its own characteristics, but also by contrasting it with other concepts of the partition. Thus, to test the hypothesis that an object $O$ must be attributed to a concept $C$, the Suitability Criterion uses :

in a *positive* fashion :  – the similarity between the description of $O$ and $C$

– the dissimilarity between the descriptions of $O$ and the other concepts

*and*  in a *negative* fashion :  – the similarity between the descriptions $O$ and the other concepts

– the dissimilarity between the descriptions of $O$ and $C$.

Each of the characteristics of a concept contributes to the calculation of the score as a function of its relevance $(w_j)$ in the concept description. In ADECLU2 and /S, this relevance will be all the greater when the characteristic is discriminating for the concept. In ADECLU/S, the selection of typical values (from the values observed in the concept) occurs with the aim of increasing the relevance of characteristics. It increases the contrast between concept descriptions, by extracting from the typical set $Vj$ (and transfering to $^cVj$) the values which are too frequently observed in the other concepts. This typicality is thus of a statistical nature and is "acquired' from the data provided to ADECLU. To learn it correctly, it is necessary to have a sufficient number of objects. If not, ADECLU2 is preferable.

After experimentation, it appears that the use of "contrasted" descriptions among concepts is beneficial not only for the quality of data classification (cf (Decaestecker, 1990)), but equally for the predictive power of the conceptual hierarchies, especially in the presence of noise.

Other definitions of typicality can be envisaged (cf (Lebbe & al, 1988)). ADECLU/S uses a "strong" typicality ("frequency in $C$" > "frequency in $P\backslash\{C\}$"), which generalises the notion of "discriminant value" ("frequency in $P\backslash\{C\}$" = 0). This definition of typicality implies that a value be selected in at most one concept. Studies are underway on the different ways of dropping this constraint, aiming at a less draconian selection of values. Initial results are encouraging.

The work on ADECLU can be related to other Conceptual clustering methods. For example, WITT (Hanson & al. 86), a non incremental system, is also related to the notion of "concept contrasting", mentioned above. The concept representation also uses contingency tables but one for each pair of attributes. This necessitates considerable storage costs ( $A[A-1]/2$ tables for $A$ attributes - too high for incremental processes). ADECLU(2 and /S) each requires only $A$ (2x2) contingency tables with easy updating.

COBWEB (Fisher, 1987) and CLASSIT (Gennary & al, 1989) are similar to ADECLU in their clustering processes (hill climbing search with operators), but differ in their concept representations and do not select attribute and typical values. Hence, COBWEB and ADECLU(2 and /S) store the same basic knowledge : the frequencies of observed values in each concept, but ADECLU uses this knowledge to select relevant characteristics to classify new objects and to predict unknown values. CLASSIT2 (Gennari, 1989) is an extension of CLASSIT that includes a mechanism to focus attention upon a subset of attributes that are more "salient". Attributes are inspected in sequence, where the inspection order is determined by a "salience" measure, which is the contribution of one attribute to his evaluation measure (category utility). Attribute inspection stops when the remaining attributes cannot change the clustering decision.

In (Fisher, 1989), the author presents a pruning method of hierarchy (for noise-tolerant Conceptual Clustering), which uses past-performance (number of times the attribute was correctly predicted during training). During test, classification is stopped in a node that has historically outperformed its descendants (in terms of predicting missing attribute). We have compared this method with our cutoff method in ADECLU. First experiments (Decaestecker, 1991) show that Fisher method does not ameliorate our results in noisy domains.

## REFERENCES

Anderberg M.R. "Cluster analysis for applications", Academic Press, New York, 1973.

Decaestecker C. "Formation incrémentale de concepts par un critère d'adéquation". Proceedings of "4èmes Journées Française d'Apprentissage", 1989 (a).

Decaestecker C. "Incremental Concept Formation with Attribute Selection", Proceedings of the 4th EWSL (European Working Session on Learning), pp 49-58, 1989 (b).

Decaestecker C. "Description Contrasting in ADECLU : ADECLU/S", Technical Report IA-01-90, CADEPS (CAIRU), Université Libre de Bruxelles, Belgium, 1990.

Decaestecker C. Thesis, in preparation, Université Libre de Bruxelles, Belgium, 1991.

Fisher D.H. "Knowledge acquisition via incremental conceptual clustering", Machine Learning, 2, pp 139-172, 1987.

Fisher D.H. "Noise-Tolerant Conceptual Clustering", Procceedings of IJCAI-89, pp 825-830, 1989.

Gennari J.H., Langley P. and Fisher D. "Models of Incremental Concept Formation", Artificial Intelligence, vol. 40, No 1-3, 1989.

Gennari J.H. "Focused Concept Formation", Proceedings of the 6th International Workshop on Machine Learning, pp 379-382, 1989.

Goodman L.A. and Kruskal W.H. "Measures of association for cross classifications", J.of the American Stat. Assoc., vol. 49, pp 732-764, 1954.

Hanson S.J and Bauer M. "Machine Learning, Clustering and Polymorphy". In L.N. Kanal & J.F. Lemmer (Eds), Uncertainty in Artificial Intelligence, North-Holland, 1986.

Lebbe J., Vignes R., Darmoni S. "Les objets symboliques qualifiés, Application au diagnostic médical", Proceedings of the "2èmes Journées Symbolique-Numérique", Report n° 487, LRI, Université Paris-Sud (Orsay), 1988.

Lebowitz M. "Experiments with incremental concept formation : UNIMEM", Machine Learning, 2, pp 103-138, 1987.

Michalski R.S. and Chilausky R.L. "Learning by being told and learning from examples ...", Policy analysis and Information Systems, vol.4, No 2, June 1980.

Quinlan J.R. "Induction of decision trees", Machine Learning, 1, pp 81-106, 1986.

# System *FLORA*: Learning from Time-Varying Training Sets

Miroslav KUBAT, Jirina PAVLICKOVA

Computer Center, Technical University of Brno, Udolni 19, Brno, Czechoslovakia

**Keywords:** Learning from Examples, Incremental Learning, Forgetting

*FLORA* is a system for building production rules out of a set of *objects* - examples and counterexamples of a concept *T*. Objects are characterized by attributes.

The specific feature of *FLORA* is that it is able to learn concepts with time-varying meaning. A straightforward way to do it is to combine incremental learning and *forgetting*. The description of the concept is organized in the form of a decision tree similar to that of *ID3*. Each branch of the tree forms a rule. *FLORA* works with 2 possible rules: deterministic and non-deterministic. The deterministic rules are considered the output of the learning process (*accepted description*) while the non-deterministic ones are just stored for future use.

A relatively fixed number of objects (*window*) are kept in the memory. Each new increment can result in the modification of the knowledge base. After the modification, the system considers whether or not the oldest objects in the window can be trusted. The idea is that old pieces of knowledge can become, as a result of aging, unreliable. The result of adding a new object into the window is that a deterministic rule can become non-deterministic and thus be deleted from the set of accepted descriptions. The result of deletion of an object from the window is that a non-deterministic rule may become deterministic and thus be added to the set of accepted descriptions. Only accepted descriptions are output.

Experiments with *FLORA* have shown that in those aplications where the meaning of concept varies in time, the example-driven forgetting brings improvement over classical "static" approaches such as AQ-algorithms or incremental versions of ID3 .

# Message-Based Bucket Brigade: An Algorithm for the Apportionment of Credit Problem

MARCO DORIGO

MP-AI Project, Dip.Elettronica, Politecnico di Milano,
P.za Leonardo da Vinci 32 - 20133 Milano - Italy
E-mail: dorigo@ipmel1.polimi.it

## Abstract

This paper considers some issues related to the apportionment of credit problem in Genetic Based Machine Learning systems (GBML). A GBML system is composed of three major subsystems. The first one, the performance subsystem, is a parallel adaptive rule-based system where the knowledge base is a set of rules expressed in a low-level syntax. The second subsystem, called Genetic Algorithm (GA), is a procedure that searches in the rule space by means of genetic operators modelled according to natural genetic operators (e.g. reproduction, crossover, mutation). The third subsystem faces the apportionment of credit problem, i.e. how to evaluate the quality of existing rules. In this paper we propose an apportionment of credit algorithm, called *Message-Based Bucket Brigade*, in which messages instead of rules are evaluated. A rule quality is then a function of the value of the messages matching the rule conditions, of the rule conditions specificity and of the value of the message the rule tries to post. This approach gives a solution to the *default hierarchy formation* problem, i.e. the problem of creating set of rules in which default rules cover broad categories of system responses, while specific ones cover situations in which default rules are incorrect. A comparison with other approaches to default hierarchy formation is presented. The final section presents conclusions and suggests directions for further research.

## 1 Introduction

A GBML system is an adaptive system that learns to accomplish a task by means of interaction with an environment. It belongs to the class of *reinforcement learning* systems, i.e. systems in which learning is guided by rewards coming from environment. The system is composed of three main parts

- the performance subsystem
- the apportionment of credit subsystem
- the rule discovery subsystem

In figure 1 the typical structure of these systems is shown

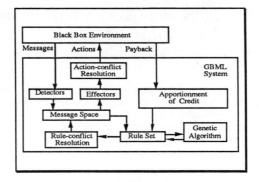

Figure 1 - Structure of a GBML system

- the performance subsystem (detectors, effectors, message space, rule set, conflict resolution)
- the apportionment of credit subsystem
- the rule discovery subsystem (genetic algorithm)

The overall GBML system resulting from the interaction of these three subsystems (see Figure 1) is a parallel production system with the following peculiarities

- rules are strings of symbols over a three-valued alphabet ($A=\{0,1,*\}$) with a condiction→action format (in our system every rule has two conditions that have to be contemporaneously satisfied in order to activate the rule)
- rules fire in parallel
- there is no need for a truth maintenance system (inconsistent set of rules do not survive)
- rules are evaluated to find out their relative importance in the problem solving task to be learned
- new rules are generated using information extracted from the rules considered to be the best by the evaluation mechanism
- if properly designed the system forms rule structures called default hierarchies, i.e. general, but imperfect, rules that cover a broad category of possible system responses plus layers of more specific ones that handle specific situations where default rules are incorrect.

As a brief introduction we present in the following the three subsystems. A review of current solutions to the apportionment of credit problem is included. Then we introduce our algorithm and subsequently compare it with the classical Bucket Brigade (BB), with particular attention to the creation of default hierarchies. The final section includes some discussion on results obtained and hints for future research.

# 2 The performance subsystem

The performance subsystem is composed of
- a set of rules, called classifiers
- a list of messages, used to collect messages sent from classifiers and from the environment to other classifiers
- an input and an output interface with the environment (detectors and effectors) to receive/send messages from/to the environment
- a payback mechanism to reward the system when a useful action is performed and to punish it when a wrong action is done.

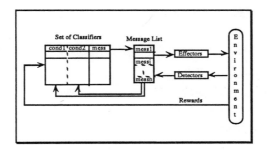

Figure 2 - The performance system

At time zero a set of classifiers is created (they may be generated randomly or by some algorithm that takes into account the structure of the problem domain) and the message list is empty. At time 1 environmental messages are appended to the message list, then they are matched against the condition part of classifiers and matched classifiers are set to status active. At time t messages coming from environment and messages sent by classifiers active at time t-1 are appended to the message list; they are then matched against classifiers in the classifiers set and matched classifiers become activated. The message list is then emptied and the cycle repeated.

The algorithm described would work only in case the message list could become infinite in length. In practical systems the message list length has some fixed finite length and therefore some kind of mechanism has to be introduced to decide which classifiers have the right to post messages when the number of messages is bigger than the message list dimensions (this mechanism is implemented in the rule-conflict resolution box, see fig.1). The need for a rule-conflict resolution system is one of the reasons for the introduction of an apportionment of credit algorithm that redistribute environmental payoff to the rules that caused the performed actions. This allows the performance subsystem to choose which rules to fire in accordance to some measure of their usefulness. Conflict resolution must also be used to solve conflict when effectors propose inconsistent actions (e.g. "go right" and "go left").

In order to better explain the nuances of this performance subsystem, let us introduce some genetic based machine learning terminology.

- a **classifier** (rule) is a string composed of three *chromosomes*, two chromosomes being the condition part[1], the third one being the message/action part; we will call a classifier an *external classifier* if it sends messages to the effectors, an *internal classifier* if it sends messages to other classifiers
- a **chromosome** is a string of n positions; every position is called *gene*
- a **gene** can assume a value, called *allelic value*, belonging to an alphabet that is usually A={0,1,*} (the reasons underlying this choice are to be found in the rule discovery algorithm used, namely the Genetic Algorithm; in fact it has been demonstrated (Holland,1975) that the lower the cardinality of the alphabet, the higher the efficiency of the algorithm in processing useful information contained in the structure of the chromosomes)

Consider for example the following classifier

$$* 1 *; \ 0 \ 1 \ 1 \rightarrow \ 0 \ 1 \ 0$$

here the second condition is matched only by the message 0 1 1, while the first one is matched by any message with a 1 in second position. The * symbol stays for "don't care", that means both symbols, 0 or 1, match the position. If both the positions are matched by some message, then the rule is activated and the message/action part, i.e. the chromosome 0 1 0 in the example, is appended to the message list at the following step (if it was to be interpreted as a message) or is sent to the effectors (if it was to be interpreted as an action).

## 3 The Genetic Algorithm

GAs are a computational device inspired by population genetics that can be used both as a function optimization device and as a rule discovery system. In GBML they work applying to the set of classifiers some operators, called *genetic operators*, that recombinant them and promote the survival of best fitted ones (where the best classifiers are those with the highest strength).

To use GAs as a rule-discovery system means to hypothesize that new and more useful rules can be created by recombination of other less useful ones. In order to preserve the system performance the GA is applied only to a subset of the rules: the m best rules (those with higher strength) are selected to form the initial population, while the worst m ones are replaced by those created by the application of the GA on the initial population. After the application of the GA only a portion of the rules are replaced. The new rules will be tested by the combined action of the performance and credit apportionment algorithms. As to test a rule requires many time steps, GAs are applied with a lower frequency than the two other subsystems.

---

[1] Although we use in our example only two chromosomes , it is in general possible to utilize any number n of chromosomes in the conditions part of a classifier (n≥2), without changing the representational power of the resulting system.

# 4 The apportionment of credit subsystem

We have said that the main task of the apportionment of credit algorithm is to classify rules in accordance with their usefulness. In words, the algorithm works as following: to every classifier $C_i$ a real value called *strength*, $Str_{C_i}(t)$, is assigned. At the beginning each classifier has the same strength. When an external classifier causes an action on the environment a payoff is generated depending on how good the action performed was with respect to the system goal. This reward is then transmitted backward to internal classifiers that caused the external classifier to fire. The backward transmission mechanism, examined in detail later, causes the strength of the classifiers to change in time and to reflect their relevance to the system performance (with respect to the system goal).

Clearly it is not possible to keep track of all the paths of activation actually followed by the rule chains (a rule chain is a set of rule activated in sequence, starting with a rule activated by environmental messages and ending with a rule performing an action on the environment) because the number of these paths grows exponentially. It is then necessary to have an appropriate algorithm that solves the problem using only local, in time and in space, information.

Local in time is meant to say that the information used at every computational step is coming only from a fixed recent temporal interval. Space locality means that changes in a classifiers strength are caused only by classifiers directly linked to it (we say that classifiers $C_1$ and $C_2$ are linked if the message posted by $C_1$ matches a condition of $C_2$).

The classical algorithm used to this purpose is the *Bucket Brigade* algorithm. This algorithm models the classifier system as an economic society, in which every classifier pays an amount of its strength to get the privilege of appending a message to the message list and receives a payment by all classifiers activated because of the presence in the message list of the message it appended during the preceding time step. In this way payoff flows backward from the environment again to the environment through a chain of classifiers. The net result is that classifiers that participate in chains that cause high rewarded actions tend to increase their strength.

We present here a formulation of the classical Bucket Brigade algorithm

Step 0 •   associate an initial strength to every classifier, clear the message list and set all the classifiers to status not-active; then append all the environmental messages

Step 1 •   set to status active every classifier which has both conditions matched by messages on the message list and then empty the message list

Step 2 •   for every active classifier compute the quantity $Bid_{C_i}(t)$

Step 3 •   auction step: choose with a probability proportional to $Bid_{C_i}(t)$ the messages to be posted until the message list is full (every message posted memorizes the name of the posting classifier for step 4 purposes)

Step 4 •   every classifier that has successfully posted a message pays the quantity $Pay_{C_i}(t)$ to the classifier that caused its activation

Step 5 • the status of all classifiers is set to not-active

Step 6 • new environmental messages are read and appended to the message list and the algorithm repeated from step 1

The quantities used in the algorithm are so defined

• $Bid_{Ci}(t) = f(Str_{Ci}(t), \rho(Spe_{Ci}), Sup_{Ci}(t))$

is the quantity offered from classifier $C_i(t)$ to compete in the auction where $Str_{Ci}(t)$ is the strength of classifier $C_i$ at time t, $Spe_{Ci}$ is the specificity of classifier $C_i$, $\rho(x)$ is a monotonic function of x with $0 \leq x \leq 1$, $0 \leq \rho(x) \leq 1$, and $Sup_{Ci}(t)$ is the support of classifier $C_i$ at time t. Specificity is defined as follows

$$Spe_{C_i} = \frac{\text{number of non-* positions in } C_i}{\text{length of classifier } C_i}$$

• $Pay_{Ci}(t) = f(Str_{Ci}(t))$

is the quantity actually paid by classifiers that are allowed to post messages

• $Str_{Ci}(t) = Str_{Ci}(t-1) - Pay_{Ci}(t)$ is a value intended to be proportional to the classifier usefulness

• $Sup_{Ci}(t)$ is a function of the support of matching messages. Message support is usually considered to be equal to the bid offered by the classifier that posted it. Support measures indirectly how useful a message is, indirectly because the measure uses the classifier strength as a reference.

One of the effects of the apportionment of credit algorithm should be to contribute to the formation of default hierarchies, i.e. set of rules that categorizes the set of environmental states into equivalence classes to be treated alike. Default hierarchies have some nice properties. They can be used to build quasi-homomorphic[2] models of the environment which generally require far fewer rules than equivalent homomorphic ones (Riolo,1987). Moreover their performance can be improved adding more exceptions and the whole system can learn gracefully, i.e. the performance of the system is not too strongly influenced by the insertion of new rules. An example of default hierarchy is given in figure 3.

Specificity has been introduced in the bid computation in order to promote default hierarchies formation. Consider the situation in which $Bid_{Ci}(t) = k\rho(Spe_{Ci})Str_{Ci}(t)^3$, where k is the bid constant (k<1, usually set to a value between 0 and 0.2). Default hierarchies formation requires then that more specific rules should offer an higher bid than default ones. This approach results in the following problem (Wilson,1988; Goldberg & Wilson,1989).

---

[2] If E is the set of environmental states that the learning system has to learn to categorize, then the system could either try to find a set of rules that partition the whole set E never making mistakes, or build a default hierarchy. With the first approach a homomorphic model of the environment is built, with the second a quasi-homomorphic one.

[3] We do not consider here support because it is a variable not controlled by the performance of the single classifier and so we set it to a constant value.

| non-hierarchical set | hierarchical set |
| :---: | :---: |
| (homomorphic set) | (quasi-homomorphic set) |
| 00;10→11 | 00;10→11 |
| 01;10→00 | **;10→00 |
| 10;10→00 | |
| 11;10→00 | |

Figure 3 - The hierarchical set implement the
same state categorisation with fewer rules.

If we examine the steady-state behaviour of the classifier strength for a single default exception pair we find that $Str_{C_d}^{ss}=\dfrac{R}{k\rho(Spe_{C_d})}$ and $Str_{C_e}^{ss}=\dfrac{R}{k\rho(Spe_{C_e})}$ where d and e suffixes stays for default and exception and R is the mean reward received from environment.

The steady-state bid is then $Bid_{C_e}^{ss}=Bid_{C_d}^{ss}=R$ and, being independent of specificity, does not promote default hierarchy creation.

A proposed solution has been to factor out specificity from the amount actually paid by an activated classifier: this results in effective separation between bids. The problem with this solution is that separation is fixed for a given ratio of default to exception specificity: problems may then arise in the presence of noise, because of taxation policies (taxes are strength losses a classifier undergoes every time it is not activated during a cycle) and because of delays in rewards distribution.

To overcome these problems another approach has been proposed based on the *necessity auction* idea (Goldberg,1990): a winning classifier pays only the amount that was offered as bid from its nearest competitor. If we limit our considerations to a two classifiers hierarchy, precedent problems are overcome with this model; unluckily it seems difficult to generalize it to more complex hierarchies.

After a careful study of the proposed hierarchy-forming algorithms we have decided to change the model in a more radical way, in such a way to make default hierarchies formation an inherent property of the model.

# 5 Message-Based Bucket Brigade

We present now a modification of the BB algorithm in which only messages strength and specificity, without any classifier strength, are enough to evaluate the system performance. We show that, using messages strength instead of classifiers strength, default hierarchies formation is an inherent property of the algorithm. This Bucket Brigade algorithm (hereafter MBB - Message-Based Bucket Brigade) has the following characteristics

- a strength $M_i$ is associated to every message i $mess_i(t)$
- during the competition phase every matched classifier $C_j$ offers a bid $\text{M-Bid}_{Cj}(t) = Str_{Maj}(t) + \rho_1 Str_{Mc1j}(t) + \rho_2 Str_{Mc2j}(t)$ where $Str_{Maj}(t)$ is the strength associated to the action part of classifier j, $Str_{Mc1j}(t)$ and $Str_{Mc2j}(t)$ are respectively the averages of the strength associated to the messages matching the first and second conditions of classifier $C_j$, $\rho_1$ and $\rho_2$ are the specificities of the two classifier conditions
- a winning message pays an amount proportional to its strength ($kM_i$, where k is the payout constant) to both the set of messages that have matched the conditions of the classifier that posted it; for example say that $mess_r$ and $mess_s$ have matched the first condition of classifier $C_k$ and $mess_t$ the second one and that, as a consequence, $mess_y$ was posted; then $mess_y$ pays the amount $kM_y$ (that is it decreases its strength of $kM_y$), $mess_t$ increases its strength of $kM_y$ and $mess_r$ and $mess_s$ increase their strength of $kM_y/2$
- in the genetic phase the classifier strength is calculated in the same way as bid is computed in the competition phase, except that the value of the two conditions is averaged on the value of all the messages that can match them and that have been generated

The MBB algorithm is then

Step 0 • create a list of all the generable messages and associate them an initial strength (a message is said to be generable if it is in the action part of some classifier of the classifier set); clear the message list, set all the classifiers to status not-active and then append all the environmental messages

Step 1 • set to status active every classifier which has both conditions matched by messages on the message list and then empty the message list; two lists containing the messages that matched the two conditions are maintained for step 4 purposes

Step 2 • for every active classifier compute the quantity $\text{M-Bid}_{Ci}(t)$ as defined above

Step 3 • choose with a probability proportional to $\text{M-Bid}_{Ci}(t)$ the messages to be posted until the message list is full

Step 4 • every message successfully posted pays the quantity $kM_i$ to the messages that caused its activation (according to the rule explained above)

Step 5 • the status of all the classifiers is set to not-active

Step 6 • new environmental messages are read and appended to the message list and the algorithm is repeated from Step 1.

# 6 Steady-state Analysis

From the following formula we get the steady-state value of a message (R is the mean value of the reward received by $mess_c$)

$$M_c^{i+1} = M_c^i - kM_c^i + R \Rightarrow M_c^{ss} = \frac{R}{k}$$

The steady-state strength $M_c^{ss}$ of message $mess_c$ is clearly independent of specificity, while the bid a classifier offers depends on specificity. As a consequence default hierarchies support is an inherent property of the system. Consider the following example

$$\boxed{010;\ 111\ \rightarrow\ 101}$$

$$\boxed{**0;\ 11*\ \rightarrow\ 010}$$

if messages 010 and 111 are in the message list both classifiers become active but the second one will always, independently of how well the strength of matching messages reflects their usefulness, bid less than the more specific one [4].

We can then state the major property of MBB as follows:

*A classifier with low specificity conditions will be activated with lower probability than one with high specificity, this property being independent of activating messages strength.*

Another useful feature of the MBB algorithm is that the value of a rule is context dependent, i.e. it depends on the value of matching messages. This means that a classifier can be more precisely tuned than it is in the classical model. A problem with the classical model is that a default classifier can be matched by very different messages and that the resulting action can be only partially (by means of pass-through characters, i.e. characters that repeat in the action part the value found in the corresponding position of one of the conditions) influenced by them. Our MBB algorithm transcends this problem using rules whose strength is a function of matching messages strength.

# 7 Conclusions and further work

In this paper we have presented the apportionment of credit problem in GBML systems. The problem of having an appropriate credit apportionment algorithm capable of forming hierarchies of rules has been introduced and an algorithm, called Message-Based Bucket Brigade, has been presented. Default hierarchies, a powerful way of categorize the environmental states, are inherently supported by this algorithm.

We are now investigating the effects of the proposed shift from a system in which actions are guided by rules strength to one in which messages strength leads the computation. In particular we are now examining the influences that this shift has on the rule discovery system and we are developing a

---

[4] Although the probability of posting a message is dependent also from the action message, our approach works correctly because either the value of the action message is equal or higher for the more specific rule, and then there is no problem, or it is lower and then it could be sensible to apply a less specific rule that results in a more useful action.

system in which the number n of chromosomes in the condition part of a classifier can be variable (n≥2).

## Acknowledgements

This research was supported in part by a grant from CNR - Progetto finalizzato robotica - Sottoobiettivo 2 - Tema: ALPI and from CNR - Progetto finalizzato sistemi informatici e calcolo parallelo - Sottoprogetto 2 - Tema: Processori dedicati.

We would like to thank Enrico Sirtori, who performed most of the implementation work on the transputer system.

## References

Goldberg D.E. & Wilson S.W., "A Critical Review of Classifier Systems", Proceedings of the Third International Conference on Genetic Algorithms, June 4-7 1989, Morgan Kaufmann (pp.244-255).

Holland J.H., "Adaptation in natural and artificial systems", Ann Arbor: The University of Michigan Press, 1975.

Riolo R.L., "Bucket Brigade Performance: II. Default Hierarchies" Proceedings of the Second International Conference on Genetic Algorithms, July 28-31 1987, Lawrence Erlbaum (pp.196-201).

Wilson S.W., "Bid Competition and Specificity Reconsidered", Complex Systems, 2(6), 1988, pp. 705-723.

# Acquiring Object-Knowledge for Learning Systems

Luc De Raedt, Johan Feyaerts and Maurice Bruynooghe

Department of Computer Science, Katholieke Universiteit Leuven
Celestijnenlaan 200A, B-3001 Heverlee, Belgium
email : lucdr@cs.kuleuven.ac.be

## Abstract

A novel approach to interactively acquire knowledge about new objects in a logic environment is presented. When the user supplies an unknown fact containing unknown objects (constants), the system will ask interesting membership and existential queries about the objects. The answers to these questions allow the system to update its knowledge base. Two basic strategies are implemented: one that examines existing Horn-Clauses for the predicate and another one that uses types. Furthermore, a powerful heuristic, based on analogy, to pose the most interesting questions first is presented.

**Keywords** : learning by being told, knowledge acquisition, analogy, concept-learning.

## 1   Introduction

It is a well known cliche that the power of artificial intelligence systems is — to a large degree — due to the knowledge they possess. The acquisition of the knowledge, necessary to build intelligent systems, is a difficult and time-consuming process. These difficulties explain the current intrest in knowledge acquisition tools [Gaines and Boose], which assist the knowledge engineer in his task. Related research issues are concerned with the so-called learning systems [Michalski, Carbonell and Mitchell 83, Michalski, Carbonell and Mitchell 86, Kodratoff and Michalski 90, Kodratoff 88], which promise to contribute to the widening of the knowledge acquisition bottleneck. The knowledge about objects and relations that hold among them constitutes the main part of the domain specific knowledge in intelligent systems. Therefore, an important subtask in knowledge acquisition as well as in learning systems is the acquisition of knowledge regarding objects. In learning systems this knowledge is often a prerequisite for success. Indeed, many systems require that the domains of variables are completely known [Michalski 83, Quinlan 86]. Other approaches, like [De Raedt and Bruynooghe 89, Wirth 88, Quinlan 90] cannot learn if they are not provided with basic knowledge about the different objects. In learning apprentice systems such as Disciple [Kodratoff and Tecuci 87, Tecuci and Kodratoff 90], some knowledge about objects is acquired as a side-effect of the learning, while in other systems as Blip [Morik 89, Wrobel 88], knowledge about objects is derived by the system from the facts which are input.

We take a different approach. When the user inputs a true fact containing an unknown object, an attempt is made to gather as much knowledge about the object as possible. To this purpose, the knowledge base is examined and interesting membership and existential queries [Angluin 88, Shapiro 83] are formulated to the user. The answers to these questions allow to update the knowledge base. Two main methods are employed: analysing existing definitions (Horn-Clauses) for the predicate and using types or sorts of predicates. The methods are completely implemented in BIMprolog. They can easily be integrated in other systems like e.g. Disciple [Kodratoff and Tecuci 87, Tecuci and Kodratoff 90], Clint [De Raedt and Bruynooghe 89], LFP [Wirth 88], Cigol [Muggleton and Buntine 88] and Blip [Morik 89, Wrobel 88]. It is also feasible to regard the approach as a form of learning by being told, and in this sense, there is some resemblance with e.g. [Haas and Hendrix 83].

This paper is organized as follows : in section 2, we define the basic notions and a problem specification; in section 3, the algorithms are presented while in section 4, an example of the algorithms at work is shown; in section 5, as a case study, it is indicated how the algorithms can be integrated in the Clint system [De Raedt and Bruynooghe 89] and finally, in section 6 we conclude and touch briefly upon related work. Before going through section 2 and/or 3, it may be useful to have a look at the example session in section 4.

# 2   Problem-specification

We use a logical framework[Genesereth and Nilsson 87]. Within this framework, a predicate-definition is a set of Horn-Clauses for the predicate (as in PROLOG [Sterling and Shapiro 86, Bratko 86]). For the sake of simplicity, we restrict ourselves to function free predicates and Horn-Clauses without recursion. We distinguish different kinds of predicates : on the one hand, *stable* and *modifiable* predicates and on the other hand, *base*, *view* and *mixed* predicates.

**Definition 2.1** *A stable predicate is assumed to be correct. It may not be modified.*

**Definition 2.2** *A modifiable predicate may contain errors. It may be modified.*

**Definition 2.3** *A base predicate is defined by a set of ground facts.*

**Definition 2.4** *A view predicate is defined by a set of non-unit Horn-Clauses.*

**Definition 2.5** *A mixed predicate is a predicate that is neither a view nor a base predicate.*

We assume that the system has access to an oracle that is willing to answer membership and existential questions.

**Definition 2.6** *([Shapiro 83, Angluin 88])*
*A membership question queries an oracle about the truth in the intended interpretation of a ground atom $p(a_1, ..., a_n)$, where $p$ is a predicate and the $a_i$ are constants (objects). The oracle must answer 'yes' if the relation $p$ holds among the constants $a_1, ..., a_n$ in the intended interpretation; otherwise, it must answer 'no'.*

**Definition 2.7** *( [Shapiro 83, Angluin 88] )*
*An existential question queries an oracle about the truth in the intended interpretation of a non-ground atom $p(x_1, ..., x_n)$, where $p$ is a predicate, at least one of the $x_i$ is a variable and at least one of the $x_i$ is a constant (an object). The oracle must return all ground substitutions $\theta$ such that $p(x_1, ..., x_n)\theta$ is true in the intended interpretation or if there are no such substitutions, it must answer 'no'.*

When the oracle answers 'no' to a question $q$, the question $q$ is added to the set of facts F. F contains all the facts that are known to be false in the intended interpretation. This set is used to prune the search and to prevent the assertion of false facts.

By now, the problem can be specified more formally as :

- **Given :**

  - a knowledge base KB of predicate definitions
  - a set of facts F, such that $\forall f \in$F there is no substitution $\theta$ for which $f\theta$ is true in the intended interpretation
  - a fact $p(o_1, ..., o_n)$ such that KB $\not\models p(o_1, ..., o_n)$ and at least one of the $o_i$ is a constant, not occurring in the knowledge base KB, i.e. $o_i$ does not occur in the Herbrand-domain of KB.
  - an oracle willing to answer existential and membership questions.

- **Find :** a set S of facts, true in the intended interpretation, such that KB $\cup$ S $\models p(o_1, ..., o_n)$ and there is no $s \in S$ for which there is an $f \in F$ and a substitution $\theta$ such that $f\theta = s$; the set S will be called the update.

### Problem Statement.

In this problem-specification, we have a fact $p(o_1, ..., o_n)$, that is not implied by the knowledge base KB, but which should. Furthermore, there is the set of known false facts F. The aim is then to find a set of true facts S such that $p(o_1, ..., o_n)$ is implied by the knowledge base KB $\cup$ S. We will sometimes refer to this problem as the *update* problem; furthermore, if the predicate $p$ is a view predicate it will be referred to as the *view update* problem; if $p$ is a base predicate, the problem becomes the *base update* problem. These notions are illustrated in example 1.

In example 1, it is rather clear which questions should be posed to the oracle as `drives` is a view predicate. However, suppose we want to add a new type of car ( a base predicate). Then it would be harder to decide which questions to generate. Of course, one could assert the fact itself. This is not desirable as the amount of knowledge acquired in this way is minimal. We will present two approaches to generate *interesting* questions

## Example 1: Illustrating the problem-specification.

Suppose we have the following definitions in our knowledge base :

```
owns(yves, peugeot) ←
owns(katharina, mercedes) ←
owns(maurice, renault) ←
owns(luc, plume) ←

car(peugeot) ←
car(mercedes) ←
car(renault) ←

bicycle(plume) ←

vehicle(X) ← car(X)
vehicle(X) ← bicycle(X)

drives(X,Y) ← owns(X,Y) ∧  car(Y) ∧  has_license(X)
drives(X,Y) ← owns(X,Y) ∧  bicycle(Y)

has_license(katharina) ←
has_license(yves) ←
has_license(maurice) ←
```

In this knowledge base, the predicates drive and vehicle are view predicates, the others are base predicates. Suppose that all predicates are modifiable and that we want to make the fact drives(luc, citroen) true. There are several possibilities to realize this :

```
S₁ = { drives(luc, citroen) }
S₂ = { owns(luc, citroen), has_license(luc), car(citroen) }
S₃ = { owns(luc, citroen), bicycle(citroen) }
```

Given the available information, we only know that $S_1$ is correct w.r.t. the intended interpretation. However, if one of the other possible updates is correct, it is not interesting to assert $S_1$ in the knowledge base. The reason is very obvious : by asserting $S_1$, much potential information would be lost. Indeed, it would no longer be possible to derive e.g. vehicle(citroen) from the knowledge base. Furthermore, the structure of our knowledge base would become more clumsy : the view predicate drives would become mixed. In order to be sure that one of the other possible updates is correct we have to query the oracle for the truth-value of the facts in the updates $S_2$ and $S_3$.

to the oracle. In these approaches, we attempt to maximize the acquired knowledge while keeping the number of questions to the user acceptable.

Note that the above sketched problem is a *machine learning* problem. It is a form of learning by being told [Carbonell, Michalski and Mitchell 83], where new information is to be transformed before it can be added to the knowledge base. It is also a form of induction : in example 1, one could imagine that the definition of vehicle was inductively learned by a concept-learner as e.g. Clint [De Raedt and Bruynooghe 89]. By asserting car(citroen) it becomes possible to induce vehicle(citroen).[1] Furthermore, it is essential that inductive concept-learners address the sketched problem. Without addressing it, they are often unable to learn. Consider e.g. the concept-learner Clint [De Raedt and Bruynooghe 89]. In order to process the true fact (positive example) drives(luc,citroen), it first derives a starting clause for drives by looking for the relations that hold among the objects (luc and citroen). Clearly if nothing is known about these objects, Clint will fail to derive the starting clause and nothing will be learned. In this situation, Clint cannot make the necessary modifications to its knowledge base to make the fact drives(luc,citroen) implied. In section 5, we show how Clint can be extended with the methods described in this paper. This allows Clint to learn even if there is nothing known about the objects, occurring in an example. Similar situations arise in other concept-learners, as e.g. LFP [Wirth 88], Blip [Morik 89, Wrobel 88] and Disciple [Kodratoff and Tecuci 87, Tecuci and Kodratoff 90]. LFP suffers from the same problem as Clint, whereas Blip and Disciple take the minimal approach, i.e. they would assert the facts containing the new objects. However, in both cases, an important opportunity to gather additional knowledge about the involved objects is missed.

# 3 The algorithms

In this section, we present two algorithms to handle updates. We first show how updates in view predicates can be handled and then how mixed and base predicates should be treated.

## 3.1 Updating view predicates

Our algorithm to handle view updates relies on the following notion of dependency :

**Definition 3.1** *A literal $l$ of a modifiable predicate in a goal $g$ depends on a constant $c$ iff (1) $c$ occurs in $l$ or (2) there is a variable $v$ occurring in $l$, that also occurs in a literal $l'$ of $g$, such that $l'$ depends on the constant $c$.*
*If $l$ does not depend on a constant $c$, it is independent of $c$.*

Dependancy means that a literal $l(..., c, ...)$ in a goal depends on the constant $c$ and also that $l(..., v, ...)$ depends on the constant $c$ if $l(..., v, ...) \wedge ... \wedge l'(..., v, ..., c, ...)$ occur in the goal where $v$ is a variable.

---

[1] One might argue that the inference of vehicle(citroen) is deduction rather than induction because the fact follows from the clauses for vehicle and the fact car(citroen). This argument is false, because the clauses for vehicle are derived by induction. As a consequence, the inference of vehicle(citroen) is an inductive (falsifiable) conclusion.

The set of subgoals of a goal $g$ that are independent of new objects in the goal will be written as $I(g)$; whereas the set of subgoals that depend on new objects is $D(g)$. A new object is an object that does not yet occur in the knowledge base, or one that is currently being added to the knowledge base by one of the algorithms presented below.

The notion of dependency is essential for our approach because our algorithm is based on the following assumption :

**Assumption 1** *The success or failure of query* $q = \leftarrow g_1 \wedge g_2 \wedge \ldots \wedge g_k$ *can be determined by applying algorithm 1 on the goal.*

---

### Algorithm 1: Solving a goal.

**procedure** solve( $\leftarrow g_1 \wedge \ldots \wedge g_n$: goal ) **returns** success or failure
    $L = \{ \leftarrow g_1 \wedge \ldots \wedge g_n \}$
    **repeat**
        delete a goal $g$ from $L$
        **if** $I(g) \neq \emptyset$
        **then for all** $\theta$ such that KB $\models I(g)\theta$ **do**
            add $D(g)\theta$ to $L$
        **endfor**
        **else if** $D(g) \neq \emptyset$
        **then** delete a literal $l$ from $g$ such that $l \in D(g)$ and
            $l$ contains a new object
            ask the question $l$ to the oracle
            **for all** $\theta$ returned by the oracle such that $l\theta$ is true **do**
                add $g\theta$ to $L$
            **endfor**
        **endif**
        **endif**
    **until** $L$ contains the empty goal or $L = \emptyset$
    **if** $L$ contains the empty goal
    **then return** success
    **else return** failure
    **endif**
**endproc**

---

This assumption implies that for the independent literals, the knowledge base is supposed to be correct. In other words, for these literals, the intended interpretation is the same as the one according to the knowledge base. Therefore independent subgoals are solved by querying the knowledge base and dependent ones by querying the user. The algorithm solve works as follows : it adds the original goal to its list of goals; then it repeatedly deletes a goal from the list and attempts to solve a subgoal of the goal. In order to solve a goal, the algorithm splits the goal in a dependent and an independent part. The independent part is run on the knowledge base. The remaining subgoal is then added to the list of goals. If the independent part of the goal is empty, then the algorithm will query the oracle for the truthvalue of a literal containing a new object. The remaining subgoal is − of course − also added to the list of goals. The process continues until the list of goals contains the empty goal and returns success or until the list of goals is empty and returns failure. Example 2 makes the involved notions clearer.

---

### Example 2: Illustrating dependency.

If we have e.g. the goal ← person(jeff) ∧ has_license(jeff) ∧ works_for(jeff,C) ∧ air_line_company(C)∧owner(C,concorde−7)∧plane(concorde−7) where concorde-7 is a new object and all predicates are modifiable, then we can verify whether the goal is true by first checking whether the independent literals are implied by the knowledge base : person(jeff) and has_license(jeff) ; if they are the existential question corresponding to owner(C,concorde-7) can be posed to the oracle; in case the oracle returns 'yes' for a substitution $\theta$ = { C = air_france } , where air_france is not a new object, then the answer to the query follows from the query ← air_line_company(air_france) ∧ works_for(jeff,air_france) to the knowledge base, because air_line_company(air_france) and works_for(jeff, air_france) are independent.

---

In algorithm 2, we summarize how to realize view updates under our assumption. The algorithm starts from a fact $p(o_1, ..., o_n)$ for a view predicate that contains a new object and that is not implied by the knowledge base. The algorithm will assert facts making $p(o_1, ..., o_n)$ implied. During the session, the system also acquires knowledge about other objects and predicates.

In algorithm 2, L contains the list of goals $g$ fulfilling the property that if $g$ is true in the intended interpretation, there is a clause in the knowledge base that covers the fact $p(o_1, ..., o_n)$.

**Definition 3.2** *A clause c covers a fact f if there is a substitution $\theta$ such that head$(c)\theta$ = f and body$(c)\theta$ is true in the intended interpretation.*

F is the set of facts, that are false in the intended interpretation. These facts are obtained by answers to previous oracle questions. The procedure Handle_View first initializes the list L with the goals corresponding to the instantiated bodies of clauses in the knowledge base.

In the repeat-loop, the most interesting goal (see section 3.3. and below) is deleted from L. The inner part of the repeat loop verifies whether the goal contributes to the coverage of the fact. Clearly, if one of the literals in such a goal is false in the intended interpretation (i.e. belongs to the set F), then it cannot contribute to the coverage of the fact. As in example 2 and algorithm 1, to determine the truthvalue of the goal, the independent part of the goal is solved by querying the knowledge base. If there are no independent subgoals in the goal, a dependent literal is used to generate a question to the oracle. The solutions $\theta$ making the subgoals true are propagated to the rest of the original goal, which is added to L. Notice that in case there is more than one true substitution for the selected subgoal(s), more than one goal will be added to L.

The heuristic to delete the most interesting goal from L will always select goals according to the clauses from which they are derived. In this way, the heuristic considers the goal corresponding to the body of one clause, and continues to work on subgoals of this clause until a solution has been found or it is certain that the clause does not cover the fact. At that point, a new clause will be selected according to the heuristic presented in section 3.3. So, within one clause, a depth-first strategy is realized and in between different clauses, a best-first strategy.

Of course, if the repeat-loop stops on the condition $L = \emptyset$, it means that there is no clause in the knowledge base covering the fact. Therefore, the fact has to be asserted in the knowledge base. This can be realized by invoking algorithm 3 (see section 3.2.) on this fact. On the other hand, if the loop terminates because the empty goal is found, we still have to assure that the literals contributing to the coverage of the fact are implied by the knowledge base. This explains why the procedure Handle_Base or Handle_View is called for all these facts.

## 3.2  Updating Base Predicates

We first define the very important notion of a type. Types in our approach are treated as in Blip [Kietz 88, Morik 89, Wrobel 89].

**Definition 3.3** *The type $T_p{}^i$, the type corresponding to the $i$-th argument position of the predicate $p$ is defined as follows :*
$$T_p{}^i = \{o \text{ is an object} \,|\, \exists x_1, ..., x_{i-1}, x_{i+1}, ..., x_n \text{ for which } KB \models p(x_1, ..., x_{i-1}, o, x_{i+1}, ..., x_n)\}$$
*We will assume that all types are finite !*

So, the type $T_p{}^i$ is the set of all objects occurring at the $i$-th position in a fact for $p$, implied by the knowledge base. Since types are sets of objects, they are partially ordered by the subset relation. Hence, they can be represented in a typegraph with at the top the universal type, containing all possible objects and at the bottom the empty type, containing no objects. We will assume here that types are represented in a graphstructure, as in Blip. The explicit representation of types from a knowledge base can be automatically computed using the techniques of [Kietz 88]. Furthermore, as in Blip's approach, we assume that non-empty intersection types are explicitly represented in the graph.

**Definition 3.4** *An intersection type $T$ is a type such that $T = T_1 \cap T_2$ where $T_1$ and $T_2$ are either intersection types or types corresponding to an argument position of a predicate.*

**Definition 3.5** *The typegraph of a knowledge base represents all types corresponding to an argument position of a predicate, the empty type, the universal type and all resulting intersection types.*

## Algorithm 2: Realizing view updates.

procedure Handle_View( $p(o_1, ..., o_n)$ : true fact containing a new object $o_i$)

    L = { $body(c)\rho$ | $c$ is a clause for $p$ in KB and

      most general unifier($head(c)$, $p(o_1, ..., o_n)$) = $\rho$ }

   repeat

        delete the most interesting goal $g$ from L

        if there is no literal $t$ in $g$ for which there is a fact $f \in F$

          and a substitution $\tau$ such that $t = f\tau$

        then if $I(g) \neq \emptyset$

           then  for all $\theta$ such that $KB \models I(g)\theta$ do

                add $D(g)\theta$ to L

             endfor

          else  if $D(g) \neq \emptyset$

             then  delete a literal $l$ from $g$ such that $l \in D(g)$

                and $l$ contains a new object

                ask the oracle for the intended interpretation of $l$

                for all $\theta$ returned by the oracle such that $l\theta$ is true do

                  add $g\theta$ to L

                endfor

             endif

          endif

        endif

   until L = $\emptyset$  or L contains the empty goal

   if L $= \emptyset$

   then  call Handle_Base($p(o_1, ..., o_n)$)

   endif

   for all answers $\theta$ from the oracle to questions $q$ obtained in the repeat loop

      such that $q\theta$ is in the intended interpretation do

        if $KB \not\models q\theta$

        then  if $q$ is a view or mixed predicate

             then  call Handle_View( $q\theta$ )

             else  call Handle_Base( $q\theta$ )

             endif

        endif

     endfor

endproc

The advantage of explicitly representing intersection types is that it is easy to determine the supertype(s) and subtype(s) of a certain type and to decide whether two types are equal, disjoint or overlapping.

**Definition 3.6** *A supertype S of a type T w.r.t. a certain typegraph G is a type occurring in G such that S is a proper superset of T.*

**Definition 3.7** *A subtype S of a type T w.r.t. a certain typegraph G is a type occurring in G such that S is a proper subset of T.*

In example 3, we illustrate types.

---

### Example 3: Types.

The types for the knowledge base of example 1 are the following :

$T_{owns}^1 = \{$ yves, katharina, maurice, luc $\}$
$T_{owns}^2 = \{$ peugeot, mercedes, renault, plume $\}$
$T_{car}^1 = \{$ peugeot, mercedes, renault $\}$
$T_{bicycle}^1 = \{$ plume $\}$
$T_{vehicle}^1 = T_{owns}^2$
$T_{drives}^1 = T_{owns}^1$
$T_{drives}^2 = T_{owns}^2$
$T_{has\_license}^1 = \{$ yves, katharina, maurice$\}$
Furthermore, we have a universal type and the empty type :
$T_{universal} = \{$ yves, katharina, maurice, luc, peugeot, mercedes, renault, plume $\}$
$T_{empty} = \{\}$
There are also some intersection types. However, these do not give rise to additional types. Indeed, all intersection types as e.g. $\{$ plume $\}$ already occur as a regular type. The resulting typegraph is shown in figure 1.

---

The main assumption underlying algorithm 3 is the following :

**Assumption 2** *If a new object o is inserted in type T of the typegraph, there is a high probability that it should also be inserted in the supertypes of T.*

Notice that this assumption is a plausible one. Given the typegraph of figure 1, it states for instance that when a new car is encountered, it is interesting to ask for its owner. The assumption will be satisfied when the typegraph is stable enough to represent the true relations among types of the domain. Clearly, the more stable the typegraph, the more clever questions algorithm 3 will generate. The assumption explains why algorithm 3 queries the oracle for the truthvalue of $q(x_1, ..., x_{j-1}, o, x_{j+1}, ..., x_n)$ if $o$ has to be inserted in a type $T \subset T_q^j$. Algorithm 3 is more complicated than this because different kinds of predicates and types have to be taken into account.

## Algorithm 3: Realizing Base Updates.

**procedure** Handle_Base( $p(o_1, ..., o_n)$ ) : true fact containing a new object $o_j$)

    **assert** $p(o_1, ..., o_n)$

    **for** all positions $i$ for which $o_i$ is a new object in $p(o_1, ..., o_n)$ **do**

        **call** Handle_Supertypes($T_p{}^i$, $o_i$)

        L = { T | T is a maximal subtype of $T_p{}^i$ in the typegraph }

        Fa = $T_p{}^i$ ; *Fa always refers to the father type of the types in L and $o_i \in P$*

        **repeat**

            delete the most interesting type T from L

            **case** $T = T_q{}^j$ for a modifiable predicate $q$ **do**

                **call** Insert_in_type($q,j,o_i$)

            **case** $T$ is an intersection type and there is a supertype $T_q{}^j$ of $T$

                such that $q$ is modifiable and $T_q{}^j \cap Fa = T$ **do**

                **call** Insert_in_type($q,j,o_i$)

            **case** otherwise **do**

                L = { T' | T' is a maximal subtype of $T$ in the typegraph }

                Fa = T

            **endcase**

        **until** L = $\emptyset$

        *Fa is the smallest type such that $o_i \in Fa$*

        **for** all types $T_q{}^j \supset Fa$, for which q is modifiable and (mixed or view) **do**

            **if** $\neg \exists \theta$ : KB $\models q(x_1, ..., x_{j-1}, o_i, x_{j+1}, x_k)\theta$ for some substitution $\theta$

            **then call** Query( $q(x_1, ..., x_{j-1}, o_i, x_{j+1}, x_k)$)

            **endif**

        **endfor**

    **endfor**

    Reconfigure the typegraph

**endproc**

## Algorithm 4: Procedures used in algorithm 3.

**procedure** Handle_Supertypes( T : type, o : new object)
    **for all** supertypes $T_q{}^j$ of T that correspond to a modifiable base predicate q
        and have not been handled yet **do**
           call Query($q(x_1, ..., x_{j-1}, o_i, x_{j+1}, x_k)$)
    **endfor**
**endproc**

**procedure** Query( $q(x_1, ..., x_{j-1}, o_i, x_{j+1}, x_k)$ : fact)
    ask the oracle for the intended interpretation of $q(x_1, ..., x_{j-1}, o_i, x_{j+1}, x_k)$
    **for all** substitutions $\theta$ returned by the oracle
        such that $q(x_1, ..., x_{j-1}, o_i, x_{j+1}, x_k)\theta$ is in the intended interpretation **do**
           **if** $q$ is a base or a mixed predicate
           **then** assert $q(x_1, ..., x_{j-1}, o_i, x_{j+1}, x_k)\theta$
           **else** call Handle_View( $q(x_1, ..., x_{j-1}, o_i, x_{j+1}, x_k)\theta$)
           **endif**
    **endfor**
    **if** the oracle returned 'no'
    **then** add $q(x_1, ..., x_{j-1}, o_i, x_{j+1}, x_k)$ to the set F
    **endif**
**endproc**

**procedure** Insert_in_type($q$ : modifiable predicate, $j$ : argument position, $o_i$ : object)
    **if** $\neg\exists\theta$ : (KB $\models q(x_1, ..., x_{j-1}, o_i, x_{j+1}, x_k)\theta$ or $q(x_1, ..., x_{j-1}, o_i, x_{j+1}, x_k)\theta \in$ F)
    **then** call Query( $q(x_1, ..., x_{j-1}, o_i, x_{j+1}, x_k)$)
    **endif**
    **if** $\exists\theta$ : KB $\models q(x_1, ..., x_{j-1}, o_i, x_{j+1}, x_k)\theta$
    **then** call Handle_Supertypes( $T_q{}^j$, $o_i$)
        L = { T | T is a maximal subtype of $T_q{}^j$ in the typegraph}
        Fa = $T_q{}^j$
    **endif**
**endproc**

# Figure 1: The typegraph of the knowledge base in example 2.

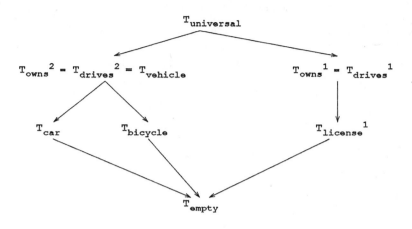

Algorithm 3 works as follows : for each new object $o_i$ occurring in the given fact, the type where the object has to be inserted is located. Following the assumption, the algorithm verifies whether the object also has to be inserted in its supertypes. In order to do so, the procedure **Handle_Supertypes** (see algorithm 4) is invoked. This procedure generates a question for all supertypes that contain a base predicate as to decide whether the object should be inserted in the supertype or not. The questions are handled by the procedure **Query**, which adds the corresponding fact to F if there are no true substitutions for the fact in the intended interpretation; otherwise, it calls the procedure of algorithm 2 in order to update the corresponding view predicate or it asserts the answers to the questions as facts in the knowledge base. The procedure **Handle_Supertypes** does not ask questions about mixed or view predicates. The reason is very simple : by asserting facts for base predicates in the knowledge base, the mixed and view predicates may also be affected. Therefore, algorithm 3 and procedure **Handle_Supertypes** first modify the base predicates and will only later verify whether questions about view and/or mixed predicates are needed. This is achieved in the inner for-loop of algorithm 3.

After treating the supertypes of the type where the object has to be inserted, algorithm 3 verifies whether the object has to be inserted in one of the subtypes of the type. Testing whether an object has to be inserted in a subtype is done by calling the procedure **Insert_in_type**. This procedure first tries to deduce whether the object belongs to the type or not. If it cannot deduce this, it will generate a query to the oracle in order to find out the answer anyway. When the object has to be inserted in a certain subtype, the procedure **Insert_in_type** will also attempt to insert the object in the supertypes of the subtype and will also consider the subtypes of the current type. This is realized by calling **Handle_Supertypes** and by modifying the current list of subtypes L.

In order to determine whether an object has to be inserted in one of the subtypes of a current type, there are three different cases to consider (the three cases in the repeat-loop of algorithm 3).

- the subtype corresponds to the argument position of a modifiable predicate : the system will verify whether the object should be inserted in the subtype by calling `Insert_in_type`

- the subtype is an intersection type : the system will verify whether there is a parent type of the intersection type that corresponds to a modifiable predicate and that is − together with the parent type already considered − responsible for the intersection type. If there is such a parent type, the system will verify whether the object has to be inserted in the parent type. If the object has to be inserted in the parent type, it will also belong to the intersection type.

- in the other case : the system is unable to generate relevant questions about the currently considered subtype. Therefore it will go one step deeper into the typegraph.

When the object cannot be inserted in any of the maximal subtypes of the current type $Fa$, the repeat loop terminates and the algorithm examines the relevant modifiable view predicates.

## 3.3  A heuristic to select the most interesting candidates first

To be able to select the most interesting candidates first in the above algorithms, the system keeps track of a set $analog(n)$ of analogous objects $o$ for each new object $n$. Furthermore, for each object $o \in analog(n)$ it computes a score, consisting of two numbers: the number of tests $t$ on analogy in which the analogous object was involved and the number of times $st$ a test has been successful. For each answer to an oracle question (the initial new term is treated as an answer to an oracle question) $q(x_1, ..., x_{j-1}, n, x_{j+1}, ..., x_k)$ involving the new object $n$, the set $analog(n)$ is modified as follows:

If the answer was 'yes' for a substitution $\theta$, then (1) the set $analog(n)$ is augmented with all objects $o$, that did not yet occur on the set and for which KB $\models q(x_1, ..., x_{j-1}, o, x_{j+1}, ..., x_k)\theta$ holds. The number of tests $t$ for these objects $o$ is initialized to 0. (2) The number of succesful tests $st$ of all objects $n$ on the new set satisfying KB $\models q(x_1, ..., x_{j-1}, n, x_{j+1}, ..., x_k)\theta$, is increased by 1. (3) The number of tests $t$ of all objects on the set is increased by 1.

If the oracle's answer was 'no', then the number of tests $t$ of all members of the set is increased by 1 and the number of successful tests $st$ of all objects $o$ for which there is no $\theta$ such that KB $\models q(x_1, ..., x_{j-1}, o, x_{j+1}, ..., x_k)\theta$, is increased by 1.

By taking subsets of the set of analogous objects, it becomes possible to detect the most interesting candidate. In order to do so, one takes a subset corresponding to each candidate and calculates the average ratio $st/t$ for each considered candidate. The most interesting candidate is then the one whose average ratio is maximal.

In algorithm 2, the heuristic can be used to choose among the clauses. This is done by associating to each clause the subset of objects from $analog(n)$ that are provable using that clause.

For the selection of the most interesting subtype in algorithm 3, the same method is used. The subset is then the intersection of the set *analog(n)* with the type itself.

The heuristic works very well in practice. Its only drawback is that when there are many elements in the set, it requires much computation. Of course, the number of elements in the set could be kept within certain bounds, by storing only a representative sample of the analogous objects.

# 4 An example session with the system

The algorithms specified in section 3, are completely implemented in BIMprolog. Below, we show a trace of a session with the implemented system. Part of the knowledge base used in the session is shown in example 4 and part of the typegraph is shown in figure 2. Comments are in *italic*, and user input is in **bold**.

---

**Example 4: Part of the knowledge base used in the session.**

```
is_allowed_to_fly(X,Y) ← person(X) ∧ owner(X,Y) ∧ has_license(X) ∧
        plane(Y)
is_allowed_to_fly(X,Y) ← person(X) ∧ has_license(X) ∧ works_for(X,C)
        ∧ air_line_company(C) ∧ owner(C,Y) ∧ plane(Y)
is_allowed_to_fly(X,Y) ← person(X) ∧ works_for(X,C) ∧ air_force(C) ∧
        owner(C,Y) ∧ military_plane(Y)

person(X) ← man(X)
person(X) ← woman(X)

plane(X) ← passengers_plane(X)
plane(X) ← military_plane(X)
plane(X) ← carrier(X)
```

The other relevant part of the knowledge base for this session, contains only facts.

---

```
?-add_fact( is_allowed_to_fly(john,concorde) ).
```
*The user inputs a new fact, it contains two unknown objects :* john *and* concorde.
*Since,* is_allowed_to_fly *is a view predicate, procedure* Handle_View *is invoked. The analogy heuristic identifies the second clause as the most interesting one, and the system proceeds.*
Is person(john) true ? **yes.**
*as* person *is a view predicate, it will be examined later*
Is has_license(john) true ? **yes.**
has_license(john) asserted ...
has_license is a base predicate
Is plane(concorde) true ? **yes.**

*as* plane *is a view predicate, it will be examined later*

Is works_for(john,X) *true for some* X ? **X = air_france.**

air_france *is a known object.*

works_for(john, air_france) *asserted ...*

works_for *is a base predicate*

Are there other X *for which* works_for(john,X) *holds* ? **no.**

Is owner(air_france,concorde) *true* ? **yes.**

owner(air_france,concorde) *asserted ...*

owner *is a base predicate*

*At this point, the system only needs to determine the truthvalue of*
air_line_company(air_france) *in order to derive that the second clause covers the original fact. However, as* air_france *is a known object, the oracle is not questioned but the knowledge base is queried. Fortunately, the fact is implied by the knowledge base, so the clause covers the original fact. Now, the system proceeds with the new facts for* person *and* plane. *These two predicates are view predicates, whereas* man *and* passengers_plane *are base predicates. Is* man(john) *true* ? **yes.**

man(john) *asserted ...*

*Because* man *is a base predicate, algorithm 3 is invoked on* man(john). *However, as* john *belongs to all supertypes of* $T_{\text{man}}$ *(* $T_{\text{person}}$ *) and to all other possible intersecting types in the typegraph (* $T^1_{\text{is\_allowed\_to\_fly}}$, $T^1_{\text{has\_license}}$ *and* $T^1_{\text{works\_for}}$ *), no further questions about* john *are generated. The system continues with* plane(concorde)

Is passenger_plane(concorde) *true* ? **yes.**

passenger_plane(concorde) *asserted ...*

*As* passenger_plane *has an intersection type with* subsonic, *the system asks :*

Is subsonic(concorde) *true* ? **no.**

*As* passengers_plane *has also an intersection type with* jet, *it asks :*

Is jet(concorde)*true* ? **yes.**

jet(concorde) *asserted ...*

*Because* supersonic *is a subtype of* jet *:*

Is supersonic(concorde) *true* ? **yes.**

supersonic(concorde) *asserted ...*

*Now, the last step of the algorithm is executed : the system checks that* concorde *belongs to all relevant supertypes. Since this is the case, no further questions are generated to the user.*


# 5   Integrating the methods in Clint

The algorithms can easily be integrated into other knowledge acquisition and learning systems. As a case study, we show how to integrate them into the learning system Clint [De Raedt and Bruynooghe 88, De Raedt and Bruynooghe 89, De Raedt and Bruynooghe 90]. Clint is a user-friendly concept-learner that combines several interesting features : it constructs its own examples, uses knowledge, copes with indirect relevance, shifts its bias and learns conjunctive as well as disjunctive concepts. Basically, it learns Horn-Clauses from incorrectly handled facts. To achieve this aim, it generates membership questions

**Figure 2: The typegraph of the knowledge base in example 2.**

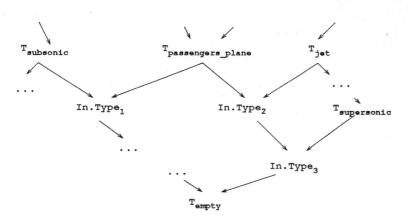

to an oracle. One problem, which occurs in Clint is that it cannot learn something about true facts that contain unknown objects. The reason is that in order to learn, it first derives a clause covering the fact by looking for all properties and relations between the objects that occur in the true fact. Clearly, if nothing is known about some of these objects, this fails. However, by using the above presented methods, Clint can easily be enhanced to cope with this situation. How this is realized is shown in algorithm 5. The algorithm is straightforward. The procedure Clint corresponds to the algorithms described in [De Raedt and Bruynooghe 89].

# 6    Conclusions and Related Work

The presented work is related to work in learning apprentices such as Disciple [Tecuci and Kodratoff 90, Kodratoff and Tecuci 87] and Blip [Morik 89, Wrobel 89], learning by being told [Haas and Hendrix 83] and knowledge base revision (e.g. [Tomasovic 88]).

The learning apprentices Disciple and Blip have some facilities to help the user to input new facts. Basically these facilities are such that the system shows the user some situation and that the user is required to enter some new facts about this situation. In Disciple this occurs when the system is in its weak theory mode and that part of an explanation is needed by the system. If the system is unable to generate this explanation the user is supposed to help the sytem by inputting some facts. In Blip the user inputs facts and gets immediate feedback about the consequences of the input facts. If the user notices that not all desired facts concerning a certain object are consequences she can enter additional facts.

The type formalism used in this paper is the same as in Blip [Kietz 88]. In Blip, the type graph is automatically modified when the user enters new facts. Also, if the type

**Algorithm 5: Enhancing Clint.**

```
procedure Enhanced_Clint( p(o_1, ..., o_n) : fact, t : truthvalue of p(o_1, ..., o_n) )
    if  (1) KB ⊭ p(o_1, ..., o_n) and
        (2) t = true and
        (3) p(o_1, ..., o_n) contains a new object o_k
    then if p is a view predicate
         then  call Handle_View(p(o_1, ..., o_n))
         else  call Handle_Base(p(o_1, ..., o_n))
         endif
    else  call Clint( p(o_1, ..., o_n), t)
    endif
endproc
```

structure should be modified, the user is told so. In this way the user is provided with additional hints about possibly missing knowledge [Kietz 88].

[Haas and Hendrix 83] present an approach to interactively acquire knowledge about a certain domain. Their approach gathers knowledge in a very similar way to ours. However, there are also some important differences : they have a natural language interface, determine the structure of the type graph by asking questions to the user and use a rather specific knowledge representation formalism. Furthermore it is not clear how to integrate their approach in concept-learning systems because of the different formalism.

The approaches to knowledge base updating such as [Tomasovic 88] attempt to automatically find the transactions needed to accomodate new facts in the data base. However, they do not try to obtain as much knowledge as possible about the new objects.

As a conclusion, our technique is different from the above mentioned ones in the sense that it attempts to acquire in a systematic way as much knowledge as possible about new objects. In this respect, we go further than the knowledge base updating and learning apprentice approaches. Also because we automatically acquire the type graph as in [Kietz 88] and show how to integrate our methods in existing concept-learners, we believe that the presented method integrated with a system as Clint is very useful for learning apprentices.

# References

[Angluin 88] Dana Angluin. Queries and concept-learning. *Machine Learning*, 1988.

[Bratko 86] I. Bratko. *Prolog Programming for Artificial Intelligence*. Addison-Wesley, 1986.

[Carbonell, Michalski and Mitchell 83] J.G. Carbonell, R.S. Michalski, and T.M. Mitchell. An overview of machine learning. In R.S. Michalski, J.G. Carbonell, and T.M. Mitchell, editors, *Machine Learning : an artificial intelligence approach*, volume 1. Morgan Kaufmann, 1983.

[De Raedt and Bruynooghe 88] L. De Raedt and M. Bruynooghe. On interactive concept-learning and assimilation. In D. Sleeman, editor, *Proceedings of the 3rd European Working Session On Learning*, pages 167–176. Pitman, 1988.

[De Raedt and Bruynooghe 89] L. De Raedt and M. Bruynooghe. Towards friendly concept-learners. In *Proceedings of the 11th International Joint Conference on Artificial Intelligence*, pages 849–856. Morgan Kaufmann, 1989.

[De Raedt and Bruynooghe 90] L. De Raedt and M. Bruynooghe. Indirect relevance and bias in inductive concept-learning. *Knowledge Acquisition*, 1990. to appear.

[Gaines and Boose] B. Gaines and J. Boose. The knowledge acquisition journal. Academic Press.

[Genesereth and Nilsson 87] M. Genesereth and N. Nilsson. *Logical foundations of artificial intelligence*. Morgan Kaufmann, 1987.

[Haas and Hendrix 83] N. Haas and G. Hendrix. Learning by being told : acquiring knowledge for information management. In R.S. Michalski, J.G. Carbonell, and T.M. Mitchell, editors, *Machine Learning : an artificial intelligence approach*, volume 1. Morgan Kaufmann, 1983.

[Kietz 88] J.U. Kietz. Incremental and reversible acquisition of taxonomies. In M. Linster, B. Gaines, and J. Boose, editors, *Proceedings of the 2nd European Knowledge Acquisition for Knowledge Based Systems Workshops*, 1988.

[Kodratoff 88] Y. Kodratoff. *Introduction to Machine Learning*. Pitman, 1988.

[Kodratoff and Michalski 90] Yves Kodratoff and R.S Michalski, editors. *Machine Learning : an artificial intelligence approach, Volume 3*. Morgan Kaufmann, 1990.

[Kodratoff and Tecuci 87] Y. Kodratoff and G. Tecuci. Disciple-1 : interactive system in weak theory fields. In *Proceedings of the 10th International Joint Conference on Artificial Intelligence*. Morgan Kaufmann, 1987.

[Michalski 83] R.S. Michalski. A theory and methodology of inductive learning. In R.S Michalski, J.G. Carbonell, and T.M. Mitchell, editors, *Machine Learning : an artificial intelligence approach*, volume 1. Morgan Kaufmann, 1983.

[Michalski, Carbonell and Mitchell 83] R.S Michalski, J.G. Carbonell, and T.M. Mitchell. *Machine Learning : an artificial intelligence approach, Volume 1*. Morgan Kaufmann, 1983.

[Michalski, Carbonell and Mitchell 86] R.S Michalski, J.G. Carbonell, and T.M. Mitchell. *Machine Learning : an artificial intelligence approach, Volume 2.* Morgan Kaufmann, 1986.

[Morik 89] Katharina Morik. Sloppy modeling. In Katharina Morik, editor, *Knowledge Representation and Organization in Machine Learning,* volume 347 of *Lecture Notes in Artificial Intelligence.* Springer-Verlag, 1989.

[Muggleton and Buntine 88] S. Muggleton and W. Buntine. Machine invention of first order predicates by inverting resolution. In *Proceedings of the 5th International Conference on Machine Learning.* Morgan Kaufmann, 1988.

[Quinlan 86] J.R. Quinlan. Induction of decision trees. *Machine Learning,* 1:81–106, 1986.

[Quinlan 90] J.R. Quinlan. Learning logical definition from relations. *Machine Learning,* 5:239–266, 1990.

[Shapiro 83] Ehud Y. Shapiro. *Algorithmic Program Debugging.* The MIT press, 1983.

[Sterling and Shapiro 86] Leon Sterling and Ehud Shapiro. *The art of Prolog.* The MIT press, 1986.

[Tecuci and Kodratoff 90] G. Tecuci and Y. Kodratoff. Apprenticeship learning in non-homogeneous domain theories. In Y. Kodratoff and R.S. Michalski, editors, *Machine Learning : an artificial intelligence approach,* volume 3. Morgan Kaufmann, 1990.

[Tomasovic 88] A. Tomasovic. View update translation via deduction and annotation. In *Proceedings 2nd International Conference on Database Theory.* Lecture Notes in Computer Science, Volume 326, Springer-Verlag, 1988.

[Wirth 88] R. Wirth. Learning by failure to prove. In D. Sleeman, editor, *Proceedings of the 3rd European Working Session on Learning.* Pitman, 1988.

[Wrobel 88] S. Wrobel. Automatic representation adjustment in an observational discovery system. In Sleeman D., editor, *Proceedings of the 3rd European Working Session on Learning.* Pitman, 1988.

[Wrobel 89] S. Wrobel. Demand driven concept-formation. In K. Morik, editor, *Knowledge Representation and Organization in Machine Learning,* volume 347 of *Lecture Notes in Artificial Intelligence.* Springer-Verlag, 1989.

# LEARNING NONRECURSIVE DEFINITIONS OF RELATIONS WITH LINUS

Nada Lavrač, Sašo Džeroski and Marko Grobelnik
Jožef Stefan Institute, Jamova 39
61000 Ljubljana, Yugoslavia
Phone: (+38)(61) 214 399, Fax: (+38)(61) 219 385
E-mail: nada@ijs.ac.mail.yu

## Abstract

Many successful inductive learning systems use a propositional attribute-value language to represent both training examples and induced hypotheses. Recent developments are concerned with systems that induce concept descriptions in first-order logic. The deductive hierarchical database (DHDB) formalism is a restricted form of Horn clause logic in which nonrecursive logical definitions of relations can be expressed. Having variables, compound terms and predicates, the DHDB formalism allows for more compact descriptions of concepts than an attribute-value language. Our inductive learning system LINUS uses the DHDB formalism to represent concepts as definitions of relations. The paper gives a description of LINUS and presents the results of its successful application to several inductive learning tasks taken from the machine learning literature. A comparison with the results of other first-order learning systems is given as well.

## 1  Introduction

The general framework for machine learning can be stated as follows. Given a set of *positive training examples* $E_T$, a (possibly empty) set of *negative training examples* $E_F$, and *background knowledge* $B$, find an *hypothesis* or *concept description* $H$ such that $B, H \vdash E_T$ and $B, H \not\vdash E_F$.

The development of inductive learning systems can focus on different problems, such as restricted representation language, inability to make use of background knowledge, noise in training examples, and bias of vocabulary. Our work deals with the first three problems. Our system LINUS can effectively use background knowledge ($B$) in inducing hypotheses ($H$). Hypotheses have the form of DHDB (deductive hierarchical database) clauses, i.e., typed nonrecursive Horn clauses with negation, and represent logical definitions of relations.

Many successful inductive learning systems use a propositional attribute-value language to represent training examples and concept descriptions, for example, the members of the AQ (e.g., Michalski et al. 1986) and TDIDT (top-down induction of decision trees, e.g., Quinlan 1986) families of inductive learning programs. Recent developments are concerned with systems that induce concept descriptions in first-order logic. Very promising approaches are used in CIGOL (Muggleton & Buntine 1988), GOLEM (Muggleton & Feng 1990) and FOIL (Quinlan 1989, 1990), which induce descriptions of complex relations in Horn clause logic.

Our approach can be best compared to FOIL, since both systems are based on ideas that have proved effective in attribute-value learning programs. Each extends these ideas to a more expressive first-order logical formalism in its own way. The idea in LINUS is to incorporate existing attribute-value learning programs into the DHDB environment. LINUS now incorporates ASSISTANT (Cestnik, Kononenko & Bratko 1987), a member of the TDIDT family, and NEWGEM (Mozetič 1985), a member of the AQ family, which are used in learning attribute-value descriptions. The incorporation into the DHDB environment is done by a special interface implemented in Prolog. The DHDB formalism is used to enhance the expressiveness of the propositional attribute-value languages used in ASSISTANT and NEWGEM. In DHDB, a typed language is used; the increase in expressiveness is due to universally quantified variables, compound terms, and utility predicates and functions, which can be used in the induced hypotheses. Despite the fact that recursively defined predicates and infinite terms (i.e., terms which can take a value from an infinite set) are not allowed in concept descriptions, the formalism is appropriate for a large scale of real-life problems.

An initial algorithm for learning in the DHDB formalism is a part of QuMAS (Qualitative Model Acquisition System, Mozetič 1987). Its further development is described in (Mozetič & Lavrač 1988, Lavrač & Mozetič 1988). The algorithm was first used to learn functions of components of a qualitative model of the heart in the KARDIO system (Bratko, Mozetič & Lavrač 1989). A detailed description of its successor LINUS and results of a number of other experiments can be found in (Lavrač 1990).

The aim of this paper is to show how LINUS can be used to learn nonrecursive logical definitions of relations. Section 2 introduces the DHDB formalism, gives an overview of the system, and describes the learning algorithm. Section 3 gives results of the successful application of LINUS to several inductive learning tasks taken from machine learning literature. Our results are compared to the results obtained by FOIL (Quinlan 1989, 1990). In the chess endgame domain, we compare the classification accuracy and efficiency with FOIL, DUCE and CIGOL (Muggleton et al. 1989).

# 2    Learning in the DHDB formalism

## 2.1    The DHDB formalism

A *deductive database* is a finite set of typed *Horn clauses with negation* of the form:

$$A \leftarrow L_0, \ldots, L_n$$

where $A$ is an atom (predicate symbol applied to terms) and each $L_i$ is a literal (positive or negative atom).

A deductive database is called *hierarchical* if its predicates can be partitioned into levels so that the bodies of the clauses in the definitions of higher level predicates contain only lower level predicates (Lloyd 1987). Consequently, recursive predicate definitions are not allowed in *deductive hierarchical databases* (DHDB).

In deductive databases a *typed language* is used. Types provide a natural way of specifying the domain of a database. We emphasize that, in contrast to the usual restriction in deductive databases, in our formalism compound terms are allowed to appear as arguments of predicates in a database and in queries. However, only hierarchical (nonrecursive) types are allowed. This restriction bans recursive data types, which means that there are only a finite number of ground (non-variable) terms of each type, and consequently, that each query can only have a finite number of answers (Lloyd 1987). A comparison of DHDB to other logical formalisms is given in (Mozetič & Lavrač 1988).

## 2.2   Learning in LINUS

In attribute-value learning, given is a set of training instances (given as n-tuples of values of a fixed collection of *attributes*), each belonging to exactly one of the possible *classes*. Classes are values of the *decision* or *dependent variable* and attributes are called *independent variables*. The learning task is to find a rule, called a *hypothesis* or a *concept description*, that can be used to predict the class of an unseen object as a function of its attribute values.

In DHDB, a set of training instances is given as a set of ground facts specifying a *relation* between $n$ domain entities. By analogy with an object's *class*, each ground fact is labeled ⊕ or ⊖ to indicate whether or not it is in the relation, i.e., whether it is to be treated as a positive or as a negative instance for learning.

In LINUS, hypothesis $H$ (i.e., the description of the *target* relation to be learned), has the form of a predicate definition (a set of typed nonrecursive Horn clauses with negation, having the same predicate in the head); positive examples $E_T$ are given ground facts; negative examples $E_F$ are either given or generated ground facts; and background knowledge $B$ consists of predicate definitions in the form of typed (possibly recursive) Horn clauses with negation.

The main idea in LINUS is to incorporate existing attribute-value learning programs into a more powerful DHDB environment. This is done by a special DHDB interface, consisting of over 2000 lines of Prolog code. The structure of the system is shown in Figure 1. The DHDB interface transforms positive instances (given facts) and negative instances (possibly generated by the DHDB interface) from the DHDB form into attribute-value tuples and vice versa, from induced if-then rules into the DHDB form. The most important feature of this interface is that, by taking into account type theory, utility predicates and functions are considered as possible new attributes for learning by an attribute-value learning program.

Currently LINUS incorporates two attribute-value learning programs, ASSIS-TANT and NEWGEM. In our environment it is easy to incorporate other learning algorithms, e.g., GINESYS (Gams 1989) and CN2 (Clark & Niblett 1989), which were already used in some of our experiments. Having different systems in the same DHDB environment, the idea (promoted in GINESYS and LOGART (Cestnik & Bratko 1988)) that multiple knowledge can increase system performance can naturally be further exploited.

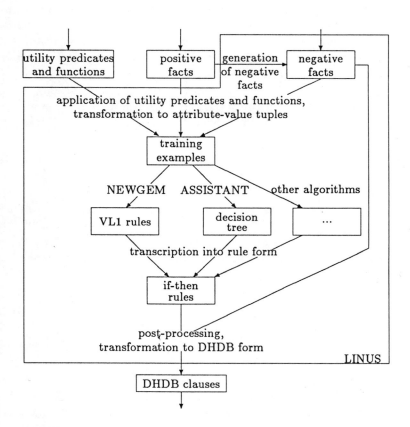

Figure 1: An overview of the LINUS system

## 2.3  Training examples and domain knowledge

We briefly describe the input to LINUS and illustrate it on a simple example.

Given are training instances in the form of ground facts determining a *relation* between $n$ domain entities. Suppose that relation r(a,b,c) is defined by the following three ground facts labeled $\oplus$:

```
r(a1,b1,b1).
r(a1,b2,b2).
r(a2,b1,b2).
```

Facts labeled $\ominus$, not belonging to the relation, may also be provided. Associated with relation r(a,b,c) is the declaration of the names and the *types* of its arguments, stating that the first argument of relation r named a is of type_a, and the other two arguments named b and c are of type_b. Each type has an associated set of possible values, e.g., {a1,a2} for type_a, and {b1,b2} for type_b. In general, values are constants or compound terms with constant arguments. The use of compound terms allows for the description of compound or structured objects. Values can be nominal, linear, continuous, or structured (hierarchical). The type boolean is defined by default.

Background knowledge consists of predicate definitions specifying relations between domain entities. These predicate definitions can be recursive. We distinguish between what we call *utility predicates* and *utility functions*. Utility functions are predicates with an annotation which determines the *input* and *output* arguments, while utility predicates only have *input* arguments. This is similar to mode declarations in GOLEM (Muggleton & Feng 1990). Utility predicates can be declared *symmetric* in certain pairs of arguments of the same type. For example, a binary predicate $q(X, Y)$ is symmetric in $X$ and $Y$ if they are both of type $T$ and $q(X, Y) = q(Y, X)$ for every value of $X$ and $Y$. A built-in symmetric utility predicate *equality* $(=/2)$ is defined by default on arguments of the same type.

For each relation, utility predicate and utility function there is a definition of the *types* of arguments. In our example, a binary utility predicate p is defined on arguments of type_a and type_b, respectively.

```
p(a1,b1).
p(a1,b2).
p(a2,b2).
```

The form of examples to be used in learning is determined by the so-called *dependence* relation. We may select any subset of the $n$ arguments of the given relation for learning the target relation. Apart from the $k_{Arg}$ selected arguments, we can also select $k_{Util}$ utility predicates and functions as interesting for the given learning task. In this way we have $k = k_{Arg} + k_{Util}$ selected arguments. In our example, the dependence relation states that all arguments (a, b and c) are selected, and that the possible applications of the utility predicates p and equality $(=/2)$ should be considered as new attributes for learning $(k = 3 + 2 = 5)$.

Having selected the $k$ arguments, some of them can be treated as *dependent* variables (analogous to *class* variables) and the others as *independent* variables (analogous to attributes in attribute-value learning). This distinction is important since LINUS can be used both for learning definitions of relations (*relation* learning mode) and for inducing descriptions of particular classes (*class* learning mode). In *class* learning mode, dependent variables are not used for learning, but are only used to determine the different *classes*, where a *class* is a combination of values of the dependent variables. In *relation* learning mode, on the other hand, the two classes to be learned are $\oplus$ and $\ominus$, denoting whether the arguments do or do not satisfy the target relation. When generating negative examples (see Section 2.4) we also need to distinguish between dependent and independent variables. In the paper we restrict our scope only to relation learning.

## 2.4   The learning algorithm

The outermost level of the LINUS learning algorithm consists of the following steps:

- establish the set of positive and negative facts,
- transform facts from the DHDB form into attribute-value tuples,
- induce a concept description by an attribute-value learning program,
- transform the induced if-then rules into the form of DHDB clauses.

Below is a short description of the individual steps illustrated by an example.

In the **first step**, the sets of positive and negative facts are determined. Positive facts are always given explicitly, while negative facts may be either given explicitly, or generated automatically. In *class* learning mode, where examples from different classes are provided, no negative examples are needed. On the other hand, in *relation* learning mode, where there are only two classes ($\oplus$ and $\ominus$), negative examples are necessary. Consequently, if they are not given explicitly, they have to be generated. The generation of negative facts takes into account the type theory. In LINUS, there are several options for generating negative examples.

- When generating negative facts under the *closed-world assumption* (cwa mode), all possible combinations of values of $k_{Arg}$ arguments of the target relation are generated.
- In *partial closed-world assumption* (pcwa) mode, for a given combination of values of the $k_{ArgInd}$ independent variables all combinations of values of the $k_{ArgDep}$ dependent variables are generated.
- In near-misses mode, facts are generated by varying only the value of one of the $k_{Arg}$ variables at a time, where $k_{Arg} = k_{ArgDep} + k_{ArgInd}$.

The generated facts are used as negative instances of the target relation, except for those given as positive. In our example, negative facts are generated under the closed-world assumption. The following facts labeled $\ominus$ are generated:

```
r(a1,b1,b2).
r(a1,b2,b1).
r(a2,b1,b1).
r(a2,b2,b1).
r(a2,b2,b2).
```

In the **second step** of the algorithm, positive and negative facts are transformed into an attribute-value form. The algorithm first checks which are the possible applications of the utility predicates and functions on the arguments of the target relation.

Next, attribute-value tuples are generated by assigning values to the enlarged set of attributes. Values true or false are assigned to each application of a utility predicate on the argument values of the target relation. Similar computation is performed for utility functions, except that values of all output arguments of a function are computed (instead of only assigning values true or false).

In our simple example, the possible applications of predicate p are p(a,b) and p(a,c); for the equality predicate the only possible application is b=c on arguments of the same type type_b. Positive tuples of the form $\langle$ a, b, c, (b=c), p(a,b), p(a,c) $\rangle$ are then generated.

$\langle$ a1, b1, b1, true, true, true $\rangle$
$\langle$ a1, b2, b2, true, true, true $\rangle$
$\langle$ a2, b1, b2, false, false, true $\rangle$

A similar computation is performed for the negative facts.

To show the complexity of the so obtained learning task, let us consider the number of attributes to be used for learning. The total number of attributes $k_{Attr}$ equals:

$$k_{Attr} = k_{Arg} + \sum_{s=1}^{k_{Util}} k_{New,p_s}$$

where $k_{Arg}$ is the number of arguments of the target relation, and $k_{New,p_s}$ is the number of new attributes, resulting from the possible (with regard to given types) applications of one of the $k_{Util}$ utility predicates/functions $p_s$ on the arguments of the target relation.

Suppose that the arguments of a $n$-ary utility predicate $p_s$ are of types $T_i$, $i = 1,\ldots,u$. $k_{New,p_s}$ is then equal to the product of the numbers of variations (with repetition) of the numbers of arguments of the same type:

$$k_{New,p_s} = \prod_{i=1}^{u} (k_{ArgT_i})^{n_i}$$

where $k_{ArgT_i}$ is the number of arguments of type $T_i$ in the target relation, $n_i$ is the number of arguments of type $T_i$ in the utility predicate, and $u$ is the number of different types of arguments in the utility predicate ($n = \sum_{i=1}^{u} n_i$). Since a relation where two arguments are identical can be represented by a relation of a smaller arity, we could restrict the arguments of a utility predicate to be different. In this case the following formula would hold:

$$k_{New,p_s} = \prod_{i=1}^{u} \binom{k_{ArgT_i}}{n_i} \cdot n_i! \tag{1}$$

Utility predicates can be declared as *symmetric* in certain pairs of arguments. In case that $p_s$ is symmetric in all pairs of arguments, the number of variations (without repetition) in (1) is replaced by the number of combinations:

$$k_{New,p_s} = \prod_{i=1}^{u} \binom{k_{ArgT_i}}{n_i}$$

For example, the number of possible applications of the built-in symmetric utility predicate *equality* (=/2) equals to:

$$k_{New,=} = \prod_{i=1}^{r} \binom{k_{ArgT_i}}{2} = \prod_{i=1}^{r} \frac{k_{ArgT_i} \cdot (k_{ArgT_i} - 1)}{2}$$

where $k_{ArgT_i}$ denotes the number of arguments of the same type $T_i$, and $r$ is the number of different types in the target relation. Similar formulas hold for utility functions.

The **third step** of the algorithm is the induction of the concept description which depends on the choice of the learning algorithm. Training examples in the form of tuples are transformed into the appropriate input form for learning by ASSISTANT or NEWGEM, learning by the chosen attribute-value algorithm is invoked and the obtained concept description (in the form of a decision tree or VL1 rules) is transcribed into the form of if-then rules.

In the **fourth step**, the induced if-then rules are transformed into DHDB form. Before this transformation is performed, a special post-processor checks whether rules can be made more compact by eliminating irrelevant literals and by discarding redundant clauses. A literal in a clause is *irrelevant* if, after it has been eliminated, the clause does not cover any new negative examples. A clause is *redundant* if it is covered by some more general clause. Post-processing is especially effective when transforming decision trees into rules (Quinlan 1987).

In our example, the if-then rules induced by NEWGEM are the following:

```
class = ⊕  if  a=a1 ∧ (b=c) = true.
class = ⊕  if  c=b2 ∧ p(a,b) = false.
```

The DHDB interface transforms these rules into the DHDB clauses below.

```
r(A,B,C) ← A=a1, B=C.
r(A,B,C) ← C=b2, not p(A,B).
```

For comparison, the description induced by LINUS using NEWGEM without background relations $p$ and *equality* (which is equivalent to NEWGEM itself) was exactly the same as the set of ground facts given as positive examples.

# 3 Experimental results and comparison with other approaches

This section discusses the performance of LINUS on three learning tasks taken from the machine learning literature. The descriptions of the domains are taken from Quinlan (1989,1990) and our results are compared to the ones obtained by his system FOIL.

LINUS was used in *relation* learning mode to learn definitions of relations from examples of the relation and background relations given as utility predicates. No predicates of the form *Attribute = Value* for binding a variable to a constant were allowed in concept descriptions; this was achieved by selecting only applications of background relations as independent variables for learning ($k_{Attr} = \sum_{s=1}^{k_{Util}} k_{New,p_s}$, $k_{Arg} = 0$).

The arguments of the background relations used in FOIL are not typed and the same relations are sometimes used for different types of arguments which can be confusing. In LINUS, each such relation was replaced by several relations, one for each combination of types, e.g., the precedes relation in the Eleusis example was replaced by the two relations precedes_rank and precedes_suit.

Using two algorithms ASSISTANT and NEWGEM, we typically got slightly different results on the same domain; they were all comparable to the results obtained by FOIL. In the chess endgame domain we were able to compare the classification accuracy and efficiency. Our results are also compared to the ones obtained by DUCE and CIGOL (Muggleton et al. 1989).

## 3.1   Learning the concept of an arch

In this example, taken from Winston (1975) and described by Quinlan (1990), four objects are given. Two of them are arches and two are not, as shown in Figure 2.

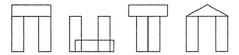

Figure 2: Arches and near misses, from Winston (1975) and Quinlan (1990)

For the target relation arch(A,B,C), stating that A, B and C form an arch with columns B and C and lintel A, the following background relations were used: supports(X,Y), left_of(X,Y), touches(X,Y), brick(X), wedge(X) and parallelepiped(X).

LINUS was first run with explicitly given (two) negative examples, and then with negative examples generated in the *closed-world assumption* mode. Results of LINUS and FOIL are listed below.

```
% LINUS                             % FOIL
% negative examples: explicitly     % negative examples: explicitly
arch(A,B,C) ←                       % no clauses generated because
 supports(B,A),                     % of encoding length restriction
 not touches(B,C).
% negative examples: cwa            % negative examples: cwa
arch(A,B,C) ←                       arch(A,B,C) ←
 left_of(B,C),                       left_of(B,C),
 supports(B,A),                      supports(B,A),
 not touches(B,C).                   not touches(B,C).
```

The definition induced with explicitly given negative examples can be paraphrased as follows: "A, B and C form an arch if B supports A and B does not touch C". Note that this definition is more general than the one obtained in cwa mode; the latter has an additional condition stating that B must be left of C.

With explicitly given negative instances FOIL was unable to learn the concept description because of the encoding length restriction. Namely, a heuristic used in FOIL restricts the total length of the concept description to the number of bits needed to enumerate the training instances explicitly. Our result in cwa mode is the same as the one by FOIL.

On an enlarged set of training instances containing two more negative examples (Lavrač, Džeroski & Grobelnik 1990) the result using both ASSISTANT and NEWGEM was essentially the same as reported by Winston (1975):

arch(A,B,C) ← supports(B,A), supports(C,A), not touches(B,C).

## 3.2 Eleusis - Learning rules that govern card sequences

The Eleusis learning problem was originaly attacked by the SPARC/E system (Dietterich & Michalski 1986). The description here is taken from Quinlan (1990). In the Eleusis card game, the dealer invents a secret rule specifying a condition under which a card can be added to a sequence of cards. The players attempt to add a card to the current sequence. If a card is a legal successor it is placed to the right of the last card, otherwise it is placed under the last card. The horizontal *main line* represents the sequence as developed so far, while the vertical *side lines* show incorrect plays. Three layouts, reproduced from Quinlan (1990), are given in Figure 3.

Each card other than the first in the sequence provides an example for learning the target relation can_follow. The example is labeled ⊕ if the card appears in the main line, and ⊖ if it is in a side line. The target relation can_follow(A,B,C,D,E,F) states that a card of rank A and suit B can follow a sequence ending with: a card of rank C and suit D; E consecutive cards of suit D; and F consecutive cards of the same color. Background relations that can be used in induced rules are the following: precedes_rank(X,Y), precedes_suit(X,Y), lower_rank(X,Y), face(X), same_color(X,Y), odd_rank(X), and odd_num(X).

In the first layout, the intended dealer's rule was: "Completed color sequences must be odd and a male card may not appear next to a female card". Neither FOIL nor LINUS could discover the intended rule, because no information on the sex of cards was encoded in the background relations. LINUS using ASSISTANT with post-processing induced the clauses given below.

can_follow(A,B,C,D,E,F) ← same_color(B,D).
can_follow(A,B,C,D,E,F) ← odd_num(F), not precedes_suit(D,B).
can_follow(A,B,C,D,E,F) ← odd_num(F), not precedes_rank(C,A).

While the clauses induced by LINUS using both ASSISTANT and NEWGEM cover all positive examples, the ones induced by FOIL are not complete: they do not cover

| main line | A♡ | 7♣ | 6♣ | 9♠ | 10♡ | 7♡ | 10◇ | J♣ | A♢ | 4♡ | 8◇ | 7♣ | 9♠ |
|---|---|---|---|---|---|---|---|---|---|---|---|---|---|
| side lines |  | K◇ |  |  |  | 5♣ |  | Q◇ |  | 3♠ |  |  | 9♡ |
|  |  | J♡ |  |  |  |  |  |  |  |  |  |  | 6♡ |
| main (ctd) | 10♣ | K♠ | 2♣ | 10♠ | J♠ |
| side (ctd) |  | Q♡ |
|  |  | A◇ |

| main line | J♣ | 4♣ | Q♡ | 3♠ | Q◇ | 9♡ | Q♣ | 7♡ | Q◇ | 9◇ | Q♣ | 3♡ | K♡ |
|---|---|---|---|---|---|---|---|---|---|---|---|---|---|
| side lines | K♣ | 5♠ |  |  |  | 4♠ |  | 10◇ |  |  |  |  |  |
|  |  | 7♠ |  |  |  |  |  |  |  |  |  |  |  |
| main (ctd) | 4♣ | K◇ | 6♣ | J◇ | 8◇ | J♡ | 7♣ | J◇ | 7♡ | J♡ | 6♡ | K◇ |

| mainline | 4♡ | 5◇ | 8♣ | J♠ | 2♣ | 5♠ | A♣ | 5♠ | 10♡ |
|---|---|---|---|---|---|---|---|---|---|
| side line | 7♣ | 6♠ | K♣ | A♡ |  | 6♣ | A♠ |  |  |
|  | J♡ | 7♡ | 3♡ | K◇ |  |  |  |  |  |
|  | 4♣ | 2♣ |  | Q♠ |  |  |  |  |  |
|  | 10♠ | 7♠ |  |  |  |  |  |  |  |
|  | 8♡ | 6◇ |  |  |  |  |  |  |  |
|  | A◇ | 6♡ |  |  |  |  |  |  |  |
|  | 2◇ | 4♣ |  |  |  |  |  |  |  |

Figure 3: Three Eleusis layouts, from Dietterich and Michalski (1986) and Quinlan (1990)

the positive example can_follow(10,heart,9,spade,1,3). This is due to the encoding restriction, which prevents further search for clauses. Although this might be useful when dealing with noisy data, it is unsuitable for exact domains. The application of the encoding restriction could be controlled by a parameter: it should be applied if the domain is noisy or inexact, but should not be applied to exact domains with no noise, such as the domains presented in this paper. Here are the clauses induced by LINUS using NEWGEM, and by FOIL:

```
% layout 1
% negative examples: explicitly
% LINUS using NEWGEM
can_follow(A,B,C,D,E,F) ←
  same_color(B,D).
can_follow(A,B,C,D,E,F) ←
  odd_num(F),
  odd_rank(A).
can_follow(A,B,C,D,E,F) ←
  not face(A),
  lower_rank(C,A).
```

```
% negative examples: explicitly
% FOIL
can_follow(A,B,C,D,E,F) ←
  same_color(B,D).
can_follow(A,B,C,D,E,F) ←
  odd_num(F),
  odd_rank(A).
```

In layout 2 both LINUS using NEWGEM and FOIL correctly induced the intended rule: "Play alternate face and non-face cards". ASSISTANT's rule set contains a superfluous clause which was not removed in post-processing.

```
% layout 2
% LINUS using NEWGEM                    % FOIL
can_follow(A,B,C,D,E,F) ←               can_follow(A,B,C,D,E,F) ←
  face(A),                                face(A),
  not face(C).                            not face(C).
can_follow(A,B,C,D,E,F) ←               can_follow(A,B,C,D,E,F) ←
  face(C),                                face(C),
  not face(A).                            not face(A).
```

```
% LINUS using ASSISTANT (after post-processing)
can_follow(A,B,C,D,E,F) ← face(C), not face(A).
can_follow(A,B,C,D,E,F) ← face(A), not face(C).
can_follow(A,B,C,D,E,F) ← not odd_num(E).
```

In layout 3 the intended rule was: "Play a higher card in the suit preceding that of the last card; or, play a lower card in the suit following that of the last card". FOIL discovered only one clause, approximately describing the first part of the rule. LINUS using ASSISTANT discovered an approximation of the whole rule: "Play a higher or equal card in the suit preceding that of the last card; or, play a lower card in the suit following that of the last card". The DHDB clauses are given below.

```
can_follow(A,B,C,D,E,F) ← lower_rank(A,C), precedes_suit(D,B).
can_follow(A,B,C,D,E,F) ← precedes_suit(B,D), not lower_rank(A,C).
```

Again, the descriptions induced by LINUS are complete, while FOIL's is not. Using NEWGEM, LINUS generated exactly the intended dealer's rule.

```
% layout 3
% LINUS using NEWGEM                    % FOIL
can_follow(A,B,C,D,E,F) ←
  lower_rank(A,C),
  precedes_suit(D,B).
can_follow(A,B,C,D,E,F) ←               can_follow(A,B,C,D,E,F) ←
  lower_rank(C,A),                        precedes_suit(B,D),
  precedes_suit(B,D).                     not lower_rank(A,C).
```

## 3.3  Learning illegal positions in a chess endgame

The domain of this learning task, described in Muggleton et al. (1989) and Quinlan (1990), is the chess endgame White King and Rook versus Black King. The target relation illegal(A,B,C,D,E,F) states whether the position in which the White King is at (A,B), the White Rook at (C,D) and the Black King at (E,F) is not a legal White-to-move position. In FOIL, the domain knowledge is represented by the two relations adjacent(X,Y) and less_than(X,Y) indicating that rank/file X is adjacent to rank/file Y and rank/file X is less than rank/file Y, respectively.

LINUS uses the following utility predicates: adjacent_rank(X,Y), adjacent_file(X,Y), less_rank(X,Y), less_file(X,Y) and equality X=Y. Their arguments are of type rank (with values 1 to 8) and file (with values a to h), respectively.

The training and testing sets used in our experiments were the ones used by Muggleton et al. (1989). There are altogether ten sets of positions (examples), five of 100 examples each and five of 1000 examples each. Each of the sets was used as a training set for the three systems FOIL, LINUS using ASSISTANT, and LINUS using NEWGEM. The sets of clauses were then tested as described in Muggleton et al. (1989). The clauses obtained from a small set were tested on the 5000 examples from the large sets and the clauses obtained from each large set were tested on the remaining 4500 examples.

| System | 100 training instances | | 1000 training instances | |
|---|---|---|---|---|
| | Accuracy | Time | Accuracy | Time |
| CIGOL | 77.2% | 21.5 hr | N/A | N/A |
| DUCE | 33.7% | 2 hr | 37.7% | 10 hr |
| FOIL on different sets | 92.5% sd 3.6% | 1.5 sec | 99.4% sd 0.1% | 20.8 sec |
| FOIL | 90.8% sd 1.7% | 31.6 sec | 99.7% sd 0.1% | 4.0 min |
| LINUS using ASSISTANT | 98.1% sd 1.1% | 55.0 sec | 99.7% sd 0.1% | 9.6 min |
| LINUS using NEWGEM | 88.4% sd 4.0% | 30.0 sec | 99.7% sd 0.1% | 4.3 min |

Table 1: Results on the chess endgame tasks

Table 1 gives the results in the chess endgame task. The classification accuracy is given by the percentage of correctly classified testing instances and by the standard deviation (sd), averaged over 5 experiments. The first two rows are taken from Muggleton et al. (1989), the third is from Quinlan (1990) and the last three rows present the results of our experiments. Note that the results reported by Quinlan (1990) were not obtained from the same training and testing sets. The times in the first two rows are for a Sun 3/60, in the third for a DECStation 3100, in the fourth for a Sun 3/50 and in the last two rows CPU times are given for a VAX-8650 mainframe. The times given for LINUS include transformation to attribute-value form, learning and transformation into DHDB clauses.

In brief, on the small training sets LINUS using ASSISTANT with post-processing outperformed FOIL. According to the T-test for dependent samples, this result is significant at the 0.5% level. Although LINUS using NEWGEM was sligtly worse than FOIL, his result is not significant (even at the 20% level). The clauses obtained with LINUS are as short and understandable (transparent) as FOIL's. On the large training sets both systems performed equally well. Although LINUS is slower than FOIL, it is much faster than DUCE and CIGOL. LINUS is slowed down mainly by the parts implemented in Prolog, that is the DHDB interface and especially the post-processor. More efficient implementations would significantly improve LINUS' speed. For illustration, for the small training sets, the average time spent on transforming to attribute-value form, learning and transforming to DHDB form was 16, 6 and 36 seconds for ASSISTANT, and 16, 11 and 3 seconds for NEWGEM, respectively.

Our latest measurements on noisy data indicate that for large and noisy training sets FOIL is much slower than LINUS. Namely, on the training set consisting of the 5000 examples with artificially added noise (30%), it took LINUS less than 20 minutes of VAX 8650 CPU time to generate the hypothesis while FOIL on Sun 3/50 did not complete the induction in 24 hours.

As an example, the clauses induced by LINUS using ASSISTANT (with post-processing) from one of the sets of 100 examples are:

illegal(A,B,C,D,E,F) ← C=E.
illegal(A,B,C,D,E,F) ← D=F.

illegal(A,B,C,D,E,F) ← adjacent_file(A,E), B=F.
illegal(A,B,C,D,E,F) ← adjacent_file(A,E), adjacent_rank(B,F).
illegal(A,B,C,D,E,F) ← A=E, adjacent_rank(B,F).

illegal(A,B,C,D,E,F) ← A=E, B=F.

These may be paraphrased as: a position is illegal if the Black King is on the same rank or file as (i.e., is attacked by) the Rook, or the White King and the Black King are next to each other, or the White King and the Black King are on the same square. Although these clauses are neither consistent nor complete, they correctly classify 98.5% of the 5000 unseen cases.

# 4  Summary and discussion

Compared to attribute-value learning, our approach has a number of advantages. It allows for relational descriptions; use of compound terms; compact description of concepts; use of utility predicate definitions and utility functions (background knowledge) in concept descriptions; and inclusion of existing successful attribute-value learning programs into the logic programming environment. LINUS can be used both for learning definitions of relations and for inducing descriptions of individual classes (possibly considering more than one decision variable). In LINUS, we use attribute-value learning programs that embody years of research work, that are known to perform well and that were tested and evaluated on a number of real-life domains. We add to their advantageous features (e.g., mechanisms for handling noisy data in ASSISTANT) the ability of learning logical definitions of relations in a more expressive first-order representational formalism.

For the sake of efficiency, all systems that learn in first-order logic restrict the hypotheses language. For example, FOIL uses function-free and CIGOL negation-free Horn clause logic. LINUS uses an even more restricted language, i.e., the deductive hierarchical database formalism. All variables in the body of a DHDB clause must appear in its head. This is the main reason why LINUS can not learn recursive definitions of relations, while FOIL and CIGOL can. On the other hand, the efficiency of attribute-value learning algorithms is preserved which is extremely important in large real-life domains.

In this paper we have shown that LINUS can induce concept descriptions similar to the ones obtained with other systems that learn definitions of relations in first-order logic. The results of the experiments in learning nonrecursive definitions are equal to or better than the ones obtained with FOIL. The descriptions generated by LINUS are more general and more accurately represent the intended relations. In the 'arches' domain less training examples were needed and the generation of negative examples in the closed-world assumption mode was unnecessary. In the task of learning rules that govern card sequences, in layout 3 LINUS, unlike FOIL, induced the intended (correct) definition, and in the first layout it induced a more general definition. In the chess endgame, LINUS using ASSISTANT achieved better classification accuracy than FOIL. LINUS using NEWGEM achieved comparable results. LINUS and FOIL were both much better than CIGOL.

To summarize, in our experiments, LINUS performed slightly better than FOIL. Having parts implemented in Prolog, LINUS was slightly slower than FOIL, implemented in C. However, both LINUS and FOIL were substantially more efficient than DUCE and CIGOL. Our latest measurements on noisy data indicate that for large and noisy training sets FOIL is much slower than LINUS.

# Acknowledgements

This research was supported by the Slovene Research Council and is part of the ESPRIT II Basic Research Action No. 3059, Project ECOLES. We are grateful to Ross Quinlan for making available his system FOIL and the data used in the experiments, and Michael Bain for the chess endgame data. We wish to thank Igor Mozetič for his contribution in the development of LINUS, Dunja Mladenič for the implementation of ASSISTANT in the VAX/VMS environment, and Ivan Bratko and Igor Kononenko for their comments on an earlier draft of the paper.

# References

Bratko, I., Mozetič, I. & Lavrač, N. (1989) KARDIO: A study in deep and qualitative knowledge for expert systems. Boston, MA: The MIT Press.

Cestnik, B. & Bratko, I. (1988) Learning redundant rules in noisy domains. Proc. European Conference on Artificial Intelligence, ECAI-88, Muenchen, Germany.

Cestnik, B., Kononenko, I. & Bratko, I. (1987) ASSISTANT 86: A knowledge-elicitation tool for sophisticated users. In: Bratko, I. & Lavrač, N. (eds.) Progress in machine learning. Wilmslow: Sigma Press.

Clark, P. & Niblett, T. (1989) The CN2 induction algorithm. Machine Learning 1 (3), 261-284. Kluwer Academic Publishers.

Dietterich, T.G. & Michalski, R.S. (1986) Learning to predict sequences. In: Michalski, R.S., Carbonell, J.G. & Mitchell, T.M. (eds.) Machine learning: An artificial intelligence approach (Volume 2). Los Altos: Morgan Kaufmann.

Gams, M. (1989) New measurements highlight the importance of redundant knowledge. Proc. European Working Session on Learning, EWSL 89. Montpellier, France: Pitman.

Lavrač, N. (1990) Principles of knowledge acquisition in expert systems. PhD Thesis, Maribor University, Yugoslavia.

Lavrač, N., Džeroski, S. & Grobelnik, M. (1990) Experiments in learning nonrecursive definitions of relations with LINUS. Report IJS-DP-5863, Jožef Stefan Institute, Ljubljana, Yugoslavia.

Lavrač, N. & Mozetič, I. (1988) Experiments with inductive learning programs NEWGEM and ASSISTANT in the DHDB environment. Report IJS-DP-5029, Jožef Stefan Institute, Ljubljana, Yugoslavia.

Lloyd, J.W. (1987) Foundations of logic programming (Second edition). Springer-Verlag.

Michalski, R.S., Mozetič, I., Hong, J. & Lavrač, N. (1986) The multi-purpose incremental learning system AQ15 and its testing application on three medical domains. Proc. National Conference on Artificial Intelligence, AAAI-86. Philadelphia, PA: Morgan Kaufmann.

Mozetič, I. (1985) NEWGEM: Program for learning from examples - Technical documentation and user's guide. Report, University of Illinois at Urbana-Champaign, Department of Computer Science. Also: Report IJS-DP-4390, Jožef Stefan Institute, Ljubljana, Yugoslavia.

Mozetič, I. (1987) Learning of qualitative models. In: Bratko, I. & Lavrač, N. (eds.) Progress in machine learning. Wilmslow: Sigma Press.

Mozetič, I. & Lavrač, N. (1988) Incremental learning from examples in a logic-based formalism. Proc. Int. Workshop on Machine Learning, Meta-reasoning and Logic, Sesimbra, Portugal.

Muggleton, S.H. & Buntine, W. (1988) Machine invention of first-order predicates by inverting resolution. Proc. Machine Learning Conference, Ann Arbor, Michigan.

Muggleton, S.H., Bain, M., Hayes-Michie, J. & Michie, D. (1989) An experimental comparison of human and machine learning formalisms. Proc. Sixth International Workshop on Machine Learning. Ithaca, NY: Morgan Kaufmann.

Muggleton, S.H. & Feng, C. (1990) Efficient induction of logic programs. Proc. First Conference on Algorithmic Learning Theory. Tokyo: Ohmsha.

Quinlan, J.R. (1986) Induction of decision trees. Machine Learning 1 (1), 81-106. Kluwer Academic Publishers.

Quinlan, J.R. (1987) Generating production rules from decision trees. Proc. Int. Joint Conference on Artificial Intelligence, IJCAI 87. Milano, Italy: Morgan Kaufman.

Quinlan, J.R. (1989) Learning relations: Comparison of a symbolic and a connectionist approach. Technical Report 346, Basser Dept. Comp. Sc., University of Sydney, Sydney, Australia.

Quinlan, J.R. (1990) Learning logical definitions from relations. To appear in Machine Learning. Kluwer Academic Publishers.

Winston, P.H. (1975) Learning structural descriptions from examples. In: Winston, P.H. (ed.) The psychology of computer vision. New York: McGraw-Hill.

# Extending Explanation-Based Generalization by Abstraction Operators

Igor Mozetič

Austrian Research Institute for Artificial Intelligence

Schottengasse 3, A-1010 Vienna, Austria

igor@ai-vie.uucp


Christian Holzbaur

Austrian Research Institute for Artificial Intelligence, and

Department of Medical Cybernetics and Artificial Intelligence

University of Vienna

Freyung 6, A-1010 Vienna, Austria

christian@ai-vie.uucp

### Abstract

We present two contributions to the explanation-based generalization techniques. First, the operationality criterion is extended by abstraction operators. These allow for the goal concept to be reformulated not only in terms of operational predicates, but also allow to delete irrelevant arguments, and to collapse indistinguishable constants. The abstraction algorithm is presented and illustrated by an example. Second, the domain theory is not restricted to variables with finite (discrete) domains, but can deal with infinite (e.g., real-valued) domains as well. The interpretation and abstraction are effectively handled through constraint logic programming mechanisms. In the paper we concentrate on the role of $CLP(\Re)$ — a solver for systems of linear equations and inequalities over reals.

# 1 Introduction

Explanation-based generalization (EBG) is a technique to formulate general concepts on the basis of an individual example and a domain theory (Mitchell *et al.* 1986). The domain theory is used to explain the training example, and the resulting explanation is generalized and reformulated in operational terms. Specifically, the input to the EBG algorithm consists of:

- Domain theory,

- Goal concept — concept to be learned,

- Training example — an instance of the goal concept,

- Operationality criterion — easily evaluable predicates from the domain theory in terms of which the goal concept should be reformulated.

It has been shown (Van Harmelen & Bundy 1988) that in the context of logic programming, EBG is essentially equivalent to partial evaluation. The domain theory is represented by a logic program, and the explanation is a proof that the example logically follows from the program. The goal concept is the partially evaluated program, i.e., it is reformulated in terms of leaves of the proof tree which contain only operational predicates. Further, the training example can be either ground, partially instantiated, or even omitted, since its role is just to restrict the search for the proof. In the case that no example is provided, the resulting goal concept is equivalent to the original one, but expressed just in terms of operational predicates and therefore more efficient for subsequent use.

In the paper we push further the idea of performing EBG by partial evaluation. In EBG the operationality criterion refers just to predicates — procedure calls of non-operational predicates are unfolded. We extend the criterion to abstraction operators which refer to all parts of atomic formulae. For example, predicates can become operational by deleting some arguments, or different constants can be collapsed into singletons. More systematically, if $P$ is a domain theory represented by a logic program then it can be abstracted into $P'$ in the following ways:

- by unfolding non-operational predicates throughout $P$ (like in EBG),

- by deleting some arguments of functions and predicates throughout $P$,

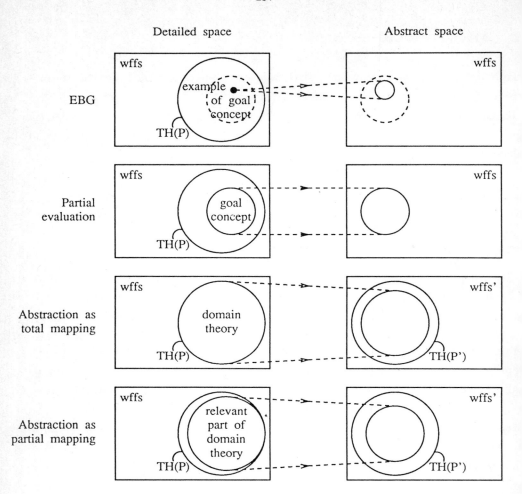

Figure 1: Relation between EBG, partial evaluation, and abstractions. $P$ and $P'$ denote a detailed and an abstract domain theory, respectively, and $TH(P)$ is the set of well formed formulae provable from $P$.

- by renaming constant, function, and predicate symbols throughout $P$ (the renaming is typically many-to-one).

In contrast to partial evaluation (without training example), the abstracted goal concept and domain theory are no longer equivalent to the original ones, but are their logical consequences, respectively (Figure 1). The equivalence is lost due to the arguments deletion and many-to-one renaming. As a consequence, a non-theorem from th detailed space can be abstracted into a theorem in the abstract space. Each theorem is abstracted into a theorem, however. A specific type of abstractions with this property are so-called *truthful* or *TI-abstractions* (theorem increasing, Giunchiglia & Walsh 1989). In general, an abstraction is a *partial* and not a total mapping (Mozetic 1990a) since one wants to ignore irrelevant features of the domain theory for the task at hand. Note also that in contrast to EBG and partial evaluation, an abstraction might introduce a different language into the abstract space.

The abstracted domain theory can be used either to answer the queries more efficiently and less precisely, or in conjunction with the original domain theory as a falsity preserving filter. Abstractions turned out to be useful in reducing the search space in theorem proving (Plaisted 1981, Giunchiglia & Walsh 1990), planning (Sacerdoti 1974, Korf 1987), and model-based diagnosis (Gallanti *et al.* 1989, Mozetic 1990b, Mozetic & Holzbaur 1991).

Section 2 motivates the introduction of abstraction operators by an example. Given is a domain theory for a numerical model of an inverter. In section 3 the three abstraction operators which replace the operationality criterion are defined. The numerical model is first abstracted to a qualitative model, and then to a binary-logic model of an inverter. Section 4 describes the abstraction algorithm and its Prolog implementation. In section 5 constraint logic programming inference over real-valued variables is outlined and its application is illustrated by the inverter example.

# 2  Motivating example: a model of an inverter

We represent a domain theory by a constraint logic program (CLP, Jaffar & Michaylov 1987) which is a logic program extended by interpreted functions. A proper implementation of a CLP scheme allows for an easy integration of specialized problem solvers into the logic programming framework. For example, in Metaprolog (an extension of C-Prolog, Holzbaur 1990) specialized solvers communicate with the standard Prolog interpreter via extended semantic unification and are implemented in Prolog themselves. So far, three solvers have been implemented: constraint propagation over finite domains by forward checking, CLP($\mathcal{B}$) — a solver over boolean expressions, and CLP($\Re$) — a solver for systems of linear equations and inequalities over reals (Holzbaur 1990). In the paper we concentrate on the role of CLP($\Re$) in the interpretation and abstraction of a domain theory.

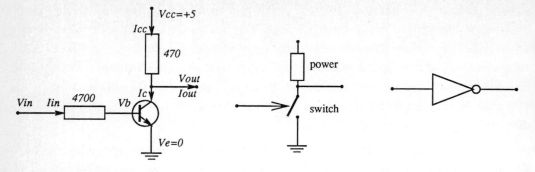

Figure 2: A numerical, qualitative, and logical model of an inverter

We illustrate the EBG algorithm, realized by partial evaluation and without a training example, on a model of an inverter. The initial domain theory consists of a numerical model of an inverter (predicate $inv_n$), which is later simplified into a qualitative ($inv_q$), and finally into a logical model ($inv_l$, Figure 2). The inverter is realized by an npn transistor and two resistors. The description of an npn transistor is from Heinze, Michaylov & Stuckey (1987). The transistor operates in three states: *cutoff*, *saturated*, and *active*. In digital circuits only the cutoff and saturated states are of interest, and therefore the active state, interesting in amplifier circuits, is omitted. $Vx$ and $Ix$ denote the real-valued voltages and currents for the base, collector and emmiter, respectively. Constants *Beta*, *Vbe*, and *Vcesat* are device parameters.

**Domain theory:**

$inv_n($ $S$, $b(Vin,Iin)$, $b(Vout,Iout)$ $)$ $\leftarrow$
    $switch_n($ $S$, $Vin$, $Iin$, $Vout$, $Ic$ $)$,
    $power_n($ $Ic$, $Vout$, $Iout$ $)$.

$switch_n($ $S$, $Vin$, $Iin$, $Vc$, $Ic$ $)$ $\leftarrow$
    $Ve=0$, $Beta=100$, $Vbe=0.7$, $Vcesat=0.3$,
    $resistor($ $Vin$, $Vb$, $Iin$, $4700$ $)$,
    $transistor($ $S$, $Beta$, $Vbe$, $Vcesat$, $Vb$, $Vc$, $Ve$, $Iin$, $Ic$, $Ie$ $)$.

$power_n($ $Ic$, $Vout$, $Iout$ $)$ $\leftarrow$
    $Vcc=5$, $Ic+Iout=Icc$,
    $resistor($ $Vcc$, $Vout$, $Icc$, $470$ $)$,
    $0 \leq Iout$, $Iout \leq 0.006$.

$resistor($ $V1$, $V2$, $I$, $R$ $)$ $\leftarrow$ $R>0$, $V1-V2=I*R$.

*transistor( cutoff, Beta, Vbe, Vcesat, Vb, Vc, Ve, Ib, Ic, Ie )* ←
$\quad$ *Vb < Ve + Vbe, Ib=0, Ic=0, Ie=0.*
*transistor( saturated, Beta, Vbe, Vcesat, Vb, Vc, Ve, Ib, Ic, Ie )* ←
$\quad$ *Vb = Ve + Vbe, Vc = Ve + Vcesat, Ib≥0, Ic≥0, Ie=Ic+Ib.*

**Goal concept:** *$inv_n$( State, In, Out ).*

**Operational predicates:** $=, <, \leq, >, \geq.$

Partial evaluation of the goal concept unfolds procedure calls of non-operational predicates, propagates constant values, and branches out conditionals. Using Metaprolog with CLP($\Re$), this yields the following operational definition of the inverter.

**Reformulated goal concept** (through partial evaluation):

*$inv_n$( cutoff, b(Vin,Iin), b(Vout,Iout) )* ←
$\quad$ *Vin < 0.7,*
$\quad$ *Iin = 0,*
$\quad$ *Vout = −470\*Iout + 5,*
$\quad$ *Iout ≤ 0.006, Iout ≥ 0.*
*$inv_n$( saturated, b(Vin,Iin), b(Vout,Iout) )* ←
$\quad$ *Vin = 4700\*Iin + 0.7,*
$\quad$ *Iin ≥ 0,*
$\quad$ *Vout = 0.3,*
$\quad$ *Iout ≤ 0.006, Iout ≥ 0.*

The reformulated definition of the inverter is structureless and refers just to easily evaluable arithmetic operators. However, it is still unnecessarily detailed for a number of tasks. For diagnosis, for example, it does not really matter if the voltage is 4.4 or 4.6, but whether it is qualitatively *high* or *low*, and whether the transistor properly operates as a switching device. If we specify the transistor state and currents as irrelevant arguments, and voltages 0–0.7 and 2–5 as indistinguishable, we can derive the following alternative reformulation of the domain theory.

**Alternative reformulation** (through abstractions):

*$inv_l$( low, high ).*
*$inv_l$( high, low ).*

In the following section we specify abstraction operators more precisely. We illustrate their applicability by showing a two-step abstraction: a qualitative model of the inverter is derived first, and then abstracted into the above logical model.

# 3    Abstraction operators

Underlying the formulation of abstractions is a typed logic program (Lloyd 1987). Types provide a natural way of expressing the concept of a domain and are convenient for specifying abstraction operators in a compact form. We assume that variables and constants have types such as $\tau$. Functions have types of the form $\tau_1 \times \ldots \times \tau_n \to \tau$, and predicates have types of the form $\tau_1 \times \ldots \times \tau_n$.

The following three abstraction operators replace and extend the EBG operationality criterion. Since they do not change the structure of formulae but refer just to atoms they define a class of *atomic abstractions* (Giunchiglia & Walsh 1990). We use a binary predicate $h_\tau$ to denote abstractions of constants and functions of range type $\tau$, and a binary predicate $h$ to denote predicate abstractions.

1. Collapsing constants.

   Different constants can be renamed into a single constant. For example, assume that $a_1$ and $a_2$ are of type $\tau$, and that they are collapsed into a single constant $a'$:

   $$h_\tau(a_1, a'). \qquad h_\tau(a_2, a').$$

2. Function abstractions.

   Functions can be renamed and irrelevant arguments deleted. For example, let $f$ be of type $\tau_1 \times \ldots \times \tau_n \to \tau$, its first argument be deleted, and $f$ be renamed to $f'$:

   $$h_\tau(f(X_1, X_2 \ldots, X_n), f'(X_2', \ldots, X_n')) \leftarrow h_{2\tau}(X_2, X_2'), \ldots, h_{n\tau}(X_n, X_n').$$

3. Predicate abstractions.

   Operational predicates can be renamed and some arguments deleted. For example, let $p$ be of type $\tau_1 \times \ldots \times \tau_n$, its first argument be deleted, and $p$ be renamed to $p'$:

   $$h(p(X_1, X_2 \ldots, X_n), p'(X_2', \ldots, X_n')) \leftarrow h_{2\tau}(X_2, X_2'), \ldots, h_{n\tau}(X_n, X_n').$$

The abstraction operators degenerate to the EBG operationality criterion as a special case. In EBG one specifies just the predicate abstractions by adding, for each operational predicate $p$, a unit clause of the form:

$$h(p(X_1, \ldots, X_n), p(X_1, \ldots, X_n)).$$

Predicates for which no abstraction is specified are assumed to be non-operational and their definitions are unfolded.

The following specifies the extended operationality criterion for the inverter example.

**Collapsing constants:**

$h_s(cutoff, ok)$.

$h_s(saturated, ok)$.

$h_i(0, zero)$.

$h_i(I, pos) \leftarrow I>0$.　　　% *negative I has no abstraction*

$h_v(V, low) \leftarrow 0\leq V, V<0.7$.
$h_v(V, high) \leftarrow 2\leq V, V\leq 5$.

**Function abstraction:**

$h_b(b(V,\_I), V') \leftarrow h_v(V,V')$.　　　% *I is deleted*

**Predicate abstractions:**

$h(inv_n(S,X,Y), inv_q(S',X',Y')) \leftarrow$
　　　$h_s(S,S'), h_b(X,X'), h_b(Y,Y')$.

$h(switch_n(S,Vin,\_Iin,Vc,Ic), switch_q(S',Vin',Vc',Ic')) \leftarrow$　　% *Iin is deleted*
　　　$h_s(S,S'), h_v(Vin,Vin'), h_v(Vc,Vc'), h_i(Ic,Ic')$.

$h(power_n(Ic,Vout,\_Iout), power_q(Ic',Vout')) \leftarrow$　　% *Iout is deleted*
　　　$h_i(Ic,Ic'), h_v(Vout,Vout')$.

From the numerical model of the inverter and the above abstractions, a qualitative model was automatically derived through term rewriting and partial evaluation. Predicates, for which no abstractions are specified (*resistor, transistor*) are treated as non-operational and their definitions are unfolded. The remaining predicates and terms are rewritten according to the abstraction specifications.

**Reformulated goal concept** (qualitative model of the inverter):

$inv_q( S, Vin, Vout ) \leftarrow$
　　　$switch_q( S, Vin, Vout, Ic ),$
　　　$power_q( Ic, Vout )$.

$switch_q( ok, low, \_, zero )$.
$switch_q( ok, high, low, zero )$.
$switch_q( ok, high, low, pos )$.

$power_q( zero, high )$.
$power_q( pos, low )$.
$power_q( pos, high )$.

In the next step $switch_q$ and $power_q$ are treated as non-operational, $inv_q$ is renamed to $inv_l$, and the argument $S$ which denotes the internal state of the inverter is deleted.

**Predicate abstraction:**

$h(inv_q(\_S,X,Y),\ inv_l(X,Y))$.        *% S is deleted*

The abstraction algorithm yields the binary-logic model of the inverter.

**Reformulated goal concept** (logical model of the inverter):

$inv_l($ *low, high* $)$.
$inv_l($ *high, low* $)$.

# 4    The abstraction algorithm

The algorithm takes as an input a goal concept, a domain theory, and abstraction operators. The goal concept is an explicit parameter to the algorithm, while the domain theory and abstraction operators are implicit inputs, accessible through the Prolog built-in *clause/2* and *call/1* predicates. A training example can be represented as a partially instantiated goal concept, e.g., $inv_n(S,b(0.5,Iin),b(Vout,0.001))$. However, we do not address the advantages and disadvantages of providing an example here — the algorithm works in both cases.

The output of the algorithm is an abstracted goal concept in the form of a predicate definition, i.e., a set of clauses with the same head. The procedure is run in a failure-driven loop. At each iteration a clause defining the goal concept is selected, abstracted, and written to the output:

*abstract_goal( Goal )*   ←
     *abstract_clause( Goal, Clause' )*,
     *write_clause( Clause' )*,
     *fail.*
*abstract_goal( Goal )*.

The procedure *write_clause( Clause' )* extracts residual constraints over relevant variables, adds them to the body of the abstracted clause, and outputs the clause (see next section). A clause is abstracted by first unfolding definitions of non-operational predicates, abstracting the remaining atoms in the body, and finally abstracting the head of the clause. For brevity, we omit recursive definitions of predicates which traverse a list of atoms (*unfold_atoms*, *abstract_atoms*) and present just the base cases (*unfold_atom*, *abstract_atom*):

> *abstract_clause( Head, (Head' ← Body') )* ←
>     *clause( Head, Body ),*
>     *unfold_atoms( Body, Leaves ),*
>     *abstract_atoms( Leaves, Body' ),*
>     *abstract_atom( Head, Head' ).*

> *unfold_atom( Atom, Leaves )* ←
>     *not clause( h(Atom, _), _ ), !,    % non-operational predicate*
>     *unfold( Atom, Leaves ).*
> *unfold_atom( Atom, Atom ).*

> *unfold( Atom, true )* ← *builtin( Atom ), !,    % evaluate built-ins*
>     *call( Atom ).*
> *unfold( Atom, Leaves )* ←
>     *clause( Atom, Body ),*
>     *unfold_atoms( Body, Leaves ).*

> *abstract_atom( Atom, Atom' )* ←    *% predicate abstractions*
>     *clause( h(Atom, Atom'), Arguments ),*
>     *abstract_terms( Arguments ).*

A predicate is abstracted by referring to the abstraction operator $h$ which defines the new name and arity, and then by abstracting the arguments. A term abstraction depends on its type: a variable is 'abstracted' to the same variable, a constant of type $\tau$ is renamed according to the $h_\tau$ abstraction operator, and a function of range type $\tau$ is abstracted by referring to the abstraction operator $h_\tau$ and by recursively abstracting its arguments:

> *abstract_term( $h_\tau$(Variable, Variable) )* ← *var( Variable ), !.*
> *abstract_term( $h_\tau$(Constant, Constant') )* ← *constant( Constant ), !,*
>     *call( $h_\tau$(Constant, Constant') ).*
> *abstract_term( $h_\tau$(Term, Term') )* ←    *% structured term*
>     *clause( $h_\tau$(Term, Term'), Arguments ),*
>     *abstract_terms( Arguments ).*

> *constant( X )* ← *atomic( X ).    % constant or number*
> *constant( X )* ← *ismeta( X ).    % constrained variable in Metaprolog*

Note that a variable is treated as a constant if it is constrained and the constraints are satisfiable, i.e., if it can be substituted by a constant. See the next section for an example.

The following example illustrates the algorithm for a simple case when just predicates and functions are renamed and some arguments deleted. A standard Prolog interpreter suffices for such abstractions. The next section presents a more involved example where a Prolog interpreter has to be augmented by the CLP($\Re$) solver in order to collect linear constraints over reals and verify their satisfiability.

**Example.** Assume that the following clause is to be abstracted:

$inv_n(\ S,\ b(Vin,Iin),\ b(Vout,Iout)\ )\ \leftarrow$
$\quad switch_n(\ S,\ Vin,\ Iin,\ Vout,\ Ic\ ),$
$\quad power_n(\ Ic,\ Vout,\ Iout\ ).$

Both atoms in the body are operational and no unfolding takes place. $Switch_n$ is abstracted to $switch_q$ with the argument $Iin$ deleted, and $power_n$ is abstracted to $power_q$ with the argument $Iout$ deleted:

$inv_n(\ S',\ b(Vin',Iin),\ b(Vout',Iout)\ )\ \leftarrow$
$\quad switch_q(\ S',\ Vin',\ Vout',\ Ic'),$
$\quad power_q(\ Ic',\ Vout'\ ).$

The head of the clause $inv_n$ is abstracted to $inv_q$ by abstracting its arguments. The variable $S'$ remains a variable, and both terms $b(V,I)$ are abstracted according to the function abstraction specified by the $h_b$ clause. As a result, currents $I$ are dropped and only voltages $V'$ remain:

$inv_q(\ S',\ Vin',\ Vout'\ )\ \leftarrow$
$\quad switch_q(\ S',\ Vin',\ Vout',\ Ic'),$
$\quad power_q(\ Ic',\ Vout'\ ).$

# 5  The role of CLP($\Re$) in abstractions

Whereas the previous abstraction of the $inv_n$ clause did not rely on any CLP($\Re$) functionality, the abstraction of $switch_n$ to $switch_q$ does, however. All atoms in the body of $switch_n$ are non-operational so that $unfold\_atoms$ in the abstraction algorithm essentially calls $switch_n(S,Vin,Iin,Vc,Ic)$ and returns the following two answer substitutions with residual constraints:

$switch_n(\ cutoff,\ Vin,\ 0,\ Vc,\ 0\ )$
   Constraints: $Vin<0.7$ ;

$switch_n(\ saturated,\ Vin,\ Iin,\ 0.3,\ Ic\ )$
   Constraints: $Vin=4700^*Iin+0.7,\ Vin\geq0.7,\ Ic\geq0$

**Abstraction of the first solution.** The abstraction algorithm proceeds with the abstraction of the head of $switch_n$ for there are no body goals left. The constant *cutoff* is abstracted into *ok* through an application of $h_s$. The next argument *Vin* is a constrained variable and there are two $h_v$ clauses that specify the abstraction rules for voltages. The first clause succeeds as the combined set of constraints $\{\ Vin<0.7,\ 0\leq Vin,\ Vin<0.7\}$ is satisfiable. *Vin* is abstracted to *low*. The argument *Iin* is deleted through predicate abstraction. The fourth argument *Vc* is again a voltage. It remains unchanged in the abstraction since it is unconstrained. The last argument *Ic* is instantiated to 0 which is abstracted to *zero* in turn. This yields the first defining clause of the abstract $switch_q$ predicate:

$switch_q(\ ok,\ low,\ Vc,\ zero\ )$.

During backtracking the abstraction of *Ic* to *pos* fails as this is incompatible with the constraint $Ic>0$. Backtracking proceeds until *transistor* and therefore $switch_n$ delivers the second solution.

**Abstraction of the second solution.** Again the abstraction algorithm proceeds with the head of $switch_n$ for there are no body goals left. The constant *saturated* is abstracted into *ok* through an application of $h_s$. The next argument *Vin* is a constrained variable and there are two $h_v$ clauses that specify the abstraction rules for voltages:

$h_v(V,\ low)\ \leftarrow\ 0\leq V,\ V<0.7.$
$h_v(V,\ high)\ \leftarrow\ 2\leq V,\ V\leq5.$

The first clause fails as the combined set of constraints $\{\ Vin\geq0.7,\ 0\leq Vin,\ Vin<0.7\}$ is unsatisfiable. The second clause, however, succeeds with the abstraction of *Vin* to *high*. The argument *Iin* is deleted through predicate abstraction. The fourth argument *Vc*, a voltage, is instantiated to 0.3. This value satisfies the constraints of the first clause of $h_v$ and *Vc* is abstracted to *low*. The last argument *Ic* is a constrained variable and there are two $h_i$ clauses that specify the abstraction rules for currents:

$h_i(0,\ zero)$.
$h_i(I,\ pos)\ \leftarrow\ I>0.$

The residual constraint $Ic\geq0$ from $switch_n$ is compatible with both clauses of $h_i$, and therefore we get the final two defining clauses of the abstract *switch$_q$* predicate:

*switch$_q$( ok, high, low, zero ).*
*switch$_q$( ok, high, low, pos ).*

The role of CLP($\Re$) in this derivation is manyfold. First, it allows to compute with a domain theory over real-valued variables at the numerical level of the model. Second, it admits the specification of abstraction operators that share the computational domain with the numerical model. The third function is to guarantee the satisfiablity of the constraints collected during partial evaluation and abstraction. The ability to deal with partially instantiated constraints is vital if we want to apply EBG in the *absence* of an example — in particular if we operate in an infinite domain.

One traditional method for deciding linear inequalities is the simplex method. The simplex method works by turning inequalities into equations through the introduction of so-called 'slack variables'. This leads to a 'contamination' of the equation system with artificial variables from the user's point of view. In our experience, the amount of code that is needed to compute a human readable form of the (in)equation system is unproportionally high in comparison to the code that does the actual job. Therefore, we rather selected the Shostak's 'Loop Residue' method (Shostak 1981). Besides being better suited for small inequalities, this method operates with a 'direct' representation of inequalities. For each set of inequalities a graph is constructed whose vertices correspond to the variables and edges to the inequalities. Kraemer (1989) proves the equivalence between a satisfiable set of inequalities and the corresponding closed graph without any infeasible loop.

As far as the derivation of the abstract model is concerned, the residual set of constraints that are *not* related to the variables in the abstract model are not used any longer. They *can* be added to the numerical model, however. This leads to a specialization of the model or a *relevance projection* with respect to the abstractions. In analogy to the traditional EBG framework we can thereby prune irrelevant computations when the *numerical* model is used for diagnosis, say.

Our Metaprolog implementation of CLP($\Re$) is preferred over other existing implementations of CLP($\Re$) (Heintze *et al.* 1987, Jaffar 1990) since it allows for the simultaneous use of solvers for different domains in a consistent framework. In this respect Metaprolog is very well suited for the computational demands that arise in the context of hierarchical abstractions. The numerical level of the model can be formulated with CLP($\Re$) for example, and successive qualitative abstractions thereof typically utilize constraint propagation over finite domains. The implementation of the specialized solvers is based on the user-definable[1] extended unification. As the solvers themselves are written in Prolog they can easily be customized to specific demands. The choice of Prolog as an implementation language for the equation solver leads to a reduction in code size by an order of magnitude. On the other hand, the CLP($\Re$) solver implemented in *interpreted* Prolog is about six times slower than a dedicated C implementation (Holzbaur 1990). More important, however, is the fact that the solvers operate on the same data structures — Prolog terms in fact. Therefore it is easy to combine different, independent solvers in the same program. Additionally, the user is supplied with an external representation of the residual constraints which can be manipulated further (printed, for example).

# 6    Conclusion

The paper makes two contributions to the EBG techniques. First, the proposed scheme is less dependent on a training example. We can even get away without an example and still perform nontrivial and useful computations at the partial evaluation time. If we accept that one intention behind the EBG is to derive specialized, and therefore more efficient reformulations of the domain theory, it is obvious that the choice of a richer computational domain contributes to this aspect. If the examples of this paper were to be partially evaluated in an empty semantic theory (pure Prolog with the Herbrand interpretation) one would have to declare all relational operators and equations over real-valued variables of the domain theory as operational. This results in specializations where the set of collected constraints (operational predicates) is neither minimal, nor is it guaranteed to be satisfiable. The choice of a richer computational domain allows for the resolution of some constraints at the EBG time already.

The second contribution are abstraction operators which extend the standard EBG operationality criterion. Further, abstractions perform a kind of 'relevance projection' of the domain theory even in the absence of an example. Through this explicit specification, the usual problem of estimating the relevance of training examples is circumvented. In the case of a domain theory over infinite domains, it is only the combination of abstractions with a powerful computational domain that allows for the application (a partial or complete resolution) of the abstraction operators at the EBG time.

---

[1]In Metaprolog, CLP($\Re$), CLP($\mathcal{B}$), and forward checking over finite domains are provided as libraries.

# Acknowledgements

This work was supported by the Austrian Federal Ministry of Science and Research. Thanks to Bernhard Pfahringer for valuable comments and to Robert Trappl for making this work possible.

# References

Gallanti, M., Roncato, M., Stefanini, A., Tornielli, G. (1989). A diagnostic algorithm based on models at different level of abstraction. *Proc. 11th IJCAI*, pp. 1350-1355, Detroit, Morgan Kaufmann.

Giunchiglia, F., Walsh, T. (1989). Abstract theorem proving. *Proc. 11th IJCAI*, pp. 372-377, Detroit, Morgan Kaufmann.

Giunchiglia, F., Walsh, T. (1990). Abstract theorem proving: mapping back. IRST Technical Report 8911-16, Istituto Ricerca Scientifica e Tecnologica, Trento, Italy.

Heintze, N., Jaffar, J., Michaylov, S., Stuckey, P., Yap, R. (1987). The CLP($\Re$) programmer's manual. Dept. of Computer Science, Monash University, Australia.

Heintze, N., Michaylov, S., Stuckey, P. (1987). CLP($\Re$) and some electrical engineering problems. *Proc. 4th Intl. Conference on Logic Programming*, pp. 675-703, Melbourne, Australia, The MIT Press.

Holzbaur, C. (1990). Specification of constraint based inference mechanisms through extended unification. Ph.D. Thesis, Technical University of Vienna, Austria.

Jaffar, J. (1990). CLP($\Re$) version 1.0 reference manual. IBM Research Division, T.J. Watson Research Center, Yorktown Heights, NY.

Jaffar, J., Michaylov, S. (1987). Methodology and implementation of a CLP system. *Proc. 4th Intl. Conference on Logic Programming*, pp. 196-218, Melbourne, Australia, The MIT Press.

Korf, R.E. (1987). Planning as search: a quantitative approach. *Artificial Intelligence 33*, pp. 65-88.

Kraemer, F.-J. (1989). A decision procedure for Presburger arithmetic with functions and equality. SEKI working paper SWP-89-4, FB Informatik, University of Kaiserslautern, Germany.

Lloyd, J.W. (1987). *Foundations of Logic Programming* (Second edition). Springer-Verlag, Berlin.

Mitchell, T., Keller, R., Kedar-Cabelli, S. (1986). Explanation-based generalization: A unifying view. *Machine Learning 1 (1)*, pp. 47-80.

Mozetic, I. (1990a). Abstractions in model-based diagnosis. Report TR-90-4, Austrian Research Institute for Artificial Intelligence, Vienna, Austria. *Proc. Automatic Generation of Approximations and Abstractions, AAAI-90 Workshop*, pp. 64-75, Boston.

Mozetic, I. (1990b). Reduction of diagnostic complexity through model abstractions. Report TR-90-10, Austrian Research Institute for Artificial Intelligence, Vienna, Austria. *Proc. First Intl. Workshop on Principles of Diagnosis*, pp. 102-111, Stanford University, Palo Alto.

Mozetic, I., Holzbaur, C. (1991). Integrating qualitative and numerical models within Constraint Logic Programming. Report TR-91-2, Austrian Research Institute for Artificial Intelligence, Vienna, Austria. *Workshop on Qualitative Reasoning about Physical Systems*, Genova, Italy.

Plaisted, D.A. (1981). Theorem proving with abstractions. *Artificial Intelligence 16*, pp. 47-108.

Sacerdoti, E.D. (1974). Planning in a hierarchy of abstraction spaces. *Artificial Intelligence 5*, pp. 115-135.

Shostak, R. (1981). Deciding linear inequalities by computing loop residues. *Journal of the ACM 28 (4)*, pp. 769-779.

Van Harmelen, F., Bundy, A. (1988). Explanation-based generalisation = partial evaluation. *Artificial Intelligence 36*, pp. 401-412.

# STATIC LEARNING FOR AN ADAPTATIVE THEOREM PROVER

C. BELLEANNEE   J. NICOLAS

IRISA-INRIA, Campus de Beaulieu, 35042 Rennes cedex.  France. Email : jnicolas@irisa.fr

## Abstract

An adaptative theorem prover is a system able to modify its current set of inference rules in order to improve its performance on a specific domain. We address here the issue of the generation of inference rules, without considering the selection and deletion issues. We especially develop the treatment of repeating events within a proof. We specify a general representation for objects to be learned in this framework, that is macro-connectives and macro-inference-rules and show how they may be generated from the primitive set of inference rules. Our main contribution consists to show that a form of analytical, static learning, is possible in this domain.

**Key-words**   Theorem proving. Macro-operators. Sequent calculus. Generalization to N.

## 1 Introduction

Our aim is to improve the performance of the theorem prover on a given domain, given some representative sample of theorems on this domain. A theorem prover may be characterized by its set of inference rules and its set of axioms. Our methodology is to produce automatically an auxiliary new set of macro-inference rules for the prover, rendering the specificity of the semantics of the domain.

It seems that there has been very little work addressing the issue of adapting a general automated prover on a specific domain  (Cohen, 1987; O'Rorke, 1987; Pastre 1989). We present these works in the last section. At a first sight, theorem proving is just a particular case of problem solving and one may wonder why known learning methods in problem solving are not widely used in theorem proving. The mutual ignorance of each research field is only a partial answer to this situation. In order to explain the specificity of theorem proving, we need a more accurate view of each domain.

One of the most common views of problem solving is to conceive it as a search in a state space. The transitions in the space are formalized as applications of operators. To solve a problem is to find a path between an initial state and a final goal state. If we want to describe theorem proving within this framework, states are sets of formulas, the goal state being the theorem to be proven (or its negation if we are looking for unsatisfiability). Operators are rules of inference.

Learning in problem solving consists of building a new, more abstract state space. That is, learning either produces clusters of states, or/and sequences of operators (paths in the space). The first case corresponds to the learning of preconditions of operator applications. The second case describes macro-operator learning.

What makes the learning of preconditions effective in problem solving is that each step is meaningful. Each operator represents a transition between two worlds with a clear semantics conveyed by the action. In theorem proving, one faces the issue of transformations that are too atomic to represent significative steps and allows the production of uninteresting intermediate states (sets of formulas). Unlike problem solvers where operators are problem-dependent, theorem provers need a complete and general set of inference rules in order to draw their conclusions, which does not capture the semantic of the domain.

The definition of a strategy is the main problem in theorem proving. We reduce it to the learning of useful sequences of elementary steps, that is, learning of macro-inference rules. The principle is to produce a redundant set of inference rules, making up for the increase in the branching factor during the choice of an inference rule step, with a sensible decrease of the number of steps needed to achieve a proof. The formation of macro-rules has been a subject of interest since the development of problem solvers and planning systems. An early and famous study is the MACROPS system of Fikes, Hart and Nilsson (1972). More recent studies include (Porter, 1984; Korf 1983, 1985; Minton 1988; Iba 1989). The specificity of the problem for theorem provers lies in the fact that elementary operators have a very poor semantics, independant of the domain. However, it is possible to build useful macros if we consider some proof traces of known theorems. This dynamic form of learning has been previously explored. However, it seems that **static** learning, a form of learning studied by Korf (1983,1985) in the framework of problem solving, has not lead to any work in theorem proving. Static learning produce macro-operators while analysing operators themselves, without considering any trace of resolution. Since operators are very general in theorem proving, one may believe that such a technique is of no help for the problem at hand. This paper aims to show that some kind of static learning is nontheless possible. We first present a quick view of our prover.

# 2 Automated Theorem Proving

Automated deduction methods may be split into two main streams. Resolution style methods deal with formulas in a standard form by means of a single inference rule. Natural like methods accept formulas in their original form but require at least as many inference rules as connectives in the original language.

This paper deals with the second kind of methods, since we claim that keeping formulas in a more structured form allows one to reason at different levels of abstraction, which is a fundamental requirement for learning methods.

Amongst natural-like methods, we have chosen the system G, a sequent calculus defined by Gentzen (Gallier, 1986), which is well suited to mechanisation because of the convergence of its set of inference rules (due to the subformula property of the system). A sequent (SA,SB) is a pair of possibly empty sets of formulas, noted SA $\rightarrow$ SB or $A_1, ...,A_m \rightarrow B_1, ...,B_n$ if SA = $\{A_1, ...,A_m\}$ and SB = $\{B_1, ...,B_n\}$. The semantics associated to this notation is that $A_1, ...,A_m \rightarrow B_1, ...,B_n$ is true iff the formula $A_1 \wedge ... \wedge A_m \Rightarrow B_1 \vee ... \vee B_n$ is true. The inference rules of the system G directly reflect the semantics of the logical connectives. There are two inference rules for each connective, corresponding respectively to the treatment of an occurence of the connective in the left and in the right part of the sequent. For example, the following rules govern the occurences of the *and* connective:

$$\frac{A_1, A_2, SA \rightarrow SB}{A_1 \wedge A_2, SA \rightarrow SB} \qquad \frac{SA \rightarrow SB, B_1 \quad SA \rightarrow SB, B_2}{SA \rightarrow SB, B_1 \wedge B_2}$$

In the framework of the system G, a deduction of a sequent S consists in splitting up the semantics of S, by means of the inference rules. As an example, here is a deduction tree for the sequent " $\rightarrow (p \Rightarrow q) \Rightarrow (\neg q \Rightarrow \neg p)$" (It is a proof tree for the formula F= $(p \Rightarrow q) \Rightarrow (\neg q \Rightarrow \neg p)$ )

$$\rightarrow (p \Rightarrow q) \Rightarrow (\neg q \Rightarrow \neg p)$$
$$|$$
$$p \Rightarrow q \rightarrow \neg q \Rightarrow \neg p$$
$$\diagup \qquad \diagdown$$
$$\rightarrow p, \neg q \Rightarrow \neg p \qquad q \rightarrow \neg q \Rightarrow \neg p$$
$$| \qquad\qquad |$$
$$\neg q \rightarrow p, \neg p \qquad q, \neg q \rightarrow \neg p$$
$$| \qquad\qquad |$$
$$\neg q, p \rightarrow p \qquad q \rightarrow \neg p, q$$

# 3 When to build a new macro

Four issues have to be addressed when considering macros :
- a) When to build a new macro.
- b) How to build a new macro.
- c) When to cancel an old macro.
- d) When to select a given macro.

The focus of this paper is on the first two points. Point a) raises the issue of defining the concept of *interestingness* of a sequence of rules or operators. It is the subject of this section. Point b) addresses the issue of *composing* a sequence of rules or operators and is developed in section 4.

The generation of macros requires the prior definition of formal criteria leading to the specification of the concept of an interesting sequence of rules. This work proposes to tackle with domains where repeated applications of a same sequence of rules of inference occur during the proof of theorems. In fact, this covers three kinds of situations. First, a given theorem may have a regular structure, with repeated sequences of connectives, leading to a repeated application of some sequence of rules in the proof tree. Next, the proof of the theorem itself may be structured, leading to the natural elaboration of lemmas whose proofs may be reused for the construction of the global proof. And last, one may want to prove several instantiations of a generic formula, thus using the same sequence of rules for different theorems sharing a same structure. In this last case, the prover becomes able to solve complex theorems (problems), training itself on a set of simpler but complex similar theorems of growing complexity, thus exhibiting an ability to learn from experience. In each case, macro-rules may be detected upon an empirical basis : the observation of regularities in the data.

The problem is referred to as the "generalization to N" problem since the work of Shavlick and Dejong (1987), and is a subject of growing interest in the Machine Learning community (see, e.g., (Cheng &Carbonell, 1986; Cohen, 1987,1988; Prieditis, 1986)). It involves the extension of a given procedure accepting a fixed number of arguments, in order to obtain a new looping procedure, able to handle an arbitrary finite number of arguments. The aim of this transformation is to keep the computation inside reasonable bounds of complexity with the growing number of arguments.

We now define more precisely this notion of regularity in the framework of theorem proving. We introduce for this purpose the basic concept of homogeneity, which roughly corresponds to the invariance with permutation on the components of a logical object. The motivation for this choice comes from the observation of classical "hard" logical puzzles like the placing of queens on a board, the colouring of a complete graph (Greenwood and Gleason 1955) or the Schurr lemma (Schur 1916). They all include homogeneous formulas, and the difficulty of their proofs stems from the incapability of general theorem provers to handle such a global property. As a consequence, the size of their proofs depends exponentially on the number of "objects" in the problem (number of queens, of nodes...). We developed a semantical and a syntaxical version of the homogeneity criterion. The detection of syntactical homogeneity leads to a form of static learning, in the sense that no proof is needed in order to build macros.

## 3.1   Basic definitions

> **Definition** : A *macro-operator of arity n*  M is a $\lambda$abstraction of a logical object w.r.t. n variables $F_1,...F_n$, i.e. of the form    $\lambda F_1,...F_n\ M(F_1,...F_n)$

This definition is primarily designed for formulas, where operators are connectives and we will focus on formulas in the rest of the paper. But the definition may be easily instantiated to handle sets of formulas, by means of a special connective ",". Finally, we represent a proof in the same way, rules of inference being treated as connectives of arity 2.

**Examples:**  Id $= \lambda\ F.F$ is the identity macro operator, of arity 1.

Equiv $= \lambda\ A,B.(A\Rightarrow B)\wedge(B\Rightarrow A)$  is a macro-connective of arity 2 corresponding to the usual equivalence relation.

> **Definition** : A formula F is *semantically homogeneous with respect to the components* $S_c$ if $S_c$ is a set of sub-formulas occurring in F such that F is invariant for every permutation on these objects (i.e every permutation on $S_c$ leads to logically equivalent formulas). The cardinality of $S_c$ is the *arity* of homogeneity.

(Macro-)connectors themselves may be viewed as generic formulas. We say that a connector of arity 2 is *extendable*  iff it is associative and homogeneous of arity 2, that is  iff it is associative and commutative.

**Examples:**

$\{p\vee q\vee r, \neg p\vee\neg q, \neg p\vee\neg r, \neg q\vee\neg r\}$ is a set of formulas homogeneous of arity 3 with respect to the components p,q,r.

The $\vee$ connective is extendable.

We now provide a syntactical, stronger notion of homogeneous logical objects. This provides a **practical** definition of homogeneity. We first define the notion of homogeneous block, which is a syntactical characterization of the elementary (smallest) homogeneous objects.

---

**Definition** : A formula F is a *homogeneous block with respect to a set of components* $S_C$, denoted $<C,M>$ if there exists a redex of F= $(F_A \quad F_I)$, such that

a) the only operator of $F_A$ is the extendable connective C, the *link* of the block

b) each formula $f_i \in F_I$ is an instance of the macro-operator M, the *pattern* of the block

c) the set $\{f_i\}$ is invariant (unaltered) for every permutation of its components $S_C$.

---

**Proposition1**: If there exists a redex (FA FI) representing a formula F such that the formulas $f_i$ of FI are homogeneous blocks with respect to a set of components $S_C$, then F is semantically homogeneous with respect to $S_C$. We say that F is a *connection of the blocks FI* , with the *block structure* FA.

**Examples:**

F1 = $p \vee q \vee r$ = $((\lambda x,y,z . x \vee y \vee z) \ p \ q \ r)$ = $<\vee,Id>$ is a homogeneous block with respect to $\{p,q,r\}$. The extendable connective $\vee$ is the link and $\lambda x. x$ = Id is the pattern of the block.

F2 = $(\neg p \vee \neg q) \wedge (\neg p \vee \neg r) \wedge (\neg q \vee \neg r)$ = $((\lambda x,y,z . x \wedge y \wedge z) \ \neg p \vee \neg q \ \neg p \vee \neg r \ \neg q \vee \neg r)$ = $<\wedge,\lambda x \lambda y. \neg x \vee \neg y>$ is a homogeneous block with respect to $\{p,q,r\}$.

F3 = $(\neg p \vee \neg q) \wedge (\neg p \vee \neg r)$ is not homogeneous with respect to $\{p,q,r\}$. Indeed, given the permutation $\{p \leftarrow q, q \leftarrow p\}$, the formula becomes $(\neg p \vee \neg q) \wedge (\neg q \vee \neg r)$ which is clearly not equivalent.

F = $(p \vee q \vee r) \wedge (\neg p \vee \neg q) \wedge (\neg p \vee \neg r) \wedge (\neg q \vee \neg r)$ is not a homogeneous block with respect to $\{p,q,r\}$, but it is a homogeneous formula with respect to $\{p,q,r\}$. It is a connection of the blocks $\{F1,F2\}$ whose block structure is $\lambda x \lambda y. x \wedge y$.

The converse of the proposition is clearly false. For example, $(p \Rightarrow q) \wedge (p \vee \neg q)$ is homogeneous with respect to $\{p,q\}$ but is not decomposable in homogeneous blocks. We assume that syntactical regularities are the only relevant regularities at the formula level and that the detection of equivalences occurs at the proof level. Thus, we obtain a practical, efficient way to test for homogeneity. Moreover, we have proved in (Belleannée, 1991) the following result, showing the expression power of the syntactical criterion:

**Proposition2:** for every semantically homogeneous formula of the propositional calculus, there exists at least one logically equivalent formula syntactically homogeneous.

The next step consists in generalizing the number of parameters a same macro-operator is able to handle, leading to the construction of an homogeneous concept.

## 3.2 Macro-operators of variable arity

> **Definition** : A *macro-operator of variable arity* M(L) is an abstraction of variable length such that L denotes the set of variables occurring in the macro.

The expression of these macro-operators requires the definition of a language of operators handling sets of logical objects. We have designed for this purpose a general *set operator schema*. In order to improve the readability of paper, we only present a restriction of our schema, sufficient for the current description. In this schema, "logical object" means formula or sequent:

$\overset{\infty}{M}$( (Macro-)Operator, Structure_of_selections, Set_of_logical_objects), where

$\overset{\infty}{M}(M_d, \text{Struct}(V_1..., V_d), L) \equiv \{M_d(\sigma V_1..., \sigma V_d) / \sigma \text{ instanciates Struct}(V_1..., V_d) \text{ in } L\}$

A structure with variable arity is based on a notion of repetition of patterns.

In our schema, in terms of control structures the macro is a for loop producing instances of the macro-operator $M_d$. $\text{Struct}(V_1..., V_d)$ may be viewed as the condition part of a while loop on the set of primitive components L.

In the schema:

-The macro-operator $M_d$ is either a simple macro operator or a primitive macro-operator of variable arity (that is, the extension of an extendable macro of arity 2 to greater arities by means of a repeated application of it). For instance, we define $\overset{\infty}{\wedge}(L)$ to be the repeated application of $\wedge$ on the elements of L.

-The selector $\text{Struct}(V_1, ..., V_d)$ designates the set of variables $\{V_1, ..., V_d\}$ with a particular structure (i.e. a partial ordering on the variables).

Based on this schema, we introduce simplified notations for some default values of set operator arguments such as: $\overset{\infty}{M}(M_d, L) = \overset{\infty}{M}(M_d, \text{Var}(L), L)$, where $\text{Var}(L)$ returns a pattern of different variables the length of which is the cardinal of L, and we define primitive operators such as: $\text{AND}(S, L) = \overset{\infty}{M}(\wedge, S, L)$ ).

**Example** : At-least-2(L) = $\overset{\infty}{M}(\vee, \overset{\infty}{M}(\wedge, <A,B>, L)) = \overset{\infty}{\vee}(\text{AND}(<A,B>, L))$ is a macro-connective of variable arity.

At-least-2($\{p,q,r\}$) $\equiv \{(p \wedge q) \vee (p \wedge r) \vee (q \wedge r)\}$.

## 3.3 From homogeneous formula to homogeneous concepts

The defined language allows the user to introduce his own macro-connectives in the theorem prover. However, some macro-connectives of variable arity may be automatically derived from simple ones. So, the homogeneity concept aims at specifying the simple macro-operators that may be extended to handle an arbitrary number of arguments. We now define this mapping.

The process consists in generalizing to N the number of arguments of the macro, *preserving the block structure* of this macro. Indeed, our fundamental claim is that preserving this block structure preserves the underlying semantical interesting features of the operator and hence allows it to be efficiently treated.

Formally, let F be a fixed arity homogeneous logical object for a set of components S, and let P = (FA FI) be a redex of F where $f_i \in F_I$ are homogeneous blocks. The corresponding macro-operator of variable arity is P except that

each block $f_i = <C,M_d>$ is replaced with $\overset{\infty}{f_i} = \overset{\infty}{M}(C, \overset{\infty}{M}(M_d, structure(M_d), L))$,

where structure is a recursive function whose result is a partially ordered set of variables depending on the primitive connectives of $M_d$.

**Example:** Let F be the homogeneous formula F of the previous section:
F = (p∨q∨r)∧(¬p∨¬q)∧(¬p∨¬r)∧(¬q∨¬r), whose block structure is F= F1∧F2, with
S={p,q,r}, F1 = <∨, Id> and F2 = <∧, λxλy.¬x∨¬y>.

The corresponding macro-connective of variable arity is

$\overset{\infty}{F}(L) = \overset{\infty}{F_1}(L) \wedge \overset{\infty}{F_2}(L)$ with

$\overset{\infty}{F_1}(L) = \overset{\infty}{M}(\vee, \overset{\infty}{M}(Id,<x>,L)) = \overset{\infty}{M}(\vee,L) = \overset{\infty}{V}(L)$.

$\overset{\infty}{F_2}(L) = \overset{\infty}{M}(\wedge, \overset{\infty}{M}(\lambda x\lambda x.\neg x\vee\neg y, <P,Q>,L)) = \overset{\infty}{\wedge}(\{\lambda x\lambda x.\neg x\vee\neg y, <P,Q>,L)\})$.

That is $\overset{\infty}{F}(L) = \overset{\infty}{V}(L) \wedge \overset{\infty}{\wedge}(\{\lambda x\lambda x.\neg x\vee\neg y, <P,Q>, L)\})$.

For instance, $\overset{\infty}{F}(\{a,b,c,d\}) = (a \vee b \vee c \vee d) \wedge (\neg a\vee\neg b) \wedge (\neg a\vee\neg c) \wedge (\neg a\vee\neg d) \wedge (\neg b\vee\neg c) \wedge (\neg b\vee\neg d) \wedge (\neg c\vee\neg d)$.

From a semantic point of view, the instance F expresses the meaning 1-among-3, and the generalized formula $\overset{\infty}{F}$ represents the concept 1-among-N. Actually, the generalization preserving the block structure also preserves the homogeneity property.

We do not claim that this mapping is the only interesting one. It has been considered for its simplicity, and in our opinion it exhibits the concept the more naturally induced from the instance, within the bias of homogeneity. But it must be clear that other transformations have to be considered in order to fully benefit from the expressiveness of the language of macros of variable arity.

# 4 How to build a new macro-rule

This section deals with the integration of the new macro-connectives in the framework of the system G (see section 2), according to a *partial evaluation principle*. The problem is the following: given a macro-connective, we would like the system to be able to take it into account directly through associated macro-rules. For each macro-connective, two inference rules may be generated, one operating on a macro occurring in the left part of a sequent and the other one in the right part. A macro-rule is produced by synthesizing the deduction tree of the macro-connective. The method used to process the inference rules assigned to a macro-connective MC may be featured by the following algorithm.

---

func construct-the-inference-rules (MC):

        construct-one-rule (MC $\rightarrow$ )  construct-one-rule ( $\rightarrow$ MC)

func construct-one-rule (Sequent):

      Deduction-tree := expand-tree (Sequent)

      Leaves:= extract-the-leaves (Deduction-tree)

$$\frac{\text{Leaves}}{\text{Sequent}}$$

---

We precise now the construction of the rules for the simple and the variable arity cases.

For a macro-connective MC *with fixed arity*, the function "expand-tree" processes the deduction tree associated to the sequent MC$\rightarrow$ (or $\rightarrow$ MC) applying inference rules of the system G to the sequent. The development is achieved when all the operators occurring in the partition of MC have been completely expanded, that is, when the resulting sequents contain only logical objects of the initial partition (those sequents are the *leaves* of the tree). Then, the second procedure "extract-the-leaves" simplify the proof, removing redundant leaves such as axioms and subsumed leaves. The resulting macro-rule consists of the optimized leaves as its premise, and in the macro-connective as its conclusion.

**Example:** Given the macro-connective MC defined by MC(A,B,C) = (B$\Rightarrow$C)$\Rightarrow$((A$\Rightarrow$B) $\wedge$ (B$\Rightarrow$A)), the following figure illustrates the processing of the right macro-rule for MC:

deduction tree resulting from expand-tree ($\rightarrow$MC(A,B,C)):

$$\rightarrow(B\Rightarrow C)\Rightarrow((A\Rightarrow B)\wedge(B\Rightarrow A))$$
$$|$$
$$B\Rightarrow C \rightarrow (A\Rightarrow B)\wedge(B\Rightarrow A)$$
$$\diagup \qquad\qquad \diagdown$$
$$B\Rightarrow C\rightarrow A\Rightarrow B \qquad\qquad B\Rightarrow C\rightarrow B\Rightarrow A$$
$$| \qquad\qquad\qquad\qquad |$$
$$B\Rightarrow C,A\rightarrow B \qquad\qquad B\Rightarrow C,B\rightarrow A$$
$$| \qquad\quad | \qquad\qquad | \qquad\quad |$$
$$A\rightarrow B,B \quad A,C\rightarrow B \quad B\rightarrow A,B \quad B,C\rightarrow A$$

right macro-rule for MC resulting from construct-1-rule($\rightarrow$MC(A,B,C)):

$$\frac{A\rightarrow B \quad B,C\rightarrow A}{\rightarrow MC(A,B,C)}$$

In order to derive the deduction tree of a macro-connective *with variable arity*, according to the system G, the function "expand-tree" needs extended derivation rules dealing with the variable arities. For illustration purpose, we just present one of them, treating the occurence of a variable arity AND in the left part of a sequent (for more information see (Belleannée, 1991)):

$$\frac{\overset{\infty}{M}([SA\rightarrow SB,X],<X>,L)}{SA\rightarrow SB,\overset{\infty}{\wedge}(L)}$$

# 5 An example

We show an example of a homogeneous formula handled by the system. The first step consists in detecting the simple homogeneous formula and then learning the corresponding macro-rule with variable arity. The second step illustrates the use of the learned structure.

## 5.1 Learning step

- Given the formula $F=(a\wedge b)\vee(\neg a\wedge\neg b)$, the system detects whether it is homogeneous with respect to its components $\{a,b\}$. The resulting block structure is $F=F_1\vee F_2$ with $F_1=(a\wedge b)=<\wedge,Id>$ and $F_2=(\neg a\wedge\neg b)=<\wedge,\lambda x.\neg x>$

- Then, the application of the generalization to N algorithm produces the homogeneous formula with variable arity $\overset{\infty}{F}$: $\quad \overset{\infty}{F}(L)=\overset{\infty}{F_1}(L)\vee\overset{\infty}{F_2}(L)$

with $\overset{\approx}{F}_1(L) = \overset{\approx}{M}(\wedge, \overset{\approx}{M}(Id,<A>,L)) = \overset{\approx}{M}(\wedge,L) = \overset{\infty}{\wedge}(L)$

and $\overset{\approx}{F}_2(L) = \overset{\approx}{M}(\wedge, \overset{\approx}{M}(\lambda x.\neg x ,<A>,L)) = \overset{\infty}{\wedge}(\{\lambda x.\neg x , <A>, L\})$

-Both macro-rules associated to $\overset{\approx}{F}$ are established applying on $\overset{\approx}{F}$ variable arity rewriting rules (see section 4). Notation: PROD is a product on sets of sequents.

---

a- Left rule:

derivation tree:                                  synthesized rule:

$$\overset{\infty}{\wedge}(L) \vee \overset{\infty}{\wedge}(\{\lambda x.\neg x ,<A>,L\}) \to$$

         $/$                     $\backslash$                       $\dfrac{L \to \qquad \to L}{\overset{\approx}{F} \to}$

$\overset{\infty}{\wedge}(L) \to$               $\overset{\infty}{\wedge}(\{\lambda x.\neg x ,<A>,L\}) \to$

    |                           |

PROD $(\overset{\approx}{M}(\lambda x.[x \to ] , <A>, L))$     PROD $(\overset{\approx}{M}(\lambda x.[\neg x \to ] ,<A>, L))$

    |                           |

    $L \to$                 PROD $(\overset{\approx}{M}(\lambda x.[ \to x ] , <A>, L))$

                                        |

                                     $\to L$

---

b- Right rule:

derivation tree:                                    synthesized rule:

$$\to \overset{\infty}{\wedge}(L) \vee \overset{\infty}{\wedge}(\{\lambda x.\neg x ,<A>,L\})$$

                   |                         $\dfrac{\overset{\approx}{M}(\lambda x \lambda y. x \to y, <A1;A2>,L)}{\to \overset{\approx}{F}}$

PROD $(\{\to \overset{\infty}{\wedge}(L) , \to \overset{\infty}{\wedge}(\{\lambda x.\neg x , <A>, L\})$

                   |

PROD $(\{\overset{\approx}{M}(\lambda x.[ \to x ] ,<A>, L) , \overset{\approx}{M}(\lambda x.[ \to \neg x ] , <A>, L)\})$

                   |

PROD $(\{\overset{\approx}{M}(\lambda x.[ \to x ] ,<A>, L) , \overset{\approx}{M}(\lambda x.[x \to ] , <A>, L)\})$

                   |

$\overset{\approx}{M}(\lambda x \lambda y. x \to y, <A_1;A_2> L)$

## 5.2 Using the learned rules

From now on, when the system detects that a formula F is an instance of $\overset{\infty}{F}$, it directly derives F by means of both previous rules. For instance, the formula $F_2 = (p \wedge q \wedge r) \vee (\neg p \wedge \neg q \wedge \neg r)$ matches the formula $\overset{\infty}{F}$, with the instanciation $L = \{p,q,r\}$, so the immediate derivation of "$F_2 \rightarrow$" using the macro-rule "$\overset{\infty}{F} \rightarrow$" is (while an indirect derivation of "$F_2 \rightarrow$" would have produced a derivation tree with 10 nodes and 7 levels):

$$(p \wedge q \wedge r) \vee (\neg p \wedge \neg q \wedge \neg r) \rightarrow$$

$$\diagup \qquad \diagdown$$

$$p,q,r \rightarrow \qquad \rightarrow p,q,r$$

# 6 Related Work

Amongst the systems addressing the issue of adapting a general automated theorem prover on a particular domain, one can distinguish two main approaches.

The system Muscadet (Pastre, 1989) is a representative of the first approach. In this system, the learning component may be classified as performing knowledge acquisition. Indeed, learning proceeds by transforming some declarative knowledge into a procedural, deductive one.

Muscadet is a general theorem prover with an expert system architecture. It is dedicated to mathematical fields requiring a lot of knowledge and know-how, like set theory, relations, topology... Specific knowledge is given to the system as facts and rules. Then some meta-rules automatically translate mathematical definitions into inference rules.

The second approach is related to explanation based learning in order to build an operational knowledge guiding deductions.

The system realized by O'Rorke consists in applying an EBL learning system to propositional calculus problems from Principia Mathematica (O'Rorke, 1987). The system generalizes the already proven theorems in order to forget the extraneous details and to remember only the main features of the specific theorems.

The generalized theorems are then stored to be reused for future proofs. For instance, the theorem $\neg (p \lor q) \Rightarrow (p \Rightarrow q)$ gives rise to the theorem $\neg (A \lor B) \Rightarrow (A \Rightarrow D)$.

In this system, the learning process consists in learning particular lemmas, characteristic to the domain, in order to augment the set of basic axioms of the theorem prover.

The system ADEPT (Acquisition of DEterministic Proof Tactic) (Cohen, 1987, 1988) performs a more sophisticated kind of EBL. It acquires some control knowledge, that is, search strategies for a theorem prover on a particular domain, given instances of "good proofs".

The method consists in analysing the inputs proofs in order to find which inference rule was used in which situation. This learned knowledge is represented in a finite state automaton, and is used to guide the choice of the inference rule to employ in future proofs, when similar situations occur. Learning belongs to generalization to N methods, which allows recognition and generalization of looping constructs in the proof instances.

Our method shares with all these systems the common concern to "operationalize" some knowledge about the kind of proofs that are requested from the prover. ADEPT is the nearest system from ours. But, we are working on the structure of the theorems themselves rather than the proofs. Both approaches are not concurrent and the full treatment of homogeneity requires a work at the proof level. However, homogeneity is a *global* criterion, and requires to work on the whole proof. The regularity criterion in ADEPT (two rules of inference belongs to a same class if they are immediately followed by identical rules) is more local and thus, potentially captures more and shortest macros.

# 7 Conclusion

This paper proposes a framework enabling one to introduce learning abilities in an automated theorem prover. It is founded on the detection of regular structures within formulas and proofs. We provide a representation, that is a language and operators to deal with such structures

We have not yet addressed the important issue of determinating when to cancel an old macro. Iba (1989) has developed a general framework to describe system managing sets of macro-operators. In this view, the set of macro-operators is pruned by two types of filters. Static filters are applied at the creation of a new macro to decide on analytical criteria which macro may be kept. Dynamic filters are applied after an execution requiring some macro-operators to decide on empirical criteria which macro may be kept.

In the framework of theorem proving, according to this work, we plan to experiment with the following filters:

static filters: a) Keep macros of polynomial complexity (analytical measure). b) Check for each new macro if it is not redundant with some old ones. Remove the most specific.

dynamic filters: c) Keep macros of polynomial complexity (empirical measure). d) Retain macros in an ordered list of bounded size. Remove the least frequently used.

## References

Belleannée C. "Improving deduction in a sequent calculus". Proc of the 8th biennal conference of the CSCSI",  pp 220-226, Ottawa, may 1990.

Belleannée C. "Vers un démonstrateur adaptatif". Thèse de l'Université de RennesI, Jan 1991.

Cheng P. & Carbonell J. "The FERMI system: Inducing Iterative Macro-operators from Experience". Proc. of AAAI, 1986 .

Cohen W. "A Technique for Generalizing Number in Explanation Based Learning". ML TR 19,  Rutgers University , Sept 1987.

Cohen W. "Generalising Number and Learning from Multiple Examples in Explanation Based Learning". Proc. of 5th ICML, pp256-269,  Morgan Kaufmann, Los Altos, Calif. 1988.

Fikes R., Hart P. & Nilsson N.  "Learning and Executing Generalized Robot Plans ". A.I. 3,  pp 251-288,  1972.

Gallier J.H. "Logic for Computer Science: Foundations of Automatic Theorem Proving". Harper & Rown, New York, 1986.

Greenwood R.E. & Gleason A.M. "Combinatorial relations and chromatic graphs" Combinatorial Journal 7, 1955

Iba G. "A Heuristic Approach to the Discovery of Macro-operators". Machine Learning 3, pp 285-317,  1989.

Korf R. "Learning to Solve Problems by searching for macro-operators". PhD Thesis  Carnegie Mellon University, 1983.

Korf R.  "Macro-operators : A Weak Method for Learning". A I 26,  pp35-77,  1985.

Minton S.  "Learning Effective Search Control Knowledge: an Explanation Based Approach". PhD Thesis  Carnegie Mellon University , 1988.

O'Rorke P. "LT revisited : Experimental results of applying explanation-based learning to the logic of principia mathematica". 4th IWML  Irvine,1987.

Pastre.D "Muscadet : An Automatic Theorem Proving System Using Knowledge and Meta-knowledge in Mathematics". Artificial Intelligence,  vol 38, 1989  pp 257-318.

Porter.B "Learning Problem Solving". PhD Thesis University of California, Irvine 1984.

Prieditis A. "Discovery of Algorithms from Weak Methods". Proc. of International Meeting on Advances in Learning, Les Arcs  France, 1986.

Schur I. "Über die kongruenz $x^m + y^m = z^m$ mod p"   Jber Deutsch Verein 25, pp114-116. 1916

Shavlik J. & Dejong G.  "An Explanation-Based Approach to Generalising Number". Proc. of IJCAI-87, Milan, Italy, pp236-238,  1987.

# EXPLANATION-BASED GENERALIZATION AND CONSTRAINT PROPAGATION WITH INTERVAL LABELS

Kai Zercher

Siemens AG, ZFE IS INF 33,
Otto-Hahn-Ring 6, D-8000 München 83

TU München, Institut für Informatik
Orleanstr. 34, D-8000 München 80
Germany

zercher@ztivax.uucp

## Abstract

Two ways of applying EBG to constraint propagation with interval labels are presented. The first method, CP-EBG-1, is described by a straightforward use of a Prolog EBG implementation. The second, CP-EBG-2, performs two phases: First constraint propagation is done and, using EBG, a generalized final labelling is derived but no extra conditions are learned. Second, constraint propagation is again performed using the final labellings of phase 1 as the initial labelling. This time, conditions are learned which form the desired concept description.

It is shown that CP-EBG-2 learns more general concept descriptions than CP-EBG-1. A proof is outlined that CP-EBG-2 produces correct concept descriptions for the class of constraints using linear equations and interval arithmetic. Central to this proof - and to possible proofs for other constraint classes - is the notion of *moderate* generalization. It guarantees that a generalization which was learned from one instance and which is now used in a new situation, does not lead to the exclusion of any solution for this new situation.

## Keywords

Explanation-based generalization, constraint propagation, interval labels, moderate generalization.

# 1. Introduction

Constraint propagation is a popular and widely used inference technique in AI (Davis, 1987). It operates on a constraint network, i.e., a set of variables (nodes) interconnected by constraints which express relations among variables. The most common type of constraint propagation is label inference: Every variable is assigned a set of possible values, and constraints are evaluated in order to restrict this set. This sort of constraint propagation is also called local constraint propagation (Güsgen & Hertzberg, 1988) or simply, as we will do throughout this paper, constraint propagation.

Given a constraint network, typical questions are whether a locally consistent solution (labeling of all variables) exists or what a particular value of such a solution is. Sometimes, the constraint network is fixed but some inputs vary and we have to determine the answer to these questions for various possible inputs. This is a situation which we faced in an application of model-based diagnosis for robot operations. Since constraint propagation turned out to be too slow for this application, we applied explanation-based generalization (EBG) to it. Thereby we learned general rules which, if applicable, derived the same results as constraint propagation would do. When we compared the execution time of constraint propagation for a specific instance with the time needed to match a rule learned by EBG from constraint propagation and this example, the latter was faster by two orders of magnitude. With the help of conditions learned from constraint propagation, we could construct rules for error diagnosis whose usage reduced the average diagnosis time considerably (Zercher, 1988, 1990 a).

In the next section we present a straightforward way to apply EBG to constraint propagation and illustrate it with a small example; this is the method used in the above mentioned literature. In Section 3, we propose a new, two phase approach, which learns a more general but still correct concept description. Properties of both methods are discussed in Section 4. We show in Section 5 that one can also learn concept descriptions from inconsistencies detected by constraint propagation. Section 6 introduces the notion of a *moderate* generalization, and we will show that, together with the monotonicity property of constraints, this is sufficient to guarantee that the new method yields correct generalizations. In the final section, we present our conclusion.

## 2. EBG and constraint propagation: First approach

EBG is a powerful, knowledge intensive learning technique (Mitchell et al., 1986; DeJong & Mooney, 1986). It is able to learn a correct generalization from a single training instance. Utilizing an available domain theory, EBG constructs an explanation why the given example belongs to the target concept. This explanation is then generalized and a conjunction of conditions, which forms a sufficient condition for the target concept, is extracted from it. EBG guarantees that the learned description fulfills an operationality criterion (Keller, 1987) that tries to ensure that the description can be efficiently evaluated. Some authors put EBG in a theorem proving framework and consequently speak about proofs, proof trees, and so forth; other authors put it in a problem solving framework where an explanation is a sequence of operators which transform an initial state into a goal state. As (Mooney & Bennett, 1986) have shown, both are two views of the same coin since the proposed, different generalization algorithms yield basically the same results.

Table 1 shows a simple Prolog implementation of constraint propagation along with some of the predicates needed for interval arithmetic. We normally work with a CommonLisp implementation, however, we use Prolog here since it is the de facto standard language for describing EBG research. Constraint propagation works by repeatedly evaluating constraints. Whenever a value used by a constraint is changed, this constraint must be reprocessed. This can mean that the same constraint is executed several times. Constraint propagation stops - reaches quiescence - when no constraint can change the value of a variable. Termination of constraint propagation is guaranteed for some classes of constraints, e.g., linear equations with unit coefficient, but not for all (Davis, 1987).

For the purpose of EBG, an explanation (proof) is a sequence of constraint propagation steps which transforms an initial variable labelling into a final labelling which is consistent, i.e., every constraint is fulfilled. Such a sequence is exactly what cp__consistent/3 (the '/3' is a Prolog notation which means that the predicate has 3 arguments) will produce provided the predicate succeeds. In (Kedar-Cabelli & McCarty, 1987) a clear and concise EBG implementation is given. Their predicate prolog__ebg/3 has as arguments, the goal clause, the generalized goal, and a list of learned conditions (the operational concept definition). By applying it to cp__consistent/3, we have the desired combination of EBG and constraint

```
/*   cp__consistent( + Constraints, + StartLabelling, -FinalLabelling ) :-        */
/*       succeeds if constraint propagation terminates with a consistent final labelling.   */
cp__consistent( [Constraint|RConstraints], StartLabelling, FinalLabelling ) :-
     constraint(Constraint, StartLabelling, NewLabelling, AffectedConstraints),
     /* Applies a constraint and produces a new labelling. If a value of a variable   */
     /* was changed then all constraints which must be reused are contained in      */
     /* AffectedConstraint.  Fails if an empty interval was derived.                */
     append(RConstraints, AffectedConstraints, UpdatedConstraints),
     cp__consistent(UpdatedConstraints, NewLabelling, FinalLabelling).
cp__consistent( [], FinalLabelling, FinalLabelling ).

constraint(c4, [x(X__Int), y(Y__Int)), a(A__Int), b(B__Int), c(C1__Int) ],
              [x(X__Int), y(Y__Int)), a(A__Int), b(B__Int), c(C2__Int) ], [] ) :-
     /* The simple constraint  C ← X + [-2, 2] + A taken from Table 2.              */
     interval__plus(X__Int, [-2, 2], H__Int), interval__plus(H__Int, A__Int, CNew__Int),
     interval__intersection(C1__Int, CNew__Int, C2__Int).

interval__intersection([A1,A2], [B1,B2], [C1,C2]) :-
     maximum(A1, B1, C1),  minimum(A2, B2, C2),  C1 ≤ C2.

interval__plus([A1,A2], [B1,B2], [C1,C2]) :-
     C1 is  A1 + B1,   C2 is  A2 + B2.

maximum(- ∞, Y, Y) .
maximum(X, Y, X) :-  Y ≤ X.
maximum(X, Y, Y) :-  X ≤ Y.
```

Table 1: Pieces of the Prolog code for constraint propagation

propagation; it will be called CP-EBG-1. However, we perform a few modifications, which we will explain after the following examples.

We first look at what happens if we apply prolog__ebg/3 to the predicate interval__intersection/3. Provided that arithmetic operations and comparisons are declared as being operational, calling

```
prolog__ebg( interval__intersection([1,5], [2,6], Int3),
             interval__intersection([X,Y], [U,V], GInt3),
             LearnedConditions ).
```

will succeed with the following bindings:

Int3 = [2,5] , GInt3 = [U,Y],  LearnedConditions = [ X ≤ U,  Y ≤ V, U ≤ Y]

The first condition guarantees that the lower bound of the result interval is the lower bound of the second interval, the second condition guarantees that the upper bound of the result interval is the upper bound of the first interval, and the third condition guarantees that the result interval is well defined.

Table 2 shows an extremely simple constraint propagation problem. It is atypical in the sense that there is no feedback, i.e., no constraint must be executed twice, but it is sufficient for demonstration purposes. The training example is defined by $X = 5$ and $Y = 7$. If we call

```
prolog__ebg( cp__consistent([c1, ... ], [ x([5,5]), y([7,7]), a([-∞, ∞]), ... ], Labelling),
            cp__consistent([c1, ... ], [ x([X,X]), y([Y,Y]), a([-∞, ∞]), ... ], GenLabelling),
            LearnedConditions ).
```

it will succeed with the following bindings:

```
Labelling = [ x([5,5]), y([7,7]), a([1,2]), b([2,3]), c([6,9]) ],
GenLabelling = [ x([X,X]), y([Y,Y]), a([1, 2]), b([2, 3]), c([Y-1, X + 4]) ],
LearnedConditions = [ X ≤ 6,  6 ≤ Y, -5 ≤ X-Y]     /* simplified result */
```

This means, that we have learned the general rule (we use '←' instead of ':-' in order to distinguish Prolog code from learned rules):

```
cp__consistent([c1, c2, c3, c4, c5], [x([X,X]), y([Y,Y]), a([-∞, ∞]), b([-∞, ∞]), c([-∞, ∞]) ],
              [ x([X,X]), y([Y,Y]), a([1, 2]), b([2, 3]), c([Y-1, X + 4]) ])
     ← X ≤ 6,  6 ≤ Y, -5 ≤ X-Y.
```

In some cases, we might not be interested in computing the consistent final labelling but only in determining whether it exists depending on the values of X and Y. With the definition

```
cp__consistent__problem1(X, Y) :-
    cp__consistent([c1, c2, c3, c4, c5], [ x([X,X]), y([Y,Y]), a([-∞, ∞]), b([-∞, ∞]), c([-∞, ∞]) ], _ ).
```

we would get the rule:

```
cp__consistent__problem1(X, Y)  ←  X ≤ 6,  6 ≤ Y, -5 ≤ X-Y.
```

Table 2 shows in detail what happens; it lists the constraint propagation steps, their grounded and generalized results and the learned conditions. Some expressions have been simplified in order to enhance readability. The conditions are constructed when $C_{i-1}$ and $C_{new,i}$ are intersected in order to get $C_i$. This is done in the same fashion as demonstrated above in the example for the predicate interval__intersection/3. In Figure 1, the dark shaded area shows the space covered by the learned concept definition.

To the the standard EBG approach, we have applied the following modifications:

- Predicates which are used for control purposes do not cause any conditions to enter the learned concept description. We took append/3 as an extremely simple strategy to control constraint propagation. Other strategies (Davis, 1987) could also be used as long as they are "fair" (Güsgen & Hertzberg 1988).
- The list of learned conditions is simplified. After conditions have been individually simplified, e.g., $X + Y - 2 ≤ Y + 5$ becomes $X ≤ 7$, redundant conditions are

A Simple Constraint Propagation Problem:

$A \leftarrow [1, 2]$, $\quad B \leftarrow [2, 3]$, $\quad C \leftarrow [5, 16]$, $\quad C \leftarrow X + [-2, 2] + A$, $\quad C \leftarrow Y + [-3, 3] + B$

Training example: $X = 5$, $Y = 7$

Trace of CP-EBG-1 for the variable C

| Name | Interval | Generalized Interval | Learned Conditions or Comment |
|---|---|---|---|
| $C_0$ | $[-\infty, \infty]$ | $[-\infty, \infty]$ | - |
| $C_{new,1}$ | $[5, 16]$ | $[5, 16]$ | constraint $C \leftarrow [5, 16]$ |
| $C_1$ | $[5, 16]$ | $[5, 16]$ | $5 \le 16$ |
| $C_{new,2}$ | $[4, 9]$ | $[X-1, X+4]$ | constraint $C \leftarrow X + [-2, 2] + A$ |
| $C_2$ | $[5, 9]$ | $[5, X+4]$ | $X-1 \le 5$, $X+4 \le 16$, $5 \le X+4$ |
| $C_{new,3}$ | $[6, 13]$ | $[Y-1, Y+6]$ | constraint $C \leftarrow Y + [-3, 3] + B$ |
| $C_3$ | $[6, 9]$ | $[Y-1, X+4]$ | $5 \le Y-1$, $X+4 \le Y+6$, $Y-1 \le X+4$ |

Learned conditions (simplified): $X \le 6$, $6 \le Y$, $-5 \le X-Y$

Trace of phase 2 of CP-EBG-2 for the variable C

| Name | Interval | Generalized Interval | Learned Conditions or Comment |
|---|---|---|---|
| $C_0$ | $[6, 9]$ | $[Y-1, X+4]$ | result of phase 1 |
| $C_{new,1}$ | $[5, 16]$ | $[5, 16]$ | constraint $C \leftarrow [5, 16]$ |
| $C_1$ | $[6, 9]$ | $[Y-1, X+4]$ | $5 \le Y-1$, $X+4 \le 16$, $Y-1 \le X+4$ |
| $C_{new,2}$ | $[4, 9]$ | $[X-1, X+4]$ | constraint $C \leftarrow X + [-2, 2] + A$ |
| $C_2$ | $[6, 9]$ | $[Y-1, X+4]$ | $X-1 \le Y-1$, $X+4 \le X+4$, $Y-1 \le X+4$ |
| $C_{new,3}$ | $[6, 13]$ | $[Y-1, Y+6]$ | constraint $C \leftarrow Y + [-3, 3] + B$ |
| $C_3$ | $[6, 9]$ | $[Y-1, X+4]$ | $Y-1 \le Y-1$, $X+4 \le Y+6$, $Y-1 \le X+4$ |

Learned conditions (simplified): $X \le 12$, $6 \le Y$, $-5 \le X-Y$, $X-Y \le 0$

Table 2: Constraint propagation and EBG

removed. A condition is redundant if it is either always true like $0 \le 2$ or if it is implied by the remaining conditions. For instance, $X \le 7$ is implied by $X \le 5$. For the general case of linear inequalities, this test can be performed with the well known Simplex method (e.g., Papadimitriou & Steiglitz, 1982). In our experiments, simplification drastically decreased the size of the learned concept description. This is one of the major causes why the learned concept

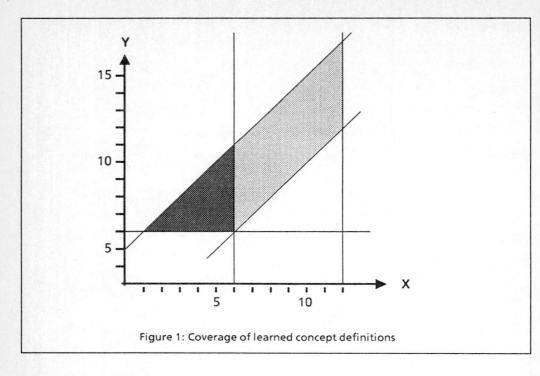

Figure 1: Coverage of learned concept definitions

description can be executed much faster than constraint propagation on the same example. See also (Minton, 1988) on the importance of simplification for EBG.

- We handle the predicate is/2 differently. Instead of getting the generalized interval [Y-1, X + 4], standard EBG would produce something like [U, V] plus the conditions U is Y-1 and V is X + 4. We achieve our type of generalization with a simple change: When prolog_ebg/3 performs is/2 on the grounded data, = /2 is done for the generalized data (in addition, the use of clause/2 must be altered slightly). This modification causes in fact only a syntactic change in the EBG result. However, it has several small advantages, the main being that it makes the presentation of EBG and its results simpler and easier to read.

## 3. EBG and constraint propagation: Second approach

We will call the new approach CP-EBG-2. From a given example it is able to learn a more general concept description than CP-EBG-1. CP-EBG-2 consists of two phases: First, we do constraint propagation and use EBG to construct a generalized final labelling but we do not learn any $\leq/2$ conditions. Second, with the consistent labelling and its generalization produced in phase 1, we again perform constraint propagation and apply EBG to it. Off course, the labelling and its generalization will not be changed by any constraint (after all, this is the property of a consistent labelling). This time, however, we will learn conditions and form the desired concept description. For our example these steps are illustrated in Table 2. We have learned the general rule

cp__consistent([c1, c2, c3, c4, c5], [x([X,X]), y([Y,Y]), a([-∞, ∞]), b([-∞, ∞]), c([-∞, ∞]) ],
     [ x([X,X]), y([Y,Y]), a([1, 2]), b([2, 3]), c([Y-1, X + 4]) ])

← X ≤ 12, 6 ≤ Y, -5 ≤ X-Y, X-Y ≤ 0.

or as an alternative

cp__consistent__problem1(X, Y)  ←  X ≤ 12, 6 ≤ Y, -5 ≤ X-Y, X-Y ≤ 0.

The area covered by the learned concept description is depicted in Figure 1 by the light and dark shaded areas. As we can see, the concept description found by the new method is more general (covers a larger area) than the one learned by the old method (only the dark shaded area). In Section 6 we will show that CP-EBG-2 always produces correct concept descriptions. The Prolog code of CP-EBG-1, CP-EBG-2, and the examples presented here is available from the author upon request.

Why can CP-EBG-2 learn a more general concept description than CP-EBG-1 for the same generalized labelling? A formal argument is presented in Section 6, but the following trivial example should help to get an intuitive understanding: Assume we want to find the maximum of the list [1,2,3]. We do this in the usual sequential fashion and after we have determined that $1 \leq 2$ and $2 \leq 3$ we conclude that 3 is the maximum. A generalization of these reasoning steps would be that Z is the maximum of [X,Y,Z] if $X \leq Y$ and $Y \leq Z$. However, the antecedent '$X \leq Z$ and $Y \leq Z$' would obviously be more general and still be correct. We could get this antecedent if we generalize the verification that 3 is indeed the maximum, i.e., $1 \leq 3$ and $2 \leq 3$. By generalizing the verification of the solution instead of generalizing the steps which led to the solution, a more general concept description was found.

As an effect of our modified EBG, all functional expressions, e.g., Y-1, needed to compute the final labelling are included in the final generalized labelling. If we use standard EBG this is not the case; we just get generalized intervals like [U,V]. Consequently, starting phase 2 of CP-EBG-2 only with such a generalized labelling would not produce a useful result; the connection to the parameters of the initial labelling - here X and Y- would be lost. To perform CP-EBG-2 correctly with standard EBG, we keep after phase 1 all predicates which compute the final labelling, i.e., the is/2 predicates, and remove all others, i.e., the ≤/2 predicates. Phase 2 is then performed as before. Both methods will produce equivalent results. In this paper one should read 'generalized labelling' as either the result of our modified EBG or as the result of standard EBG plus the conditions which are needed to compute the labelling. When we talk about 'generalized solution' this should be understood the same way.

At first one might think that the result of CP-EBG-2 could also be achieved by first computing the final consistent labelling and then presenting this as a training example to EBG. EBG would proof that the labelling is consistent and would then derive a general condition for this. But this idea is flawed since all connections to the initial labelling and its parameters are lost. The two phases of CP-EBG-2 are really required.

## 4. Properties of CP-EBG-1 and CP-EBG-2

The training example used by CP-EBG-1 and CP-EBG-2 guides the generalization process. It thereby determines which generalized final labelling is constructed and when constraint propagation and its generalization is stopped . The latter point is not apparent in our example, but as soon as there are feedback loops, e.g., introduced by the constraint B ← C - A, this becomes important. When feedback loops are present, it is difficult to imagine how generalization could be done without the help of examples. This is similar to the problem partial evaluation faces with recursive rules.

Phase 2 of CP-EBG-2 is conveniently described as doing EBG. Note however, in this phase the example is not really required since the outcome of all constraint propagation steps, i.e., no change, is known in advance.

One question is whether two phases are sufficient. The rule learned by CP-EBG-2 describes the largest possible coverage of the determined generalized labelling. Consequently, another phase which would try to change the learned ≤/2 conditions could not be of any help.

Whenever an interval intersection is generalized three ≤/2 conditions are produced. Consequently, CP-EBG-1 will initially produce a number of conditions equal to three times the number of constraint propagation steps. On the other hand, with CP-EBG-2 it is just three times the number of existing constraints. The number only depends on the problem size and not on the number of inference steps performed. Usually, this means that CP-EBG-2 initially produces far fewer conditions than CP-EBG-1. Therefore, less time must be spent by CP-EBG-2 on simplification. Consequently, CP-EBG-2 will usually - despite the need for a second phase - be much faster than CP-EBG-1.

When constraint propagation does not terminate, CP-EBG-1 or CP-EBG-2 are obviously not possible. In such a situation one must resort to other inference techniques. If the task is to decide the consistency of constraints which are linear equalities or inequalities, a sound technique is the Simplex method. We can even apply EBG to it (Zercher, 1990b).

Finally, a note on implementation seems in place. The predicate prolog_ebg/3 is a general EBG implementation based on a Prolog meta-interpreter and is therefore quite slow. A much better speed is achieved with a specialized implementation: All predicates are augmented by extra parameters for generalized values. The generalization operations are explicitly coded. We experienced that Lisp is better suited than Prolog. One reason is that Lisp has efficient array operations which are needed to implement the Simplex method (required for simplification).

# 5. Learning from inconsistencies

Sometimes, we want to learn a concept description for the inconsistency of a constraint network depending on the input variables. An inconsistency is present when the intersection of two intervals, e.g., [1,2] and [4,5], is empty. CP-EBG-1 learns conditions for such a case by doing the same as before with the one exception that the detection of an inconsistency, i.e., the upper bound of one interval is lower than the lower bound of the other, produces a corresponding general $</2$ condition and immediately stops constraint propagation. With the training example $X = 5$, $Y = 15$ we learn the rule

cp_inconsistent_problem1(X, Y) $\leftarrow$ X-Y < -5, $1 \leq X$, $X \leq 6$.

In the case of CP-EBG-2, we stop phase 1 as soon as an inconsistency has been found and in phase 2, we just generate the one condition capturing the inconsistent interval intersection. In effect this means that we take just the one

$<$ /2 condition from phase 1 and ignore all $\leqq$ /2 conditions. For the same training example, CP-EBG-2 learns the rule

cp__inconsistent__problem1(X, Y)  $\leftarrow$  X-Y $<$ -5.

CP-EBG-2 will always produce just one single condition which implies an inconsistency. This is quite surprising at first. If we look at the space defined by the extra input variables (here X and Y), one can easily show that the subspace of all consistent variable values is convex. Consequently, an inconsistent subspace can be described by just one hyperplane (linear inequality).

For a given instance, we expect that the one condition concept description learned from this example can be executed much faster than constraint propagation on this example. We can even proof this statement with precise complexity results. If linear equations and unit coefficients are used as constraints the time complexity of constraint propagation is already $O(nE)$ where n is the number of variables and E is the total size of all constraints (Davis, 1987). In contrast to this, executing one learned condition has a complexity of just $O(n)$.

## 6. Correctness of CP-EBG-2

We will try to keep this section as brief and as informal as possible. We will heavily use (Güsgen & Hertzberg, 1988) for which we will henceforth take the short form (G&H); for those who want to get a deeper understanding we highly recommend this paper. Since prolog__ebg is a correct method and cp__consistent implements a fair constraint propagation strategy (Def. 8 G&H), our first approach CP-EBG-1 is guaranteed to learn a correct concept description. Correct means, that if an instance fulfills the learned conditions then the labelling, which we get by instantiating and evaluating the generalized labelling, is identical to the final labelling produced by constraint propagation.

The concept descriptions constructed by both approaches guarantee that the final generalized labelling is consistent. However, the CP-EBG-1 concept description in addition assures that, for a new instance, all constraint propagation steps yield results analog to the one produced by the training instance. Consequently, CP-EBG-2 learns a more general concept description than CP-EBG-1. We must however show that the CP-EBG-2 concept description is also correct.

A labelling L assigns every variable of a constraint network an interval, i.e., a description of a set of possible values. A labelling $L_1$ is a subset ( $\subseteq$ ) of a labelling

$L_2$ , iff the subset relation holds for every variable value. A constraint c is a mapping from a labelling to a new labelling. A constraint includes computing a new value and intersecting it with the old one. We only deal with monotonic constraints (Def. 2 G&H), i.e., $c(L_1) \subseteq L_1$ and $[ L_1 \subseteq L_2 \rightarrow c(L_1) \subseteq c(L_2) ]$. Almost all types of constraints, including the one we are using (linear equations with intervals), are monotonic. An instantiation h is a function which maps a generalized labelling to a grounded labelling by replacing certain variables with a value and evaluating all expressions. For instance, if h instantiates X with 5 and Y with 7, then $h([Y-1, X + 4]) = [6,9]$.

Def. 1: Let c be a constraint, h an instantiation, $L_1$ a labelling, $GL_1$ a generalized labelling such that $L_1 = h(GL_1)$. A generalization gen is a function which produces a new generalized labelling $GL_2$ given c, $L_1$, and $GL_1$ such that $GL_2 = gen(c, L_1, GL_1)$ and $c(L_1) = h(GL_2)$.

Def. 2: Let $h_1$ be one particular instantiation, $L_1 = h_1(GL_1)$, $GL_2 = gen(c, L_1, GL_1)$, and H be the set of all possible instantiation functions.

A generalization gen is *moderate*, iff $\forall h_i \in H: c(h_i(GL_1)) \subseteq h_i(GL_2)$.

Moderateness means that if we derive a general labelling from a constraint execution of a specific instance and then use this labelling for a different instance (instantiation), the resulting instantiated labelling will be a superset of what executing the constraint will give us. Moderateness prevents us from ruling out possibly consistent values from a labelling.

For linear equations and interval arithmetic, the generalizations we perform are all moderate. The rational is the following: When we generalize arithmetic operations like + /2 there is no loss of precision. When we generalize interval__intersection/3 we have to generalize maximum/3 (responsible for the lower bound) and minimum/3 (responsible for the upper bound). For instance if we compute the minimum of 9 and 13 we get 9; if the generalized values are X + 4 and Y + 6 the generalized result is X + 4. Even if this result is not correct for a different instantiation (e.g., X = 8, Y = 5), it can only cause an interval to be larger than it should be (but never smaller).

Prop. 1: Let cp be a mapping from an initial labelling to a final consistent labelling (if it exists) as it is computed by constraint propagation. Let $GL_S$ be a general start labelling. If $GL_F$ is a generalized final labelling constructed by moderate generalizations of the constraint propagation for some $h_1$, then $\forall h_i \in H: cp(h_i(GL_S)) \subseteq h_i(GL_F)$.

This can be easily proved by induction. It already gives us the correctness of CP-EBG-2 in the case of inconsistency: If a superset of the labelling achievable with constraint propagation is already inconsistent, then constraint propagation would also detect an inconsistency.

Prop. 2: *Same requirements as Proposition 1.*

If $h_i(GL_F)$ is consistent, i.e., $h_i(GL_F) = cp(h_i(GL_F))$ ,

then $h_i(GL_F) = cp(h_i(GL_S))$.

This can be proved using the uniqueness property of constraint propagation (Prop.2 G&H). Proposition 2 guarantees that if the CP-EBG-2 concept description is fulfilled then constraint propagation would terminate with a consistent labelling identical to the instantiated generalized final labelling constructed by CP-EBG-2. Consequently, this proposition gives us the correctness of CP-EBG-2.


# 7. Conclusions

We have presented two ways of combining EBG with constraint propagation. The first, CP-EBG-1, is described by a straightforward use of prolog__ebg/3 and it is obviously a correct method. The second, CP-EBG-2, performs two phases: First, a generalized final labelling is derived but no conditions are learned. Second, constraint propagation is again performed using the final labellings of phase 1 as the initial labelling. Now conditions are learned which form the desired concept description. This concept description is more general than the one constructed by CP-EBG-1. The reason is that although both descriptions guarantee that the final labelling is consistent, the CP-EBG-1 description in addition assures that the final labelling is reached with equivalent intermediate labellings. Or, to express it differently, a CP-EBG-2 description only guarantees that a particular solution is correct, whereas a CP-EBG-1 description requires that the solution is reached on a specific path with specific intermediate results.

We have proved the correctness of CP-EBG-2 for the class of constraints using linear equations and interval arithmetic. Central to this proof - and to possible proves for other constraint classes - is the notion of a *moderate* generalization. It guarantees that a generalization which was learned from one instance and which we now used in a new situation, does not lead to the exclusion of any solution for this new situation. The propositions outlined in Section 6 are very general and do not depend on the use of interval labels; they are applicable whenever variables are labelled with (the description of) a set of possible values.

We have applied CP-EBG-2 in an example application where we had originally used CP-EBG-1 (Zercher 1990a). CP-EBG-2 led to clear improvements, i.e., for a given set of training examples, the number of rules needed to be learned was decreased, the coverage of the learned rule set increased, and the average matching time for the rule set also decreased.

We think that a two phase EBG approach, i.e., first derive a generalized solution and then justify this solution again in order to learn a concept description, will also be useful in other domains. In fact, we first discovered the two phase principle when we tried to apply EBG to the Simplex method (Zercher 1990b). Here it was obviously the correct and better approach. This then triggered a reconsideration of our first combination of EBG and constraint propagation. Clearly, whenever we want to apply the two phase approach to a new inference technique, we have to put in extra efforts in order to determine whether we will still learn correct concept descriptions.

## Acknowledgements

I would like to thank Angelika Hecht, Peter Struss, and my advisor Prof. Bernd Radig for many fruitful discussions and useful suggestions on earlier versions of this paper. Special thanks go to the anonymous referees for their helpful comments. The author thankfully acknowledges the support by a Ph.D. grant from Siemens AG.

## References

Davis, E., (1987). Constraint propagation with interval labels. *Artificial Intelligence, 32,*281-331.

DeJong, G., & Mooney,R. (1986). Explanation-based learning: An alternative view. *Machine Learning, 1,* 145-176.

Güsgen, H.-W., & Hertzberg, J. (1988). Some fundamental properties of local constraint propagation. *Artificial Intelligence, 36,* 237-247.

Kedar-Cabelli, S. T., & McCarty, L. T. (1987). Explanation-based generalization as resolution theorem proving. *Proceedings of the Fourth International Workshop on Machine Learning* (pp. 383-389). Irvine,CA: Morgan Kaufmann.

Keller, R. M. (1987). Defining operationality for explanation-based learning. *Proceedings of the Sixth National Conference on Artificial Intelligence* (pp. 482-487).

Minton, S., (1988). Quantitative results concerning the utility of explanation-based learning. *Proceedings of the Seventh National Conference on Artificial Intelligence* (pp. 564-569).

Mitchell, T. M., Keller, R., & Kedar-Cabelli, S. (1986). Explanation-based generalization: a unifying view. *Machine Learning, 1*, 47-80.

Mooney, R. J., & Bennett, S. W. (1986). A domain independent explanation-based generalizer. *Proceedings of the Fifth National Conference on Artificial Intelligence* (pp. 551-555). Philadelphia, PA: Morgan Kaufmann.

Papadimitriou, C. H., & Steiglitz, K. (1982). *Combinatorical Optimization: Algorithms and Complexity*. Englewood Cliffs, NJ: Prentice-Hall.

Zercher, K., (1988). Model-based learning of rules for error diagnosis. In Hoeppner, W. (Ed.), *Proceedings of the 12th German workshop on artificial intelligence (GWAI 88)* (pp. 196-205). Springer.

Zercher, K., (1990 a). Constructing decision trees from examples and their explanation-based generalizations. In Marburger, H., (Ed.), *Proceedings of the 14th German workshop on artificial intelligence (GWAI 90)* (pp. 267-276). Springer.

Zercher, K., (1990 b). Learning efficient rules and decision trees for error diagnosis of robot operations. Unpublished working paper.

# Learning By Explanation of Failures

Paulo Urbano[1]
Laboratório de Informática e Sistemas
Universidade de Coimbra
Quinta da Boavista, lote 1, 1ª
3000  Coimbra
Portugal

## Abstract

The EBG learning technique has been mainly used in learning processes based on positive examples and successful experiences. However, several authors have demonstrated that failed proofs revealed to be quite useful as a form of avoiding future failures. The first attempts to learn from failure were based on the axiomatization of the problem-solver and on the creation of a specific meta-theory for all possible failures. Whenever there is a positive example of a failure, EBG is used to make operational the meta-theory.
Siqueira & Puget designed a new technique with a different philosophy to learn from counter-examples using only the domain theory. Their method finds a sufficient generalized condition from the failed proof of a goal. EBGF is still a fragile and incomplete technique as it doesn't cover all cases. The failure of a proof has specific characteristics which are not considered when we deal with positive proofs. In this paper we show the weaknesses of EBGF and we propose an improved technique to learn from failures in the presence of a counter-example. Our method is implemented in Prolog and its efficiency is currently under analysis.

**Keywords** Explanation based learning, failure.

## 1  Introduction

Learning from unsuccessful experiences can be as important in a deduction or planning task as it is the current approaches to learning from positive examples (Minton & Carbonell, 1987; Gupta, 1987;

---

[1]  Current adress: Departamento de Informática da Universidade de Lisboa, Avª 24 de Julho, 131, 7º, P-1200 Lisboa Portugal.

Hammond, 1987). Learning from failures can be very useful in presence of default knowledge and, generally, whenever we reason with incomplete knowledge. As Hirsh showed (Hirsh, 1987), if we want to apply the EBG method (Mitchell, Keller & Kedar-Kabelli, 1986) using a default rule of some goal (Goal), we have to introduce in the domain theory a particular predicate of the kind "unknown(Goal)", which will also appear in the learned rule. The problem with this procedure is that this predicate is not operational and so the EBG technique is not fully effective. Therefore, we also have to make operational the predicate which represents the incomplete information. This is an example of the large domain of applications suited for learning from failures in presence of counter-examples.

The first attempts to learn from failures were based on the definition of a meta-theory representing all possible failures. EBG was then applied to make operational the failure's theory using positives examples of a failure. This approach can be inefficient because we have to define all possible failures in the meta theory.

Siqueira & Puget developed a new technique and an algorithm called EBGF (Siqueira & Puget, 1988), in the universe of logic programming, that learns from counter-examples using only the domain theory. The method is similar to EBG but uses a counter-example rather than an example. EBGF, from a failed proof, finds a generalized condition which satisfies the counter-example, is sufficient to warrant the failure of the goal, covering similar counter-examples.

This method is still incomplete and ambiguous. There are some cases in which it cannot even make the failure operational. The different quality of literals deserves an importance that has been ignored because there are literals which demand that at least one of their variables should be instantiated before tested. EBGF is only able to deal with literals that make no demands on their variables Moreover, the order of the literals in a conjunction can be very important and cannot be changed without the risk of aborting the process.

We have developed a learning technique that is a revision and a major extension of EBGF, and is able to solve the problems found.

In section (2) we describe EBGF illustrated with an example; in (3) we analyze its insufficiencies; in section(4) we present our method and finally in section (5) we present an example showing the functioning mode of our method.

## 2 Explanation Based Generalization of Failures (EBGF)

Siqueira & Puget's algorithm is situated in the universe of logic programming. Its aim is to find the minimal sufficient conditions for failure during the process of classifying a counter-example. The failure is then generalized in a way to cover similar counter-examples.

## 2.1 Logical framework of EBGF

The logical framework supporting this method depends on the Negation As Failure assumption (NAF). It also depends on the notion of Completed Data Base (CBD) - each concept is rewritten in its complete form. EBGF uses first order predicate logic restricted to Horn clauses and the interpreter is SLD-resolution.

The method is based on Clark's conclusion that using NAF inference rule is equivalent to make deductions from the completed domain theory. We rewrite the theory so that the right part of each clause of the target concept G is a conjunction of atomic literals $CL_j$ (literals that cannot be defined through other literals). We can expand this notion of atomic to different operationality criterion as in EBG (Hirsh, 1988). We have then a theory in which every clause of the target concept G is compiled - each $CL_j$ is formed by atomic or operational literals .The process is described in (Siqueira & Puget, 1988).

$$G \leftarrow CL_1 \vee CL_2 \vee \ldots \vee CL_m$$

The negation of G corresponds to the rule:

$$\neg G \leftarrow \neg CL_1 \wedge \neg CL_2 \wedge \ldots \wedge \neg CL_m$$

However, this rule is not in general an operational rule since it is too complex and may have redundant literals - literals that are not responsible for the failure. Moreover, the process of transforming any theory in its complete form can be a difficult task, especially in the presence of recursive clauses.

The idea of EBGF is to simplify each conjunction of literals $CL_j$ so that in the end we have only sufficient literals for the failure.

## 2.2 General description of EBGF

Given a domain theory, a target concept, an operationality criterion and a counter-example, EBGF finds an operational definition for the negation of the target concept, increasing the problem-solver efficiency. For that purpose it builds a negative explanation of why the counter-example is not an example of the target concept. The explanation is generated from the failed proof and it is generalized covering a larger number of similar counter-examples.

EBGF is divided in three steps which we will describe:

a) Finding the generalized conjunctions CLj

The manipulation of the completed data base can be too complex and expensive, so the system tries to prove the goal using the domain theory and the counter-example. When the proof is not possible it can collect one of the generalized conjunctions CLj mentioned above; the system backtracks and collects every generalized conjunction. The generalization is done in parallel, taking as input a generalized version of the target concept and performing SLD-resolution as done in (Kedar-Kabelli & Mc Carty, 1987).The role of the counter-example is to bias the search and to avoid recursivity problems.

b) Simplification of every conjunction CLj

The next step consists in the simplification of each generalized conjunction using the counter-example. The simplification method relies on the rightmost literal heuristics. Siqueira & Puget give an intuitive definition of the rightmost literal of a conjunction: it is the one that always fails and doesn't allow the proof to go further to the right. This method deletes, from the original conjunction, every literal which is redundant.
We will describe in detail the simplification algorithm:

Input: a conjunction of literals $CL = \Lambda_i L_i$ $(i = 1..n)$.
Output: a conjunction of literals CS, sufficient for the failure.

0- Initially, the simplified conjunction CS has no literals.

1- Let $L_d$ be the rightmost literal of $\Lambda_i L_i$. We remove it from $\Lambda_i L_i$ and insert it on the end of the simplified conjunction CS.

2- If CS is true for the counter-example, all the literals from CS are satisfied by an instantiation I; we apply I to the variables of $\Lambda_i L_i$ and return to step 1. Otherwise, if S is false for the counter-example then CS is the final simplified conjunction.

c) Operational rule of failure

The learned operational rule representing the negation of the target concept is:

$$\neg G \leftarrow \neg CS_1 \wedge \ldots \wedge \neg CS_m$$

where $CS_j$ is the result of simplifying each $CL_j$.

## 2.3  Example of EBGF

The following example, representing the game of Othelo (Siqueira & Puget, 1988), will illustrate the EBGF technique.

We have a theory expressing the conditions in which a square, with a particular colour and occupying a particular position on the game board (8*8), can be flipped. "status" defines the square's situation; "pos" defines a relation of distance between two board positions. Each position is represented by a number (1...64). The surrounding of any square is made by symmetric distances and is represented by "surr1" and "surr2".

Example 1
- theory
  flips_to(P,C1) ← opponent(C1,C0) ∧ surr1(P,D,C0) ∧ surr2(P,D,C0)
  surr1(P,D,C1) ← pos(P,P1,D) ∧ status(P1,empty)
  surr1(P,D,C1) ← pos(P,P1,D) ∧ status(P1,C1) ∧ surr1(P1,D,C1)
  surr2(P,D,C1) ← pos(P2,P,D) ∧ status(P2,empty)
  surr2(P,D,C1) ← pos(P2,P,D) ∧ status(P2,C1) ∧ surr2(P2,D,C1)

- target concept
  flips_to(P, C1)

- Operationality criterion
  operational(pos(_,_,_))          operational(status(_,_))

- Counter-example
  opponent(black,white)            opponent(white,black)
  pos(1,2,1)                       pos(1,9,8)
  pos(1,10,9)                      pos(2,3,1)
  pos(2,1,-1)
  status(1,white)                  status(2,black)
  status(3,empty)                  status(9,empty)
  status(10,empty)

We cannot prove "flips_to(1,white)".
One of the generalized conjunctions obtained from the failed proof, when the resolution couldn't go further, is:

CL$_1$=opponent(C1,C0) ∧ pos(P,P1,D) ∧ status(P1,empty) ∧ pos(P2,P,D) ∧ status(P2,empty)

We will show, in detail, the simplification algorithm, taking $CL_1$ as input:

    0- $CS_1$ initially has no literals.

    cycle1
    1- We apply the instantiation of the target concept, [P=1,C1=white], to $CL_1$. The rightmost literal of $CL_1$ is "pos(P2,P,D)"; we delete it from $CL_1$ and we insert it in $CS_1$.
    2- $CS_1$=pos(P2,P,D) is true for the counter-example; we can apply the instantiation [P2=2, P=1, D=-1] to the variables of $CL_1$ and return to step 1.

    cycle 2
    1- $CL_1$=opponent(white,C0) ∧ pos(1,P1,-1) ∧ status(P1,empty) ∧ status(P2,empty);
       the rightmost literal of $CL_1$ is "pos(P,P1,D)"; we delete it from $CL_1$ and insert it in $CS_1$.
    2- $CS_1$=pos(P2,P,D) ∧ pos(P,P1,D) is false for the counter-example and it is the final simplified conjunction.

When we apply the simplification algorithm to the other conjunctions $CL_j$ we obtain exactly the former simplified conjunction $CL_1$.

At the end, the system will learn the operational rule:

$$\neg flips\_to(P,C1) \leftarrow \neg[pos(P2,P,D) \wedge pos(P,P1,D)]$$

This learned rule represents the fact that square P cannot be fliped if it is a corner.

# 3  Insufficiencies detected in EBGF

The two limitations we found in EBGF are in the second step: the process of simplification of the original conjunctions.

The first is an error detected in the rightmost heuristics due to the dependance upon the choice of instantiations. In fact, the algorithm can output different answers depending on the chosen instantiations.

The second limitation reveals EBGF to be unprepared to deal with the particularities of the failure universe. In a conjunction there are literals that are responsible for the first instantiations of some variables, given the atomic attributes of the counter-example, and the consequent value propagation to the right. Other literals need to receive decisive instantiations from the left and cannot be tested otherwise. The order of the literals in a conjunction can, for this reason, be very important and cannot be altered when we transform one conjunction into another. EBGF is only capable to deal with literals which make no demands on the instantiations of their variables making the method limited.

In the following two sections we are going to describe these two limitations in more detail by means of examples.

## 3.1 Incorrectness of EBGF

We are going to analyze how EBGF deals with the following example adapted from (Siqueira & Puget, 1988).

Example 2
- Theory

$$a(X,Y) \leftarrow b(X,Z) \wedge c(X) \wedge d(Z,Y)$$
$$a(X,Y) \leftarrow e(X) \wedge f(Y)$$
$$b(X,Y) \leftarrow g(X,Y)$$
$$b(X,Y) \leftarrow h(X,Y)$$

- Target concept

$$a(X,Y)$$

- Every attribute from the counter-example is operational.

- Counter-example

$$c(2), d(1,2), d(3,2), f(1), g(2,2), g(1,1), h(2,2)$$

We cannot prove "$a(X,Y)$". Let´s initiate the failure analysis:

$CL_1 = g(X,Z) \wedge c(X) \wedge d(Z,Y)$ is one of the generalized conjunctions returned after the first step.

Now, we will apply the rightmost heuristics to $CL_1$ to find the conjunction of literals which is the sufficient condition for $CL_1$'s failure:

0- $CS_1$ is initially empty of literals.

cycle 1

1- "d(Z,Y)" is the rightmost literal of $CL_1$. We delete it from $CL_1$ and insert it in the sufficient conjunction $CS_1$.

2- $CS_1$ is true for the counter-example: there are two instantiations that satisfy $CS_1$: $I_1=[Z=1,Y=2]$ and $I_2=[Z=3,Y=2]$. We can apply $I_1$ or $I_2$ to $CL_1$.

cycle 2

1- the rightmost literal of $CL_1$ after $I_1$ is "c(X)". the rightmost literal of $CL_1$ after $I_2$ is "g(X,Z)", which is not a correct one.

This case demonstrates that the simplification algorithm is ambiguous and can output wrong answers. The simplification process cannot depend on a casual choice of instantiations of the current sufficient condition.

## 3.2 Incompleteness of EBGF

Let us consider the following example taken from (Mitchell & Kedar-Kabelli, 1986):

Example 3

- Theory

    safe_to_stack(X,Y) $\leftarrow$ lighter(X,Y)

    lighter(X,Y) $\leftarrow$ weight(X,Px) $\land$ weight(Y,Py) $\land$ <(Px,Py)

    weight(X,Px) $\leftarrow$ volume(X,Vx) $\land$ density(X,Dx) $\land$ ×(Vx,Dx,Px)

    weight(X,5) $\leftarrow$ isa(X,table)         (default rule)

- Target concept

    safe_to_stack(X,Y)

- Operationality criterion

    operational(volume(_,_))               operational(density(_,_))

    operational(isa(_,_))                 operational(<(_,_))

    operational(×(_,_,_))

- Counter-example

    volume(box1,2)                 volume(table1,3)

    density(box1,4)                density(table1,2)

    isa(box1,box)                  isa(table1,table)

After the first step of the algorithm, one of the operational conjunctions that causes the failure of "safe_to_stack(box1,table1)" is:

$$CL_1 = volume(X,Vx) \land density(X,Dx) \land \times(Vx,Dx,Px) \land isa(Y,table) \land <(Px,5)$$

Now, we will apply the rightmost heuristics to $CL_1$ to find the conjunction of literals which is the sufficient condition for $CL_1$'s failure:

0- $CS_1$ is initially empty of literals.

1- The rightmost literal of $CL_1$ is "$<(Px,5)$"; we delete it from $CL_1$ and insert it in the sufficient conjunction $CL_1$.

2- When we try to test if $CS_1 = <(Px,5)$ is satisfied for the counter-example we detect an error: literal "$</2$" demands its first variable instantiated before tested.

In this way, we conclude that it is not enough to find the rightmost literal of a conjunction. The simplification algorithm has to be changed to cover the case in which there are literals that demand at least one of its variables previously instantiated. We have to put other literals in the sufficient condition to warrant the necessary instantiations. Note that when we put literals in the sufficient conditions $CS_j$ we have to maintain their original order in $CL_j$ because if not there is the risk of breaking the original link of variables that guaranteed the propagation of instantiations.

## 4 Alternative method

Our method has also three steps as EBGF. We have reviewed and expanded EBGF on two points: we have a different and improved process of finding the initial generalized conjunctions from the failed proof, and we have reformulated the rightmost literal heuristics in a way to solve both limitations analyzed above.

## 4.1 Finding the initial generalized conjunctions

In EBGF, we initially obtain the generalized conjunctions responsible for the failure. However, these conjunctions might be too complex and redundant, which made us think in a way of simplifying them.

The advantage is that we can directly obtain a conjunction with the first rightmost literal in the end. To accomplish this goal we built a special interpreter adapted to failures.

The interpreter is quite simple: the explanation of the failure of a literal which is not operational and is the head of a clause, is the explanation of the failure of the clause's body. The explanation of the failure of an operational literal which fails is just the literal. The explanation of the failure of a conjunction of literals $\Lambda_i N_i$ (i=1...x...n), is based on the first conjunction $\Lambda_i N_i$ (i=1...x) which does not satisfy the counter-example because of its last literal $N_x$. That is, $\Lambda_i N_i$ (i=1...x) is false but $\Lambda_i N_i$ (i=1...x-1) is true. We operationalize the conjunction $\Lambda_i N_i$ (i=1...x-1) using EBG and concatenate it with the explanation of the failure of the literal $N_x$.

That way, when we fail to prove a goal we always obtain an explanation represented by a conjunction of operational literals in which the last one is the first rightmost literal. In conclusion, our initial generalized conjunctions represent a first direct simplification to the initial generalized conjunctions of EBGF. We do the generalization process in parallel, maintaining a generalized version of the goal. If there is more than one clause for some literal then the system backtracks, collecting every explanation. This interpreter has to ignore all control symbols he finds traversing every possible path, otherwise it could ignore other clauses that could fail.

Now we will show the difference between our method and EBGF, using example 3 with the following counter-example:

Example 4
  - Counter-example

|  |  |
|---|---|
| isa(box3,box) | density(box4,4) |
| volume(box3,2) | isa(box4,box) |

In this case EBGF outputs $CL_1$ as one of the initial generalized conjunctions for the failure of "safe_to_stack(box3,box4)":

$$CL_1 = volume(X,Vx) \wedge density(X,Dx) \wedge \times(Vx,Dx,Px) \wedge weight(Y,Py) \wedge <(Px,Py)$$

Let´s apply our method:

- safe_to_stack(box3,box4) fails because weight(box3,Px) $\wedge$ weight(box4,Py) $\wedge$ <(Px,Py) fails.
- weight(box3,Px) $\wedge$ weight(box4,Py) $\wedge$ <(Px,Py)] fails because weight(box3,Px) fails.
- weight(box3,Px)] fails because volume(box3,Vx) $\wedge$ density(box3,Dx) $\wedge$ ×(Vx,Dx,Px) fails.
- volume(box3, Vx) $\wedge$ density(box3, Dx) $\wedge$ ×(Vx, Dx, Px) fails because volume(box3,Vx) $\wedge$ density(box3,Dx) fails; volume(box3,Vx) is true.

We conclude that the failure of volume(box3,Vx) ∧ density(box3,Dx), which is already composed by operational literals, explains the failure of the target concept. Therefore, the generalized conjunction is:

$$CL_1 = \text{volume}(X,Vx) \wedge \text{density}(X,Dx)$$

When we try to prove the goal we simplify directly the conjunction wich is obtained by EBGF. If the rightmost literal is the last to be responsible for the failure then the literals which are positioned on its right are redundant for the failure.

## 4.2  Reformulation of the simplification algorithm

We begin by formally defining the concept of the rightmost literal of a conjunction.

Definition 1
The rightmost literal of a conjunction $CL = \wedge_i L_i$ $(i=1...n)$ is:
- $L_1$ if $L_1$ is always false.
- $L_d$ if $\wedge_i L_i$ $(i=1...d-1)$ is true and $\wedge_i L_i$ $(i=1...d)$ is always false.

Next, we will present two algorithms that solve the two insufficiencies detected in EBGF.
The former algorithm solves the first problem: the next rightmost literal of a conjunction CL during the simplification process cannot depend on the different instantiations that satisfy the conjunction formed by the past rightmost literals CS.
The final algorithm expands the first as it is capable to deal with literals that demand at least one of their variables previously instantiated to be correctly applied.

## 4.2.1  First simplification algorithm

When we want to output the rightmost literal of a conjunction in any moment of the simplification algorithm, we must take into account every literal of the original conjunction. EBGF separates the sufficient literals and looks for the next rightmost literal in the remaining conjunction, making the process dependent on the instantiations of the separated literals, as we have shown above. To solve this problem, what we do is to change the order of the several rightmost literals, putting them on the left of the remaining conjunction. Then we look for the next rightmost literal in the conjunction formed by every original literal where the past rightmost literals have changed order.

This way the choice of the rightmost literal is not ambiguous, giving as output the only rightmost literal of a conjunction of literals.

## The algorithm

We consider that the initial conjunction CL is composed by two kinds of literals: those which are decisive for failure and belong to the sufficient conjunction CS and those which are redundant.and belong to the redundant conjunction CR.

> Input: a conjunction of literals $CL=\wedge_i L_i$ $(i = 1..n)$.
> Output: a sufficient conjunction of literals CS.
>         a conjunction of redundant literals CR.
>
> 0- initially CR = CL; CS has no literals.
>
> 1- Find the rightmost literal of the ordered concatenation of conjunctions CS and CR (CS∧CR); delete it from CR and put it in the end of CS.
>
> 2- If CS is false for the counter-example then CS is the final simplified conjunction, else return to step 1.

## Example

Now we are going to apply the simplification algorithm to the conjunction of example 2 that created problems to EBGF.

> $CL=g(X,Z) \wedge c(X) \wedge d(Z,Y)$
>
> 0- CR=CL; CS is a conjunction with no literals.
>
> cycle 1
> 1- The rightmost literal of CS∧CR is "d(Z,Y)". CR=g(X,Z) ∧ c(X); CS=d(Z,Y).
> 2- d(Z,Y) is true for the instantiation [Z=1,Y=2]; we return to step 1.

cycle 2

1- CS∧CR=d(Z,Y) ∧ g(X,Z) ∧ c(X). By definition 1, the rightmost literal of CS∧CR is "c(X)".

The literals from CS always have to take part in the conjunction where every rightmost literal is sought - this conjunction has always the same literals, their order only being changed during the aplication of the algorithm.

## 4.2.2   The final simplification algorithm

## Type of literals

We consider two types of literals: those which do not need any of its variables previously instantiated and those which demand that at least one of their variables should be previously instantiated.
The first is the general case. The second type of literals have to be declared in the domain theory.

For instance, if we want to assert that the literal with symbol "×" and arity 3 needs its first two variables instantiated before it is applied, we declare:

$$instantiated(\times \backslash 3, [1,2])$$

The former version of the rightmost literal algorithm we designed is only able to deal with the first type literals. To deal with all kinds of literals, we have to be sure that when we test the successive rightmost literals conjunction CS, there are always literals that supply them with the necessary instances. We have thus to formalize the notion that a literal receives its necessary instances from a conjunction of other literals. The following section is entirely dedicated to this formalization.

## Definitions

Definition 2
A literal $L_X$ is a <u>basic literal</u> if
- it is a literal that does not need any of its variables previously instantiated
or if
- it is a literal in which every variable that needs instantiation is instantiated.

Definition 3

A literal $L_x$ is <u>supported</u> in a conjunction of literals $\Lambda_i L_i$ (i =1...x...n) if

-it is a basic literal

or if

- x>1 and each variable in $L_x$ that needs instantiation and it is not instantiated, belongs to some literal in $\Lambda_i L_i$ (i=1...x-1) wich is <u>supported</u> in $\Lambda_i L_i$ (i=1...x...n).

## The algorithm

Now, we can expand the first version of the rightmost literal algorithm:

Input: A conjunction of literals CL.

Output: CS - sufficient conjunction of literals for the failure of CL.

CR - conjunction of redundant literals.

0- Initially CR=CL and CS is empty of literals.

1- Find $L_d$,the rightmost literal of the ordered concatenation of conjunctions CS and CR (CS$\Lambda$CR). Delete $L_d$ from CR and insert it in CL.

2- Case1: if Ld is supported in CS goto 3, else

Case 2: Look for a minimum set of literals of CR that once inserted in CS result in Ld being now supported in CS. Delete the set of literals found from CR and goto to 3.

3- If CS is false then ¬CS is the sufficient condition; else goto step 1.

Note that, whenever we insert any literal in CS we have to maintain its original position in LC. If we change the order we might break the link between variables that allows the propagation of decisive values.

## Example

We are going to show how this algorithm deals with the following generalized conjunction taken from example 3.

$CL_1$=volume(X,Vx) $\Lambda$ density(X,Dx) $\Lambda$ ×(Vx,Dx,Px) $\Lambda$ isa(Y,table) $\Lambda$ <(Px,5)

We have to add the following literals to the original theory.

      instantiated($<\backslash2[1,2]$)
      instantiated($\times\backslash3,[1,2]$)

Let's apply our method to simplify $CL_1$.

0- $CR_1=CL_1$; $CS_1$ has no literals.

1- The rightmost literal in $CS_1 \wedge CR_1$ is $L_d$="$<(Px,5)$". We inserte it in $CS_1$.

2- "$<(Px,5)$" is not a basic literal because, by definition 2, it needs Px previously instantiated. $L_d$ is the only literal in $CS_1$ and so, by definition 3, it is not supported in $CS_1$. We have to find a minimum set of literals from $CR_1$ so that when inserted in $CS_1$, $L_d$ will be supported in $CS_1$:

[volume(X,Vx),density(X,Dx),$\times$(Vx,Dx,Px)] is the minimum set of literals from $CR_1$ so that when inserted in $CS_1$, maintaining their original positions in $CL_1$, $L_d$ will be supported in $CS_1$. Next, we are going to prove it:

The sufficient condition will be:

$CS_1$=volume(X,Vx) $\wedge$ density(X,Dx) $\wedge$ $\times$(Vx,Dx,Px) $\wedge$ $<(Px,5)$

"$<(Px,5)$" is supported in $CS_1$: it is not a basic literal but Px belongs to the literal "$\times$(Vx,Dx,Px)" which is supported in $CS_1$.

"$\times$(Vx,Dx,Px)" is supported in $CS_1$: It is not a basic literal ( it needs Vx and Dx instantiated); however, Vx and Dx belong respectively to the literals "volume(X,Vx)" and "density(X,Dx)" which are both supported in $CS_1$, because they are basic literals.

3- Finally, $CS_1$ is false for the counter-example and the redundant conjunction is $CR_1$=isa(Y,table). At the end we have $\neg$[volume(X,Vx) $\wedge$ density(X,Dx) $\wedge$ $\times$(Vx,Dx,Px) $\wedge$ $<(Px,5)$] as the sufficient condition for the failure of $CL_1$.

## 5  Example of our technique

Let us illustrate our method solving example 3 in order to obtain the operational rule for the failure of "safe_to_stack(box1,table1)".

After the first step we have as the initials conjunctions for failure:

$CL_1$=volume(X,Vx) $\wedge$ density(X,Dx) $\wedge$ ×(Vx,Dx,Px) $\wedge$ volume(Y,Vy) $\wedge$ density(Y,Dy) $\wedge$
    ×(Vy,Dy,Py) $\wedge$ <(Px,Py)

$CL_2$=volume(X,Vx) $\wedge$ density(X,Dx) $\wedge$ ×(Vx,Dx,Px) $\wedge$ isa(Y,table) $\wedge$ <(Px,5)

$CL_3$=isa(X,table)

The final operational rule the system learns is:

$\neg$safe_to_stack(X,Y) $\leftarrow$

$\neg$[volume(X,Vx) $\wedge$ density(X,Dx) $\wedge$×(Vx,Dx,Px) $\wedge$ volume(Y,Vy) $\wedge$
    density(Y,Dy) $\wedge$ ×(Vy,Dy,Py) $\wedge$ <(Px,Py)]

$\wedge$

$\neg$[volume(X,Vx) $\wedge$ density(X,Dx) $\wedge$ ×(Vx,Dx,Px) $\wedge$ <(Px,5)]

$\wedge$

$\neg$[isa(X,table)]

## 6  Conclusion

We have developed a revision and a major extension of the method EBGF which learns from failures. EBGF is a method that on the contrary of the current approaches doesn't need a meta-theory specific for failures. We found insufficiencies in EBGF in which the most serious was the fact that it was not capable to deal with literals which demand at least one of their variables previously instantiated. These problems limited EBGF making learning inefficient. We have developed and implemented a technique which solves the insufficiencies limiting EBGF.

# Acknowledgments

I would like to thank Prof. Ernesto Costa for all his support.

# References

Siqueira, J. CL. e Puget, J. F., Explanation-Based Generalization of Failures, *Proceedings of the* ECAI-88, pp 339-344, 1988.

Mitchell T. M., Keller R. M.,& Kedar-Kabelli S. T., Explanation-based Generalization: a unifying view, *Machine Learning* 1:1, pp 47-80, 1986.

Minton, S. and Carbonell, J. G., Strategies for Learning Search Control Rules: An Explanation-based Approach. *Proceedings of the* 10th. IJCAI, Milan, pp 228-235, 1987.

Gupta, A., Explanation-Based Failure Recovery, *Proceedings* AAAI- 87, pp 606-610, 1987.

Hirsh, H., Explanation-based generalization in a logic-programming environment. *In Proceedings of the* 10th. IJCAI, Milan, pp 221-227, 1987.

Hirsh H., Reasoning about operationality for Explanation-based Learning. *In Proceedings of the Fourth International Workshop on Machine Learning* , pp 214-220, 1988.

Kedar-Kabelli, S. T.& Mc Carty, CL. T., Explanation-Based Generalization as Resolution Theorem Proving, *Proceedings of the Fourth International Workshop on Machine Learning*, pp 383-389, 1987.

Hammond, J. K., Explanation and Repairing Plans that Fail, *Proceedings of the* 10th. IJCAI, Milan, pp 109-114, 1987.

# PANEL : Logic and Learnability

Luc De Raedt

Department of Computer Science, Katholieke Universiteit Leuven
Celestijnenlaan 200A, B-3001 Heverlee, Belgium
email : lucdr@cs.kuleuven.ac.be

**Panellists (tentative) :** Francesco Bergadano, Luc De Raedt, Achim Hoffman,
Stephen Muggleton and Jean-Francois Puget

## Abstract

This abstract outlines some of the topics to be addressed in the panel on *Logic and Learnability*. The panel is concerned with the inductive logic programming area of research and the place of theories of the learnable in it. Note that I do not wish to take position here, I only want to raise some questions.

- Is logic (and logic programming) a good formalism for constructing theories of the learnable and if so, why is it preferable to other formalisms ?

- Are theories of the learnable important and if so, why ?

- Theories of the learnable are based on complex mathemathical principles. It requires much work to prove that an algorithm satisfies a theory. Does this mean that current theories of the learnable are too complex to be practically relevant ?

- At the moment there are basically two paradigms for theories of the learnable : identification in the limit and probably approximate correct identification. While some approaches in the inductive logic programming field prove properties in the first paradigm (e.g. Shapiro's Model Inference System and De Raedt and Bruynooghe's Clint), there are only few techniques that address the second one. It also has been argued that the identification in the limit paradigm is too simple as a model for empirical learning. Do these two observations imply that the current paradigms are not feasible for the inductive logic programming area ? Is another notion of identification needed ?

- Since the Muggleton-Buntine paper in 1988, there has been much interest in *inverse resolution* and related research topics. People have hoped that inverse resolution could become the basis for induction just as resolution does for deduction. Will this hope become reality ?

Panel on :
# CAUSALITY AND LEARNING

### Coordinator: L. Saitta
### Participants: I. Bratko, Y. Kodratoff, K. Morik, W. Van de Velde

This panel has the goal of stimulating a discussion on the very nature of the knowledge that has been the focus of Machine Learning up to now.

The panelists shall think about questions of the kind reported below and will give their (I expect and hope controversial) answers at the panel. Everyone who believes he/she has something to say is welcome to do so.

**Question 1 :** **Do we really need to learn "why" knowledge and not only "how" knowledge ? If yes, why ?**
In philosophy of science there is a distinction between descriptive knowledge and explanatory knowledge. Descriptive knowledge aims mostly at predicting future outcome on the basis of the past history, whereas explanatory knowledge aims at understanding, and hence mastering, phenomena. How does machine learning locate itself today?

**Question 2 :** **What is the role you think causality could play in learning? Does there exist a "deep" knowledge which does not make any reference to causality? What definition of causal relation would you be glad to see universally accepted?**
This point involves a wider issue, such as to define what does "deepness" mean in knowledge. Moreover, are causes only "physical" causes? What about teleological causes, probabilistic causes, functional causes? What about mathematical equations?

**Question 3 :** **Is a causal theory nothing else than a special case of domain theory, deductively exploitable as in EBL, or are other reasoning mechanisms, such as abduction, unavoidable?**
{Can abductive reasoning allow something really new to be learned? Is there something which can be learned by abduction and which cannot be learned by deduction only?

**Question 4 :** **Can you suggest a concrete way of exploiting causality (or, more in general, deep knowledge) in machine learning ?**

# SEED SPACE AND VERSION SPACE:
# GENERALIZING FROM APPROXIMATIONS

Jacques NICOLAS

INRIA  Campus de Beaulieu 35042 Rennes cedex France. jnicolas@irisa.fr  ☎ (33) 99362000

## Abstract

This work stands in the continuation of Mitchell's Candidate Elimination Algorithm (Mitchell 82). Practical applications of this algorithm need the design of a useful "bias", constraining the size and shape of the Version Space. Our approach strives towards an inclusion of bias at an **empirical** level. We are working on a conceptual clustering application (Lebbe 89). Our statistical module builds clusters and provides information about attributes involved in the emergence of each cluster, which can be combined to build some approximate generalizations. Thus, we have elaborated on the assumption that we know approximations (the bias) of the concept definitions to be produced. The issue then becomes:

1)How to formalize an approximation in the Version Space prospect? Approximations are represented with a **seed set**, a set of descriptions comparable with the initial boundary sets for the specificity ordering. The "projection" of the seed set on the version space leads to a **focus set**. It is an extension of Mitchell's boundary sets S and G, i.e. a set of consistent descriptions such that every target definition is "attainable" by at least one of these.

2) How to make profit of these approximations in the C.E.A. prospect? A version space may be viewed as a collection of paths between elements of S and G. The focus set simply restricts the allowed paths by giving intermediate nodes along these paths. The algorithm searches generalizations between two comparable points of the focus set. Since we have no idea of how accurate are the approximations, the algorithm includes a "repair" strategy, loosening the bias until consistency for the whole set of instances. For a detailled report, see (Nicolas 90).

**Keywords**   Concept Learning . Generalization. Candidate Elimination Algorithm. Bias.

## References

J. Lebbe &al "Conceptual Clustering in Biology: Application and Perspectives" Proc. of Data Analysis and Learning. Antibes. Sept 1989. Diday Ed.  Nova Science Pub.
T. Mitchell   "Generalization as search"  Artificial Intelligence 18  pp 203-226  1982.
J. Nicolas   "An Informed Generalization Algorithm " Intern. Report  INRIA Rennes  Jan 91.

# INTEGRATING EBL WITH AUTOMATIC TEXT ANALYSIS

S. DELISLE, S. MATWIN, L. ZUPAN*

Department of Computer Science, University of Ottawa,Ottawa, Ontario, K1N 6N5 Canada
*Ecole Nationale Supérieure des Télécommunications, Paris, France
email: stan@csi.uottawa.ca

## Abstract

Existing text analysis systems (TAS) and systems for knowledge acquisition from expository texts do not process examples in a satisfactory manner, if they do at all. This is clearly a limitation since examples in texts are usually meant to show the reader how to integrate the declarative part of the text into an operational concept or procedure. On the other hand, EBL seems to fill this gap as it explains the example within the domain theory, generalizes the explanation and operationalizes the concept definition by compiling necessary knowledge from the domain theory into the definition. Not using examples to the fullest extent in knowledge acquisition from text is a drawback. Expository texts rely on examples to show to the reader how to integrate different rules contained in the declarative part of the text into an operational concept or procedure. The writers of expository texts often expect their readers to use examples to generate reasonable abstractions for using a concept or procedure.

On the other hand, Explanation-Based Learning seems to fill perfectly the gap in the existing text analysis systems. EBL links an example with the underlying domain theory by explaining the example within the domain theory, and compiling, into the example itself, parts of the domain theory necessary to operationalize the example. Moreover, the explanation and its operational part are generalized, so that the result is usable not only for the single example but for any case that has the same justification.

In this paper, we study the synergistic combination of automatic text analysis and EBL. We assume that the texts processed by TAS have the following components:

- the narrative text describing the domain
- examples, which illustrate rules, concepts, and procedures defined in the declarative part
- captions, which accompany examples and highlight their contents. Captions name the concept, or procedure, described in the example. They do not provide the details of the concept or procedure definition. Captions link the example with the narrative text.

We propose initially to use EBL on the examples, with the following mapping of parts of the expository text into EBL:

- the declarative part is converted into a domain theory. This is done by a TAS, perhaps with assistance of the human operator (e.g. in removing certain types of natural language ambiguities)
- examples of concepts or procedures from the expository text are used as EBL's training examples
- captions are used as non-operational definitions of concepts and procedures

The result of EBL, i.e. the operationalized and generalized concept or procedure, is then added to the knowledge base that has been acquired by TAS from the expository text. Although the learning that has been achieved is of the "deductive" type, it enhances the knowledge base with new and potentially useful rules that cannot be obtained from the analysis of the declarative part alone. Full account of our work describes a prototype system for INtegration of Text analysis with ExpLanation-based LeArning (INTELLA)[1] and shows its application on the text of the Canadian Income Tax Guide. We also discuss the necessary extensions of EBL's concept of operationality and show INTELLA's preliminary architecture. This prototype Prolog-based system consists of four prinicipal components: NL Simplifier, Parser, Case-to-Fact Transducer, and the EBG module.

---

[1] Integrating EBL with Automatic Text Analysis, TR-90-41, University of Ottawa, October 1990

# ABDUCTION
# for EXPLANATION-BASED LEARNING

Béatrice DUVAL

Equipe Inférence et Apprentissage, L.R.I. Bât 490, Université Paris Sud 91405 ORSAY Cedex France
Email : bd@lri.lri.fr
Université d'Angers, 2 Boulevard Lavoisier 49045 ANGERS Cedex France

**Abstract**

Explanation-based Learning has raised many studies in Machine Learning community but the original process proposed by Mitchell suffers of a major drawback, the necessity to deal with a complete, correct and tractable theory, since learning results from a complete explanation, that means a complete proof, of a training instance. In this paper, we propose to learn when only a partial explanation can be found. Our idea is to extend the resolver that explains examples so that plausible completions of partial proofs can be proposed to the user. To achieve such completions, abductive and analogical inferences are used. We do not detail in this paper each step of our system processing but we want to show how our work is related to abductive techniques, why it is faced to some similar problems and how solutions proposed for abduction can be adapted for EBL.

**Keywords** Explanation-Based Learning, Abduction, Analogy

## 1 Introduction

In Machine Learning III (Michalski & Kodratoff, 1990), learning processes are classified into synthetic and analytic on the basis of their main goal. "Synthetic learning aims primarily at creating new or better knowledge, and analytic learning aims primarily at reformulating given knowledge into a better form." Explanation-based learning (EBL) presented in (Mitchell et al., 1986) and (DeJong & Mooney, 1986) is an analytic method guided by an example and its purpose is reformulating existing knowledge into an operational form. Its computational mechanism is purely deductive and requires a complete, consistent and tractable background knowledge. To deal with incomplete theories, it is necessary to extend EBL by synthetic learning processes that enable to modify the deductive closure of the knowledge base. We present in this paper how abduction and analogical reasoning can be used to complete a failed deductive proof. More details about other steps of our learning process, namely generalization and proposition of new rules, can be found in (Kodratoff, 1990) and (Duval, 1990).

## 2   Explanation-based learning and deduction

The key idea of EBL is to generalize an example proof to obtain a sufficient condition for the concept under study, called target concept. So in the EBL context, the word "explanation" is a synonymous of "proof". An example explanation is defined as a proof that shows how the example features satisfy the concept definition. Applying EBL requires that the initial domain theory provides a definition of the target concept and that this definition and other rules enable to recognize all interesting examples. This constraint has been denominated as the complete theory requirement and is a major drawback for EBL aplications.

Such a limitation has raised a discussion about the notion of explanation used in EBL framework. For many authors (DeJong, 1990 ; Josephson, 1990), it seems too restrictive to consider explanation and proof as equivalent notions. Even if we agree that from a general point of view, explanation is a broader concept than proof, in our system inspired from EBL, we use proofs as explanations of examples. To answer to some counter example provided in (Josephson, 1990), we must be more precise about which kinds of proofs we accept as explanations. Let us consider the assertions "John leaves today or tomorrow" and "John doesn't leave today" ; from these sentences, we can **prove** that "John leaves tomorrow", but nobody will accept that proof as an explanation. On the contrary, if we say "John leaves today or tomorrow" and "John has a date today at office", we can prove that "John leaves tomorrow", because "John has a date today" implies that "John does not leave today" and everybody would recognize the explanatory meaning of this proof. The main point in this latter case is that the proof uses some domain knowledge, namely the rule "somebody cannot leave when he has a date", while the first proof uses only a logical axiom, namely that from "A v B" and "¬A" we can infer "B". So our point of view is that only knowledge-based proofs, that means proofs that use domain-dependent rules for at least one inference step, can be considered as explanations. Proofs that use only logical axioms have no real explanatory power : they are either trivial, either complex formal manipulations very far from human understanding and intuition.

This remark helps to discard some non interesting cases but the fundamental discussion about the relationships between explanation and proof subsists and would constitute a full paper.

In the following, our aim is to study how EBL, which studies deductive proofs, can be adapted to incomplete theories. For many real situations, it is impossible to provide or to formalize the whole knowledge necessary to recognize (to explain) all situations illustrating a concept. So dealing with incomplete theories may be achieved by two means. One is to accept a broader and more flexible notion of explanation. Arguing for this solution, DeJong rejects logical proofs as explanations because of the "qualification" problem : an implication like $(\forall X, Bird(X) \Rightarrow Flies(X))$ would have to include a great number of qualifications to be interpreted as an accurate statement about the world. DeJong's proposal (DeJong, 1990) is to change rule semantics to perform plausible inferences that take into account contexts in which the rules occur. But the contexts can never be known or represented or reasoned about. So it seems that DeJong's work is particularly suited to treatment of inconsistent examples, that means examples that contradicts the initial theory.

The other possibility we have studied is rather adapted to incomplete knowledge ; our proposal is to extend the inferencer so that it can complete failed deductive proofs. The type of problems we want to solve can be stated as follows :

```
Given :
        - a target concept C
        - a domain theory TH which provides a definition of target concept C
        - a set of facts F describing a situation Ex, instance of the concept C, so that
        TH U F I-/- C(Ex)
we search
        a set of hypotheses H so that
        H I-/- C
        and
        TH U F U H I— C
        and
        TH U F U H is consistent.
```

*EBL in incomplete theories*

Hypotheses H are a set of rules that refine the initial domain theory TH. Acceptance of these hypotheses will be submitted to the user but the aim of our system is to limit the user's interventions and to select "good" hypotheses. Induction of a new theory is realized in two steps. First, the system determines partial proofs for the example, and searches completion of a partial proof by elementary inference processes as abduction and analogical reasoning. The second step is then to generalize the completed explanation, which induces a new theory, more powerful than the initial theory since it enables to recognize more examples. Section 3 explains how abductive inference can be integrated into an EBL system. In Section 4, we present another type of reasoning, based on analogy, which enables also to propose plausible completions of a failed proof. The generalization process is inspired from EBG algorithm proposed by Kedar-Cabelli and McCarty (1987). This generalization step can also be realized by inversion of resolution (Muggleton & Buntine, 1988) and particularly by intraconstruction which enables to introduce new terms in the description language. This point, described in (Duval, 1990) is not developped here.

# 3 Explanation-based learning and abduction

## 3.1 Abduction

Abduction has been defined by Peirce (1965) as a particular form of explanatory hypothesis generation that can be summarized by the following sentence : "The surprising fact C is observed ; but if A were true, C would be a matter of course, hence there is reason to suspect that A is true." In a context of cause-to-effect relations, abduction can be defined as reasoning from effects to causes and plays an important role in diagnosis systems (Cox & Pietrzykowski, 1986 ; Ayel et al., 1990). When relations are represented by implications, abductive inference can be characterized as an inversion of modus ponens represented by the following schema :

$A \Rightarrow B$

B

———

A

A theory generally provides several rules that conclude on B, so a major interest for automated abduction is the selection of plausible hypotheses to explain B. That is the reason why Artificial Intelligence researchers understand abduction with the broader meaning : "inference to the best explanation". Different criteria can be proposed to define what is a "good" explanation : they depend on the domain of application and on the aim of the abductive mechanism (Stickel, 1990). But some requirements are common to all abductive systems. The first is that hypotheses must be consistent with the initial theory. The second requirement which is often used is that the set of explanatory hypotheses must be minimal in some sense. This property aims at ruling out facts that are not relevant to explain the observations. In fact, if A entails B, every conjonction of facts containing A and consistent with A will entail B ; but we are only interested in hypotheses that have a causality connection with B.

So the reader can notice that abduction and EBL in incomplete theories as we have formalized it in section 2 have a common goal, which is to produce a set of consistent hypotheses that, together with the theory, entails the example or the observations. But the types of hypotheses we search are different. In this paper, the term "abduction" represents an elementary inference process which is an inversion of modus ponens. Abduction aims at proposing a set of plausible hypotheses about initial situations to explain a set of observations ; in our problem, that means a set of instanciated features which, added to the example description, explains the target concept. But, as it will be explained in section 4, abductive inference is not always sufficient to explain examples. We also use analogical reasoning to propose other hypotheses. So the hypotheses we propose are not limited to an inversion of modus ponens. Moreover, the aim of learning in EBL framework is to generalize constraints about example features to produce some general rules that can be applied to other examples. In our system, when satisfactory hypotheses are found to complete an example proof, they are generalized into new rules that refine or extend the domain theory. This is also a reason why our hypotheses are more general than those proposed by "pure" abduction.

In the following of this section, we examine how abductive techniques can be adapted to the particular task of EBL.

## 3.2   Partial proofs for EBL in incomplete theories

The EBL system we use works with Horn clauses and resolution ; a concept is represented by a predicate and a clause is a concept definition. An explanation of a training instance is a refutation of the target concept. There is a great similarity between backward construction of a deductive proof in EBL systems (Kedar-Cabelli & McCarty, 1987) and backward tracing from effects to causes used in abduction. So a natural idea is to propose abductive inferences to complete failed proofs of examples in an incomplete theory (Kodratoff, 1990). Abductive inference can be implemented as an extension of Prolog resolution as it is proposed in (Stickel, 1988). When the theory cannot explain an example, Prolog backward chaining is applied as much as possible to produce partial proofs. In our method, we define a **partial proof** as a refutation tree in which some leaves are labelled by "Failure" to indicate that there is no way to prove these litterals. The abductive or analogical reasoning will then focus on these failure nodes to propose completion hypotheses. Before speaking of this completion mechanism, we must precise what kinds of partial proofs are needed and how they can be computed.

The most important computational problem is that we must search all partial explanations, that is to say all the incomplete refutation trees produced by different rules or different instanciations of subgoals. Prolog resolution which is performed with a fixed computation rule is not suited to such a task as it is illustrated by the following example.

We consider the following theory that describes family relationships.

Théorie TH

| | | |
|---|---|---|
| (1) grandfather(X,Y) | :- | father(X,Z), mother(Z,Y). |
| (2) father(X,Y) | :- | child(Y,X), man(X). |
| (3) mother(X,Y) | :- | child(Y,X), woman(X). |

Let us notice that this theory defines the concept "maternal grandfather" but not the concept "paternal grandfather".

We consider the example "grandfather(john,andy)" described by the following facts :

(4) child(andy,liz).

(5) child(andy,ben).

(6) child(ben,john).

(7) man(john).

(8) man(ben).

(9) man(andy).

(10) woman(liz).

Prolog resolution fails to prove the goal "grandfather(john,andy)" since John is the paternal grandfather of Andy. A missing definition for "grandfather" is the cause of incompleteness. But we can find a partial proof that can be represented by the following tree:

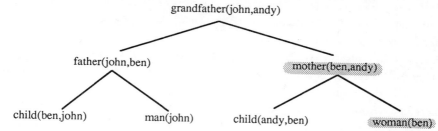

*Figure 1 : first partial proof*

In this proof, failed subgoals are shadowed. The subgoal "mother(ben,andy)" fails since the leaf "woman(ben)" cannot be proved.

We must notice that another partial proof tree can be found if we try other instanciations for subgoals. This second partial proof is represented below :

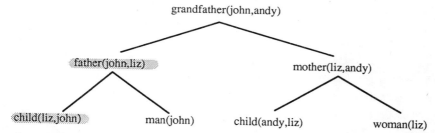

*Figure 2 : second partial proof*

This last partial proof cannot be found by Prolog resolution which selects always the leftmost litteral in a list of subgoals and stops at the first failure : using clause (1) which defines "grandfather", resolution of the first subgoal "father(john,Z)" will select Z=ben as the only possible substitution. Prolog uses a fixed computation rule which chooses always the leftmost litteral in a subgoal list ; we can also say that resolution is ordered : the first goal of the list of current goals is resolved with the first litteral (head) of a clause. This is a correct strategy because one can prove that for a given program and a given goal, there is a bijective mapping between success sets obtained by two different computation rules (Lloyd, 1984). But, as illustrated by the preceding example, this is not the case for failure branches of resolution trees and when dealing with incomplete theories, we are particularly interested in failure branches. To produce all partial proof trees, we must use a linear but non ordered resolution that enables to consider alternative instanciations for subgoals. Unordered resolution is very expensive because each list of n subgoals gives n! lists of subgoals to consider. When implementing our resolver, we have limited the research by noticing that permutations of subgoals are no longer necessary when resolution of a subgoal cannot influence resolution of the others. This happens in two cases : when subgoals are completely instanciated or when subgoals are independent, that is when they contain no common variables.

This computational complexity is not inherent to abduction but to a particular kind of abduction called most specific abduction by Stickel. We find in (Stickel, 1988) an interesting classification about abduction based on the kind of computed hypotheses. In fact, if we only say that an abductive hypothesis must entail the observation, the observation itself constitutes an hypothesis and every clause generated during backward chaining from the goal is also an hypothesis. But explaining the observed situation S by fact S is not always very interesting. The aim of abductive inference must be more precisely stated by defining what kinds of litterals are abducible hypotheses. Stickel distinguishes three types of abduction. Stickel speaks of **predicate specific abduction** when hypotheses must belong to a set of predicates defined by the user. This is particularly suited to planning and design synthesis tasks where abducible predicates may correspond to executable actions or elementary components. In natural language processing, **least specific abduction** looks for the most simple and general explanation  by allowing only litterals in the initial formula to be assumed. This a case where explaining situation S by fact S is interesting. These two types of abduction can be implemented by ordered resolution because they give a precise indication about which properties can be "abduced". Consequently, when an abducible litteral is encountered during resolution of a list of subgoals, the resolver can assume it and pursue resolution of other subgoals. On the opposite, **most specific abduction**, which is used in diagnosis, searches the most basic causes, causes that cannot be reduced by backward chaining (Cox & Pietrzykowski, 1986).

The type of abduction we have chosen for extending EBL is most specific abduction. The most obvious reason for this choice is that we must reach "dead-ends", that is litterals for which no resolution is possible, to check that the proof fails. On the other hand, least specific abduction is not suited to our task since it would limit research to the initial target concept definition and would give no new rule. But an alternative to our choice would be to consider predicate specific abduction. In order to apply predicate specific abduction, we must  know precisely a set of abducible predicates. This requirement is very similar to the operationality criterion used in EBL. An EBL system can use a static operationality criterion that specifies which predicates are easily computable or easily evaluable ; in such a case, we can decide that abducible predicates are operational predicates. But studies in EBL have shown that a static definition of operationality is not very convenient (Segre, 1987) and the same can be said about a static definition of abducible predicates (Stickel, 1988). Moreover, the aim of our learning process is not reexpression of a concept into a more operational form but rather refinement of existing incomplete rules. So we have not considered the application of predicate specific abduction in our system.

## 3.3   Consistency  of  hypotheses

We have noticed above that consistency with the theory is a fundamental requirement for abductive hypotheses. We have introduced consistency checking in our learning system in order to discard some hypotheses. Let us recall that we work with a theory expressed by Horn clauses on which the resolver performs linear resolution. The user can also provide integrity constraints that express some fundamental properties of the domain. The only form of constraints we consider is denials, that is pure negative Horn clauses.

Let us consider again the family example. The knowledge base (theory and example description) consists of the following clauses :

(1) grandfather(X,Y)    :-  father(X,Z), mother(Z,Y).
(2) father(X,Y)      :-  child(Y,X),man(X).
(3) mother(X,Y)      :-  child(Y,X), woman(X).
(4) child(andy,liz).
(5) child(andy,ben).
(6) child(ben,john).
(7) man(john).
(8) man(ben).
(9) man(andy).
(10) woman(liz).

We can use the following denials to express basic contradictions between predicates used in this theory.

Integrity constraints

(IC1)           :-  man(X), woman(X).
(IC2)           :-  father(X,Y), mother(X,Z).

The first clause means that nobody can be man and woman and the second that nobody can be father and mother. We have implemented a very simple mechanism based on Prolog resolution to test the consistency of an hypothesis. An hypothesis has always the form of an instanciated litteral : it is a node of the failed proof tree. Interested readers can consult (Sadri & Kowalski, 1987) which presents a procedure for checking consistency with a general form of integrity constraints and a general form of updates.

Let us explain on the example how this checking can prune the space of possible assumptions.

We have found two partial proofs for the example "grandfather(john,andy)". In the first partial proof presented in Figure 1, the subgoals "mother(ben,andy)" and "woman(ben)" cannot be proved.

Our procedure for consistency checking examines every subgoal in the failure branch. We assume that the initial knowledge base is consistent. To test a failed litteral, this litteral is added to the knowledge base and for each integrity constraint, a Prolog resolution is performed with this constraint as the goal. If this Prolog session leads to a success, that means that the hypothesis contradicts some integrity constraint.

To test if the property "woman(ben)" is coherent, we add this property to the knowledge base and we submit the first constraint

(IC1)           :-  man(X), woman(X).

as a goal for Prolog resolution. This goal can be proved by using fact (8) and the hypothesis "woman(ben)". So "woman(ben)" is inconsistent and cannot be accepted as a plausible assumption.

It is not illustrated by the preceding example but we may have to deal with several hypotheses to complete several failures in a partial proof. What happens for consistency checking in such cases ? Let us suppose that the same partial proof contains two failure nodes "man(ben)" and "woman(ben)". The first failure leads to propose "man(ben)" as a possible hypothesis. If the user agree with this proposition, the fact "man(ben)" is added to our knowledge base. So, when dealing with the second failure, hypothesis "woman(ben)" leads to an inconsistency because of constraint IC1 and of hypothesis "man(ben)" that is now considered as a true fact. When our system has to examine another hypothesis for the first failure node or another partial proof, the fact "man(ben)" is deleted from the knowledge base. So our system can consider several hypotheses and interaction with the user enables to avoid non monotony of abductive inference : when an hypothesis is accepted by the user, it becomes a true fact and is not reconsidered until the system backtracks to another possible hypothesis or another partial proof.

Consistency checking provides also information about inappropriate rules in a partial proof. We consider incomplete theories where some rules are missing. When a failure occurs in a proof tree, failure is detected when a leaf cannot be proved, but we do not know which rule is responsible of the failure. In the proof tree of figure 1, the failure branch interacts with two rules :

(1) grandfather(X,Y)                          :-        father(X,Z), mother(Z,Y).

and

(3) mother(X,Y)                              :-        child(Y,X), woman(X).

To determine the fautive or missing rule in a proof tree, the usual way is to ask an oracle about each node (Shapiro, 1983 ; Wirth, 1988). In order to limit queries to the user, our idea is to use consistency to focus on the problem source. We test every subgoal in a failure branch of the refutation tree in order to detect inconsistent nodes that must necessarily be changed in the completed proof.

For the first partial tree of grandfather example (fig. 1), we test consistency of the failed subgoal "mother(ben,andy)". A Prolog session with goal

  (IC2)                                  :-        father(X,Y), mother(X,Z).

leads to a success by using the hypothesis "mother(ben,andy)" and by using rules (2), (5), (8) to prove that "father(ben,andy)" is true. So this failed subgoal "mother(ben,andy)" is inconsistent and it would be useless to search a completed proof containing it ; this node and the rule that have produced this node in the proof tree must be replaced. Inducing a plausible rule to replace this unsuitable rule is the aim of our method.

Of course, the second proof tree shown in Figure 2 is tested in the same way and we leave it to the user to check that no inconsistent node is found in this tree.

So, if the user provides some general knowledge about domain inconsistencies, the system can avoid some misleading assumptions by checking consistency of failed nodes in the partial proof tree.


## 4  Explanation-based learning and analogical reasoning


Let us summarize what happens for the grandfather example. A first step has computed two partial proof trees. Then consistency checking has shown that the failed nodes in the first partial proof are inconsistent. So abductive inferences, that is assuming that the failed properties are true, cannot be applied to this proof. The second partial proof contains no inconsistency ; abductive inference is applied and the system asks to the user if the failed property "child(liz,john)" is a correct hypothesis. The user rejects this hypothesis ; so for this example, abduction cannot propose a completed proof.

When abduction is not possible or when an abductive completion is not accepted by the user, we propose to search other completion hypotheses by analogical reasoning upon explanations.

More precisely, if A is a failed leaf of a partial proof tree, we propose to search in the example description a property A' that can replace A. Let us suppose that a rule $A \Rightarrow B$ occurs in the partial proof tree, our aim is to replace this implication by the rule $A' \Rightarrow B$. We have seen that abduction is an inversion of modus ponens, the reasoning we propose to complete a proof can also be considered as an inversion of modus ponens and represented by the schema :

A

B

———

$A \Rightarrow B$

but such a schema is underconstrained : we could as well infer $B \Rightarrow A$ from the observations of facts A and B ; moreover, the main problem is that the example description may contain irrelevant features which must not be considered during this process. In order to reduce the number of possibilities, we use an analogy criterion to select plausible hypotheses for completion of a partial proof. Our reasoning can be summarized by the following schema :

$A \Rightarrow B$

A' analogous to A

B

———

$A' \Rightarrow B$

This analogical bias means that we search minor repairs to our theory : our method looks for refinement of the initial theory on the form of analogous rules because we suppose that the right explanation is not so far from the failed explanation. If this is not the case, our system is not suited to the problem.

For the grandfather example presented above, abduction of failed properties does not lead to an acceptable proof. So our system performs a search by analogy for each of the two partial proofs. Let us recall that the first partial proof is the following :

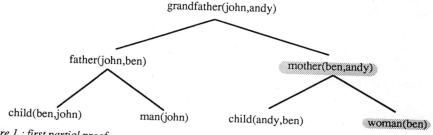

*Figure 1 : first partial proof*

Search of a property analogous to "woman(ben)" is based on a syntactic criterion.

*Definition :*

Two litterals L and L' are analogous if

    - predicates of L and L' have the same arity

and

    - list of arguments of L and L' are identical.

This analogy criterion is very simple but it is domain independent. When domain knowledge provides information about concept taxonomy, we define a distance between predicates that is considered during evaluation of analogous litterals (Duval, 90). For particular domain knowledge, one can propose semantical definition of analogical proofs ; it is done for example in (Genest et al., 1990) where two actions are analogous if they share the same goal.

From the example description, our syntactic criterion selects the property "man(ben)" as analogous to "woman(ben)".

But as we have seen previously, consistency checking has revealed that the property "mother(ben,andy)" is incoherent. In such a case, we try to revise the proof tree by a limited phase of forward reasoning. Focusing on the facts used at the leaves of the proof tree and the selected analogous property "man(ben)", we try to replace the incoherent subgoal "mother(ben,andy)".

With the property "child(andy,ben)" and "man(ben)", clause (2) enables to prove "father(ben,andy)".

So the following completed proof tree is proposed to the user :

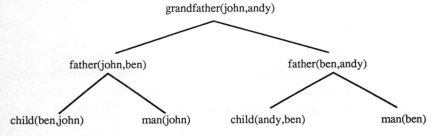

*Figure 3 : completed proof*

The last result of our process is to propose a new rule

    grandfather(X,Y)                        :-father(X,Z), father(Z,Y).

in order to extend the initial theory.

More details about selection of hypotheses and generalization of rules by intraconstruction can be found in (Kodratoff, 1990) and (Duval, 1990). The aim of this paper is to show that our process has many similarities with abductive inference and is faced to the same problems, as for example determination of partial proofs and test of consistency. Others problems encountered in abduction could be studied in the context of EBL, we think to the problem of variables in hypotheses for instance (Poole, 1987).

# 5 Conclusion

To apply EBL techniques to incomplete theories, our method is to study partial proofs of a training instance, where a partial proof is a refutation tree in which some subgoals are left unproved. From these partial proofs, we try to propose completion hypotheses and new rules that refine the initial domain knowledge. During this work, the main problem is that a great number of completions are possible. Automated abduction, which tries to propose a set of plausible hypotheses explaining observations, is faced to the same problem. The aim of this paper is to point out some interesting aspects of abduction that can be applied to EBL in incomplete theories. We have studied particularly what kinds of partial proofs are needed for EBL and how they can be computed. Moreover, consistency, which is a fundamental requirement for automated abduction, can be introduced in a learning system to prune the search space of possible completions. For Horn clause logic, we have implemented a simple mechanism to test that an hypothesis does not contradict constraints expressed as pure negative clauses. Abductive inferences are not always sufficient to complete a failed proof ; we also use analogy to search inductive hypotheses that propose refinements of initial rules.

# Acknowledgements

This work has been partially sponsored by PRC/GRECO-IA of "CNRS" and "Ministère de la Recherche et de la Technologie". We would like to thank our thesis supervisor Yves Kodratoff for his ideas and support about this work, Christel Vrain for her suggestions about this paper and all the members of the Inference and Learning group at LRI.

# References

Ayel B.E., Marquis P., Rusinowitch M., "Deductive/Abductive Diagnosis : The DA-Principles", Proceedings of ECAI 1990. pp.47-52.

Cox P.T., Pietrzykowski T., "Causes for Events : their computation and applications", Proceedings of the 8th Conference on Automated Deduction, pp.608-621. Oxford, July 1986.

DeJong G., Mooney R., "Explanation-Based Learning : An Alternative View", in *Machine Learning 1,* pp. 145-176. Kluwer Academic Publishers. 1986.

DeJong G., "Plausible Inference vs. Abduction", Proceedings of AAAI Spring Symposium on Automated Abduction. pp.48-51. Standford University. March 1990.

Duval B., "Abduction guidée par les Analogies entre Explications", *Revue d'Intelligence Artificielle.* Vol.4 N°2. pp.11-27. Eds Hermès. 1990.

Genest J., Matwin S.,Plante B., "Explanation-Based Learning with Incomplete Theories : A Three-Step Approach", Proceedings of the International Workshop on Machine Learning. pp.286-294. Austin 1990.

Josephson J.R., "On the "Logical Form" of Abduction", Proceedings of the AAAI Spring Symposium on Automated Abduction. Standford University. pp.140-144. March 1990.

Kedar-Cabelli S.T., McCarty L.T., "Explanation-Based Generalization as Resolution Theorem Proving", Proceedings of the Fourth International Machine Learning Workshop. pp.383-389. Irvine 1987.

Kodratoff Y., "Using Abductive Recovery of Failed Proofs for Problem Solving by Analogy", Proceedings of the International Workshop on Machine Learning. pp.295-303. Austin 1990.

Lloyd J.W., *Foundations of Logic Programming* Springer-Verlag. 1984.

Michalski R.S., Kodratoff Y., "Research in Machine learning : Recent Progress, Classification of Methods and Future Direction" in *Machine Learning: An Artificial intelligence Approach, Volume III*, Y. Kodratoff and R.S. Michalski (Eds.), Morgan Kaufmann, San Mateo, 1990, pp. 3-30.

Mitchell T., Keller R., Kedar-Cabelli S.T., "Explanation-Based Generalization : A Unifying View", in *Machine Learning 1*, pp.47-80. Kluwer Academic Publishers. 1986.

Muggeleton S., Buntine W., "Machine Invention of First Order Predicates by Inverting Resolution", Proceedings of 5th International Machine Learning Workshop, pp.287-292. Morgan Kaufmann. 1988.

Peirce C.S., "Elements of Logic" in *Collected Papers of Charles Sanders Peirce (1839-1914)*, C.H.Hartshone and P.Weiss (Eds), The Belknap Press Harvard University Press, Cambridghe, MA. 1965.

Poole D., "Variables in Hypotheses" Proceedings of the Tenth International Joint Conference on Artificial Intelligence. pp.905-908. Milan. Los-Altos, Ca: Morgan Kaufmann. 1987.

Sadri F., Kowalski R., "A Theorem-Proving Approach to Database Integrity", in *Foundations of Deductive Databases and Logic Programming* pp.313-362. Jack Minker (Ed). Morgan Kaufmann Publishers, Los Altos, CA. 1987.

Segre A.M., "On the Operationality/Generality Trade-off in Explanation-Based Learning", Proceedings of the Tenth International Joint Conference on Artificial Intelligence. pp.242-248. Milan. Los-Altos, Ca: Morgan Kaufmann. 1987.

Shapiro E., *Algorithmic Program Debugging*, MIT Press, Cambridge, London. 1983.

Stickel M.E. "A Prolog-like Inference System for Computing Minimum-Cost Abductive Explanations in Natural-Language Interpretation", Proceedings of the International Computer Science Conference '88, Hong Kong. Decembre 1988.

Stickel M.E., "A Method for Abductive Reasoning in Natural Language Interpretation", Proceedings of the AAAI Spring Symposium on Automated Abduction. pp.5-9. Standford University. March 1990.

Wirth R., "Learning by Failing to Prove" Proceedings of European Working Session on Learning, pp.237-251. Pitman. 1988.

# CONSISTENT TERM MAPPINGS, TERM PARTITIONS, AND INVERSE RESOLUTION

SHAN HWEI NIENHUYS-CHENG (*)   PETER A. FLACH (**)

(*) Erasmus University, POBox 1738, 3000 DR Rotterdam, Netherlands

(**) Tilburg University, POBox 90153, 5000 LE Tilburg, Netherlands. Email: flach@kub.nl.

## Abstract

We formalize the notion of inverse substitution, used in the context of inverse resolution, by means of consistent term mappings. An inverse substitution from a clause to a more general clause can also be characterized by means of a term partition. We can generate clauses more general than a given clause by taking an *admissible* subset of its term occurrences, and constructing a term partition of this subset. We show that these term partitions can be partially ordered. This ordering coincides with the generality of the induced clauses. Similar partitions have been used by Muggleton and Buntine for describing their absorption operator. We show that their absorption algorithm is incomplete, and we give an alternative, complete algorithm, based on our definitions of admissible subset and term partition. We show that under certain conditions, clauses generated by absorption are incomparable with respect to generality. Finally, we relate this to a recent result about least general absorption obtained by Muggleton.

**Keywords**       Inverse resolution, absorption, substitution.


# 1. Introduction

Muggleton and Buntine (1988) introduced inverse resolution in machine learning. Operators like absorption and intra-construction are used to generalize given first-order clauses, and to invent new predicates. They implement the absorption operator in a system GIGOL such that for given clause C and positive literal $C_1$, $C_2$ can be found as the resolvent of $C_1$ and $C_2$. They present also an algorithm, which we call MB-absorption, to find $C_2$ non-deterministically. They consider a subset TP' of the set of all term occurrences in $C\vee{\sim}C_1$. This subset is partitioned in blocks. Every block looks like

$$B=\{(r,p_1),\dots, (r,p_n)\}\cup\{(s,q_1),\dots, (s,q_m)\}$$

where $(r,p_i)$ is a term occurrence in C and $(s,q_j)$ is a term occurrence of ${\sim}C_1$. Furthermore, there is a substitution $\theta_1$ from ${\sim}C_1$ which brings s to r. Every such block corresponds to a new variable in $C_2$. That means, all the terms $(r,p_i)$ and $(s,q_j)$ are changed to a new variable. To understand what this algorithm can do or cannot do, we give a few examples.

(*i*)    Let $C_1=P(x)$, $C=Q(v,g(v))$ and $C_2=Q(v,g(v))\vee{\sim}P(h(v))$. Although C is the resolvent of $C_1$ and $C_2$, yet we cannot find $C_2$ with MB-absorption. A block which contains the term occurrence of x from $C_1$ has to correspond to a variable. It cannot be changed to h(v). Hence, MB-absorption is *incomplete*: it does not find all $C_2$ such that C is the resolvent of $C_1$ and $C_2$.

(*ii*)    Another example of the incompleteness of MB-absorption: let $C_1=P(x,y)$, $C=Q(u,f(w))$ and $C_2=Q(u,f(w))\vee{\sim}P(u,u)$. It is clear that C is the resolvent of $C_1$ and $C_2$. On the other hand, we cannot find $C_2$ with MB-absorption. In that algorithm, the term occurrences $(s,q_j)$ from $C_1$ in a block have to be the same term s. Here x, y from $C_1$ are different but they have to be in the same block in order to go to the same variable u in $C_2$.

(*iii*)    Let $C=Q(f(a),f(b))$, $C_1=P(f(u),f(v))$, then $C_2=Q(x,y)\vee{\sim}P(x,y)$ can be constructed by MB-absorption if we define $\theta_1=\{u/a, v/b\}$. The resolvent of $C_1$ and $C_2$ is $Q(f(u),f(v))$, which is more general than C. Thus, MB-absorption is also *unsound*: It constructs $C_2$ such that C is not the resolvent of $C_1$ and $C_2$.

Besides the incompleteness and unsoundness of the MB-algorithm there are still the following questions:

- What kind of subsets of terms are used for partitions and which partitions are allowed for a given subset?
- Different partitions induce different clauses. Is it possible to see that one induced clause is more general than another, just by comparing the associated partitions?

To improve the MB-algorithm and to answer the two questions above we need a formal basis so as to discuss problems and prove theorems easily and more precisely. To this end, we introduce consistent term mappings in section 2. A consistent term mapping is defined on a subset of all term occurrences in a clause. A term occurrence is identified not only by the term but also by the position where this term occurs. In fact the position determines the term in the clause and we can use positions to prove several properties and theorems. A consistent term mapping has the effect of replacing a term occurrence in a clause by new ones and thus induces a new clause. We can also formulate substitutions and inverses of substitutions as special consistent term mappings and thus we have generalized these two concepts. The generalizations go beyond these aspects. For example, a substitution is defined on variables, now we can consider a consistent mapping which coincides with this substitution in variables but has a different domain. The flexibility of domains makes many mathematical formulations and proofs possible and easier. Consistent term mappings have been introduced (under the name consequent functions) in a report by the first author (Nienhuys-Cheng, 1990), which examines in more detail the properties of consistent term mappings in general.

In section 3 we consider partitions which are defined on some subsets of term occurrences in a clause. Such a partition induces a more general clause by constructing an inverse substitution with respect to this partition. We can compare two partitions by an order relation. This order relation between partitions coincides with the generality relation between the induced clauses. The advantages of comparing term partitions instead of clauses is that we do not have to construct the induced clauses and the substitutions explicitly.

In section 4 we apply the theory in the first two sections to absorption. The problem with MB-absorption is that they consider $C \vee \sim C_1$ when they want to construct $C_2$ and they distinguish the term occurrences from C and from $C_1$. This approach is not general enough to construct all $C_2$'s. Our approach considers first a fixed substitution $\theta_1$ and then $C \vee \sim C_1 \theta_1$ as a whole, thus we can apply the theory of section 3 about partitions which are based on one clause (i.e. $C \vee \sim C_1 \theta_1$) without taking into account which term occurrences comes from C and which ones comes from $C_1$. Thus we establish a new algorithm. If we let $\theta_1$ change, then we have all possible $C_2$'s.

However, if we do consider $C \vee \sim C_1 \theta_1$ as combination of C and $\sim C_1 \theta_1$, we can compare $C_2$'s with respect to different $\theta_1$'s by using C as a bridge. If $C_2$ is induced on the basis of $C \vee \sim C_1 \theta_1$ and $C_2'$ is induced on the basis of $C \vee \sim C_1 \theta_1'$, then a substitution from $C_2$ to $C_2'$ implies that $\theta_1 = \theta_1'$ under not very constraining conditions. Thus for a fixed substitution $\theta_1$, we can build a partial ordering of $C_2$'s on $C \vee \sim C_1 \theta_1$ according to their generalities. For different $\theta_1$'s, the $C_2$'s are incomparable. The theorem about comparing $C_2$'s with respect to different $\theta_1$'s has as a corollary a result of (Muggleton, 1990).

For the sake of brevity, we omit most proofs of theorems; the interested reader is referred to (Nienhuys-Cheng, 1990).

# 2. Consistent term mappings

In this paper we use a language of first order logic. The *constants* are denoted by a, b, c,... and the variables are denoted by x, y, z, u, v, w, ... . The letters P, Q, R, ... are used to denote *predicates* and the letters f, g, h, ... are used to denote *functions*. A *term* is either *simple*, i.e. a constant or variable, or *compound* which has the form of $f(t_1, t_2, ..., t_n)$ where $t_i$'s are terms and f is n-ary. An *atom* has the form of $P(t_1,...,t_n)$ where P is an n-ary predicate and $t_i$'s are terms. The negation of an atom has the form ~M where M is an atom and we call an atom or the negation of an atom a *literal*. A *clause* has the form $L_1 \vee L_2 \vee ... \vee L_n$ where every $L_i$ is a literal.

## 2.1 Term occurrences

Let P(x,y) be a given clause. A mapping which maps x to f(u) and y to f(u) can be used to denote the action of substituting x and y in this clause both by f(u). The result is P(f(u),f(u)). If we want to do this action reversely, the function to map f(u) to x or y is not enough and we have to specify that the first f(u) is mapped to x and the second f(u) is mapped to y. Thus we need to define positions of terms. This notation is also used in (Plotkin, 1970; Muggleton & Buntine, 1988).

**Definition.** A *position* is a sequence $<n_1, n_2,..., n_j>$ of positive integers. Let X be a term, literal or a non-unit clause. We use <> to denote the position of X related to itself. If $X = L_1 \vee L_2 ... \vee L_n$, $n \geq 2$ is a clause, then $<i>$ is used to denote the position of $L_i$ in X. If $Y(t_1,...,t_n)$ is a term or a literal in X with position $<p_1, p_2,..., p_k>$, then $t_i$ has the position $<p_1, p_2,..., p_k, i>$. A *term occurrence* in X is a pair (t,p) which is used to denote the term t found at position p in X.

For example, if $X = P(f(x),y) \vee Q(f(x))$, the position of P(f(x),y) is <1>, the position of y in P(f(x),y) is <2> but in X is <1,2>.

Notice that in one term or clause the position determines the term occurrence completely. If (t,p) and (s,q) are term occurrences in X where $p = <p_1,...,p_k>$ and $q = <p_1,...,p_k,q_1,...,q_j>$, then in position $q' = <q_1,...,q_k>$ of t we find the term s, i.e. (s,q') is a term occurrence in t. In this situation (s,q) is called a *subterm occurrence* of (t,p) and we denote the relation by (t,p)≥(s,q). We also say that p is a *subsequence* of q, and we can use q-p to denote q' and pq' to denote q. If p=q, then (t,p)=(s,q); if q is longer than p, then (s,q) is called a *proper subterm occurrence* of (t,p), denoted by (t,p)>(s,q). Notice that a variable or a constant occurrence has longest position specification because they do not have proper subterm occurrences.

## 2.2 Consistent term mappings

If a clause C is given, it is easy to construct the set T(C) of all term occurrences of C. We can ask the following reverse question: what kind of set K of pairs of term and position (t,p) can be used to construct a clause C which has K as a subset of T(C)? For example, the set $K=\{(f(x,g(y)),<1>),\ (h(y),<2>),\ (g(y),<1,2>\}$ can be used to construct a clause P(f(x,g(y)),h(y)) for a 2-ary predicate P. A set $K'=\{(f(x,g(y)),<1>),\ (h(y),<2>),\ (k(y),<1,2>)\}$ cannot be used to construct a clause because <1> and <1,2> are nested but in position <2> of f(x,g(y)) is not k(y). In a way we can say a new clause can be constructed only if we can glue the terms together so that the terms coincide if the positions coincide. For a given clause C, we can also replace some term occurrences by new term occurrences and hence construct a new clause. For this purpose we define consistent term mappings.

**Definition.** An *abstract term occurrence* is a pair of term and position (t,p) which is not yet associated to a special clause. For a given clause C, a mapping θ from a subset of T(C) to a set of abstract term occurrences is called *consistent term mapping* (abbreviated as *CTM*) if the following condition is satisfied:

1) For every (t,p) in the domain of θ, (t,p)θ=(s,p). That is to say θ preserves positions.
2) If (t,p) and (s,q) are in the domain and (t,p)≥(s,q), then (t,p)θ≥(s,q)θ. That is, if (t,p)θ=(t',p) and (s,q)θ=(s',q), then in t' we find s' in position q-p.

We say that a CTM has *minimal set* as domain, if for every two different (t,p), (s,q) in the domain, p is not a subsequence of q and q is not a subsequence of p. In other words, one is not a subterm occurrence of the other. If we have a CTM θ defined on $\{(t_1,p_1),...,(t_n,p_n)\}$ and $(t_i,p_i)θ=(t_i',p_i)$ for all i, we can denote this mapping also by $\{(t_1/t_1',p_1),...,(t_n/t_n',p_n)\}$. Such a CTM with minimal domain can be used to construct a new clause. We just replace every $(t_i,p_i)$ in the original clause by $(t_i',p_i)$. Because $p_i$ is not a subsequence of $p_j$ for different i, j, the replacement of such term occurrences do not interfere with each other. We can consider construction of new clauses also for more general CTM's. For example, let C=P(f(g(u),v),g(u)) and the CTM be $\{(f(g(u),v)/k(x,y),<1>)\}$, then the new clause is C'=P(k(x,y),g(u)). We can also consider C' to be the induced clause by a CTM with bigger domain, namely, $\{(f(g(u),v)/k(x,y),<1>), (g(u)/x,<1,1>)\}$ because in $<1,1>$ of C' is x and in $<1,1>$ of C is g(u). A CTM $\{(g(u)/x,<1,1>)\}$ induces a different clause $P(f(x,v),g(u))$.

**Theorem 1.** Let $\theta$ be a CTM defined on a subset T of T(C). Let T$\theta$ be the set of images of $\theta$. Then there is a subset S of T which is minimal and $\theta$ restricted to S induces a clause C' such that $T(C')\supset T\theta$.

**Proof.** Let S be the subset of T which consists of occurrences with shortest position specification, i.e. $(t,p)\in S$ iff there is no other $(t',p')$ in T such that $(t',p')>(t,p)$. For every $(t,p)$ in S, we replace $(t,p)$ in C by $(t,p)\theta$. The result is a clause C'. The proof proceeds by showing that every $(t,p)\theta$ for $(t,p)$ in T is a term occurrence in C'.

From now on we use C$\theta$ for the clause C' defined as in this theorem and we say it is induced by $\theta$. Notice that the inverse $\theta^{-1}$ of a CTM $\theta$ is also a CTM. Thus, if C$\theta$=C', then C=C'$\theta^{-1}$. This theorem tells us every CTM can be reduced to a CTM with minimal domain. Why not define CTM's with the restriction of minimal domains? In following sections we compare two clauses induced by different mappings. There we need to consider CTM's with bigger domains. Although we can derive many properties about CTM's in general (Nienhuys-Cheng, 1990), here we pay attention to two special kinds of CTM's: substitutions and inverse substitutions, and CTM's which induce the same clauses as them.

## 2.3 Substitutions and inverse substitutions

Let C be a clause. A *substitution* $\theta$ from C is a CTM defined on the set of all variable occurrences which maps the same variable to the same term. That is to say: if $(v,p)\theta=(t,p)$ and $(v,q)\theta=(t',q)$, then t=t'. A substitution induces a mapping defined on the set of all variables. For convenience we use $\theta$ also for this mapping and we write $(v,p)\theta=(v\theta,p)$. We define substitution with domain on all variable occurrences for the convenience of term partition in the following section. Under this definition a variable can also be mapped to itself. We use often $\{v_1/t_1, v_2/t_2,..., v_n/t_n\}$ to denote a substitution where v/v can be omitted if we want. If $\theta$ is a substitution, then the inverse $\theta^{-1}$ of $\theta$ is called *inverse substitution*. We can define inverse substitution without first considering the existence of a substitution. A CTM $\sigma$ defined on a subset of T(C) for a clause C is an inverse substitution iff the following conditions are satisfied: the domain is minimal; the images are variable occurrences; if $(t,p)\sigma=(v,p)$ and $(t',q)\sigma=(v,q)$, then t=t'; for every variable occurrence $(w,q)$ of C, there is a $(t,p)$ in the domain of $\sigma$ such that $(t,p)\geq(w,q)$. The last condition guarantees that the inverse $\sigma^{-1}$ of $\sigma$ is defined on all variable occurrences, to ensure that the inverse of an inverse substitution is a substitution. Notice that both substitutions and inverse substitutions have minimal domains. A substitution $\theta$ from C can be extended to a CTM $\underline{\theta}$ with maximal domain, i.e. T(C). We define $(t,p)\underline{\theta}=(t',p)$ where t' is obtained by replacing all variable occurrences in t by their images. An inverse substitution $\sigma$ from C can also be extended to a CTM $\underline{\sigma}$ with a maximal domain. If (t,p) is in T(C) and there is a (s,q) in the domain of $\sigma$ such that $(t,p)\geq(s,q)$, then define $(t,p)\underline{\sigma}=(t',p)$ where t' is obtained by replacing all subterm occurrences in (t,p) which are also in the domain by their image variable occurrences. If (t,p) in T(C) contains no element from the domain of $\sigma$ as subterm occurrence and is also not a subterm occurrence of such an element, then $(t,p)\underline{\sigma}=(t,p)$.

There are still other extensions of a substitution which have domains between the maximal domain and the original domain. All such extensions induce the same clause as the original substitution. In fact these are not the only CTM's which induce the same clause. For example, consider $C=P(g(f(x)),y)$ and a substitution $\theta=\{x/h(u,v)\}$. It induces the clause $C'=P(g(f(h(u,v))),y)$. A CTM defined by $\{f(x)/f(h(u,v)),<1,1>\}$ induces the same clause. With these ideas in mind we can prove theorem 2 and 3. Theorem 3 is used to prove theorem 5.

**Theorem 2.** Let $\mu$ be a substitution from C to C$\mu$ and $\underline{\mu}$ be the maximal extension of $\mu$ defined on T(C). Let $\theta$ be another CTM on a subset T of T(C) which is the same as $\underline{\mu}$ restricted to T. Furthermore, suppose that for every variable occurrence (v,q) in T(C), there is a (t,p) in T such that $(t,p)\geq(v,q)$, then $\theta$ induces also C$\mu$, i.e. C$\mu$=C$\theta$.

**Theorem 3.** Let $\mu$ be an inverse substitution from C and it induces C$\mu$. Let $\underline{\mu}$ be the maximal extension of $\mu$. If $\theta$ is a CTM, defined on a subset T of T(C) which is the same as $\underline{\mu}$ restricted to T, and for every (s,q) in the domain of $\mu$ there is a (t,p) in T such that $(t,p)\geq(s,q)$, then C$\mu$=C$\theta$.

# 3. Term partitions and their comparisons

In this paper the role of inverse substitutions is important because we want to generalize clauses. We can divide the domain of an inverse substitution into a partition according to the the image variables. For example, for $P(f(x),g(f(x)),h(x))$ we can define inverse substitution $\{(f(x)/v,<1>), (f(x)/v,<2,1>), (h(x)/w,<3>)\}$ and it induces $P(v,g(v),w)$. Thus we have a partition $\{(f(x),<1>), (f(x),<2,1>)\}$ and $\{(h(x),<3>)\}$ of the domain which corresponds to the variables v and w.

Let C be a clause and $\mu$ be an inverse substitution defined on T. We can define a partition $\Pi$ in T by dividing T in blocks. A block B defined by the variable v is the set

$$B=\{(t,p)\in T|(t,p)\mu=(v,p)\}.$$

We use B/v to denote that B is defined by v.

Let $\mu$ and $\partial$ be two inverse substitutions which define the same partition $\Pi$. Then the clauses $C\mu$ and $C\partial$ differ only in the name of variables. If we are only interested in the structure of the induced clauses without concern for the names of variables, then we can use $C(\Pi)$ to denote one of such clauses. We want to define a partial ordering in partitions $\geq$ such that $\Pi\geq\Omega$ iff $C(\Pi)\geq C(\Omega)$, i.e. there is a substitution $\sigma$ from $C(\Pi)$ to $C(\Omega)$. If $C_1\geq C_2$, then for every $(w,q)$ variable in $C_2$, there must be a $(v,p)$ in $C_1$ such that $(v,p)\sigma$ contains $(w,q)$ as subterm. In this situation w has relative position q-p in $(v,p)\sigma$. If there is also $(v,p')$ in $C_1$, then $(v,p')\sigma$ contains also a variable w in the position q-p(=q'-p'). We try to translate such concepts to relations between partitions. For example,

$C=P(f(g(h(x),y))),\ g(h(x),y),k(a,h(x)))$

$C_2=P(f(g(w,y)),\ g(w,y),\ k(a,w))$

$C_1=P(f(u),u,v)$

To find $C_2$, we need the following partition $\Omega$:

$D_1=\{(h(x),<1,1,1>),\ (h(x),<2,1>),\ (h(x),\ <3,2>)\},\ D_1/w;$

$D_2=\{(y,<1,1,2>),(y,<2,2>)\},D_2/y$

To find $C_1$, we need the following partition $\Pi$:

$B_1=\{(g(h(x),y),<1,1>),\ (g(h(x),y),<2>)\},\ B_1/u;$

$B_2=\{(k(a,h(x)),<3>)\},\ B_2/v.$

Notice that $(u,<1,1>)\sigma=(g(w,y),<1,1>)$ and $(u,<2>)\sigma=(g(w,y),<2>)$ and $(v,<3>)\sigma=(k(a,w),<3>)$. The first two elements in $D_1$ are related to $B_1$. For $(h(x),<1,1,1>)$ in $D_1$ there is $(g(h(x)),<1,1>)$ in $B_1$ to contain it as subterm in position $<1>$ and for $(h(x),<2,1>)$ in $D_1$ there is $(g(h(x)),<2>)$ in $B_1$ to contain it as subterm in position $<1>$. This is also the position of w in $v\sigma$. For $(h(x),<3,2>)$ in $D_1$ there is $(k(a,h(x)),<3>)$ in $B_2$ which contains it as subterm in position $<2>$. This is also the position of y in $v\sigma$. We can find similar relation between elements in $D_2$ and elements in $B_1$. Thus, first we want to define a partition without an explicit inverse substitution and then define the partial order relation $\geq$ for partitions:

**Definition.** Let C be a given clause. An *admissible* subset T of T(C) satisfies the following conditions:

1) T is minimal.

2) If $(w,q)$ is an variable occurrence in C, then there is a $(t,p)$ in T such that $(t,p)\geq(w,q)$.

A *term partition* of an admissible subset T is a set of disjoint non-empty subsets $B_1,..., B_k$ such that $B_1 \cup ... \cup B_k = T$, and every *block* $B_i$ contains occurrences of only one term. Notice that every partition defined by an inverse substitution is also a term partition. On the other hand, we can define an inverse substitution $\mu$ from T such that $\Pi$ is also the partition induced by $\mu$. We just define $(t,p)\mu = (v_i, p)$ if $(t,p_i)$ is in $B_i$. Thus we can call the partition induced by an inverse substitution also term partition.

**Definition.** Let C be a given clause and T, S be admissible subsets of T(C). Let $\Pi$ be a term partition defined on T and $\Omega$ be a term partition defined on S. We say $\Pi \geq \Omega$ if

1) For every $(s,q)$ in S, there is a $(t,p)$ in T such that $(t,p) \geq (s,q)$.
2) Let $(t,p)$ be in a block B of $\Pi$ and $(s,q)$ be in a block D in $\Omega$. If $(t,p) \geq (s,q)$, and $B = \{(t,p_1),...,(t,p_n)\}$, $D = \{(s,q_1),...,(s,q_m)\}$, then $m \geq n$ and by reordering the indices, we have $p_1 = p$, $q_1 = q$ and $q_i - p_i = q - p$ for every $i = 1,...,n$.

**Theorem 4.** Let C be a given clause. Let $\partial$ and $\mu$ be two inverse substitutions which induce term partitions $\Pi$ and $\Omega$ on T and S, admissible subsets of T(C), respectively. If there is a substitution from $C\partial$ to $C\mu$, then $\Pi \geq \Omega$.

To prove that $\Pi \geq \Omega$ implies also $C(\Pi) \geq C(\Omega)$, we use theorem 3 of the last section which tells when a CTM induces the same clause as the inverse substitution. As an example, let $C = P(f(g(x)))$. Let $C(\Pi) = P(u)$ and $\partial$ be the inverse substitution from C to $C(\Pi)$. Let $C(\Omega) = P(f(w))$ and let $\mu$ be the inverse substitution from C to $C(\Omega)$. Let $\underline{\mu}$ be also the maximal extension of $\mu$ and $\partial^{-1}$ be the substitution which is the inverse of $\partial$. We can use the composition of $\partial^{-1}: u \rightarrow f(g(x))$, $\underline{\mu}: f(g(x)) \rightarrow f(w)$ to define the composition $\sigma: u \rightarrow f(w)$. This CTM induces a clause based on $C(\Pi)$ and we can prove it is just $C(\Omega)$. That means $\sigma$ is the substitution which we are looking for. The following diagram illustrates the situation. In the right diagram we left the letter T out to make things look more transparant.

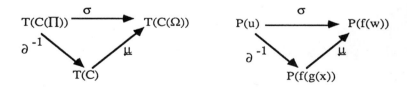

**Theorem 5.** Let C be a given clause and let $\Pi$ and $\Omega$ be two term partitions defined on S and T, admissible subsets of T(C), respectively. Let $C(\Pi)$ and $C(\Omega)$ be two clauses induced by $\Pi$ and $\Omega$, respectively. If $\Pi \geq \Omega$, then there is a substitution $\sigma$ from $C(\Pi)$ to $C(\Omega)$.

For the given clause C, the relation $\geq$ forms a partial ordering on all term partitions which are defined on subsets of $T(C)$. The minimal term partition under this ordering induces the clause C itself. The ordering coincides with the generality ordering on clauses, which allows us to compare clauses without actually building them. The absorption algorithm, discussed in the next section, is based on such term partitions. A related problem is the construction of minimal generalizations of a given clause, and of the supremum of clauses (Plotkin, 1970; Reynolds, 1970). In (Nienhuys-Cheng, 1991) we consider all partitions based on C and we give algorithms for building the least higher partitions (w.r.t. $\geq$) for a given partition and the supremum of two partitions.

# 4. Absorption

We briefly review the basic concepts related to resolution. Let $L_1$ and $L_2$ be two literals. A *unifier* of the $L_1$ and $L_2$ is a pair of substitutions $(\theta_1, \theta_2)$ such that $\theta_1$ is defined on all variable occurrences of $L_1$ and $\theta_2$ is defined on all variable occurrences of $L_2$ and $L_1\theta_1 = L_2\theta_2$. A unifier $(\theta_1, \theta_2)$ is called a *most general unifier (mgu)* if for any unifier $(\sigma_1, \sigma_2)$ for $L_1$, $L_2$ there is a substitution $\gamma$ such that $L_1\theta_1\gamma = L_2\theta_2\gamma = L_1\sigma_1 = L_2\sigma_2$ where $L_i\theta_i\gamma$ is the clause induced by $\gamma$ based on $L_i\theta_i$.

To define the resolution principle we need to know first how to extend a substitution from a literal to a clause which contains this literal. If C is a clause such that $C = C' \vee L$ where L is a literal, then a substitution $\theta$ on L can be extended to a substitution on the entire clause C. If $v\theta = t$, then for every $(v, p)$ in C we can define $(v, p)\theta = (t, p)$. Let $C_1 = C_1' \vee L_1$, $C_2 = C_2' \vee L_2$ be two clauses. If $(\theta_1, \theta_2)$ is a mgu of $\sim L_1$ and $L_2$, then the resolution principle allows to infer $C_1'\theta_1 \vee C_2'\theta_2$. This is called a *resolvent* of $C_1$ and $C_2$.

## 4.1 MB-absorption and a new algorithm

In the introduction, we demonstrated the incompleteness and unsoundness of MB-absorption. On the other hand, (Muggleton, 1990) demonstrates that for any $C_2$ constructed by MB-absorption from $C_1$ and C, there are substitutions $\theta_1$ and $\theta_2$ such that $C_2\theta_2 = C \vee \sim C_1\theta_1$. Thus, the resolvent of $C_1$ and $C_2$ is either C, or some clause more general than C. Because in machine learning we are looking for generalizations, we may take this as an alternative soundness condition. We have a sound and complete absorption algorithm, if it can construct all, and only those, $C_2$'s such that $C_2\theta_2=Cv\sim C_1\theta_1$. Essentially, such an algorithm first constructs $\theta_1$ from $C_1$ and then constructs an inverse substitution $\theta_2^{-1}$ from an admissible subset of $T(Cv\sim C_1\theta_1)$ by means of a term partition.

> **Algorithm.** *A non-deterministic, sound and complete absorption algorithm.*
> Input: clauses C and $C_1$, where $C_1$ is a positive literal.
> Output: $C_2$ such that $C_2\theta_2=Cv\sim C_1\theta_1$ for some $\theta_1$ and $\theta_2$.
> Construct a substitution $\theta_1$ from $C_1$;
> Construct an admissible subset T of $T(Cv\sim C_1\theta_1)$;
> Construct a term partition of T;
> Construct an inverse substitution and an induced clause $C_2$ from this partition.

To find an admissible subset T, we can begin with considering a set S of all variable occurrences plus some constant occurrences (optional). Initially, $T:=\varnothing$. For every $(s,q)$ in S, find a $(t,p)$ in $T(Cv\sim C_1\theta_1)$ such that q contains p as a subsequence. If this $(t,p)$ is not already in T, and there is no $(t',p')$ in T with the property that p and p' have subsequence relationship, let $T:=T\cup\{(t,p)\}$. When all elements in S have been considered, we have an admissible set. We define the partition in the following way. Let $(t,p)$ in T, find some elements in T such that they are occurrences of the same term t. Define a block B by including these elements and $(t,p)$. We repeat the same process for elements in $T:=T-B$. The partition is ready when there is no element in T left.

$C_2$'s based on the same $\theta_1$ can be compared by means of the term partitions of section 3. Notice that $Cv\sim C_1\theta_1$ is the least general $C_2$ which can be constructed by using the same $\theta_1$; it will be called an *LG-absorption*. The algorithm above is not directed and therefore inefficient. This can partly be remedied by constructing partitions which are least higher (w.r.t. $\geq$) compared to a given partition based on $Cv\sim C_1\theta_1$, and constructing the supremum of some partitions based on $Cv\sim C_1\theta_1$ (Nienhuys-Cheng, 1991).

# 4.2 Comparison of $C_2$ induced by different $\theta_1$'s

Let $C=P(f(x))$ and $C_1=Q(y)$ and $\theta_1=\{y/f(x)\}$, then we have $Cv\sim C_1\theta_1=P(f(x))v\sim Q(f(x))$. For some term partition $\Pi$ we have $C_2(\Pi)=P(u)v\sim Q(u)$. For any other $\theta_1'$, we have $Cv\sim C_1\theta_1'=P(f(x))v\sim Q(X)$, with X an unknown term. Suppose there is a term partition $\Omega$ on a subset of $T(Cv\sim C_1\theta_1')$ such that $C_2(\Omega)=P(f(v))v\sim Q(Y)$ and a substitution from $C_2(\Pi)$ to $C_2(\Omega)$, then it must bring u to $f(v)$; hence $Y=f(v)$. The variable v determines a block in the term partition $\Omega$, and from C we know $(x,<1,1,1>)$ must be in the block. Therefore, $X=f(x)$ and $\theta_1=\theta_1'$. In general, $C_2$'s are incomparable if they are built on different $\theta_1$'s which satisfy a certain condition.

**Lemma.** Let C be a clause and $C_1$ be a literal. Consider two substitutions $\theta_1$, $\theta_1'$ from $C_1$. Let $\Pi$ be a term partition defined on a subset of $T(C\vee\sim C_1\theta_1)$, and let $\Omega$ be a term partition defined on a subset of $T(C\vee\sim C_1\theta_1')$. Let $\theta_2$ and $\theta_2'$ be the substitution from $C_2(\Pi)$ to $C\vee\sim C_1\theta_1$ and $C_2(\Omega)$ to $C\vee\sim C_1\theta_1'$, respectively. Suppose there is a substitution $\sigma$ from $C_2(\Pi)$ to $C_2(\Omega)$ and suppose a block B, B/v of $\Pi$ contains both terms from C and $\sim C_1\theta_1$, then if $(t,p)$, a term occurrence in $T(C\vee\sim C_1\theta_1)$, is in B, then $(t,p)$ is also in $T(C\vee\sim C_1\theta_1')$ and $(t,p)=(v\sigma,p)\underline{\theta_2}'$ where $\underline{\theta_2}'$ is the maximal extension of $\theta_2'$.

**Proof.** The relations between different mappings can be seen in the following diagram:

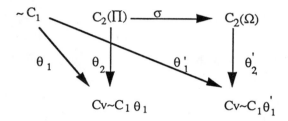

Let us consider the following block of $\Pi$: $B=\{(t,p_1),...,(t,p_n),(t,q_1),...,(t,q_m)\}$, B/v where $(t,p_i)$ are term occurrences of C and $(t,q_j)$ are term occurrences of $\sim C_1\theta_1$. From the given condition about a block of $\Pi$ we know $m>0$ and $n>0$. We consider the set

$$B'=\{(v\sigma\underline{\theta_2}',p_1),...,(v\sigma\underline{\theta_2}',p_n),(v\sigma\underline{\theta_2}',q_1),...,(v\sigma\underline{\theta_2}',q_m)\}$$

B is a subset of $T(C\vee\sim C_1\theta_1)$ and B' is a subset of $T(C\vee\sim C_1\theta_1')$. Furthermore, $(t,p_i)$ is the $p_i$-th term of C and so is $(v\sigma\underline{\theta_2}',p_i)$. Thus if the set of $(t,p_i)$'s in B is not empty, then $t=v\sigma\underline{\theta_2}'$. Thus $(t,q_j)$ is also a term occurence in $C\vee\sim C_1\theta_1'$.

**Theorem 6.** Let C, $C_1$, $\theta_1$, $\theta_1'$, $C_2$, $C_2'$, $\Pi$, $\Omega$, $\theta_2$ and $\theta_2'$ be defined as in the lemma. Suppose there is a substitution $\sigma$ from $C_2(\Pi)$ to $C_2(\Omega)$ and every block in $\Pi$ which contains term occurrences from $\sim C_1\theta_1$ contains also term occurrences from C. Then for every variable w in $C_1$, we have $w\theta_1=w\theta_1'$.

The proof goes as follows. If w is a variable such that there is a $(t,q_j)$ in block B such that $(t,q_j)\geq(w,q)\theta_1$, then $(w,q)\theta_1'$ is the same subterm of $(t,q_j)$ with position $q-q_j$ because $\theta_1'$ preserves positions and $(t,q_j)$ is also in $T(C\vee\sim C_1\theta_1')$ from the lemma. If $(w,q)\theta_1$ contains

$t_1,p_1),...,(t_k,p_k)$ which belong to blocks $B_1,...,B_k$, then $(t_i,p_i)$ are also in $T(C\vee\sim C_1\theta_1')$ from he lemma and they are subterms of $(w,q)\theta_1'$ and in fact $(w,q)\theta_1=(w,q)\theta_1'$.

Let us define two conditions, V: $C_1\theta_1$ *should contain only variables occurring in C* and W: *if a block B in a partition to define $C_2$ contains a term in $\sim C_1\theta_1$ then it contains also term occurrences in C*. If for some $\theta_1$ there is a $C_2$ which satisfies W, then $\theta_1$ satisfies V because every variable occurrence in $\sim C_1\theta_1$ is contained in a term occurrence in a block and the same erm occurs also in C. On the other hand, if $\theta_1$ satisfies V, then we can take the trivial $Cv\sim C_1\theta_1$ as a $C_2$ which satisfies W. Thus, V for $\theta_1$ is equivalent with the existence of a $C_2$ atisfying W.

Consider the set of all $C_2$'s satisfying W, based on some $\theta_1$ satisfying V: this set is partially ordered, but $C_2$'s based on different $\theta_1$'s cannot be compared. In fact, we can prove hat $Cv\sim C_1\theta_1$ for $\theta_1$ satisfying V is least general, i.e. there exists no substitution from it to a $C_2$ based on another $\theta_1$ (not necessarily satisfying V). If $\theta_1$ does not satisfy condition V, then t may result in a $C_2$ which is not least general.

## 4.3 Related work

Muggleton (1990) investigates how to construct a least general $C_2$ if $C_1$ is not a literal. Let $C_1=C_1'\vee L_1$, $C_2=C_2'\vee L_2$, $L_1$ (positive) and $L_2$ (negative) are the literals resolved upon and $\theta_1,\theta_2)$ is the mgu. Muggleton argues that $C_2'\theta_2$ should contain every literal in $C_1'\theta_1$, hence $C_2'\vee L_2)\theta_2=Cv\sim L_1\theta_1$. Furthermore, $\theta_1$ can partly be derived by comparing literals in $C_1'$ and C, because $C_1'\theta_1$ must be a part of C. Therefore, he requires the variables in the head of $C_1$ to be in its body, to assure $Cv\sim L_1\theta_1$ is least general. On the other hand, for us to construct such a $C_2$ means to construct a term partition on $Cv\sim L_1\theta_1$, and the condition concerning the variables n $C_1$ implies $\theta_1$ satisfies V. Thus, his result is a corollary of our theory. We allow in addition $C_1$ to be a unit clause.

Unlike what is implicitly suggested in (Muggleton, 1990), such a $\theta_1$ is not necessarily unique. For instance, let $C=P(x,y)\vee\sim R(x)\vee\sim R(y)$ and $C_1=Q(z)\vee\sim R(z)$, then we can take $\theta_1=\{z/x\}$ resulting in $C_2=P(x,y)\vee\sim R(x)\vee\sim R(y)\vee\sim Q(x)$, but also $\theta_1'=\{z/y\}$ which yields $C_2'=P(x,y)\vee\sim R(x)\vee\sim R(y)\vee\sim Q(y)$. Both $C_2$ and $C_2'$ are least general.

(Rouveirol & Puget, 1989) present an approach to inverse resolution, based on a representation change. Before applying an inverse resolution step to clauses, they are *flattened* to clauses containing no function symbols (the functions are transformed to predicates). This simplifies the process of inverse resolution. For instance, an inverse substitution on a flattened clause amounts to dropping some literals from the clause. Within our framework, the completeness of their Absorption operator could be analysed as well.

# 5. Conclusions

In this paper, we have formalized the language for discussing problems about inverse resolutions by using consistent term mappings; we compare the clauses by comparing the partitions and we have improved the absorption algorithm. Finally, we have extended Muggleton's result about least general absorption by allowing $C_1$ to be a unit clause.

# References

Stephen Muggleton. Inductive Logic Programming. First Conference on Algorithmic Learning Theory, Ohmsha, Tokyo, October 1990.

Stephen Muggleton & Wray Buntine. Machine Invention of First-order Predicates by Inverting Resolution. Proceedings of the 5th International Conference on Machine Learning, Morgan Kaufmann, pp. 339-351, 1988.

Shan-Hwei Nienhuys-Cheng. Consequent Functions and Inverse Resolutions. Report Eur-CS-90-03, Erasmus University, Rotterdam, Netherlands, May 1990.

Shan-Hwei Nienhuys-Cheng. Term Partitions and Minimal Generalizations of Clauses. Report, Erasmus University, Rotterdam, Netherlands, 1991.

Gordon D. Plotkin. A Note on Inductive Generalisation. *Machine Intelligence 5*, B. Meltzer & D. Michie (eds.), Edinburgh University Press, 1970.

John C. Reynolds. Transformational Systems and the Algebraic Structure of Atomic Formulas. *Machine Intelligence 5*, B. Meltzer & D. Michie (eds.), Edinburgh University Press, 1970.

Céline Rouveirol & Jean-Francois Puget. A Simple Solution for Inverting Resolution. EWSL-89, Pitman, London, pp. 201-210, 1989.

# LEARNING BY ANALOGICAL REPLAY IN PRODIGY: FIRST RESULTS

Manuela M. VELOSO          Jaime G. CARBONELL
mmv@cs.cmu.edu               jgc@cs.cmu.edu
School of Computer Science
Carnegie Mellon University
Pittsburgh, PA 15213

## Abstract

Robust reasoning requires learning from problem solving episodes. Past experience must be compiled to provide adaptation to new contingencies and intelligent modification of solutions to past problems. This paper presents a comprehensive computational model of analogical reasoning that transitions smoothly between case replay, case adaptation, and general problem solving, exploiting and modifying past experience when available and resorting to general problem-solving methods when required. Learning occurs by accumulation and reuse of cases (problem solving episodes), especially in situations that required extensive problem solving, and by tuning the indexing structure of the memory model to retrieve progressively more appropriate cases. The derivational replay mechanism is briefly discussed, and extensive results of the first full implementation of the automatic generation of cases and the replay mechanism are presented. These results show up to a 20-fold performance improvement in a simple transportation domain for structurally-similar problems, and smaller improvements when a rudimentary similarity metric is used for problems that share partial structure in a process-job planning domain and in an extended version of the STRIPS robot domain.

## Keywords

Analogy, general-purpose problem solving, learning.

# 1 Introduction: Motivation and Substrate

Derivational analogy is a general form of case-based reconstructive reasoning that replays and modifies past problem solving traces to solve problems more directly in new but similar situations [Carbonell, 1986]. While generating a solution to a problem from a given domain theory, the problem solver accesses a large amount of knowledge that is not explicitly present in the final solution returned. One can view the problem solving process as a troubled (messy) search for a solution where different alternatives are generated and explored, some failing and others succeeding. Local and global reasons for decisions are recorded incrementally during the search process. A final solution represents a sequence of operations that correspond only to a particular successful search path. Transformational analogy [Carbonell, 1983] and most case-based reasoning systems (as summarized in [Riesbeck and Schank, 1989]) replay past solutions by modifying, *tweaking* the retrieved past solution. Derivational analogy, on the other hand, aims at capturing that extra amount of knowledge present at search time, by compiling the justifications at each decision point and annotating these at different steps of the successful path. When replaying a solution, the derivational analogy engine reconstructs the reasoning process underlying the past solution. Justifications are tested to determine whether modifications are needed, and when they are needed; justifications provide constraints on possible alternative search paths. In the derivational analogy framework, the compilation of the justifications at search time is done naturally without extra effort, as that information is directly accessible by the problem solver. In general, the justifications are valid for the individual problem. No costly attempt is made to infer generalized behavior from a unique problem solving trace. Generalization occurs incrementally as the problem solver accumulates experience in solving similar problems when they occur. In this way we differ from the eager-learning approach of EBL and chunking [Laird *et al.*, 1986].

This work is done in the context of the nonlinear problem solver of the PRODIGY research project. The PRODIGY integrated intelligent architecture was designed both as a unified testbed for different learning methods and as a general architecture to solve interesting problems in complex task domains. The problem solver is an advanced operator-based planner that includes a simple reason-maintenance system and allows operators to have conditional effects. All of PRODIGY's learning modules share the same general problem solver and the same domain representation language. Learning methods acquire domain and problem specific control knowledge.

A domain is specified as a set of operators, inference rules, and control rules. Additionally the entities of the domain are organized in a type hierarchy. Each operator (or inference rule) has a precondition expression that must be satisfied before the operator can be applied, and an effects-list that describes how the application of the operator changes the world. Search control in PRODIGY allows the problem solver to represent and learn control information about the various problem solving decisions. A problem consists of an initial state and a goal expression. To solve a problem, PRODIGY must find a sequence of operators that, if applied to the initial state, produces a final state satisfying the goal expression.

The derivational analogy work in PRODIGY takes place in the context of PRODIGY's **nonlinear** problem solver [Veloso, 1989, Veloso *et al.*, 1990 forthcoming]. The system is called NoLIMIT, standing for **Nonlinear** problem solver using casual commitment. The basic search procedure is, as in the linear planner [Minton *et al.*, 1989], means-ends analysis in backward chaining mode. Basically, given a goal literal not true in the current world, the planner selects one operator that adds (in case of a positive goal, or deletes, in case of a negative goal) that goal to the world. We say that this operator is *relevant* to the given goal. If the preconditions of the chosen operator are true, the operator can be *applied*. If this is not the case, then the preconditions that are not true in the *state*, become *subgoals*, i.e., new goals to be achieved. The cycle repeats until all the conjuncts from the goal expression are true in the world. NoLIMIT's nonlinear character stems from working with a **set** of goals in this cycle, as opposed to the top goal in a goal stack. The skeleton of NoLIMIT's search algorithm is shown in Figure 1. Dynamic goal selection enables NoLIMIT to interleave plans, exploiting common subgoals and addressing issues of resource contention.

---

1. Check if the goal statement is true in the current state, or there is a reason to suspend the current search path.

     If yes, then either, show the formulated plan, backtrack, or take appropriate action.
2. Compute the *set* of *pending goals* $G$, and the set of possible *applicable operators* $A$.
3. Choose a goal $G$ from $G$ or select an operator $A$ from $A$ that is directly applicable.
4. If $G$ has been chosen, then
     - *expand goal* $G$, i.e., get the set $O$ of *relevant instantiated operators* for the goal $G$,
     - choose an operator $O$ from $O$,
     - go to step 1.
5. If an operator $A$ has been selected as directly applicable, then
     - *apply* $A$,
     - go to step 1.

---

Figure 1: A Skeleton of NoLIMIT's Search Algorithm

The algorithm in Figure 1 describes the basic cycle of NoLIMIT as a *mental* planner. *Applying* an operator means *executing* it in the *internal* world of the problem solver, which we refer to, simply by *world* or *state*. Step 1 of the algorithm checks whether the top level goal statement is true in the current state. If this is the case, then we have reached a solution to the problem. Step 2 computes the set of pending goals. A goal is *pending*, iff it is a precondition of a *chosen* operator that is not true in the state. The *subgoaling* branch of the algorithm continues, by choosing, at step 3, a goal from the set of pending goals. The problem solver *expands* this goal, by getting the set of *instantiated operators* that are relevant to it (step 4). NoLIMIT now *commits* to a relevant operator. This means that the goal just being expanded is to be achieved by applying this *chosen* operator. Step 2 further checks for the *applicable* chosen operators. An operator is *applicable*, iff all its preconditions are true in the state. Note that we can apply several operators in sequence by repeatedly choosing step 5 in case there are multiple applicable operators. Such situations occur when fulfilling a subgoal satisfies the preconditions of more than one pending operator. The *applying* branch continues by choosing to apply this operator at step 3, and applying it at step 5, by updating the state. A search path is therefore defined by the follwoing regular expression:

(*goal chosen-operator applied-operator*\*)\*.

PRODIGY's general problem solver is combined with several learning modules. The operator-based problem solver produces a complete search tree, encapsulating all decisions – right ones and wrong ones – as well as the final solution. This information is used by each learning component in different ways: to extract control rules via EBL [Minton, 1988], to build derivational traces (cases) by the derivational analogy engine [Veloso and Carbonell, 1990], to analyze key decisions by the Apprentice knowledge acquisition interface [Joseph, 1989], or to formulate focused experiments [Carbonell and Gil, 1990]. The axiomatized domain knowledge is also used to learn abstraction layers [Knoblock, 1990], and statically generate generate control rules [Etzioni, 1990].

The remainder of this paper is organized as follows. Section 2 discusses the automatic case generation, as fully annotated derivational traces. Section 3 presents the replay mechanism for case utilization, illustrated with results obtained by derivational replay in three different domains. In section 4 we briefly describe the case memory we are developing to address dynamically the indexation and organization of cases. Finally section 5 draws conclusions on this work.

# 2 The Derivational Trace: Case Generation

The ability to replay previous solutions using the derivational analogy method requires that the problem solver be able to introspect into its internal decision cycle, recording the justifications for each decision during its extensive search process. These justifications augment the solution trace and are used to guide the future reconstruction of the solution for subsequent problem solving situations where equivalent justifications hold true.

Derivational analogy is a *reconstructive* method by which *lines of reasoning* are transferred and adapted to the new problem [Carbonell, 1986]. It is, therefore, necessary to extract and store these lines of reasoning from the search process in an explicit way. The goal is to identify and capture the reasons for the decisions taken by the problem solver at the different choice points encountered while searching for a solution. We identify the following types of choice points [Veloso, 1989]:

- What *goal* to subgoal, choosing it from the set of pending goals.
- What *operator* to choose in pursuit of the particular goal selected.
- What *bindings* to choose to instantiate the selected operator.
- Whether to *apply* an applicable operator or continue *subgoaling* on a pending goal.
- Whether the search path being explored should be *suspended*, continued, or abandoned.
- Upon failure, which *past choice point* to backtrack to, or which *suspended path* to reconsider for further search.

Justifications at these choice points may point to user-given guidance, to preprogrammed control knowledge, to automatically-learned control rules responsible for decisions taken, or to previous cases used as guidance (more than one case can be used to solve a complete problem). They also represent links among the different steps and their related generators, in particular capturing the subgoaling structure. We record failed alternatives (explored earlier) and the cause of their failure. Note that "cause of failure" here refers to the reason why the search path starting at that alternative failed. It does not necessarily mean that the failed alternative is directly responsible for the failure of the global search path. It may be an indirect relationship, but this is the least costly attribution to determine. The current reasons for failure in NoLIMIT follow from to PRODIGY's search philosophy [Minton *et al.*, 1989]:

**No Relevant Operators** - When NoLIMIT reaches an *unachievable* goal, i.e. a goal that does not have any relevant operator that adds it as one of its effects, given the current state and control rules.

**State Loop** - If the application of an operator leads into a previously visited state, then NoLIMIT abandons this path, as a redundant sequence of operators was applied.

**Goal Loop** - When NoLIMIT encounters an unmatched goal that was already previoulsy posted in the search path (i.e. when a pending goal bccomes its own subgoal).

NoLIMIT abandons a search path either due to any of these failures, or at a situation that is heuristically declared not promising (e.g. a search path that is too long).

A search path follows the sequence of decisions presented in the algorithm of Figure 1. Hence, a step of the search path can only be either a goal choice, an operator choice, or the application of an operator. To generate a case from a search tree episode, we take the successful solution path annotated with both justifications for the successful decisions taken, and record of the remaining alternatives that were not explored or that were abandoned and their corresponding reasons. We show below the different justifications annotated at a goal, operator, and applied operator decision nodes.

## 2.1  Justifications at the Different Decision Nodes

According to the search algorithm presented in Figure 1, a goal is selected from the set of pending goals. NoLIMIT may either apply an operator whose preconditions are satisfied (if any), i.e. its left hand side is true in the current state, or continue subgoaling in an unmatched precondition of a different chosen operator. Figure 2 (a) shows the skeleton of a goal decision node.

```
Goal Node                        Applied Operator Node            Chosen Operator Node
   :step                            :step                            :step
   :sibling-goals                   :sibling-goals                   :sibling-relevant-ops
   :sibling-applicable-ops          :sibling-applicable-ops          :why-this-operator
   :why-subgoal                     :why-apply                       :relevant-to
   :why-this-goal                   :why-this-operator
   :precond-of
      (a)                              (b)                              (c)
```

Figure 2: Justification Record Structure: (a) At a Goal Decision Node; (b) At a Chosen Operator Decision Node; (c) At an Applied Operator Decision Node

The different slots capture the context in which the decision is taken and the reasons that support the choice:

**Step** shows the goal selected at this node.

**Sibling-goals** enumerates the set of pending goals, i.e. goals that arose from unmatched preconditions of operators chosen as relevant to produce previous goals; the goal at this node was selected from this set; the other goals in this set were therefore sibling goals to work on. NOLIMIT annotates the reason why these alternatives were not pursued further according to its search experience (either not tried, or abandon as described above).

**Sibling-applicable-ops** shows the relevant operators that could have been applied instead of subgoaling on this goal.

**Why-Subgoal** presents the reason why NOLIMIT decided to subgoal instead of applying an operator (in case there was one).

**Why-This-Goal** explains why this particular goal was selected from the set of alternative sibling goals.

**Precond-of** captures the subgoaling structure; it refers to the operator(s) that gave rise to this goal as an unmatched precondition.

The reasons annotated at the slots *why-subgoal* and *why-this-goal* can range from arbitrary choices to a specific control rule or guiding case that dictated the selection. These reasons are tested at replay time and are interpretable by NOLIMIT.

An operator may be applied if previously selected as relevant for a pending goal and all its preconditions are satisfied in the current state. Figure 2 (b) shows the skeleton of an applied operator decision node. The different slots have an equivalent semantics to the ones at a goal decision node.

An operator is chosen because it is relevant to a pending goal. Figure 2 (c) shows the skeleton of a chosen operator decision node. Alternative instantiated relevant operators are listed in the slot *sibling-relevant-ops*. The slot *why-this-operator* captures reasons that supported the choice of both the current operator and instantiated bindings. The subgoaling link is kept in the slot *relevant-to* that points at the pending goal that unifies with an effect of this operator.

To illustrate the automatic generation of an annotated case, we now present an example.

## 2.2 Example

Consider the set of operators in Figure 3 that define the *ONE-WAY-ROCKET* domain.

```
(LOAD-ROCKET                        (UNLOAD-ROCKET                     (MOVE-ROCKET
 (params ((<obj> OBJECT)             (params ((<obj> OBJECT)           (params nil)
         (<loc> LOCATION))                   (<loc> LOCATION))        (preconds
 (preconds                           (preconds                         (at ROCKET locA))
  (and                                (and                            (effects
   (at <obj> <loc>)                    (inside <obj> ROCKET)           (add (at ROCKET loc)
   (at ROCKET <loc>)))                 (at ROCKET <loc>)))             (del (at ROCKET loc
 (effects                            (effects
  (add (inside <obj> ROCKET))         (add (at <obj> <loc>))
  (del (at <obj> <loc>))))            (del (inside <obj> ROCKET))))
```

Figure 3: The *ONE-WAY-ROCKET* Domain

Variables in the operators are represented by framing their name with the signs "<" and ">". In this domain, there are variable objects and locations, and one specific constant ROCKET. An object can be loaded into the ROCKET at any location by applying the operator LOAD-ROCKET. Similarly, an object can be unloaded from the ROCKET at any location by using the operator UNLOAD-ROCKET. The operator MOVE-ROCKET shows that the ROCKET can move only from a specific location *locA* to a specific location *locB*. Although NoLIMIT will solve much more complex and general versions of this problem, the present minimal form suffices to illustrate the derivational analogy procedure in the context of nonlinear planning.

Suppose we want NoLIMIT to solve the problem of moving two given objects *obj1* and *obj2* from the location *locA* to the location *locB* as expressed in Figure 4.

```
Initial State:                Goal Statement:
    (at obj1 locA)                (and (at obj1 locB)
    (at obj2 locA)                     (at obj2 locB))
    (at ROCKET locA)
```

Figure 4: A Problem in the *ONE-WAY-ROCKET* World

Without any control knowledge the problem solver searches for the goal ordering that enables the problem to be solved. Accomplishing either goal individually, as a linear planner would do, inhibits the accomplishment of the other goal. A precondition of the operator LOAD-ROCKET cannot be achieved when pursuing the second goal (after completing the first goal), because the ROCKET cannot be moved back to the second object's initial position (i.e. *locA*). So interleaving of goals and subgoals at different levels of the search is needed to find a solution. An example of a solution to this problem is the following plan: (LOAD-ROCKET obj1 locA), (LOAD-ROCKET obj2 locA) (MOVE-ROCKET), (UNLOAD-ROCKET obj1 locB), (UNLOAD-ROCKET obj2 locB).

NoLIMIT solves this problem, because it switches attention to the conjunctive goal *(at obj2 locB)* before completing the first conjunct *(at obj1 locB)*. This is shown in Figure 5 by noting that; after the plan step 1 where the operator (LOAD-ROCKET obj1 locA) is applied as relevant to a subgoal of the top-level goal *(at obj1 locB)*, NoLIMIT suspends processing and changes its focus of attention to the other top-level goal and applies, at plan step 2, the operator (LOAD-ROCKET obj2 locA) which is relevant to a subgoal of the goal *(at obj2 locB)*. In fact NoLIMIT explores the space of possible attention foci and only after backtracking does it find the correct goal interleaving. The idea is to learn next time from its earlier exploration and reduce search dramatically.

While solving this problem, NoLIMIT automatically annotates the decisions taken with justifications that reflect its experience while searching for the solution. As an example, suppose that the correct decision of choosing to work on the goal *(inside obj1 ROCKET)* was taken after having failed when working first on *(at ROCKET locB)*. The decision node stored for the goal *(inside obj1 ROCKET)* is annotated with sibling goal failure as illustrated in Figure 6. *(at ROCKET locB)* was a sibling goal that was abandoned because NoLIMIT encountered an unachievable predicate pursuing that search path, namely the goal *(at ROCKET locA)*.

The problem and the generated annotated solution become a *case* in memory. The case corresponds

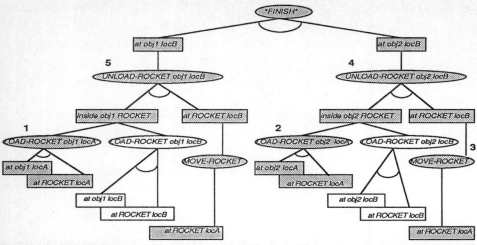

Figure 5: The Complete Conceptual Tree for a Successful Solution Path. The numbers at the nodes show the execution order of the plan steps. Shaded nodes correspond to the choices to which the problem solver committed.

```
Frame of class goal-decision-node
  :step   (inside obj1 ROCKET)
  :sibling-goals (((inside obj2 ROCKET) not-tried)
                    ((at ROCKET locB) (:no-relevant-ops (at ROCKET locA))))
  :sibling-applicable-ops NIL
  :why-subgoal NIL
  :why-this-goal NIL
  :precond-of   (UNLOAD-ROCKET obj1 locB)
  step of next-decision-node   (LOAD-ROCKET obj1 locA)
```

Figure 6: Saving a Goal Decision Node with its Justifications

to the search tree compacted into the successful path annotated with the justifications that resulted in the sequence of correct decisions that lead into a solution to the problem. In essence, a case is a sequence of decision nodes such as the one illustrated in Figure 6.

# 3   The Derivational Replay: Case Utilization

When solving new problems similar to past cases, one can envision two approaches for derivational replay:

- **A.** *The satisficing approach* - Minimize planning effort by solving the problem as directly as possible, recycling as much of the old solution as permitted by the justifications.
- **B.** *The optimizing approach* - Maximize plan quality by expanding the search to consider alternatives of arbitrary decisions and to re-explore failed paths if their causes for failure are not present in the new situation.

At present we have implemented in full the satisficing approach, although work on establishing workable optimizing criteria may make the optimizing alternative viable (so long as the planner is willing to invest the extra time required). Satisficing also accords with observations of human planning efficiency and human planning errors.

In the satisficing paradigm, the system is fully guided by its past experience. The syntactic applicability of an operator is always checked by simply testing whether its left hand side matches the current state. Semantic applicability is checked by determining whether the justifications hold (i.e. whether there is still a *reason* to apply this operator). In case the choice remains valid in the current problem state, it is merely copied, and in case it is not valid the system has three alternatives:

1. Replan at the particular failed choice, e.g. re-establishing the current subgoal by other means (or to find an equivalent operator, or equivalent variable bindings) substituting the new choice for the old one in the solution sequence,

2. Re-establish the failed condition by adding it as a prioritized goal in the planning, and if achieved simply insert the extra steps into the solution sequence, or

3. Attempt an experiment to perform the partially unjustified action anyway; if success is achieved the system refines its knowledge according to the experiment. For instance, if the justification for stacking blocks into a tower required objects with flat top and bottom surfaces, and there were none about (so the first fix does not work) nor is there a way to make surfaces flat (so the second fix also fails), the robot could attempt to forge ahead. If the objects were spherical it would fail, but if they were interlocking LEGO$^{TM}$ pieces, it would learn that these were just as good if not better than rectangular blocks for the purpose of stacking objects to build tall towers. Thus, the justification could be generalized for future reference.

In the first case (substitution), deviations from the retrieved solution are minimized by returning to the solution path after making the most localized substitution possible.

The second case occurs, for example, when the assumptions for the applicability of an operator fail. The system then tries to overcome the failed condition, and if it succeeds, it returns to the exact point in the derivation to proceed as if nothing had gone wrong earlier. Failures however, can be serious. Consider as an example, applying to the context of matrix calculus, some previously solved problems on scalars that rely on commutativity of multiplication. Facing the failure to apply a commutation operator in the matrix context, the system may try to overcome this difficulty by checking whether there is a way of having two matrices commute. In general this fails; the case must be abandoned; and a totally different approach is required.

The experimentation case enables uncertain attempts to perform the same action with partially unjustified conditions, or can digress from the problem at hand to perform systematic relaxation of justifications, and establish whether a more general (more permissive) set of conditions suffices for the instance domain. Then, returning to the problem at hand, it may find possible substitutions or perhaps even re-establishments of these looser conditions via steps 1 or 2 above.

The fact that these different situations can be identified by the problem solver when trying to replay a past case is the motivation and support for our proposed memory model. Memory organization is in a closely coupled dynamic relationship with the problem solving engine.

## 3.1 The One-Way-Rocket Domain, An Example

Let us return to the *ONE-WAY-ROCKET* problem shown in section 2.2 to illustrate the derivational replay process. We show the results obtained in the problems of moving three objects and four objects from *locA* into *locB* in Tables 1 and 2. Each row of the tables refers to one new problem, namely the two- (2objs), three- (3objs), and four-object (4objs) problems. We show the number of search steps in the final solution, the average running time of NOLIMIT without analogy (blind search), and using analogical guidance from one of the other cases.

| New Problem | Blind Search (s) | Following Case 2objs (s) | Impro-vement | Following Case 3objs (s) | Impro-vement | Following Case 4objs (s) | Impro-vement |
|---|---|---|---|---|---|---|---|
| 2objs (18 steps) | 18 | 8 | 2.3x | 8 | 2.3x | 8 | 2.3x |
| 3objs (24 steps) | 59 | 31 | 1.9x | 13 | 4.5x | 13 | 4.5x |
| 4objs (30 steps) | 470 | 110 | 4.3x | 58 | 8.1x | 23 | 20.4x |

Table 1: Replaying Direct Solution

Table 1 shows the results obtained when the justifications are not fully tested. The solution is simply replayed whenever the same step is possible (but not necessarily desirable). For example, if using the two-object case as guidance to the three- (or four-) object problem, after two objects are loaded into the rocket, the step of moving the rocket is tested and replayed because it is also a syntatically possible step. This is not the right step to take, as there are more objects to load into the rocket in the new extended cases. NOLIMIT must backtrack across previously replayed steps, namely across the step of moving the rocket.

On the other hand, in Table 2, we show the results obtained from further testing the justifications before applying the step. In this case, the failure justification for moving the rocket - "no-relevant-ops" - is tested and this step is not replayed until all the objects are loaded into the rocket. Testing justifications shows maximal improvement in performance when the case and the new problem differ substantially (two-objects and four-objects respectively).

From these results we also note that it is better to approach a complicated problem, like the four-object problem, by first generating automatically a reduced problem [Polya, 1945], such as the two-object problem, then gain insight solving the reduced problem from scratch (i.e. build a reference case), and

| New Problem | Blind Search (s) | Following Case 2objs (s) | Impro- vement | Following Case 3objs (s) | Impro- vement | Following Case 4objs (s) | Impro- vement |
|---|---|---|---|---|---|---|---|
| 2objs (18 steps) | 18 | 8 | 2.3x | 8 | 2.3x | 8 | 2.3x |
| 3objs (24 steps) | 59 | 19 | **3.1x** | 13 | 4.5x | 13 | 4.5x |
| 4objs (30 steps) | 470 | 30 | **15.2x** | 30 | **15.2x** | 23 | 20.4x |

Table 2: Testing the Justifications: no-relevant-ops

finally solve the original four-object problem by analogy with the simpler problem. The running time of the last two steps in this process is significantly less than trying to solve the extended problem directly, without analog for guidance. (18 seconds + 30 seconds = 48 seconds – see Table 2 – for solving the two-objects from scratch + derivational replay to the four-object case, versus 470 seconds for solving the four-object case from scratch.)

We note that whereas we have implemented the nonlinear problem solver, the case formation module, and the analogical replay engine, we have not yet addressed the equally interesting problem of automated generation of simpler problems for the purpose of gaining relevant experience. That is, PRODIGY will **exploit** successfully the presence of simpler problems via derivational analogy, but cannot **create** them as yet.

## 3.2 Process-Job Planning and extended-STRIPS Domains, More Examples

We also ran two other experiments to test empirically the benefits of the replay mechanism. We ran NoLimit without analogy in a set of problems in the process-job planning and in the extended-STRIPS domains [1]. We accumulated a library of cases, i.e. annotated derivational solution traces. We then ran again the set of problems using the case library. In particular, if the set of cases is $C$, and the new problem is $P$, corresponding to case $C_P$, then we searched for a similar case in the set $C - C_P$. We used a rudimentary fixed similarity metric that matched the goal predicates, allowed substitutions for elements of the same type, and did not consider any relevant correlations. Figures 7 and 8 show the results for these

---

[1]This set is a sampled subset of the original set used by [Minton, 1988].

two domains. We plotted the average cumulative number of nodes searched.

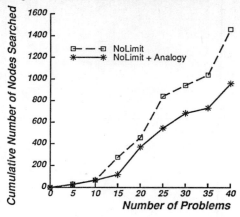

Figure 7: Comparison in the Process-Job Planning and Scheduling Domain

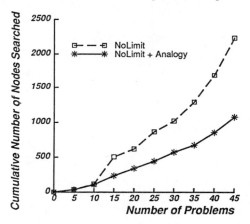

Figure 8: Comparison in the Extended-STRIPS Domain

We note from the results that analogy showed an improvement over basic blind search: a factor of 1.5 fold up for the process-job planning and scheduling domain and 2.0 fold for the extended-STRIPS domain. We noticed few individual problems in the case library that provided bad guidance. In general, however, the simple similarity metric lead to acceptable results. We expect to achieve even better results when a more sophisticated metric is used through dynamic memory organization, as discussed below. We also expect faster indexing than the current linear comparison search, and therefore expect higher performance improvements after completing the implementation of the more sophisticated memory model.

# 4 Towards an Integrated Memory Model

We view the ultimate desired behavior of the analogical reasoning system to emerge from the interaction of two functional modules, namely the *problem solver* and *the memory manager*. We call the memory manager, SMART, for Storage in Memory and Adaptive Retrieval over Time. NOLIMIT and SMART communicate as shown in Figure 9, where $W_i$ is the initial world, $G$ is the goal to be achieved, $W_f$ is the final world, *Analogs* are the retrieved candidate cases, and *Feedback* represents both the new solved problem and information about the utility of the candidate cases in reaching a solution.

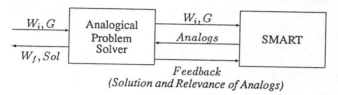

Figure 9: Interaction of the Problem Solver and the Memory Manager

In encoding the utility of the guidance received from SMART, we foresee four different situations that can arise, as shown in Figure 10.

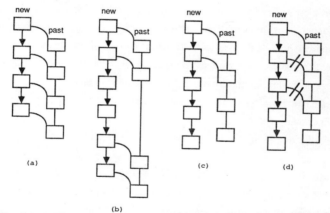

Figure 10: Four Situations to Encode the Utility of the Guidance Received: (a) Fully-sufficient: past case is fully copied; (b) Extension: past case is copied but additional steps are performed in the new case; (c) Locally-divergent: justifications do not hold and invalidate copying part of the past case; (d) Globally-divergent: extra steps are performed that undo previously copied steps.

These four situations determine the reorganization of memory when the new case is to be stored in memory. We are exploring algorithms to address each of these situations. If a case was *fully-sufficient* under a particular match, SMART will generalize its data structure over this match updating the indices to access these cases [Veloso and Carbonell, 1989, Veloso and Carbonell, 1990]. If the new case is an *extension* of the previous case, the conditions that lead into the adaptation and extension work are used to differentiate the indexing of the two cases. Generalization will also occur on the common parts of the case. The situations where the two cases diverge represent a currently incorrect metric of similarity or lack of knowledge. The fact that the retrieval mechanism suggested a past case as most similar to the new problem and the problem solver could not fully use the past case or even extend it, indicates either the sparsity of better cases in memory, or a similarity function that ignores an important discriminant condition. SMART will have to either specialize variables in the memory data structures due to previous overgeneralization or completely set apart the two cases in the decision structure used for retrieval. We plan to extract memory indices from the justification structure, and use them at retrieval time to more adequately prune the set of candidate analogs.

# 5 Conclusion

Whereas much more work lies ahead in reconstructive problem solving exploiting past experience, the results reported here demonstrate the feasibility of derivational analogy as a means to integrate general problem solving with analogical reasoning.

The research into full-fledged case-based reasoning and machine learning in the context of the PRODIGY nonlinear planner and problem solver, however, is far from complete. The full implementation of the SMART memory model, for instance, must be completed. This will enable us to scale up from the present case libraries of under a hundred individual cases to much larger case libraries numbering in the thousands of cases. We are investigating domains such as logistics and transportation planning whose inherent complexity requires large case libraries and sophisticated indexing methods.

Finally, we summarize new contributions in this work beyond the original derivational analogy framework as presented in [Carbonell, 1986]:

- Elaboration of the model of the derivational trace, i.e. identification and organization of appropriate data structures for the justifications underlying decision making in problem solving episodes. Justifications are compiled under a lazy evaluation approach.
- Development of a memory model that dynamically addresses the indexation and organization of cases, by maintaining a closely-coupled interaction with the analogical problem solver.
- Full implementation of the refined derivational analogy replay and memory model in the context of a nonlinear planner (as opposed to the original linear one). Hence the refined framework deals with a considerably larger space of decisions and with more complex planning problems.

# Acknowledgments

The authors thank the whole PRODIGY research group for helpful discussions: Daniel Borrajo, Yolanda Gil, Robert Joseph, Dan Kahn, Craig Knoblock, Dan Kuokka, Steve Minton, Alicia Pérez, and Mei Wang. This research was sponsored in part by the Defense Advanced Research Projects Agency (DOD), ARPA Order No. 4976, Amendment 20, under contract number F33615-87-C-1499, monitored by the Avionics Laboratory, Air Force Wright Aeronautical Laboratories, Aeronautical Systems Division (AFSC), United States Air Force, Wright-Patterson AFB, Ohio 45433-6543, and in part by the Office of Naval Research under contracts N00014-86-K-0678. The views and conclusions contained in this document are those of the authors and should not be interpreted as representing the official policies, either expressed or implied, of the Defense Advanced Research Projects Agency or the US Government.

# References

[Carbonell and Gil, 1990] J. G. Carbonell and Y. Gil. Learning by experimentation: The operator refinement method. In R. S. Michalski and Y. Kodratoff, editors, *Machine Learning: An Artificial Intelligence Approach, Volume III*. Morgan Kaufmann, Palo Alto, CA, 1990.

[Carbonell, 1983] J. G. Carbonell. Learning by analogy: Formulating and generalizing plans from past experience. In R. S. Michalski, J. G. Carbonell, and T. M. Mitchell, editors, *Machine Learning, An Artificial Intelligence Approach, Volume I*. Tioga Press, Palo Alto, CA, 1983.

[Carbonell, 1986] J. G. Carbonell. Derivational analogy: A theory of reconstructive problem solving and expertise acquisition. In R. S. Michalski, J. G. Carbonell, and T. M. Mitchell, editors, *Machine Learning, An Artificial Intelligence Approach, Volume II*. Morgan Kaufman, Los Altos, CA, 1986.

[Etzioni, 1990] O. Etzioni. Why Prodigy/EBL works. In *Proceedings of AAAI-90*, 1990.

[Joseph, 1989] R. L. Joseph. Graphical knowledge acquisition. In *Proceedings of the 4th Knowledge Acquisition For Knowledge-Based Systems Workshop*, Banff, Canada, 1989.

[Knoblock, 1990] Craig A. Knoblock. Learning abstraction hierarchies for problem solving. In *Proceedings of Eighth National Conference on Artificial Intelligence*, Boston, MA, 1990.

[Laird et al., 1986] J. E. Laird, P. S. Rosenbloom, and A. Newell. Chunking in SOAR: The anatomy of a general learning mechanism. *Machine Learning*, 1:11–46, 1986.

[Minton et al., 1989] S. Minton, C. A. Knoblock, D. R. Kuokka, Y. Gil, R. L. Joseph, and J. G. Carbonell. PRODIGY 2.0: The manual and tutorial. Technical Report CMU-CS-89-146, School of Computer Science, Carnegie Mellon University, 1989.

[Minton, 1988] S. Minton. *Learning Effective Search Control Knowledge: An Explanation-Based Approach*. PhD thesis, Computer Science Department, Carnegie Mellon University, 1988.

[Polya, 1945] G. Polya. *How to Solve It*. Princeton University Press, Princeton, NJ, 1945.

[Riesbeck and Schank, 1989] C. K. Riesbeck and R. C. Schank. *Inside Case-Based Reasoning*. Lawrence Erlbaum Associates, Inc., Hillsdale, New Jersey, 1989.

[Veloso and Carbonell, 1989] M. M. Veloso and J. G. Carbonell. Learning analogies by analogy: The closed loop of memory organization and problem solving. In *Proceedings of the Second Workshop on Case-Based Reasoning*. Morgan Kaufmann, May 1989.

[Veloso and Carbonell, 1990] M. M. Veloso and J. G. Carbonell. Integrating analogy into a general problem-solving architecture. In Maria Zemankova and Zbigniew Ras, editors, *Intelligent Systems*, 1990.

[Veloso *et al.*, 1990 forthcoming] M. M. Veloso, D. Borrajo, and A. Perez. NoLimit - the nonlinear problem solver for Prodigy: User's and programmer's manual. Technical report, School of Computer Science, Carnegie Mellon University, 1990, forthcoming.

[Veloso, 1989] M. M. Veloso. Nonlinear problem solving using intelligent casual-commitment. Technical Report CMU-CS-89-210, School of Computer Science, Carnegie Mellon University, 1989.

# Analogical Reasoning for Logic Programming

Birgit Tausend    Siegfried Bell

Institut für Informatik, Universität Stuttgart

Forststr. 86, D-7000 Stuttgart 1, Germany

email: tausend@informatik.uni-stuttgart.de

## Abstract

Analogical reasoning is useful to exploit knowledge about similar predicates to define new ones. This paper presents MARs[1], a tool that supports the definition of new Prolog predicates with respect to known ones. Starting from similar examples, one of the known predicate and one of the new, the tool proposes a definition for the new predicate. The algorithm for constructing this new definition by analogy includes four main steps that will be described in detail in this paper.

## 1 Introduction

Analogical reasoning is concerned with finding a solution for a new problem by making use of the known solution of a similar problem. Basically, analogical reasoning aims at mapping knowledge from a well understood domain, the so called source domain, to a new domain called the target domain in order to solve the new problem. According to this terminology the new problem is called *target problem* and the solved one *source problem*.

The process of analogical reasoning includes four main steps, *recognition*, *elaboration*, *evaluation*, and *consolidation*, as described in [Hall 89]. First, recognition determines a minimal set of source problems that are analogical to a given target problem. The next step is to elaborate a mapping between the source and the target problem and to make analogical inferences. Then the mapping and the inferences have to be evaluated in a particular context and in addition justified, extended or repaired if necessary. The last step concerns the consolidation of the result of the analogical reasoning process to make further use of it.

Most of the machine learning approaches to analogical reasoning can be described and compared within this framework, as shown in [Hall 89]. They mainly differ in the particular method preferred in each step and in the application domain.

The organization of this paper is as follows: in the first section we introduce basic terms and a four step model of analogical reasoning. The next section presents the learning situation of MARs. Section 3 describes each of the four steps of the analogical reasoning process of MARs in detail. The last section discusses briefly some limitations of the existing approach and concludes with the goals of further work.

---

[1]MARs is an acronym for Model of Analogical Reasoning

## 2 Learning Situation

Machine learning approaches to analogical reasoning aim at solving problems in very different domains, as shown in [Hall 89]. Some apply to physical domains [Greiner 88], [Gentner 88], others are concerned with concept learning [KedarCabelli 88],[Burstein 86] or planning [Carbonell 83].

The application problem we address is the analogical definition of a new Prolog predicate according to a known one. This is a task novices in programming language are often involved with. In exercises they are told to find a solution for a problem that is similar to one solved before. Thus, they are requested to slightly modify a known piece of code instead of programming the solution from scratch.

The task of MARs is nearly the same as the students task. Starting from an example of the source predicate and a similar of the target predicate MARs should construct a definition of the new predicate by analogical reasoning. Figure 1 shows an example where the Prolog predicate *member* should be defined analogically to the predicate *append*.

---

**Target and source example:**
   member(2,[1,2,3]) ~ append([1],[2,3],[1,2,3])

**Source problem:** append([1],[2,3],[1,2,3])

**Knowledge base:** append([],L,L)
   append([X|T],L,[X|T1]) ←append(T,L,T1)

**New definition:** member(L,[L|T1])
   member(L,[X|T1]) ← member(L,T1)

---

Figure 1: Analogical definition

Before explaining how MARs constructs the new predicate we have to clarify which problems we consider to be analogical.

In general the hint that two problems are analogical can address two different kinds of similarity. In one case the problems are similar because they can be programmed in a similar way. So the Prolog predicates *member* and *append* could be defined analogically because their structure and their arguments are similar. In the other case similarity concerns the meaning that is the relation of input and output of the program pieces and disregards any structural similarity. For instance the Prolog predicates *first* and *last* could be said to have a similar meaning because they cut one element off a list, *first* at the beginning and *last* at the end of the list, but they have to be programmed in a different way. MARs deals with the first kind of similarity that is the source and the target problem are supposed to have a both similar structure and arguments.

## 3 A Model of Analogical Reasoning

MARs intends to support the definition of new Prolog predicates with respect to similar known predicates. The input required includes two analogical examples and a knowledge base. Both examples have to be ground literals. The knowledge base is supposed to store at least all rules and facts needed to prove the source example. The target example can not be solved directly according to the knowledge base, but it is required to be provable in a similar way. The output of MARs consists of the rules and facts necessary to prove the target problem. This knowledge has to be justified by an oracle before it is added to the knowledge base for further use.

The construction of the missing rules and facts involves four basic steps. First, the recognition step compares the arguments of the source and the target example. In addition, the proof tree of the source example is constructed. The elaboration step maps the ground literals of the proved source example onto the target problem. During evaluation MARs uses forward chaining to construct a proof tree for the target problem. The last step generalizes the proof tree in order to get the missing predicates.

## 3.1  Recognition

Recognition starts with the determination of the analogical argument terms of the examples. In general, there are many possibilities to map argument terms but we assume that the user has given the most similar examples. Therefore, we prefer identical terms to be mapped first and then try to find further similarities between the unmapped terms with the help of other relations, e.g. subset or membership. Thus, the mapping relations are ranked where the identity relation has the highest rank. The term mapping $M_{term}$ is stored in a replacement list with the following structure:

$$\{(p_t, p_s)(\ldots, (arg_{t_i}, i, arg_{s_j}, j), \ldots))\}$$

where $p_t$ is the target predicate symbol, $p_s$ is the source predicate symbol. The 4-tuples $(arg_{t_i}, i, arg_{s_j}, j)$ describe the term mappings where $arg_{t_i}$ is the $i$th argument of the target example, $arg_{s_j}$ is the $j$th argument of the source example, and $i$ and $j$ are the argument positions needed for later recovery of the term mappings.

Figure 2 shows an example of two analogical predicates, where six mappings of terms are possible. Given a ranking of the candiate mapping relations, we use the highest ranking relation, identity, to correlate the third argument of *append* with the second argument of *member*. Also, using the same ranking, the membership relation is established between the first term of *member* and the second of *append*. This term mapping is choosen for further processing and only if the analogical reasoning fails MARs tries to establish another term mapping with lower ranked relations.

---

**Example of analogy:**
member(2,[1,2,3]) ~ append([1],[2,3],[1,2,3])

**Source problem:** append([1],[2,3],[1,2,3])

$M_{term}$: $\{(member, append)$
$((2, 1, [2, 3], 2), ([1, 2, 3], 2, [1, 2, 3], 3))\}$

Figure 2: A recognition step

In addition to the term mapping the refutation tree of the *append* example has to be constructed. The refutation tree is built up using resolution.

A single resolution step can be represented by a **V** representing an inverted tree, as shown in Figure 3. The clause $Res_{i+1}$ is inferred from the two given clauses $Res_i$ and $Cl_i$ with the particular substitutions $\Theta_{Res_i}$ and $\Theta_{Cl_i}$. The refutations are established using a special kind of resolution, the SLD resolution, that applies to a negative clause, the so called resolvent, and a positive clause to transform them into a negative clause.

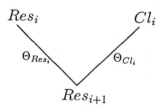

Figure 3: A single resolution step

**Resolvent:** Let $Res_i$ and $Cl_i$ be two clauses with no variables in common. Let $L_1 \in Res_i$, $L_2 \in Cl$ and $\Theta$ is the most general unifier or *mgu* such that $L_1\Theta = \overline{L_2}\Theta$. We write the resolvent as

$$Res_{i+1} = (Res_i \setminus \{L_1\})\Theta \cup (Cl_i \setminus \{L_2\})\Theta$$

The result of recognition includes the term mapping and the refutation tree. For further work we have to extend the refutation tree so that the resolvent and the positive clauses of each particular resolution step together with their substitutions are contained. We use the following structure of a refutation tree where the symbol □ stands for an empty clause:

$$Tree = \{ \langle Res_1, Cl_1, \Theta_1 \rangle, \ldots,$$
$$\langle Res_{n-1}, Cl_{n-1}, \Theta_{n-1} \rangle,$$
$$\langle \square \rangle \}$$

where $\Theta_i = \Theta_{Cl_i}$, because $Res_i$ are instantiated clauses and $\Theta_{Res_i}$ is empty.

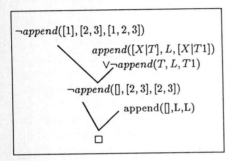

Figure 4: The refutation tree

The following tree is generated of the example of figure 4.

$Tree =$
$\{ \langle$ (¬append([1],[2,3],[1,2,3])),
$\quad$ (append([X|T],L,[X|T1])
$\qquad$ ∨¬append(T,L,T1)),
$\quad$ (X→1, T→[], L→[2,3], T1→[2,3])⟩,
$\langle$ (¬append([],[2,3],[2,3])),
$\quad$ (append([],L,L)),
$\quad$ (L→[2,3]) ⟩,
$\langle \square \rangle \}$

## 3.2 Elaboration

Elaboration maps all ground literals of the proof tree into the domain of the target example. Two cases can be distinguished depending on the ground literals and the term mapping $M_{term}$: if the predicate symbol occurs in $M_{term}$, then, the argument mapping can be used simply in

reverse. The other case is more complicated because we do not have any information about the corresponding literal in the target domain. So, only the argument terms will be replaced but the predicate symbols will not be changed.

The definition for determining the ground literals needed to prove the target example is given by the following replace mapping $M_{repl}$ where $f$ is a mapping relation like identity, inclusion or subset:

$$M_{repl}(p_s(\ldots, arg_{s_j}, \ldots)) =$$

$$\begin{cases} p_t(\ldots, arg_{t_i}, \ldots) & : (p_t, p_s) \in M_{term} \\ \quad and \quad (arg_{t_i}, i, arg_{s_j}, j) \in M_{term} \\ p_t(\ldots, arg_{t_i}, \ldots) & : (p_t, p_s) \in M_{term} \\ \quad and \quad (f(arg_{t_i}), i, f(arg_{s_j}), j) \in M_{term} \\ p_t(\ldots, arg_{t_j}, \ldots) & : (p_t, p_s) \notin M_{term} \\ \quad and \quad (arg_{t_j}, j, arg_{s_j}, j) \in M_{term} \\ p_t(\ldots, arg_s, \ldots) & : otherwise \end{cases}$$

$M_{repl}$ transforms the ground literal $p_s(\ldots, arg_{s_j}, \ldots)$ of the source proof tree into the ground literal needed for the target proof tree according to the information about term mappings stored in $M_{term}$. Figure 5 shows an example of elaboration where the terms and the predicate symbol of the ground literal of the source refutation tree, $append([], [2,3], [2,3])$, are mapped onto $member(2, [2,3])$. For example, the first rule of $M_{repl}$ applies to the second argument of $append([], [2,3], [2,3])$ and the second rule to the third argument.

$M_{term}$: {$(member, append)$
$\quad ((2, 1, [2,3], 2), ([1,2,3], 2, [1,2,3], 3))$}

**Ground literal:** $append([],[2,3],[2,3])$

$M_{repl}(append([], [2,3], [2,3]))$
$\quad = member(2, [2,3])$

Figure 5: An elaboration step

## 3.3 Evaluation

The evaluation step uses the mapped ground literals and the refutation tree of the known example to construct a refutation tree for the target example. Starting from the ground literals the missing nodes of the new refutation tree are determined by forward chaining. In general, the search space of this problem is large but the structure of the known proof tree restricts it considerably because the new proof tree should be as similar as possible.

Forward chaining can be done by simply inverting the resolution step as described in [MuggletonBuntine 88],[Wirth 89]. With this mechanism, called inverse resolution, we can determine clause $Res_i$ from the clauses $Cl_i$ and $Res_{i+1}$ in a configuration like it is shown in figure 3.

The formula of the inverse resolution $Res_i$ is a simple algebraic manipulation of the resolution formula with five unknown parameters in the general case as shown in [Wirth 89]:

$$[Res_{i+1} \setminus Cl_i \Theta_{Cl_i} \cup \{\overline{L_2}\Theta_{Cl_i}\} \cup S\Theta_{Cl_i}]\Theta_{Res_i}^{-1}$$

Here, we make the assumption for $Res_i$ that we only use instantiated clauses and that $S$ is empty. Therefore, the formula used for forward chaining in the source domain is defined by:

$$Res_{s_i} = (Res_{s_{i+1}} \setminus Cl_{s_i}\Theta_{Cl_{s_i}} \cup \{\neg l_{s_i}\Theta_{Cl_{s_i}}\})$$

where all parameters are known and $l_{s_i} \in Cl_{s_i}$. The formula of the target domain is:

$$Res_{t_i} = (Res_{t_{i+1}} \setminus Cl_{t_i} \cup \{\neg l_{t_i}\})$$

where $l_{t_i} \in Cl_{t_i}$. $l_{t_i}$ and $Cl_{t_i}$ are instantiated. $Cl_{t_i}$ can be conjectured by $M_{repl}$ and the resolution literal can be effectively determined.

Figure 6 shows one forward chaining step for each example. For efficient construction of the refutation tree it is useful to tie together both refutation resolvents into one. Figure 7 shows the same example resolvents as figure 6 but tied together in a double resolvent.

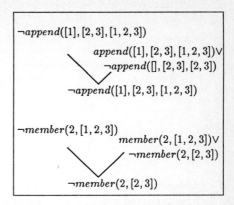

Figure 6: A forward chaining step

The double resolvent of $n$ resolution steps is determined by:

$$Res_{d_n} = \{(\neg t_{i_j}, \neg s_{i_j})\}$$

where $s_{i_j}$ represents the $j$ ground literals included in the refutation tree of the source domain and $t_{i_j}$ are the $j$ resulting ground literals of the elaboration step.

$$Res_{d_i} = Res_{d_{i+1}} \setminus \{(t_{i_j}, s_{i_j})\} \cup \{(\neg l_{t_i}, \neg l_{s_i})\}$$

where $s_{i_j} \in Res_{s_{i+1}}$, $Cl_{s_i}\Theta_{Cl_i} = l_{s_i} \vee \neg s_{i_1} \ldots \vee \neg s_{i_k}$, $\langle Res_{s_i}, Cl_{s_i}, \Theta_{Cl_i} \rangle \in Tree$ and $0 < i < n$.

Forward chaining suceeds if the resolvent $Res_{d_1}$ contains both examples.

The unknown clauses $Cl_{t_i} = l_{t_i} \vee \neg t_{i_1}, \ldots, \neg t_{i_k}$ are conjectured using $M_{repl}$

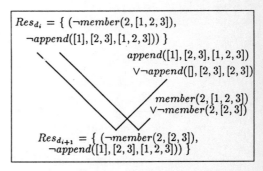

Figure 7: Refutation with a double resolvent

and the instantiated clauses $Cl_{s_i}$.

$$M_{repl}(l_{s_i} \vee \neg s_{i_1} \ldots \vee \neg s_{i_k}) =$$

$$l_{t_i} \vee \neg t_{i_1}, \ldots, \vee \neg t_{i_k}$$

The result of the evaluation step is a refutation tree of the target example with the instantiated clauses $Cl_{t_i}$. Figure 7 shows an example of a forward chaining step.

## 3.4 Consolidation

The last step called consolidation generalizes the conjectured rules of the previous step. For this purpose we use the term replacement set $M_{term}$ and the substitutions of the refutation tree generated during the recognition step. Thus, generalization is performed through inverse substitution as defined by

$$\Theta_{is_k}(\Theta_{Cl_k}) =$$

$$\Theta_{is_k}(\{\ldots, X_j \rightarrow arg_{s_j}, \ldots\}) =$$

$$\begin{cases} \{\ldots, ((arg_{t_i}, i) \rightarrow X_i) \ldots\} \\ \quad : \quad (arg_{t_i}, i, arg_{s_j}, j) \in M_{term} \\ \{\ldots, ((arg_{t_i}, i) \rightarrow X_i) \ldots\} \\ \quad : \quad (f(arg_{t_i}), i, f(arg_{s_j}), j) \in M_{term} \\ \{\ldots, (), \ldots\} \quad : \quad otherwise \end{cases}$$

where $\Theta_{Cl_k}$ are the substitutions of the recognition step and $M_{term}$ is the term replacement set. $f$ is a mapping relation for two argument terms.

---

$M_{term}$: $\{(member, append)$
$((2, 1, [2,3], 2), ([1,2,3], 2, [1,2,3], 3))\}$

$\Theta_{Cl_k}$:
$\{$ X→1, T→[], L→[2,3], T1→[2,3])$\}$

$\Theta_{is_k}(\Theta_{Cl_k}) =$
$\{((2,1)\rightarrow L),((1,2)\rightarrow X),(([2,3],2)\rightarrow T1)\}$

---

Figure 8: The inverse substitution

Figure 8 shows an example of establishing the inverse substitution. For instance, the application of the first rule of $\Theta_{is_k}$ to

the substitution (X→1) of $\Theta_{Cl_k}$ results in the inverse substitution $((2,1)\rightarrow L)$.

The inverse substitution is applied in order to generalize each literal of the conjectured clauses of the target domain as shown in figure 9. Using this procedure the *member* clause of the example is constructed. For instance, the inverse substitution $\Theta_{Cl_k}$ applied to member(2,[2,3]) results in member(L,T1).

---

$\Theta_{is_k}(\Theta_{Cl_k}) =$
$\{((2,1)\rightarrow L),((1,2)\rightarrow X),(([2,3],2)\rightarrow T1)\}$

$(\Theta_{is}\Theta_{Cl_k})(member(2,[1,2,3])) =$
  member(L,[X|T1])

$(\Theta_{is}\Theta_{Cl_k})(member(2,[2,3])) =$
  member(L,T1)

**Result:**
  member(L,[X|T1]) ← member(L,T1)

---

Figure 9: A consolidation step

## 4 Concluding Remarks

In this paper we introduced MARs, a tool for defining new Prolog predicates by analogy. Particular methods are presented for each of the four steps of the analogical reasoning process. The main contribution of MARs is that it is a logically well founded but simple model of analogical reasoning. However, MARs has to be evaluated in more detail and to be extended to be applicable for more complex kinds of analogy.

We plan to improve MARs along serveral lines. First, applying MARs to other analogical pairs of predicates, e.g. *union* ~ *intersection* or *sumlist* ~ *multlist*, has shown that it is useful to submit more than one example or to use an oracle. In many cases the information included in the term mappings and the source proof tree is not sufficent to determine the correct target literals. For instance, using more examples, e.g. $union([], [2,3], [2,3])$, $union([1,2], [2,3], [1,2,3])$, in addition to the analogical example $union([1,2], [2,3], [1,2,3]) \sim intersection([1,2], [2,3], [2])$ makes it possible to define $union$ analogically to $intersection$ without asking an oracle.

Second, we intend to resolve the limitations on the structure of the known predicates that have to be very similar. Especially the treatment of the predicates appearing in the proof tree of an example but not in the replacement list has to be investigated in more detail.

Third, we plan to apply MARs to other domains like language processing in order to define new grammar rules analogically. Comparing grammar rules shows that they are often very similar especially in their structure so that an analogical definition will succeed in many cases. Using the DCG formalism to describe grammar rules makes it possible to use MARs because the grammar rules can be treated in a similar way as logical predicates.

# References

[Burstein 86] M. Burstein. Incremental learning from multiple analogies. In R. Michalski, J. Carbonell und T. Mitchell (Hrsg.), *Machine Learning: An Artificial Intelligence Approach*. Morgan Kaufmann, 1986.

[Carbonell 83] J. Carbonell. Learning by analogy: Formulating and generalizing plans from past experience. In R. Michalski, J. Carbonell und T. Mitchell (Hrsg.), *Machine Learning: An Artificial Intelligence Approach*. Tioga, 1983.

[Gentner 88] D. Gentner. Analogical inference and analogical access. In A. Prieditis (Hrsg.), *Analogica*. Morgan Kaufmann, 1988.

[Greiner 88] R. Greiner. *Learning by understanding analogies*. PhD thesis, Stanford University, 1988.

[Hall 89] R. P. Hall. Computational approaches to analogical reasoning: A comparative analysis. *Artificial Intelligence*, 39:3–120, 1989.

[KedarCabelli 88] S. Kedar-Cabelli. Towards a computational model of purpose-directed analogy. In A. Prieditis (Hrsg.), *Analogica*. Morgan Kaufmann, 1988.

[MuggletonBuntine 88] S. Muggleton und W. Buntine. Machine invention of first-order predicates by inverting resolution. In A. Arbor (Hrsg.), *Fifth International Conference on Machine Learning*. Morgan Kaufmann, 1988.

[Wirth 89] R. Wirth. *Lernverfahren zur Vervollständigung von Hornklauselmengen durch inverse Resolution*. Doktorarbeit, Institut für Informatik, Universität Stuttgart, 1989.

# CASE-BASED LEARNING OF STRATEGIC KNOWLEDGE

BEATRIZ LOPEZ  ENRIC PLAZA
Institut d'Investigació en Intel·ligència Artificial
CEAB-CSIC, Camí de Santa Bàrbara, 17300 Blanes, Catalunya, Spain
bea@ceab.es, plaza@ceab.es

*Research partially supported by CICYT 801/90 Massive Memory Project and Esprit II 2148 Valid Project.*

## Abstract

In this paper we describe BOLERO, a case-based reasoner that learns strategic knowledge (plans) to improve the problem-solving capabilities of an expert system. As a planner, BOLERO is a reactive planner that when gathering new observations can immediately generate a new plan to cope with the new situations. As a learner, BOLERO is capable of learning strategies from observation of the problem-solving performed by a teacher. From this experience, BOLERO plans strategies that solve new problems. BOLERO learns from success and failure during its problem-solving process. An evaluation to measure the efficiency of BOLERO is performed by comparing the system's results against both the correct solution of a case and the solutions provided by different domain experts. BOLERO has been proved useful in acquiring strategic knowledge and in refining existing strategies, in a real-life expert system for pneumonia diagnosis.

**Keywords:** Strategy learning, case-based learning, planing, control knowledge.

## 1. Introduction

When approaching the application of machine learning techniques to the knowledge acquisition process of expert systems it is important to know what are the main problems today for building expert systems. In a recent study developed at Carnegie Group on the building of expert systems the surprising result was that the major effort (50%) of knowledge engineers was dealing with the uncontrolable interaction among rules and assuring that the proper sequence of goals and rule chainings is achieved during problem solving (Carbonell 1990). In this paper we show how this issue can be solved through the automatic acquisition of strategies that control the behavior of a rule-base. Strategies are acquired by case-based learning techniques by observing the problem-solving behavior of an expert and by learning from the system's own case-based problem-solving.

In this paper we describe BOLERO, a system that learns strategies to improve solving capabilities in expert systems. Problem solving strategies avoid to explore the whole search space for a problem, focus the process to the most likely solutions (as human experts are able to do), and reduce the number of observations or questions made to the user (low cost solution). Thus learning strategies means to learn efficient ways of solving problems.

Usually strategies are present in expert systems as control knowledge. Control knowledge is in charge of the goal/subgoal decomposition of a task, the detection of an end-condition, etc. For example, in pneumonia diagnosis, to validate the hypothesis *anemia* control knowledge splits the search in several subgoals as *hypoproliferates*, *hyperproliferates*, and *maturing defect*. Control knowledge can be explicitly separated from domain knowledge (e.g. using meta-level rules as in TEIRESIAS (Davis, 84), MILORD (Godo et al., 89), and MU (Cohen, 87)) or implicitly coded in the ordering of rules. The aim of BOLERO is to provide an expert system with the capability of learning a strategic knowledge base, in order to control the execution of the problem solving of that expert system. An overview of BOLERO is shown in figure 1. Learning in BOLERO has two modes: the training mode and the performance mode. In the training mode BOLERO learns strategies from observation of a teacher solving a set of problems. The goal of the training mode is that BOLERO acquires an initial set of strategies from a teacher. Learned strategies are organised in a dynamic memory as we will see in section 2.

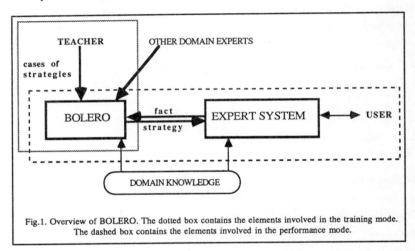

Fig.1. Overview of BOLERO. The dotted box contains the elements involved in the training mode. The dashed box contains the elements involved in the performance mode.

During the performance mode, BOLERO builds up strategies to solve a new problem. A new strategy is the result of the combination of one or more strategies of cases in memory. Strategies are constructed dynamically, according to the observable data provided for the current problem, and they are executed by an expert system[1]. Two new opportunities to learn are possible in the performance mode when solving a problem: (i) when BOLERO succeeds in solving the current problem and incorporates it in memory for future use, and (ii) when the strategy fails to achieve a good solution. The performance mode is described in section 3.

---

[1]The expert system only contains domain knowledge, and no strategic knowledge whatsoever is provided. The architecture of the expert system (based on MILORD [Godo et al., 89]) is linked to BOLERO via a plan interpreter that schedules the problem solving of the domain knowledge sources accordingly.

The performance mode needs some criteria to know how good is a strategy (solution) planned by BOLERO. This has lead us to develop an evaluation process where BOLERO results are compared against the teacher results as well as other domain experts. With this multi-expert evaluation we avoid to mimetize the teacher's behavior. BOLERO's evaluation is described in section 4. Finally in section 5 we sketch some implementation considerations and in section 6 a discussion of the system is performed.

## 1.1. BOLERO framework

The objects that play the main role in BOLERO are strategies, and cases. An strategy is represented by a sequence of goals considered along the problem solving and that lead to a problem solution. A case is a sequence of steps (problem states) performed to solve a problem. A step $S(t)$ consists of the observed facts $F(t)$ known up to time $t$, and the current goal $G(t)$ the problem solver (human or machine) is considering at time $t$ given $F(t)$ (see table 1). The problem solver chooses, at each step, which information to ask or gather from the environment such that is the most useful for achieving the most recent goal $G(t-1)$. Figure 2 summarises a case using two conventions: first, only the steps where the current goal is changed are shown, and second, only the new data gathered during the interval in which a given goal is current are shown.

$$S(t) = <F(t), G(t)>$$
$$F(t) = \{f \mid f \in \text{Facts and } f \text{ is known at time } t\}$$
$$F(t+1) \supset F(t) \qquad |F(t+1)| = |F(t)| + 1$$
$$G(t) \in \text{Goals}$$

**Table 1.** Definition of a step

As an example, case *C05v1* of figure 2 is a case of pneumonia diagnosis, where in step 2 the goal *pneumococcus* was considered, and in step 3 *injured lobes* was asked, allowing the teacher to conclude the goal: *(pneumococcus very-possible)*. Immediately, the teacher focuses on a new goal, namely *enterobacteriaceae*, as suggested by the data available up to *t=3* (see step 3 in figure 2). A special step 0 is required in order to start the diagnostic process. Step 0 contains a default goal (the *acquire-general-data* goal, used to start gathering data from the user). We will distinguish between *training-cases* and *problem-cases*. Training-cases are problems already solved (i. e.past experiences). Problem-cases are cases being solved.

Two assumptions should be made before using BOLERO. The first one is that we assume that a domain knowledge base (DKB) is already existing in the expert system for which BOLERO learns strategic knowledge. No new learning is performed on domain knowledge and the DKB organisation is known and used by BOLERO in both training and performance modes. The second one is that we have a kind of oracle, as for example a teacher, a domain expert, a book, etc., that can be used by BOLERO as a model of performance.

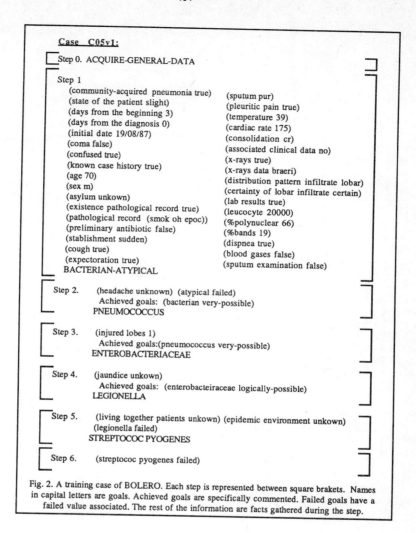

Fig. 2. A training case of BOLERO. Each step is represented between square brakets. Names in capital letters are goals. Achieved goals are specifically commented. Failed goals have a failed value associated. The rest of the information are facts gathered during the step.

## 2. Learning by observation

The training mode aim is to provide a knowledge base of strategies to BOLERO. The training set consists of training-cases. Training-cases are organised in BOLERO's memory as a tree where each node keeps information about a step, i. e. Node(i) = <F(i), G(i)>. Training-cases are split along the tree in such a way that to recover them it is necessary to follow the paths from the root to the leaves of the tree (see figure 3). A strategy associated with a node is the sequence of goals found in the path from the root to that node. For example, the strategy associated with the node <N5> of figure 3 is the sequence of the goals from *acquired-general-data* goal to the goal *legionella* stored in node <N5>, i. e. (*acquire-general-data, bacterian-atipical, pneumococcus. enterobacteriaceae, legionella*). Facts of nodes are used as indexes to remind nodes from facts. These indexes will play an important role when retrieving past experiences to solve new problems (see section 3.1).

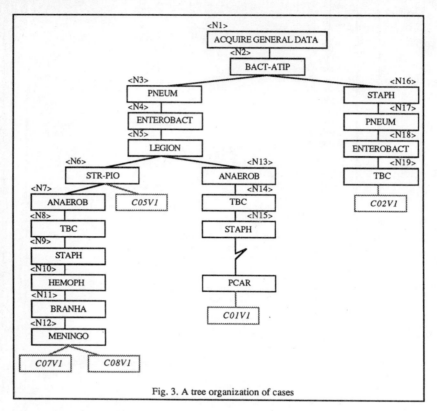

Fig. 3. A tree organization of cases

The learning by observation consists of two main processes: the incorporation process and the generalisation process. The incorporation process is in charge of the incorporation of a single training-case in memory, re-organizing the current memory. The generalisation process helps the incorporation process when different facts present in the training-case and other nodes need to be generalised. Before processing any training-case the tree is empty. During learning by observation, the incorporation of training-cases is performed incrementally training-case by training-case, for a set of training-cases provided by the teacher.

## 2.1 Incorporation process

BOLERO incorporates the problem solving it observes from a training-case into the memory tree. Before incorporating a training-case, BOLERO analyses the strategy in order to assure that goals only appears once along the strategy. Very often goals are tried but abandoned because some evidence focuses the problem solving to a different goal and afterwards these goals are retrieved and achieved. The incorporation process rationalises the sequences of goals, erasing duplicate goals and maintaining each goal in the last place where it occurs. Failed goals are kept in the strategy because their failure may be relevant. The result of this rationalisation is the strategy incorporated to the system´s memory.For example suppose that the original strategy of a training-case is the following: $(g_a, g_b, g_a, g_c, g_d)$. $g_a$ is tried, $g_b$ is tried and achieved, $g_a$ is tried again and achieved this time,$g_c$ is tried and failed, and $g_d$ is tried and achieved. Then BOLERO rationalises the strategy as $(g_b, g_a, g_c, g_d)$ and incorporates it to the memory as a training case. [2]

```
Procedure Incorporate-Case(C)
Let C be the current training-case with steps {S1, ... Sk}
     where Si=<Fc(i), Gc(i)>
Let N={Root}
Let i=1
While ∃ n ∈ N such that Gc(i)=Gn(i) for n=<Fn(i), Gn(i)>
     Let Fn(i) = Generalize(Fc(i),Fn(i))
     Let i = i+ 1
     Let N = sons(n)
Let n' = Create-Node(parent(p), Si) where p∈N
∀j, k≥j≥i+1
     Let n'=Create-Node(n', Sj)

Procedure Create-Node(parent, Sj)
     Let M be a new node  with <Fc(i), Gc(i)>
     Let Parent(M)=parent
     Return M
```

**Table 2.** Incorporation of a training-case in memory

A training-case is added to the tree by successively comparing the goal of its $i$-step against any node at the $i$-level of the tree. If no node $n$ (of the $i$-level) has a goal that matches the goal of the $i$-step, then the facts of the $i$-step and the facts of the node $n$ are generalised, and the result is updated in the node $n$. Then the process continues with the step $i+1$ of the training-case and the nodes in the level $i+1$ of the memory tree the ancestor of which is the node $n$. This process is performed for all steps of the current training-case. If any node is found that matches the goal of step $i$ of the training-case, then a new branch of the tree is started from the level $i-1$, and the rest of the steps of the training-case become new nodes from level $i$ to level $k$ where step $k$ is the last step of the tree. Each new node is created from a step of the training-case. In table 2 the algorithm is shown.

## 2.2 Generalisation process

The construction of the memory tree involves a generalisation process such that facts stored on each node are the result of a generalisation of the facts of the nodes that are placed under that node. The generalisation process is based on the hierarchies defined in the domain knowledge that establish different kinds of relations between facts. For example the facts *cardiocirculatory clinical data*, , *hematopoietical clinical data, neurological clinical data, cutaneous scars* (and others) are of type *associated clinical data*

---

[2]The rationalization process reduces the case storage in memory since different strategies are mapped to the same memory representation. Nevertheless, this simplification does not affect the capability of generating new strategies which restart abanded goals due to BOLERO´s reactive planning, as explained in section 4.1.

and can be generalised to *(associated clinical data true)*. Values of facts are generalised depending on its type. Integers are generalised by using intervals relevant to the application. The generalisation of two enumerated values is the union of the values. The generalisation of two uncertain values is the lowest value. Most of the generalisations are performed as in the ARC system (Plaza & López de Mantaras, 90).

## 3. BOLERO's problem solving

Once BOLERO has some knowledge about strategies in the memory tree, the system is applied to solve new problems. As a case-based reasoner, the basic mechanism of BOLERO is as follows:

0. Start with a default strategy (the strategy associated to the root of the tree) until new evidence is found.
1. Retrieve from memory the nodes more similar to the current situation (i. e. the facts known up to a time $t$ of the current problem-case). If the retrieved nodes coincide with the last retrieved nodes then go to 3.
2. Construct a new strategy by adapting the strategies of the retrieved nodes.
3. Execute the constructed strategy onto the problem-case (until $t+\partial$ where new evidence is achieved), then go to 1.
4. Stop when the current strategy has been completed.

Notice that BOLERO acts as a reactive planner: anytime the current situation changes, the strategy executed by the system can be interrupted by the activation of new nodes in memory which suggest a better strategy, the new strategy is then constructed and executed immediately. When solving problems, BOLERO acts as the control knowledge component of the cycle of execution of an expert system. It proposes to the expert system a strategy to follow, and the expert system executes it until a new fact is obtained. BOLERO analyzes the new fact and decides whether to proceed with the same strategy or change to a new one.

BOLERO´s problem solving strongly depends on how the retrieval of nodes are performed and how the strategies of the retrieved nodes are adapted to solve the current problem-case. The following subsections explain how retrieval and strategy adaptation is performed.

### 3.1 Retrieval

The retrieval of nodes is performed by matching the known facts of the current problem-case $F(t)$ against facts stored in nodes. This matching is performed incremented for the most recently obtained fact *(current fact)*. The matching is the same as the matching of the generalisation process in the training mode. Facts are indexes to nodes, as has been stated in (section 2), and this allows BOLERO to retrieve only the nodes that contain the current-fact or the facts that match the current fact. The matching score for a node is computed as follows:

1. For each fact that exactly matches the current fact in a node it scores 1.

```
1.   Let A = {e₁, e₂, ..., eₙ} such that
     ∀ eᵢ, score(eᵢ) > threshold (threshold is given) and
     ∀ eᵢ, eⱼ, if  i < j, then score(eᵢ) > score(eⱼ).
3.If e₁ is a node, and
          ∀ eᵢ ∈ A, i > 1, score(e₁) >> score(eᵢ)
     then return strategy(e₁)
4.   Otherwise,
     Let B = {e₁, e₂, ..., eᵦ} where ß is given.
     If ∃ a node nₖ, such that
          ∀ eᵢ ∈ B, strategy(eᵢ) ⊃ strategy(nₖ)
     then return strategy(nₖ).
5.   Otherwise return strategy(e₁).
```

**Table 3**. Adaptation of a new strategy

2. A score $\lambda$ is assigned to facts of a node that partially match the current fact (Plaza & López de Mántaras, 90)

3. Finally for all nodes activated a normalised total score is computed based on the scores of their facts.

In order to elaborate the current strategy only one node or few ones are chosen to construct the strategy. This second selection is based on the following criteria:(a) select a node if it has a score far higher than the rest, and (b) if neither one is found, then select only the first ß nodes (ß is given)

## 3.2 Strategy adaptation

Once BOLERO has one or ß nodes most similar to the current problem-case, it constructs the strategy adapting the strategies of the selected nodes. Adaptation is performed as follows: if there is only one node selected, the strategy of such node is applied to the current problem-case. Otherwise BOLERO looks for a common ancestor for the ß nodes in the memory tree. The strategy of the node identified as the lowest common ancestor is taken as a partial strategy to be followed in the current stage of problem-solving. However, the strategy of the common ancestor may be already executed, and therefore there is no guarantee that the common ancestor can propose a strategy useful for the current stage of problem-solving. If a useful common ancestor cannot be found, then the strategy of the highest score node is applied. Table 3 sketches the algorithm followed.

This process is performed for each new fact available for the current problem-case. So a different and better strategy can be decided anytime the system obtains new information. The problem solving process stops when the selected strategy finishes executing the current problem-case. Then the expert system gives a *domain solution* (e. g. the solution shown in figure 4). This domain solution has been achieved following a strategy that we will call from now on the *solution strategy*.

Once BOLERO has solved the current problem-case, it is incorporated in the memory organisation of cases by using the incorporation process described in section 2.1, as it was a training-case. If the problem-case has been solved according to a strategy of a node already in memory, this incorporation will cause only new generalisations of facts attached to nodes. However BOLERO's knowledge of strategies is refined when the solution strategy was not already in memory.

```
Solution set for case B13v1
        Bacterian pneumonia          Quite possible
        Pneumococcus pneumonia       Possible
        Clamydia                     Slightly possible
        Hemophylus                   Very low chance
        Tuberculosis                 Very low chance

        Fig. 4. A domain solution of the expert system
```

# 4. Learning by BOLERO´s own experience

BOLERO learns from success and failure through strategic memory refinement. To know the success of BOLERO performance we have developed an evaluation process that will be described in section 4. Refinement from success occurs when the solution of the problem-case is successful and the solution strategy is different of any other in memory. Refinement from failure occurs when the domain solution of the problem is rejected in the evaluation process.

## 4.1 Learning from success

As we have seen, BOLERO solves a new problem by dynamically adapting strategies of nodes according to the data known at each problem solving state. As a result of this reactive planning, the strategy $Str(C)$ constructed for solving a problem-case $C$ is the sequence of the effective followed parts of the strategies BOLERO generated during problem solving. This emergent strategy $Str(C)$, although based on past strategies, can be a *novel strategy* (i. e. $Str(C)$ is different from any past strategy in memory). BOLERO can therefore learn new strategies from its own successful problem solving when including the new strategies in memory.

For instance, suppose that in a given moment BOLERO´s strategic knowledge is represented as in figure 5(a). A new problem-case $Cn$ is being solved. At the beginning a strong match was produced against node $<N5>$ (corresponding to the training-case $C1$), but progressively the match against node $<N9>$ (corresponding to the training-case $C2$ ) increases, and the final execution of the case $Cn$ follows that of node $<N5>$ (fig 5(b)). Finally the execution of case $Cn$ is completed and the strategy followed by $Cn$ is the sequence of parts of the strategies of both nodes, $<N5>$ and $<N9>$. That is *(acquire-general-data, bacterian-atypical, pneumococcus, enterobacteriaceae)* from $<N5>$ and *(staphilococcus, tuberculosis)* from $<N9>$. Note that when a change of strategy is performed, goals already achieved are not repeated (in the example: *pneumococcus* and *enterobacteriaceae*). So in the problem-case $Cn$ BOLERO has followed a strategy not explicitly known before. Therefore when the problem-case $Cn$ is incorporated in memory, BOLERO´s organisation of past experiences is refined as shown in figure 5(c).

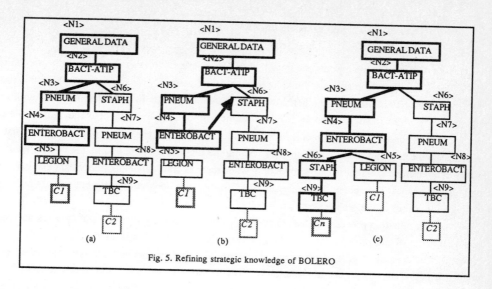

Fig. 5. Refining strategic knowledge of BOLERO

## 4.2 Learning from failure

The second opportunity to learn arises when the solution of the current problem-case is rejected. A strategy is evaluated as a bad solution and rejected, as we will see in section 5, when a set of goals that should have been pursued were not considered in the solution strategy. BOLERO has two options to correct the failure and avoid it in the future. The first option is using the training mode: BOLERO asks to the teacher for the correct strategy solution and the problem-case is incorporated in memory. The second option is goal exploration: BOLERO continues generating a new strategy for achieving goals that have not yet been tried but should have been tried and achieved. BOLERO´s method to learn from failure is to select a strategy from the set of nodes activated in the performance mode but whose strategy has not yet been executed for the current problem-case. A new strategy is generated and BOLERO tries to prove new goals until the solution is accepted by the evaluation process. When the solution strategy is accepted it is incorporated in BOLERO's memory. Although the new strategies generated by BOLERO are based on past experience, the search performed (i. e. the goals that are pursued) is less focussed in goal exploration than usual. For this reason, when incorporating the problem-case into memory, the goals that have been tried but not successfully established after the failure are not incorporated into memory as part of the problem-solving strategy of the current problem-case. Note that BOLERO assumes domain knowledge in DKB correct, i. e., goals achieved by the solution strategy cannot be false positives. Although the system does not store the negative results of failing it learns from failure in the sense that repairs the wrong solution (using the teacher advice or thru goal exploration) and therefore prevents those failures to occur again.

## 5. Evaluation of BOLERO´s strategies

As we stated in the introduction, BOLERO has some criteria to evaluate the domain solution of the current problem-case. One solution could be to ask to the teacher for his opinion. However this method will lead to mimetize the teacher´s behavior. Our approach consists in providing BOLERO with a gold standard with which it can compare its results with the help of a teacher. The gold standard can be either the known correct domain solution or different solutions given by several domain experts. The first kind of gold standards is not always available. In pneumonia diagnosis, for example, the correct solution is rarely known. In fact, diagnoses are known only when there is conclusive laboratory data that isolates the pathogenic agent[3]. The second kind of gold standard involves consulting different experts opinions to evaluate the results of the problem-cases solved by BOLERO.

The evaluation process consists in comparing the solution provided by BOLERO against the gold standard. First of all, the success or failure of BOLERO's solution is assessed. If successful, we also evaluate the focusing degree of the solution strategy. Success in problem solving is assessed by two conditions: (1) if the correct domain solution is available, BOLERO's solution is correct when it includes all the domain solutions established by the gold standard[4], and (2) also it is mandatory that the set of achieved goals of the solution strategy provided by BOLERO includes the achieved goals of the solution strategy suggested by the teacher.

Once BOLERO gets past this first stage of the evaluation, the system's solution is accepted and it is possible to measure the focusing degree of the solution strategy. We can have different degrees of focussing depending on the solution strategy of BOLERO:

•Loss of focusing: when BOLERO has considered some goals not considered by any expert and no result is obtained, then we can say that BOLERO has lost focusing

•Averaged solution: when the domain solutions proposed by BOLERO are not identical to those established by the teacher, but the goals not present in the solution have been considered by other domain experts, then we can say that the solution strategy of BOLERO is an averaged solution.

## 6. Implementation

The first application chosen to develop BOLERO is a pneumonia diagnosis expert system, Pneumon-IA, built using the MILORD shell[5].. The pneumonia application has been implemented by a

---

[3]But most of the clinical cases of the application we have use to develop BOLERO do not contain this data, because most patients can be cured by expert physicians without lab tests, which are expensive and slow. The set of cases with correct solution is highly biased towards dangerous cases due to a complicated evolution of patients.

[4] We assume that the expert system to which BOLERO plans strategies deals with uncertain information. So instead of a unique solution, the result of the system is a set of possible solutions with different degrees certainty (see for a example fig. 4).

[5]Briefly described MILORD is an expert system shell whose main features are its multilevel architecture and its uncertainty management method [Godo et al., 89].The modularity of having separate

knowledge engineer along all the different knowledge levels of MILORD. We have taken Pneumon-IA as a whole and used it as a teacher for BOLERO. Moreover, when we disable the strategic knowledge of Pneumon-IA, the expert system is useful to test the strategies generated by BOLERO. Pneumon-IA was validated in 1989 by comparing its results against other five domain experts and Pneumon-IA scored as the second best expert among them (Verdaguer, 89). Of the 86 cases the results of 10 cases where exactly known due to the patients lab tests. The evaluation criteria described in section 5 has been applied using the 86 pneumonia cases and the diagnoses of the five expert physicians on all those cases.

BOLERO has been developed using PCL in a SUN machine. The mechanism of indexing in BOLERO is implemented using a spreading-activation mechanism that simulates the parallelism of marker-passing techniques (see Kolodner, 87). Our future research agenda includes implementing the parallelism of marker-passing techniques in an hypercube IPSC/2 multicomputer for memory search and retrieval.

Table 4 shows some evaluation results on the behavior of BOLERO after testing 10 problem-cases. We can say that BOLERO performance is as good as Pneumon-IA but tens to be less focused. That is, BOLERO learns to consider all the goals Pneumon-IA would have pursued (see first row in Table 4). Moreover sometimes BOLERO considers some goals not pursued in Pneumon-IA. Some are irrelevant but but others were indeed considered by other experts, and whose processing have produced positive results (row 2 in Table 4). The exact goal ordering used in Pneumon-IA is not respected by BOLERO; but they are generally very close in their execution order, so the change of order does not have meaningful consequences.

| Training Cases | 16 | 36 | 46 | 76 |
|---|---|---|---|---|
| Successes | 40% | 40% | 40% | 90% |
| Missing goals | 2.33 | 2.16 | 2 | 2 |
| Averaged Solution | 30% | 20% | 20% | 30% |
| Averaged goals | 2.66 | 3 | 2 | 1.3 |
| Loss of focus | 5.62 | 5.10 | 4.50 | 4.31 |

**Table 4**. Evaluation of BOLERO for four suites of training cases and 10 problem-cases. Success measures the cases in which BOLERO achieves the correct domain solution. Missing goals are the mean number of missed goals in a failed case. Averaged solution measures the number cases where bolero achived goals relevant to other experts but not considered by the teacher. Averaged goals are the mean number of those goals. Loss of focus measures the number of goals in a case considered by BOLERO but could not be achieved. The averaged length of the teacher solution provided for the same 10 problem-cases is 17,3 goals. Pneumon-IA has a total of 35 goals.

levels for different kinds of knowledge (strategic & plan levels for strategic knowledge, metarules & domain levels for domain knowledge) allows the connection of BOLERO´s strategic reasoning and learning with the domain level of MILORD in a clean way.

# 7. Conclusion and discussion

Most of the methods developed in machine learning deal with concept learning. In this paper, however, we introduce a system that learns strategies to solve problems in expert systems. A previous work on acquiring strategic knowledge is ASK (Gruber, 89), an acquisition tool to elicit strategic knowledge from experts. Although ASK learns strategic rules, the kernel of ASK is based on an interactive dialogue between the system and the domain expert. Besides, ASK has been proved efficient when refining an existing strategic knowledge base but it is hard to build strategic knowledge from scratch. The method to acquire strategic knowledge we propose is useful both for learning strategies from scratch and for refining strategies already learned as we have seen along the paper. Moreover, BOLERO learns from success and failures while ASK only learns from failure. Learning control knowledge has also been done using machine learning techniques like explanation-based learning (EBL) in (Minton, Carbonell, Etizioni, Knoblock & Kuokka, 87). Although there is much research in EBL with imperfect theories, EBL seems to impose strict conditions on the type of knowledge needed. Our case-based approach is more germane to AI research on planing and does not require any of those strong requirements.

We can view strategies as plans, and from this perspective we can relate BOLERO with the CHEF system (Hammond, 89) CHEF is a case-based planning system whose aim is to reuse plans. CHEF learns by correctly indexing its planning experiences in memory as BOLERO does. Both systems generalise the features used to index cases in order to make plans applicable in similar but not identical situations. However, the mechanism of indexing in CHEF is based on a pre-selected group of features, while in BOLERO all features are used. Another important difference between CHEF and BOLERO is that the former constructs one-shot plans. Instead, BOLERO is a reactive planner: as gathering new observations the system can generate a new plan to cope with the new situation. This difference stems from the need of CHEF to work only with complete information (i. e. CHEF starts planning only when all information is available to the system). BOLERO is instead designed to plan in uncertain environments: information is usually incomplete, and the information is gathered (as specified by domain knowledge) only if it is relevant for the goals the system has decided to be worth pursuing.

In the future we plan to apply BOLERO to the learning of strategies for a rheumatology diagnosis expert system. We are also thinking to use the prototypicality of exemplars defined in PROTOS and ARC (Plaza & López de Mantaras., 90) in the definition of the matching function of the performance mode. Another improvement we are planning is to identify sub-strategies, that is, a very similar (but not exact) sequence of goals that appears quite often as a part of different strategies.

ACKNOWLEDGEMENTS

We are indebted with Ramon López de Mántaras and Walter van de Welde who red previous versions of this paper, providing a lot of useful suggestions and comments. Research partially supported by CICYT 801/90 Massive Memory Project and Esprit II 2148 Valid Project.

# References

Bareiss E.R., Porter B.W.& Wier C.C. Protos: An exemplar-based learning apprentice, *Proc. 4th International Workshop on Machine Learning*, University of California, Irvine, 1987.

Carbonell J., Personal Communication, 1990.

Cohen P.R. The control of reasoning under uncertainty: A discussion of some programs, COINS Technical Report 87-81, University of Massachusetts, Amherst, 1987.

Davis R. Interactive transfer of expertise, *Rule-Based Expert Systems.*, Edited by B.G. Buchanan & E.H. Shortliffe, Addison-Wesley, 1984.

Godo L., López de Màntaras R., Sierra C.& Verdaguer A. MILORD: The architecture and the management of linguistically expressed uncertainty, *International Journal of Intelligent Systems*, Vol. 4, Num. 4, Winter 1989.

Gruber T.R. *The acquisition of strategic knowledge*, Academic Press, Inc., 1989.

Hammond K.J. *Case-Based Planning*. Academic Press Inc., 1989.

Kodratoff Y.& Ganascia J.G. Improving the generalization step in learning, *Machine Learning*, Vol. II, Morgan Kaufmann Pub., 1986.

Kolodner J.L. Retrieving events from a case memory: A parallel implementation, *DARPA Workshop on Case-Based Reasoning*, 1987.

Minton S., Carbonell J.G., Etzioni O., Knoblock C.A.& Kuokka D.R. Acquiring effective search control rules: Explanation-based learning in the PRODIGY system, *Proc. 4th International Workshop on Machine Learning*, University of California, Irvine, 1987.

Plaza E.& López de Màntaras R. ARC: Learning typicality knowledge from fuzzy examples, In Ras, Zemankova, Emrich (Eds.), *Methodologies for Intelligent systems 5*, p. 420-427. North-Holland, 1990.

Verdaguer, A. *PNEUMON-IA: Desenvolupament i validació d'un sistema expert d'ajuda al diagnòstic mèdic*, PhD. Thesis, Universitat Autònoma de Barcelona, July 1989.

# Learning in Distributed Systems
# and Multi-Agent Environments

### P. Brazdil[1]   M. Gams[2]   S. Sian[3]
### L.Torgo[1]   W. van de Velde[4] *

[1] LIACC-CIUP, Rua Campo Alegre, 823, 4100 Porto, Portugal
E-mail: pbrazdil@nccup.ctt.pt  (later pbrazdil@liacc.up.pt)

[2] Jozef Stefan Institute, Jamova 39, 61000 Ljubljana, Yugoslavia
E-mail: mezi@ijs.ac.mail.yu

[3] Imperial College, Department of Computing, 180 Queen´s Gate
London SW7 2BZ, UK.  E-mail: sss@doc.ic.ac.uk

[4] Vrije Universitaet, AI Lab., Pleinlaan 2, B-1050 Brussels, Belgium
E-mail: walter@arti.vub.ac.be

## Abstract

The paper begins with the discussion on why we should be concerned with machine learning in the context of distributed AI. The rest of the paper is dedicated to various problems of multi-agent learning. First, a common framework for comparing different existing systems is presented. It is pointed out that it is useful to distinguish *when* the individual agents communicate. Some systems communicate during the learning phase, others during the problem solving phase, for example. It is also important to consider *how,* that is in what language, the communication is established. The paper analyses several systems in this framework. Particular attention is paid to previous work done by the authors in this area. The paper covers use of redundant knowledge, knowledge integration, evaluation of hypothesis by a community of agents and resolution of language differences between agents.

**Keywords:** learning in distributed systems, multi-agent learning, evaluation of hypotheses, knowledge integration, use of redundant knowledge, resolution of language differences.

---

(*) This paper has been prepared with a specific purpose in mind - to provide a basis for the *Panel on Learning in Distributed Systems.* It was edited by P.Brazdil on the basis of the individual contributions received and/or papers made available. The names of the authors are shown in the alphabetic order.

# 1. Introduction

As Sian (1991) has pointed out many real world problems are best modelled using a set of cooperating intelligent systems (agents). There are many reasons that we could give to justify our position. First, our society consists of many interacting entities and so if we are interested to model some aspects of our society, our model needs to be structured. Also, as data often originates at different physical locations, centralized solutions are often inapplicable or inconvenient. Recent work in the field of *Distributed Artificial Intelligence* (DAI) and multi-agent systems (Huhns, 1987; Bond and Gasser, 1988; Durfee et al., 1989; Demazeau et al., 1991, etc.) has addressed the issues of organization, coordination and cooperation. The problems of multi-agent learning has, however, been largely ignored. One purpose of this paper is to address some issues that arise when studying ML in multi-agent systems.

Two rather different questions can be formulated in this context. First, how can multi-agent systems benefit from machine learning. Second, how can machine learning benefit from considering multi-agent set-up. As multi-agent systems are by nature complex, machine learning techniques may be the only way to achieve a robust and versatile system. The advantages of ML cannot be taken for granted, but rather have to be demonstrated in terms of its effects on cost, time, resources and product quality. One may envisage advantages defined in terms of ease of programming, maintenance, scope of application, efficiency and coordination of activity.

One may wonder why the researchers in machine learning should venture into an area so difficult as distributed AI. We believe that multi-agent learning will touch upon some of the fundamental issues of intelligence and learning that can be only understood in this context. Although communication seems to play an important role in human learning, so far this has not been studied much in ML.

Studying multi-agent learning may help us to design systems that are faster, thanks to the possibility of parallelism. Furthermore, the systems may become more robust when compared to single-agent systems. As has been shown by various authors (e.g. Gams, 1989; Buntine, 1989; Brazdil and Torgo, 1990 etc.) cross checking of results between different methods provides more reliable results.

The study of multi-agent learning poses new questions that need to be answered. For example, when should the individual systems cooperate and how. The purpose of this paper is to discuss several different approaches that have been taken. This discussion will not attempt to be exhaustive, but rather concentrate mainly on the work done in this area by the authors of this paper. However, an attempt will be made to present this work in a unified perspective and suggest directions for further work.

The paper is organized as follows. In Section 2 we shall briefly discuss autonomous agent learning. Section 3 will be dedicated to multi-agent learning. It will describe certain criteria that we can use when comparing different systems. This section describes several existing systems and approaches and is mainly oriented towards some earlier work done by the authors. The last section will discuss new horizons and future work.

# 2. Autonomous Agent Learning

Multi-agent learning could be seen as an extension of autonomous agent learning. But could the study of multi-agent learning really benefit from the results that have been achieved in autonomous learning?

The application of symbolic AI to robotics reveals one of its major weaknesses, namely that low-level processes are taken for granted. Much work on *learning robots* has therefore concentrated on learning the details of action execution and its effects, and on learning about the semantic relation between symbolic representations and reality which they represent[1]. Most of this work has been concerned with a single agent. There are some exceptions, however. For example, Alberto Segre´s ARMS system learns how to plan from observations of plan executions of a teacher agent. Furthermore, John Laird´s *Robo-Soar,* apart from being an application of SOAR to a real world and object manipulation task, permits accepting advice from another agent. In the *World Modellers Project* the goal was to experiment with learning from observations of another agent. The other agent appears solely in the role of a teacher and hence communication between the agents is of a somewhat special kind. Although the investigations into learning robots on a number of important issues, the questions related to communication, cooperation and goal definition have, in general, been left aside. This does not mean that this work is not of potential interest.

Mitchell (1990) describes an autonomous agent (THEO) as having three learning goals: becoming more perceptive, more correct and more reactive. At the moment there is no consensus as to how to map the learning goals to learning methods. Future work could provide some of the answers not only to the questions we have mentioned, but also to the following related issues. When is it better to reason and when to act? When should the system initiate learning and how long should it continue?

---

[1] The reader could consult (van de Velde, 1991) This collection of papers describes some recent advances in the area of autonomous agent learning.

# 3. Multi-Agent Learning Systems

Multi-agent systems which include one or more learning agents share some of the concerns of autonomous agent learning. For example, the issue of when to reason, or when to act is even more pertinent in this context. There are important distinctions between the two approaches. Multi-agent learning offers radically different solution to some of the problems in learning. A robot can become more correct (or more reactive) not only by learning from experience, but by communicating with other agents (artificial or human agents). No wonder that the attention of several researchers working in this area has turned to various architectural issues, all of which have something to do with communication. The design should determine *when*, *how* and *with what purpose* should the individual agents communicate. Various systems differ in how they approach these questions. Basically, the learning agents can communicate:

- before the learning / problem solving phase,
- during the problem solving phase,
- before the problem solving phase, but after the individual learning phase,
- during the individual learning phase.

Expressed differently, the agents can be involved in *distributed data gathering, distributed problem solving* or *distributed learning*. Of course various hybrid solutions may exist too.

## Distributed Data Gathering + Individual Learning and Problem Solving

Let us finally consider one rather trivial method that enables a number of agents to work on a learning task. All agents are involved in collecting data, but only one system is involved in learning. That is, all the data is transferred to the learning agent that incrementally updates its theory. As the purpose of this paper is not to discuss incremental learning methods, but rather systems with more complex interactions between agents, we shall let the interested reader consult appropriate literature (see e.g. Schlimmer and Fisher, 1988; Utgoff, 1988; Janikow, 1989).

## Individual Learning + Distributed Problem Solving

The system described in (Gams, 1989) exploits *redundant knowledge,* and is involved in *distributed problem solving*. It admits several agents with a learning capability, but these do not really communicate while learning is in progress. Different knowledge bases are taken into account when problems are being solved. As has been shown by Gams, this mode achieves a superior performance when compared to a system containing just one knowledge base.

An important issue in this work is how to combine the opinions of different agents. Generally certain confidence factor is associated with each decision and then some method is used to generate the final decision on the basis of the individual decisions.

We notice that distributed solutions need not necessarily involve weighing opinions of different agents. If agent $A_i$ is capable of dealing with a subset of given problems, and if this agent can be considered "sufficiently reliable", we do not need to worry about redundancy at all. The answer of one agent $A_i$ is sufficient. As in Shannon and Weaver's (1964) information theory, the amount of redundancy that is necessary seems to be related to the level of noise present in the data, and the level of uncertainty introduced in its processing. This argument has been put forward by Gams et al. (1990) and is supported by experimental results.

## Individual Learning + Knowledge Integration + Individual Problem Solving

The system described by Brazdil and Torgo (1990) attempts to integrate the knowledge acquired by individual agents. The integrated theory is then used by one of the agents to resolve problems.

The system works in three phases. In the first phase the agents go through individual learning. There are no interactions between the agents then. This phase is followed by knowledge integration. This process involves all agents in principle. Knowledge integration can be regarded as a special form of distributed (re-)learning. This process involves characterization of individual theories (or rules) on the basis of experimental tests. These provide the system with estimates of quality or utility of individual theories (rules). This method could be compared with the one used by Gams et al. mentioned earlier employing confidence factors. The quality estimates determine which theories (rules) should be included in the integrated theory.

Experimental results have shown that, in general, the integrated theory had a significantly better performance than the individual theories. We believe that this is due to the fact that redundant knowledge is properly exploited by this system. The knowledge integration method can be seen as a kind of "symbolic filter" for noisy knowledge (imperfect theories and noisy test data).

This approach differs from the one described earlier in several aspects. First, the system can resort to individual problem solving mode. Problems can be directed to the agent that has assembled the integrated theory (although this theory could be given to other agents too).

Problem solving is thus simpler and hence the whole system is more "reactive" if we use the term from autonomous agent learning. It is not necessary to consult the whole community of agents before giving an answer. It is interesting to ask question why this should be so.

As we have mentioned earlier, different agents are called upon many times, but this is done at knowledge integration time. The result of knowledge integration is stored for future use. Consequently one need not consult different agents later. The system of Gams does not attempt to construct such a theory, and so it is necessary to solicit opinions of other agents at problem solving time.

There are arguments for and against each approach. The system described by Gams retains structured representation of knowledge. As individual agents update their knowledge, this immediately bears some effects on the opinion of the group. This is not true of the integrated theory. If one of the individual theories has been altered, the integrated theory may need to be revised. In a certain sense, the first approach has similar advantages as *interpreting*, while the second one has the advantages of *compiling*.

Sometimes it may be difficult or outright impossible to construct an integrated theory. Difficulties can arise particularly when the agents use different (and possibly incompatible) ways of representing knowledge.

Integrated theory represents a more compact representation of knowledge than the structured representation discussed earlier. Compact representations have obvious advantages. Simple theories are easier to communicate to other agents (including humans) than complex ones. They can also serve as a useful starting point in further learning.

Alternative theories are no doubt useful both in science and politics. Alternative theories often find their adepts, and it would be wrong to try to come up with one integrated theory that would explain everything. However, people would generally agree that there is a limit as to how many theories should be taken into account. Some theories may be just minor variants of others. In our view methods are needed that would determine whether some particular theory is worth keeping around as a useful alternative.

## Distributed Learning + Individual Problem Solving

Sian´s system (1990a, 1991b) is involved in both individual and distributed learning. Each system learns individually, but if certain conditions arise interaction is initiated with other agents. The interaction is established via an *interaction board*, which plays a similar as in blackboard architecture systems. Here the agents can, for example, propose a hypothesis to the the interaction board.

Communication between the learning agents is whenever one of the agents has obtained a hypothesis and has sufficient confidence in it. This is considered as a good candidate to put to test. Opinions of the other agents are solicited with the objective of establishing a consensus. The rules can remain as they are, or they can be modified, or they can be withdrawn. The rules that have been agreed upon represent a *consensus* of the group and appear in the "integrated theory".

This work differs form the other two presented earlier in various aspects. First, the author has elaborated an interface through which the individual agents communicate. Introduction and retraction of hypotheses to/from the interaction board is achieved using the operators

> PROPOSE, ASSERT, WITHDRAW, ACCEPT

Evaluation of hypotheses is accomplished using the operators

> CONFIRM, DISAGREE, MODIFY, NOOPINION,

while AGREED modifies a state. Each hypothesis is characterized by a NET-VALUE calculated on the basis of the opinions of different agents (CONFIRM, DISAGREE, MODIFY, NOOPINION) and the confidence values associated with each operator.

We notice that all three systems discussed in this section (i.e. Gams´s, Brazdil & Torgo´s and Sian´s) use some particular method for assessing the usefulness of a given rule on the basis of evidence presented by different agents. Further work could be done to present a more detailed comparative study.

As we have mentioned earlier Sian´s system differs from Brazdil and Torgo´s in one important aspect. The agents are allowed to interact in the learning phase. This seems to make sense, particularly if we are interested to save some agents´ effort associated with learning. The earlier a potentially good hypothesis is put to test and possibly accepted, the better.

When considering testing in a multi-agent environment, it is necessary to distinguish between centralized testing (done by one agent) and distributed testing. Testing against all data available does not necessarily imply a centralized solution. A particular hypothesis can be sent to different agents. Each can then update the information received. A global view can be thus built up by passing a hypothesis from one agent to another.

In Sian´s system each agent tests the proposed rule against his *own data*. A global view of each rule is then built up on the basis of a number of local views. A question arises whether this built-up view is equivalent to the global view that could be obtained by centralized testing. Brazdil and Torgo´s system seems to satisfy this criterion. Each agent could update the qualitative and quantitative characterixation of the given rule and then pass this information to the next agent. This information is the same as the one generated during centralized testing.

Further work could be done here. A study of cost-effectiveness of the two methods could be made, taking into account:

- the effort of transferring the local views / instances to one agent,
- the effort of evaluating a given hypothesis (using instances / local views),
- net increase of confidence for some particular method.

# 4. Some Aspects of Communication between Agents

As has been suggested in the previous sections, communication plays rather an important role in multi-agent learning systems. It may supply the agent with valuable information and thus avoid "re-discovering the wheel". Communication need not, however, bring about benefits. It is thus important to study this topic in its own right. Although this topic exceeds the objective of this paper, we would like to make several observations here.

It is important to distinguish between the issues related to *form of the language* used between agents and the actual *statements* in that language. Here we make a similar distinction as when talking about natural language. There is a difference between problems related to structure of English and particular piece of text.

The issues related to the language itself could be viewed as issues of interfaces between agents. It is necessary to decide what kind of statements the agents should be able to generate and comprehend. For example, one could decide that the operator PROPOSE(H,C) should have a certain meaning. In Sian´s system this operator adds hypothesis H (and the associated confidence C) to the interaction board.

Obviously, the design of interfaces is closely related to the design of the architecture of the whole system. The operator PROPOSE plays a specific role in the system for which it was designed. A question arises whether some set of basic communication primitives could be found that would be generally useful in multi-agent learning. This would have the advantage that it would make it easier to compare different approaches. Of course, one could always add extra primitives, or define other constructs in terms of the existing core primitives, if this was required in some specific system.

The second kind of issues are related to the problems of interpretation and meaning of agent's statements. As Shaw and Gaines (1989) have pointed out, same term can have different meaning for different agents. This situation is called a *conflict*. Different terms may, however, have similar meaning. This situation is called a *correspondence*.

Work of Brazdil and Muggleton (1991) is concerned with the problem of resolving certain language differences between agents. The agents are not only presented with different situations from which they can learn, but also, employ a somewhat different terms in their description of the (simulated) world. For example, one agent uses the predicate *father(..)* while the other *parent(..)*. If we use Shaw and Gaines's terminology, there is a problem of correspondence. Brazdil and Muggleton show how these language differences can be overcome. It is shown that standard machine learning techniques can be used to acquire the meaning of undefined concepts.

There are interesting relationships between inductive learning and communication. There interplay mentioned here is of a different kind than the one discussed in Section 3. There we have discussed different ways communication can supplement learning. Here we are concerned with the possibility of resolving certain problems of communication using learning.

## 5. Role of Learning in a Community of Agents

### Utility of Learning

Learning in distributed systems opens new horizons. It makes us consider issues that have not been looked at earlier in machine learning. For example, it forces us to consider the question why a particular agent (in a community of agents) should want to learn? Designing agents that would learn about anything in the world goes against the basic philosophy of distributed AI.

We believe it is thus necessary to reason about the *utility of learning*. We notice that in most general architectures of intelligence (SOAR, THEO, PRODIGY, ICARUS) this issue has not really been paid attention to. This may be the reason why some systems are ill-behaved (the more they learn, the slowed they perform). We believe that addressing this point in the context of DAI will make it easier to find the appropriate answer(s).

## Community Goals and Agent Goals

An important capacity of an agent in a multi-agent world is the ability to define one´s own goals. The agent´s goals are often affected by (and in some cases determined by) the goals of other agents.

The process of *goal definition* seems to subsume goal selection. Mitchell (1990) has defined *perception* as a process linking the state of the world to the appropriate goals to attend to. This process involves selecting the most pertinent goal and trying to achieve it in preference to others.

So far not much work has been done in the area of goal definition. Most work done has concentrated on goals of two agents only. Baker´s system KANT (1991), for example, incorporates reasoning mechanisms for determining which set of goals are to be *negotiated* in a tutorial interaction.

When considering the relationships between individual goals and community goals two issues arise. First, how the satisfaction of individual goals affects the satisfaction of community goals. Then, how the satisfaction of community goals leads to the satisfaction of individual goals.

It is also possible to envisage that agents could *learn which goals to pursue* in order to achieve some overall goals. Perhaps the agents would follow a scheme of gradual differentiation that is common in human society. The agents start with similar goals, but differences in local conditions and agent-specific skills gradually differentiate the agents´ goals so as to function better in a community. Ideally this process lets the community evolve from a fairly uniform group to a differentiated highly competent society.

## Learning Tasks in a Community

As we have mentioned earlier, Mitchell (1990) ascribes three learning goals to an agent: becoming more perceptive, more correct, and more reactive. These are the goals that an external observer might ascribe to an agent when observing its behaviour over time.

If an observer were to observe a multi-agent system, which learning goals could he ascribe to individual agents? We believe that the list of learning goals mentioned by Mitchell could be extended to include at least one additional requirement. We could require that the agent should become increasingly *more integrated,* that is, play its proper role in the community of agents.

This involves being called upon by other agents, recognizing when to delegate a problem to others and exploiting these opportunities.

## Acknowledgments

The work of P. Brazdil and L. Torgo discussed in this paper was supported by Esprit 2 Project Ecoles (3059). The authors wish to thank the Commission of European Communities for their support.

# References

Baker M. (1991): "A Model for Negotiation in Intelligent Tutoring Dialogs", in *New Directions for ITS*, E.Costa (ed.), to be published by Springer Verlag.

Bond A. and Gasser. L. (eds.) (1988): *Readings in DAI*, Morgan Kaufmann Publishers, San Mateo.

Brazdil P. and Torgo L. (1990): "Knowledge Acquisition via Knowledge Integration", in *Current Trends in Artificial Intelligence, B. Wielinga et al. (eds.)*, IOS Press, Amsterdam, 1990.

Brazdil P. and Muggleton S. (1991): "Learning to Relate Terms in Multiple Agent Environment", in this volume.

Buntine W. (1889): "Learning Classification Rules Using Bayes", in *Proceedings of 6th International Workshop on Machine Learning*, Ithaca, New York.

Demazeau Y. and J.-P. Mueller (eds.) (1991): *Proceedings of the 2nd European Workshop on Modelling Autonomous Agents and Multi-Agent Worlds (MAAMAW 90)*, Saint-Quentin-en-Yvelines, France, August 1990, Elsevier Science Publishers.

Durfee E., Lesser V.R. and Corkill D.D. (1989): "Cooperative Distributed Problem Solving", in *The Handbook of Artificial Intelligence, Volume IV*, Barr A., Cohen P.R. and Feigenbaum E.A. (eds.), Addison Wesley, 1989.

Gams M. (1989): "The Measurement Highlight the Importance of Redundant Knowledge", in *Proceedings of 4th European Working Session on Machine Learning (EWSL-89)*, K. Morik (ed.), pp. 71-80, Pitman - Morgan Kaufmann.

Gams M., Bohanec M. and Cestnik B. (1990): A Schema for Using Multiple Knowledge, Working Paper, Jozef Stefan Institute, Ljubljana, Yugoslavia.

Huhns M. (ed.) (1987): *Distributed AI Vol.1*, Pitman and Morgan Kaufmann, 1987.

Janikow C.Z. (1989): "The AQ16 Inductive Learning Program: Some Experimental Results with AQ16 and Other Symbolic and Nonsymbolic Programs", Rep. of AI Center, George Mason University.

Mitchell T. (1990): "Becoming Increasingly Reactive", in *Proceedings of 8th National Conference on Artificial Intelligence (AAAI-90)*, Morgan Kaufmann, pp. 1051-1058.

Oliveira E., Camacho R. and Ramos C. (1990): A Multi-Agent Environment in Robotics, Working Paper, Fac. of Engineering, Univ. of Porto, (also LIACC, Univ. of Porto), Portugal.

Schlimmer J.C. and Fisher D. (1986): "A Case Study of Incremental Concept Induction", in *Proceedings of the Fifth National Conference on Artificial Intelligence*, pp. 496-501, Morgan Kaufmann.

Sian S. (1991a): "Adaptation Based on Cooperative Learning in Multi-Agent Systems", in *Proceedings of the 2nd European Workshop on Modelling Autonomous Agents and Multi-Agent Worlds (MAAMAW 90)*, Demazeau Y. and J.-P. Mueller (eds.), Saint-Quentin-en-Yvelines, France, August 1990, Elsevier Science Publishers.

Sian S. (1991b): Extending Learning to Multiple Agents: Issues and a Model for Multi-Agent Machine Learning (MA-ML), in this volume.

Shaw M. and Gaines B. (1989): Knowledge Acquisition: Some Foundations, manual Methods and Future Trends, in *Proceedings of Third European Workshop on Knowledge Acquisition for Knowledge-Based Systems*, J. Boose, B. Gaines and J.G. Ganascia (eds.), Paris, July 1989.

Utgoff P.E. (1988): "ID5: An Incremental ID3", in *Proc. of 5th International Workshop on Machine Learning*, J. Laird (ed.), Ann Harbour, Morgan Kaufmann Inc.

van de Velde W.(ed.) (1990): *Towards Learning Robots*, North Holland, Amsterdam.

# Learning to Relate Terms in a Multiple Agent Environment

## P. Brazdil (*) S. Muggleton (**)

(*) LIACC-CIUP, Rua Campo Alegre, 823, 4100 Porto, Portugal
E-mail: pbrazdil@nccup.ctt.pt ; Later: pbrazdil@liacc.up.pt

(**) The Turing Institute, 36 North Hanover Street, Glasgow G1 2AD, UK
E-mail: steve@turing.ac.uk

**Abstract**

In the first part of the paper we describe how different agents can arrive at different (but overlapping) views of reality. Although the agents can cooperate when answering queries, it is often desirable to construct an integrated theory that explains 'best' a given reality. The technique of knowledge integration based on an earlier work is briefly reviewed and some shortcomings of this technique are pointed out. One of the assumptions underlying the earlier work was that all agents must use the same predicate vocabulary. Here we are concerned with the problems that can arise if this assumption does not hold. We also show how these problems can be overcome. It is shown that standard machine learning techniques can be used to acquire the meaning of other agent´s concepts. The experiments described in this paper employ INTEG.3, a knowledge integration system, and GOLEM, an inductive system based on relative least general generalization.

**Keywords:** knowledge integration, language differences, learning concept definitions, learning unknown concepts, predicate vocabulary, learning in distributed systems.

# 1. Introduction

Many AI applications are inherently distributed. Consider, for example, the problem of developing a large expert system in some domain (e.g. medicine). This process usually involves consultations with various experts. The knowledge of these experts may often be quite complementary. In each consultation one could cover a somewhat different part of the domain. Facilities are needed for elicitation and analysis of knowledge from multiple experts (Boose et al., 1989). Moreover, it is necessary to develop cooperative mechanisms that enable multiple systems to work together to solve common problems. We would like also the system to improve the overall problem solving performance. As Durfee et al. (1989, p.103) have pointed out, improvements of performance may often be achieved by transferring certain knowledge (operators) from one system to another.

Whenever knowledge is generated and transferred from one subsystem to another, conflicting information can easily be generated. So far relatively little work has been done in the area of how one potential conflicts could be resolved.

The objective of our earlier work (Brazdil and Torgo, 1990) was to partly cover this gap. In our scenario we admitted the existence of several different agents, each of whom was capable of constructing theories on the basis of given data. The objective of system INTEG.3 was to construct an integrated theory from the individual theories. Our experiments have shown that the integrated theory had in general better performance that the original theories. In that work we have, however, assumed that all agents use the same predicate vocabulary. The purpose of this paper is to show what we can do if this assumption does not hold. That is, we will show how agents can overcome certain language differences automatically, without human intervention. As we shall see standard machine learning techniques can be used to acquire the meaning of other agents´ concepts.

The purpose of the method described here could be stated as follows: Given two or more theories (which are assumed to belong to different agents), construct a *new theory* that includes the essential parts of the original theories, while trying to minimize possible inconsistencies and redundancies on the basis of experimental tests.

Other people have adopted a somewhat different stand. Gams (1989), for example, maintains all apparently redundant rules (or theories) within the system. He has shown that when redundant rules are taken into account, this can lead to improvements of performance. Theories that contain many redundant rules have, however, certain disadvantages over those that have been trimmed down. They are more difficult to understand and consequently they are also more difficult to modify.

## Organization of the Paper

The rest of this paper is organized as follows. First we discuss some other related work in this area. Section 2 is devoted to the description of how different agents can arrive at different (but overlapping) views of reality.

Section 3 discusses the functioning of a distributed system. It shows that whenever different agents have overlapping but non-identical knowledge, it is advantageous for the agents to cooperate. One disadvantage of the distributed solution, however, is that all agents must be ready to step in and act. The functioning of the distributed system will be impaired if one agent is non-operational.

An alternative, centralized solution is described in Section 4. This section reviews the method of knowledge integration (more details are in (Brazdil and Torgo, 1990)) and identifies some problems that can arise whenever agents use different predicate vocabulary. Section 5 describes how these problems can be overcome.

## Relation to Other Work

The problem of language differences typically arises when knowledge is elicited from several (human) experts. As Shaw and Gaines (1989) have pointed out, the *same* term can have *different* meaning in different systems. They call this situation a *conflict*. *Different* terms may, however, have *identical* meanings. Shaw and Gaines call this situation a *correspondence*.

Our system INTEG.3 (Brazdil and Torgo, 1990) deals with the problem of *conflict*, but not of correspondence. The system uses empirical evidence to decide whose definition of a given concepts is 'best'. In this paper we are concerned with the problem of correspondence. Although, the meanings of *parent* and *father* are not identical, the system will establish how they are related.

Murray and Porter (1989) have developed a system PROTOKI (a prototype of a larger system KI). The system is intended to provide support when new piece of information is integrated in the existing knowledge base. The process of integration involves three main steps: recognition, elaboration and adaptation. The third step is concerned with resolution of anomalies. These arise, for example, when conflicting solutions can be reached using different chains of reasoning. The prototype system inspects the explanation that lead to the anomaly and tries to determine the weakest premise. This premise is then modified.

On one hand Murray and Porter's work goes further than ours. So far we have not tried to integrate knowledge consisting of rules that are chained. On the other hand PROTOKI requires a great deal of domain dependent knowledge, and besides, does not attempt to deal with the problem of *correspondence*. It does not try to establish relationships between similar concepts that may already exist within the system.

## 2. World of Agents

Here we will be involved with a distributed system, similar to the ones discussed by Durfee et al., (1989). We assume that the system consists of a number of separate agents that can communicate. We will assume *loose coupling* between agents in the sense defined by Durfee et al., implying that the communication costs between agents are significant. This assumption has the following important implication for us: It is worth trying to integrate related pieces of knowledge within one system.

Here we will assume that each agent has certain perceptive, communicative and reasoning capabilities, but also that it is capable of inductive reasoning and integrating pieces of knowledge into one theory. That is, the agents will be capable of:

- perceiving a portion of the given world (or simulated world),
- accepting facts and rules from another agent,
- formulating queries and supplying them to another agent,
- responding to queries formulated by another agent,
- interpreting answers provided by another agent,
- inducing rules on the basis of facts,
- integrating knowledge.

The last two capabilities differentiate our agents from those discussed by Durfee at al. Here we shall adopt a particular form of knowledge representation. All agents' knowledge will be represented in the form of facts and/or rules. This, however, does not mean that the agents must represent their knowledge in this way. Our simulation merely places certain constraints on what the agents can or cannot do.

## 2.1 Our Scenario

The experiments described in later sections involve two agents (A, B) and the user. The user can be viewed as another agent. Our scenario also includes a micro-world of family relations. Actually, we will distinguish various views of this micro-world. All of these views are shown in Fig.1. Note that this figure shows how *we see* the domain. The agents´ representation of this domain will be shown later.

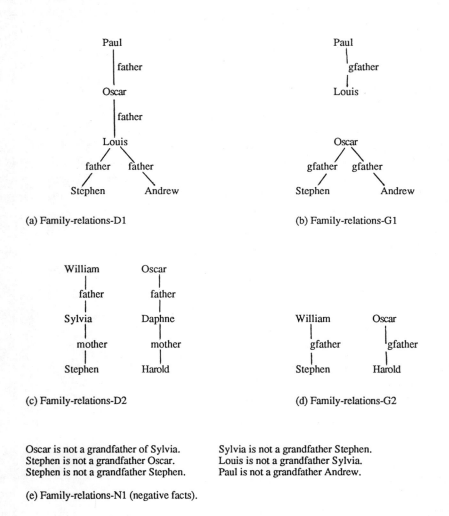

(a) Family-relations-D1

(b) Family-relations-G1

(c) Family-relations-D2

(d) Family-relations-G2

Oscar is not a grandfather of Sylvia.     Sylvia is not a grandfather Stephen.
Stephen is not a grandfather Oscar.     Louis is not a grandfather Sylvia.
Stephen is not a grandfather Stephen.     Paul is not a grandfather Andrew.

(e) Family-relations-N1 (negative facts).

Fig.1 The given micro-world of family relations and its views

The interpretation of this figure is rather obvious. The link between *Paul* and *Oscar*, for example, with the label *"father"* represents the fact that *"Paul is a father of Oscar"*. The term *gfather* is an abbreviation of *grandfather*. The microworld *Family-relations-N2* is assumed to be identical to *Family-relations-N1*.

## 2.2 Agent´s Differing Views of Reality

Perceptive actions provide the agents with a *description* of the relevant part of the world. This description consists of a set of predicates that are part of A´s vocabulary. Here we will assume that A´s predicate vocabulary includes the following predicates:

father (X,Y), mother (X,Y), gfather (X,Y).

After agent A has executed a perceptive action, its knowledge base will include instances of the three predicates mentioned. If A´s perceptive action has been directed towards the micro-world of *Family-relations-D1*, its knowledge base will contain the assertions:

| | |
|---|---|
| father ( "Paul", "Oscar"). | father ( "Louis", "Stephen"). (D1A) |
| father ( "Oscar", "Louis"). | father ( "Louis", "Andrew"). |

Similarly, perception of *Family-relations-G1* will give:

| | |
|---|---|
| gfather ( "Oscar", "Stephen"). | gfather ( "Paul", "Louis"). (G1A) |
| gfather ( "Oscar", "Andrew"). | |

The set G1A represents "conclusions" that we would like the agent to derive on the basis of its rules and D1A. Agent A´s view of the negative facts available *(Family-relations-N1)* will be identified by N1A.

In our scenario agent B has a somewhat different view of reality. First, let us assume that B´s predicate vocabulary includes:

parent (X,Y), male (X), female (X), gfather (X,Y),

but not *father(X,Y)* or *mother(X,Y)*. Second, let us assume that B´s attention is directed towards *Family-relations-D2*. B´s representation of the corresponding facts is:

| | |
|---|---|
| parent ( "William", "Sylvia"). | parent ( "Oscar", "Daphne"). (D2B) |
| parent ( "Sylvia", "Stephen"). | parent ( "Daphne", "Harold"). |
| male ( "William"). | male ( "Oscar"). |
| male ( "Stephen"). | male ( "Harold" ). |
| female ( "Sylvia"). | female ( "Daphne"). |

Agent B´s representation of *Family-relations-G2* will similarly be:

| | |
|---|---|
| gfather ( "William", "Stephen"). | gfather ( "Oscar", "Harold"). (G2B) |

Agent B´s view of the negative facts *(Family-relations-N2)* will give assertions called N2B.

## 2.3   Construction of Different Theories of Reality

As we have mentioned earlier our agents are capable of inducing theories on the basis of given (observed) facts. The outcome of inductive process depends on a number of factors, such as:

- inductive method employed,
- the facts available,
- background knowledge,
- predicate vocabulary adopted,
- other "inductive biases".

Here we will assume that both agents use the same inductive method called GOLEM. The method is based on *Relative Least General Generalization* and is described in detail in (Muggleton & Feng, 1990).

We would like to point out that the assumption concerning the agents´ inductive method simplifies somewhat the points we want to make here. However, the methods described here are in no way based on (or limited by) this assumption.

The facts contained in the set (D1A) and the correct answer set (G1A) and the negative facts (N1A) enable agent A to generate the following definition of *´gfather´* :

$$\text{gfather}(X,Y) :\text{- father}(X,Z), \text{father}(Z,Y). \tag{R1A}$$

Rule (R1A) covers all A´s positive examples of *´gfather´,* and so the facts

$$\begin{array}{ll} \text{gfather ( "Oscar", "Stephen").} & \text{gfather ( "Paul", "Louis").} \\ \text{gfather ( "Oscar", "Andrew").} & \end{array} \tag{G1A}$$

are no longer necessary for answering queries.

As B uses a different set of initial facts, and also, different predicate vocabulary, the rule generated by B is different from A´s:

$$\text{gfather}(X,Y) :\text{- parent}(X,Z), \text{male}(X), \text{parent}(Z,Y), \text{female}(Z). \tag{R2B}$$

This rule covers B´s positive examples of *´gfather´* and so the facts

$$\text{gfather ( "William", "Stephen").} \qquad \text{gfather ( "Oscar", "Harold").} \tag{G2B}$$

are no longer necessary for answering queries.

We notice that A´s concept of *gfather(..)* is defined in terms of A´s vocabulary, that is, using the concept of *father(..)*. Similarly B´s concept is defined in terms of B´s vocabulary. In our case this vocabulary includes the concepts *parent(..)*, *male(..)* and *female(..)*. This is the reason why agent A fails to prove, for example, the following fact (this fact appears in G2B):

gfather ( "William",  "Stephen")

using

gfather(X,Y) :- father(X,Z), father(Z,Y)                                    (R1A)

and

parent ( "William", "Sylvia").
parent ( "Sylvia", "Stephen").
male ( "William").

that is certain relevant facts from (D2B). A´s definition of *gfather(..)* contains the reference to *father(..)*, but B´s data uses the concepts *parent(..)*, *male(..)* and *female(..)*. As agents A and B use a somewhat different vocabulary, A´s definition cannot be applied to B´s data. In the next section we will see how this problem can be overcome.


# 3. Distributed Problem Solving

As we have seen in the previous section both agents A and B were capable of answering certain queries concerning *gfather(..)* after certain training. However, neither A nor B could answer correctly all the queries that A and B were presented with during the training phase. This suggests that something could be gained by letting both agents try to work together. In this section we will analyze this mode of operation in more detail.

In order to be able to function together as one system the agents need to be able communicate. Communication between agents is achieved using a special communication layer obeying certain rules. Its purpose is to determine when the given problem (query) should be resolved by the recipient agent (Ai) (i.e. the agent that received the query), and when it should be sent to someone else. For simplicity of exposition the user will be regarded as another agent.

Let us adopt the following rather simple rules to control the communication between agents:

(Com1)  Agent Ai should attempt to solve problem P before sending it to another agent.

(Com2)  If Ai succeeded in solving P, the answer should be returned to the agent that issued P.

(Com3)  If Ai failed to solve P and if there is some agent Aj that has not yet attempted to solve P, P should be sent to Aj. If Aj succeeded in solving P the answer should be sent to the agent that issued P.

(Com4)  If Ai failed to solve P and if all agents available have attempted to solve P without success, failure should be returned to the agent that issued P.

(Com5)  Each agent should use his own theories and data when solving P (it is not allowed to interchange of theories or data at run-time).

The rules shown above assure that the given problem is not passed around unnecessarily from one agent to another. The rules have another purpose, however. They determine how a particular agent should act when trying to resolve the given problem.

The rules shown above can be used to control the behavior of the agents A and B. In the following we will use the symbols "A+B" to identify a *distributed system* with agents A and B obeying the rules (Com1)-(Com5). Let us see how this system handles one query. Suppose the user has asked agent A to determine whether

gfather ( "William", "Stephen")

is true. Agent A by himself cannot answer this query, but thanks to the fact that A and B can communicate, correct answer can be given. The query is simply sent to agent B and then a positive answer is sent back to A. This answer is then returned to the user. It is easy to show that, here, the problem solving performance of the distributed system  A+B  exceeds the performance of individual agents.

The rules (Com1)-(Com5) do not take into account relative success rates of individual agents or the quality of individual rules. Whenever one agent has succeeded in answering the given query, its answer is returned (Com2). No attempt is made to check which answer the other agents would give. Different agents could however give conflicting answers and so some strategy is needed to decide which answer should be chosen. Some people have proposed and used a kind of voting scheme (Gams, 1989). Our method (Brazdil and Torgo, 1990) attempts to select a subset of rules which appear to be most reliable.

Distributed systems have other disadvantages, however. If we cannot a priory determine to which agent particular queries should be attributed to, all agents must be operational and ready to step in. This affects the costs involved in obtaining the answer(s). This suggests that all the rules acquired individually could be collected by one of the agents and then this agent could act alone to answer the user´s queries. In the next section we will discuss this process in detail, and also, analyze some problems that can arise whenever agents use different vocabulary.

# 4. Theory Integration

The aim of knowledge integration could be defined as follows. Consider all theories available and construct an integrated theory taking into account performance criteria of various constituents. The details of this algorithm are in (Brazdil and Torgo, 1990).

Suppose agent A has been designated to construct an integrated theory on the basis of the individual theories acquired earlier by agents A and B. As each theory consists of only one rule, the candidate rules set will contain the following two rules:

gfather(X,Y) :- father(X,Z), father(Z,Y).                    (R1A)
gfather(X,Y) :- parent(X,Z), male(X), parent(Z,Y), female(Z).    (R2B)

The integration algorithm needs to be supplied with available data (D1A,D2B) and required answers (G1A,G2B). Assuming that both agents have kept all the initial data, agent A needs to get only B's data to proceed. The integration algorithm will then test the given rules on available data. In our case there are just two rules. As each rule covers only a part of the data without covering any negative examples, both rules will appear in the integrated theory.

The integrated theory enables the agent to answer correctly any query selected from set G1A or G2B. For example, the query

gfather ( "William", "Stephen")

will succeed. Despite this apparent success, one important issue has remained unresolved. Agent A is unable to perceive B's micro-world and act correctly.

Let us assume that agent A has the rules R1A and R2B. Let us further assume that all data is obtained using direct observations (perceptive actions). The perceptive action directed towards the micro-world *Family-relations-D2* will update A's knowledge base with:

father ( "William", "Sylvia").     father ( "Oscar", "Daphne").     (D2A)
father ( "Sylvia", "Stephen").     father ( "Daphne", "Harold").

It can be verified that the goal

gfather ( "William", "Stephen")

will fail. The failure is due to the fact that A's rules and his data use *different vocabulary*. Rule R2B, for example, contains the predicates

parent(X,Z), male(X), parent(Z,Y), female(Z)

all of which are unknown concepts (for A). They do not figure among A´s primitive concepts, and moreover, agent A has no definition showing what these concepts mean. In the next section we will show how standard ML techniques can be used to acquire the definitions of such concepts.

## 5. Acquiring the Meaning of Unknown Concepts

In the previous section we have shown that when theories integrate knowledge of different agents, care must be taken to avoid failures. Failures are likely when agents use a somewhat different vocabulary. The rules acquired by communication can contain concepts that are simply unknown to the recipient agent.

In this section we will describe a technique that can be used to overcome these problems. We will show how agents can acquire the required definitions of unknown concepts. As we shall see standard machine learning techniques can be used to construct such definitions. One of the crucial steps in this process will be the following. The agents will attempt to describe the same "situation" so as to be able to formulate the relationships between different concepts.

The technique used here seems to be quite common in human learning. Consider, for example, mother and a child. The mother will often describe the situation the child can see. The child is able to learn the meaning of her mother´s concepts by relating the mother´s description to its own experience.

Let us apply this strategy to our scenario. Here we will use the micro-world of *Family-relations-D2* to try to define the unknown concepts. As we have seen agent A´s view of this micro-world is:

| | | |
|---|---|---|
| father ( "William", "Sylvia"). | father ( "Oscar", "Daphne"). | (D2A) |
| mother ( "Sylvia", "Stephen"). | mother ( "Daphne", "Harold"). | |

B´s view of this micro-world is:

| | | |
|---|---|---|
| parent ( "William", "Sylvia"). | parent ( "Oscar", "Daphne"). | (D2B) |
| parent ( "Sylvia", "Stephen"). | parent ( "Daphne", "Harold"). | |
| male ( "William" ). | male ( "Oscar" ). | |
| male ( "Stephen" ). | male ( " Harold" ). | |
| female ( "Sylvia"). | female ( "Daphne" ). | |

The concepts that are unknown to A and whose meaning is to be defined are:

parent(X,Z), male(X), female(Z).

These facts will enable the agent A to generate the required definitions. Given these facts the inductive system will generate[1]:

| | | |
|---|---|---|
| parent (X,Z) | :- father (X,Z). | (RI1) |
| parent (X,Z) | :- mother (X,Z). | (RI2) |
| male (X) | :- father (X,_). | (RI3) |
| female (Z) | :- mother (Z,_). | (RI4) |

The rules shown above relate B´s concepts (e.g. *parent(..)*) to A´s own concepts (i.e. *father(..)*). The new definitions enable the agent A to overcome the problem mentioned earlier. It can be verified that the goal

gfather ( "William", "Stephen")

no longer fails. The solution of this goal requires rule R2B. Application of this rule generates the subgoals

parent("William",Z), male("William"), parent(Z,"Stephen"), female(Z),

all of which can be interpreted correctly thanks to the new definitions (RI1-RI4). The application of rule RI1 to the subgoal *parent("William,Z)*, for example, will produce the subgoal *father("William",Z)*. In other words, B´s concept of *parent(..)* will be substituted by the concept of *father(..)*, which is one of A´s primitive concepts.


## 5.1  Role of Interface Theory

In this paper we have been concerned with the problem of composing theories from different constituents generated by different agents. Let us come back to our scenario and examine these constituents in more detail. In particular let us look at A´s theory which was completed in the last section. It consists of the following rules:

| | | |
|---|---|---|
| gfather(X,Y) | :- father(X,Z), father(Z,Y). | (R1A) |
| gfather(X,Y) | :- parent(X,Z), male(X), parent(Z,Y), female(Z). | (R2B) |
| | | |
| parent (X,Z) | :- father (X,Z). | (RI1) |
| parent (X,Z) | :- mother (X,Z). | (RI2) |
| male (X) | :- father (X,_). | (RI3) |
| female (Z) | :- mother (Z,_). | (RI4) |

Rule R1A was generated by agent A´s inductive subsystem on the basis of its data. Rule R2B was obtained from agent B using a process of communication.

---

[1] The present version of GOLEM is unable to generate the definitions of *male(X)* and *female(Z)* shown here. The point is that the system cannot learn clauses with arbitrary existential quantification, such as $\exists y \forall x \; male(x) \leftarrow father(x,y)$. It is expected that a solution to this problem can, however, be found.

Rule R1A was initially generated by B, and then B has simply supplied this rule to A. Sometimes this type of learning is called "learning by being told". Agent A was spared the effort of generating the rule.

Rules (RI1-RI4) represent a kind of *interface theory* that establishes relationships between concepts. In our case, these rules provide the definition of some unknown concepts that appeared in the rule supplied by B. These definitions enable agent A to interpret correctly B´s theory.

## 6. Representation of Agent´s Beliefs

In all experiments described here the agents´ beliefs have been represented using assertions of the form *bel(Ag1, P1)* where *Ag1* represents an agent and *P1* some predicate. Rules of the form

    bel(Ag1, P1) :- bel(Ag2, P2)

relate beliefs of one agent to beliefs of another agent. Note that if *Ag1* and *Ag2* are the same, we get a special case of this rule relating different agent´s beliefs. Here we will call this representation *meta-level representation*.

For example, A´s belief set D1A is represented using the following meta-level assertions:

    bel("A", father("Paul", "Oscar"))                          (D1A*)
    bel("A", father("Oscar", "Louis"))
    etc.

All other facts are represented in a similar manner. This representation affects the form of the rules generated by GOLEM. The system did not generate rule R1A shown earlier, but rule R1A* which has the following form:

    bel("A", gfather(X,Y) ) :- bel("A", father(X,Z )) , bel("A", father(Z,Y ))      (R1A*)

As this represension is somewhat less readable, we have decided to the simpler form throughout in this paper, without the meta-predicate bel(..). Notice that there is no loss of information as long as we deal with one particular agent only. That is, all rules Ri belonging to the simplified representation system can be automatically transformed into more complex rules Ri* (and vice versa) if we assume that all beliefs belong to one agent only (e.g. A).

As our scenario involves two agents, the issue concerning representation of beliefs deserves more attention. Let us analyse the final theory generated by the system:

| | | |
|---|---|---|
| bel("A", gfather(X,Y)) | :- bel("A", father(X,Z)), bel("A",father(Z,Y)). | (R1A*) |
| bel("A", P) | :- bel("B", P). | (RI0*) |
| bel("B", gfather(X,Y)) | :- bel("B", parent(X,Z)), bel("B", male(X) | (R2B*) |
| | bel("B", parent(Z,Y)), bel("B", female(Z)). | |
| bel("B", parent (X,Z)) | :- bel("A", father (X,Z)). | (RI1*) |
| bel("B", parent (X,Z)) | :- bel("A", mother (X,Z)). | (RI2*) |
| bel("B", male (X)) | :- bel("A", father (X,_)). | (RI3*) |
| bel("B", female (Z)) | :- bel("A", mother (Z,_)). | (RI4*) |

Rule RI0 is a kind of interface rule that has been added manually to the rules shown above. When interpreted in the Prolog style, we can say that it transforms the goal *bel("A",P)* into *bel("B",P)*. Looking at it from a different angle, this rule enables agent A to interpret goal P using rules of B. Rule R2B* is the rule generated by agent B. The remaining rules (RI1*-RI4*) represent the interface theory. Rule RI1*, for example, enables the system to transform the goal *bel("B", parent (X,Z))* into *bel("A", father (X,Z))*.


## 7.  Discussion


Most earlier work in ML has been concerned with the problem of constructing (and improving) a theory on the basis of examples. The problem of integrating two or more theories has been largely ignored. Perhaps it has reminded people of "learning by being told" which has usually been dismissed as "too easy" and of no real interest to ML community.

The purpose of our earlier work was to partly fill in this gap. The system described in (Brazdil and Torgo, 1990) consisted of several learning agents, and it tried to minimize possible inconsistencies and redundancies on the basis of experimental tests. The experiments have shown that this strategy can lead to performance gains. In this paper we have shown how agents can overcome certain language differences that can arise in communication between them. As has been demonstrated, standard machine learning techniques can be used to acquire the meaning of other agents´ concepts. The theory consisting of concept definitions represents a kind of "interface theory". It relates concepts of different agents, providing them with meaning.

Some people argue that although different theories are useful, these should be retained as separate entities. Gams (1989), for example, maintains all apparently redundant rules (theories) within the system. Improvements of performance can be achieved by taking these redundant rules into account. Theories containing redundant rules are, however, more difficult to understand and consequently also more difficult to modify.

Knowledge integration is concerned with issues that are related to those in *incremental learning* systems. There are some important differences between the two approaches, however. When employing some incremental version of a given learning algorithm only *one* system is constructing theories. Knowledge integration, on the other hand, involves *several* systems all of which try to construct their own theories on the basis of their own experience. Knowledge integration tends to <u>capitalize on the results</u> obtained by different systems.

In our scenario both agent A and B attempt to generate the definition of *grandfather*. As they fail to cover some cases (for example A´s definition fails on B´s data), agent A attempts to complete his knowledge using the method of knowledge integration. As we have seen this process may involve additional learning (i.e. generation of new concept definitions). If we were not interested to exploit the results obtained by B (that is B´s original definitions) we could have simply supplied agent A with B´s data. Agent A could have revised his definitions on the basis of the additional data. We believe that agent A would have been able to generate the correct definitions this way (i.e. by incremental learning). However, does not try to capitalize on the results obtained by agent B earlier.

More work could be done to evaluate the two approaches. Obviously communication and generation of the interface theory has certain costs, too. It would be interesting to quantify the effort associated with each alternative. Moreover, it would be useful to define a set of rules (or heuristics) that would enable us to decide which approach would be most appropriate in a new domain.

## Acknowledgments

This work was supported by Esprit 2 Project Ecoles (3059). The authors wish to thank Commission of European Communities for their support.

The authors wish to thank also Thomas Hoppe for carrying out some experiments with *ancestors* and *parents* at The Turing Institute in Glasgow and also for various helpful comments. Thanks also to anonymous referees for their helpful remarks. These have taken into account when preparing the final version of this paper.

# References

Boose J., Bradshaw J., Kitto C. and Sherma D. (1989): "From ETS to Acquinas: Six Years of Knowledge Acquisition Tool Development," in *Proceedings of Third European Workshop on Knowledge Acquisition for Knowledge-Based Systems*, J. Boose, B. Gaines and J.G. Ganascia (eds.), Paris, July 1989.

Brazdil P. and Torgo L. (1990): "Knowledge Acquisition via Knowledge Integration", in Current Trends in Artificial Intelligence, B. Wielinga et al. (eds.), IOS Press, Amsterdam, 1990.

Durfee E., Lesser V.R. and Corkill D.D. (1989): "Cooperative Distributed Problem Solving", in *The Handbook of Artificial Intelligence, Volume IV,* Barr A., Cohen P.R. and Feigenbaum E.A. (eds.), Addison Wesley, 1989.

Gams M. (1989): "The Measurement Highlight the Importance of Redundant Knowledge", in *Proceedings of 4th European Working Session on Machine Learning (EWSL-89)*, K. Morik (ed.), pp. 71-80, Pitman - Morgan Kaufmann.

Muggleton S. and Feng C. (1990): "Efficient Induction of Logic Programs", in Proceedings of the First Conference on Algorithmic Learning, Tokyo, Japan, October 1990, Ohmsha Publ., Tokyo.

Murray K.S. and Porter B.W. (1989): "Controlling Search for the Consequences of New Information During Knowledge Integration", in *Proceedings of 6th International Workshop on Machine Learning*, A.M. Segre (ed.), Ithaca, New York, Morgan Kaufmann Inc.

Shaw M. and Gaines B. (1989): Knowledge Acquisition: Some Foundations, manual Methods and Future Trends, in *Proceedings of Third European Workshop on Knowledge Acquisition for Knowledge-Based Systems*, J. Boose, B. Gaines and J.G. Ganascia (eds.), Paris, July 1989.

# Extending Learning to Multiple Agents: Issues and a Model for Multi-Agent Machine Learning (MA-ML)

SATI S. SIAN

Dept. of Computing, Imperial College, 180 Queen's Gate, London SW7 2BZ
Email: sss@doc.ic.ac.uk

## Abstract

Many real world situations are currently being modelled as a set of cooperating intelligent agents. Trying to introduce learning into such a system requires dealing with the existence of multiple autonomous agents. The inherent distribution means that effective learning has to be based on a cooperative framework in which each agent contributes its part. In this paper we look at the issues in multi-agent machine learning and examine what effect the presence of multiple agents has on current learning methodologies. We describe a model for cooperative learning based on *structured dialogue* between the agents. MALE is an implementation of this model and we describe some results from it.

**Keywords**        Multiple Agents, Distributed Learning, Support Combination.

## 1  Introduction

Current Machine Learning (ML) research deals primarily with one single learning agent [Michalski et. al., 1983; Michalski et. al., 1986; Kodratoff, 1988]. However many real world problems are modelled better as a set of cooperating intelligent agents. In addition, even agents who are not explicitly part of cooperative framework will, in many real world situations, have to deal with other agents in their operating environment. Recognising this situation, recent work in the field of Distributed Artificial Intelligence (DAI) [Huhns, 1987; Bond & Gasser, 1988; Gasser & Huhns, 1989] has examined the problems of coordination and cooperation associated with such multi-agent systems. The problem of learning when multiple agents are present, however, has not received much attention.

Our primary objective in this paper is to look at *multi-agent machine learning* (MA-ML) by examining:

- the motivation for multiple agents in learning
- the problems introduced by the presence of multiple agents
- the effect on current methodologies
- a framework and model for MA-ML based on structured dialogue between the agents

In addition we have carried out some investigations with an implementation of the model called MALE (Multi-Agent Learning Environment) and some results from this are described.

## 2   Attributes of Multi-Agent Systems

We will start by looking at the various attributes of multi-agent learning systems such as the reasons for trying to construct such systems, the problems that occur and the specific issues that have to be tackled.

### 2.1   The Motivation

The reasons for modelling a system using multiple intelligent agents range from improvements in speed to autonomous agents providing a better 'fit' to the problem [Bond & Gasser, 1988]. At the very least therefore, the existence of such systems and the requirement of having learning within them motivates the study of MA-ML. More positively however multiple agents may bring the following benefits to the learning task itself :

- *Scalability* : Individual agents in a system will have bounds on the resources available to them. Scaling up the learning task beyond a certain level will require the use of multiple agents and cooperation between these agents.
- *Speed* : Where it is possible to parallelise the learning process, the use of multiple agents may give advantages of speed and efficiency. However this has to be weighed against the overhead due to cooperation.
- *Fault Tolerance* : Distributed systems in general provide a more graceful degradation in performance in the presence of failures. In addition the use of cross-checking of results between agents may provide more reliable results.
- *Encapsulation* : A system of multiple agents allows the encapsulation of specific learning knowledge or expertise in particular agents. Such encapsulation gives advantages in development, management, understandability and reliability.

The increased availability of distributed platforms has allowed these rationales to be tested in distributed processing and increasing now in distributed AI. This work has led to the development of numerous methodologies some of which will be useful when building MA-ML systems.

## 2.2 The Problems

The problems associated with multi-agent systems all arise from the fact that the existence of multiple agents implies a distribution of information. Where the solution of a particular problem requires the availability of all such information (or as much as possible), effective ways of overcoming the distribution are required. Learning is one such problem where this distribution has important consequences.

Other than the learning algorithm, the main factor in deciding the quality of what an agent learns is the quality of the data on which the learning is based. For a learning agent, distribution of this data implies two possible problems:

- *Completion* : Consider a situation where the distribution is based on a partitioning of information into parts which are distinct but coupled. If.an agent has access to data only from one part and what has to be learned requires knowledge from other parts then this agent is unable to learn as its local data is incomplete. We shall call this the *completion problem*. An example of this would occur in a distributed manufacturing system in which individual agents are assigned the construction of distinct sub-parts and the learning task consists of finding attributes of sub-solutions that make a good overall component. Since these parts have interrelationships between them, the learning process of individual agents is constrained by the information held by other agents.

- *Confidence* : A well known problem when using induction is that the resulting hypothesis cannot be completely validated. However the confidence in a particular hypothesis increases as we obtain more and more data that is correctly explained by the hypothesis. Distribution of this data may therefore mean that an agent is unable to reach a level of confidence in its hypothesis sufficient to allow it to make use of it even though such data exists in the system. This we shall call the *confidence problem*.

These problems necessitate that we develop some means of cooperation between the agents in the system.

## 2.3 The Issues

We can quickly discount the possibility of simply collecting the source information of the multiple agents at one special point and using available methods of learning as one solution to the distribution. Other than the sheer volume of data, we would loose all the advantages that we previously outlined. What is required is a more cooperative framework where the participating agents perform local processing as far as possible and cooperate when necessary. Such an approach means the following issues must be handled:

- Recognising when to cooperate : One may adopt the approach that the agents always cooperate. This will be necessary when the agents do not have knowledge of the specific abilities of the other agents. Rather what exists in the system is implicit knowledge that there are other agents and that these agents are potentially useful. Where agents are aware of the other agents' abilities, more focused cooperation may be possible. The goal of such cooperation is always to overcome the completion and/or confidence problems.

- How to cooperate : Cooperation based on communication requires the use of some interaction language, a protocol for structuring the use of this language and associated semantics to allow the agents to make sense of the interaction. In complex systems such a language may hide representational differences between the agents and require agents to find a translation mechanism for expressing hypotheses in a common form. This is necessary to allow other agents to evaluate these hypotheses. The cooperation scheme also needs a mechanism for integrating the learning of the participating agents.

- Dealing with conflict : Having autonomous intelligent agents introduces the possibilities of conflict in the views of these agents. This requires having methods for recognising and resolving conflict.

In general we have to revise the prevalent procedure for a learning agent from a (get data → form best generalisation) to one of (get data → form best generalisation → confer with other agents → revise hypothesis).

## 3   The Effect on Current Methodologies

We can now look at the existing paradigms in ML [Michalski, 1987] and see what affect the presence of multiple agents has, viewing the changes necessary on both the algorithmic and structural level.

### Learning by being told

The presence of multiple agents may be reflected as an extension to one or both parts of the teacher/learner scenario in learning-by-being-told i.e multiple teachers and/or multiple learners. The multiple learners case poses no new problems. The one-to-one interaction is simply extended to a one-to-many interaction. Additional problems may however occur for the teaching agent if it is biasing its teaching based on knowledge of the learning agent. In this case the existence of multiple learners means that the teaching agent has to maintain multiple contexts.

The multiple teachers scenario requires additional capabilities on the part of the learning agent. The main problems arise when there is a conflict between the knowledge received from two teachers. Since the assumption in this form of learning is that the teacher's knowledge is correct, conflict has to be attributed to contextual differences. However if the assumption of correctness is relaxed then some framework for conflict resolution has to exist between the teaching agents.

## Learning by Deduction

In analytical or explanation-based learning [Mitchell et. al, 1986] the presence of multiple agents becomes significant when, as in many real-world domains, the domain knowledge is distributed amongst more than one agent. In such a situation the first step in the learning process, that of constructing a logical proof of why an instance is an example of a concept, may not be within the means of a single agent. What is required is a process of distributed search. [Kitamura & Okumoto, 1990] present a method that they call *diffused inference* in which each agent performs local search as far as possible and solicits help from the other agents when necessary. The subsequent step of generalisation may also require the use of more than one agent.

One useful attribute of the use of multiple agents in EBL is that one may be able to specify different operationality criteria for the different agents. As is quite often the case, an abstract domain theory is useful to different agents in different ways. Consider for example a domain theory describing the operation of a vehicle. The operationality criteria for this theory will be different for an agent that wishes to use it for learning how the vehicle functions from one who wishes to use it for diagnosis of faults. Such differences may be effectively captured in a multi-agent scenario.

## Learning by Analogy

Analogical learning transfers well between single and multi-agent systems. The process of recognising a similarity between two problems at some abstract level is the same inter-agent as it is intra-agent. Derivational analogy is more problematic as derivations are local to an agent.

## Learning by Induction

In the presence of multiple agents, the inductive learning suffers from the two problems of completeness and confidence that we described earlier. These problems occur in learning-from-examples where due to the examples being distributed each agent can only form a partial hypothesis and in learning-from-observation where different agents may form different concepts due to different foci of attention.

## 4  A Cooperative Framework for MA-ML

From the large space of problems in multi-agent learning we have concentrated our attention on the problem of learning by induction in peer group agents. Using models of human peer group learning as a basis, a framework for cooperative learning is proposed. An analyses of how the compositional structure of multi-agent systems affects the role of cooperation in learning has been reported by us in [Sian, 1990a] and the use of this cooperative framework to get adaptation in Distributed AI systems is reported in [Sian, 1990b]. Here we will give details of the model itself and how the model can be used to get group induction. Results from an implementation of the model are also shown. Our model consists of the following components:

- Agents that learn from their experience
- An interaction board for negotiation between agents
- An interaction language for talking about hypotheses
- An integration function for combining the opinions of the agents

In the model each agent first learns locally. When an agent has constructed a hypothesis in which it has reasonable confidence (a parameter to the system) it proposes it to the other agents via the interaction board. Other agents use their own experience to evaluate the hypothesis and may make changes to it. The net confidence value of each such hypothesis is used to select the one that should be accepted by the agents. The following sections give details of this process and the components of the model.

We make the following two assumptions:

- The cooperation paradigm is one of consensus with agents accepting the hypotheses that have the greatest support.
- The hypothesis representation and generation is the same in all agents.

### 4.1 The Learning Agent

Agents in our model consist of the following parts:

- Performance component : This is the part that is responsible for carrying out whatever problem solving activity the agent is assigned within a multi-agent system. This component will contain domain knowledge and expertise about the agent's task. A significant attribute of this knowledge is that it is necessarily non-monotonic so that the learning sub-system can add or modify information contained within it. Such changes are monitored by a simple belief maintenance component.

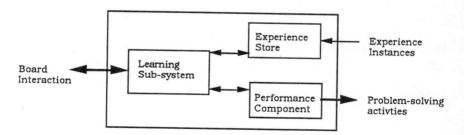

**Fig 1: Agent Structure**

- Experience store : During its problem-solving activities the agent receives information about the events and state of the external environment. This forms the source data for the learning system. The learning may be restricted to certain issues by filtering this data so that only data regarding that which has to be learnt arrives in the experience store. The store is organised as a hierarchy in which the instances form the lowest level and successively higher levels contain generalisations that classify these instances at the first level and classify lower level generalisations at successive levels. Maintenance of the hierarchy is controlled by the learning algorithm.

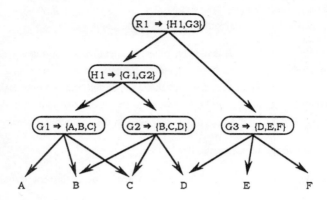

**Fig 2: Experience Store Hierarchy**

- Learning sub-system : This has three primary tasks; learning by induction on the data in the experience store, maintaining the store and interaction with the board for cooperative learning. The learning algorithm is incremental and is described in detail in the next section. The experience store is the 'workspace' of the algorithm and the learning process makes changes in this hierarchy. Additional maintenance of the store essentially consists of removing instances that are covered by a concept description which has been agreed and in which the agent has sufficient confidence. A full-memory model is impractical in most domains. Interaction using the board is the process by which the agents cooperate with the other agents to get the other agents' opinions about hypotheses that the proposer has learnt locally. This serves to both modify a hypothesis based on another agent's experience and increase confidence in it based on concurrence from the other agents.

Note that there is no direct connection between the experience store and the performance component. The data in the experience store must be processed by the learning sub-system before being made available to the performance component.

**Learning Algorithm**

The learning process consists of an incremental learning algorithm that constructs a generalisation hierarchy with successively lower levels being more specific. The lowest level consists of individual instances. Each generalisation has associated with it two values; *in-conf* and *out-conf*. The value in-conf is a measure of how many instances the generalisation correctly covers and out-conf is a measure of how many instances argue against the generalisation (*net-conf* is the difference between the two). The algorithm proceeds as follows:

```
For each new instance I
   If I is correctly explained by current knowledge
      Then increase confidence in this knowledge
   Else
      For all generalisations G in heirarchy that cover this instance
         Check( G,I )

   For all instances not now covered
      Create new generalisation and insert in heirarchy

   If net-conf > threshold for any generalisation G
      Propose G on board

Check( G,I ):
   If +ve instance
      Then increase in-conf of G
   If -ve instance
      Then If specialisation( G,I ) does not succeed
            Then increase out-conf of G
```

The basic goal of the algorithm is to create a generalisation hierarchy with maximum *net-conf* values at each node. Each new instance is first checked against what the agent already knows. This is to stop the agent from spending effort in learning previously agreed hypotheses. Instances that agree with these hypotheses simply increase their confidence. All other instances are added to the hierarchy. The first step is to check the current generalisations starting with the most specific. An instance correctly covered by one of these generalisation need not be checked against those at a higher level. If an instance is incorrectly covered then the we first try and specialise the generalisation so as to include as many as possible of the originally covered set but exclude the new instance. The specialisation procedure uses both attributes of the instances and domain knowledge to change the generalisation. If no specialisation can be found then the out-conf value of the generalisation is increased. Generalisations with a net-conf value too low are removed. At the end of this stage we may have a number of instances not covered by any generalisation. Where possible new generalisations are created to cover these instances and linked into the hierarchy. The preference when creating these generalisations is to find more generalised versions of existing ones in an incremental fashion to cover these instances.

Additional changes to the hierarchy may occur as a result of the interaction with the other agents and we shall discuss these after looking at the the cooperative activity in the system. This algorithm has some similarity to the UNIMEM algorithm [Lebowitz, 1987] in that it also constructs a hierarchy of generalisations. However in the UNIMEM hierarchy each instance may only have one parent. Each instance is unique and consists of attribute-value pairs. UNIMEM attaches confidence values to each attribute rather then the generalisation as a whole.

### Hypothesis evaluation

In addition to learning from its own environment, a cooperative framework requires agents to evaluate other agents' hypotheses with respect to their local data. This may consist in the first instance of agreement or disagreement with a hypothesis. However a more useful form is for the evaluating agent to itself propose ways of making the hypothesis more acceptable. This leads to a negotiation process that we will examine in the next section. Here we will look at how an agent evaluates a hypothesis proposed by another agent.

The goal of the evaluation as we have said is for the evaluating agent to check if the proposed hypothesis is consistent with its own data. From the evaluating agent's perspective it would prefer to do this as efficiently as possible. Trying to check a hypothesis against individual instances is prohibitive. Instead the agent can use the generalisation hierarchy to get much more effective evaluation. The result of this evaluation can be one the following four cases. If P is the proposal then

- *Totally Consistent* if the agent has no data against P
- *Totally Inconsistent* if the agent has data against P and can find no way of specialising P to exclude this data
- *Partially Consistent* if a specialisation of P is consistent with the agent's data
- *Disjoint* if the agent has no relevant data regarding P

The result will decide what response an agent gives to a proposal. We will see this when looking at the operators available to an agent for talking about hypothesis.

## 4.2 Interaction Board and Language

The interaction board is a multi-level shared structured which the agents use to communicate. Peer agents are connected to one level. Higher levels are necessary to cope with hierarchical organisations in multi-agent systems. Agents at one level are able to influence the interaction at lower-levels. The structural similarity to a blackboard architecture [Erman et. al., 1980] is obvious. The role of our agents is not however to opportunisticly transform a problem but to express an evaluated opinion as regards proposed hypotheses. Such a centralised structure is appropriate in peer groups as it is not known *a priori* which agent will be of benefit.

The interaction language consists of a set of operators for hypotheses. These operators allow agents to introduce/remove hypotheses, express the results of local evaluation and change the status of hypotheses based on the integration of the evaluations.

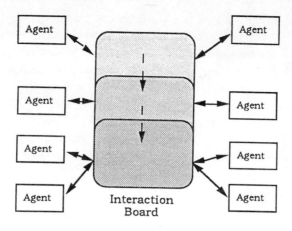

**Fig 3: Shared Interaction Board Structure**

The following is the definition of the operators:

- Introduction & Removal :
    PROPOSE( H,C ), ASSERT( H ), WITHDRAW( H ), ACCEPT( H )
- Evaluation :
    CONFIRM( H,C), DISAGREE( H,C ), MODIFY( H,H',C,S ), NOOPINION( H )
- Status modifiers :
    AGREED( H,T )

where        H is the hypothesis in question

H' is a modified H

C is the confidence value (range 0..1)

T is the resultant confidence value (range 0..1)

S is a similarity measure (range 0..1)

As can be seen from the definitions, most of these operators have an associated confidence value. This allows the agents to give a measure of how many instances the response is based on. A CONFIRM based on lots of instances is obviously more powerful that one based on just a few. The resultant confidence value for H is given by the integration function described in the next section. The similarity measure S is a measure of the number of instances that motivate the specialisation of H to H'. The mapping from the number of instances to the confidence value is dependent on the context of the system. So, for example, if within a particular situation the existence of 5 instances indicates near certainty then this would map to a value close to 1. Other situations may need hundreds of instances to approach this value. The exact numbers are less important then the mapping being consistent across agents.

The protocol that structures the use of this language consists of a set of rules that specify the order in which the operators must occur. Essentially once an agent proposes a hypothesis it waits for the other agents to respond. Each agent evaluates the proposal and returns a CONFIRM if it is totally consistent, DISAGREE if it is totally inconsistent, MODIFY if it is partially consistent and NOOPINION if it is disjoint relative to its data as defined in the previous section. These responses are combined using their associated confidence values and the integration function to give T. Any modified H (H') has to be reevaluated by the other agents. Once this process is complete, the version with the highest T value is agreed and the subsequent ACCEPT from the agent removes it from the board. The other versions are withdrawn by the proposers. If the highest T value is below a threshold then no hypothesis is accepted.

## 4.3 The Integration Function

In order to judge the relative merits of a hypothesis against other versions of that hypothesis we have to be able to give each hypothesis a net value based on the responses and their associated confidence values that it received from the participating agents. In general this can be a difficult problem since the confidence values represent a measure of belief on the part of the agent. Use of Bayesian functions is inappropriate as these values are certainly not probabilities. A confidence value of C in H does not imply a confidence value of $1-C$ in $\neg$H. Similar problems resulting from trying to combine the belief values of two rules were encountered in the MYCIN project [Shortliffe & Buchanan, 1980]. The situation is even more difficult in our case as the more recent work on the Shafer-Dempster theory [Shafer, 1976] (which deals adequately for the MYCIN problems) requires knowing the complete set of possible hypotheses suggested by the evidence which is a condition that we cannot meet in our general situation.

We have adopted an extension of the approach in [Stefanyuk 87] in which he presents an axiomatisation of a combination function and derives the function from these axioms. This work considers only confidence values in support of a hypothesis and our extension has been to use Stefanyuk's Formula for the combination of confidence values of one kind (either in support-of or support-against), provide an axiomatisation of a combination function that handles both kinds of confidence values and finally to derive this function from these axioms. Let $x_1$ and $x_2$ be two confidence values of one kind, $c(x_1,x_2)$ be a function that combines these values, $\alpha_n$ and $\beta_n$ be the total confidence for and against a hypothesis respectively and $C(\alpha_n,\beta_n)$ be the function that gives the resultant confidence in the hypothesis. Then the following axiomatic definitions apply:

A1:    $0 \le x_1 < 1, 0 \le x_2 < 1, 0 \le c(x_1,x_2) < 1, 0 \le C(\alpha_n,\beta_n) < 1$

A2:    $c(x,0) = x$

A3:    $c(x_1,x_2) = c(x_2,x_1)$

A4:    $C(0,\beta_n) = 0, C(\alpha_n,0) = \alpha_n$

A5:    As $\alpha_n \to 1$ then $C(\alpha_n,\beta_n) \to 1-\beta_n$, as $\beta_n \to 1$ then $C(\alpha_n,\beta_n) \to 0$

A6:    $c(x_1,x_2)$ and $C(\alpha_n,\beta_n)$ can be expanded as a power series in $x_1,x_2$ and $\alpha_n,\beta_n$ respectively

From these we derive the following functions ([Sian, 1990c] gives the rational for the axioms and the derivation):

$$c(x_1, x_2) = x_1 + x_2 - x_1 x_2 \quad \text{(Stefanyuk's Formula)}$$
$$C(\alpha_n, \beta_n) = \alpha_n - \alpha_n \beta_n$$

Within our interaction framework CONFIRM represents confidence in a hypothesis, DISAGREE confidence against the hypothesis, MODIFY partial confidence in the hypothesis (with the similarity measure determining the level of partiality and NOOPINIONs representing neither. The combination function is therefore defined as follows:

$$\textbf{Net-Val( H ) = Total\_Confidence( supporting,H) [ 1 - Total\_Confidence( against,H ) ]}$$

Let Count( T ) give the number of responses of type T. Then given n agents if:

Count( CONFIRM ) = c, Count( DISAGREE ) = d,
Count( MODIFY ) = m, Count( NOOPINION ) = p and
$n = c + d + m + p$

then

$$\text{Total\_Confidence( supporting,H)} \quad = V_{c+m}$$
$$\text{Total\_Confidence( against,H )} \quad = V_d$$

where

$$V_x = V_{x-1} + C_x(1 - V_{x-1})$$
$$V_0 = 0.$$

in which

$C_x$ = Confidence of xth agent giving response.

Consider an example with 4 responses; 2 confirms with values $c_1$ and $c_2$, 1 modify with value $m_1$ and 1 disagree with value $d_1$. If the similarity measure of the modify response is $s_1$ then the response can be considered a confirm $c_3 = m_1 s_1$. Then:

$$\text{Total\_Confidence( supporting,H)} \quad = c_1 + c_2 + c_3 - c_1 c_2 - c_1 c_3 - c_2 c_3 + c_1 c_2 c_3.$$
$$\text{Total\_Confidence( against,H )} \quad = d_1$$
$$\text{Net-Val( H ) =} \quad = (c_1 + c_2 + c_3 - c_1 c_2 - c_1 c_3 - c_2 c_3 + c_1 c_2 c_3)(1 - d_1)$$

## 4.4 An Example

We can now tie all these parts together and illustrate the functioning of the model with an example. We will consider a system with three agents operating in the domain of commodities trading. Each agent is responsible for trading within a particular area. Each agent receives information on events that occur in the area and how the prices of various commodities change with these events. The goal of the learning is to create generalised descriptions of how prices fluctuate due to various classes of events. To aid the learning process agents have domain knowledge about these commodities available to them. First let us see how one agent learns locally. Given the following data agent 1 constructs the generalisation hierarchy shown below:

```
I1:    Price(Coffee,Rising),Weather(Kenya,Frost)
I2:    Price(Coffee,Rising),Weather(Kenya,Drought)
I3:    Price(Tea,Rising),Weather(Kenya,Frost)
I4:    Price(Tea,Rising),Weather(Kenya,Drought)
```

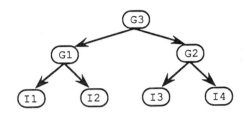

where

```
G1:    Price(Coffee,Rising) if Weather(Kenya,Adverse)
G2:    Price(Tea,Rising) if Weather(Kenya,Adverse)
G3:    Price(Crop,Rising) if Weather(Kenya,Adverse)
```

The relationship between (coffee,tea) and crop and between (frost,drought) and adverse is part of a is-a hierarchy that forms part of the agent's domain knowledge. When a new instance I5 arrives the hierarchy changes as shown:

```
I5:    Price(Cocoa,Steady),Weather(Kenya,Flood)
G3':   Price(Crop,Rising) if Weather(Kenya,Adverse),Affects(Adverse,Crop)
```

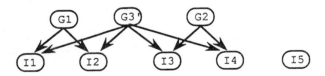

G3 has had to be specialised since it incorrectly covered I5. This is achieved by finding an attribute that distinguishes I5 from as many as possible of the original set. The agent uses its domain knowledge to find that cocoa is unaffected by floods whereas the others are affected by frost and drought.

Other agents use this same procedure to construct their own hierarchies based on the data they receive. Let us assume that Agent 3 has enough confidence in one of its generalisations to propose it on the board. The other agents will then use the evaluation procedure described previously to check this proposal against their own experiences. Note that the objective of the interaction is to find the most specific version of the proposal that has the maximum support. Therefore agents not only indicate confirmation or disagreement with a proposal but also modifications that make it more consistent with their experiences. In this case the interaction proceeds as follows:

Agent 3: **PROPOSE**( P1,0.7 )         [P1 = Price( Cocoa,Rising ) if Weather( Brazil,Adverse )]
Agent 2: **MODIFY**( P1,P2,0.6,0.6 )   [P2 = Price( Cocoa,Rising ) if Weather( Country,Adverse )]
Agent 1: **MODIFY**( P1,P3,0.8,0.63 )  [P3 = Price( Crop,Rising ) if   Weather( Country,Adverse),
                                                          Affects( Adverse,Crop )]

Agent 1: **MODIFY**( P2,P3,0.8,0.63 )
Agent 3: **CONFIRM**( P2,0.7 )
Agent 3: **CONFIRM**( P3,0.7 )
Agent 2: **MODIFY**( P3,P4,0.6,0.54 ) [P4 = Price( Crop,Rising ) if   Weather( Country,Adverse),
                                                          Affects( Adverse,Crop ),
                                                          Produces( Country,Crop )]

Agent 1: **CONFIRM**( P4,0.8 )
Agent 3: **CONFIRM**( P4,0.7 )

[ Net-Val( P1 ) = 0.9556, Net-Val( P2 ) = 0.9556, Net-Val( P3 ) = 0.9724, Net-Val( P4 ) = 0.976 ]

Agent 2: **AGREED**( P4,0.976 )
Agent 3: **WITHDRAW**( P1 ), **ACCEPT**( P4 )
Agent 1: **WITHDRAW**( P3 ), **ACCEPT**( P4 )
Agent 2: **WITHDRAW**( P2 )

Agent 2 generalises P1 with regard to country. Agent 1 generalises with regard to crop but adds the specialisation of 'Affects' which its data has suggested. The same response is also appropriate for P2. The original proposer Agent 3 has no data against either and therefore confirms both with its original confidence value. The interesting response is Agent 2's **MODIFY** to P3. This is based on it having an instance in which the price of tea is unaffected by drought in its region. Since it only has a very small number of instances to back a modification its the difference between its similarity measure and proposal value is very low (0.06). However on evaluating P4 the other agents find it consistent with their data and its resultant net value is highest. Note that our main interest is in the relative values rather than the actual numbers. Studies in psychology show that such convergence to the correct hypothesis once it has been suggested by one agent also occurs in human group induction [Laughlin & Shippy, 1983]. The other proposals are withdrawn and P4 accepted (an agreed hypothesis such as P4 is automatically removed once it has been accepted by all the other agents).

The net result of this cooperation is that agents are amalgamating their experience at a high level. Each agent is benefiting from the experience of the other agents. This results in hypotheses being corrected when necessary and further confirmed when possible.

## 4.5 Some experiments

The above model has been implemented in a system called MALE (multi-agent learning environment) in PROLOG with agents as processes that interact with the interaction board via message passing. We have tested the model using examples from a commodities trading domain as the source data. This data contains various sorts of events such as changes in weather, changes in political situation, announcement of alternatives to some commodities, changes in economic conditions plus how these events were followed by changes to the prices of various commodities such as crops, metals and oil. The goal of the system is to get the maximum average performance from the agents where performance is measured by the ability to correctly predict the price change given an event.

We have tried to evaluate the performance based on a number of scenarios:

1) Single agent receiving all the data compared to a multi-agent system with the data spread equally (both systems using the learning algorithm defined in the model)
2) Multi-agent system with single agent learning only (no interaction)
3) Multi-agent system no-learning
4) The effect of varying the number of agents participating in the interaction
5) Varying the spread of the data with some agents getting more data

For this paper the significant test is the first (results of the others are more relevant to the design of multi-agent systems and are reported in [Sian, 1990b]). The predictive ability of single versus multi-agent systems with the same data showed no difference if the agents interact after receiving each new instance. Otherwise the multi-agent system catches up the single agent after each interaction session.

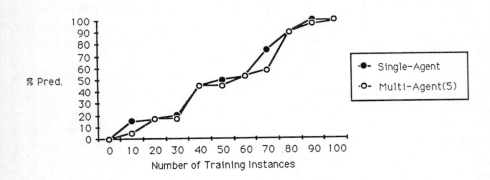

**Fig 4: Predictive performance of single versus multi-agent learning**

Predictive performance was measured against a test set. The multi-agent systems had 5 agents which interacted after receiving 2 new instances each. This result leads us to propose the following for our model:

*Proposition 1 : The predictive ability of a learning system is unaffected by the use of multiple agents.*

The difference in the two systems occurs in the speed with which they perform the inductive generalisation. In tests the single agent system outperforms the multi-agent system in the initial stages as the later has the overhead of cooperation. However as the number of instances increases the parallelisation of the learning process rapidly overcomes this overhead. On average with 5 agents the multi-agent system on a SUN 4 for this data was 3 times faster.

From this we propose the following:

*Proposition 2: In the presence of large amounts of data, a multi-agent learning system will give advantages in speed over a single agent system.*

We have are now trying MALE with the soya-bean disease data used in incremental AQ [Riene & Michalski, 1987]. A multi-agent scenario can be envisaged for this data if we assume that the data was collected from different autonomous agricultural centres. A cooperative approach to finding discriminant descriptions for these diseases can then be applied.

# 5 Conclusion

Consideration from both a pragmatic point of view i.e. multi-agent systems exist and therefore we must study learning within these systems and from a technological point of view i.e. looking for benefits to the learning process from the use of multiple agents warrants the study of the hitherto unexplored area of MA-ML. In this paper we have described the problems and issues in MA-ML and how the presence of multiple agents may affect current paradigms in ML. We have proposed a cooperative framework and studied its use in a sample domain. As the results show, MA-ML can give considerable benefits to learning systems. Further work needs to look at the use of different algorithms in the agents, richer forms of dialogue between the agents and ways of formulating the belief combination in agents.

# References

[Bond & Gasser, 1988]  -  Bond A. & Gasser L. [Eds], *Readings in DAI*, Chapter 1, Morgan Kaufmann Publishers, San Mateo, CA 1988.

[Erman et. al, 1980]  -  Erman L. et. al, *The Hearsay II Speech Understanding System*, Computing Surveys 12(2), p213-253, June 1980

[Gasser & Huhns, 1989]  -  Gasser L. & Huhns M. [Eds], *Distributed AI II*, Pitman, London, 1989.

[Huhns, 1987]  -  Huhns M. [Ed], *Distributed AI*, Pitman, London, 1987.

[Kitamura & Okumoto, 1990]  -  Kitamura Y. & Okumoto T., *Diffusing Inference: A Inference Method for Distributed Problem Solving and Its Property*, in Proceeding of

First International Working Conference on Cooperating KBS, University of Keele, Oct 1990.

[Kodratoff, 1988] - Kodratoff Y., *Introduction to Machine Learning*, Pitmann Publishers, London, 1988.

[Laughlin & Shippy, 1983] - Laughlin P. & Shippy T., *Collective Induction*, Journal of Personality and Social Psychology 45(1), p 94-100, 1983.

[Lebowitz, 1987] - Lebowitz M., *Experiments with Incremental Concept Formation: UNIMEM*, Machine Learning 2(2), p103-138, 1987.

[Michalski et. al, 1983] - Michalski R. et. al., *Machine Learning: An AI Approach*, Morgan Kaufmann Publishers, Los Altos, CA, 1983.

[Michalski et. al., 1986] - Michalski R. et. al., *Machine Learning: An AI Approach Vol 2*, Morgan Kaufmann Publishers, Los Altos, CA, 1983.

[Michalski, 1987] - Michalski R., *Learning Strategies and Automated Knowledge Acquisition: An Overview*, in Computational Models of Learning, Bolc L. [Ed.], Springer-Verlag, Germany, 1987.

[Mitchell et. al., 1986] - Mitchell T. et. al., *Explanation-based Generalisation: A Unifying View*, Machine Learning 1(1), p 47-80, 1986.

[Riene & Michalski, 1987] - Riene R. & Michalski R., *Incremental Learning of Concept Descriptions*, in Machine Intelligence Vol 11, Hayes J. et. al. [Eds.], p263-288, Morgan Kaufmann, San Mateo, 1987.

[Shafer, 1976] - Shafer G., *A Mathematical Theory of Evidence*, Princeton, New Jersey, Princeton University Press, 1976.

[Shortliffe & Buchanan, 1980] - Shortliffe & Buchanan, *Rule-Based Expert Systems*, MIT Press, 1980.

[Sian, 1990a] - Sian S., *The Role of Cooperation in Multi-Agent Learning*, in Proceeding of First International Working Conference on Cooperating KBS, University of Keele, Oct 1990.

[Sian, 1990b] - Sian S., *Adaptation based on Cooperative Learning in Multi-Agent Systems*, in Proceedings of Second Workshop on Modelling Autonomous Agents (MAAMAW 90), ONERA, Paris, August 1990.

[Sian, 1990c] - Sian S., *Learning in Distributed AI Systems*, Ph. D Thesis, Imperial College, University of London, London (forthcoming).

[Stefanyuk 87] - Stefanyuk V. L., *Some Aspects of the Theory of Expert Systems*, Soviet Journal of Computing Science 25(5), p110-116, 1987.

# Applications of Machine Learning: Notes from the Panel Members

Peter Clark (Turing Institute, Glasgow, UK)
Bojan Cestnik (Jozef Stefan Institute, Ljubljana, Yugoslavia)
Claude Sammut (Univ. New South Wales, Australia)
Joachim Stender (Brainware GmbH, Berlin, Germany)

## 1  Introduction

Machine learning (ML) is devoted to the study and computer modelling of learning processes in their multiple manifestations. Although ML research started with the advent of computers, it is only relatively recently that its results have left the research laboratories and found their way into real-world applications.

The motivation for applying ML techniques to real-world tasks is strong: the problems of manually engineering a knowledge base are now well known, and ML offers a technology for assisting in this task; there is vast potential for automatically discovering new knowledge in the recent explosion of available on-line databases, too large for humans to manually sift through; and the ability of computers to automatically adapt to changing expertise would offer huge benefits for the maintenance and evolution of expert systems.

Despite this, the success of ML applications varies tremendously. There are some spectacular successes to its credit, but also the number of mature real-world applications reported in the literature is limited.

The fact ML has been highly successful in some instances deserves emphasising, to dispel the myth that ML has yet to achieve serious real-world success. Two notable examples are GASOIL and BMT, expert systems engineered using inductive tools with massive time savings (see Table 1). GASOIL was constructed in 1986 [Slocombe et al., 1986], and reported to be in regular use at four company sites in 1987 [Hertz, 1987]. BMT was constructed by Brainware GmbH, and is currently being deployed [Hayes-Michie, 1990]. A third example is Westinghouse's process control system [Leech, 1986], constructed with the aid of the inductive tool ExpertEase. By using ExpertEase along with other traditional means of analysis, Westinghouse achieved increased throughput in one important factory to the extent of increasing business volume by more than ten million dollars per annum, a result considered unlikely to have been achieved without ExpertEase [Barry, 1984]. Brief reports on around 25 other real-world ML applications can be found in [Hayes-Michie, 1990] and [Mowforth, 1986], and the number continues to grow.

| System | Application | No. of rules | Development (man-years) | Maintenance (man-years) | Inductive tools |
|--------|-------------|--------------|------------------------|-------------------------|-----------------|
| Mycin | Medical diagnosis | 400 | 100 | n/a | n/a |
| XCon | VAX computer configuration | 8,000 | 180 | 30 | n/a |
| GASOIL | Hydrocarbon separation system configuration | 2,800 | 1 | 0.1 | Yes |
| BMT | Configuration of fire-protection equipment in buildings | >30,000 | 9 | 2.0 | Yes |

Table 1: Tabulation from [Slocombe et al., 1986] and augmented by Michie with BMT data [Michie, 1990]

These achievements are substantial. However, it is also true that the number of such successes reported in the literature is limited. While this is partly because companies are either reluctant or see no reason to make public their progress, part of the reason must also be attributed to the need for ML research to mature further to extend the class of real-world problems that can be handled. It is thus worth reflecting on the current state of ML application: What type of applications have been successfully tackled by ML? Which ML techniques have been most successful in application? How well does the current research in ML match the requirements of application-builders? and what directions of further research are pointed to by those experienced in building applications?

The panel, all who have had substantial experience of constructing real-world ML applications, will be discussing these issues. Here, as a prelude to the panel meeting, some initial comments are offered from the panel members.

# 2 Comments

## 2.1 from Joachim Stender

Machine Learning research has resulted mainly in algorithms which handle synthetic data. This data has the following properties:

- The 'fields' are either carefully separated beforehand into conditions and conclusions by human experts or this can easily be done afterwards. This separation is semantically unique or is at least interpreted as such

- The examples are always carefully selected with the help of a human expert

- Very frequently these examples show the semantic properties of rules (through the extensive use of "Don't Care" or wildcard characters "*")

- The scope of the data samples is relatively small and it is easy to get an overview

- The data are typically free of noise; "Clashing Examples" are as a rule interpreted as input errors

- Very frequently, the examples cover the complete state space

Such synthetic databases are mostly artificial. i.e., they have been carefully constructed at a specific point in time.

The solution of real world problems usually requires the handling of analytic data. This data has the following properties:

- The state space is not completely covered by the given data samples

- The data are usually very noisy

- The hidden regularities within the data are not known by a human expert

- Conventional methods of data analysis cannot successfully be used due to (a) the complexity of the relations to be considered and (b) the size of the dataset

- Popular machine learning algorithms (in particular ID3-based algorithms) cannot be used due to the size of the dataset and the degree of noise in the data

- The separation of the 'fields' into conditions and conclusions is not simple and there is no single 'correct' way to do so

We call datasets with such properties analytic. Such datasets typically evolve through "natural evolution" which has normally taken place through years of additions and changes. Examples are customer databases or machine-acquired data.

Some ML researchers have responded to this discrepancy by attempting to extend their algorithms so that they can handle analytic data more easily (Tree pruning, statistical criteria etc). However, this is the wrong approach! Such algorithms were originally designed for something different, namely for the solution of artificial problems and through necessity have been extended. These extensions frequently do not reflect the original structure of the algorithm and sometimes represent a completely different philosophy, namely that of statistics.

Instead, the required approach is designing algorithms for the handling of large-scale, analytic data. These algorithms regard synthetic data as a special case.

## 2.2   from Bojan Cestnik

I would like to make two general points about the relation of ML research to ML applications. Firstly, most of the ML methods developed so far (e.g. ID3 and its successors, AQ, CN2, DUCE, FOIL) are general in the sense that they can be applied to a variety of different domains. On the other hand, the incorporation of domain-specific properties in the acquired knowledge has not been sufficiently considered yet in the ML research. Among the domain-specific properties, I would like to specifically mention the monotonicity of an attribute that can, when encountered, serve many useful purposes. It can be, for example, used in checking consistency of learning examples, or in generating additional learning examples if they are required. And more importantly, it is reasonable to believe that the quality of acquired knowledge can be substantially improved by taking the monotonicity into account within a learning method.

Secondly, for the applications of machine learning methods in real-world domains it seems important that several methods are applied and combined together. Since every single method generates only an approximation of domain knowledge, the main benefits of the combination are expected to be the following:

- Due to different methods, the acquired domain knowledge can be observed form different perspectives, in different knowledge representation formalisms, etc,; therefore the understandability of acquired knowledge from a user viewpoint can be substantially improved

- The performance of a reasonable combination of applied methods, in terms of classification accuracy, can be improved with respect to every single method.

## 2.3    from Claude Sammut

### 2.3.1    Where have practical ML successes occurred?

Almost certainly, the most successful learning program so far has been Quinlan's C4. What have been the reasons for its success?

- It can cope with noisy data

- It's representation allows continuous-valued attributes.

- The domains in which it has been use only require simple feature vector representations.

Donald Michie has conjectured that feature vectors seem to be a characteristic representation for one of the major application areas of expert systems, viz, finance. However, scientific and engineering domains tend to require more structured representations. Why should this be so?

### 2.3.2    Representations and structure

Perhaps one explanation is that many current expert systems capture 'seat of the pants' knowledge that is not governed by any deep model but purely by experience. However, if we are trying to discover laws governing natural phenomena then it is likely that a deep model is required. This implies that research in constructive induction and learning relations is central to learning in scientific domains. We might also mention the importance of qualitative models since they are useful in capturing relations.

Does the above also endorse research in explanation-based learning, since it too can deal with structured representations? I do not believe so. EBL (or more correctly, automatic programming) seeks to 'operationalise' an already acquired concept. While there is good reason to wish to do this, learning is not one of them since it is not possible to make any justifiable generalisation from one example. Learning by induction is still likely to be the most productive method for acquiring knowledge. This leads us to a consideration of how data for learning are collected.

### 2.3.3   Noisy data and non-determinism

The real world is messy! It is noisy, non-deterministic and not at all well behaved. We are familiar with noise in data sets such as those obtained from pathology laboratories, etc. However, even this data has been extensively filtered before being input to a learning program. Useful attributes and even higher-level features are chosen for the program.

A much more difficult task for machine learning is to place a learning program in control of an agent in a reactive environment and have the program learn how to achieve some desired result. In this case the program alone is responsible for collecting data. This situation arises in manufacturing and robotics when we would like some processes to tune itself automatically. The difficulties in this kind of task are: finding an appropriate representation, especially finding threshold values for variables; dealing with non-deterministic behaviour when the representation is inadequate.

Very little research into learning in this kind of domain has been conducted and it is vital if learning programs are to be of any use in real- time applications. Neural-net enthusiasts will immediately claim that they are making progress in this area. However, most research has been in the form of designing programs with almost no understanding of how or why they should work. A theory for this style of learning is essential. Interestingly, this is likely to bring statistics and learnability theory even more into mainstream machine learning.

## 2.4   from Peter Clark

It is tempting to try and generalise about which applications are most suitable for a ML approach. However, while some guidelines can be given, it should also be noted that the success of a ML application depends as much on the skill of the 'ML expert' as on the ML technique used. For example, in order to apply ID3, a suitable way of converting the problem into a classification-of-examples task must be selected; a suitable way of describing examples must be designed, requiring careful consideration and imagination to ensure the essential information is captured in the attributes; appropriate class values must be chosen; and initial runs of ID3 might reveal the data needs to be reorganised, or more data collected, or the definition of some attributes changed. This process may iterate several times until an acceptable solution is produced.

Thus the skills required to apply ML are quite considerable. For those seeking a ML solution to a real-world problem, the cost of obtaining the necessary ML expertise to use the ML algorithm frequently exceed the costs of the algorithm itself. In a nutshell, the 'unsupervised learning' of a tool such as ID3 is never unsupervised.

The implication of this for someone interested in a ML application to their problem is that ML expertise as well as the algorithm itself should be sought. The implication for ML research is that there is considerable activity in 'learning' to solve a problem which is not yet conducted by machines. Study of these extra areas of activity must be essential for further progress to be made in addressing real-world problems. Two practical ways forward for this are as follows. Firstly, critical study of the application as well as the development of ML techniques should be encouraged, and should be viewed as an important area of research. Secondly, as the ML expert's skill involves the use of substantial domain knowledge, the integration of ML with other knowledge-rich AI techniques (eg. qualitative modelling, causal reasoning, handling uncertainty) will become increasingly more important.

# References

Barry, R. Personal communication, 1984.

Hayes-Michie, J. E., editor. *Pragmatica: Bulletin of the Inductive Programming Special Interest Group*, volume 1. Turing Institute Press, Glasgow, UK, 1990.

Hertz, D. B., editor. *Applied AI Reporter*, volume 4 (4). Univ. of Miami, NJ, 1987.

Leech, W. J. A rule-based process control method with feedback. *Advances in Instrumentation*, 41:169–175, 1986.

Michie, D. Machine executable skills from 'silent' brains. In Addis, T. R. and Muir, R. M., editors, *Research and Development in Expert Systems VII*, pages 1–24. Cambridge Univ. Press. (Proc. ES90, the 10th BCS Specialist Group on Expert Systems), 1990.

Mowforth, P. Some applications with inductive expert system shells. TIOP 86-002, Turing Institute, Glasgow, UK, 1986.

Slocombe, S., Moore, K., and Zelouf, M. Engineering expert system applications. In *Annual Conference of the BCS Specialist Group on Expert Systems*, 1986.

# EVALUATION OF LEARNING SYSTEMS : AN ARTIFICIAL DATA-BASED APPROACH[1]

## H. LOUNIS  G. BISSON

LRI, Equipe Inférence et Apprentissage
Université Paris-Sud, Bâtiment 490
91405 Orsay Cedex France
email : lounis@lri.lri.fr, bisson@lri.lri.fr, phone : (33) 69-41-64-09

## Abstract

Experimentation has an important role in determining the capacities and restrictions of machine learning (ML) systems. In this paper we present the definition of some sensitivity and evaluation criteria which can be used to perform an evaluation of learning systems. Moreover, in order to overcome some of the limitations of real data sets, we introduce the specification of a parametrable generator of artificial learning sets which allows us to make easily complete experiments to discover some empirical rules of behavior for ML algorithms. Finally, we give some results obtained with different algorithms, showing that artificial data bases approach is an interesting direction to explore.

**Keywords** : Evaluation of Machine Learning Algorithms, Sensitivity Criteria, Evaluation Criteria, Artificial Data Base, Parametrable Generator, Modelization of Learning Domains.

# 1 Introduction

In Machine Learning and more generally in Artificial Intelligence domains, it is very difficult to completely evaluate a system through previous theoretical reasoning (Kibler, Langley 1988 ; Rendell 1989 ; Bisson, Laublet 1989&1990). This drawback comes mainly from the large utilization of heuristics in AI, the behavior of which is difficult to predict. Thus, information such as the actual complexity of an algorithm, is rarely provided by the authors and when it is, it often concerns the best and worst cases only. Nevertheless, the knowledge of its complexity is fundamental for those who

---

[1] This work is partially supported by CEC through the ESPRIT-2 contract MLT 2154 ("Machine Learning Toolbox") and also by MRT through PRC-IA.

want to use a system. On the other hand, some concepts such as the quality of learning, are subjective and very hard to define. In this context, the main goal of experimentation is to point out some relations between behaviors of learning systems and the conditions under which they occur.

In order to experiment we must set the characteristics of the output data (evaluation criteria) that we would like to measure and what are the relevant variables for these measures (sensitivity criteria). In this way, we determine a measure space that is characterized by the set of pairs [criterion (i), variable (j)]. However, for a given learning system, only a subset of these measures are feasible : for instance, the tests evaluating the bias influence or the degree of incrementality (Martin 1989), are feasible only if the system has these features. Moreover, according to the learning techniques and the goals of the system (diagnostic, problem solving, ...), the criteria change : in this way, for planning problems, the problem solving time is an important criterion that allows one to quantify the efficiency of the learned knowledge, however, this criterion is not very significant for classification problems.

In practice, it is useless to work out all the theoretically feasible tests, because this would cost too much time or would not be relevant when considering the purpose of the evaluation. So, the experimenter must decide the most useful tests in respect to this evaluation purpose. This paper is organized in three parts. In the first one, we detail how to execute an experimental study of learning systems by relating some of the sensitivity and evaluation criteria. In the second one, in order to establish correlations between the two types of criteria and to bring some answers to the limitations of real data sets, an artificial data base generator is proposed and its specifications are given. Finally, we show some results obtained with five different systems belonging to the supervised learning approach : CN2 (Boswell 1990 a), NewID (Boswell 1990 b), NewBOOLE (Bonelli 1990), LVQ (Mc-Dermott 1989) and MLP (Rumelhart 1986). We want to emphasize that the current work was partially done as part of the EEC ESPRIT contract "Machine Learning Toolbox". It has been integrated in the work package 7, whose goal is to develop an evaluation methodology of ML algorithms. The reader could find more details in the Deliverable 7.2 (MLT 1990) of this project.

# 2 Sensitivity criteria

The most important problem in inducing suitable knowledge is the problem of defining a "good" set of attributes and a "good" set of examples to represent a problem to be learned. The ML algorithms are sensitive to various characteristics of the information provided as input and they do not have the same behavior ; for example, some are more or less noise resistant, or more or less sensitive to the input order of the examples. The description and the choice of examples for a domain problem is of very great importance for the user of a ML algorithm. The sensitivity criteria correspond to the parameters on which depend the quality of the learned knowledge.

*Information quantity* : One of the main experimentations is concerned with the study of observable relations between the performance measures and the information quantity. On the one hand, they are relatively easy to achieve, if we limit ourselves to syntactic criteria. On the other hand, they are particularly informative about the main properties and limitations of the learning system. The size of the training set can be defined by several parameters such as the number of examples or descriptors, the number of concepts to learn or the quantity of available background knowledge ...

*Problem complexity* : In addition to the quantitative variables just described, we would like to define more qualitative criteria such as the difficulty of the problem that the learned knowledge must help to solve. These criteria are more domain dependent. For instance, in the case of concept recognition, the complexity can be measured by the number of conjunctions and disjunctions in the recognition functions (Rendell 1989). The presence of noise is another complexifying factor. Moreover, if the studied system types the descriptors or the data, it will be relevant to evaluate the learning results according to the types manipulated in the training data (nominal, ordered, ...).

*Relevance of descriptors* : In complex domains, the determination of the relevant descriptors is a very difficult problem (Cannat 1988). Thereby, the expression of knowledge can not be immediately suitable and there are often a lot of irrelevant descriptors in the initial training set. The system's capacity to learn in such an environment must be evaluated. We distinguish this variable from those about noise : here, all the needed information to learn are present and undamaged.

*Information order* : The use of pruning heuristics can modify the result of learning according to the input order of information within the training set. The study of its influence provides some information about the *learning stability* . These tests are different from those about the incrementality : the measure of stability is defined as soon as a learning step uses several set of data *simultaneously*. A low stability is awkward : the reliability of learned knowledge becomes questionable. Moreover in this case, it is probable that the learning process is very noise sensitive because a lack of stability reveals that the system does not use the data globally but incrementally when it builds its hypothesis.

*Noise influence* : These tests aim at measuring the noise sensitivity of the studied learning system. Indeed, in the real world domains, the noise is very difficult to erase because it is often linked to the acquisition process : for instance, the uncertainty on the measure instruments. There can be multiple sources for noisy data in a learning set (Manago, Kodratoff 1987) such as the uncertainty or imprecision of the valuation of the descriptors or a miss-classification of some examples.

*Incrementality degree* : These tests are very close to those effected to evaluate the stability of learning ; however, the conclusions are different. With an incremental system, we can accept that the order of information in the training set has some consequences for the quality of learning. During these measures it is also interesting to quantify the problem of *forgetting*. With this aim in view, we shall verify if the problems solved by the learned knowledge at time (t) are always solved at (t+1).

*Learning bias and heuristics* : When the system provides the possibility of changing the learning strategies (heuristics or bias), the experimenter must test their influences on the results of the learning process. During these measures, some empirical relations between the domain characteristics and the parameter values could be profitably established.

## 3 Evaluation criteria

Evaluation criteria were elaborated in order to exploit the notion of having a "good" result for a ML algorithm. In fact, "good" means that a result succeeds in a selection of tests of performance. Generally, the criteria which are most frequently used for evaluating ML algorithms involve the study of learning efficiency, since the main interest of a learning system is to build up a knowledge base able to effect accurate prediction. Nevertheless, the other criteria are also important : for instance, the understandability to a human user of "what is learned" is often crucial in order to improve the learning set ; similarly, the constraints of time can restrain the application domains. We can classify the learning evaluation criteria into five major categories which are :

*Cost of the learning set* : Learning can be an expensive process, particularly to constitute the training set. Therefore, it is very important to evaluate the cost of this preliminary phase. Independently of specific domain costs (medical tests for instance), this cost is obtained by measuring the amount of data required for learning (number of examples, ...), as well as by evaluating the required quality of these data (no noise, domain theory needed, ...). In the case of learning apprentice systems, the cost also takes into account the number and the relevance of questions asked.

*Time and memory constraints* : The measures of learning rapidity allow us to evaluate empirically the actual complexity of algorithms as a function of different parameters : the amount of data, the used heuristics, ... In practice, with this information, users will avoid making use of systems that are O(number of examples[3]) on very large training sets. In the case of systems that learn by successive refinements, connectionist systems for example, this criterion and the previous will also depend on the time and the number of observations required to obtain a specified accuracy level of the learned knowledge. In EBL we will measure the time to generalize a specific problem's solution (Shavlik 1989). The memory measure is less important. Nevertheless, the quantity of memory used during the learning phase indicates the usable computers for these learning techniques. Moreover, this criterion is related to the efficiency of the learning.

*Effectiveness of the learned knowledge* : When the purpose of learning is to obtain knowledge usable for classification or diagnosis, the main feasible measure concerns the predictive accuracy. Most empirical research on induction has focused on improving this criterion that measures the capability of the system to match a new situation with the learned expertise (Quinlan 1986). For planning problems, the quality of a solution will be evaluated by the number and the cost of operations used in the solutions of the problems. In the case of EBL, as the quality of learning is very time gain dependant, we have to take into account the memory used and the processing time. As a matter of fact, the learned knowledge can let the system resolve some problems that were too "expensive" to solve before learning. During the use of the test set, the predictive systems can provide three kinds of answers : right prediction, wrong prediction or no answer. Generally, the authors are just interested by the correct predictions, nevertheless, the study of the two other kinds of answers is also relevant and they must not be mixed. For example, in the case of wrong predictions, it would be useful for the experimenter to know the "distance" existing between the different concepts to identify in order to evaluate the "severity" of an erroneous answer.

*Efficiency of the learned knowledge* : The time required to solve a problem, corresponds to the indexation quality of learned knowledge (rules ...). In others terms, it reflects the structure of the knowledge base. Most analytical work has focused on efficiency. In fact, for planning systems and especially for EBL, the time is the most important measure because the purpose of learning is to accelerate problem solving. Another measure will be the number of searched nodes (Minton 1985). In decision tree systems, the indexing quality can be roughly linked to some syntactical criteria such as the height, the breadth and the number of nodes in the produced trees.

*Intelligibility of results* : One of the main advantages of symbolic learning systems consists in that the learnt knowledge is in a readable form. This property helps the system users to understand the results, and also to find and to rapidly correct mistaken or missing information in the training set. The intelligibility of the learned knowledge may be appreciated syntactically and semantically. The number of disjunctions and conjunctions may be a measure of the intelligibility. For decision trees, the smaller and more well balanced the tree produced, the more it will be readable and understandable. Another measure, attempting to consider the semantics of the results, is based on the type of analysis a human expert does when he looks at the induced knowledge base. The more an expert can identify prototypical situations, the more the knowledge is understandable.

# 4 The artificial data base generator

## 4.1 Introduction

The problem to solve for the experimenter is to choose the data sets that will be used for the experiments. A great number of different data sets are currently available in the published literature such as : soja diseases, iris features, thyroid cancer symptoms, lymphography ... These bases are useful for the designers to compare homogeneously the learning systems, however, this kind of approach presents four drawbacks that we are going to explain below.

*Availability of the data base for experiment* : In order to experiment, we must find data sets simultaneously available, usable by the system and, above all, carefully acquired. They must, for instance, contain enough examples or a domain theory. However, at the beginning of an experimental phase, it can be difficult to know exactly the type and amount of information needed. Moreover, in order to be significant, an experimentation must use several data sets taken from different domains.

*Translation of the data into the studied system representation* : Generally, the syntax of the found data is different from that used by the studied system, so a translation phase is needed. However, there are two problems : firstly, the translation is time consuming ; secondly when the translation is done by a non-expert of the domain, some information of the initial base can be damaged because the syntactic level and the semantic one are often linked.

*Difficulties in the modification of the data in the course of experimentation* : Even if an expert is available, it is not so easy to modify real data sets. Therefore, during the experimentation, it is not always possible to study a specific aspect of the behavior of the system unless a more adequate data set is available. On the other hand, the characteristics of the examples are not often well known. For instance, the noise quantity and its localization are generally ignored.

*Difficulties in the correct evaluation of the learned knowledge* : Usually, for evaluating the results of learning, as in data analysis, the researcher splits the experiment set in two parts : a training set for learning and a test set. However, by using the data sets from real domains, the evaluation can lack in precision without an expert (Ganascia, Helft 1988). For instance, in medical domain, an expert system under-estimating the gravity of a disease in 20% of cases, is far more dangerous that another one over-estimating the disease in the same proportion !

To take into account these problems that restrict strongly the benefits of real data sets, we propose the use of artificial data sets. This approach is not completely new (Quinlan 1988 ; Martin 1989), but its use was limited mainly to randomly introducing noise into data. Our approach is more general since we would like to simulate the many different learning domains in which a ML algorithm might be applied, by using a generator (Bisson, Laublet 1989&1990) that the user could tune with parameters. This method allows to bring some answers to the limitations of real data sets. Firstly, the availability of data is no longer a problem : the data sets are generated in case of need and these data sets are homogeneous and give reliable criteria of comparison. Secondly, the translation stage becomes very simplified : One translator is enough to transform the generator outputs into inputs of the learning system, instead of a specific translator for each real data set. Finally, it is easier to answer the question : "what happens if the application domain was different ?", by changing the values of parameters and therefore the modeling of the domain performed by the generator. Moreover in this approach, the interpretation of the results can be easily done by the experimenter himself.

However, two questions become apparent. The first one concerns the validity of the evaluations obtained by this bias. The answer depends completely on the degree of realism of artificial data sets in comparison with the real data sets. In other terms, it depends on the fitness of the model of application domain. The second question obviously relates to the generator feasibility.

## 4.2 Generation algorithm

In this study, we have limited ourselves to the supervised learning approach. Algorithms within this learning paradigm cover a large number of current realizations. Broadly speaking, in this field, the learning problem is always the same : from a set of classified examples, the system must learn characteristic or discriminant functions that will be used to associate a class (or expertise), with each situation (or context) of the domain. All the recognition functions that were acquired in this way are elements of a knowledge base usable as a part of an expert-system. For generating the artificial data sets, the starting idea is that this inductive process could be inverted :

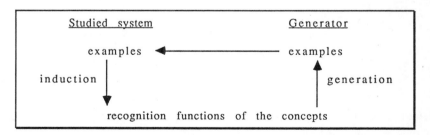

In the first stage, recognition functions of concepts are fixed by the experimenter himself or randomly produced by the generator whose parameters are tuned by the user. Then, this tool generates a set of examples from these recognition functions. The control parameters of the generator allow us to simulate an application domain and correspond logically to the previously seen sensitivity parameters such as : the number and types of the descriptors, the number of conjunctions and disjunctions in the class descriptions, the noise intensity and its localization , ...

Currently, we have implemented two versions of the generator, the first one is working in attribute value logic and the second one is a predicate logic version. For both systems, the generation process is divided into four steps. We are going to detail these steps :

1) *Creation of a vocabulary* : This stage consists of creating the descriptors used to describe the learning set (concepts, examples and domain theory) and for each of them to associate a type and a set of possible values. This process can be performed automatically by a random generator or manually ; when it is manual, the users chooses the name, the type and the domain of each descriptor.

Ex : *descriptors randomly produced by the generator :*
        *$att_1$, $att_2$, $att_3$, ...*       *(attribute value logic)*
        *$P(?x1, ?x2)$, $Q(?x1)$, ...*     *(predicate logic)*

        *descriptors fixed by the experimenter :*
        *height, hair, ...*
        *height ($?x1, ?x2$), hair ($?x1, ?x2$), ...*

2) *Creation of the recognition functions* : When the descriptors are generated, with respect to the given parameters, the generator builds up the logical functions which characterize the set of generated concepts. The logical operators used are AND ($\Lambda$) and OR (V) and the recognition functions RFi are written under normal disjunctive form. In the current release, for a given attribute (or argument of predicate) the values are selected randomly following a uniform distribution law.

$$RF_i = V_{j=1..Nd}\, CT_j$$
$$\text{with } CT_j = \Lambda_{k=1..Nc}\, (att_k\ sel_k\ val_k) \qquad \text{(attribute value logic)}$$
$$or \quad CT_j = \Lambda_{k=1..Nc}\ [not]\ P_k\,(v_1, v_2, ..., v_n). \quad \text{(predicate logic)}$$
$$v_i : \text{variable or constant, } Nc = \text{number of conjunctions, } Nd = \text{number of disjunctions}$$

However, the main problem to solve during this stage, is that the generator must assume that two different functions $RF_1=V_jCT_j$ and $RF_2=V_kCT_k$ could not be verified at the same time by confirming that : $\forall j$, $\forall k$, not ($CT_j \Rightarrow CT_k$) $\Lambda$ not ($CT_k \Rightarrow CT_j$). Like in the previous stage, the experimenter can define himself his own recognition functions. The algorithm used for creating automatically a recognition function is divided into the following steps.

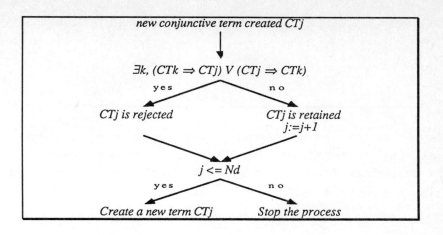

$$\textit{new conjunctive term created CTj}$$

$$\exists k,\ (CTk \Rightarrow CTj)\ V\ (CTj \Rightarrow CTk)$$

yes               no

*CTj is rejected*        *CTj is retained*
$$j:=j+1$$

$$j <= Nd$$

yes               no

*Create a new term CTj*     *Stop the process*

*Examples : RFi : (att$_1$ = val$_{11}$ $\wedge$ att$_4$ = val$_{42}$) V (att$_5$ > val$_{52}$)*     *(attribute value logic)*
*RFj : height (?x1, tall) $\wedge$ eyes (?x1, brown)*     *(predicate logic)*

3) *Generation of the examples* : For constructing an example, firstly, the generator randomly chooses one concept Ci, then it selects one conjunctive term CT in the recognition function of Ci. The example is built up around CT by adding some new terms to the conjunction. As during the elaboration of the recognition function, the system must take care that the new example belongs to one concept only ; the criteria to verify are the same as previous.

*Examples (the recognition functions RFi and RFj are the same as previously) :*
  *ei $\in$RFi : < class = Ci>*
                 **att$_1$ = val$_{11}$ $\wedge$ att$_2$ = val$_{22}$ $\wedge$ att$_3$ = val$_{31}$ $\wedge$ att$_4$ = val$_{42}$ $\wedge$ att$_5$ = val$_{51}$**
  *ej $\in$RFj : <class = Cj>*
                 **height (Paul, tall) $\wedge$ eyes (Paul, brown) $\wedge$ hair (John, dark)**

4) *Generation of a domain theory* : Even if the construction of a domain theory is not needed in all cases, it will be interesting to perform for some other systems such as CHARADE (Ganascia 1987) or KBG (Bisson 1991). In the current release, the generator is able to build up a domain theory in the form of a set of rules. The method used is very simple : we assume that the previously produced examples result from the virtual application (by forward chaining) of a domain theory on the initial examples ; this corresponds to the following scheme :

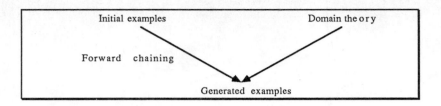

Then the idea is to "reverse" this process ; the method for creating one rule is as follows. Firstly, the generator chooses randomly a term T appearing in one or several examples ; this one will constitute the conclusion of the rule. Secondly, the system randomly builds the premises $T_1$, $T_2$, ... of this rule, taking notice of the two following constraints:

    1) The premises of the rule do not verify an existing recognition function.
    2) The premises of the rule do not subsume and are not subsumed by the premises of the previously generated rules.

Next, when the rule is created, the examples containing the term T are rewritten by applying the rule in backward chaining. Finally, these rewritten examples and the rules constitute the initial set of examples and the domain theory.

Ex :  *Example $e_i$ : $att_1 = val_{11} \wedge att_2 = val_{22} \wedge att_3 = val_{31} \wedge att_4 = val_{42} \wedge att_5 = val_{51}$*
    *Rule k : $att_7 <= val_{74} \wedge att_6 = val_{62} \rightarrow att_2 = val_{22}$*
    *The rewritten example $e_i$ :*
    *$att_1 = val_{11} \wedge att_7 = val_{72} \wedge att_6 = val_{62} \wedge att_3 = val_{31} \wedge att_4 = val_{42} \wedge att_5 = val_{51}$*

    *Example ej : height (Paul, tall) $\wedge$ eyes (Paul, brown) $\wedge$ hair (Paul, dark)*
    *Rule l : eyes (?x1, brown) --> hair (?x1, dark)*
    *The rewritten example ej :*
    *height (Paul, tall) $\wedge$ eyes (Paul, brown)*

## 4.3 Parameters of the generator

For this first version of the generator, we have chosen a set of parameters mainly based on syntactic criteria described during the presentation of the sensibility criteria in a previous section. However, in the future, it would be possible to increase their number and to introduce some more semantic criteria. The parameters of the attribute value logic version are the following :

*Number and type of descriptors* : the generator provides five standard types to the users which are : nominal, ordered, taxonomy, integer and real. Here are the description, for the attribute value generator, of the semantics of each one and the list of authorized selectors. The predicative logic version works similarly, indeed, each argument of each predicate is typed :

| | | |
|---|---|---|
| Nominal | : set of different values | : =, <> |
| Ordered | : set of ordered values | : =, <>, <, <=, >, >= |
| Taxonomy | : tree of values | : =, <>, <, <=, >, >= |
| Integer | : interval of number | : =, <>, <, <=, >, >= |
| Real | : interval of number | : =, <>, <, <=, >, >= |

So, the user can specify the employed descriptors as following :

*att1 nominal (red blue green)*
*att2 ordered (small medium large)*
*att3 taxonomy (shape (rectangle (square)) circle)*
*att4 integer (0 100)*

*Number of classes* : The user gives the number of possible classes for the examples ; for each class, the generator creates a symbol and its recognition function. In the current version of the generator, it is also possible to choose "by hand" the recognition function : in that case the system will just check there are no subsuming links between the different recognition functions.

*Number of conjunctions and disjunctions* : these two parameters guide the generator to elaborate the recognition function of the different concepts. Both numbers are described as an interval setting the lowest and highest possible values. So, the user can say for example that the conjunctive (or disjunctive) parts of the recognition functions must have between two and four terms.

*Constraints on the variables* : for the predicative logic version of the generator, there are two additional parameters, which control the generation of the variables into the predicates during the elaboration of the recognition functions (RF). The first parameter gives the repartition percentage between the variables and the constants in the RF. The second parameter controls the number of occurrencse of each variable in the RF. It corresponds to the probability of creation of new variables.

*Number of examples* : the number of classified examples that the generator must build up. Generally, the set of examples is split in two parts, corresponding to the training set and the test set.

*Size of the examples* : this parameter corresponds to the number of descriptors in the examples. This parameter is directly linked to the sensitivity criterion concerning the irrelevant information : indeed, when you increase the number of terms, you add some irrelevant parameters too.

*Noise intensity* : the user can introduce some noise into the examples. For instance, if the user sets this parameter to the value 10, he assumes that 10% of the generated examples are noisy. Here, the word "noise" has a very precise meaning : we say that an example is noisy when it can simultaneously belong to two different concepts. Several other types of noise remain to be implemented such as the attribute errors and the value errors.

*Unknown and Don't care values* : the generator handles the "unknown" and "dont'care" values. They correspond to an existential (respectively universal) quantification of the concerned attribute (Boswell 1990 a&b)). The user can choose the name of the attributes which have these kind of values and also the percentage of unknown and dont'care values for each one.

*Number of rules and size of premises* : the user fixes the number of rules that he wants in the domain theory and the size of the premises in the rules (number of terms).

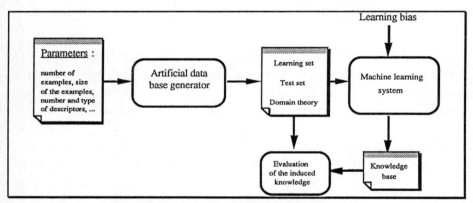

Working of the generator with a ML system

# 5 Application to some learning algorithms

The goal of experimenting learning systems is to vary sensitivity parameters in order to determine the algorithm's behavior over a range of situations. We have tested our generator with five learning systems. All of them use the attribute value representation :

| Algorithms | Authors | Learning method |
|---|---|---|
| CN2 | Boswell 1990 a | Rule induction program based on the AQ algorithm |
| NewID | Boswell 1990 b | ID3 program which can generate a pruning tree |
| NewBOOLE | Bonelli 1990 | Genetic based learning system |
| LVQ | Mc Dermott 89 | Classifier based on the Euclidian distance |
| MLP | Rumelhart 1986 | Multi layer perceptron using back propagation |

For all the experimentations, we have fixed the different parameters of the generator in order to compare the five algorithms to the following values :

- Number of attributes     : 10 nominal attributes
- Number of classes     : 3
- Number of conjunctions     : [2 .. 4]
- Number of disjunctions     : [1 .. 2]
- Size of the examples     : 10
- Number of examples     : 200 (100 for learning and 100 for testing)
- No domain theory

Number of possible values (which the distribution is uniform) for each attribute:

| a1 | a2 | a3 | a4 | a5 | a6 | a7 | a8 | a9 | a10 |
|----|----|----|----|----|----|----|----|----|-----|
| 2  | 5  | 5  | 4  | 2  | 4  | 7  | 4  | 6  | 3   |

The recognition functions randomly set for each concept (class) are :

*Class C1* : $att_2 = val_{22} \land att_6 = val_{62}$
*Class C2* : $att_1 = val_{11} \land att_4 = val_{41} \land att_5 = val_{52}$
*Class C3* : $(att_{10} = val_{102} \land att_4 = val_{43} \land att_6 = val_{63}) \lor (att_9 = val_{92})$

The measures that are consigned in the following table are the following :

NR  = number of induced rules      %RP     = % Right Prediction
N    = number of nodes      %WP     = % Wrong Prediction
L    = number of leaves      %NP     = % No Prediction
H    = mean of the way heights

## 5.1 Learned knowledge as a function of the size of the learning set

These experiments aim at defining an empirical relation between the size of the learning set (for a given set of recognition functions) and the effectiveness and the size of the learned knowledge. Two tests have been done, the first one is performed with noise free examples, and the second one in an environment in which 10% of the attributes coding the class of the examples are noisy.

1) Results with 0% noise :

| | 25 learning examples | | | | | 50 learning examples | | | | | 75 learning examples | | | | | 100 learning examples | | | | |
|---|---|---|---|---|---|---|---|---|---|---|---|---|---|---|---|---|---|---|---|---|
| | CN2 | NewID | NBOOL | LVQ | MLP | CN2 | NewID | NBOOL | LVQ | MLP | CN2 | NewID | NBOOL | LVQ | MLP | CN2 | NewID | NBOOL | LVQ | MLP |
| NR | 6 | | | | | 5 | | | | | 5 | | | | | 4 | | | | |
| N | | 17 | | | | | 33 | | | | | 38 | | | | | 44 | | | |
| L | | 13 | | | | | 27 | | | | | 28 | | | | | 32 | | | |
| H | | 2.58 | | | | | 3.22 | | | | | 3.32 | | | | | 3.32 | | | |
| % RP | 100 | 74 | 97 | 72 | 71 | 100 | 94 | 100 | 76 | 86 | 100 | 95 | 100 | 78 | 93 | 100 | 95 | 100 | 78 | 97 |
| % WP | 0 | 13 | 3 | 28 | 29 | 0 | 0 | 0 | 24 | 14 | 0 | 0 | 0 | 22 | 7 | 0 | 0 | 0 | 22 | 3 |
| % NP | 0 | 13 | 0 | 0 | 0 | 0 | 6 | 0 | 0 | 0 | 0 | 5 | 0 | 0 | 0 | 0 | 5 | 0 | 0 | 0 |

The obtained results seem reasonable. They show that the correct prediction depends logically on the size of the learning set. We can remark that CN2 and NewBOOLE obtain comparable good results and that the results obtained by the back propagation based neural net MLP are better than those obtained by the classifier LVQ.

2) Results with 10% noise :

| | 25 learning examples | | | | | 50 learning examples | | | | | 75 learning examples | | | | | 100 learning examples | | | | |
|---|---|---|---|---|---|---|---|---|---|---|---|---|---|---|---|---|---|---|---|---|
| | CN2 | NewID | NBOOL | LVQ | MLP | CN2 | NewID | NBOOL | LVQ | MLP | CN2 | NewID | NBOOL | LVQ | MLP | CN2 | NewID | NBOOL | LVQ | MLP |
| NR | 8 | | | | | 9 | | | | | 11 | | | | | 12 | | | | |
| N | | 24 | | | | | 47 | | | | | 64 | | | | | 62 | | | |
| L | | 17 | | | | | 36 | | | | | 48 | | | | | 47 | | | |
| H | | 2.75 | | | | | 3.31 | | | | | 3.38 | | | | | 3.86 | | | |
| % RP | 21 | 20 | 50 | 44 | 67 | 82 | 66 | 55 | 47 | 69 | 91 | 69 | 83 | 47 | 69 | 95 | 82 | 88 | 59 | 78 |
| % WP | 79 | 58 | 50 | 56 | 33 | 18 | 21 | 45 | 53 | 31 | 9 | 16 | 17 | 53 | 31 | 5 | 13 | 12 | 41 | 22 |
| % NP | 0 | 22 | 0 | 0 | 0 | 0 | 13 | 0 | 0 | 0 | 0 | 15 | 0 | 0 | 0 | 0 | 5 | 0 | 0 | 0 |

This table displays that learning in a noisy environment (error on the class information) makes the correct prediction of the different systems worse. In such an environment, CN2 and NewBOOLE also obtain the best results and we confirm that the correct prediction of MLP (based on back propagation) is better than LVQ one. In other respects, in the case of NewID we can improve the prediction capacity of the system by the use of a pruning algorithm. We obtain these results :

1) Without pruning = an average of 57% of correct prediction.
2) With pruning = an average of 62.7% of correct prediction.

However, in a noisy environment, the size of the learned knowledge (number of rules in the case of CN2 and tree size for NewID) increases. Nevertheless, the use of the pruning algorithm of NewID reduces considerably the size of this tree without damaging the correct prediction criterion.

## 5.2 Learning time as a function of the size of the learning set

We have also studied, the learning time of CN2 and NewID as a function of the size of the learning set (the three other systems are too slow to be compared to the two previous ones and the stopping criteria are too different). The obtained results are the following :

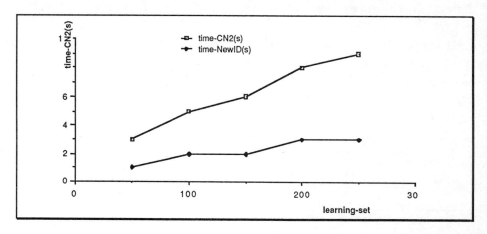

We remark that NewID takes less time to learn then CN2. The curve shows also that both are usable with large learning sets. These results confirm that a induction algorithm based on producing rules is inherently more time consuming than a tree-induction algorithm (Elomaa 1989).

## 5.3 Effect of the descriptor type on learning process

CN2 and NewID both are able to treat real attributes, so we will now examine their effect on the learning process by varying the number of real descriptors from 2 to 8 (let us recall that the total number of descriptors is 10). We obtain the following results :

|  | 2 real descriptors | | 4 real descriptors | | 6 real descriptors | | 8 real descriptors | |
|---|---|---|---|---|---|---|---|---|
|  | CN2 | NewID | CN2 | NewID | CN2 | NewID | CN2 | NewID |
| number of rules | 5 | | 7 | | 7 | | 8 | |
| N = number of nodes | | 17 | | 36 | | 44 | | 80 |
| L = number of leaves | | 13 | | 25 | | 30 | | 60 |
| H = mean of the way heights | | 2.33 | | 2.92 | | 3.18 | | 3.34 |
| % right prediction | 96 | 97 | 88 | 79 | 87 | 68 | 73 | 64 |
| % wrong prediction | 4 | 3 | 12 | 17 | 13 | 32 | 27 | 25 |
| % no prediction | 0 | 0 | 0 | 4 | 0 | 0 | 0 | 11 |

It appears that the two learning systems are sensitive to the proportion of numeric attributes present in the learning set. The number of correct predictions of the two algorithms decreases and the size of the induced knowledge (number of rules and number of nodes) increases when the number of numeric descriptors increases. It is interesting to note that such an experiment would have been very difficult to make using real data sets.

## 5.4 Effect of Unknown and Don't care values on learning process

CN2 and NewID provide the possibility of treating Unknown values which correspond to an existantially quantified variable, or Don't care values which correspond to a universally quantified variable. Then, we study their effect on the learning process by fixing the proportion of Unknown values (respectively Don't care values) to 25 %. After several runs, we obtain the following results :

| % RP | CN2 | NewID |
|---|---|---|
| Without Unknown or Don't care values | 98 | 83 |
| The corrupted descriptor with don't care value do not belong to the recognition function. | 92.25 | 76.5 |
| The corrupted descriptor with unknown value do not belong to the recognition function. | 96 | 81 |
| The corrupted descriptor with don't care value belongs to the recognition function. | 85 | 62.5 |
| The corrupted descriptor with unknown value belongs to the recognition function. | 94 | 74.25 |

First, we remark that the effect of Don't care and Unknown values is logically more marked in the case of a corrupted descriptor belonging to the recognition function. Secondly, we notice the difference between the results obtained with Don't care values and those obtained with Unknown values. The explanation is that, in the case of an Unknown value, the system splits the concerned example into a set of examples, with weights distributed according to the value distribution at that node ; in the case of a Don't care value, it replaces the concerned example by as many examples as there are possible values, but the weight of each new example is the same as that of the original (the concerned descriptor is transformed into an irrelevant one). So, in this way, we can consider that by introducing Don't care and Unknown values in the learning base, we have also introduced noise in this learning set, but the effect is less marked in the case of Unknown values.

## 5.5 Comparison with real world data bases

Finally, in order to show that our approach is realistic, we have compared the results obtained with two medical data sets (lymphography and breast cancer) to the results obtained with two artificial data sets having the same syntactic characteristics than the real ones :

1) *Lymphography* : 18 descriptors (all of them are nominal), 4 classes and 109 examples.

| | Medical data set | | | | | Artificial data set | | | | |
|---|---|---|---|---|---|---|---|---|---|---|
| | CN2 | NewID | NBOOLE | LVQ | MLP | CN2 | NewID | NBOOLE | LVQ | MLP |
| Time (s) | 17 | 2 | | | | 15 | 2 | | | |
| NR | 14 | | | | | 17 | | | | |
| number of premises | 3 | | | | | 3 | | | | |
| N | | 78 | | | | | 72 | | | | |
| L | | 61 | | | | | 53 | | | | |
| H | | 4.27 | | | | | 3.54 | | | | |
| %RP | 87 | 67 | 82 | 83 | 70 | 87 | 57 | 80 | 47 | 42 |
| %WP | 13 | 26 | 18 | 17 | 30 | 13 | 28 | 20 | 53 | 58 |
| %NP | | 7 | | | | | 15 | | | | |

The main difference between the two learning sets is that the distribution of the examples is different. This distribution is better in the artificial data set : both classes 1 (normal findings) and 4 (malignant lymphoma) in the medical data set contain respectively only one pattern. This feature has an effect on the results obtained with the two neural nets MLP and LVQ which are not significant. For the other systems it is interesting to notice that both the structure of the learned knowledge (size of tree, number of rules) and the experimentation results are very similar between these two bases.

2) *Breast cancer* : 10 descriptors, 2 classes and 269 examples.

| | Medical data set | | | | | Artificial data set | | | | |
|---|---|---|---|---|---|---|---|---|---|---|
| | CN2 | NewID | NBOOLE | LVQ | MLP | CN2 | NewID | NBOOLE | LVQ | MLP |
| Time (s) | 19 | 3 | | | | 19 | 3 | | | |
| NR | 32 | | | | | 31 | | | | |
| number of premises | 5 | | | | | 4 | | | | |
| N | | 177 | | | | | 152 | | | | |
| L | | 132 | | | | | 108 | | | | |
| H | | 6.03 | | | | | 4.08 | | | | |
| %RP | 72.2 | 69.4 | 77 | 65.12 | 75 | 75.5 | 70 | 82.5 | 75.5 | 63.95 |
| %WP | 27.8 | 25.1 | 23 | 34.88 | 25 | 24.5 | 22.5 | 17.5 | 24.5 | 36.05 |
| %NP | | 5.5 | | | | | 7.5 | | | | |

The distribution of the examples in this second medical base is more homogeneous. This is why we notice that the obtained results (both structure of the induced knowledge and predictive accuracy) are similar between the real world data set and the artificial one.

# 6  Conclusion

The aim of this paper has been to present an approach based on the use of a parametrable generator of learning sets to discover the effect of the learning environment on system performance. This generator resolves also some limitations of real data sets for such experiments and it represents a useful tool for exploring capacities of ML algorithms using different learning methods (symbolic algorithms, genetic based algorithms and neural networks in this first contribution).

In our study of the five previous learning algorithms, we have verified with our approach some known results like the effect of noise on concept learning. We have also pointed out some new more specific informations. For example, CN2 and NewID are sensitive to the proportion of numeric attributes and that CN2 is more resistant to the unknown values than to the don't care ones. It is important to notice that the discovery of these results by using real data sets would have been *more difficult* . Indeed, the types of the descriptors are fixed in a real data base and even if an expert is available, it is not so easy to modify them. So, the experimenter can not study the effect of the descriptor type on the behavior of the system unless more adequate data sets are available.

At present time, we have restricted our study to inductive approaches such as classification and diagnosis. However, this generation method of learning sets is probably transposable to other approaches of machine learning, like learning by discovery for instance. We think that it will be desirable that a future version of our generator builds up "maquettes" of real domains in order to test ML systems with more parameters than in the present version. The next step of our work will consist in introducing some semantic parameters, such as vocabulary constraints to inhibit or authorize the creation of some conjunctive terms in the recognition functions. These semantic parameters will allow us to simulate real domains with more accuracy.

## Acknowledgments

We would like to thank Yves Kodratoff, our thesis supervisor, for the support he gave to this work and all the members of the Inference and Learning group at LRI, particularly, Karine Causse, Adrian Gordon, P.Bonnelli, and also J.J.Cannat, N.Chaourar, P.Laublet, A.Mellouk.

## References

**Bisson, Laublet 1989**, Méthode d'évaluation des systèmes d'apprentissage, Rapport de fin d'étude, ONERA-GIA, August 1989.

**Bisson, Laublet 1990**, Theoritical and empirical study of learning systems, Cognitiva 1990 Madrid, 1990.

**Bisson 1991**, Learning of Rule Systems in a First Order Representation, LRI Internal report 1991

**Bonelli 1990**, A.PARODI, S.SEN, S.WILSON, NewBOOLE : A fast GBML system, 7th ICML, Austin, 1990.

**Boswell 1990 a**, Manual for CN2, The Turing Institute, January 1990.

**Boswell 1990 b**, Manual for NewID version 2.1, The Turing Institute, January 1990.

**Cannat 1988**, Machine Learning Applied to Air Trafic Control, Proc. Human-Machine Interaction Artificial Intelligence Aeronautics & Space, pp.265-274, Toulouse, 1988.

**Elomaa 1989**, N.HOLSTI, An experimental comparison of inducing decision trees and decision lists in noisy domains, EWSL Montpellier, 1989.

**Ganascia 1987**, AGAPE et CHARADE: deux techniques d'apprentissage symbolique appliquées à la construction de bases de connaissances, Thèse d'état soutenue 4/87,Université Paris Sud.

**Ganascia, Helft 1988**, Evaluation des Systèmes d'Apprentissage, 3éme Journées Françaises de l'Apprentissage 1988 Cassis, p 3-20.

**Kibler, Langley 1988**, Machine Learning as an Experimental Science, EWSL 1988, Glasgow, pp 81-92.

**Manago, Kodratoff 1987**, Noise and Knowledge Acquisition, Proceeding of 10th IJCAI, Los Altos, 1987

**Martin 1989**, Reducing Redundant Learning, in Proceedings of the 6° International Workshop on Machine Learning , Ithaca 1989, p 396-99.

**Minton 1985**, Selectively Generalizing Plans for Problem Solving, IJCAI 85 p596-599.

**MLT 1990**, Laboratoire de Marcoussis, British Aerospace, Université de Paris-Sud, Evaluation Methods for Attribute-Based Algorithms, Deliverable 7.2, Projet ESPRIT 2154, Aout 1990.

**Quinlan 1986**, The effect of noise on concept learning, Machine learning 2 an artificial intelligence approach, TIOGA 1986.

**Quinlan 1988**, Symplifying decision trees, in B.Gaines, J.Boose Knowledge Acquisition for Knowledge-Based Systems, Academic Press 1988.

**Rendell 1989**, H.CHO, R. SESHU Improving the Design of Similarity-Based Rule-Learning Systems, International Journal of Expert System, pp 97-133, volume 2, Number 1, 1989.

**Rumelhart 1986**, G.E.HINTON, R.J.WILLIAMS, Learning internal representation by error propagation. Parallel distributed processing : Explorations in the microstructures of cognition, MIT Press, vol 1, pp 318-362, 1986.

**Shavlik 1989**, An Empirical Analysis of EBL Approaches for Learning Plan Schemata, in Proceedings of the 6° International Workshop on Machine Learning , Ithaca 1989, p183-87.

# SHIFT OF BIAS IN LEARNING FROM DRUG COMPOUNDS: THE FLEMING PROJECT

L. DI PACE (*)  F. FABROCINI (*)  G. BOLIS (**)

(*) IBM Rome Scientific Center, AI Group, via Giorgione 159, 00147 Rome. Italy
(**) Farmitalia Carlo Erba srl Erbamont Group, R&D/CAMD, via dei Gracchi 35, 20146 Milan. Italy

## Abstract

In this paper we will illustrate the results of a machine learning application concerning drug design. Dynamic bias management, in this context, will be presented as a critical mechanism to deal with complex problems in which good representations are unavailable even to human experts. A number of domain-dependent and domain-independent operators which allow automatic bias adjustment will be discussed with the mechanisms used to decide when and how to vary bias. Finally, we will summarize the results that a system named FLEMING adopting these techniques has obtained on the domain of the inhibitors of the thermolysin enzyme.

*Keywords*:  bias management, constructive learning, learning from discovery, computer-aided molecular design.

## Introduction

A fascinating aspect of machine learning techniques is their use to discover knowledge unavailable even to human experts.  We will describe a system named FLEMING that discovers explanatory theories from a set of experimental observations concerning compounds synthesized during the drug design process. Therefore, our investigation falls into the category of the task-oriented studies; even so the need to deal with a real-world problem suggested a number of theoretically-oriented considerations. This paper is intended to be a report on our experience in applying machine learning techniques to a complex problem.

Firstly, we will briefly outline the learning problem; the limits of the approaches traditionally adopted to face this problem will be also illustrated. Then, we will sketch the general methodology used to deal with the learning task previously described.  The remainder of the paper will concentrate on FLEMING's approach to dynamic bias management. We will illustrate, as regards our application, where the need for automatic bias adjustment comes from and the solutions adopted to decide when and how to vary bias. Specifically, dynamic bias management will be presented as a necessity in real-world problems which typically exhibit a large number of distinct disjuncts (see Rendell & Cho, 1990). Finally, a summary of FLEMING's results on the system of the inhibitors of the thermolysin enzyme will be presented and discussed.

## The domain problem

The study of the correlations between pharmacological activity and molecular structure is a central issue in the drug design process. Such a study is based on the concept that a biological (or pharmacological) effect caused by a given molecule (drug) is a function of structural or electronic properties of that molecule. Conventional approaches to the Structure-Activity Relationship (SAR) problem make use of statistical techniques in order to relate the activity of the compound to substructures and/or properties used to describe the compound itself (see, for instance, Martin, 1978). The great difficulty in all the SAR studies is the selection of the molecular descriptors as their number is very large. Such a choice introduces a strong bias on the results of the analysis insofar as it abstracts secondary objects to be the "real" objects from which the learning system generalizes. The bias comes from an assumption behind this choice which says that no considerations useful to capture the target concept have been omitted from the language used to represent the instances.

Klopman's CASE program is presented as an attempt to overcome such difficulty (see Klopman, 1984). CASE is capable of manipulating a molecular structure in order to generate all the fragments that can be formed by breaking the molecule. In this way, the selection of the descriptors would not be constrained by the prejudices of the investigators. Once the fragments have been collected, they are analyzed statistically to discover those fragments relevant to the activity of the compounds. CASE, however, suffers from other drawbacks common to most of the SAR studies. Firstly, the functional dependence existing betweeen the experimental observations and the pharmacological activity of the compound is assumed to be the sum of independent contributions of the most relevant activating/deactivating fragments automatically selected by the program. Yet, context cannot be ignored when talking about molecular structures since the relevance of the compound fragments is heavily dependent on the relative positions in the compound itself. Moreover, the properties characterizing the fragments play a fundamental role in determining the binding between compound and receptor. In this sense, statistical frequency does not appear a meaningful approximation of the relevancy of the fragments. Indeed, medicinal chemists while visually analyzing a set of compounds for determining their structure-activity relationship do not constrain the investigation at the identification of a number of fragments deemed to be invariant in the active compounds. Instead, they attempt to build a theoretical model suitable to explain the nature of the binding between active compounds and biological receptor. A set of notions that actually make the basic knowledge of a medicinal chemist about molecules and their properties such as, for instance, hydrophobicity, polarity, hydrogen bonding, etc. play an important role during the explanation process. Our attempt was to devise a computational tool which could support medicinal chemists to reduce the complexity of the problem without suffering from the drawbacks of the more traditional approaches.

## Learning methodology

FLEMING's input is a database of compounds and their inhibitory activity as reported in Figure 1. Specifically, molecules are formalized in terms of a set of atoms and their connectivity. The atoms are characterized as atom types, i.e. there is an attempt to define their electronic state.

## $K_i$ Values of Inhibitors of Thermolysin

| No. | Compound† | $K_i$ ($\mu$M) |
|-----|-----------|------|
| 1 | Z-NHNH-CS-NHNH2 | 6700 |
| 2 | Z-Agly-Leu-NHNH2 | 380 |
| 3 | Z-Gly-Leu-NHNH2 | 1100 |
| 4 | Ac-Ala-Aphe-Leu-NHNH2 | 6500 |
| 5 | Ac-Ala-Ala-Aala-Leu-NHNH2 | 7900 |
| 6 | L-Leu-NHOH | 190 |
| 7 | Z-L-Leu-NHOH | 10 |
| 8 | Z-Gly-L-Leu-NH2 | 21000 |
| 9 | Z-Gly-L-Leu-NHOH | 13 |
| 10 | Z-Gly-L-Leu-N(CH3)OH | 2230 |
| 11 | Z-Gly-L-Leu-NHOCH3 | No Inhib. |
| 12 | Z-Agly-L-Leu-NHOH | 27 |
| 13 | Z-Gly-Gly-NHOH | 940 |
| 14 | Z-Gly-Gly-L-Leu-NHOH | 39 |
| 15 | HONH-Bzm-OEt | 20 |
| 16 | HONH-Bzm-L-Ala-Gly-NH2 | 0.66 |
| 17 | HONH-Bzm-L-Ala-Gly-OH | 0.65 |
| 18 | HONH-Ibm-L-Ala-Gly-NH2 | 0.48 |
| 19 | HONH-Mal-L-Ala-Gly-NH2 | 1100 |
| 20 | HO-Bzm-L-Ala-Gly-NH2 | 420 |
| 21 | CHO-HOLeu-L-Ala-Gly-NH2 | 3.8 |
| 22 | Ac-HOLeu-L-Ala-Gly-NH2 | 3400 |
| 23 | P-NH-Et | No Inhib. |
| 24 | P-Leu-NH2 | 1.3 |
| 25 | P-Phe-OH | 73 |
| 26 | P-Ala-Ala-OH | 88 |
| 27 | P-Ile-Ala-OH | 0.36 |
| 28 | P-Leu-Phe-OH | 0.019 |
| 29 | Z-Phe-Gly-NH2 | 350 |
| 30 | Z-Phe-Gly | 4500 |
| 31 | Phe-Gly-NH2 | 10900 |
| 32 | Phe-Gly | 10300 |
| 33 | Z-Leu-Gly-NH2 | 3070 |
| 34 | Z-Leu-Gly | 4030 |
| 35 | Leu-Gly-NH2 | 8300 |

† Z, benzyloxycarbonyl; Agly, -NHNHCO-; Aala, -NHN(CH3);
Aphe, -NHN(CH2C6H5)CO-; P, phosphoryl group (HO)2PO-;
Bzm, benzylmalonyl -COCH(CH2C6H5)CO-; Ibm,
Isobutylmalonyl -COCH(CH2CH(CH3)2)CO-; Mal, malonyl; Ac,
Acetyl; Et, ethyl.

Figure 1. THE SET OF COMPOUNDS. THE ACTIVITY IS EXPRESSED IN TERMS OF $K_i$ VALUES DETERMINED BY DIXON PLOTS.

We will now briefly outline the operation of the system. It mirrors the strategy actually used by the medicinal chemist during the drug design process. Yet, because of the "cognitive overload" problem, the medicinal chemist is forced to reason locally while the nature of the problem would require spanning over a large number of variables. At the very beginning, the program identifies a set of active/inactive pairs deemed to be useful to make the learning process effective. Specifically, the system looks for compound pairs which, on the one hand, maximize the difference in activity, $\Delta (K)$, and, on the other, minimize the difference in structure, $\Delta (S)$. Usually such a set is quite large because the medicinal chemist proceeds step-by-step via small modifications to the previously experimented compounds. Although methods for quantifying differences in structure exist, at the present time two molecules are regarded as structurally similar whenever they have at most one difference in terms of residues.

Once the pairs which appear to be more informative have been defined, each compound in each pair is matched against the other in order to generate the fragments supposed to be responsible for the $\Delta(K)$. We will refer to the fragment appearing in the active compound $c_i$ as Required ($REQ_{ij}$) and the fragment in the inactive compound $c_j$ as Forbidden ($FOR_{ji}$). One problem, here, was the definition of the level of abstraction more appropriate for detailing such a fragment. FLEMING automatically makes the choice of the level of representation considered to be more adequate. Whenever the difference between the compounds in each pair is made of only one residue (as it is by definition), the system will attempt at reformulating such a difference in terms of functional groups. Yet, the reformulation step will be accomplished only when satisfied the condition that the functional groups which actually make the difference also make a connected region. The same holds as concerns the functional group level. In this case, when the difference is expressed in terms of at most one functional group, the system will reformulate such a difference in terms of atom types on the condition quoted above. The description of the molecules, then, is appropriately shifted so as to allow $REQ_{ij}$ and $FOR_{ji}$ being encoded explicitly in the representation of the compounds $c_i$ and $c_j$. What we get is an abstraction space deductively derived from the domain knowledge in which a number of clues useful to speed up the learning task have been marked inside the compound which they come from after being opportunely reformulated. This process can be regarded as a form of constructive induction in which domain-dependent knowledge is used to derive a "useful" instance representation suitable to facilitate the inductive task (see Flann & Dietterich, 1986; see also Drastal, Czako & Raatz, 1989). Specifically, because by assumption the active/inactive molecules of each pair differ at most for one fragment, we think of REQs as the fragments necessary to the activity of the compound while FORs must be considered as "forbidden" insofar as they involve a decrease in the activity.

FLEMING's learning strategy will be illustrated as follows. Let $C$ be the set of compounds. At the beginning of each iteration, a $K$ number of compounds $c_u$ deemed to be useful for improving the current model $PMODEL$ is selected from $C$. The system will evaluate a compound as useful when sufficiently similar to $PMODEL$, so as to reduce the ambiguities of matching, and when including a number of REQs and FORs, so as to maximize the information content. Whenever $c_u$ is a maximally active compound, FLEMING generalizes on the compound as a whole. In this case, FLEMING will consider all the substructures which the molecule is made of as noise-immune and, therefore, equally relevant to the inhibitory activity. Otherwise FLEMING will take into account only the REQs and the FORs included in $c_u$. Specifically, the system will generalize $PMODEL$ whenever encountering REQs and specialize whenever encountering FORs. A quality function is used to evaluate each of the new models. FLEMING will accord its preference to those models that minimize the predictive error. In other words, the system will prefer the models that predict, for each compound $c_i$, an activity value $\bar{a}_i$ as close as possible to the real one $a_i$. The new models so generated are merged into a K-limited OPEN list of current partial models and only the best K models are maintained for further expansions.

## Selecting the most appropriate bias

Mitchell defined bias as any information for controlling the complexity of the learning problem that can be considered as "extra-evidential" in the sense that it does not come from the objects or events to be described by the target concept (see Mitchell, 1980; see also Utgoff, 1986 and Rendell, Seshu & Tcheng, 1987). The satisfactory performance that researchers get from learning programs are often due to the bias previously "hard-coded" in the program. What they do, then, is to test the program and eventually shift the bias "by hand" to move to a better bias. This methodology allows inductive systems to control the combinatorial explosion of hypotheses; yet, in this way, the learning task is reduced to find a "trick" for discarding inconsistent hypotheses as instances are examined.

The use of a highly restricted hypothesis space is a very common method for focussing the search on the set of preferred hypotheses. This kind of bias has been named "restriction-type bias" (see Russell & Grosof, 1989). The most common way to control the dimensions of the hypothesis space is to restrict the object description to an abstraction of the complete observation (instance-language bias). Such an approach is successful when the objects are described in a form suitable to capture the target concept, but when the most appropriate language to describe the objects is not known a priori, then learning can be impossible using selective methods.

Our problem falls into this class. As we have seen above, all the traditional SAR methods presuppose some knowledge of the chemical or electronic properties that make the binding between molecule and receptor feasible. In other words, what these approaches presuppose is the very answer to the problem at hand. FLEMING's approach is to start the search from a restricted hypothesis space and eventually to shift to a less restricted one (see also Utgoff, 1986). The nature of the problem itself suggested this approach. As Rendell and Cho have stressed, real-world problems and, especially, complex problems in which even human experts lack understanding typically exhibit a very large number of distinct disjuncts (see Rendell & Cho, 1990). In our case, the low-level descriptors used to represent the compounds are not sufficient to derive the explanatory model we look for. What we need is a more theoretically-oriented language exploiting higher-level regularities suitable to compact the problem (i.e. suitable to produce class membership functions having at most few disjuncts). A number of operators which result in the introduction of new descriptors will accomplish the mapping between the problem definition in the initial space and its definition in an abstraction space more appropriate for capturing the target concept.

Shift of bias is closely related to constructive induction. Specifically, when we apply a set of operators to one or more existing descriptors to generate new descriptors intended for use in describing the target concept, we also shift the concept-language bias. One problem we faced was to identify exactly when and how to shift bias.

FLEMING makes use of three constructive operators. We distinguish:

- **Domain-dependent operators**:

  - **R-operators**: Allow the introduction of multiple levels of abstraction; specifically they take the form:

$$R_i: \ S_i \ \rightarrow \ G(\{S_{i\,1}, \dots, S_{i\,n}\}, \{A_{i\,1}, \dots, A_{i\,m}\})$$

where $S_i$ is a generic fragment and $G$ is the graph defined by the set of nodes $\{S_{ik}\}$ and the set of arcs $\{A_{il}\}$ such that each $S_{ik}$ is a substructure of $S_i$. The R-operators work selectively via the identification of compound subunits. Thus, the same molecule can be formalized as a hierarchy of representations that proceeds from a very detailed formalization of the compound to a coarse one as illustrated in Figure 2.

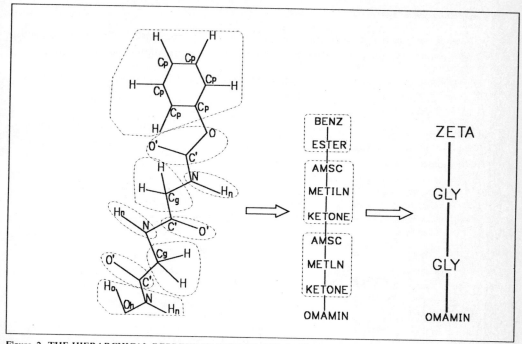

Figure 2. THE HIERARCHICAL REPRESENTATION OF THE COMPOUNDS

Specifically, atomic entities, as we have just said above, are used to represent the compound at the lower level; in the following one, the molecule is represented in terms of larger fragments named functional groups (for instance, a carboxil group); at the next level up, the compound is described in terms of residues (taken in a broad sense, for example, an amino acid in a peptide); finally it is always possible to represent the molecule as a whole with some properties associated with the compound such as, for instance, the molecular weight.

—  *I-operators*: Allow switching from the observation language used to describe the compounds to a more theoretically-oriented language of chemical properties associated with the hierarchy of molecular substructures $S_i$; I-operators have been formalized as follows:

$$I_i: S_i \rightarrow P_{i1}, P_{i2}, \dots, P_{in}$$

Thus, the system, for instance, is told that a hydroxyl group is a hydrophobic group with the property of being electron donor. Some of these properties such as, for instance, volumes and partial charges are computed via a set of domain-dependent procedures.

Both the R-operators and the I-operators make the prior knowledge used by the system for guiding the inductive process.

• *Domain-independent operators*:

    — *U-operators*: Such operators are defined as boolean combinations of other terms previously defined in the system; thus, for instance, FLEMING makes use of the following operator:

$$U_1: \; S_i = G(\{S_{ik}\}\{A_{ij}\}) \; \cup \; S_w = G(\{S_{wk}\}\{A_{wj}\}) \; \rightarrow \; S_z = G(\{S_{ik}\} \cup \{S_{wk}\}, \{A_{ij}\} \cup \{A_{wj}\})$$

Thus, the fragment $R_1$ is a *new* descriptor previously unknown to the system resulting from the application of the operator $U_1$ to $F_1$ and $F_2$ (see Figure 3). $R_1$ will also inherit the properties common to $F_1$ and $F_2$.

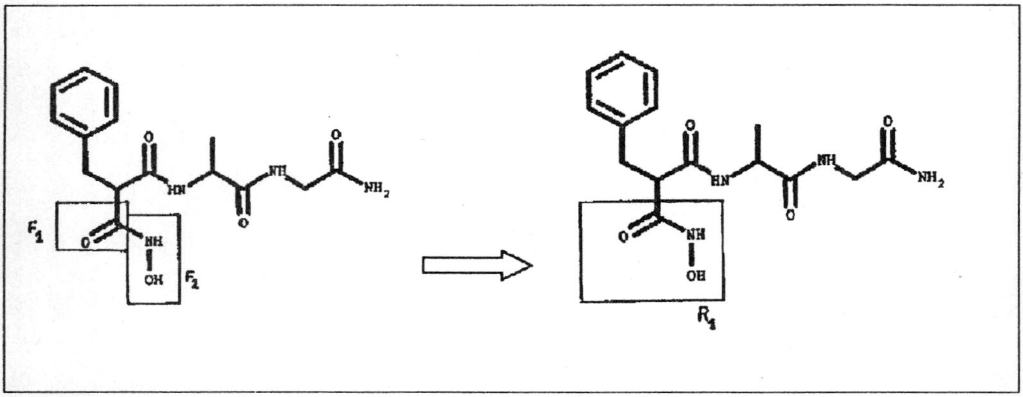

**Figure 3.** AN APPLICATION OF THE U-OPERATOR: (F1,F2) => R1

Rendell has identified four aspects considered to be inherent to the constructive induction problem (see Matheus & Rendell, 1989; see also Wrobel, 1988):

1. detection of when construction is required;
2. selection of the constructive operators;
3. generalization of the new descriptors;
4. evaluation of the new features so derived.

1. *Detection*: Detection, in our approach, is triggered via a set of evaluation functions. Because of their nature, these functions introduce a meta-reasoning mode dedicated to control the adequacy of the representational level. Specifically, constructive induction is performed either in a *demand-driven* fashion whenever the model building process faces an impasse as when the system

does not appear successful in finding a matching between $c_u$ and *PMODEL* or in a *tentative* way as when FLEMING applies the R-operators in the attempt at finding the level of abstraction more adequate for detailing REQs and FORs.

2. *Selection*: our system makes use of a two-step approach to select the useful constructors:

   - firstly FLEMING uses the domain knowledge as a set of heuristics for focussing on the class of useful operators;
   - then it completes the selection process with the selection of the appropriate operator by using information in the data set.

We are now ready to discuss one of the detection mechanisms used by FLEMING and the selection procedure adopted to choose the most appropriate constructor among the set of candidate operators. The function used in this example is triggered as a latter resource to overcome an impasse whenever the R-operators have been already exhaustively applied to the description of the compound (the attempt, here, is at finding a match between an $c_u$ and *PMODEL* ). We call $G_u$ the graph used to represent $c_u$ and $G_m$ the graph representing *PMODEL* where $G_u = (\{S_u\}, \{A_u\})$ and $G_m = (\{S_m\}, \{A_m\})$. Then let us define $P_{ki} = \{p_{k1}, \dots, p_{kn}\}$ as the set of properties appended to the $i$ -th node $S_{ki}$ of $G_k$ by the application of the I-operators. Moreover, let $MATCH(G_k, G_z)$ be the function matching the graph $G_k$ onto the graph $G_z$. $MATCH(G_u, G_m)$ produces as output a set of pairs $(S_{ui}, S_{mj})$. Then, the evaluation function can be stated as follows:

$$EF_1: \ \forall (S_{ui}, S_{mj}) \ \ni (S_{ui} \neq S_{mj}) \wedge (P_{ui} \cap P_{mj}) = \emptyset \ \rightarrow \ U_i(S_{ui}, x)$$

in which the condition-part asserts that whenever a pair of fragments $S_{ui} \neq S_{mj}$ do not also match in terms of properties, the set of the U-operators must be selected. Now FLEMING must select the fragment $x$ more useful to construct the new descriptor when joined with $S_{ui}$. The construction of the new descriptor should finally allow the generalization between $c_u$ and *PMODEL*. Specifically, FLEMING will prefer those descriptors and, therefore, those operators that maximize the number of common properties between $(S_{ui}, x)$ and the corresponding fragment $(S_{mj}, y)$. A simple inspection of the data at hand will finally produce the selection of the appropriate operator.

3. *Generalization*: The application of the standard selective methods such as dropping condition, turning constants into variables, closing interval, etc., allows the generalization of the new descriptors (Michalski, 1983). Yet, constructive induction, in our case, is successful only insofar as FLEMING encodes domain knowledge which works as selection bias. FLEMING, actually, utilizes domain heuristics to prune the space of the U-operators (the boolean operators) to a candidate set far more tractable. Such heuristics, specifically, will narrow the search to those operators which generate new descriptors consisting of adjacent fragments.

4. *Evaluation*: as other systems such as STAGGER (see Schlimmer, 1987) and CITRE (see Pagallo, 1989), FLEMING is completly autonomous in the evaluation of the quality of new descriptors. This methodology must be contrasted with DUCE's oracle-based approach in which the evaluation is delegated to the user (see Muggleton, 1987). In FLEMING's case, the quality of the new descriptors is assessed with the results of the generalization process itself. Yet, such an approach

results in an increase of complexity for the system insofar as it also carries out an increase in the number of models to be considered by the system. We are studying, at the moment, more powerful evaluation mechanisms to deal with this problem.

## Results and Discussion

In order to test FLEMING's performance we have chosen the system of the inhibitors of the thermolysin enzyme for which 3D-structural information of the complex enzyme-inhibitor is available from the Brookhaven Protein Data Bank. Thermolysin is a thermostable metalloprotease involved in several important physiological processes and, like other metalloproteases, contains a zinc ion essential for activity. It is also known that thermolysin is very specific for hydrophobic aminoacids. The data concerning the inhibitory activity of a number of thermolysin inhibitors were taken from literature and reported in Figure 1. The activity is expressed in terms of $K_i$ values determined by Dixon plots (see, for further details, Bolis, Di Pace & Fabrocini, forthcoming).

To start with, FLEMING reformulates the description of the compounds so as to allow REQs and FORs being encoded explicitly. In this way, the instance space is trasformed into a more abstract space which exploits higher-order regularities in order to improve concept concentration. Thus, the pair (16)/(20) is selected from the compound database. Such a pair satisfies the similarity constraint we adopted, insofar as compound (16) differs from compound (20) only because of one fragment (i.e. the fragment named HONH). In other words, given the same context (i.e. * - BZM - L - ALA - GLY - NH2, where the star denotes the variable), then the substitution of the HO fragment (20) with the HONH fragment (16) causes a major change in the activity of the compound. At this point, FLEMING attempts to detail as much as possible such a difference. In this case, the system will finally generate as difference between compounds (16) and (20) the atom type $n'$ (see Figure 4).

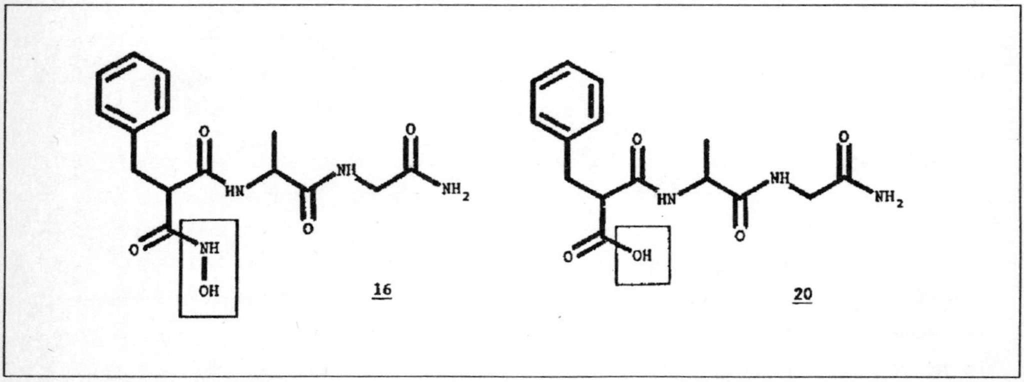

Figure 4. A CASE OF REFORMULATION. THE STRUCTURAL DIFFERENCE EVIDENTIATED BY FLEMING BETWEEN COMPOUNDS 16 AND 20.

A schematic representation of the explanatory model generated by FLEMING, as concerns our problem, is illustrated in Figure 5 where the inhibitor is depicted as composed by a number of generalized fragments named as $R_0, \ldots, R_n$.

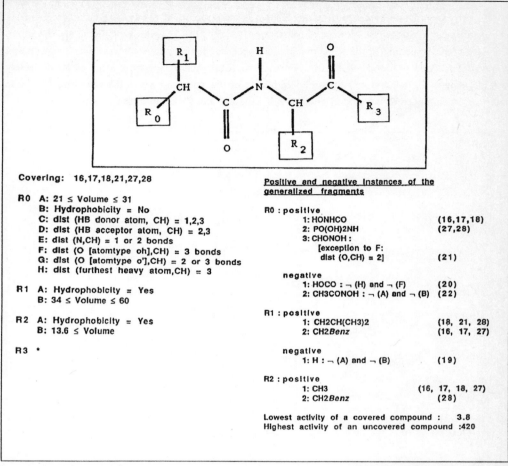

Covering: 16,17,18,21,27,28

RO  A: 21 ≤ Volume ≤ 31
    B: Hydrophobicity = No
    C: dist (HB donor atom, CH) = 1,2,3
    D: dist (HB acceptor atom, CH) = 2,3
    E: dist (N,CH) = 1 or 2 bonds
    F: dist (O [atomtype oh],CH) = 3 bonds
    G: dist (O [atomtype o'],CH) = 2 or 3 bonds
    H: dist (furthest heavy atom,CH) = 3

R1  A: Hydrophobicity = Yes
    B: 34 ≤ Volume ≤ 60

R2  A: Hydrophobicity = Yes
    B: 13.6 ≤ Volume

R3  *

Positive and negative instances of the generalized fragments

R0 : positive
    1: HONHCO          (16,17,18)
    2: PO(OH)2NH      (27,28)
    3: CHONOH :
       [exception to F:
        dist (O,CH) = 2]    (21)

   negative
    1: HOCO : ¬ (H) and ¬ (F)    (20)
    2: CH3CONOH : ¬ (A) and ¬ (B)  (22)

R1 : positive
    1: CH2CH(CH3)2      (18, 21, 28)
    2: CH2Benz         (16, 17, 27)

   negative
    1: H : ¬ (A) and ¬ (B)    (19)

R2 : positive
    1: CH3          (16, 17, 18, 27)
    2: CH2Benz     (28)

Lowest activity of a covered compound :  3.8
Highest activity of an uncovered compound :420

Figure 5. THE FINAL MODEL. $R_0$, $R_1$ AND $R_2$ ARE THE BINDING LOCATIONS DISCOVERED BY FLEMING DESCRIBED IN TERMS OF PROPERTIES (ON THE LEFT) AND FRAGMENT INSTANCES (ON THE RIGHT).

The same figure illustrates their characterization where, for each $R_i$ , a number of properties labelled with a capital letter and a number of positive and negative instances of fragments that the model is covering are associated to the fragment. The model covers six among the most active compounds of Figure 1, namely no. 16, 17, 18, 21, 27 and 28. Wherever the inductive process did not lead to the definition of a generalized fragment, such a fragment is reported in the model as it is; in our case the CH, NH and C=O groups. Thus, in FLEMING's model, the fragment $R_0$ is defined as hydrophylic, hydrogen bond donor and acceptor while the fragment $R_1$ is described as hydrophobic with volume values between 34 and 60. Both fragments $R_0$ and $R_1$ are supposed to be essential for activity. Fragment $R_2$ is also hydrophobic while fragment $R_3$ does not seem to be very relevant for any change of activity of the compounds considered.

These results obtained via the machine learning techinques previously described are fully in accord with experimental observations made on the crystal structure of thermolysin complexed with an hydroxamic acid inhibitor (see Holmes & Matthews, 1981). In this complex (see Figure 6), the group HONHCO (corresponding to the $R_0$) is making hydrogen bond interactions with the active site Zn and with residues ALA 13 and GLU 143. Furthermore, the benzyl group in the malonyl moiety corresponding to $R_1$ is found in a hydrophobic pocket of the active site while the following ALA side chain corresponding to $R_2$ is found in proximity of LEU 202 and PHE 130 of the enzyme.

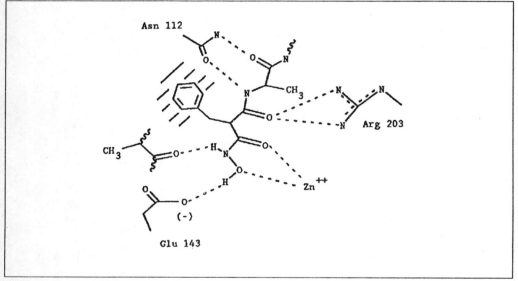

Figure 6. A SCHEMATIC VIEW OF THE ACTIVE SITE. THE ACTIVE SITE OF THERMOLYSIN WITH A FRAGMENT OF A HYDROXAMIC ACID DERIVATIVE INHIBITOR.

## Conclusions

We have presented a system named FLEMING that discovers explanatory theories from a set of experimental observations concerning drug compounds. Dynamic bias management has been presented as a critical mechanism to deal with complex structured objects such as molecules. In this case, the use of low-level descriptors appears inadequate to capture the target concept while the adoption of high-level predicates introduces a too strong bias on the results of the analysis. Because of the close integration between bias management system and learning system, we could not easily apply standard induction algorithms, notably the AQ family (Michalski, 1983). FLEMING has been successfully applied to the domain of the inhibitors of the thermolysin enzyme, where it automatically generated an explanatory model containing structural relations between generalized fragments described in terms of binding properties. In the next future we plan to test the FLEMING system on a number of problems currently under study in pharmaceutical research laboratories.

# References

[1]     Bolis, G., Di Pace, L., Fabrocini, F., **A Machine Learning Approach to Computer Aided Molecular Design,** in *International Journal of Computer Aided Molecular Design,* (forthcoming).

[2]     Drastal, G., Czako, G., Raatz, S., **Induction in an Abstraction Space: A Form of Constructive Induction,** in *Proceedings of the Eleventh International Joint Conference on Artificial Intelligence, IJCAI,* 1989.

[3]     Flann, N., Dietterich, T. G., **Selecting Appropriate Representations for Learning from Examples,** in *Proceedings of the Fifth National Conference on Artificial Intelligence, AAAI,* 1986.

[4]     Holmes, M. A., Matthews, B. W., in *Biochemistry, 20,* 1981.

[5]     Klopman, G. J., Bendale, R. D., **Computer Automated Structure Evaluation (CASE): A Study of Inhibitors of the Thermolysin Enzyme,** in *J. Theor. Biol., 136,* 1989.

[6]     Martin, Y. C., **Quantitative Drug Design,** *New York, Marcel Dekker,* 1978.

[7]     Matheus, C. J., Rendell, L. A., **Constructive Induction on Decision Trees,** in *Proceedings of the Eleventh International Joint Conference on Artificial Intelligence, IJCAI,* 1989.

[8]     Michalski, R. S., **A Theory and Methodology of Inductive Learning,** in *Michalski, R. S., Carbonell, J. G., Mitchell, T. M., eds., Machine Learning: An Artificial Intelligence Approach, vol. I, Palo Alto, Tioga Publishing Company,* 1983.

[9]     Mitchell, T. M., **The Need for Biases in Learning Generalizations,** *Tech. Rep. CBM-TR-117, Computer Sc. Dep., Rutgers University,* 1980.

[10]    Muggleton, S., **Duce, an oracle based approach to constructive induction,** in *Proceedings of the Tenth International Joint Conference on Artificial Intelligence, IJCAI,* 1987.

[11]    Pagallo, G., **Learning DNF by Decision Trees,** in *Proceedings of the Eleventh International Joint Conference on Artificial Intelligence, IJCAI,* 1987.

[12]    Rendell, L., Cho, H., **Empirical Learning as a Function of Concept Character,** in *Machine Learning, 5,* 1990.

[13]    Rendell, L., Seshu. R., Tcheng, D., **Layered Concept-Learning and Dynamically-Variable Bias Management,** in *Proceedings of the Tenth International Joint Conference on Artificial Intelligence, IJCAI,* 1987.

[14]    Russell, S. J., Grosof, N. B., **Delarative Bias: An Overview,** in *Benjamin, P., ed., Proceedings of the Philips Workshop on Reformulation and Inductive Bias, Boston, Kluwer Academic,* 1989.

[15]    Schlimmer, J. C., **Incremental Adjustment of Representations in Learning,** in *Proceedings of the International Workshop on Machine Learning,* 1987.

[16]    Utgoff, P. E., **Shift of Bias for Inductive Concept Learning,** in *Michalski, R. S., Carbonell, J. G., Mitchell, T. M., eds., Machine Learning: An Artificial Intelligence Approach, Los Altos, Morgan Kaufmann Publishers,* 1986.

[17]    Wrobel, S., **Automatic Representation Adjustment in an Observational Discovery System,** in *Proceedings of the Third European Working Session on Learning,* 1988.

# Learning Features by Experimentation in Chess

Eduardo Morales

The Turing Institute, 36 North Hanover St., Glasgow G1 2AD

Email: eduardo@turing.ac.uk

## Abstract

There are two main issues to consider in an inductive learning system. These are 1) its search through the hypothesis space and 2) the amount of provided information for the system to work. In this paper we use a constrained relative least-general-generalisation (RLGG) algorithm as method of generalisation to organise the search space and an automatic example generator to reduce the user's intervention and guide the learning process. Some initial results to learn a restricted form of Horn clause concepts in chess are presented. The main limitations of the learning system and the example generator are pointed out and conclusions and future research directions indicated.

Keywords: LGG, experimentation, chess, Horn clause

## 1 Introduction

Suppose we want a system to learn the definition of the concept of a piece threatening another piece in chess, neither of which is a king. We provide the system with a description of a position where a piece is threatening another one, but we do not tell the system what concept we want to learn or which arguments are involved in the new concept.

The position of Figure 1 can be completely described by a three-place predicate (contents/3) stating the position of each piece in the board.

$$contents(black,king,square(1,8)).$$
$$contents(black,rook,square(4,4)).$$
$$contents(white,king,square(1,1)).$$
$$contents(white,pawn,square(4,7)).$$

The system uses the above description with its current background knowledge to recognise a set of "features" and construct a possible definition. If the background vocabulary of the system consists of:

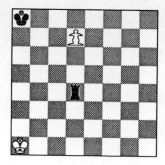

Figure 1: Example Position

| | |
|---|---|
| contents(Side,Piece,Place). | Describes the position of each piece. |
| sliding_piece(Piece). | Piece is a rook, bishop or queen. |
| straight_slide(Piece). | Piece is a rook or queen. |
| all_but_K(Piece). | Piece is anything but king. |
| other_side(Side1,Side2). | Side1 is the other side of Side2 |
| legal_move(Side,Piece,Place,NewPlace). | Piece of Side in Place can move to NewPlace. |

Then the system produces the following highly specialised definition for that particular example:

```
concept(black,king,square(1,8),black,rook,square(4,4),
        white,king,square(1,1),white,pawn,square(4,7)) ←
            contents(black,king,square(1,8)),
            ...
            other_side(black,white),
            other_side(white,black),
            all_but_K(pawn),
            all_but_K(rook),
            straight_slide(rook),
            sliding_piece(rook),
            legal_move(black,king,square(1,8),square(2,8)),
            ...
            legal_move(black,rook,square(4,4),square(1,4)),
            ...
            legal_move(white,king,square(1,1),square(2,1)),
            ...
            legal_move(white,pawn,square(4,7),square(4,8)).
```

The system then follows an experimentation process by automatically generating positive and negative examples (validated by the user) from which other features are deduced and similar definitions constructed. Following a generalisation process between definitions, eventually, the system recognises that the two kings are irrelevant to the concept and arrives to the following definition:

```
concept(A,B,square(C,D),E,F,square(G,H)) ←
        contents(A,B,square(C,D)),
        contents(E,F,square(G,H)),
        other_side(E,A),
        other_side(A,E),
        all_but_K(B),
        all_but_K(F),
        legal_move(A,B,square(C,D),square(G,H)).
```

We have built a system which arrives to the same definition after generating 21 positive and 11 negative examples. It has been able to learn a more general definition of threat, forks, possible attacks and possible checks in chess. It learns concepts expressed in a subset of Horn clauses after generating a small number of examples.

Section 2 describes the generalisation method based on an RLGG algorithm. Section 3 discusses the automatic example generator method based on "perturbations". The learning algorithm is summarised in Section 4 and some examples in chess are presented in Section 5. Finally, Section 6, summarises and suggests future research directions.

# 2   Constrained RLGG

## 2.1   Introduction

Due to the requirements of searching a large hypothesis space, systems that induce first-order predicates have been of limited success since they have been forced to constrain their search space in such a way that only simple concepts can be learned. More recently, a model of generalisation based on relative least-general-generalisation (RLGG) [Plotkin, 1971a] has been used successfully to learn new concepts using a Horn clause framework ([Muggleton & Cao, 1990]).[1]

Plotkin [Plotkin, 1971b, Plotkin, 1969] describes how to construct the least general generalisation (LGG) of two clauses in terms of $\Theta$-subsumption. Clause $C_1$ is more general than clause $C_2$ if $C_1$ $\Theta$-subsumes $C_2$ (i.e., $C_1\sigma \subseteq C_2$ for some substitution $\sigma$). The least general generalisation of two clauses is a generalisation which is less general than any other generalisation. The LGG of two

---

[1]Muggleton [Muggleton, 1990] provides a unified framework for his Inverse Resolution method [Muggleton & Buntine, 1988] and Plotkin's RLGG.

clauses $C_1$ and $C_2$ is defined as: $\{l : l_1 \in C_1 \text{ and } l_2 \in C_2 \text{ and } l = LGG(l_1, l_2)\}$. The LGG of two terms or literals is defined for two terms or literals with the same predicate name and sign (compatible). The algorithm proceeds as follows: If $L_1$ and $L_2$ are compatible, then find terms $t_1$ and $t_2$ that have the same place in $L_1$ and $L_2$ such that $t_1 \neq t_2$ and both $t_1$ and $t_2$ either begin with different function letters or at least one of them is a variable. If there is no such pair $t_1, t_2$, then finish. Else replace $t_1$ and $t_2$ by a new variable V and, whenever $t_1$ and $t_2$ appear in $L_1$ and $L_2$ in the same place, replace them by V.

Plotkin [Plotkin, 1971a, Plotkin, 1971b] also introduces a notion of LGG relative to some background knowledge $\mathcal{K}$. Given $\mathcal{K}$, two examples $e_1$ and $e_2$ for which $\mathcal{K} \not\vdash e_1$ and $\mathcal{K} \not\vdash e_2$. C is the LGG of $e_1$ and $e_2$ relative to $\mathcal{K}$ whenever C is the least general clause for which $\mathcal{K} \wedge C \vdash e_1 \wedge e_2$. We can construct C by replacing $\mathcal{K}$ with a set of ground atoms $a_1 \wedge a_2 \wedge \ldots$, representing a model of $\mathcal{K}$ (see also [Buntine, 1988, Muggleton & Cao, 1990]), and taking the LGG (as described above) of two clauses $C_1$ and $C_2$ defined as:

$$C_1 = (\overline{a_1} \vee \overline{a_2} \vee \ldots) \vee e_1$$

$$C_2 = (\overline{a_1} \vee \overline{a_2} \vee \ldots) \vee e_2$$

## 2.2 Constraints on the Background Knowledge

In general, if $e_1$ and $e_2$ are unit clauses and only a finite number of ground atoms (constructed with symbols in $\mathcal{K}$, $e_1$ and $e_2$) are logical consequences of $\mathcal{K}$, then the LGG of $e_1$ and $e_2$ relative to $\mathcal{K}$ exists. A key issue in RLGG is how to choose adequate constraints to produce a finite set of "relevant" atoms derived from $\mathcal{K}$. Buntine [Buntine, 1988] suggests using a finite subset of the least Herbrand model of $\mathcal{K}$. Muggleton and Feng [Muggleton & Cao, 1990] substitute $\mathcal{K}$ by an h-easy model constructed from a restricted form of Horn clauses. Rather than generating and storing a large number of relevant atoms, we use a restricted form of Horn clauses, supported by a variable-typed logic, from which only a finite number of ground atoms can be derived.[2]

## 2.3 Knowledge Representation

Our final research direction aims to use a learning strategy in conjunction with a planning system to deal with reactive environments such as chess [Morales, 1990]. We assume that the planning skills of a chess player are linked to the number of "features" he/she can recognise from a chess position and that their skills can improve when learning to recognise new features. With this aim in mind, our research is oriented towards learning new feature definitions from existing ones. The learning algorithm relies on an oracle which provides an initial example description and classifies

---

[2]Our clauses are more restricted than Muggleton and Feng's [Muggleton & Cao, 1990].

the examples generated by the perturbation algorithm (described in Section 3). Depending on the initial background knowledge and on the particular example description, the system is able to derive (recognise) more or less atoms (features). We propose to start with some basic background knowledge and incrementally extend the domain knowledge by learning "simple" concepts first.

Unlike other systems, the relevant arguments of the target concept do not need to be pre-defined. We define a feature as an atom which is true for the current board position description. A board position or example description is specified by a set of ground unit clauses. A feature definition is a restricted Horn clause which takes the example description to test for particular features. A feature definition has the following format:

$$H \leftarrow D_1, D_2, ..., D_n, F_1, F_2, ..., F_n.$$

where $D_i$s are "input" predicates used to describe positions and $F_i$s are "feature" predicates which are either provided as background knowledge or learned by the system. We define as input predicates those which are used to describe the current example but which depend on at most one piece. In the example of Section 1, all the predicates except `legal_move` are input predicates. Feature predicates are dependent on the position of other pieces or provided as background knowledge. For example, legal moves, checks, check mates, ..., etc.

This format instantiates the arguments required by the clause with arguments of the current example description constraining the possible instantiations of the head and producing only relevant atoms to the current example.

For example, the following feature definition is used to recognise checks in chess. The input predicates are contents/3 and other_side/2 and the feature predicate is piece_move/4.

in_check(Side,KPlace,OPiece,OPlace) ←
        contents(Side,king,KPlace),
        contents(OSide,OPiece,OPlace),
        other_side(Side,OSide),
        piece_move(OSide,OPiece,OPlace,KPlace).

The example description is included to the theory and a set of relevant atoms are derived from the feature definitions (representing a model). These atoms constitute a feasible body of the new concept definition. Since we do not specify exactly which arguments are involved in the concept definition, a "tentative" head is constructed with the arguments used in the "input" predicates. This initial clause is gradually generalised using an LGG algorithm between this clause and similar clauses constructed from other example descriptions generated by the perturbation algorithm (Appendix 1 has a complete sequence of gradual generalisations produced when learning a special case of the concept of fork in chess).

Given a new example description (ground input predicates),

and a set of feature definitions (representing the domain theory)

Add the description to the domain theory and

Construct a new clause

    The body being the set of atoms derived from the feature definitions
with the input predicates

    The head constructed with the arguments used in the input predicates

Make an LGG between this clause and the current concept clause

    the resulting clause being of the form $H \leftarrow D_1, D_2, ..., D_n, F_1, F_2, ..., F_n$.

    where $D_i$s are input predicates

Remove the arguments in the head that do not appear in any $F_i$

Remove any literal with a variable argument which do not appear in any
other place of the concept definition

Table 1: Generalisation Algorithm

Once a generalisation is produced, the system tries to reduce the number of arguments involved in the head of the new concept by keeping only those which appear in a literal (different than the input predicates) in the new concept definition. New compatible heads are constructed taking into account the current concept head.

Even if we produce a finite set of atoms to construct a clause, the RLGG algorithm can generate clauses with a large number of literals. The length of the clauses is constrained by deleting all the literals whose variable arguments do not appear on any other place in the concept definition (see Table 1).

The constrained RLGG algorithm has been able to learn concept like forks and attacks in chess. The knowledge representation syntax, which follows our intuitive definition of a feature in chess, can produce only a finite set of relevant atoms for an example description.

# 3  Perturbation Method

## 3.1  Introduction

One key issue to consider is the information on which the system relies for its "correct" behaviour. In some cases, the learning process is highly dependent on the user's intervention. This is more noticeable in an incremental learning system, where the user often has to be careful in selecting the examples or training instances to ensure that the system will succeed on its learning task (e.g. [Winston, 1977, Sammut & Banerji, 1986]). This dependency or *hidden knowledge*, requires a good understanding of the system's internal characteristics and severely questions the system's learning capabilities. Experimentation (or active instance selection) has been employed in several machine learning systems [Feng, 1990, Carbonell & Gil, 1987, Dietterich & Buchanan, 1983, Lenat, 1976, Porter & Kibler, 1986] to reduce this dependency and guide the learning process.

There are several strategies that can be adopted to generate an example. Ruff and Dietterich [Ruff & Dietterich, 1989] argue that there is no essential difference between an example generator that uses a "clever" (although computationally expensive) strategy to divide the hypothesis space and a simple example generator that randomly selects examples. As we construct clauses from positive examples only, a random strategy is of very little use, especially when the target concept covers a small part of the example space, as it can generate a huge number of negative examples before generating a positive, slowing down the learning process. Another alternative is to provide a hierarchy of concepts and generate new examples from instances of concepts higher or at the same level of the hierarchy [Porter & Kibler, 1986, Lenat, 1976]. While applicable in some domains, some others domains are not so easily structured and alternative methods must be employed. Feng [Feng, 1990] provides the theoretical basis for choosing a new example based on information theory. His next-best-verification algorithm chooses the next example which is the best to verify a hypothesis based on information content. In practice, he requires a set of heuristics to define a sequential number for the examples (the best example being the one which follows in the sequence), which in general is not easy to do as several "sequences" along different "dimensions" can exist.

## 3.2    A Framework for Describing the Example Space

In an automatic example generator, the space of examples depends on the number of arguments required to describe an instance of the target concept and on the size of their domains. If an example can be described by instantiating N arguments, we can have $2^N$ - 1 different perturbation classes distributed in N perturbation levels. Each perturbation level represents the number of arguments to change at the same time to generate a new example and each perturbation class shows the particular arguments to change, representing a class of instances. For example, if we can describe an instance of the concept of threat between two pieces with four arguments, e.g., threat(P1,L1,P2,L2) (meaning that piece P1 in place L1 threatens piece P2 in position L2), we can structure the perturbation space in four levels (see Figure 2).

At each perturbation class, we can generate $D_i \times D_j \times \ldots \times D_n$ examples, where each $D_k$ is a particular argument domain at that level. For instance, the perturbation class [L1,P2] represents the class of examples that can be generated by changing the position of the attacking piece and the piece which is being threatened. In the example of Section 1, the attacking piece (rook) can be in 60 different legal positions and the piece being attacked can be changed for knight, bishop, rook or

| 4 | | | P1,L1,P2,L2 | |
|---|---|---|---|---|

| 3 | P1,L1,P2 | P1,L1,L2 | P1,P2,L2 | L1,P2,L2 |

| 2 | P1,L1 | P1,P2 | P1,L2 | L1,P2 | L1,L2 | P2,L2 |

| 1 | | P1 | L1 | P2 | L2 |

Figure 2: Pertubation Space

queen. Clearly the example space grows exponentially with the number of arguments involved.

We can apply several domain constraints to reduce this space. In particular, not all the perturbations generate legal examples. For instance, the first (last) rank can be eliminated from the domain of the positions of the white (black) pawns, we can use the knowledge that two and only two kings (one on each side) must be at any position to constrain the domains on the possible values for the pieces and avoid changing sides on one king without changing in the other, ..., etc. We can choose a particular order in which to traverse this space. Like changing all the arguments that involve the sides of the pieces first (this corresponds to a particular perturbation class). Similarly, in other domains like the 8-puzzle, we can constrain the perturbation space to perturbation classes that involve only "swapping" tiles. Despite these constraints, the example space can still be huge (e.g., in chess, two kings alone can be in 3612 different legal positions, which corresponds to a perturbation class at level 2).

## 3.3 A Perturbation Algorithm

Our example generation strategy is guided by the current concept definition, starting the perturbation process at the lower levels of the previously described structure and moving gradually upwards trying to reduce the arguments and their domains in the process. The perturbation classes are generated dynamically, i.e., we do not produce a new perturbation class unless required. After exploring a perturbation class (this is described below), only its immediate perturbation classes above are generated. Similarly, if an argument is eliminated from the head of the concept definition (as described in Section 2) or when its domain is reduced to the empty list, all the perturbation classes where the argument appears are removed from the perturbation space.

For example, following the hypothetical concept of a threat with 4 arguments, the perturbation space will initially consist of 4 perturbation classes:

$$[[P1], [L1], [P2], [L2]]$$

As soon as we finish exploring the possible places of the attacking piece [P1], the new perturbation space becomes:

$$[[L1], [P2], [L2]], [[P1,L1], [P1,P2], [P1,L2]]$$

Similarly, after exploring the possible attacking pieces [P1], we have:

$$[[P2], [L2]], [[P1,L1], [P1,P2], [P1,L2], [L1,P2], [L1,L2]].$$

If the attacked piece "P2" is removed from the head of the concept or if its domain becomes empty, then the new perturbation space becomes:

$$[[L2]], [[P1,L1], [P1,L2], [L1,L2]]$$

Recognising irrelevant arguments is important since they represent significant cuts in the search space.[3]

The perturbation algorithm picks the first perturbation class and generates new examples by picking new values from the domains of the arguments involved. If no new values can be generated (i.e., it has finished exploring a perturbation class), it changes the perturbation space (as described above), otherwise it checks which literals (features) from the concept definition fail with the new values. After selecting new values, if none of the literals fail, it considers those values as irrelevant and removes them from the domain. If at least one literal fails, it constructs a new example with the new values. When a negative example is generated, the system tries to construct an example that will succeed on an least one of the literals that failed on that example. Whenever an argument is eliminated from the head of the concept definition or if its domain becomes empty, it is removed from the perturbation space. The perturbation process ends when there are no more perturbation classes left (see Table 2).

Following the example given in Section 1, at the first level of perturbation, a new example can be generated by replacing the attacked piece (pawn) with a knight. This perturbation fails the literal: legal_move(white,knight,square(4,7),square(4,8)) and a new clause is constructed. However, if the attacker (rook) is replaced with a knight, generating a negative example, then the system will try to construct an example that will succeed on at least one of the failed features (e.g., replacing the attacker with a queen).

The perturbation method has been used to guide the learning process of the RLGG algorithm described in Section 2. In general, this strategy will converge faster to a concept definition than a random example generator, especially in concepts where a small number of positive examples exist in a large example space. It has a clear termination criterion to stop the generation of examples and produces a smaller set of examples because it can reduce the example space during the learning process.

---

[3]An argument which is removed from the perturbation space is not necessarily removed from the definition.

```
DO UNTIL all the perturbation classes has been explored
      or stopped by the user
      IF a new definition is constructed
      THEN pick the first perturbation class and try to generate an
          example that will fail on at least one of its literals
      IF a negative example is generated
      THEN see which literals failed with that example and try to
          generate an example which that succeed on at least one
          of them
      IF we cannot generate a new example that will fail
          (or succeed) on any literal,
      THEN generate the next perturbation classes and continue
END DO
```

Table 2: Perturbation Algorithm

# 4  The Learning Algorithm

We can now summarise the learning method using the description of the previous two sections. Initially, the system is provided with some background knowledge, the domain values of the arguments involved to describe an example, and a description of a "typical" example of the target concept. The system first constructs an initial concept definition and an initial perturbation level. The system then calls the example generator method to create new examples (see Section 3). Each time a positive example is created the system uses the constrained RLGG algorithm (see Section 2) to create a new concept definition. The example generator tries to fail on at least one of the concept literals by changing (perturbing) the arguments involved in the current perturbation class. If the perturbation method generates a negative example, then the system analyses which literals failed on that example and tries to construct a new example that will succeed on at least one of them. If the system cannot generate a new example (i.e., a new generalisation of the current definition will require producing an example that involves changing different arguments), then it changes the perturbation space and continues. The process ends when there are no more levels left, or when the user decides to terminate it.

Each new definition is checked against the current negative examples (the user is also asked for confirmation). This is to avoid over-generalisations, which can occur when learning disjunctive definitions. If a definition covers a negative example, then it is rejected and the example is stored. When the perturbation process finishes, the final definition is checked against the stored examples,

Given an initial example description

Construct an initial clause (as described in Section 2) and

an initial perturbation level (as described in Section 3)

DO UNTIL no more perturbation levels or stopped by the user

    CALL PERTURBATION-METHOD to generate a new example

    IF the example is positive

    THEN CALL RLGG

        IF the new definition covers a negative example

        (or if it is rejected by the user)

        THEN reject the definition and store that example

END DO

Check the final definition with the stored examples

IF some examples are not covered,

THEN start again

ELSE add the new definition to the background knowledge

and finish

Table 3: Learning Algorithm

those which cannot succeed are tried again and the whole process is repeated. In this way the systems is able to learn disjunctive concepts although each clause is learned separately (see Table 3).

# 5 Examples

We applied the previously described system to learn some concepts in chess. We provide the system with the same background knowledge described in the introduction. The input predicates being for each example, contents/3, straight_slide/1, sliding_piece/1, all_but_K/1 and other_side/2. Feature predicates definitions to recognise legal moves, checks and check-mates were also given. We provided as well domain values for the arguments used in the input predicates (i.e., Side, Piece, Place),

```
domain(piece,[pawn,knight,bishop,rook,queen,king]).
domain(side,[black,white]).
domain(place,[square(1,1),square(1,2),...,square(8,8)]).
```

and specification of which arguments have which domain.

This time, we decided to broaden the concept of a threat and accept as positive examples those which include as well a king threatening a piece. Using the same description of the initial example given in the introduction, the system produces the following definition (which follows our more general definition) after generating 48 positive and 14 negative examples:

threat(A,B,square(C,D),E,F,square(G,H)) ←
    contents(A,B,square(C,D)),
    contents(E,F,square(G,H)),
    other_side(E,A),
    other_side(A,E),
    all_but_K(B),
    all_but_K(F),
    legal_move(A,B,square(C,D),square(G,H)).


threat(A,B,square(C,D),E,king,square(F,G)) ←
    contents(A,B,square(C,D)),
    contents(E,king,square(F,G)),
    other_side(E,A),
    other_side(A,E),
    all_but_K(B),
    legal_move(E,king,square(F,G),square(C,D)).

The first clause is the same one given in the introduction and represents a threat between two pieces. The second clause represents a threat between a king and a piece. The system can learn in the same way a threat between a piece and a king (i.e., a check), but since the concept of being in check was initially given as a feature definition the examples where a check occurred were classified as negative instances. The total number of examples generated by the system compares very favourable against an example space of approximately $\approx 10^8$ possible examples.

Similarly the learning algorithm produced the following definition of the concept of a *fork* after learning the concept of threat and after generating 13 positive and 27 negative examples. This is a restricted version of a fork in chess which occurs whenever a piece threatens another piece and checks the king at the same time. Appendix 1 describes the learning sequence involved to learn this concept showing only the positive examples generated by the system and all the intermediate generalisations:

fork(A,king,square(B,C),A,D,square(E,F),G,H,square(I,J)) ←
    contents(A,king,square(B,C)),
    contents(A,D,square(E,F)),

contents(G,H,square(I,J)),

in_check(A,square(B,C),H,square(I,J)),

other_side(G,A),

other_side(A,G),

all_but_K(D),

all_but_K(H),

legal_move(G,H,square(I,J),square(E,F)),

threat(G,H,square(I,J),A,D,square(E,F)).

Although not implemented, we can use the definition of threat to reduce this definition to:

fork(A,king,square(B,C),A,D,square(E,F),G,H,square(I,J)) ←

contents(A,king,square(B,C)),

contents(A,D,square(E,F)),

contents(G,H,square(I,J)),

in_check(A,square(B,C),H,square(I,J)),

threat(G,H,square(I,J),A,D,square(E,F)).

Again the total number of generated examples is several orders of magnitude smaller than the example space.

The learning algorithm as it stands has several limitations. In particular, it cannot deal with exceptions or negation (i.e., it cannot learn things like "without feature")[4]. It also cannot learn recursive concepts. This is partly due to the example representation, although in principle we could include previously generated heads into the list of relevant atoms to allow it to learn recursive concepts (although they will have to be updated with changes in the current number of arguments).

# 6    Conclusions and Future Research Directions

In an inductive learning system we need to consider the search through the hypothesis space and the amount of information provided by the user. We have addressed both problems by using a constrained RLGG algorithm as a model of generalisation coupled with an automatic example generator to learn a restricted form of Horn clauses. The problem of selecting a relevant set of atoms derived from the background knowledge for the RLGG algorithm has been solved by using a restricted form of Horn clauses which follows closely to our intuitive notion of a feature definition in domains like chess. We have also relaxed the example representation used in other systems by describing each example with a list of features, rather than specifying which of the arguments are relevant to the concept definition. We have reduced the user's intervention over the system for its

---

[4]Although negation is used in one of the concepts of the background knowledge

"correct" behaviour by presenting an automatic example generator which converges rapidly to the concept definition. The examples space is structured dynamically, allows to include domain rules if necessary to explore particular perturbations and is fairly independent of the learning algorithm. Finally, we have demonstrated the feasibility of the approach with some initial results in chess. We plan to continue this research by learning concepts which involve one or more moves, like in discovery attacks.

Acknowledgements.

I would like to thank Tim Niblett, Steve Muggleton and Peter Clark for helpful comments in the development of this work. This research was made possible by a grant from CONACYT (México).

# References

Buntine, W. (1988). Generalised subsumption an its applications to induction and redundancy. *Artificial Intelligence*, (36):149–176.

Carbonell, F. and Gil, Y. (1987). Learning by experimentation. In *Proceedings of the Fourth International Workshop on Machine Learning*, pages 256–265.

Dietterich, T. and Buchanan, B. (1983). The role of experimentation in theory formation. In *Proceedings of the Second International Workshop on Machine Learning*, pages 147–155.

Feng, C. (1990). *Learning by Experimentation*. PhD thesis, Turing Institute - University of Strathclyde.

Lenat, D. B. (1976). *AM: an artificial intelligence approach to discovery in mathematics as heuristic search*. PhD thesis, Stanford University, Artificial Intelligence Laboratory. AIM-286 or STAN-CS-76-570.

Morales, E. (1990). Thesis proposal. (unpublished).

Muggleton, S. (1990). Inductive logic programming. In *First International Workshop on Algorithmic Learning Theory (ALT90)*, Tokyo, Japan.

Muggleton, S. and Buntine, W. (1988). Machine invention of first-order predicates by inverting resolution. In *Proceedings of the Fifth International Conference on Machine Learning*, pages 339–353. Kaufmann.

Muggleton, S. and Cao, F. (1990). Efficient induction of logic programs. In *First International Workshop on Algorithmic Learning Theory (ALT90)*, Tokyo, Japan.

Plotkin, G. (1969). A note on inductive generalisation. In *Machine Intelligence 5*, pages 153–163. Meltzer B. and Michie D. (Eds).

Plotkin, G. (1971a). *Automatic Methods of Inductive Inference*. PhD thesis, Edimburgh University.

Plotkin, G. (1971b). A further note on inductive generalisation. In *Machine Intelligence 6*, pages 101–124. Meltzer B. and Michie D. (Eds).

Porter, B. and Kibler, D. (1986). Experimental goal regression. *Machine Learning*, (1):249 – 286.

Ruff, R. and Dietterich, T. (1989). What good are experiments? In *Proc. of the Sixth International Workshop on Machine Learning*, pages 109–112, Conell Univ., Ithaca New York. Morgan Kaufmann.

Sammut, C. and Banerji, R. (1986). Learning concepts by asking questions. In *Machine Learning: An artificial intelligence approach (Vol 2)*. R. Michalski, J. Carbonell and T. Mitchell (eds).

Winston, P. (1977). Learning structural descriptions from examples. In *The Psychology of computer vision*. Winston, P.H. (Ed), MacGraw-Hill.

**Appendix 1** This is the sequence for learning a restricted concept of fork. Only the positive examples generated by the perturbation method are shown.

|?- go.

tmp(A,king,square(3,4),A,queen,square(3,6),
   B,king,square(6,7),B,knight,square(1,5)) ←
   contents(A,king,square(3,4)),
   contents(A,queen,square(3,6)),
   contents(B,king,square(6,7)),
   contents(B,knight,square(1,5)),
   in_check(A,square(3,4),knight,square(1,5)),
   other_side(B,A),
   other_side(A,B),
   all_but_K(queen),
   all_but_K(knight),
   diagonal_slide(queen),
   straight_slide(queen),
   sliding_piece(queen),
   legal_move(A,king,square(3,4),square(4,5)),
   legal_move(A,king,square(3,4),square(2,5)),
   legal_move(A,king,square(3,4),square(4,3)),
   legal_move(A,king,square(3,4),square(3,5)),
   legal_move(A,king,square(3,4),square(3,3)),
   legal_move(A,king,square(3,4),square(4,4)),
   legal_move(A,king,square(3,4),square(2,4)),
   legal_move(B,king,square(6,7),square(7,8)),
   legal_move(B,king,square(6,7),square(6,8)),
   legal_move(B,king,square(6,7),square(7,7)),
   legal_move(B,king,square(6,7),square(5,7)),
   legal_move(B,knight,square(1,5),square(2,7)),
   legal_move(B,knight,square(1,5),square(2,3)),
   legal_move(B,knight,square(1,5),square(3,6)),
   threat(B,knight,square(1,5),A,queen,square(3,6)).

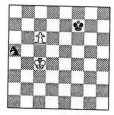

tmp(A,king,square(3,4),A,B,square(3,6),
   C,king,square(6,7),C,knight,square(1,5)) ←
   contents(C,knight,square(1,5)),
   contents(C,king,square(6,7)),
   contents(A,B,square(3,6)),
   contents(A,king,square(3,4)),

   in_check(A,square(3,4),knight,square(1,5)),
   other_side(A,C),
   other_side(C,A),
   all_but_K(knight),
   all_but_K(B),
   legal_move(C,knight,square(1,5),square(3,6)),
   legal_move(C,knight,square(1,5),square(2,3)),
   legal_move(C,knight,square(1,5),square(2,7)),
   legal_move(C,king,square(6,7),square(5,7)),
   legal_move(C,king,square(6,7),square(7,7)),
   legal_move(C,king,square(6,7),square(6,8)),
   legal_move(C,king,square(6,7),square(7,8)),
   legal_move(A,king,square(3,4),square(2,4)),
   legal_move(A,king,square(3,4),square(4,4)),
   legal_move(A,king,square(3,4),square(3,3)),
   legal_move(A,king,square(3,4),square(3,5)),
   legal_move(A,king,square(3,4),square(4,3)),
   legal_move(A,king,square(3,4),square(2,5)),
   legal_move(A,king,square(3,4),square(4,5)),
   threat(C,knight,square(1,5),A,B,square(3,6)).

tmp(A,king,square(3,4),A,B,square(3,6),
   C,king,square(D,E),C,knight,square(1,5)) ←
   contents(A,king,square(3,4)),
   contents(A,B,square(3,6)),
   contents(C,king,square(D,E)),
   contents(C,knight,square(1,5)),
   in_check(A,square(3,4),knight,square(1,5)),
   other_side(C,A),
   other_side(A,C),
   all_but_K(B),
   all_but_K(knight),
   legal_move(A,king,square(3,4),square(2,5)),
   legal_move(A,king,square(3,4),square(4,3)),
   legal_move(A,king,square(3,4),square(3,3)),
   legal_move(A,king,square(3,4),square(4,4)),
   legal_move(A,king,square(3,4),square(2,4)),
   legal_move(C,king,square(D,E),square(5,7)),
   legal_move(C,king,square(D,E),square(5,E)),
   legal_move(C,knight,square(1,5),square(2,7)),
   legal_move(C,knight,square(1,5),square(2,3)),
   legal_move(C,knight,square(1,5),square(3,6)),
   threat(C,knight,square(1,5),A,B,square(3,6)).

tmp(A,king,square(3,4),A,B,square(C,D),
   E,king,square(F,G),E,knight,square(1,5)) ←
   contents(E,knight,square(1,5)),
   contents(E,king,square(F,G)),
   contents(A,B,square(C,D)),
   contents(A,king,square(3,4)),
   in_check(A,square(3,4),knight,square(1,5)),
   other_side(A,E),

other_side(E,A),
all_but_K(knight),
all_but_K(B),
legal_move(E,knight,square(1,5),square(C,D)),
legal_move(E,knight,square(1,5),square(3,6)),
legal_move(E,knight,square(1,5),square(2,3)),
legal_move(E,knight,square(1,5),square(2,7)),
legal_move(E,king,square(F,G),square(5,G)),
legal_move(E,king,square(F,G),square(5,7)),
legal_move(A,king,square(3,4),square(2,4)),
legal_move(A,king,square(3,4),square(4,4)),
legal_move(A,king,square(3,4),square(3,3)),
legal_move(A,king,square(3,4),square(4,3)),
legal_move(A,king,square(3,4),square(2,5)),
threat(E,knight,square(1,5),A,B,square(C,D)).

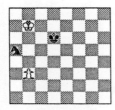

tmp(A,king,square(B,C),A,D,square(E,F),
    G,king,square(H,I),G,knight,square(1,5)) ←
    contents(A,king,square(B,C)),
    contents(A,D,square(E,F)),
    contents(G,king,square(H,I)),
    contents(G,knight,square(1,5)),
    in_check(A,square(B,C),knight,square(1,5)),
    other_side(G,A),
    other_side(A,G),
    all_but_K(D),
    all_but_K(knight),
    legal_move(G,king,square(H,I),square(5,7)),
    legal_move(G,king,square(H,I),square(5,I)),
    legal_move(G,knight,square(1,5),square(2,3)),
    legal_move(G,knight,square(1,5),square(3,6)),
    legal_move(G,knight,square(1,5),square(E,F)),
    threat(G,knight,square(1,5),A,D,square(E,F)).

tmp(A,king,square(B,C),A,D,square(E,F),
    G,king,square(H,I),G,knight,square(J,5)) ←
    contents(G,knight,square(J,5)),
    contents(G,king,square(H,I)),
    contents(A,D,square(E,F)),
    contents(A,king,square(B,C)),
    in_check(A,square(B,C),knight,square(J,5)),
    other_side(A,G),
    other_side(G,A),
    all_but_K(knight),
    all_but_K(D),
    legal_move(G,knight,square(J,5),square(E,F)),
    legal_move(G,knight,square(J,5),square(2,3)),
    legal_move(G,king,square(H,I),square(5,I)),
    legal_move(G,king,square(H,I),square(5,7)),
    threat(G,knight,square(J,5),A,D,square(E,F)).

tmp(A,king,square(B,C),A,D,square(E,F),
    G,king,square(H,I),G,knight,square(J,5)) ←
    contents(A,king,square(B,C)),
    contents(A,D,square(E,F)),
    contents(G,king,square(H,I)),
    contents(G,knight,square(J,5)),
    in_check(A,square(B,C),knight,square(J,5)),
    other_side(G,A),
    other_side(A,G),
    all_but_K(D),
    all_but_K(knight),
    legal_move(G,king,square(H,I),square(5,7)),
    legal_move(G,king,square(H,I),square(5,I)),
    legal_move(G,knight,square(J,5),square(2,3)),
    legal_move(G,knight,square(J,5),square(E,F)),
    threat(G,knight,square(J,5),A,D,square(E,F)).

tmp(A,king,square(B,C),A,D,square(E,F),
    G,king,square(H,I),G,knight,square(J,5)) ←
    contents(G,knight,square(J,5)),
    contents(G,king,square(H,I)),
    contents(A,D,square(E,F)),
    contents(A,king,square(B,C)),
    in_check(A,square(B,C),knight,square(J,5)),
    other_side(A,G),
    other_side(G,A),
    all_but_K(knight),
    all_but_K(D),
    legal_move(G,knight,square(J,5),square(E,F)),
    legal_move(G,knight,square(J,5),square(2,3)),
    legal_move(G,king,square(H,I),square(5,I)),
    legal_move(G,king,square(H,I),square(5,7)),
    threat(G,knight,square(J,5),A,D,square(E,F)).

tmp(A,king,square(B,C),A,D,square(E,F),
    G,king,square(H,I),G,knight,square(J,5)) ←
    contents(A,king,square(B,C)),
    contents(A,D,square(E,F)),
    contents(G,king,square(H,I)),
    contents(G,knight,square(J,5)),
    in_check(A,square(B,C),knight,square(J,5)),

other_side(G,A),
other_side(A,G),
all_but_K(D),
all_but_K(knight),
legal_move(G,king,square(H,I),square(5,7)),
legal_move(G,knight,square(J,5),square(2,3)),
legal_move(G,knight,square(J,5),square(E,F)),
threat(G,knight,square(J,5),A,D,square(E,F)).

tmp(A,king,square(B,C),A,D,square(E,F),
    G,king,square(H,I),G,knight,square(J,K)) ←
  contents(G,knight,square(J,K)),
  contents(G,king,square(H,I)),
  contents(A,D,square(E,F)),
  contents(A,king,square(B,C)),
  in_check(A,square(B,C),knight,square(J,K)),
  other_side(A,G),
  other_side(G,A),
  all_but_K(knight),
  all_but_K(D),
  legal_move(G,knight,square(J,K),square(E,F)),
  legal_move(G,knight,square(J,K),square(2,3)),
  legal_move(G,king,square(H,I),square(5,7)),
  threat(G,knight,square(J,K),A,D,square(E,F)).

tmp(A,king,square(B,C),A,D,square(E,F),
    G,knight,square(H,I)) ←
  contents(A,king,square(B,C)),
  contents(A,D,square(E,F)),
  contents(G,knight,square(H,I)),
  in_check(A,square(B,C),knight,square(H,I)),
  other_side(G,A),
  other_side(A,G),
  all_but_K(D),
  all_but_K(knight),
  legal_move(G,knight,square(H,I),square(2,3)),
  legal_move(G,knight,square(H,I),square(E,F)),
  threat(G,knight,square(H,I),A,D,square(E,F)).

tmp(A,king,square(B,C),A,D,square(E,F),
    G,knight,square(H,I)) ←
  contents(G,knight,square(H,I)),
  contents(A,D,square(E,F)),
  contents(A,king,square(B,C)),
  in_check(A,square(B,C),knight,square(H,I)),
  other_side(A,G),
  other_side(G,A),
  all_but_K(knight),
  all_but_K(D),
  legal_move(G,knight,square(H,I),square(E,F)),
  legal_move(G,knight,square(H,I),square(2,3)),
  threat(G,knight,square(H,I),A,D,square(E,F)).

tmp(A,king,square(B,C),A,D,square(E,F),
    G,H,square(I,J)) ←
  contents(A,king,square(B,C)),
  contents(A,D,square(E,F)),
  contents(G,H,square(I,J)),
  in_check(A,square(B,C),H,square(I,J)),
  other_side(G,A),
  other_side(A,G),
  all_but_K(D),
  all_but_K(H),
  legal_move(G,H,square(I,J),square(E,F)),
  threat(G,H,square(I,J),A,D,square(E,F)).

How would you like to call the concept? fork.

yes

| ?-

# REPRESENTATION AND INDUCTION OF MUSICAL STRUCTURES FOR COMPUTER ASSISTED COMPOSITION

Francis COURTOT (*)

(*) Bat A, 50 rue de la Fédération, 93100 Montreuil, France.Email: courtot@ircam.uucp

## Abstract

Computer assisted composition appears to be an interesting domain for Machine Learning for various reasons: the open-ended nature of music; the differences between an expert and a composer, who is not attempting to reach both truth and formalisation but artistic completion; the multilayered, multistructured nature of the music, together with the importance of time. This makes for different demands on machine learning, compared with more rigid domain.

We use a simple (functional) way to type logical terms that fits with time-embedded domains. The types are given abstract attributes such as 'circularity' that make sense for group-theory related domains. Definitions are given for type composition operators and for type relations. This representation is then used by some simple heuristics for building new types. This stage is essential in the formalisation of the language used by the composer to define his musical interesting structures.

A form of 'rules to be looked for' is specified. The rules are extension or variation of g-clauses, using typed terms. At present, two operators has been defined for learning new rules, close to Buntine and Muggleton's inversed resolution principle. An important point about this kind of approach in this particular class of domain is that the composer cannot judge wether or not a substitution is correct, although the algorithms and the typed nature of the terms cut down the search space.

## Reference

Courtot F. Representation and machine learning for Computer Assisted Composition. "Musical Intelligence", *Book on edition,* AAAI press, Menlo Park, California, 1991.

# IPSA: INDUCTIVE PROTEIN STRUCTURE ANALYSIS

S. SCHULZE-KREMER(*)  R. D. KING(**)
(*) Brainware GmbH, Gustav-Meyer Allee 25, W-1000 Berlin 65 and Free University, Dept. Crystallography, Takustr. 6, W-1000 Berlin 33, FRG, email: steffen@kristall.chemie.fu-berlin.dbp.de
(**) University of Strathclyde, Dept. Statistics, 26 Richmond Street, Glasgow G11XH, UK

## Abstract

IPSA applies machine learning to the problem of classifying and describing protein super-secondary structures. We found useful geometrical, topological and chemo-physical attributes for describing protein secondary structures, and wrote a suite of programs to calculate these attributes for 129 proteins. The attribute descriptions of these proteins were then collected together into our IPSA database. Pairs of secondary structure which aggregate together (possible examples of super-secondary structure) were collected from this database. Four separate techniques of cluster analysis (Kohonen networks, AutoClass III, Cobweb and Clustan) are being used to find clusters of these pairs, i.e. super-secondary structures. The machine learning program KET is being used to post-process these clusters to produce an explicit decision tree describing the secondary structures using biochemically meaningful terms. It is hoped that the super-secondary structures found by IPSA will be useful in solving the proteins folding problem.

The general IPSA methodology can be described in 6 steps: 1) Define a collection of the most important attributes for describing protein secondary structures and relations between pairs of secondary structure. These attributes include geometrical, topological and chemo-physical properties. 2) Write a suite of programs to calculate these attributes for secondary structures. The input to these programs are the 3-dimensional coordinates of protein from the Brookhaven database: the output is the IPSA database of protein structure. 3) Discover super-secondary structures by clustering of the multi-dimensional attribute description of pairs of secondary structure which aggregate together (unsupervised learning from observation). 4) Form symbolic descriptions of the discovered super-secondary structures which are understandable by molecular biologists (supervised learning from observation). 5) Study the 3-dimensional structure of the discovered super-secondary structures, to ensure the examples that are clustered together in the basis of their attributes also have closely related 3-dimensional structure - this helps ensure the biological relevance of the clustering. 6) Try to learn the relationships between protein primary structure and the discovered super-secondary structures. If strong relationships can be found, it would be a useful step towards solving the protein folding problem.

## References

Schulze-Kremer, S. (1990) In Stender, J. and Addis, T. (eds.), *Symbols versus Neurons?* IOS Press, Netherlands, pp. 118-151.
Schulze-Kremer, S., King, R.D. and Stender, J. (1990) (in preparation).

# FOUR STANCES ON
# KNOWLEDGE ACQUISITION AND MACHINE LEARNING

*T. R. Addis(♣), Y. Kodratoff(♦), R. L de Mantaras(♥) K. Morik(♠), & E. Plaza(♥)*

(♣)Knowledge Systems Group, School of Engineering and Information Science, University of Reading, UK.

(♦)Equipe Inference et Apprentissage, L.R.I., UA 410 du CNRS, Batiment 490, Universite Paris-Sud, France.

(♥)CEAB-CSIC, 17300 Blanes, Girona, Spain.

(♠)GMD, Postfach 1240, Schloss Birlinghoven, D-5205 SANKT AUGUSTIN 1, Germany.

## Abstract

*This paper consists of four condensed position papers given as an initial statement by five members of a panel session on Knowledge Acquisition and Machine Learning. This panel session was instigated by Yves Kodratoff in order to cover an issue that was raised in 1987 at the first workshop on knowledge acquisition for knowledge-based systems held at Reading (UK). It was at this meeting that those involved in machine learning and knowledge acquisition came to realise that a cultural gulf existed between two groups of people; people who seemed to be working in the same area. It has been the objective over the years at the meetings of both the European Working Sessions on Learning (EWSL) and the European Knowledge Acquisition Workshops (EKAW) to bridge the gap between these two cultures. This panel is intended to be a further step towards achieving this objective.*

## Keywords

Knowledge, acquisition, learning, modelling, logic, domain.

# 1. Knowledge acquisition and machine learning

*K. Morik*

Knowledge acquisition (KA) and machine learning (ML) have been closely linked by their common application field, namely building up knowledge bases for knowledge-based systems. Building up knowledge bases means to construct a model of a domain and a task. The careful analysis of modelling a domain allows for a unifying view of KA and ML. In this view, methods of KA and ML both contribute to modelling.

Differences between the methods are less clear cut than they were perceived in the beginning. For instance, the extent to which a user is involved in the modelling process is not as distinctive as was first believed. Laddering methods from KA actively ask for information from the user. But, some ML systems also query the user, e.g. CLINT (de Raedt/Bruynooghe 88). Also, building up a taxonomy automatically does not make such a clear distinction as was believed. Repertory grid methods create the taxonomy from user answers to some extent automatically. Another frequently mentioned distinction is whether task structures or domain knowledge are investigated. Again, this does not discriminate KA from ML. Only the stress is different: KA focuses on task structures but also acquires domain knowledge whereas ML concentrates more on the domain knowledge but can also be used to structure tasks. Thus, distinctions between KA and ML are hazy as long as they deal with the same application field.

However, as the strengths are different for the various methods, the combination of the two approaches and the integration of their results is promising. The input to ML can well exploit KA techniques in order to prepare the data easily. KA tools allow for structuring the overall task of the target system into subtasks. For each subtask ML tools can be applied to acquire the respective knowledge. The other way around, the knowledge acquired by KA techniques can well be enhanced by inductive inference, introduction of new terms, knowledge base refinement; techniques which have been developed within ML. Integration of KA and ML has been realized by some systems, e.g. BLIP (Morik 90). The basic assumption underlying such an integration is that KA and ML are both concerned with the same subject of knowledge construction.

But matter is more difficult. ML is not restricted to acquiring knowledge. Building macro-operators in problem solving, tuning parameter values, backtracing failures in a theory, optimizing a (logic) program, indicating some crucial consequences of a program to the user are all tasks to which ML can contribute. Whereas it would be weakening the notion of knowledge to call them "KA tasks" they can be termed "ML tasks". Thus, we may think of application fields for ML besides constructing knowledge bases. The new approach of inductive logic programming (Muggleton 90) exploits ML for programmer's support. Only if we would identify knowledge with a program we could view programming as knowledge acquisition. In fact, some software engineers describe programming as a modelling activity (Siefkes 89). In this case, the borderline between knowledge bases and programs disappears. However, to my knowledge there are no KA techniques up to now which support a user in programming or debugging. But there are ML approaches to that goal.

In the framework of knowledge-based systems all enhancements of performance are justified by increasing knowledge. This identification of performance and knowledge gives KA a broad range of applications. The broad range of possible ML applications does not rely on this identification. Thus, ML and KA are closely related in the application field of knowledge construction, i.e. modelling. The borders of this application field are fuzzy because many activities in computer science can be viewed as modelling. However, ML covers more possible application fields than its application fits but does not rely on such a view.

## 2. Learning and models of expertise

*E. Plaza & R. Lopez de Mantaras*

### 2.1. Learning and Knowledge Acquisition as Modelling Processes

We can view learning and knowledge acquisition (KA) as two processes that construct a model of a task domain, including the systematic patterns of interaction of an agent situated in a task environment. In order to elaborate this statement let us point out that:

(i)    learning of an agent involves both learning to solve new problems and learning better ways to solve old problems

(ii)   KA is interested in acquiring expertise, and expertise can be characterized by the scope of problems solved and the efficiency to solve them.

Becoming an expert therefore involves acquiring or having the knowledge necessary to solve problems and to solve them efficiently. Efficiency can only be defined with respect to the features of a task environment. These features include aspects such as:

some data can be missing, delayed, or erroneous and also aspects of resource economy play an important role in defining what is easy and what is expensive to obtain, infer or ask. Efficiency is achieved by means of adjusting (or even changing) the problem-solving method to the effects of these task environment features. In addition to these economic aspects, the pattern of interaction of the agent in the task environment involves learning expectations of events most likely to happen and the tuning of problem-solving to these expectations.

Therefore, learning and becoming an expert (system) both involve a model of the domain task and of the method appropriate for a task environment. For instance, an expert physician can focus early in the diagnosis process on the set of likely hypothesis using a small set of clinical evidence and delaying time consuming laboratory data to later stages. A novice, instead, though possessing enough domain knowledge (physiological, statistical, etc), typically uses a less focused method or even lacks the expectations of likeliness (and as a result cannot proceed to diagnose properly until some (and sometimes much) laboratory data is available) [Mantaras 90].

Another example is circuit troubleshooting: an expert uses fewer circuit checks to detect a failure using knowledge about the likeliness of component failure, economy (easiness, cost, or time) of test procedures, etc [Davis 88]. Exhaustive testing, for instance, can solve the problem. The method is 'bad' not because it is computationally expensive, but because exhaustive testing does not involve any expertise since it does not use all the knowledge resources an intelligent agent would reasonably use in troubleshooting.

## 2.2. Knowledge Level Analysis

The (excessively) short analysis we have just sketched indubitably will remind KA workers of the knowledge-level approach to expert systems (ES) analysis and construction. As a matter of fact, knowledge-level analysis of ES aims at determining problem solving methods that work efficiently for a given body of knowledge and the given features of a task environment.

The notion of knowledge-level analysis (KLA) has evolved in expert systems since Newell's definition. This evolution has been guided by the goal of using KLA as a useful intermediary step in the development of expert systems [Steels & McDermott 90]. There is a scientific rationale and a technical rationale behind KLA that can be useful for ML research. The scientific rationale of KLA is the aim of achieving a level of description of problem solving at the right level of abstraction: the description should talk about tasks, inference methods, etc, in such a way that they can be characterized independently of implementation aspects and related to features (of domain theories, of task environments) that allow methods and tasks to be applicable, useful, or efficient. Several approaches of KLA include [Chandrasekaran 86], [McDermott 89], [Steels 90]. An example of KLA in machine learning is the analysis and comparison of rule-based and case-based learning [Clarck 89]. The knowledge level analysis allows to study the issues of cognitive economy (inference vs. memory trade-offs) and relate them to task environment features (that determine when the trade-offs of a method make it efficient or even applicable) [Van de Velde 88].

The technical rationale of KLA is constructing generic components which can be reused and refined as needed, guided by features of the task and the domain (instead of by implementation and engineering considerations). This effort is very relevant for ML in its present stage. On the one hand, the relation between learning and problem-solving is explored by research on integrated architectures (SOAR, PRODIGY, THEO, ICARUS). On the other hand, as pointed out by [Langley 89], the combination of methodologies and the integration of theories for learning is imperative.

The integration of ML techniques involves the same kind of issues faced by KLA approach to expert systems, and moreover the integration of learning modules to expert-level problem-solving systems also involve these same issues. A knowledge-level analysis of learning techniques can be very usuful for ML as a discipline and for elucidating the relationship of learning techniques with problem-solving methods and expert-level performance.

## 2.3. Learning and Expertise

What role of ML can be more useful in building expertise-level problem-solving systems? Since one of the main features distinguishing expert problem-solving behaviour from novice problem-solving behaviour is the higher capability of the former to use knowledge about a domain, it is clear that ML can be used to learn this appropriate use of knowledge. Usually, the more direct relationship of ML to KA is conceptualized as an automation of domain knowledge acquisition and representation (rule induction is the classical example). However, good expert systems design approaches to knowledge representation separate domain knowledge from problem-solving strategies (strategic knowledge). In a lot of domains, domain knowledge is available while the control (strategic) knowledge acquired only by experts through their experience in solving problems is less available. Furthermore, this expert capability involves knowledge about how to deal with uncertainty and incompleteness in domain knowledge and to focus the attention to relevant goals and subgoals, to select appropiate actions to achieve these goals and to minimize the cost of interaction according to the economics of the task environment.

We think that the use of ML techniques for KA should concentrate the effort in acquiring this control knowledge rather than domain knowledge. Among the different ML techniques to do so, we think case-based learning is the most promising one. Learning control knowledge has also been approached by using EBL [Minton 87], however EBL seems to impose rather strict conditions on the need of precise and complete domain theories. Although research continues on EBL using imperfect theories, the use of EBL inside a case-based paradigm (e.g. Protos [Bareiss 89]) looks more useful as a KA tool. Case-based approaches bearing some similarities with planning do not require complete and correct domain theories to learn strategic knowledge, as the Bolero [Lopez 90] and CHEF [Hammond 90] systems show.

# 3. Knowledge and change

*T. R. Addis*

Knowledge acquisition for an Expert System relies upon the creation of a formal model that explicitly describes the 'knowledge' of an expert in a narrow domain. Machine learning also depends upon the creation and modifiction of a formal model with the additional requirement that machine learning should contain a formal model of the 'knowledge'; a model that allows a coherent change in the task domain model under the influence of 'learning' activity. In order to stand away from the technical aspects of representation and implementation so that a comparison of knowledge-based systems (of which machine learning systems are a sub-set) can be made, it is necessary to interpret the form of these sysytems in terms of a structured description of each system's knowledge content. These systems can only sensibly be compared at the knowledge level; a level that cannot be defined in absolute terms.

## 3.1. Classes of Knowledge

A taxonomy of knowledge proposed by Addis (Addis, 1989) may illustrate why 'knowledge' has defied any absolute definition. It has been difficult because knowledge is a relative notion that comes in many different forms, types and classes. Each form, type or class can only be recognised through either its origins or its use. It cannot be characterised, except in trivial cases, simply by examining its representation. Every complete

| Declarative Knowledge Class | True by: |
|---|---|
| Facts | Observation or Belief |
| Taxonomic | Definition |
| Hypotheses | Convenience |

*Table 1. The classification of declarative knowledge by its justification*

system (where a system includes the user) must contain in some form four types of knowledge. These are:

- *Tacit* - A skill or understanding that can be demonstrated but cannot be expressed; it is knowledge that resides within the user and links the system through the user with the world as it is percieved by people. Examples of tacit knowledge are motor skill, gestalt and perception.

- *Declarative* - Knowledge of a task domain that can be expressed through a formal language; a language that has a set of associated deterministic procedures and is interpreted by a user (see below on the definition of determinism). Table 1 illustrates the three major classes of declarative knowledge and how each may be recognised through the justification of its truth value.

- *Heuristic* - The knowledge of how to solve problems; it is a knowledge that is governed by purpose. Within artificial intelligence it is this knowledge that is used to control inference through the selection of declarative knowledge to solve a problem.

- *Inferential* - The knowledge of how to 'think' and draw conclusions from the declarative knowledge under the control of heuristic knowledge. There are three broad classes of inference: abduction, deduction and induction. Abduction and induction are often combined under the heading of 'induction'. However, it is clearly stated by C. S. Peirce (Peirce, 1958) that abduction was the mechanism for creating new hypotheses for consideration, deduction was the process through which the hypotheses are used and induction is the judgement through which a hypothesis is acceptable. Each of these classes of inference can be further subdivided (see Addis, 1988).

## 3.2. Incoherent Knowledge

What can be said about declarative knowledge is that it must be considered as existing in many different frameworks. The knowledge within each framework is consistent and the taxonomy clearly defines the role and type of each item of knowledge. The boundaries of each framework are expressed by taxonomic concepts and facts. The internal structure of each framework consists of a set of consistent hypotheses (theories and models).

Frameworks intersect so as to create a set of linked task domains. A framework may be visualised as a crystalline structure where each crystal is coherent, consistent and ordered. However, the complete knowledge structure may be constructed as an incoherent heap of frameworks where each framework is developing and growing in response to its use. Occasionally, a framework will merge with another to form a new structure and others will disappear.

The boundaries of the frameworks are frequently indistinct since in our use of thought we naturally move easily between task domains without noticing the shifts in perspective. It is the task of a knowledge engineer or systems analyst or system designer to identify the frameworks that can be mapped onto a machine; frameworks (the boundaries of which) contain the knowledge for the task domains and will provide a suitable interface to the users. It can mean that this task requires the synthesis of a totally new framework. In all cases there is the danger that inconsistent structures may be implemented through the inclusion of more than one framework or due to the incorrect separation of two or more frameworks. The paradigm offers guidance as to the types of knowledge to be gathered from experts and the kinds of expertise that can be implemented.

## 3.3. A Functional Representation and Deterministic Procedures

A functional language (e.g. ML, HOPE, FAITH) provides an uncommitted representation of knowledge. It is uncommitted in the sense that different views (viz. Logic, Frames, Semantic nets, Relations) of knowledge may easily be represented functionally. A functional language relates directly to knowledge in all its forms, it bridges technology and it encompasses architectures.

A functional language also provides a route to eliminating the boundaries that exist between the spheres of activity that lead to a design. The ZF function for example links the 'tuple at a time' processing to 'set at a time' processing through a pipeline (Addis &

Nowell, 1990). A functional language, in turn, links the complete range of knowledge to processes that are potentially deterministic.

A determinsitic procedure or process is a function; it is a function for which if the input parameters are known and the internal process of the function is defined then through a process of deduction the output can be predicted (i.e. determined). A simple determinsitic procedure or process is retrieval linked with a binary relation (see Addis & Nowell, 1990).

Functions for which we do not know or which we have no access to their internal mechanisms or have no explicitly defined relation (we already know about retrieval) are deemed non-deterministic. We thus resort to a constructive definition of determinism such that a mechanism that at one time is non-deterministic can become deterministic in the light of 'knowledge'. The determinism of a function is thus a relationship that exists between the function and an observer. Knowledge in this case is the 'complex' that an observer employs in order to predict an outcome of a given input to a function.

This notion of determinism is constructive and because it includes the observer this inclusion builds into the paradigm the possibility of learning right from the start. This possibility is unnatural in many of the formal systems simply because most formal systems are created on the assumption that they are independent of an observer.

# 4. Acquiring first order knowledge

*Y. Kodratoff*

We have been developing several learning-knowledge acquisition tools that manipulate first order logic knowledge, i.e., in practice, that introduce variables that can be replaced by an instance during a pattern matching process. We shall describe here some of our motivations for using 1st order knowledge representation schemes, as opposed to classical 0th order schemes, and discuss some of the difficulties met because of 1st order logic.

## 4.1. An attempt at justifying the use of first order logic

Expert Systems show a trade off between the power of expression of first order and the difficulty to implement efficient algorithms. We meet also this problem in Machine Learning. For instance, in similarity-based learning, first order knowledge enables us to represent complex events, involving different objects and their relations. However, knowledge intensive generalization tools are difficult to implement and have to face combinatorial problems. Nevertheless, we cannot give up this kind of representation, because some domains can hardly be formalized in a zeroth order representation. This is particularly true for ATC. In each example, we have at least two objects, the two planes in conflict. It would have been possible to use an attribute-value representation, but we would have to duplicate all the descriptors of the planes. Besides, it may happen that other planes could play a part in the decision of the expert.

Let us now give some more details about the problem of representation in first versus zeroth order logic representation.

### 4.1.1. Some descriptions have the same complexity in zeroth as in first order logic

Let us suppose that we have n objects, called O1, O2,..., On, which satisfy the following relations. O1 is at the left of O2 which in turn is at the left of 03, and so on until On-1 which is at the left of On. In a first order representation, we introduce a predicate "left", n constants representing each of the objects and we write

$$\text{left(O1, O2) \& left(O2, O3) \&... \& left(On-1, On).}$$

In a zeroth order representation, we introduce (n-1) propositions, that we call

$$\text{left\_Oi\_Oi+1, for i = 1,..., n-1}$$

and we write

$$\text{left\_O1\_O2 \& left\_O2\_O3 \&... \& left\_On\_1\_On.}$$

In each case, we need (n-1) atoms or (n-1) propositions.

### 4.1.2. Some descriptions are much more complex in zeroth order than in first order

Let us suppose now that we know that the relation "left" is transitive. This knowledge can be expressed in a first order representation by the following theorem,

$$\forall x \; \forall y \; \forall z \; [\text{left}(x,y) \; \& \; \text{left}(y,z) \;\tilde{}\; \text{left}(x,z)].$$

In first order, representing n objects to the left of each other takes (n-1) propositions together with this theorem. In a zeroth order representation, to express this piece of knowledge we have to introduce many new propositions, such as left_Oi_Oj, for j = i+2,..., n and we can introduce a set of theorems.

$$\text{left\_O1\_O2} \; \& \; \text{left\_O2\_O3} \;\tilde{}\; \text{left\_O1\_O3}$$
$$\text{left\_O1\_O3} \; \& \; \text{left\_O3\_O4} \;\tilde{}\; \text{left\_O1\_O4}$$
$$\text{left\_O1\_On\_1} \; \& \; \text{left\_On\_1\_On} \;\tilde{}\; \text{left\_O1\_On}$$
$$\text{left\_O2\_O3} \; \& \; \text{left\_O3\_O4} \;\tilde{}\; \text{left\_O2\_O4}$$
$$\text{left\_O2\_O4} \; \& \; \text{left\_O4\_O5} \;\tilde{}\; \text{left\_O2\_O5}$$
$$\text{left\_O2\_On-1} \; \& \; \text{left\_On-1\_On} \;\tilde{}\; \text{left\_O2\_On}$$
$$\text{left\_On-2\_On-1} \; \& \; \text{left\_On-1\_On} \;\tilde{}\; \text{left\_On-2\_On}$$

Note that this set of theorems is far from being exhaustive. Alternately, we can rewrite the description of the example as follows.

$$\text{left\_O1\_O2} \; \& \; \text{left\_O1\_O3} \; \&... \; \& \; \text{left\_O1\_On} \; \&$$
$$\text{left\_O2\_O3} \; \& \; \text{left\_O2\_O4} \; \&... \; \& \; \text{left\_O2\_On} \; \&$$
$$\text{left\_On-1\_On}$$

In the case of a first order logic representation, in order to represent p types of links amongs n objects, we need (n-1) atomic formulas and p theorems. In a zeroth order representation, we need $p*(n-1)*(n-2)/2$ propositions. Moreover, in this last case, the way to treat knowledge expressing relations between objects is neither natural nor straightforward. Since this example may seem somewhat artificial, the reader may imagine we are in the situation of representing a long organic molecule, in which "left" becomes "is_linked_to", and for which the theorem becomes

$$\forall x \; \forall y \; \forall z \; [\text{is\_linked\_to}(x,y) \; \& \; \text{is\_linked\_to}(y,z) \;\tilde{}\; \text{is\_linked\_to}(x,z)].$$

In that case, expressing that a simple butane molecule (with 4 carbon and 10 hydrogen atoms) holds, i.e.. expressing a unique very simple kind of relationship, needs to represent 3 C-C links and 10 C-H links, thus it requires $12*11/2 = 66$ relations in zeroth order logics.

## 4.1.3. Some descriptions cannot be achieved in zeroth order logic.

### 4.1.3.1. Relations between variable entities

There are relations between parts of objects such that the parts are not instantiated in advance. We know only some of the properties they must fulfill, and the actual instances must be computed on the fly. For instance, a chlorine atom at one extremity of the molecule influences a hydrogen of the "CH3" group at the other extremity of the molecule. This requires to be expressed without knowing in advance where the "extremity" of a given molecule is, knowing only a description of what should be an extremity.

### 4.1.3.2. Functions

First order logic representations enable functional expressions. For instance, consider the relation between the speed, the distance and the time. We are unable to express it in in a zeroth logic representation, whereas we can write in first order logic

$$\forall x \ \forall t \ \text{distance}(x) \ \& \ \text{time}(t) \ \tilde{} \ \text{speed}(x/t)],$$

i.e. if the distance is x and the time is t then the speed is x/t. In fact, we shall see that in the application to ATC, we did not take advantage of this last point. It is due to a limitation of the current version of our generalization tool that does not treat numeric values. Numeric values are replaced by symbolic ones and we use a kind of very naive qualitative physics to perform the computations. For instance, we replace the numeric operation "/" by a symbolic one, called "/s", defined by

$$/s(\text{high, low}) = \text{high},$$
$$/s(\text{low, high}) = \text{low},$$
$$\text{otherwise } /s(x, y) = \text{undefined}.$$

We give two theorems expressing the graph of "/s",

$$\text{distance(high)} \ \& \ \text{times(low)} \ \tilde{} \ \text{speed(high)},$$
$$\text{distance(low)} \ \& \ \text{times(high)} \ \tilde{} \ \text{speed(low)}.$$

In the application to ATC, we have only a few objects, at least the two aircraft in conflict, but we have many relations between them, i.e., the value of n (as in section 4.1.2 above) is 2 or 3, but the value of p is large. The expert will forget some of them, he will represent only the pieces of knowledge that he has in mind at present. This means that we cannot express all the knowledge in the initial representation of the examples, we need theorems that will introduce new pieces of knowledge in the examples. Most of the knowledge of the expert is first order knowledge like for instance the previous relation between speed, time and distance.

### 4.1.4. Some knowledge is useless if learned at zeroth order

We would like to pinpoint here an effect of zeroth order logics which is often underestimated since it concerns only learning systems. As we said in section 4.1.2, zeroth order increases largely the complexity of some descriptions. Moreover, the knowledge that will be learned from these descriptions is not really usable. This is true when the relation can hold between several objects. The learning system will possibly learn something about an instantiated relation, but it will be unable to apply it correctly to another new example since nothing will tell which of the objects of the new example are concerned by this relation. For instance, suppose that an ID3-like algorithm learns that a relation like left_O1_O3 is important for building a decision tree, which is quite possible. Then, when trying to apply this knowledge on a newJexample, it may well happen that the objects named O1 and O3 in the new example have nothing to do with those named O1 and O3 in the training example. As another example, consider the case of several symptoms on the leaf of a plant. Suppose that we learn "if symptom_1 is a mold then the sickness is A". Then, in an application, if the user happens to say that the mold is symptom_2, then the system will fail detecting sickness A.

In other words, the application of the learned knowledge may often demand to match the patterns of the new example with variable patterns in the learned knowledge which, therefore must be expressed in first order logics.

### 4.2. Clauses and their skolemization

First order logic is able to express a large variety of knowledge. Nevertheless, it has a well-known drawback, namely the undecidability of the proof procedure. Since we want to use a theorem prover that is efficient enough to be applied iteratively on the examples, we have to restrict ourselves to the simpler case of Horn clauses.

## 4.2.1. Clause representation, and the problem of negation

Presently, all ES making use of first order knowledge representation do not accept a disjunction in the right hand side of their if-then rules. Let us discuss a bit more this last point. An if-then rule actually works as follows. When the premisses of the if-then rule are true for a given data base then we deduce that the conclusion is true for this data base. Let us consider an if-then rule if LHS then RHS and let us suppose that RHS is the disjunction of two conjunctive formulas, say F1 and F2. When LHS is true for a given data base then one of the two formulas F1 or F2 or both are true but we do not know which one. One way to use this piece of information is to suppose that one is true and to go on until we get a contradiction. Thus, we achieve a hypothetical reasoning with all the problems involved in non-monotonous reasoning. Some generators of ES, as for instance the system ART, allow such kind of reasoning. We can also consider this production rule as the logical formula LHS . (F1 OR F2). For simplicity, suppose that there are no variables in this formula. In terms of logics, this formula is equivalent for instance to LHS & NOT F1 . F2. But, in terms of ES, the two formulations are not equivalent. Actually, the second one means "If LHS is true and if F1 is false for the given data base, then we can deduce that F2 is true." But, we have been losing the symmetry between F1 and F2, and we have to check also the formula LHS & NOT F2 . F1. Besides, we are now facing the difficult problem of the negation, for which well-known partial solutions, like negation by failure, are obviously unacceptable in the concept of a learning system that cannot be approximated by a closed universe.

## 4.2.2. The skolemization of clauses

Transforming a theorem into a set of clauses includes a step known as skolemization, which happens because, in a clause, all variables have to be universally quantified. Therefore, all existentially quantified variables have to be deleted. If the existential quantification is not under the scope of a universal quantifier, as for instance when there are only existentially quantified variables, then they must be replaced by a new constant. If the existential quantification is under the scope of one or several universal quantifiers, then the existentially quantified variables must be replaced by a new function depending on these universally quantified variables whose $\forall$ occurs ahead of the $\exists$ concerned. In other words, suppose that we have a formula of the form:

$$\forall x \; \forall y \; \exists u \; \forall z \; \exists v \; F(x, y, z, u, v)$$

then it can be transformed into:

$$\forall x \, \forall y \, \forall z \, F(x, y, z, h(x, y), g(x, y, z))$$

where h and g are new symbols of functions. Notice that u has been replaced by a function of x and y because it is under the scope of x and y, while v, which is under the scope of x, y, and z has to be replaced by a function of x, y, and z. The constant or function introduced are new symbols. This is essential to the theory, and skolemization does not transform a formula into an equivalent one. Consider now that when this operation is performed by an expert, as happens in AI, he will not introduce a new symbol which would be meaningless for him. On the contrary, he will insist on finding the "good" symbol that will keep the truth value of his clauses. In other words, the operation performed by a human is a pseudo-skolemization (hence the quotes we have been using above when speaking of skolemization) in which the pseudo-Skolem function is related to the existing knowledge. Let us exemplify the skolemization problem on the clause representation of the sentence Everybody makes mistakes. In first-order logic it reads

$$\forall x \, \exists y \, [\text{human}(x) \text{~} (\text{does}(x, y) \, \& \, \text{mistake}(y))].$$

The variable y is under the scope of the " quantifier that quantifies x, therefore y has to be skolemized as a function of x. We can bring in an arbitrary skolem function and transform our theorem into

$$\forall x \, [\text{human}(x) \text{~} \text{does}(x, g(x)) \, \& \, \text{mistake}(g(x))]$$

where g is a new function symbol. In practice, it is awkward to neglect any information we have about the function g, which tells us that what is done is a misfit action. An expert would even insist on making explicit the kind of actions that are misfit in the considered field of expertise. Suppose that we are in the context of a school class, and that the teacher wants to insist on the fact that lack of attention brings mistakes, then he would attribute these errors to unthoughtfulness, and write, instead of g(x), unthoughtful_action(x)

$$\forall x \, [\text{human}(x) \text{~} \text{does}(x, \text{unthoughtful\_action}(x)) \, \& \, \text{mistake} \, (\text{unthoughtful\_action} \, (x))].$$

To complete the example, let us point out that the expert would also dislike the presence of functions in his predicates, he would then rather give to the theorem the form

$$\forall x \, \forall y \, [(\text{human}(x) \, \& \, \text{unthoughtful\_action\_pred}(x,y)) \text{~} (\text{does}(x, y) \, \& \, \text{mistake}(y))],$$

where   unthoughtful_action_pred(x,y)   represents   the   graph   of   the   function
unthoughtful_action(x) and can be expressed in a logic with equality by

$$\forall x \, \forall y \; \text{unthoughtful\_action\_pred}(x,y) \; [\; y = \text{unthoughtful\_action}(x).$$

This last version is no longer equivalent at all to the general theorem we started from. In
theory, this is an abomination. In practice, we want the expert to be happy with the
knowledge he has been transmitting into the system. The skolemization process has
forced him to make his thought more precise than it was at the beginning, which is a very
positive feature of knowledge acquisition. The choice of an appropriate replacement for
a skolem function is a problem which nobody has envisaged an automatic solution to as
far as we know. However, as the following examples clearly show, it is quite all right to
convert a sentence expressing a feature into a theorem when its conversion into a clause
(or rule) requires a pseudo-skolemization which can only be done well by a domain
expert. Techniques for acquiring knowledge to construct ES must not fail to get the
expert to point out the right supplementary information that allow to solve the problem of
skolemization.


## 4.3.  How to represent knowledge when using predicates

In most applications, an expert describes a situation he has to face by using attributes and relations between objects. The attributes represent either global descriptors of
the context in which the situation occurs as for instance the weather, or descriptors of the
objects appearing in the situation as for instance, the temperature of the patient, the color
of an object, etc. In other terms, the description provided by the expert is composed of

- some pairs (attribute, value) characterizing the environment as for instance
  (weather, fine),

- some triplets (attribute, object, value) as for instance (temperature Bob high),

- some relations (relation, object1, object2,...) which may be oriented. In this case,
  the order of the objects occurring in the list is important. Most often, the relations
  are binary ones.

We shall study in this section how we can transpose these pieces of knowledge into a first
order representation.

We see at least four ways of transforming a pair (attribute, value) into a first order
representation but the list is not exhaustive. Let us consider first the case of global
descriptors, represented by pairs (attribute, value), as for instance the pair (weather, fine)

which means that for the given situation, the weather is fine.

- 1st representation: attribute(value), attribute becomes a predicate and value becomes a constant. This representation is the closest to the attribute-value one. In this case, the word weather becomes a predicate of the underlying first order language and the word fine becomes a constant. In terms of logics, in order to define a semantic interpretation of this formula, we have to give a non empty set D, an interpretation of the constant fine and of the predicate weather over D. Intuitively, we interpret the constant fine as an object, and this is not very natural.

- 2nd representation: value(attribute), value becomes a predicate and attribute becomes a constant. Another possible representation is to write fine(weather). In that case, weather becomes a constant and fine a predicate. Intuitively, weather is interpreted as an object which satisfies the property of being fine.

- 3rd representation: pred(attribute, value), pred is a new symbol of predicate and attribute and value are constants. In this representation, a type has been attributed to the pair (attribute, value) and pred is a new symbol of predicate that represents the type. For instance, we can say that the pair (weather, fine) represents a weather forecast by forecast(weather, fine).

- 4th representation: attribute(C) & value(C), attribute and value become predicates and C is a new symbol for a constant. This representation is close to an object-oriented one. For instance, in our example, we express that there is an object, say W, which satisfies the two following properties. W represents the weather of the given situation and W is fine. This reads weather (W) & fine(W). The words fine and weather both become predicates, and we introduce a new constant W. This idea of introducing a fictitious object is quite classical. It is used to transform facts written in first order logic into structured object representations (Nilsson, 1980). For instance, to translate the atom gives(PETER, MARY, BOOK1), we introduce a new object G which is an instance of the action give, for which the actor is Peter, the receiver is Mary, and the object is Book1 and we obtain

give(G) & actor(G, PETER) & receiver(G, MARY) & object(G, BOOK1).

We can apply these four representations to descriptions of objects, that is to say to triplets (attribute, object, value), as for instance the triplet (color_eyes, John, brown).

- 1st representation: attribute(object, value), gives color_eyes(John, brown).

- 2nd representation: value(object, attribute), gives brown(John, color_eyes).

- 3rd representation: pred(object, attribute, value), gives physical_descr(John, color_eyes, brown).

- 4th representation: attribute(object, C) & value(C) gives color_eyes (John,C) & brown(C) where C is a new symbol of constant.

First order logic is well suited to express relations between objects, as (relation, object1, object2...). Relation becomes a predicate and object1, object2,... become constants. We obtain relation(object1, object2,...).

This section shows that there are many possible choices for the transformation of the knowledge of the expert into a first order representation.

## 4.4. Conclusion

Knowledge intensive generalization techniques need even more than a generalization tool making use of the field expert's knowledge. The very use of this knowledge entails a first order logic representation, which is not friendly to the expert. Thus, besides the generalization tools, we need other tools to perform the transformation of the examples and the expert's knowledge into first order, and, once the learning has taken place, we need to translate it back into a representation that is acceptable to the expert. All these translation steps are far from trivial, as shown here, and they contain choices that must be carefully discussed with the expert since they can are strongly biasing the learning. We performed an application of this knowledge intensive generalization to knowledge acquisition in the domain of air traffic control. In this application field, knowledge intensiveness and first order logic are impossible to avoid.

# 5. References

Addis T. R., A Knowledge Organisation for Abduction, Proceedings of the Interdisplinary Information Technology Conference, Bradford Univeristy, pp 19, 1988.

Addis T. R., The Science of Knowledge. Third European Workshop on Knowledge Acquisition for Knowledge-Based Systems, Paris, July, 1989.

Addis T. R. & Nowell M. C. C., Knowledge and The Structure of Machines. *Symbols vs Neurons*, ed. Addis T. R. and Stender J., pub. IOS press, Amsterdam, October, 1990.

Bareiss R, Exemplar-based knowledge acquisition. Academic Press, 1989.

Clarck P, "A comparison of rule- and exemplar-based learning systems", in P B Brazdil & K Konolige (Eds.) "Machine Learning, Meta-Reasoning, and Logics", Kluwer Pub, 1989.

Chandrasekaran B, "Generic Tasks in Knowledge-based Reasoning: High-level building blocks for expert systems design" IEEE Expert, Vol. 1, 1986.

Davis R & Hamscher C, "Model-based reasoning: Troubleshooting". MIT AIL Memo #1059, 1988.

Hammond K. J., Explaining and repairing plans that fail, Artificial Intelligence, 45, 229-264, 1990.

Lopez B & Plaza E, Case-base learning of strategic knowledge, Research Report GRIAL 90/14, 1990.

Lopez de Mantaras R., Sierra C. & Agusti J., "COLAPSES: A modular architecture and language for modelling meta-control and uncertainty", in "New Directions for Intelligent Tutoring Systems" (E Costa, Ed.), Spriger Verlag NATO ASI Series, 1990.

Luc de Raedt & Bruynooghe M,. On Interactive Concept-Learning and Assimilation, in: Sleeman (ed) Procs. of the 3rd European Working Session on Learning, Pitman, 167 - 176, 1988.

Morik K, Integrating Manual and Automatic Knowledge Acquisition - BLIP, in: McGraw, Westphal (eds) Readings in Knowledge Acquisition - Current Practices and Trends, Ellis Horwood, 213 - 232, 1990.

Muggleton S, Inductive Logic Programming, in: Procs. of 1st Conference on Algorithmic Learning Theory, Tokyo, Ohmsha, 1990.

Peirce, C. S. Science and Philosophy. *Collected Paprs of Charles S. Peirce 7*, Harvard University Press, 1958.

Siefkes D, Prototyping is Theory Building, in: Procs. IFIP Conference on Information Systems, Work and Organization Design, Berlin, 1989.

McDermott J, "The world would be a better place if non-programmers could program", Machine Learning, 4, 337-338, 1989.

Minton S, Carbonell J, Knoblock C, Kuokka D, Etzioni & O Gil Y, Explanation Based Learning: A problem solving perspective, Artificial Intelligence, 40, 63-118, 1989.

Nilsson N, "Principles of Artificial Intelligence", Tioga Publishing Company, 1980.

Steels L, "The components of expertise", AI Magazine, August 1990.

Steels L & McDermott J, "Knowledge-Level in Action. Proceedings of the Workshop on Expert Systems Foundations" (to appear).

Van de Velde W, "The Quality of Learning", Proc. ECAI-88, p. 408-413, 1988.

# PROGRAMME of EWSL-91

## WEDNESDAY MARCH 6TH 1991

### Morning 9h30-13h30

**9h30-10h30:** Carbonell's key-note presentation:
*Scaling up knowledge-based systems via machine learning*
**10h30-11h Break**
**11h-12h30: Presentations on constructive induction and multi-strategy approaches**
A GIORDANA, D ROVERSO, and L SAITTA
Abstracting Background Knowledge for Concept Learning
G TECUCI
A Multistrategy Learning Approach to Domain Modeling and Knowledge Acquisition
G WIDMER
Using Plausible Explanations to Bias Empirical Generalizations in Weak Theory Domains
D YANG, G BLIX, and L A RENDELL
The Replication Problem: A Constructive Induction Approach

**12h30h-13h30h panel:** Evaluating and Changing Representation in Concept Acquisition
F BERGADANO (coordinator) , F ESPOSITO, C ROUVEIROL, and S WROBEL (panelists)

### Afternoon 3h-6h

**3h-4h panel:** Applications of Machine Learning
P CLARK (coordinator), B CESTIK, C SAMMUT, and J STENDER (panelists)

**4h-5h: Presentations on discovery and numeric & statistical approaches**

M MOULET
Using Accuracy in Scientific Discovery
H LOUNIS and G BISSON
Evaluation of Learning Systems: An Artificial Data-Based Approach
C SCHAFFER
Scientific Function Finding as Classification

M DORIGO
Message-Based Bucket Brigade: An Algorithm for the Apportionment of Credit Problem

**5h-6h panel:** Application of Empirical Discovery in Knowledge Acquisition
J M ZYTKOW (coordinator), P EDWARDS, and M MOULET (panelists)

## THURSDAY MARCH 7TH 1991

### Morning 9h-12h

**9h-11h: Presentations on numeric & statistical approaches**

B CESTNIK and I BRATKO
On Estimating Probabilites in Tree Pruning
P CLARK and R BOSWELL
Rule Induction with CN2: Some Recent Improvements
J CATLETT
On Changing Continuous Attributes into Ordered Discrete Attributes
C SCHAFFER
When Does Overfitting Decrease Prediction Accuracy in Induced Decision Trees and Rule Sets
C DECAESTECKER
Description Contrasting in Incremental Concept Formation

**11h-12h panel** Causality and Learning
L SAITTA (coordinator), I BRATKO, Y KODRATOFF, K MORIK, and W VAN DE VELDE
(panelists)

### Afternoon 2h-6h

**2h-4h Posters**

F ZERR and JG GANASCIA
Integrating an Explanation-Based Learning Mechanism into a General Problem Solver
C CARPINETO
Analytical Negative Generalization and Empirical Negative Generalization are not Cumulative:
A Case Study
G BISSON
KBG: A Generator of Knowledge Bases
J PAREDIS

Decision trees and Neural Nets: Two Complementary Representations for Learning
F VERDENIUS
A Method for Inductive Cost Optimization
I KONONENKO
Semi-Naive Bayesian Classifier
M KUBAT and J PAVLICKOVA
The System FLORA: Learning from Time-Varying Training Sets
P URBANO
Learning by Explanation of Failures
J NICOLAS
Seed Space and Version Space: Generalizing from Approximations
S MATWIN, S DELISLE, and L ZUPAN
Integrating EBL with Automatic Text Analysis
B LOPEZ and E PLAZA
Case-Based Learning of Strategic Knowledge
L DI PACE, F FABROCINI, and G BOLIS
Shift of Bias in learning from Drug Compounds: The Fleming Project
E MORALES
Learning Features by Experimentation in Chess
F COURTOT
Representation and Induction of Musical Structures for Computer Assisted Composition
S SCHULZE-KREMER and R D KING
IPSA: Inductive Protein Structure Analysis

**4h-5h: Presentations on theorem proving & EBL**

L DE RAEDT, J FEYAERTS, and M BRUYNOOGHE
Acquiring Object-Knowledge for Learning Systems
N LAVRAC, S DZEROSKI, and M GROBELNIK
Learning Nonrecursive Definitions of Relations with LINUS
I MOZETIC and C HOLZBAUR
Extending Explanation-Based Generalization by Abstraction Operators

**5h-6h panel**: Logic and Learnability
L DE RAEDT (coordinator), F BERGADANO, A HOFFMAN, S MUGGLETON, and J F PUGET
(panelists)

# FRIDAY MARCH 8TH, 1991

## Morning 9h-12h15

### 9h-10h30: Presentations on theorem proving & EBL

K ZERCHER
Explanation-Based Generalization and Constraint Propagation with Interval Labels
C BELLEANNEE and J NICOLAS
Static Learning for an Adaptative Theorem Prover
B DUVAL
Abduction and Induction for Explanation-Based Learning
S H NIENHUYS-CHENG and P A FLACH
Consistent Term Mappings, Term Partitions and Inverse Resolution

**10h30-11h30 panel**: Four Stances on Knowledge Acquisition and Machine Learning
T R ADDIS (coordinator), Y KODRATOFF, R L DE MANTARAS, K MORIK, and E PLAZA (panelists)

### 11h30-12h15: Presentations on analogy & case-based learning
M VELOSO and J G CARBONELL
Learning by Analogical Replay in PRODIGY: First Results
B TAUSEND and S BELL
Analogical Reasoning for Logic Programming

## Afternoon 2h-4h

### 2h-3h: Presentations on multi-agents

P BRAZDIL and S MUGGLETON
Learning to Relate Terms in a Multiple Agent Environment
S S SIAN
Extending Learning to Multiple Agents: Issues and a Model for Multi-Agent ML

**3h-4h panel**: Learning in Distributed Systems and Multi-Agent Environments
P BRAZDIL (coordinator), M GAMS, S SIAN, L TORGO, and W VAN DE VELDE (panelists)

# Lecture Notes in Computer Science